Freedom in America

Freedom in America

Kenneth Bridges, Ph. D.
South Arkansas Community College

Upper Saddle River, New Jersey 07458

Library of Congress Cataloging-in-Publication Data

Bridges, Kenneth.
  Freedom in America / Kenneth Bridges.
     p. cm.
  Includes bibliographical references.
  ISBN-13: 978-0-13-614734-3 (pbk.)
  ISBN-10: 0-13-614734-8 (pbk.)
  1. Civil rights—United States—History—Sources. 2. Liberty—History—Sources.
3. United States—History—Sources. 4. United States—Politics and government—Sources.
5. Democracy—United States—History—Sources. 6. United States—Social conditions—Sources. I.
Title.
  JC599.U5B69 2008
  323.0973—dc22

                                                                          2007006259

Editorial Director: Charlyce Jones-Owen
Senior Assistant: Maureen Diana
Senior Managing Editor: Joanne Riker
Production Liaison: Joanne Hakim
Director of Marketing: Brandy Dawson
Senior Marketing Manager: Kate Mitchell
Marketing Assistant: Jennifer Lang
Manufacturing Buyer: Benjamin Smith
Cover Art Director: Jayne Conte
Cover Design: Bruce Kenselaar
Cover Illustration/Photo: Todd Gipstein/CORBIS-NY
Manager, Cover Visual Research & Permissions: Karen Sanatar
Permissions Assistance: Warren Drabek
Full-Service Project Management: Babitha Balan/GGS Book Services
Composition: GGS Book Services
Printer/Binder: RR Donnelley & Sons Company

Credits and acknowledgments borrowed from other sources and reproduced, with permission, in this textbook appear on appropriate page within text.

Pearson Prentice Hall™ is a trademark of Pearson Education, Inc.
Pearson® is a registered trademark of Pearson plc
Prentice Hall® is a registered trademark of Pearson Education, Inc.

Pearson Education LTD., London
Pearson Education Singapore, Pte. Ltd
Pearson Education, Canada, Ltd
Pearson Education–Japan
Pearson Education Australia Pty, Limited

Pearson Education North Asia Ltd
Pearson Educación de Mexico, S.A. de C.V.
Pearson Education Malaysia, Pte. Ltd
Pearson Education, Upper Saddle River, New Jersey

10 9 8 7 6 5 4 3 2 1
ISBN 13: 978-0-13-614734-3
ISBN 10:   0-13-614734-8

Contents

Freedom in America

Introduction

Freedom is the one word that defines America. From the founding of the earliest European colonies, Americans have defined themselves by freedoms preserved and freedoms denied. The words freedom, liberty, and justice each evoke strong emotions and powerful opinions from the American people.

But what is freedom? Statesmen and philosophers have offered their opinions since the earliest days of the republic. The answer that each one gives provides an important insight into the cultural and political concerns of the day. Each generation defines freedom slightly differently, seeking to meet the challenge of the times and live up to the ideals of equality and justice.

Most of the political debates and debates over civil liberties in the history of this nation have focused on the definition of freedom. The colonies of the seventeenth century debated freedom of religion; the colonists of the eighteenth century pressed for free government, free speech, and the freedom of dissent. The Americans of the nineteenth century debated abolition of slavery and women's rights, while twentieth-century America examined civil rights and economic justice issues. Countless Americans had sought to live up to the ideal of "all men are created equal." Despite the failures and injustices the United States suffered through, generations of Americans have attempted to live up to that ideal and expand the promises of freedom to more of their countrymen.

Like so much of the nation's past, men and women both well-known and obscure contribute to these statements on human liberty. Each has tried to define in their own way what they saw as the proper relationship between the individual and the state. This anthology presents letters, essays, constitutions, and laws that seek to define American freedom. Their authors both criticize the United States for its failures to live up to its ideals and seek to inspire it to expand the benefits of freedom to ever-increasing multitudes. Overall, in spite of the tremendous obstacles at particular points in time, these authors exude a tremendous sense of optimism that the nation can overcome prejudice, repression, and whatever impediment that slows the progress of justice.

Wherever possible, the actual spellings of the words in these essays have been preserved in order to retain a flavor of the time period. In some cases, additional information has been inserted into brackets to clarify references to individuals and facts. The debate on the definition of freedom does not stop with this work or any election, but will continue as freedom evolves and the idea carries the nation into the future.

My thanks to the following reviewers whose comments were helpful in shaping the first edition of *Freedom in America*: Dr. Sheri I. David, Northern Virginia

1

Community College; Wade Shaffer, West Texas A&M University; James Seymour, Cy Fair College; Richard Elder, Bay Mills Community College; and Craig Ferguson, Oklahoma City Community College.

My thanks to my wife, Karen, sons Kaleb and Toby, friends and faculty at South Arkansas Community College, and heroes from the history books for inspiring this project. Thanks also to the editors, staff, and readers at Prentice Hall for their support and advice. It was a considerable task to decide which of these essays to include, but in the traditional disclaimer of historians, I beg the reader's forgiveness for any errors or omissions, all entirely my own.

Kenneth Bridges

1

Charter of Virginia, 1606

This first selection was written in England to establish the colony of Virginia, describing the borders, rights of landowners, and the structure of the colonial government. The structure of this government became one of the most important foundations in the history of American civil liberties. The charter called for a council to help make decisions for the colonies, similar to Parliament. Unlike the colonies of other powers, which were ruled through individual governors or viceroys, Virginia would have a representative form of government. Since England already had a 400-year-old tradition of due process of law and representative assemblies, this arrangement seemed a logical extension. From this council, the people (although limited to white, landowning men) could have a voice in the affairs of the community. The Virginia colony was not established until 1610 and the Virginia General Assembly was not established until 1619, but it would have repercussions that would last for centuries.

JAMES, by the Grace of God, King of England, Scotland, France and Ireland, Defender of the Faith, &c. WHEREAS our loving and well-disposed Subjects, Sir Thorn as Gales, and Sir George Somers, Knights, Richard Hackluit, Clerk, Prebendary of Westminster, and Edward-Maria Wingfield, Thomas Hanharm and Ralegh Gilbert, Esqrs. William Parker, and George Popham, Gentlemen, and divers others of our loving Subjects, have been humble Suitors unto us, that We would vouchsafe unto them our Licence, to make Habitation, Plantation, and to deduce a colony of sundry of our People into that part of America commonly called VIRGINIA, and other parts and Territories in America, either appertaining unto us, or which are not now actually possessed by any Christian Prince or People, situate, lying, and being all along the Sea Coasts, between four and thirty Degrees of Northerly Latitude from the Equinoctial Line, and five and forty Degrees of the same Latitude, and in the main Land between the same four and thirty and five and forty Degrees, and the Islands hereunto adjacent, or within one hundred Miles of the Coast thereof;

And to that End, and for the more speedy Accomplishment of their said intended Plantation and Habitation there, are desirous to divide themselves into two several Colonies and Companies; the one consisting of certain Knights, Gentlemen, Merchants, and other Adventurers, of our City of London and elsewhere, which are, and from time to time shall be, joined unto them, which do desire to begin their Plantation and Habitation in some fit and convenient Place, between four and thirty and one and forty Degrees of the said Latitude, alongst the Coasts of Virginia, and the Coasts of America aforesaid: And the other consisting of sundry Knights, Gentlemen, Merchants, and other Adventurers, of our Cities of Bristol and Exeter, and of our Town of Plimouth, and of other Places, which do join themselves unto that Colony, which do desire to begin their Plantation and Habitation in some fit and convenient Place, between eight and thirty Degrees and five and forty Degrees of the said Latitude, all alongst the said Coasts of Virginia and America, as that Coast lyeth:

We, greatly commending, and graciously accepting of, their Desires for the Furtherance of so noble a Work, which may, by the Providence of Almighty God, hereafter tend to the Glory of his Divine Majesty, in propagating of Christian Religion to such People, as yet live in Darkness and miserable Ignorance of the true Knowledge and Worship of God, and may in time bring the Infidels and Savages, living in those parts, to human Civility, and to a settled and quiet Government: DO, by these our Letters Patents, graciously accept of, and agree to, their humble and well-intended Desires;

And do therefore, for Us, our Heirs, and Successors, GRANT and agree, that the said Sir Thomas Gates, Sir George Somers, Richard Hackluit, and Edward-Maria Wingfield, Adventurers of and for our City of London, and all such others, as are, or shall be, joined unto them of that Colony, shall be called the first Colony; And they shall and may begin their said first Plantation and Habitation, at any Place upon the said Coasts of Virginia or America, where they shall think fit and convenient, between the said four and thirty and one and forty Degrees of the said Latitude; And that they shall have all the Lands, Woods, Soil, Grounds, Havens, Ports, Rivers, Mines, Minerals, Marshes, Waters, Fishings, Commodities, and Hereditaments, whatsoever, from the said first Seat of their Plantation and Habitation by the Space of fifty Miles of English Statute Measure, all along the said Coast of Virginia and America, towards the West and Southwest, as the Coast lyeth, with all the Islands within one hundred Miles directly over against the same Sea Coast; And also all the Lands, Soil, Grounds, Havens, Ports, Rivers, Mines, Minerals, Woods, Waters, Marshes, Fishings, Commoditites, and Hereditaments, whatsoever, from the said Place of their first Plantation and Habitation for the space of fifty like English Miles, all alongst the said Coasts of Virginia and America, towards the East and Northeast, or towards the North, as the Coast lyeth, together with all the Islands within one hundred Miles, directly over against the said Sea Coast, And also all the Lands, Woods, Soil, Grounds, Havens, Ports, Rivers, Mines, Minerals, Marshes, Waters, Fishings, Commodities, and Hereditaments, whatsoever, from the same fifty Miles every way on the Sea Coast, directly into the main Land by the Space of one hundred like English Miles; And shall and may inhabit and remain there; and shall and may also build and fortify within any the same, for their better Safeguard and Defense, according to their best Discretion, and the Discretion of the Council of that Colony; And that no other of our Subjects shall be permitted, or suffered, to plant or inhabit behind, or on the Backside of them, towards the main Land, without the Express License or Consent of the Council of that Colony, thereunto in Writing; first had and obtained.

And we do likewise, for Us, Our Heirs, and Successors, by these Presents, GRANT and agree, that the said Thomas Hanham, and Ralegh Gilbert, William Parker, and George Popham, and all others of the Town of Plimouth in the County of Devon, or elsewhere which are, or shall be, joined unto them of that Colony, shall be called the second Colony; And that they shall and may begin their said Plantation and Seat of their first Abode and Habitation, at any Place upon the said Coasts of Virginia and America, where they shall think fit and convenient, between eight and thirty Degrees of the said Latitude, and five and forty Degrees of the same Latitude; And that they shall have all the Lands, Soils, Grounds, Havens, Ports, Rivers, Mines,

Minerals, Woods, Marshes, Waters, Fishings, Commodities, and Hereditaments, whatsoever, from the first Seat of their Plantation and Habitation by the Space of fifty like English Miles, as is aforesaid, all alongst the said Coasts of Virginia and al raerica towards the West and Southwest, or towards the South, as the Coast lyeth, and all the Islands within one hundred Miles, directly over against the said Sea Coast; And also all the Lands, Soils, Grounds, Havens, Ports, Rivers, Mines, Minerals, Woods, Marshes, Waters, Fishings, Commodities, and Hereditaments, whatsoever, from the said Place of their first Plantation and Habitation for the Space of fifty like Miles, all alongst the said Coast of Virginia and America, towards the least and Northeast, or towards the North, as the Coast lyeth, and all the Islands also within one hundred Miles directly over against the same Sea Coast; And also all the Lands, Soils, Grounds, Havens, Ports, Rivers, Woods, Mines, Minerals, Marshes, Waters, Fishings, Commodities, and Hereditaments, whatsoever, from the same fifty Miles every way on the Sea Coast, directly into the main Land, by the Space of one hundred like English Miles; And shall and may inhabit and remain there; and shall and may also build and fortify within any the same for their better Safeguard, according to their best Discretion, and the Discretion of the Council of that Colony; And that none of our Subjects shall be permitted, or suffered, to plant or inhabit behind, or on the back of them, towards the main Land, without express Licence of the Council of that Colony, in Writing thereunto first had and obtained.

Provided always, and our Will and Pleasure herein is, that the Plantation and Habitation of such of the said Colonies, as shall last plant themselves, as aforesaid, shall not be made within one hundred like English Miles of the other of them, that first began to make their Plantation, as aforesaid.

And we do also ordain, establish, and agree, for Us, our Heirs, and Successors, that each of the said Colonies shall have a Council, which shall govern and order all Matters and Causes, which shall arise, grow, or happen, to or within the same several Colonies, according to such Laws, Ordinances, and Instructions, as shall be, in that behalf, given and signed with Our Hand or Sign Manual, and pass under the Privy Seal of our Realm of England; Each of which Councils shall consist of thirteen Persons, to be ordained, made, and removed, from time to time, according as shall be directed and comprised in the same instructions; And shall have a several Seal, for all Matters that shall pass or concern the same several Councils; Each of which Seals, shall have the King's Arms engraven on the one Side thereof, and his Portraiture on the other; And that the Seal for the Council of the said first Colony shall have engraven round about, on the one Side, these Words; Sigillum Regis Magne Britanniae, Franciae, & Hiberniae; on the other Side this Inscription round about; Pro Concilio primae Coloniae Virginiae. And the Seal for the Council of the said second Colony shall also have engraven, round about the one Side thereof, the aforesaid Words; Sigillum Regis Magne Britanniae, Franciae, & Hiberniae; and on the other Side; Pro Concilio primae Coloniae Virginiae:

And that also there shall be a Council, established here in England, which shall, in like manner, consist of thirteen Persons, to be for that Purpose, appointed by Us, our Heirs and Successors, which shall be called our Council of Virginia; And shall, from time to time, have the superior Managing and Direction, only of and for all Matters that shall or may concern the Government, as well of the said several Colonies, as of and for any other Part or Place, within the aforesaid Precincts of four and thirty and five and forty Degrees abovementioned; Which Council shall, in like manner, have a Seal, for matters concerning the Council or Colonies, with the like Arms and Portraiture, as aforesaid, with this inscription, engraven round about on the one Side; Sigillum Regis Magne Britanniae, Franciae, & Hiberniae; and round about on the other Side, Pro Concilio fuo Virginiae. And moreover, we do GRANT and agree, for Us, our Heirs and Successors; that that the said several Councils of and for the said several Colonies, shall and lawfully may, by Virtue hereof, from time to time, without any Interruption of Us, our Heirs or Successors, give and take Order, to dig, mine, and search for all Manner of Mines of Gold, Silver, and Copper, as well within any Part of their said several Colonies, as of the said main Lands on the Backside of the same Colonies; And to HAVE and enjoy the Gold, Silver, and Copper, to be gotten thereof, to the Use and Behoof of the same Colonies, and the Plantations thereof; YIELDING therefore to Us, our Heirs and Successors, the fifth Part only of all the same Gold and Silver, and the fifteenth Part of all the same Copper, so to be gotten or had, as is aforesaid, without any other Manner of Profit or Account, to be given or yielded to Us, our Heirs, or Successors, for or in Respect of the same:

And that they shall, or lawfully may, establish and cause to be made a Coin, to pass current there between the people of those several Colonies, for the more Ease of Traffick and Bargaining between and amongst them and the Natives there, of such Metal, and in such Manner and Form, as the said several Councils there shall limit and appoint. And we do likewise, for Us, our Heirs, and Successors, by these Presents, give full Power and Authority to the said Sir Thomas Gates, Sir George Somers, Richard Hackluit, Edward-Maria Wingfeld, Thomas Hanham, Ralegh Gilbert, William Parker, and George Popham, and to every of them, and to the said several Companies, Plantations, and Colonies, that they, and every of them, shall and may, at all and every time and times hereafter, have, take, and lead in the said Voyage, and for and towards the said several Plantations, and Colonies, and to travel thitherward, and to abide and inhabit there, in every the said Colonies and Plantations, such and so many of our Subjects, as shall willingly accompany them or any of them, in the said Voyages and Plantations; With sufficient Shipping, and Furniture of Armour, Weapons, Ordinance, Powder, Victual, and all other things, necessary for the said Plantations, and for their Use and Defence there: PROVIDED always, that none of the said Persons be such, as shall hereafter be specially restrained by Us, our Heirs, or Successors.

Moreover, we do, by these Presents, for Us, our Heirs, and Successors, GIVE AND GRANT Licence unto the said Sir Thomas Gates, Sir George Somers, Richard Hackluit, Edward-Maria Wingfield, Thornas Hanham, Ralegh Gilbert, William Parker, and George Popham, and to every of the said Colonies, that they, and every of them, shall and may, from time to time, and at all times forever hereafter, for their several Defences, encounter, expulse, repel, and resist, as well by Sea as by Land, by all Ways and Means whatsoever, all and every such Person or Persons, as without the especial Licence of the said several Colonies and Plantations, shall attempt to inhabit within the said several Precincts and Limits of the said several Colonies and Plantations, or any of them, or that shall enterprise or attempt, at any time hereafter, the Hurt, Detriment, or Annoyance, of the said several Colonies or Plantations:

Giving and granting, by these Presents, unto the said Sir Thomas Gates, Sir George Somers, Richard Hackluit, Edward-Maria Wingfield, Thornas Hanham, Ralegh Gilbert, William Parker, and George Popham, and their Associates of the said second Colony, arid to every of them, from time to time, and at all times for ever here-after, Power and Authority to take and surprise, by all Ways and Means whatsoever, all and every Person and Persons, with their Ships, Vessels, Goods, and other Furniture, which shall be found trafficking, into any Harbour or Harbours, Creek or Creeks, or Place, within the Limits ok Precincts of the said several Colonies and Plantations, not being of the same Colony, until such time, as they, being of any Realms, or Dominions under our Obedience, shall pay, or agree to pay, to the Hands of the Treasurer of that Colony, within whose Limits and Precincts they shall so traffick, two and a half upon every Hundred, of any thing so by them trafficked, bought, or sold; And being Strangers, and not Subjects under our Obeysance, until they shall pay five upon every Hundred, of such Wares and Merchandises, as they shall traffick, buy, or sell, within the Precincts of the said several Colonies, wherein they shall so traffick, buy, or sell, as aforesaid; WHICH Sums of Money, or Benefit, as aforesaid, for and during the Space of one and twenty Years, next ensuing the Date hereof, shall be wholly emploied to the Use, Benefit, and Behoof of the said several Plantations, where such Traffick shall be made; And after the said one and twenty Years ended, the same shall be taken to the Use of Us, our Heires, and Successors, by such Officers and Ministers as by Us, our Heirs, and Successors, shall be thereunto assigned or appointed.

And we do further, by these Presents, for Us, our Heirs and Successors, GIVE AND GRANT unto the said Sir Thomas Gates, Sir George Sommers, Richard Hackluit, and Edward-Maria Wingfield, and to their Associates of the said first Colony and Plantation, and to the said Thomas Hanham, Ralegh Gilbert, William Parker, and George Popham, and their Associates of the said second Colony and Plantation, that they, and every of them, by their Deputies, Ministers, and Factors, may transport the Goods, Chattels, Armour, Munition, and Furniture, needful to be used by them, for their said Apparel, Food, Defence, or otherwise in Respect of the said Plantations, out of our Realms of England and Ireland, and all other our Dominions, from time to time, for and during the Time of seven Years, next ensuing the Date hereof, for the better Relief of the said several Colonies and Plantations, without any Customs, Subsidy, or other Duty, unto Us, our Heirs, or Successors, to be yielded or payed for the same.

Also we do, for Us, our Heirs, and Successors, DECLARE, by these Presents, that all and every the Persons being our Subjects, which shall dwell and inhabit within every or any of the said several Colonies and Plantations, and every of their children, which shall happen to be born within any of the Limits and Precincts of the said several Colonies and Plantations, shall HAVE and enjoy all Liberties, Franchises, and Immunities, within any of our other Dominions, to all Intents and Purposes, as if they had been abiding and born, within this our Realm of England, or any other of our said Dominions.

Moreover, our gracious Will and Pleasure is, and we do, by these Presents, for Us, our Heirs, and Successors, declare and set forth, that if any Person or Persons, which shall be of any of the said Colonies and Plantations, or any other, which shall trick to the said Colonies and Plantations, or any of them, shall, at any time or times hereafter, transport any Wares, Merchandises, or Commodities, out of any of our Dominions, with a Pretence to land, sell, or otherwise dispose of the same, within any [of] the Limits and Precincts of any of the said Colonies and Plantations, and yet nevertheless, being at Sea, or after he hath landed the same within any of the said

Colonies and Plantations, shall carry the same into any other Foreign Country, with a Purpose there to sell or dispose of the same, without the Licence of Us, our Heirs, and Successors, in that Behalf first had and obtained; That then, all the Goods and Chattels of such Person or Persons, so offending and transporting together with the said Ship or Vessel, wherein such Transportation was made, shall be forfeited to Us, our Heirs, and Successors.

Provided always, and our Will and Pleasure is, and we do hereby declare to all Christian Kings, Princes, and States, that if any Person or Persons which shall hereafter be of any of the said several Colonies and Plantations, or any other, by his, their, or any of their Licence and Appointment, shall, at any Time or Times hereafter, rob or spoil, by Sea or Land, or do any Act of unjust and unlawful Hostility to any the Subjects of Us, our Heirs, or Successors, or any the Subjects of any King, Prince, Ruler, Governor, or State, being then in League or Amitie with Us, our Heirs, or Successors, and that upon such Injury, or upon just Complaint of such Prince, Ruler, Governor, or State, or their Subjects, We, our Heirs, or Successors, shall make open Proclamation, within any of the Ports of our Realm of England, commodious for that purpose, That the said Person or Persons, having committed any such robbery, or Spoil, shall, within the term to be limited by such Proclamations, make full Restitution or Satisfaction of all such Injuries done, so as the said Princes, or others so complaining, may hold themselves fully satisfied and contented; And, that if the said Person or Persons, having committed such Robery or Spoil, shall not make, or cause to be made Satisfaction accordingly, within such Time so to be limited, That then it shall be lawful to Us, our Heirs, and Successors, to put the said Person or Persons, having committed such Robbery or Spoil, and their Procurers, Abettors, and Comforters, out of our Allegiance and Protection; And that it shall be lawful and free, for all Princes, and others to pursue with hostility the said offenders, and every of them, and their and every of their Procurers, Aiders, abettors, and comforters, in that behalf.

And finally, we do for Us, our Heirs, and Successors, and agree, to and with the said Sir Thomas Gates, Sir George Somers, Richard Hackluit, Edward-Maria Wingfield, and all others of the said first colony, that We, our Heirs and Successors, upon Petition in that Behalf to be made, shall, by Letters Patent under the Great Seal of England, GIVE and GRANT unto such Persons, their Heirs and Assigns, as the Council of that Colony, or the most part of then, shall, for that Purpose, nominate and assign all the lands, Tenements, and Hereditaments, which shall be within the Precincts limited for that Colony, as is aforesaid, To BE HOLDEN of Us, our heirs and Successors, as of our Manor at East-Greenwich, in the County of Kent, in free and common Soccage only, and not in Capite:

And do in like Manner, Grant and Agree, for Us, our Heirs and Successors, to and with the said Thomas Hanham, Ralegh Gilbert, William Parker, and George Popham, and all others of the said second Colony, That We, our Heirs, and Successors, upon Petition in that Behalf to be made, shall, by Letters-Patent, under the Great Seal of England, GIVE and GRANT, unto such Persons, their Heirs and Assigns, as the Council of that Colony, or the most Part of them, shall for that Purpose nominate and assign, all the Lands, Tenements, and Hereditaments, which shall be within the Precincts limited for that Colony, as is aforesaid, To BE nodded of Us, our Heires, and Successors, as of our Manor of East-Greenwich, in the County of Kent, in free and common Soccage only, and not in Capite.

All which Lands, Tenements, and Hereditaments, so to be passed by the said several Letters-Patent, shall be sufficient Assurance from the said Patentees, so distributed and divided amongst the Undertakers for the Plantation of the said several Colonies, and such as shall make their Plantations in either of the said several Colonies, in such Manner and Form, and for such Estates, as shall be ordered and set down by the Council of the said Colony, or the most part of them, respectively, within which the same Lands, Tenements, and Hereditaments shall lye or be; Although express Mention of the true yearly Value or Certainty of the Premises, or any of them, or of any other Gifts or Grants, by Us or any of our Progenitors or Predecessors, to the aforesaid Sir Thomas Gates, Knt. Sir George Somers, Knt. Richard Hackluit, Edward-Maria Wingfield, Thomas Hanham, Ralegh Gilbert, William Parker, and George Popham, or any of them, heretofore made, in these Presents, is not made; Or any Statute, Act, Ordinance, or Provision, Proclamation, or Restraint, to the contrary hereof had, made, ordained, or any other Thing, Cause, or Matter whatsoever, in any wise notwithstanding. IN Wetness whereof, we have caused these our Letters to be made Patent; Witness Ourself at Westminster, the tenth Day of April, in the fourth Year of our Reign of England, France, and Ireland, and of Scotland the nine and thirtieth.

LUKIN

Per breve de private Sigillo.

2

Mayflower Compact, 1620

The Mayflower Compact was an agreement made by the settlers at Plymouth in order to preserve order in the community. The Pilgrims originally planned to settle in Virginia, but fate cast them to the north in what is now Massachusetts, then far outside the authority and protection of the British government. Such compact as these were common in New England communities to give their new villages a sense of purpose and community and became representative of the new idea of government in the English colonies: governments created by the people.

Agreement Between the Settlers at New Plymouth, 1620

IN THE NAME OF GOD, AMEN. We, whose names are underwritten, the Loyal Subjects of our dread Sovereign Lord King *James*, by the Grace of God, of *Great Britain*, *France*, and *Ireland*, King, *Defender of the Faith*, &c. Having undertaken for

Kermit Hall, ed., "Mayflower Compact," *Major Problems in American Constitutional History*, Vol. I (Lexington, MA: D. C. Heath, 1992): 35–36.

the Glory of God, and Advancement of the Christian Faith, and the Honour of our King and Country, a Voyage to plant the first Colony in the northern Parts of *Virginia*; Do by these Presents, solemnly and mutually, in the Presence of God and one another, covenant and combine ourselves together into a civil Body Politick, for our better Ordering and Preservation, and Furtherance of the Ends aforesaid: And by Virtue hereof do enact, constitute, and frame, such just and equal Laws, Ordinances, Acts, Constitutions, and Officers, from time to time, as shall be thought most meet and convenient for the general Good of the Colony; unto which we promise all due Submission and Obedience. IN WITNESS whereof we have hereunto subscribed our names at *Cape-Cod* the eleventh of November, in the Reign of our Sovereign Lord King *James*, of *England, France*, and *Ireland*, the eighteenth, and of *Scotland* the fifty-fourth, *Anno Domini*; 1620.

Mr. John Carver,	Mr. William Bradford,	Mr. Edward Winslow,
Mr. William Brewster,	Isaac Allerton,	Myles Standish,
John Alden,	John Turner,	Francis Eaton,
James Chilton,	John Craxton,	John Billington,
Joses Fletcher,	John Goodman,	Mr. Samuel Fuller,
Mr. Christopher Martin,	Mr. William Mullins,	Mr. William White,
Mr. Richard Warren,	John Howland,	Mr. Steven Hopkins,
Digery Priest,	Thomas Williams,	Gilbert Winslow,
Edmund Margesson,	Peter Brown,	Richard Britteridge,
George Soule,	Edward Tilly,	John Tilly,
Francis Cooke,	Thomas Rogers,	Thomas Tinker,
John Ridgdale,	Edward Fuller,	Richard Clark,
Richard Gardiner,	Mr. John Allerton,	Thomas English,
Edward Doten,	Edward Liester.	

3

Fundamental Orders of Connecticut, 1639

The Fundamental Orders of Connecticut served as the constitution for the colony. It specified the offices, terms, and duties for the officers of the colony. Amplifying the British concept of constitutional law and limitations on the powers of government, the Connecticut colony specified these restrictions to protect the freedoms of the people and to ensure that the powers of the government would not be abused. Although the government may make and enforce the laws, it too is subject to the law.

Kermit Hall, ed., "Fundamental Orders of Connecticut, 1639," *Major Problems in American Constitutional History*, Vol. I (Lexington, MA: D. C. Heath, 1992): 36–38.

For as much as it hath pleased Almighty God by the wise disposition of his divine providence so to order and dispose of things that we the Inhabitants and Residents of Windsor, Hartford and Wethersfield are now cohabiting and dwelling in and upon the River of Connectecotte and the lands thereunto adjoining; and well knowing where a people are gathered together the word of God requires that to maintain the peace and union of such a people there should be an orderly and decent Government established according to God, to order and dispose of the affairs of the people at all seasons as occasion shall require; do therefore associate and conjoin ourselves to be as one Public State or Commonwealth; and do for ourselves and our successors and such as shall be adjoined to us at any time hereafter, enter into Combination and Confederation together, to maintain and preserve the liberty and purity of the Gospel of our Lord Jesus which we now profess, as also, the discipline of the Churches, which according to the truth of the said Gospel is now practiced amongst us; as also in our civil affairs to be guided and governed according to such Laws, Rules, Orders and Decrees as shall be made, ordered, and decreed as followeth:

1. It is Ordered, sentenced, and decreed, that there shall be yearly two General Assemblies or Courts, the one the second Thursday in April, the other the second Thursday in September following; the first shall be called the Court of Election, wherein shall be yearly chosen from time to time, so many Magistrates and other public Officers as shall be found requisite: Whereof one to be chosen Governor for the year ensuing and until another be chosen, and no other Magistrate to be chosen for more than one year: provided always there be six chosen besides the Governor, which being chosen and sworn according to an Oath recorded for that purpose, shall have the power to administer justice according to the Laws here established, and for want thereof, according to the Rule of the Word of God; which choice shall be made by all that are admitted freemen and have taken the Oath of Fidelity, and do cohabit within this Jurisdiction having been admitted Inhabitants by the major part of the Town wherein they live or the major part of such as shall be then present.

2. It is Ordered, sentenced, and decreed, that the election of the aforesaid Magistrates shall be in this manner: every person present and qualified for choice shall bring in (to the person deputed to receive them) one single paper with the name of him written in it whom he desires to have Governor, and that he that hath the greatest number of papers shall be Governor for that year. And the rest of the Magistrates or public officers to be chosen in this manner: the Secretary for the time being shall first read the names of all that are to be put to choice and then shall severally nominate them distinctly, and every one that would have the person nominated to be chosen shall bring in one single paper written upon, and he that would not have him chosen shall bring in a blank; and every one that hath more written papers than blanks shall be a Magistrate for that year; which papers shall be received and told by one or more that shall be then chosen by the court and sworn to be faithful therein; but in case there should not be six chosen as aforesaid, besides the Governor, out of those which are nominated, than he or they which have the most writen papers shall be a Magistrate or Magistrates for the ensuing year, to make up the aforesaid number.

3. It is Ordered, sentenced, and decreed, that the Secretary shall not nominate any person, nor shall any person be chosen newly into the Magistracy which was not

propounded in some General Court before, to be nominated the next election; and to that end it shall be lawful for each of the Towns aforesaid by their deputies to nominate any two whom they conceive fit to be put to election; and the Court may add so many more as they judge requisite.

4. It is Ordered, sentenced, and decreed, that no person be chosen Governor above once in two years, and that the Governor be always a member of some approved Congregation, and formerly of the Magistracy within this Jurisdiction; and that all the Magistrates, Freemen of this Commonwealth; and that no Magistrate or other public officer shall execute any part of his or their office before they are severally sworn, which shall be done in the face of the court if they be present, and in case of absence by some deputed for that purpose.

5. It is Ordered, sentenced, and decreed, that to the aforesaid Court of Election the several Towns shall send their deputies, and when the Elections are ended they may proceed in any public service as at other Courts. Also the other General Court in September shall be for making of laws, and any other public occasion, which concerns the good of the Commonwealth.

6. It is Ordered, sentenced, and decreed, that the Governor shall, either by himself or by the Secretary, send out summons to the Constables of every Town for the calling of these two standing Courts one month at least before their several times: And also if the Governor and the greatest part of the Magistrates see cause upon any special occasion to call a General Court, they may give order to the Secretary so to do within fourteen days' warning: And if urgent necessity so required, upon a shorter notice, giving sufficient grounds for it to the deputies when they meet, or else be questioned for the same; And if the Governor and major part of Magistrates shall either neglect or refuse to call the two General standing Courts or either of them, as also at other times when the occasions of the Commonwealth require, the Freemen thereof, or the major part of them, shall petition to them so to do; if then it be either denied or neglected, the said Freemen, or the major part of them, shall have the power to give order to the Constables of the several Towns to do the same, and so may meet together, and choose to themselves a Moderator, and may proceed to do any act of power which any other General Courts may.

7. It is Ordered, sentenced, and decreed, that after there are warrants given out for any of the said General Courts, the Constable or Constables of each Town, shall forthwith give notice distinctly to the inhabitants of the same, in some public assembly or by going or sending from house to house, that at a place and time by him or them limited and set, they meet and assemble themselves together to elect and choose certain deputies to be at the General Court then following to agitate the affairs of the Commonwealth; which said deputies shall be chosen by all that are admitted Inhabitants in the several Towns and have taken the oath of fidelity; provided that none be chosen a Deputy for any General Court which is not a Freeman of this Commonwealth.

The aforesaid deputies shall be chosen in manner following: every person that is present and qualified as before expressed, shall bring the names of such, written in several papers, as they desire to have chosen for that employment, and these three or four, more or less, being the number agreed on to be chosen for that time, that have the greatest number of papers written for them shall be deputies for that Court; whose names shall be endorsed on the back side of the warrant and returned into the Court, with the Constable or Constables' hand unto the same.

8. It is Ordered, sentenced, and decreed, that Windsor, Hartford, and Wethersfield shall have power, each Town, to send four of their Freemen as their deputies to every General Court; and Whatsoever other Town shall be hereafter added to this Jurisdiction, they shall send so many deputies as the Court shall judge meet, a reasonable proportion to the number of Freemen that are in the said Towns being to be attended therein; which deputies shall have the power of the whole Town to give their votes and allowance to all such laws and orders as may be for the public good, and unto which the said Towns are to be bound.

9. It is Ordered, sentenced, and decreed, that the deputies thus chosen shall have power and liberty to appoint atime and a place of meeting together before any General Court, to advise and consult of all such things as may concern the good of the public, as also to examine their own Elections, whether according to the order, and if they or the greatest part of them find any election to be illegal they may seclude such for present from their meeting, and return the same and their reasons to the Court; and if it be proved true, the Court may fine the party or parties so intruding, and the Town, if they see cause, and give out a warrant to go to a new election in a legal way, either in part or in whole. Also the said deputies shall have power to fine any that shall be disorderly at their meetings, or for not coming in due time or place according to appointment; and they may return the said fines into the Court if it be refused to be paid, and the Treasurer to take notice of it, and to escheat or levy the same as he does other fines.

10. It is Ordered, sentenced, and decreed, that every General Court, except such as through neglect of the Governor and the greatest part of the Magistrates the Freemen themselves do call, shall consist of the Governor, or some one chosen to moderate the Court, and four other Magistrates at least, with the major part of the deputies of the several Towns legally chosen; and in case the Freemen, or major part of them, through neglect or refusal of the Governor and major part of the Magistrates, shall call a Court, it shall consist of the major part of Freemen that are present or their deputiues, with a Moderator chosen by them: In which said General Courts shall consist the supreme power of the Commonwealth, and they only shall have power to make laws or repeal them, to grant levies, to admit of Freemen, dispose of lands undisposed of, to several Towns or persons, and also shall have power to call either Court or Magistrate or any other person whatsoever into question for any misdemeanor, and may for just causes displace or deal otherwise according to the nature of the offense; and also may deal in any other matter that concerns the good of this Commonwealth, except election of Magistrates, which shall be done by the whole body of Freemen.

In which Court the Governor or Moderator shall have power to order the Court, to give liberty of speech, and silence unseasonable and disorderly speakings, to put all things to vote, and in case the vote be equal to have the casting voice. But none of these Courts shall be adjourned or dissolved without the consent of the major part of the Court.

11. It is Ordered, sentenced, and decreed, that when any General Court upon the occasions of the Commonwealth have agreed upon any sum, or sums of money to be levied upon the several Towns within this Jurisdiction, that a committee be chosen to set out and appoint what shall be the proportion of every Town to pay of the said levy, provided the committee be made up of an equal number out of each Town.

14th January 1639 the 11 Orders above said are voted.

ROGER WILLIAMS  **4**

A Plea for Religious Liberty, 1646

Roger Williams was banished in 1636 for criticizing the Puritan hierarchs who controlled the religious and political life of the Massachusetts Bay Colony. Williams, in response, founded Rhode Island as a haven for religious dissenters. It became the first of the English colonies to practice freedom of religion for individuals. The early colonies, such as Massachusetts and Plymouth (Puritan), were founded by religious communities for the purpose of expanding that particular faith. Williams called for the right of individuals to decide religious issues for themselves. Because of this, Rhode Island was freed from religious dissent and became the only colony where Jews could openly practice their faith. This tract is written as a dialogue between Truth and Peace, arguing that persecuting others for differing religious views is inherently unchristian.

First, that the blood of so many hundred thousand souls of Protestants and Papists, spilt in the wars of present and former ages, for their respective consciences, is not required nor accepted by Jesus Christ the Prince of Peace.

Secondly, pregnant scriptures and arguments are throughout the work proposed against the doctrine of persecution for cause of conscience.

Thirdly, satisfactory answers are given to scriptures, and objections produced by Mr. Calvin, Beza, Mr. Cotton, and the ministers of the New English churches and others former and later, tending to prove the doctrine of persecution for cause of conscience.

Fourthly, the doctrine of persecution for cause of conscience is proved guilty of all the blood of the souls crying for vengeance under the altar.

Fifthly, all civil states with their officers of justice in their respective constitutions and administrations are proved essentially civil, and therefore not judges, governors, or defenders of the spiritual or Christian state and worship.

Sixthly, it is the will and command of God that (since the coming of his Son the Lord Jesus) a permission of the most paganish, Jewish, Turkish, or antichristian consciences and worships, be granted to all men in all nations and countries; and they are only to be fought against with that sword which is only (in soul matters) able to conquer, to wit, the sword of God's Spirit, the Word of God.

Seventhly, the state of the Land of Israel, the kings and people thereof in peace and war, is proved figurative and ceremonial, and no pattern nor president for any kingdom or civil state in the world to follow.

Eighthly, God requireth not a uniformity of religion to be enacted and enforced in any civil state; which enforced uniformity (sooner or later) is the greatest occasion of civil war, ravishing of conscience, persecution of Christ Jesus in his servants, and of the hypocrisy and destruction of millions of souls.

Ninthly, in holding an enforced uniformity of religion in a civil state, we must necessarily disclaim our desires and hopes of the Jew's conversion to Christ.

Tenthly, an enforced uniformity of religion throughout a nation or civil state, confounds the civil and religious, denies the principles of Christianity and civility, and that Jesus Christ is come in the flesh.

Eleventhly, the permission of other consciences and worships than a state professeth only can (according to God) procure a firm and lasting peace (good assurance being taken according to the wisdom of the civil state for uniformity of civil obedience from all forts).

Twelfthly, lastly, true civility and Christianity may both flourish in a state or kingdom, notwithstanding the permission of divers and contrary consciences, either of Jew or Gentile....

TRUTH. I acknowledge that to molest any person, Jew or Gentile, for either professing doctrine, or practicing worship merely religious or spiritual, it is to persecute him, and such a person (whatever his doctrine or practice be, true or false) suffereth persecution for conscience.

But withal I desire it may be well observed that this distinction is not full and complete: for beside this that a man may be persecuted because he holds or practices what he believes in conscience to be a truth (as Daniel did, for which he was cast into the lions' den, Dan. 6), and many thousands of Christians, because they durst not cease to preach and practice what they believed was by God commanded, as the Apostles answered (Acts 4 & 5), I say besides this a man may also be persecuted, because he dares not be constrained to yield obedience to such doctrines and worships as are by men invented and appointed....

Dear TRUTH, I have two sad complaints:

First, the most sober of the witnesses, that dare to plead thy cause, how are they charged to be mine enemies, contentious, turbulent, seditious?

Secondly, shine enemies, though they speak and rail against thee, though they outrageously pursue, imprison, banish, kill thy faithful witnesses, yet how is all vermilion'd o'er for justice against the heretics? Yea, if they kindle coals, and blow the flames of devouring wars, that leave neither spiritual nor civil state, but burn up branch and root, yet how do all pretend an holy war? He that kills, and he that's killed, they both cry out: "It is for God, and for their conscience."

'Tis true, nor one nor other seldom dare to plead the mighty Prince Christ Jesus for their author, yet (both Protestant and Papist) pretend they have spoke with Moses and the Prophets who all, say they (before Christ came), allowed such holy persecutions, holy wars against the enemies of holy church.

TRUTH. Dear PEACE (to ease thy first complaint), 'tis true, thy dearest sons, most like their mother, peacekeeping, peacemaking sons of God, have borne and still must bear the blurs of troublers of Israel, and turners of the world upside down. And 'tis true again, what Solomon once spake: "The beginning of strife is as when one letteth out water, therefore (saith he) leave off contention before it be meddled with. This caveat should keep the banks and sluices firm and strong, that strife, like a breach of waters, break not in upon the sons of men."

Yet strife must be distinguished: It is necessary or unnecessary, godly or Ungodly, Christian or unchristian, etc.

It is unnecessary, unlawful, dishonorable, ungodly, unchristian, in most cases in the world, for there is a possibility of keeping sweet peace in most cases, and, if it be possible, it is the express command of God that peace be kept (Rom. 13).

Again, it is necessary, honorable, godly, etc., with civil and earthly weapons to defend the innocent and to rescue the oppressed from the violent paws and jaws of oppressing persecuting Nimrods (Psal. 73; Job 29).

It is as necessary, yea more honorable, godly, and Christian, to fight the fight of faith, with religious and spiritual artillery, and to contend earnestly for the faith of Jesus, once delivered to the saints against all opposers, and the gates of earth and hell, men or devils, yea against Paul himself, or an angel from heaven, if he bring any other faith or doctrine....

PEACE. I add that a civil sword (as woeful experience in all ages has proved) is so far from bringing or helping forward an opposite in religion to repentance that magistrates sin grievously against the work of God and blood of souls by such proceedings. Because as (commonly) the sufferings of false and antichristian teachers harden their followers, who being blind, by this means are occasioned to tumble into the ditch of hell after their blind leaders, with more inflamed zeal of lying confidence. So, secondly, violence and a sword of steel begets such an impression in the sufferers that certainly they conclude (as indeed that religion cannot be true which needs such instruments of violence to uphold it so) that persecutors are far from soft and gentle commiseration of the blindness of others....

For (to keep to the similitude which the Spirit useth, for instance) to batter down a stronghold, high wall, fort, tower, or castle, men bring not a first and second admonition, and after obstinacy, excommunication, which are spiritual weapons concerning them that be in the church: nor exhortation to repent and be baptized, to believe in the Lord Jesus, etc., which are proper weapons to them that be without, etc. But to take a stronghold, men bring cannons, culverins, saker, bullets, powder, muskets, swords, pikes, etc., and these to this end are weapons effectual and proportionable.

On the other side, to batter down idolatry, false worship, heresy, schism, blindness, hardness, out of the soul and spirit, it is vain, improper, and unsuitable to bring those weapons which are used by persecutors, stocks, whips, prisons, swords, gibbets, stakes, etc. (where these seem to prevail with some cities or kingdoms, a stronger force sets up again, what a weaker pull'd down), but against these spiritual strongholds in the souls of men, spiritual artillery and weapons are proper, which are mighty through God to subdue and bring under the very thought to obedience, or else to bind fast the soul with chains of darkness, and lock it up in the prison of unbelief and hardness to eternity....

PEACE. I pray descend now to the second evil which you observe in the answerer's position, viz., that it would be evil to tolerate notorious evildoers, seducing teachers, etc.

TRUTH. I say the evil is that he most improperly and confusedly joins and couples seducing teachers with scandalous livers.

PEACE. But is it not true that the world is full of seducing teachers, and is it not true that seducing teachers are notorious evildoers?

TRUTH. I answer, far be it from me to deny either, and yet in two things I shall discover the great evil of this joining and coupling seducing teachers, and scandalous livers as one adequate or proper object of the magistrate's care and work to suppress and punish.

First, it is not an homogeneal (as we speak) but an hetergeneal commixture or joining together of things most different in kinds and natures, as if they were both of one consideration....

TRUTH. I answer, in granting with Brentius that man hath not power to make laws to bind conscience, he overthrows such his tenent and practice as restrain men from their worship, according to their conscience and belief, and constrain them to such worships (though it be out of a pretense that they are convinced) which their own souls tell them they have no satisfaction nor faith in.

Secondly, whereas he affirms that men may make laws to see the laws of God observed.

I answer, God needeth not the help of a material sword of steel to assist the sword of the Spirit in the affairs of conscience, to those men, those magistrates, yea that commonwealth which makes such magistrates, must needs have power and authority from Christ Jesus to fit judge and to determine in all the great controversies concerning doctrine, discipline, government, etc.

And then I ask whether upon this ground it must not evidently follow that:

Either there is no lawful common earth nor civil state of men in the world, which is not qualified with this spiritual discerning (and then also that the very commonweal hath more light concerning the church of Christ than the church itself).

Or, that the commonweal and magistrates thereof must judge and punish as they are persuaded in their own belief and conscience (be their conscience paganish, Turkish, or antichristian) what is this but to confound heaven and earth together, and not only to take away the being of Christianity out of the world, but to take away all civility, and the world out of the world, and to lay all upon heaps of confusion? ....

PEACE. The fourth head is the proper means of both these powers to attain their ends.

First, the proper means whereby the civil power may and should attain its end are only political, and principally these five.

First, the erecting and establishing what form of civil government may seem in wisdom most meet, according to general rules of the world, and state of the people.

Secondly, the making, publishing, and establishing of wholesome civil laws, not only such as concern civil justice, but also the free passage of true religion; for outward civil peace ariseth and is maintained from them both, from the latter as well as from the former.

Civil peace cannot stand entire, where religion is corrupted (2 Chron. 15. 3. 5. 6; and Judges 8). And yet such laws, though conversant about religion, may still be counted civil laws, as, on the contrary, an oath cloth still remain religious though conversant about civil matters.

Thirdly, election and appointment of civil officers to see execution to those laws.

Fourthly, civil punishments and rewards of transgressors and observers of these laws.

Fifthly, taking up arms against the enemies of civil peace.

Secondly, the means whereby the church may and should attain her ends are only ecclesiastical, which are chiefly five.

First, setting up that form of church government only of which Christ hath given them a pattern in his Word.

Secondly, acknowledging and admitting of no lawgiver in the church but Christ and the publishing of His laws.

Thirdly, electing and ordaining of such officers only, as Christ hath appointed in his Word.

Fourthly, to receive into their fellowship them that are approved and inflicting spiritual censures against them that o end.

Fifthly, prayer and patience in suffering any evil from them that be without, who disturb their peace.

So that magistrates, as magistrates, have no power of setting up the form of church government, electing church officers, punishing with church censures, but to see that the church does her duty herein. And on the other side, the churches as churches, have no power (though as members of the commonweal they may have power) of erecting or altering forms of civil government, electing of civil officers, inflicting civil punishments (no not on persons excommunicate) as by deposing magistrates from their civil authority, or withdrawing the hearts of the people against them, to their laws, no more than to discharge wives, or children, or servants, from due obedience to their husbands, parents, or masters; or by taking up arms against their magistrates, though he persecute them for conscience: for though members of churches who are public officers also of the civil state may suppress by force the violence of usurpers, as Iehoiada did Athaliah, yet this they do not as members of the church but as officers of the civil state.

TRUTH. Here are divers considerable passages which I shall briefly examine, so far as concerns our controversy.

First, whereas they say that the civil power may erect and establish what form of civil government may seem in wisdom most meet, I acknowledge the proposition to be most true, both in itself and also considered with the end of it, that a civil government is an ordinance of God, to conserve the civil peace of people, so far as concerns their bodies and goods, as formerly hath been said.

But from this grant I infer (as before hath been touched) that the sovereign, original, and foundation of civil power lies in the people (whom they must needs mean by the civil power distinct from the government set up). And, if so, that a people may erect and establish what form of government seems to them most meet for their civil condition; it is evident that such governments as are by them erected and established have no more power, nor for no longer time, than the civil power or people consenting and agreeing shall betrust them with. This is clear not only in reason but in the experience of all commonweals, where the people are not deprived of their natural freedom by the power of tyrants.

And, if so, that the magistrates receive their power of governing the church from the people, undeniably it follows that a people, as a people, naturally consider (of what nature or nation soever in Europe, Asia, Africa, or America), have fundamentally and originally, as men, a power to govern the church, to see her do her duty, to correct her, to redress, reform, establish, etc. And if this be not to pull God and Christ and Spirit out of heaven, and subject them unto natural, sinful, inconstant men, and so consequently to Satan himself, by whom all peoples naturally are guided, let heaven and earth judge....

PEACE. Some will here ask: What may the magistrate then lawfully do with his civil horn or power in matters of religion?

TRUTH. His horn not being the horn of that unicorn or rhinoceros, the power of the Lord Jesus in spiritual cases, his sword not the two-edged sword of the spirit, the word of God (hanging not about the loins or side, but at the lips, and proceeding out of the mouth of his ministers) but of an humane and civil nature and constitution, it must consequently be of a humane and civil operation, for who knows not that operation follows constitution; And therefore I shall end this passage with this consideration:

The civil magistrate either respecteth that religion and worship which his conscience is persuaded is true, and upon which he ventures his soul; or else that and those which he is persuaded are false.

Concerning the first, if that which the magistrate believeth to be true, be true, I say he owes a threefold duty unto it:

First, approbation and countenance, a reverent esteem and honorable testimony, according to Isa. 49, and Revel. 21, with a tender respect of truth, and the professors of it.

Secondly, personal submission of his own soul to the power of the Lord Jesus in that spiritual government and kingdom, according to Matt. 18 and 1 Cor. 5.

Thirdly, protection of such true professors of Christ, whether apart, or met together, as also of their estates from violence and injury, according to Rom. 13.

Now, secondly, if it be a false religion (unto which the civil magistrate dare not adjoin, yet) he owes:

First, permission (for approbation he owes not what is evil) and this according to Matthew 13. 30 for public peace and quiet's sake.

Secondly, he owes protection to the persons of his subjects (though of a false worship), that no injury be offered either to the persons or goods of any....

...The God of Peace, the God of Truth will shortly seal this truth, and confirm this witness, and make it evident to the whole world, that the doctrine of persecution for cause of conscience, is most evidently and lamentably contrary to the doctrine of Christ Jesus the Prince of Peace. Amen.

5

Maryland Toleration Act, 1649

Maryland, founded in 1636 as a haven for Roman Catholics to escape persecution in Protestant England, soon discovered a growing population of Protestants within the colony. England had just completed a bitter civil war between the Puritan-dominated Parliament and the Anglican King Charles I. The war was waged over the issue of parliamentary rights to govern England, but an aspect of the dispute was anger over what Puritans saw as Charles I pushing the Church of England back toward a Roman Catholic theology. In addition, the German states of the Holy Roman Empire had just completed the bitter Thirty Years War, a war between Catholics and Protestants. Seeing the strife that religious issues continued to play in Europe, the Maryland assembly passed the Toleration Act, spelling out the rules for religious conduct in Maryland. One section mandates strict observance of the Sabbath day, but the most influential portion is the granting of the freedom of worship to all professing Christians. Under Maryland law, both Catholics and Protestants would be treated equally and could practice their faiths free from fear of persecution.

An Act Concerning Religion

Forasmuch as in a well governed and Christian Common Wealth matters concerning Religion and the honor of God ought in the first place to bee taken, into serious consideracion and endeavoured to bee settled, Be it therefore ordered and enacted by the Right Honourable Cecilius Lord Baron of Baltemore absolute Lord and Proprietary of this Province with the advise and consent of this Generall Assembly:

That whatsoever person or persons within this Province and the Islands thereunto helonging shall from henceforth blaspheme God, that is Curse him, or deny our Saviour Jesus Christ to bee the sonne of God, or shall deny the holy Trinity the father sonne and holy Ghost, or the Godhead of any of the said Three persons of the Trinity or the Unity of the Godhead, or shall use or utter any reprochfull Speeches, words or language concerning the said Holy Trinity, or any of the said three persons thereof, shalbe punished with death and confiscation or forfeiture of all his or her lands and goods to the Lord Proprietary and his heires.

And bee it also Enacted by the Authority and with the advise and assent aforesaid, That whatsoever person or persons shall from henceforth use or utter any reprochfull words or Speeches concerning the blessed Virgin Mary the Mother of our Saviour or the holy Apostles or Evangelists or any of them shall in such case for the first offence forfeit to the said Lord Proprietary and his heirs Lords and Proprietaries of this Province the summe of five pound Sterling or the value thereof to be Levyed on the goods and chattells of every such person soe offending, but in case such Offender or

Offenders, shall not then have goods and chattells sufficient for the satisfyeing of such forfeiture, or that the same bee not otherwise speedily satisfyed that then such Offender or Offenders shalbe publiquely whipt and bee imprisoned during the pleasure of the Lord Proprietary or the Lieutenant or cheife Governor of this Province for the time being. And that every such Offender or Offenders for every second offence shall forfeit tenne pound sterling or the value thereof to bee levyed as aforesaid, or in case such offender or Offenders shall not then have goods and chattells within this Province sufficient for that purpose then to bee publiquely and severely whipt and imprisoned as before is expressed. And that every person or persons before mentioned offending herein the third time, shall for such third Offence forfeit all his lands and Goods and bee for ever banished and expelled out of this Province.

And be it also further Enacted by the same authority advise and assent that whatsoever person or persons shall from henceforth uppon any occasion of Offence or otherwise in a reproachful manner or Way declare call or denominate any person or persons whatsoever inhabiting, residing, traffiqueing, trading or comerceing within this Province or within any the Ports, Harbors, Creeks or Havens to the same belonging an heritick, Scismatick, Idolator, puritan, Independant, Prespiterian popish prest, Jesuite, Jesuited papist, Lutheran, Calvenist, Anabaptist, Brownist, Antinomian, Barrowist, Roundhead, Separatist, or any other name or terme in a reproachfull manner relating to matter of Religion shall for every such Offence forfeit and loose the somme of tenne shillings sterling or the value thereof to bee levyed on the goods and chattells of every such Offender and Offenders, the one half thereof to be forfeited and paid unto the person and persons of whom such reproachfull words are or shalbe spoken or uttered, and the other half thereof to the Lord Proprietary and his heires Lords and Proprietaries of this Province. But if such person or persons who shall at any time utter or speake any such reproachfull words or Language shall not have Goods or Chattells sufficient and overt within this Province to bee taken to satisfie the penalty aforesaid or that the same bee not otherwise speedily satisfyed, that then the person or persons soe offending shalbe publickly whipt, and shall suffer imprisonment without baile or maineprise [bail] untill hee, shee or they respectively shall satisfy the party soe offended or greived by such reproachfull Language by asking him or her respectively forgivenes publiquely for such his Offence before the Magistrate of cheife Officer or Officers of the Towne or place where such Offence shalbe given.

And be it further likewise Enacted by the Authority and consent aforesaid That every person and persons within this Province that shall at any time hereafter prophane the Sabbath or Lords day called Sunday by frequent swearing, drunkennes or by any uncivill or disorderly recreacion, or by working on that day when absolute necessity doth not require it shall for every such first offence forfeit 2s 6d sterling or the value thereof, and for the second offence 5s sterling or the value thereof, and for the third offence and soe for every time he shall offend in like manner afterwards 10s sterling or the value thereof. And in case such offender and offenders shall not have sufficient goods or chattells within this Province to satisfy any of the said Penalties respectively hereby imposed for prophaning the Sabbath or Lords day called Sunday as aforesaid, That in Every such case the partie soe offending shall for the first and second offence in that kinde be imprisoned till hee or shee shall publickly in open Court before the cheife Commander Judge or Magistrate, of that County Towne or precinct where such offence shalbe committed acknowledg the Scandall and offence he hath in that respect given against God and the good and civill Governement of this Province, And for the third offence and for every time after shall also bee publickly whipt.

And whereas the inforceing of the conscience in matters of Religion hath frequently fallen out to be of dangerous Consequence in those commonwealthes where it hath been practised, And for the more quiett and peaceable governement of this Province, and the better to preserve mutuall Love and amity amongst the Inhabitants thereof, Be it Therefore also by the Lord Proprietary with the advise and consent of this Assembly Ordeyned and enacted (except as in this present Act is before Declared and sett forth) that noe person or persons whatsoever within this Province, or the Islands, Ports, Harbors, Creekes, or havens thereunto belonging professing to beleive in Jesus Christ, shall from henceforth bee any waies troubled, Molested or discountenanced for or in respect of his or her religion nor in the free exercise thereof within this Province or the Islands thereunto belonging nor any way compelled to the beleife or exercise of any other Religion against his or her consent, soe as they be not unfaithfull to the Lord Proprietary, or molest or conspire against the civill Governement established or to bee established in this Province under him or his heires. And that all and every person and persons that shall presume Contrary to this Act and the true intent and meaning thereof directly or indirectly either in person or estate willfully to wrong disturbe trouble or molest any person whatsoever within this Province professing to beleive in Jesus Christ for or in respect of his or her religion or the free exercise thereof within this Province other than is provided for in this Act that such person or persons soe offending, shalbe compelled to pay trebble damages to the party soe wronged or molested, and for every such offence shall also forfeit 20s sterling in money or the value thereof, half thereof for the use of the Lord Proprietary, and his heires Lords and Proprietaries of this Province, and the other half for the use of the party soe wronged or molested as aforesaid, Or if the partie soe offending as aforesaid shall refuse or bee unable to recompense the party soe wronged, or to satisfy such fyne or forfeiture, then such Offender shalbe severely punished by publick whipping and imprisonment during the pleasure of the Lord Proprietary, or his Lieutenant or cheife Governor of this Province for the tyme being without baile or maineprise.

And bee it further alsoe Enacted by the authority and consent aforesaid That the Sheriff or other Officer or Officers from time to time to bee appointed and authorized for that purpose, of the County Towne or precinct where every particular offence in this present Act conteyned shall happen at any time to bee committed and whereupon there is hereby a forfeiture fyne or penalty imposed shall from time to time distraine and seise the goods and estate of every such person soe offending as aforesaid against this present Act or any part thereof, and sell the same or any part thereof for the full satisfaccion of such forfeiture, fine, or penalty as aforesaid, Restoring unto the partie soe offending the Remainder or overplus of the said goods or estate after such satisfaccion soe made as aforesaid.

The freemen have assented.

6

Charter of Rhode Island and Providence Plantations, 1663

The Rhode Island colonial charter in many respects represented the standard description of the boundaries and government of the colony, written in the non-standardized spelling of seventeenth-century English. But Rhode Island went a step further. The charter defined that anyone within the colony had the same rights and liberties as any Englishman in Britain. It further declared that all colonists would have freedom of religion, going beyond what was even stated in English law at the time. This made Rhode Island a unique haven for religious dissenters. These colonists had declared that they were equal to those subjects who had stayed behind in England and had not given up any of their rights by moving to America. These became important defining principles for the colonies as time progressed and which were most fiercely contested in the years before the American Revolution.

CHARLES THE SECOND, by the grace of God, King of England, Scotland, France and Ireland, Defender of the Faith, &c., to all to whome these presents shall come, greeting: Whereas wee have been informed, by the humble petition of our trustie and well beloved subject, John Clarke, on the behalf of Benjamine Arnold, William Brenton, William Codington, Nicholas Easton, William Boulston, John Porter, John Smith, Samuell Gorton, John Weeks, Roger Williams, Thomas Olnie, Gregorie Dexter, John Cogeshall, Joseph Clarke, Randall Holden, John Greene, John Roome, Samuell Wildbore, William Ffield, James Barker, Richard Tew, Thomas Harris, and William Dyre, and the rest of the purchasers and ffree inhabitants of our island, called Rhode-Island, and the rest of the colonie of Providence Plantations, in the Narragansett Bay, in New-England, in America, that they, pursueing, with peaceable and loyall minces, their sober, serious and religious intentions, of goalie edifieing themselves, and one another, in the holie Christian ffaith and worshipp as they were perswaded; together with the gaineing over and conversione of the poore ignorant Indian natives, in those partes of America, to the sincere professione and obedienc of the same ffaith and worship, did, not onlie by the consent and good encouragement of our royall progenitors, transport themselves out of this kingdome of England into America, but alsoe, since their arrivall there, after their first settlement amongst other our subjects in those parts, Nor the avoideing of discorde, and those manic evills which were likely to ensue upon some of those oure subjects not beinge able to beare, in these remote parties, theire different apprehensiones in religious concernements, and in pursueance of the afforesayd ends, did once againe leave theire desireable stationies and habitationes, and with excessive labour and travell,

http://www.yale.edu/lawweb/avalon/states/ri04.htm

hazard and charge, did transplant themselves into the middest of the Indian natives, who, as wee are informed, are the most potent princes and people of all that country; where, by the good Providence of God, from whome the Plantationes have taken their name, upon theire labour and industrie, they have not onlie byn preserved to admiration, but have increased and prospered, and are seized and possessed, by purchase and consent of the said natives, to their ffull content, of such lands, islands, rivers, harbours and roades, as are verie convenient, both for plantationes and alsoe for buildings of shipps, suplye of pypestaves, and other merchandise; and which lyes verie commodious, in manie respects, for commerce, and to accommodate oure southern plantationes, and may much advance the trade of this oure realme, and greatlie enlarge the territories thereof; they haveinge, by neare neighbourhoode to and friendlie societie with the greate bodie of the Narragansett Indians, given them encouragement, of theire owne accorde, to subject themselves, theire people and lances, unto us; whereby, as is hoped, there may, in due tyme, by the blessing of God upon theire endeavours, bee layd a sure ffoundation of happinesse to all America:

And whereas, in theire humble addresse, they have ffreely declared, that it is much on their hearts (if they may be permitted), to hold forth a livlie experiment, that a most flourishing civill state may stand and best bee maintained, and that among our English subjects. with a full libertie in religious concernements; and that true pietye rightly grounded upon gospell principles, will give the best and greatest security to sovereignetye, and will lay in the hearts of men the strongest obligations to true loyaltye: Now know bee, that wee beinge willinge to encourage the hopefull undertakeinge of oure sayd lovall and loveinge subjects, and to secure them in the free exercise and enjoyment of all theire civill and religious rights, appertaining to them, as our loveing subjects; and to preserve unto them that libertye, in the true Christian ffaith and worshipp of God, which they have sought with soe much travaill, and with peaceable myndes, and lovall subjectione to our royall progenitors and ourselves, to enjoye; and because some of the people and inhabitants of the same colonie cannot, in theire private opinions, conforms to the publique exercise of religion, according to the litturgy, formes and ceremonyes of the Church of England, or take or subscribe the oaths and articles made and established in that behalfe; and for that the same, by reason of the remote distances of those places, will (as wee hope) bee noe breach of the unitie and unifformitie established in this nation: Have therefore thought ffit, and doe hereby publish, graunt, ordeyne and declare, That our royall will and pleasure is, that noe person within the sayd colonye, at any tyme hereafter, shall bee any wise molested, punished, disquieted, or called in question, for any differences in opinione in matters of religion, and doe not actually disturb the civill peace of our sayd colony; but that all and everye person and persons may, from tyme to tyme, and at all tymes hereafter, freelye and fullye have and enjoye his and theire owne judgments and consciences, in matters of religious concernments, throughout the tract of lance hereafter mentioned; they behaving themselves peaceablie and quietlie, and not useing this libertie to lycentiousnesse and profanenesse, nor to the civill injurye or outward disturbeance of others; any lawe, statute, or clause, therein contayned, or to bee contayned, usage or custome of this realme, to the contrary hereof, in any wise, notwithstanding. And that they may bee in the better capacity to defend themselves, in theire just rights and libertyes against all the enemies of the Christian ffaith, and others, in all respects, wee have further thought fit, and at the humble petition of the persons aforesayd are gratiously pleased to declare, That they shall have and enjoye the benefist of our late act of indempnity and ffree pardon, as the rest of our subjects in other our dominions and territoryes have; and to create and make them a bodye politique or corporate, with the powers and priviledges hereinafter mentioned.

And accordingely our will and pleasure is, and of our especiall grace, certaine knowledge, and meere motion, wee have ordeyned, constituted and declared, and by these presents, for us, our heires and successors, doe ordeyne, constitute and declare, That they, the sayd William Brenton, William Codington, Nicholas Easton, Benedict Arnold, William Boulston, John Porter, Samuell Gorton, John Smith, John Weekes, Roger Williams, Thomas Olneye, Gregorie Dexter, John Cogeshall, Joseph Clarke, Randall Holden, John Greene, John Roome, William Dyre, Samuell Wildbore, Richard Tew, William Ffeild, Thomas Harris, James Barker, Rainsborrow,- Williams, and John Nicksonj and all such others as now are, or hereafter shall bee admitted and made ffree of the companv and societie of our collonie of Providence Plantations, in the Narragansett Bay, in New England, shall bee, from tyme to tyme, and forever hereafter, a bodie corporate and politique, in fact and name, by the name of The Governor and Company of the English Colony of Rhode-Island and Providence Plantations, in New-England, in America; and that, by the same name, they and their successors shall and may have perpetuall succession, and shall and may bee persons able and capable, in the lawe, to sue and bee sued, to pleade and be impleaded, to answeare and bee answeared unto, to defend and to be defended, in all and singular suites, causes, quarrels, matters, actions and thinges, of what kind or nature soever; and alsoe to have, take, possessej acquire and purchase lands, tenements or hereditaments, or any goods or chattels, and the same to lease, graunt, demise, aliene, bargaine, sell and dispose of, at their owne will and pleasure, as other our liege people of this our realme of England, or anie corporation or bodie politique within the same, may be lawefully doe: And further, that they the sayd Governor and Company, and theire successors, shall and may, forever hereafter, have a common scale, to serve and use for all matters, causes, thinges and affaires, whatsoever, of them and their successors; and the same scale to alter, change, breake, and make new, from tyme to tyme, at their will and pleasure, as they shall thinke bitt.

And farther, wee will and ordeyne, and by these presents, for us, oure heires and successours, doe declare and apoynt that, for the better ordering and managing of the adaires and business of the sayd Company, and theire successours, there shall bee one Governour, one Deputie-Governour and ten Assistants, to bee from tyme to tyme, constituted, elected and chosen, out of the freemen of the sayd Company, for the tyme beinge, in such manner and fforme as is hereafter in these presents expressed; which sayd officers shall aplye themselves to take care for the best disposeinge and orderings of the generall businesse and adaires of, and concerneinge the lances and hereditaments hereinafter mentioned, to be graunted, and the plantation thereof' and the government of the people there. And for the better execution of oure royall pleasure herein, wee doe, for us, oure heires and successours, assign, name, constitute and apoynt the aforesayd Benedict Arnold to bee the first and present Governor of the sayd Company, and the sayd William Brenton, to bee the Deputy-Governor, and the sayd William Boulston, John Porter, Roger Williams, Thomas Olnie, John Smith, John Greene,

John Cogeshall, James Barker, William Ffeild, and Joseph Clarke, to bee the tenn present Assistants of the sayd Companye, to continue in the sayd severall offices, respectively, untill the first Wednesday which shall bee in the month of May now next comeing. And farther, wee will, and by these presents, for us, our heires and successes-sours, doe ordeyne and graunt, that the Governor of the sayd Company, for the tyme being, or, in his absence, by occasion of sicknesse, or otherwise, by his leave and per-mission, the Deputy-Governor, Ror the tyme being, shall and may, ffrom tyme to tyme, upon all occasions, give order Ror the assemblinge of the sayd Company and callinge them together, to consult and advise of the businesse and affaires of the sayd Company.

And that forever hereafter, twice in every year, that is to say, on every first Wednesday in the month of May, and on every last Wednesday in October, or oftener, in case it shall bee requisite, the Assistants, and such of the ffreemen of the Company, not exceedings six persons For Newport, doure persons ffor each of the respective townes of Providence, Portsmouth and Warwicke, and two persons for each other place, towne or city, whoe shall bee, from tyme to tyme, thereunto elected or deputed by the majour parte of the ffreemen of the respective townes or places For which they shall bee so elected or deputed, shall have a generall meetings or Assembly then and there to consult, advise and determine, in and about the affaires and businesse of the said Company and Plantations. And farther, wee doe, of our especiall grace, certayne knowledge, and meere motion, give and graunt unto the sayd Governour and Company of the English Colonie of Rhode-lsland and Providence Plantations, in New-England, in America, and theire successours, that the Governour, or, in his absence, or, by his permission, the Deputy-Governour of the sayd Company, for the tyme beinge, the Assistants, and such of the Freemen of the sayd Company as shall bee soe as aforesayd elected or deputed, or soe many of them as shall bee present aft such meetinge or assemblye, as a Boresayde, shall bee called the Generall Assemblye; and that they, or the greatest parte of them present, whereof the Governour or Deputy-Governour, and sixe of the Assistants, at least to bee seven, shall have, and have hereby given and graunted unto them, ffull power authority, Prom tyme tyme, and at all tymes hereafter, to apoynt, alter and change, such dayes, tymes and places of meetinge and Generall Assemblye, as theye shall thinke ffitt; and to choose, nominate, and apoynt, such and soe manye other persons as they shall thinke ffitt, and shall be willing to accept the same, to bee Free of the sayd Company and body politique, and them into the same to admits; and to elect and constitute such offices and officers, and to graunt such needfull commissions, as they shall thinke Ott and requisite, ffor the ordering, managing and dispatching of the affaires of the sayd Governour and Company, and their successours; and from tyme to tyme, to make, ordeyne, constitute or repeal, such lawes statutes, orders and ordi-nances, fformes and ceremonies of government and magistracye as to them shall seeme meete for the good nad wellfare of the sayd Company, and ffor the govern-ment and ordering of the lances and hereditaments, hereinafter mentioned to be graunted, and of the people that doe, or aft any tyme hereafter shall, inhabitt or bee within the same; soe as such lawes, ordinances and constitutiones, soe made, bee not contrary and repugnant unto, butt, as neare as may bee, agreeable to the lawes of this our realme of England, considering the nature and constitutions of the place and people there; and alsoe to apoynt, order and direct, erect and settle, such places and courts of jurisdiction, ffor the heareinge and determillinge of all actions, cases, matters and things, happening within the sayd collonie and plantations, and which shall be in dispute, and depending there, as they shall thinke ffit; and alsoe to distinguish and sett forth the severall names and titles, duties, powers and limitts, of each court, office and officer, superior and inferior; and alsoe to contrive and apoynt such formes of oaths and attestations, not repugnant, but, as neare as may bee, agreeable, as aforesayd, to the lawes and statutes of this oure realme, as are conveniente and requisite, with respect to the due administration of justice, and due execution and discharge of all offices and places of trust by the persons that shall bee therein concerned; and alsoe to regulate and order the wave and manner of all elections to offices and places of trust, and to prescribe, limits and distinguish the numbers and bounces of all places, townes or cityes, within the limitts and bounds herein after mentioned, and not herein particularlie named, who have, and shall have, the power of electing and sending of ffreemen to the sayd Generall Assembly; and alsoe to order, direct and authorize the imposing of lawfull and reasonable Dynes, mulcts, imprisonments, and executing other punishments pecuniary and corporal, upon offenders and delinquents, according to the course of other corporations within this oure kingdom of England; and agayne to alter, revoke, annull or pardon, under their common scale or otherwyse, such Dynes, mulcts, imprisonments, sentences, judgments and condemnations, as shall bee thought Bitt; and to direct, rule, order and dispose of, all other matters and things, and particularly that which relates to the makinge of purchases of the native Indians, as to them shall seeme meete; wherebv oure sayd people and inhabitants, in the sayd Plantationes, may be soe religiously, peaceably and civilly governed, as that, by theire good life and orderlie conversations, they may win and invite the native Indians of the countrie to the knowledge and obedience of the onlie true God, and Saviour of mankinde; willing, commanding and requireing, and by these presents, for us, oure heires and successours, ordeyneing and apoynting, that all such [awes, statutes, orders and ordinances, instructions, impositions and directiones, as shall bee soe made by the Governour, deputye-Governour, Assistants and Freemen. Or such number of them as aforesayd, and published in writinge, under theire common scale, shall bee carefully and duely observed, kept, performed and putt in execution, accordinge to the true intent and meaning of the same.

And these our letters patent, or the duplicate or exemplificationon thereof, shall bee to all and everie such officer, superiour or inferiour, From tyme to tyme, for the putting of the same orders, lawes, statutes, ordinances, instructions and directions, in due execution, against us, oure heires and successours, a sufficient warrant and discharge. And further, our will and pleasure is, and wee doe hereby, for US, oure heires and successours, establish and ordeyne, that yearelie, once in the yeare, forever hereafter, namely, the aforesayd Wednesday in May, and at the towne of Newport, or elsewhere, if urgent occasion doe require, the Governour, Deputy-Governour and Assistants of the sayd Company, and other officers of the sayd Company, or such of them as the Generall Assemblye shall thinke Bitt, shall bee, in the sayd Generall Court or Assembly to bee held from that daye or tyme, newely chosen for the year ensuring, by such greater part of the sayd Company, for the tyme beinge, as shall bee then and there present; and if itt shall happen that the present Governour, Deputy-Governour and Assistants, by these presents apoynted, or any such as shall hereafter be newly chosen into their roomes, or any of them, or any other the officers of the sayd Company, shall die or bee removed From his or their severall offices or places,

before the sayd generall day of election, (whom wee doe hereby declare, for any mis-
demeanour or default, to be removeable by the Governour, Assistants and Company,
or such greater parte of them, in any of the sayd publique courts, to bee assembled as
aforesayd), that then, and in every such case, it shall and may bee lawfull to and ffor
the sayd Governour, Deputy-Governour, Assistants and Company aforesayde, or
such greater parte of them, soe to bee assembled as is aforesayde, in any theire assem-
blyes, to proceede to a new election of one or more of their Company, in the roome
or place, roomes or places, of such officer or officers, soe dyeinge or removed,
according to theire discretiones; and immediately upon and after such elections or
elections made of such Governour, Deputy-Governour or Assistants, or any other
officer of the sayd Company, in manner and forme aforesayde, the authoritie, office
and power, before given to the fformer Governour, Deputy-Governour, and other
officer and officers, soe removed, in whose steade and place new shall be chosen,
shall, as to him and them, and every of them, respectively, cease and determine:

Provided, allwayes, and our will and pleasure is, that as well such as are by these
presents apoynted to bee the present Governour, Deputy-Governour and Assistants,
of the sayd Company, as those that shall succeede them, and all other officers to bee
apoynted and chosen as aforesayde, shall, before the undertakeinge the execution of
the sayd offices and places respectively, give theire solemn engagement, by oath, or
otherwyse, for the due and faythfull perfonnance of theire duties in their severall
offices and places, before such person or persons as are by these presents hereafter
apoynted to take and receive the same, that is to say: the sayd Benedict Arnold, whoa
is hereinbefore nominated and apoynted the present Governour of the sayd
Company, shall give the aforesayd engagement before William Brenton, or any two
of the sayd Assistants of the sayd Company; unto whome, wee doe by these presenter
give Bull power and authority to require and receive the same; and the sayd William
Brenton, whoe is hereby before nominated and apoynted the present Deputy-
Governour of the sayd Company, shall give the aforesaved engagement before the
sayd Benedict Arnold, or any two of the Assistants of the sayd Company; unto whome
wee doe by these presents give ffull power and authority to require and receive the
same; and the sayd William Boulston, John Porter, Roger Williams, Thomas Olneye,
John Smith, John Greene, John Cogeshall, James Barker, William Ffeild, and Joseph
Clarke, whoe are hereinbefore nominated apoynted the present Assistants of the sayd
Company, shall give the sayd engagement to theire offices and places respectively
belongeing, before the sayd Benedict Arnold and William Brenton, or one of them;
to whome, respectively wee doe hereby give dull power and authority to require,
administer or receive the same: and further, our will and pleasure is. that all and every
other future Governour or Deputy-Governour, to bee elected and chosen by vertue
of these presents, shall give the sayd engagement before two or more of the sayd
Assistants of the sayd Company ffor the tyme beinge; unto whome wee doe by these
presents give full power and authority to require, administer or receive the same; and
the sayd Assistants, and every of them, and all and every other officer or officers to
bee hereafter elected and chosen by vertue of these presents, from tyme to tyme, shall
give the like engagements, to their offices and places respectively belonging bofere
the Governour or Deputy-Governour for the tyme being; unto which sayd
Governour, or Deputy-Governour, wee doe by these presents give full power and
authority to require, administer or receive the same accordingly.

And wee doe likewise, for vs, oure heires and successours, give and graunt vnto the sayd Governour and Company and theire successours by these presents, that, for the more peaceable and orderly Government of the sayd Plantations, it shall and may bee lawfull ffor the Governour, Deputy-Governor, Assistants, and all other officers and ministers of the sayd Company, in the administration of justice, and exercise of government, in the sayd Plantations, to vse, exercise, and putt in execution, such methods, rules, orders and directions, not being contrary or repugnant to the laws and statutes of this oure realme, as have byn heretofore given, vsed and accustomed, in such cases respectively, to be putt in practice, untill att the next or some other Generall Assembly, special provision shall be made and ordeyned in the cases afore-sayd. And wee doe further, for vs. oure heroes and successours, give and graunt vnto the sayd Governour and Company, and theire successours, by these presents, that itt shall and may bee lawfull to and for the sayd Governour, or in his absence, the Deputy-Governour, and majour parte of the sayd Assistants, for the tyme being, aft any tyme when the sayd Generall Assembly is not sitting, to nominate, apoynt and constitute, such and soe many commanders, governours, and military officers, as to them shall seeme requisite, for the leading, conductinge and travneing vpp the inhab-itants of the sayd Plantations in martiall afiaires, and for the defence and safeguard of the sayd Plantations; and that itt shall and may bee lawfull to and for all and every such commander, governour and military officer, that shall bee soe as aforesayd, or by the Governour. or, in his absence, the Deputy-Governour, and six of the sayd Assistants, and majour parte of the Freemen of the sayd Company present att any Generall Assemblies, nominated, apoynted and constituted according to the tenor of his and theire respective commissions and directions, to assemble, exercise in arms, martiall array, and putt in warlyke posture, the inhabitants of the sayd collonie, For theire speciall defence and safety; and to lead and conduct the sayd inhabitants, and to encounter, expulse, expell and resist, by force of armes, as well by sea as by lance; and alsoe to kill, slay and destroy, by all fitting wayes, enterprises and meaner, whatsoever, all and every such person or persons as shall, aft any tyme hereafter, attempt or enter-prize the destruction, invasion, detriment or annoyance of the sayd inhabitants or Plantations; and to vse and exercise the lawe martiall in such cases only as occasion shall necessarily require; and to take or surprise, by all wayes and meanes whatsoever, all and every such person and persons, with theire shipp or shipps, armor, ammuni-tion or other goods of such persons, as shall, in hostile manner, invade or attempt the defeating of the sayd Plantations, or the hurt of the sand Company and inhabitants; and vpon just causes, to invade and destroy the native Indians, or other enemyes of the sayd Collony. Neverthelesse, our will and pleasure is, and wee doe hereby declare to the rest of oure Collonies in New England, that itt shall not bee lawfull ffor this our sayd Collony of Rhode-Island and Providence Plantations, in America, in New-England, to invade the natives inhabiting within the bounces and limitts of theire sayd Collonies without the knowledge and consent of the sand other Collonies. And itt is hereby declared, that itt shall not bee lawfull to or ffor the rest of the Collonies to invade or molest the native Indians, or any other inhabittants, inhabiting within the bounds and lymitts hereafter mentioned (they having subjected themselves vnto vs. and being by vs taken into our speciall protection), without the knowledge and consent of the Governour and Company of our Collony of Rhode-Island and Providence Plantations.

Alsoe our will and pleasure is, and wee doe hereby declare unto all Christian Kings, Princes and States, that if any person, which shall hereafter bee of the sayd Company or Plantations, or any other, by apoyntment of the sayd Governour and Company for the tyme beinge, shall at any tyme or tymes hereafter, rob or spoyle, by sea or land, or do any hurt, unlawfull hostillity to any of the subjects of vs, oure heires or successours, or any of the subjects of any Prince or State, beinge then in league with vs, oure heires, or successours, vpon complaint of such injury done to any such Prince or State, or theire subjects, wee, our hearer and successours, will make open proclamation within any parts of oure realme of England, ffitt ffor that purpose, that the person or persons committing any such robbery or spoyle shall, within the tyme lymitted by such proclamation, make full restitution or satisfaction of all such injuries, done or committed, soe as the sayd Prince, or others soe complaineinge, may bee fully satisfyed and contented; and if the sayd person or persons whoe shall commits any such robbery or spoyle shall not make satvsfaction, accordingly, within such tyme, soe to bee lymitted, that then wee, oure heires and successours, will putt such person or persons out of oure allegiance and protection; and that then itt shall and may bee lawefull and Tree ffor all Princes or others to prosecute, with hostillity, such offenders, and every of them, theire and every of theire procurers, adders, abettors and counsellors, in that behalfa; Provided alsoe, and oure expresse will and pleasure is, and wee doe, by these presents, For vs. our heirs and successours, ordeyne and apoynt, that these presents shall not, in any manner, hinder any of oure lovinge subjects, whatsoever, ffrom vseing and exercising the trade of ffishing vpon the coast of New-England, in America; butt that they, and every or any of them, shall have ffull and ffree power and liberty to continue and vse the trade of ffishing vpon the sayd coast, in an of the seas thereunto adjoyninge, or-any armes of the seas, or salt water, rivers and creeks, where they have been accustomed to ffish; and to build and to sett upon the waste land, belonginge to the sayd Collony and Plantations, such wharfes, stages and worke-houses as shall be necessary for the salting, drying and keepeing of theire dish, to be taken or gotten upon that coast. And ffurther, for the encouragement of the inhabitants of our sayd Collony of Providence Plantations to sett vpon the businesse of takeing whales, itt shall bee lawefull For them, or any of them, having struck whale, dubertus, or other greate ffish, itt or them, to pursue unto any parte of that coaste, and into any bay, river, cove, creeke or shoare, belonging thereto, and itt or them, vpon sayd coaste, or in the sand bay, river, cove, creeke or shoare, belonging thereto, to kill and order for the best advantage, without molestation, they makeing noe wilfull waste or spoyle, any thinge in these presents conteyned, or any other matter or thing, to the contrary notwithstanding. And further alsoe, wee are gratiously pleased, and doe hereby declare, that if any of the inhabitants of oure sayd Collony doe sett upon the plantings of vineyards (the soyle and clymate both seemeing naturally to coneurr to the production of wynes), or bee industrious in the discovery of ffishing banks, in or about the sayd Collony, wee will, ffrom tyme to tyme, give and allow all due and fitting encouragement therein, as to others in cases of tyke nature. And further, of oure more ample grace, certayne knowledge, and meere motion, wee have given and graunted, and by these presents, ffor vs. oure heires and successours, doe Five and graunt vnto the sayd Governour and Company of the English Collony of Rhode-Island and Providence Plantations, in the Narragansett Bay, in New-England in America, and to every inhabitant there, and to every person and persons trading thither, and to every such person or persons as are or shall bee Tree of the sayd Collony, full power and authority, from tyme to tyme, and aft all tymes hereafter, to take, shipp, transport and carry away, out of any of our realmes and dominions for and towards the plantation and defence of the sayd Collony, such and soe many of oure loveing subjects and strangers as shalt or will willingly accompany them in and to their sayd Collony and Plantation; except such person or persons as are or shall be therein restrained by vs. oureheires and succes-sours, or any law or statute of this realme: and also to shipp and transport all and all manner of goods, chattels, merchandises, and other things whatsoever, that are or shall bee vsefull or necessary ffor the sayd Plantations, and defence thereof, and vsually transported, and nott prohibited by any lawe or statute of this our realme; yielding and paying vnto vs. our heires and successours, such the rluties, customes and subsidies, as are or ought to bee payd or payable for the same.

And ffurther, our will and pleasure is, and wee doe, For us, our heires and succes-sours, ordeyn, declare and graunt, vnto the sayd Governour and Company, and their successours, that all and every the subjects of vs. our heires and successours, which are already planted and settled within our sayd Collony of Providence Plantations, or which shall hereafter Roe to inhabit within the sayd Collony' and all and every of theire children, which have byn borne there, or which shall happen hereafter to bee borne there, or on the sea, goeing thither, or retourneing from thence, shall have and enjoye all libertyes and immunityes of fires and naturall subjects within any the dominions of vs. our heires or successours, to all intents, constructions and purposes, whatsoever, as if they, and every of them, were borne within the realme of England. And ffurther, know ye, that wee, of our more abundant grace, certain knowledge and meere motion, have given, graunted and confirmed, and, by these presents, for vs. our heires and successours, doe give, graunt and confirms, vnto the sayd Governour and Company, and theire successours, all that parte of Our dominiones in New-England, in America, conteyneing the Nahantick and Nanhyganset Bay, and countryes and partes adjacent, bounded on the west, or westerly, to the middle or channel of a river there, commonly called and known by the name of Pawcatuck, alias Pawcawtuck river, and soe along the sayd river, as the greater or middle streame thereof reacheth or lyes vpp into the north countrye, northward, unto the head thereoof, and from thence, by a streight lyne drawn due north, vntill itt meets with the south lyne of the Massachusetts Collonie; and on the north, or northerly, by the aforesayd south or southerly lyne of the Massachusettes Collony or Plantation, and extending towards the east, or eastwardly, three English miles to the east and north-east of the most eastern and north-eastern parts of the aforesayd Narragansett Bay, as the sayd bay lyeth or extendeth itself from the ocean on the south, or southwardly, vnto the mouth of the river which runneth towards the towne of Providence, and from thence along the east-wardly side or banke of the sayd river (higher called by the name of Seacunck river), vp to the ffalls called Patuckett ffalls, being the most westwardly lyne of Plymouth Collony, and soe from the sayd Balls, in a streight lyne, due north, untill itt meete with the aforesayd line of the Massachusetts Collony; and bounded on the south by the ocean: and, in particular, the lands belonging to the townes of Providence, Pawtuxet, Warwicke; Misquammacok, alias Pawcatuck, and the rest vpon the maine land in the tract aforesayd, together with Rhode-Island, Blocke-Island, and all the rest of the islands and banks in the Narragansett Bay, and bordering vpon the coast of the tract aforesayd (Ffisher's Island only excepted), together with all firme lands, soyles,

grounds, havens. ports rivers, waters, ffishings, mines royall, and all other mynes, min-
eralls, precious stones, quarries, woods, wood-grounds, rocks' slates, and all and singular other commodities, jurisdictions, royalties, priviledges, franchises, preheminences
and hereditaments, whatsoever, within the sayd tract, bounds, lances, and islands,
aforesayd, or to them or any of them belonging, or in any wise appertaining: to have
and to hold the same, Into the sayd Governour and Company, and their successours,
forever, vpon trust, for the vse and benefit of themselves and their associates, ffreemen
of the sayd Collony, their heires and assignas, to be holden of vs. our heires and successours, as of the Mannor of East-Greenwich, in our county of Kent, in free and
comon soccage, and not in capite, nor by knight service; Wilding and paying therefor,
to vs. our heires and successours, only the Fifth part of all the oare of Fold and silver
which, from tyme to tyme, and att all tymes hereafter, shall bee there gotten, had or
obtained, in lieu and satisfaction of all services, duties, Dynes, forfeitures, made or to
be made, claimes and demands, whatsoever, to bee to vs. our heires or successours,
therefor or thereout rendered, made or paid; any graunt, or clause in a late graunt,
to the Governour and Company of Connecticutt Colony, in America, to the contrary
thereof in any wise notwithstanding; the aforesavd Pawcatuck river haven byn yielded,
after much debate, for the fixed and certain bounces betweene these our sayd
Colonies, by the agents thereof; w hoe have alsoe agreed, that the sayd Pawcatuck
river shall bee alsoe called alias Norrogansett or Narrogansett river; and to prevent
future disputes, that otherwise might arise thereby, forever hereafter shall bee construed, deemed and taken to bee the Narragansett river in our late Irrupt to
Connecticutt (colony mentioned as the easterly bounds of that Colony. And further,
our will and pleasure is, that in all matters of publique controversy which may fall out
betweene our Colonv of Providence Plantations, and the rest of our Colonies in New-
England, lit shall and may bee lawfull to and for the Governour and Company of the
sayd Colony of Providence Plantations to make their appeales therein to vs. our heirs
and successours. for redresse in such cases, within this our realme of England: and that
itt shall bee lawfull to and for the inhabitants of the sayd Colony of Providence
Plantations, without let or molestation, to passe and repasse with freedome, into and
thorough the rest of the English Collonies, vpon their lawfull and civill occasions, and
to converse, and hold commerce and trade, wit: such of the inhabitants of our other
English Collonies as shall bee willing to admits them thereunto, they behaveing themselves peaceably among them; any act, clause or sentence, in any of the sayd Collonies
provided, or that shall bee provided, to the contrary in anywise notwithstanding. And
lastly, wee doe, for vs. our heires and successours, ordeyne and graunt vnto the sayd
Governor and Company, and their successours, and by these presents, that these our
letters patent shall be firme, good, effectuall and available in all things in the lawe, to
all intents, constructions and purposes whatsoever, according to our true intent and
meaning hereinbefore declared; and shall bee construed, reputed and adjudged in all
cases most favorably on the behalfe, and for the benefit and behoofe, of the sayd
Governor and Company, and their successours; although empress mention of the true
yearly value or certainty of the premises, or any of them, or of any other gifts or
graunts by vs. or by any of our progenitors or predecessors, heretofore made to the
sayd Governor and Company of the English Colony of Rhode-Island and Providence
Plantations, in the Narragansett Bay, New-England, in America, in these presents is
not made, or any statute, act, ordinance, provision. proclamation or restriction,

heretofore had, made, enacted ordeyned or provided, or any other matter, cause or thing whatsoever, to the contrary thereof in anywise notwithstanding; In witnes whereof, wee have caused these our letters to bee made patent. Witnes our Selfe att Westminster, the eighth day of July, in the Fifteenth yeare of our reigne.

By the King:

HOWARD.

WILLIAM PENN **7**

Preface to the Frame of Government of Pennsylvania, 1682

As other colonies tried to define themselves and their laws, William Penn, a Quaker dedicated to peace and toleration, tried to establish a society in Pennsylvania that expanded the liberties of the people as much as possible, including into the rights of the accused, freedom of religion, and due process of law. These ideas made Pennsylvania a model for the other colonies and also made Pennsylvania an extremely attractive location for many colonists, making it one of the most successful and diverse colonies in the British Empire. These next three articles list the charter, the laws for Pennsylvania as designed under the 1682 charter, and a statement by Penn on why he framed the government of his colony in this manner. As a Quaker, Penn felt that he could not do otherwise and his faith directed him to treat all men with decency and charity and not to oppress them. Penn had to finish many legal details before establishing the government of Pennsylvania but believed that the men living under his government and enforcing the laws held the ultimate fate of the liberties of Pennsylvania colonists—that morality was the ultimate guarantee of liberty.

The frame of the government of the province of Pensilvania, in America: together with certain laws agreed upon in England, by the Governor arid divers freemen of the aforesaid province. To be further explained and confirmed there, by the first provincial Council, that shall be held, if they see meet.

The Preface

When the great and wise God had made the world, of all his creatures, it pleased him to chuse man his Deputy to rule it: and to fit him for so great a charge and trust, he did not only qualify him with skill and power, but with integrity to use them justly.

William Penn, "Preface to the Frame of Government of Pennsylvania," *Major Problems in American Constitutional History*, Vol. I, Kermit Hall, ed.: 38–40.

This native goodness was equally his honour and his happiness, and whilst he stood here, all went well; there was no need of coercive or compulsive means; the precept of divine love and truth, in his bosom, was the guide and keeper of his innocency. But lust prevailing against duty, made a lamentable breach upon it; and the law, that before had no power over him, took place upon him, and his disobedient posterity, that such as would not live comfortable to the holy law within, should fall under the reproof and correction of the just law without, in a Judicial administration.

This the Apostle teaches in divers of his epistles: "The law (says he) was added because of transgression:" In another place, "Knowing that the law was not made for the righteous man; but for the disobedient and ungodly, for sinners, for unholy and prophane, for murderers, for whoremongers, for them that defile themselves with mankind, and for man-stealers, for lyers, for perjured persons," &c., but this is not all, he opens and carries the matter of government a little further: "Let every soul be subject to the higher powers; for there is no power but of God. The powers that be are ordained of God: whosoever therefore resisteth the power, resisteth the ordinance of God. For rulers are not a terror to good works, but to evil: wilt thou then not be afraid of the power? do that which is good, and thou shalt have praise of the same." "He is the minister of God to thee for good." "Wherefore ye must needs be subject, not only for wrath, but for conscience sake."

This settles the divine right of government beyond exception, and that for two ends: first, to terrify evil doers: secondly, to cherish those that do well; which gives government a life beyond corruption, and makes it as durable in the world, as good men shall be. So that government seems to me a part of religion itself, a filing sacred in its institution and end. For, if it does not directly remove the cause, it crushes the effects of evil, and is as such, (though a lower, yet) an emanation of the same Divine Power, that is both author and object of pure religion; the difference lying here, that the one is more free and mental, the other more corporal and compulsive in its operations: but that is only to evil doers; government itself being otherwise as capable of kindness, goodness and charity, as a more private society. They weakly err, that think there is no other use of government, than correction, which is the coarsest part of it: daily experience tells us, that the care and regulation of many other affairs, more soft, and daily necessary, make up much of the greatest part of government; and which must have followed the peopling of the world, had Adam never fell, and will continue among men, on earth, under the highest attainments they may arrive at, by the coming of the blessed Second Adam, the Lord from heaven. Thus much of government in general, as to its rise and end.

For particular frames and models, it will become me to say little; and comparatively I will say nothing. My reasons are:

First. That the age is too nice and difficult for it; there being nothing the wits of men are more busy and divided upon. It is true, they seem to agree to the end, to wit, happiness; but, in the means, they differ, as to divine, so to this human felicity; and the cause is much the same, not always want of light and knowledge, but want of using them rightly. Men side with their passions against their reason, and their sinister interests have so strong a bias upon their minds, that they lean to them against the good of the things they know.

Secondly. I do not find a model in the world, that time, place, and some singular emergences have not necessarily altered; nor is it easy to frame a civil government, that shall serve all places alike.

Thirdly. I know what is said by the several admirers of monarchy, aristocracy and democracy, which are the rule of one, a few, and many, and are the three common ideas of government, when men discourse on the subject. But I chuse to solve the controversy with this small distinction, and it belongs to all three: Any government is free to the people under it (whatever be the frame) where the laws rule, and the people are a party to those laws, and more than this is tyranny, oligarchy, or confusion.

But, lastly, when all is said, there is hardly one frame of government in the world so ill designed by its first founders, that, in good hands, would not do well enough; and story tells us, the best, in ill ones, can do nothing that is great or good; witness the Jewish and Roman states. Governments, like clocks, go from the motion men give them; and as governments are made and moved by men, so by them they are ruined too. Wherefore governments rather depend upon men, than men upon governments. Let men be good, and the government cannot be bad; if it be ill, they will cure it. But, if men be bad, let the government be never so good, they will endeavor to warp and spoil it to their turn.

I know some say, let us have good laws, and no matter for the men that execute them: but let them consider, that though good laws do well, good men do better: for good laws may want good men, and be abolished or evaded [invaded in Franklin's print] by ill mend but good men will never want good laws, nor suffer ill ones. It is true, good laws have some awe upon-ill ministers, but that is where they have not power to escape or abolish them, and the people are generally wise and good: but a loose and depraved people (which is the question) love laws and an administration like themselves. That, therefore, which makes a good constitution, must keep it, vie: men of wisdom and virtue, qualities, that because they descend not with worldly inheritances, must be carefully propagated by a virtuous education of youth; for which after ages will owe more to the care and prudence of founders, and the successive magistracy, than to their parents, for their private patrimonies.

These considerations of the weight of government, and the nice and various opinions about it, made it uneasy to me to think of publishing the ensuing frame and conditional laws, forseeing both the censures, they will meet with, from melt of differing humours and engagements, and the occasion they may give of discourse beyond my design.

But, next to the power of necessity, (which is a solicitor, that will take no denial) this induced me to a compliance, that we have (with reverence to God, and good conscience to men) to the best of our skill, contrived and composed the frame and laws of this government, to the great end of all government, viz: To support power in reverence with the people, and to secure the people from the almost of power; that they may be free by their just obedience, and the magistrates honourable, for their just administration: for liberty without obedience is confusion, and obedience without liberty is slavery. To carry this evenness is partly owing to the constitution, and partly to the magistracy: where either of these fail, government will be subject to convulsions; but where both are wanting, it must be totally subverted; then where both meet, the government is like to endure. Which I humbly pray and hope God will please to make the lot of this of Pensilvania. Amen.

WILLIAM PENN.

8

Frame of Government of Pennsylvania, 1682

This second document by William Penn, the Frame of Government of Pennsylvania, essentially acted as the constitution for the Pennsylvania colony, detailing how the government would be constructed and the responsibilities of government officials. Through this document, Pennsylvania had cemented the principle of government responsibility and accountability to the people.

To all Persons, to whom these presents may come. WHEREAS, king Charles the Second, by his letters patents, under the great seal of England, bearing date the fourth day of March in the Thirty and Third Year of the King, for divers considerations therein mentioned, hath been graciously pleased to give and grant unto me William Penn, by the name of William Penn, Esquire, son and heir of Sir William Penn, deceased, and to my heirs and assigns forever, all that tract of land, or Province, called Pensylvania, in America, with divers great powers, pre-eminences, royalties, jurisdictions, and authorities, necessary for the well-being and government thereof: Now know ye, that for the well-being and government of the said province, and for the encouragement of all the freemen and planters that may be therein concerned, in pursuance of the powers aforementioned, I, the said William Penn, have declared, granted, and confirmed, and by these presents, for me, my heirs and assigns, do declare, grant, and confirm unto all the freemen, planters and adventurers of, in and to the said province, these liberties, franchises, and properties, to be held, enjoyed and kept by the freemen, planters, and inhabitants of the said province of Pensilvania for ever.

Imprimis. That the government of this province shall, according to the powers of the patent, consist of the Governor and freemen of the said province, in form of a provincial Council and General Assembly, by whom all laws shall lie made, officers chosen, and public affairs transacted, as is hereafter respectively declared, that is to say-

II That the freemen of the said province shall, on the twentieth day of the twelfth month, which shall be in this present year one thousand six hundred eighty and two, meet and assemble in some fit place, of which timely notice shall be before hand given by the Governor or his Deputy; and then, and there, shall chuse out of themselves seventy-two persons of most note for their wisdom, virtue and ability, who shall meet, on the tenth day of the first month next ensuing, and always be called, and act as, the provincial Council of the said province.

III That, at the first choice of such provincial Council, one-third part of the said provincial Council shall be chosen to serve for three years, then next ensuing;

one-third part, for two years then next ensuing; and one-third part, for one year then next ensuing such election, and no longer; and that the said third part shall go out accordingly: and on the twentieth day of the twelfth month, as aforesaid, yearly for ever afterwards, the freemen of the said province shall, in like manner, meet and assemble together, and then chuse twenty-four persons, being one-third of the said number, to serve in provincial Council for three years: it being intended, that one-third part of the whole provincial Council (always consisting, and to consist, of seventy-two persons, as aforesaid) falling oh yearly, it shall be yearly supplied by such new yearly elections, as aforesaid; and that no one person shall continue therein longer than three years: and, in case any member shall decease before the last election during his time, that then at the next election ensuing his decease, another shall be chosen to supply his place, for the remaining time, he was to have served, and no longer.

IV That, after the first seven years, every one of the said third parts, that goeth yearly off, shall be uncapable of being chosen again for one whole year following: that so all may be fitted for government, and have experience of the care and burden of it.

V That the provincial Council, in all cases and matters of moment, as their arguing upon bills to be passed into laws, erecting courts of justice, giving judgment upon criminals impeached, and choice of officers, in such manner as is hereinafter mentioned, not less than two-thirds of the whole provincial Council shall make a quorum, and that the consent and approbation of two-thirds of such quorum shall be had in all such cases and matters of moment. And moreover that, in all cases and matters of lesser moment, twenty-four Members of the said provincial Council shall make a quorum, the majority of which. twenty-four shall, and may, always determine in such cases and causes of lesser moment.

VI That, in this provincial Council, the Governor or his Deputy, shall or may, always preside, and have a treble voice; and the said provincial Council shall always continue, and sit upon its own adjournments and committees.

VII That the Governor and provincial Council shall prepare and propose to the General Assembly, hereafter mentioned, all bills, which they shall, at any time, think fit to be passed into laws, within the said province; which bills shall be published and affixed to the most noted places, in the inhabited parts thereof, thirty days before the meeting of the General Assembly, in order to the passing them into laws or rejecting of them, as the General Assembly shall see meet.

VIII That the Governor and provincial Council shall take care, that all laws, statutes and ordinances, which shall at any time be made within the said province, be duly and diligently executed.

IX That the Governor and provincial Council shall, at all times, have the care of the peace and safety of the province, and that nothing be by any person attempted to the subversion of this frame of government.

X That the Governor and provincial Council shall, at all times, settle and order the situation of all cities, ports, and market towns in every county, modelling therein all public buildings, streets, and market places, and shall appoint all necessary roads, and high-ways in the province.

XI That the Governor and provincial Council shall, at all times, have power to inspect the management of the public treasury, and punish those who shall convert any part thereof to any other use, than what hath been agreed upon by the Governor, provincial Council, and General Assembly.

XII That the Governor and provincial Council, shall erect and order all public schools, and encourage and reward the authors of useful sciences and laudable inventions in the said province.

XIII That, for the better management of the powers and trust aforesaid, the provincial Council shall, from time to time, divide itself into four distinct and proper committees, for the more easy administration of the affairs of the Province, which divides the seventy-two into four eighteens, every one of which eighteens shall consist of six out of each of the three orders, or yearly elections, each of which shall have a distinct portion of business as followeth: First, a committee of plantations, to situate and settle cities, ports, and market towns, and high-ways, and to hear and decide all suits and controversies relating to plantations. Secondly, a committee of justice and safety, to secure the peace of the Province, and punish the mar-administration of those who subvert justice to the prejudice of the public, or private, interest. Thirdly, a committee of trade and treasury, who shall regulate all trade and commerce, according to law, encourage manufacture and country growth, and defray the public charge of the Province. And, Fourthly, a committee of manners' education, and arts, that all wicked and scandalous living may be prevented, and that youth may be successively trained up in virtue and useful knowledge and arts: the quorum of each of which committees being six, that is, two out of each of the three orders, or yearly elections, as aforesaid, make a constant and standing Council of twenty-four, which will have the power of the provincial Council, being the quorum of it, in all cases not excepted in the fifth article; and in the said committees, and standing Council of the Province, the Governor, or his Deputy, shall, or may preside, as aforesaid; and in the absence of the Governor, or his Deputy, if no one is by either of them appointed, the said committees or Council shall appoint a President for that time, and not otherwise; and what shall be resolved at such committees, shall be reported to the said Council of the province, and shall be by them resolved and confirmed before the same shall be put in execution; and that these respective committees shall not sit at one and the same time, except in cases of necessity.

XIV And, to the end that all laws prepared by the Governor and provincial Council aforesaid, may yet have the more full concurrence of the freemen of the province, it is declared, granted and confirmed, that, at the time and place or places, for the choice of a provincial Council, as aforesaid, the said freemen shall yearly chuse Members to serve in a general Assembly, as their representatives, not exceeding two hundred persons, who shall yearly meet on the twentieth day of the second month, which shall be in the year one thousand six hundred eighty and three following, in the capital town, or city, of the said province, where, during eight days, the several Members may freely confer with one another; and, if any of them see meet, with a committee of the provincial Council (consisting of three out of each of the four committees aforesaid, being twelve in all) which shall be, at that time, purposely appointed to receive from any of them proposals, for the alterations or amendment of any of the said proposed and promulgated bills: and on the ninth day from their so meeting, the said General Assembly, after reading over the proposed bills by the Clerk of the provincial Council, and the occasions and motives for them being opened by the Governor or his Deputy, shall give their affirmative or negative, which to them seemeth best, in such manner as hereinafter is expressed. But not less than two-thirds shall make a quorum in the passing of laws, and choice of such officers as are by them to be chosen.

XV That the laws so prepared and proposed, as aforesaid, that are assented to by the General Assembly, shall be enrolled as laws of the Province, with this stile: By the Governor, with the assent and approbation of the freemen in provincial Council and General Assembly.

XVI That, for the establishment of the government and laws of this province, and to the end there may be an universal satisfaction in the laying of the fundamentals thereof: the General Assembly shall, or may, for the first year, consist of all the freemen of and in the said province; and ever after it shall be yearly chosen, as aforesaid; which number of two hundred shall be enlarged as the country shall increase in people, so as it do not exceed five hundred, at any time; the appointment and proportioning of which, as also the laying and methodizing of the choice of the provincial Council and General Assembly, in future times, most equally to the divisions of the hundreds and counties, which the country shall hereafter be divided into, shall be in the power of the provincial Council to propose, and the General Assembly to resolve.

XVII That the Governor and the provincial Council shall erect, from time to time, standing courts of justice, in such places and number-as they shall judge convenient for the good government of the said province. And that the provincial Council shall, on the thirteenth day of the first month, yearly, elect and present to the Governor, or his Deputy, a double number of persons, to serve for Judges, Treasurers, Masters of Rolls, within the said province, for the year next ensuing; and the freemen of the said province, in the county courts, when they shall be erected, and till then, in the General Assembly, shall, on the three and twentieth day of the second month, yearly, elect and present to the Governor, or his Deputy, a double number of persons, to serve for Sheriffs, Justices of the Peace, and Coroners, for the year next ensuing; out of which respective elections and presentments, the Governor or his Deputy shall nominate and commissionate the proper number for each office, the third day after the said presentments, or else the first named in such presentment, for each office, shall stand and serve for that office the year ensuing.

XVIII But forasmuch as the present condition of the province requires some immediate settlement, and admits not of so quick a revolution of officers; and to the end the said Province may, with all convenient speed, be well ordered and settled, I, William Penn, do therefore think fit to nominate and appoint such persons for Judges, Treasurers, Masters of the Rolls, Sheriffs, Justices of the Peace, and Coroners, as are most fitly qualified for those employments; to whom I shall make and grant commissions for the said offices, respectively, to hold to them, to whom the same shall be granted, for so long time as every such person shall well behave himself in the office, or place, to him respectively granted, and no longer. And upon the decease or displacing of any of the said officers, the succeeding officer, or officers, shall be chosen, as aforesaid.

XIX That the General Assembly shall continue so long as may be needful to impeach criminals, fit to be there impeached, to pass bills into laws, that they shall think fit to pass into laws, and till such time as the Governor and provincial Council shall declare that they have nothing further to propose unto them, for their assent and approbation: and that declaration shall be a dismiss to the General Assembly for that time; which General Assembly shall be, notwithstanding, capable of assembling together upon the summons of the provincial Council, at any time during that year, if the said provincial Council shall see occasion for their so assembling.

XX That all the elections of members, or representatives of the people, to serve in provincial Council and General Assembly, and all questions to be determined by both, or either of them, that relate to passing of bills into laws, to the choice of officers, to impeachments by the General Assembly, and judgment of criminals upon such impeachments by the provincial Council, and to all other cases bv then- respectively judged of importance, shall be resolved and determined by the ballot; -and unless on sudden and indispensible occasions, no business in provincial Council, or its respective committees, shall be finally determined the same day that it is moved.

XXI That at all times when, and so often as it shall happen that the Governor shall or may be an infant, under the age of one and twenty years, and no guardians or commissioners are appointed in writing, by the father of the said infant, or that such guardians or commissioners, shall be deceased; that during such minority, the provincial Council shall, from time to time, as they shall see meet, constitute and appoint guardians or commissioners, not exceeding three; one of which three shall preside as deputy and chief guardian, during such minority, and shall have and execute, with the consent of the other two, all the power of a Governor, in all the public affairs and concerns of the said province.

XXII That, as often as any day of the month, mentioned in any article of this charter, shall fall upon the first day of the week, commonly called the Lord's Day, the business appointed for that day shall be deferred till the next day, unless in case of emergency.

XXIII That no act, law, or ordinance whatsoever, shall at any time hereafter, be made or done by the Governor of this province, his heirs or assigns, or by the freemen in the provincial Council, or the General Assembly, to alter, change, or diminish the form, or edect, ~of this charter, or any part, or clause thereof, without the consent of the Governor, his heirs, or assigns, and six parts of seven of the said freemen in provincial Council and General Assembly.

XXIV And lastly, that I, the said William Penn, for myself, my heirs and assigns, have solemnly declared, granted and confirmed, and do hereby solemnly declare, grant and confirm, that neither I, my heirs, nor assigns, shall procure or do any thing or things, whereby the liberties, in this charter contained and expressed, shall be infringed or broken; and if any thing be procured by any person or persons contrary to these premises, it shall be held of no force or eReet. In witness whereof, I, the said William Penn, have unto this present character of liberties set my hand and broad seal, this five and twentieth day of the second month, vulgarly called April, in the year of our lord one thousand six hundred and eighty-two.

WILLIAM PENN.

Laws Agreed Upon in England, &c.

I That the charter of liberties, declared, granted and confirmed. the five and twentieth day of the second month, called April, 1682, before divers witnesses, by William Penn, Governor and chief Proprietor of Pensilvania, to all the freemen and planters of the said province, is hereby declared and approved, and shall be for ever held for fundamental in the government thereof, according to the limitations mentioned in the said charter.

II That every inhabitant in the said province, that is or shall be, a purchaser of one hundred acres of land, or upwards, his heirs and assigns, and every person who shall have paid his passage, and taken up one hundred acres of land, at one penny an acre, and have cultivated ten acres thereof, and every person, that hath been a servant, or bonds-man, and is free by his service, that shall have taken up his fifty acres of land, and cultivated twenty thereof, and every inhabitant, artifices, or other resident in the said province, that pays scot and lot to the government; shall be deemed and accounted a freeman of the said province: and every such person shall, and may, be capable of electing, or being elected, representatives of the people, in provincial Council, or General Assembly, in the said province.

III That all elections of members, or representatives of the people and freemen of the province of Pensilvania, to serve in provincial Council, or General Assembly, to be held within the said province, shall be free and voluntary: and that the elector, that shall receive any reward or gift, in meat, drink, monies, or otherwise, shall forfeit his right to elect; and such person as shall directly or indirectly give, promise, or bestow - any such reward as aforesaid, to he elected, shall forfeit his election, and be thereby incapable to serve as aforesaid: and the provincial Council and General Assembly shall be the sole judges of the regularity, or irregularity of the elections of their own respective -Members.

IV That no money or goods shall be raised upon, or paid by, any of the people of this province by way of public tax, custom or contribution, but by a law, for that purpose made; and whoever shall levy, collect, or pay any money or goods contrary "hereunto, shall be held a public enemy to the province and a betrayer of the liberties of the people thereof.

V That all courts shall be open, and justice shall neither be sold, denied nor delayed.

VI That, in all courts all persons of all persuasions may freely appear in their own way, and according to their own manners and there personally plead their own cause themselves; or, if unable, by their friends: and the first process shall be the exhibition of the complaint in court, fourteen days before the trial; and that the party, complained against, may be fitted for the same, he or she shall be summoned, no less than ten days before, and a copy of the complaint delivered him or her, at his or her dwelling house. But before the complaint of any person be received, he shall solemnly declare in court, that he believes, in his conscience, his cause is just.

VII That all pleadings, processes and records in courts, shall be short, and in English, and in an ordinary and plain character, that they may be understood, and justice speedily administered.

VIII That all trials shall be by twelve men, and as near as may be, peers or equals, and of the neighborhood, and men without just exception; in cases of life, there shall be first twenty-four returned by the sheriffs, for a grand inquest, of whom twelve, at least, shall find the complaint to be true; and then the twelve men, or peers, to be likewise returned by the sheriff, shall have the final judgment. But reasonable challenges shall be always admitted against the said twelve men, or any of them.

IX That all fees in all cases shall be moderate, and settled by the provincial Council, and General Assembly, and be hung up in a table in every respective court; and whosoever shall be convicted of taking more, shall pay twofold, and be dismissed his employment; one moiety of svllich shall go to the party wronged.

X That all prisons shall be work-houses, for felons, vagrants, and loose and idle persons; whereof one shall be in every county.

XI That all prisoners shall be bailable by sufficient sureties, unless for capital offences, where the proof is evident, or the presumption great.

XII That all persons wrongfully imprisoned, or prosecuted at law, shall have double damages against the informer, or prosecutor.

XIII That all prisons shall be free, as to fees, food and lodging.

XIV That all lands and goods shall be liable to pay debts, except where there is legal issue, and then all the goods, and one-third of the land only.

XV That all wills, in writing, attested by two witnesses, shall be of the same force as to lands, as other conveyances, being legally proved within forty days, either within or without the said province.

XVI That seven years quiet possession shall give an unquestionable right, except in cases of infants, lunatics, married women, or persons beyond the seas.

XVII That all briberies and extortion whatsoever shall be severely punished.

XVIII That all fines shall be moderate, and saving men's contenements, merchandise, or wainage.

XIX That all marriages (not forbidden by the law of God, as to nearness of blood and affinity by marriage) shall be encouraged; but the parents, or guardians, shall be first consulted, and the marriage shall be published before it be solemnized; and it shall be solemnized by taking one another as husband and wife, before credible witnesses; and a certificate of the whole, under the hands of parties and witnesses, shall be brought to the proper register of that county, and shall be registered in his office.

XX And, to prevent frauds and vexatious suits within the said province, that all charters, gifts, grants, and conveyances of and (except leases for a year or under) and all bills, bonds, and specialties above five pounds, and not under three months, made in the said province, shall be enrolled, or registered in the public enrolment office of the said province, within the space of two months next after the making thereof, else to be void in law, and all deeds, grants, and conveyances of land (except as aforesaid) within the said province, and made out of the said province, shall be enrolled or registered, as aforesaid, within six months next after the making thereof, and settling and constituting an enrolment office or registry within the said province, else to be void in law against all persons whatsoever.

XXI That all defacers or corrupters of charters, gifts, grants. bonds, bills, wills, contracts, and conveyances, or that shall deface or falsify any enrolment, registry or record, within this province, shall make double satisfaction for the same; half whereof shall go to the party wronged, and they shall be dismissed of all places of trust, and be publicly disgraced as false men.

XXII That there shall be a register for births, marriages, burials, wills, and letters of administration, distinct from the other registry.

XXIII That there shall be a register for all servants, where their names, time, wages, and days of payment shall be registered.

XXIV That all lands and goods of felons shall be liable, to make satisfaction to the party wronged twice the value; and for want of lands or goods, the felons shall be bondmen to work in the common prison, or work-house, or otherwise, till the party injured be satisfied.

XXV That the estates of capital offenders, as traitors and murderers, shall go, one-third to the next of kin to the sufferer, and the remainder to the next of kin to the criminal.

XXVI That all witnesses, coming, or called, to testify their knowledge in or to any matter or thing, in any court, or before any lawful authority, within the said province, shall there give or deliver in their evidence, or testimonly, by solemnly promising to speak the truth, the whole truth, and nothing but the truth. to the matter, or thing in question. And in case any person so called to evidence, shall be convicted of wilful falsehood, such person shall suffer and undergo such damage or penalty, as the person, or persons, against whom he or she bore false witness, did, or should, undergo; and shall also make satisfaction to the party wronged, and be publicly exposed as a false witness, never to be credited in any court, or before any Magistrate, in the said province.

XXVII And, to the end that all officers chosen to serve within this province, may, with more care and diligence, answer the trust reposed in them, it is agreed, that no such person shall enjoy more than one public office, at one time.

XXVIII That all children, within this province, of the age of twelve years, shall be taught some useful trade or skill, to the end none may be idle, but the poor may work to live, and the rich, if they become poor, may not want.

XXIX That servants be not kept longer than their time, and such as are careful, be both justly and kindly used in their service, and put in fitting equipage at the expiratiol; thereof, according to custom.

XXX That all scandalous and malicious reporters, backbiters, defamers and spreaders of false news, whether against Magistrates, or private persons, shall be accordingly severely punished, as enemies to the peace and concord of this province.

XXXI That for the encouragement of the planters and traders in this province, who are incorporated into a society, the patent granted to them by William Penn, Governor of the said province, is hereby ratified and confirmed.

XXXII * * *

XXXIII That all factors or correspondents in the said province, wronging their employers, shall make satisfaction, and one-third over, to their said employers: and in case of the death of any such factor or correspondent, the committee of trade shall take care to secure so much of the deceased party's estate as belongs to his said respective employers.

XXXIV That all Treasurers, Judges, Masters of the Rolls, Sheriffs, Justices of the Peace, and other officers and persons whatsoever, relating to courts, or trials of causes or any other service in the government; and all Members elected to serve in provincial Council and General Assembly, and all that have right to elect such Members, shall be such as possess faith in Jesus Christ, and that are not convicted of ill fame, or unsober and dishonest conversation, and that are of one and twenty years of age, at least; and that all such so qualified, shall be capable of the said several employments and privileges, as aforesaid.

XXXV That all persons living in this province, who confess and acknowledge the one Almighty and eternal God, to be the Creator, Upholder and Ruler of the world; and that hold themselves obliged in conscience to live peaceably and justly in civil society, shall, in no ways, be molested or prejudiced for their religious persuasion, or practice, in matters of faith and worship, nor shall they be compelled, at any time, to frequent or maintain any religious worship, place or ministry whatever.

XXXVI That, according to the good example of the primitive Christians, and the case of the creation, every first day of the week, called the Lord's day, people shall abstain from their common daily labour, that they may the better dispose themselves to worship God according to their understandings.

XXXVII That as a careless and corrupt administration of justice draws the wrath of God upon magistrates, so the wildness and looseness of the people provoke the indignation of God against a country: therefore, that all such offences against God, as swearing, cursing, lying, prophane talking, drunkenness, drinking of healths, obscene words, incest, sodomy, rapes, whoredom, fornication, and other uncleanness (not to be repeated) all treasons, misprisions, murders, duels, felony, seditions, maims, forcible entries, and other violences, to the persons and estates of the inhabitants within this province; all prizes, stage-plays, cards, dice, May-games, gamesters, masques, revels, bull-battings, cock-fightings, bear-battings, and the like, which excite the people to rudeness, cruelty, looseness, and irreligion, shall be respectively discouraged, and severely punished, according to the appointment of the Governor and freemen in provincial Council and General Assembly; as also all proceedings contrary to these laws, that are not here made expressly penal.

XXXVIII That a copy of these laws shall be hung up in the provincial Council, and in public courts of justice: and that they shall be read yearly at the opening of every provincial Council and General Assembly, and court of justice; and their assent shall be testified, by their standing up after the reading thereof.

XXXIX That there shall be, at no time, any alteration of any of these laws, without the consent of the Governor, his heirs, or assigns, and six parts of seven of the freemen, met in provincial Council and General Assembly.

XL That all other matters and things not herein provided for, which shall, and may, concern the public justice, peace or safety of the said province; and the raising and imposing taxes, customs, duties, or other charges whatsoever, shall be, and are, hereby referred to the order, prudence and determination of the Governor and freemen, in provincial Council and General Assembly, to be held, from time to time, in the said province.

Signed and sealed by the Governor and freemen aforesaid, the fifth day of the third month, called May, one thousand six hundred and eighty-two.

WILLIAM PENN **9**

Charter of Liberties, 1682

This third document by William Penn details some of the administrative regulations of the new Pennsylvania colony, including the duties of colonial officials and a number of the goals of the colonial government, including encouraging science and invention.

To ALL PEOPLE to whom these presents shall come WHEREAS King Charles the second by his Letters, Patents under the Great Seal of England for the Considerations therein mentioned hath been graciously pleased to give and grant unto me William Penn (By the name of William Penn Esq'r son and heir of Sr. William Penn deceased) and to my heirs and assigns forever ALL that tract of land or province called PENNSILVANIA in America with divers Great Powers Preheminencies Royalties Jurisdictions and Authorities necessary for the Well being and Government thereof NOW KNOW YE That for the Welll Being and Government of the said Province and for the Encouragement of all the Freeman and Planters that may be therein concerned in pursuance of the powers afore mentond I the said William Penn have declared Granted and Confirmed and by these presents

http://www.yale.edu/lawweb/avalon/states/pa04.htm

for me my heirs and Assigns do declare grant and Confirm unto all the flreemen Planters and Adventurers of in and to the said Province those Liberties Franchises and properties TO BE HEED Enjoyed and Kept by the Freemen Planters and Inhabitants of and in the said province of Pennsilvania forever.

"IMPRIMIS"—THAT the Government of this Province shall according to the Powers of the Patent consist of the Governour and Freemen of the said Province in the fform of a Provincial Council and General Assembly by whom all Laws Shall be made Officers Chosen and publick affairs Transacted and is hereafter Respectively declared That is to say

2. THAT the freemen of the said Province shall on the Twentieth day of the Twelfth Month which shall be in this present year One Thousand Six hundred Eighty and two Meet and Assemble in some fit place of which timely notice shall be beforehand given by the Governour or his deputies and then and there shall chuse of themselvs Seventy-Two persons of most note for their Wisdom Virtue and Ability who shall meet on the Tenth day of the ffirst month next ensuing and always be called and act as the Provincial Councill of the said province.

3. THAT at the First Choice of such Provincial Council One Third part of the said Provincial Council shall be Chosen to serve for Three years then next ensuing one Third part for Two years then next ensuing and one Third part for one year then next following such Election and no longer and that the said Third part shall go out accordingly And on the Twentieth day of the Twelfth month aforesaid yearly forever afterward the ffreemen of the said province shall in like manner Meet and Assemble together and then Chuse Twenty flour persons being one Third of the said Number to serve in provincial Council for Three years it being intended that one Third of the whole provincial Council (always consisting and to consist of seventy two persons as aforesaid) falling off yearly it shall be yearly supplied by such new yearly Eleccons as aforesaid and that no one person shall continue therein longer than Three years And in Case any member shall decease before the Last Eleccon during his time that then at the next Eleccon ensuing his decease another shall be chosen to Supply his place for the remaining time he was to have served and no longer.

4. THAT—After the First Seven Years every one of the said Third parts that goeth yearly off shall be uncapable of being Chosen again for one whole year following that so all may be fitted for the Government and have Experience of the Care and burthen of it.

5. THAT—In the provincial Council in all Cases and matters of moment as There agreeing upon Bills to be passed into Laws Exorting Courts of Justice having Judgment upon criminals Impeached and choice of Officers in such manner as is herein after menconed Not lesse than Two Thirds of the whole Provincial Council shall make a Quorum and that the Consent and approbaton of Two Thirds of said Quorum shall be had in all such Cases or matters of Moment. And moreover that in all cases and matters of lesser moment Twenty-ffour members of the said Provincial Council shall make a quorum The Majority of which flour and Twenty shall and may always determine on such Cases and Causes of Lesser moment.

6. THAT—In this Provincial Council the Governour or his deputies shall or may always preside and have a treble Voice. And the said Provincial Council shall always Continue and Sit upon its own Adjournments and Committees.

7. THAT—The Governour and Provincial Council shall prepare and propose to the General Assembly hereinafter menconed all Bills which they shall at any time think fit to be past into Laws within the said Province which Bills shall be publish" and Affixed to the most noted places in the inhabited parts thereof Thirty days before the meeting of the General Assembly in order to the passing of them into laws or Rejecting of them as the General Assembly shall see meet.

8. THAT—The Governour and Provincial Council shall take Care that all Laws Statutes and Ordinances which shall at any time be made within the said Province be duly and diligently executed.

9. THAT—The Governour and Provincial Council shall at all times have the Care of the peace and Safety of the Province and that nothing he by any person Attempted to the subversion of this Frame of Government.

10. THAT—The Governour and Provincial Council shall at all times settle and order the Situation of all Cities ports and Market towns in every County modelling therein all publick buildings Streets and Market places and shall appoint all necessary roads and highways in the province.

11. THAT—The Governour and Provincial Council shall at all times have power to inspect the management of the public Treasury and punish those who shall Convert any part thereof to any other use than what hath been Agreed upon by the Governour Provincial Council and General Assembly.

12. THAT—The Governour and Provincial Council shall Erect and order all publick Schools and incourage and Reward the Authors of usefull Science and Laudable Inventons in the said province.

13. THAT—For the better management of the powers and Trust aforesaid the Provincial Council shall from time to time divide itself into flour Distinct and proper Committees for the more Easie Administration of the Affairs of the province which divides the Seventy Two into flour Eighteens Every one of which Eighteens shall consist of Six out of each of the Three Orders or yearly Eleccons-Each of which shall have a distinct portion of business as followeth A Committee of plantatons to situate and settle cities ports and Market-towns and highways and to hear and decide all Suits and Controversies relating to Plantatons. A Committee of Justice and Safety to secure the peace of the province and punish the Male [mat-] Administration of those who subvert Justice to the prejudice of the publick and private Interest. A Committee of Trade and Treasury who Shall Regulate all Trade and Commerce according to Laws encourage Manufacture and Country-growth and defray the publick Charge of the province. And a Committee of manners Education and Arts that all Wicked and scandalous Living may be prevented and that Youth may be successively trained up in Virtue and useful Knowlledge and Arts. The Quorum of each of which Committees being six that is Two out of each of the three orders or yearly eleccons as aforesaid make a Constant or Standing Council of Four and Twenty which shall have the

power of the Provincial Council being the Quorum of it in all Cases not excepted in the ffifth Article. And in the said committees and standing Council of the Province the Governour or his deputy shall or may preside as aforesaid. And in the Absence of the Governour or his deputy if no one is by either of them appointed the said Committees or Council shall appoint a President for that time and not otherwise and what shall be Resolved at such Committees shall be reported to the said Council of the Province and shall be by them resolved and confirmed before the same shall be put in Execution And that these Respective Committees shall not sit at one and the same time except in Cases of necessity.

14. AND TO THE End that all Laws prepared by the Governour and Provincial Council aforesaid may yet have the more-full Concurrence of the Freemen of the Province It is declared granted and confirmed that at the time and place or places for the Choice of a Provincial Council as aforesaid the said FREEMEN shall yearly chuse to serve in a General Assembly as their representatives not exceeding Two hundred persons who shall yearly meet on the Twentieth day of the Second Month in the Capital Town or City of the said province where during Eight days the several members mav freely confer with one another and if any of them see meet with a Committee of the Provincial Council consisting of Three out of each of the flour Committees aforesaid being Twelve in all which shall be at that time purposely appointed to secuir from any of them proposals for the Alteration or Amendment of any of the said proposed and promulgated Bills and on the ninth day from their meeting the said General Assembly after the reading over of the proposed Bills by the Clerk of the Provincial Council and the occasion and motives for them being opened by the Governour or his Deputy shall give their Affirmative or Negative which, to them seemeth best in such manner as hereafter is express. But not less than two thirds shall make a Quorum in the passing of Laws and Choice of such Officers as are by them to be chosen.

15. THAT—The Laws so prepared and proposed as aforesaid that are Assented to by the General Assembly shall be Enrolled as Laws of the province with this stile by the Governour with the Assent and Approbation of the ffreemen in Provincial Council and General Assembly.

16. THAT—For the better Establishment of the Government and Laws of this province and to the end there may be an Universal Satisfaction in the laying of the ffundamentals thereof the General Assembly shall or may for the ffirst year consist of all the ffreemen of and in the said province and ever after it shall be yearly chosen as aforesaid. Which number of Two hundred shall be enlarged as the Country shall Increase in people So as it do not exceed dive hundred at any time The Appointment and proportoning of which as also the laying and methodizing of the choice of the Provincial Council and General Assembly in future times most equally to the Division of the Hundreds and Counties which the Country shall hereafter be divided into shall be in the power of the Provincial Council to propose and the General Assembly to resolve.

17. THAT The Governour and the Provincial Council shall from time to time erect Standing Courts of Justice in such places and number as they shall Judge Convenient for the good Government of the said province And that the Provincial

Council shall on the Thirteenth day of the First month yearly Elect and present to the Governour or his Deputy a double number of persons to serve for Judges Treasurers Masters of the Rolls within the said province for the year next ensuing. AND the ffreemen of the said province in their County Courts when they shall be erected and till then in the General Assembly shall on the Three and Twentieth day of the Second Month yearly Elect and present to the Governour or his Deputy a double number of persons to serve for Sheriffs Justices of peace and Coronors for the year next ensuing Out of which respective Eleccons and presentments the Governour or his Deputy shall nominate and Commissionate the proper number for each office the Third day after the said respective presentments or else the first named in such presentment for each office shall stand and serve for that office the year ensuing.

18. BUT for as much as the present Conditon of the Province requires some Immediate Setlement and admitts not of so quick a Revoluton of Officers and to the end the said Province may with all Convenient speed be well ordered and settled I William Penn do therefore think fit to nominate and appoint Such persons for Judges Treasurers Masters of Rolls Sheriffs Justices of the peace and Coronors as are most fitly qualified for those imployments To whom I shall make and grant Commissions for the said Offices respectively TO nod to them to whom the same shall be granted for so long time as every such person shall well behave himself in the Office or place to him respectively granted and no longer And upon the Decease or displacing of any of the said Officers the Succeeding Officer or Officers shall be chosen as before said.

19. That the General Assembly shall continue so long as may be needful to Impeach Criminals fit to be there Impeached To pass Bills into Laws that they shall think fit to pass into Laws and till such time as the Governour and Provincial Council shall declare that they have nothing further to propose unto them for their Assent and Approbation And that Declaration shall be a Dismiss to the General Assembly for that time Which General Assembly shall be notwithstanding Capable of Assemblying together upon the summons of the Provincial Council at any time during that year if the said Provincial Council shall see occasion for their so Assembling.

20. THAT—All the Eleccons of Members or Representatives of the people to serve in Provincial Council and General Assembly, and all Questions to be determined by both or either of them that relate to passing of bills into Laws to the choice of Officers to Impeachments made by the General Assembly and Judgment of Criminals upon such Impeachment by the Provincial Council and to all other Cases by them respectively Judged of Importance Shall be resolved and determined by the BALLOTT And unless on suddain and Indispensable Occasions no business in Provincial Council or its respective Committees shall be finally determined the same day that it is moved.

21. AND THAT at all times when and so often as it shall happen that the Governour shall or may be an Infant under the Age of one and Twenty years and no Guardians or Commissioners are appointed in Writing by the dasher of said Infant or that Such Guardians or Commissioners shall be deceased that during such Minority the Provincial Council shall from time to time as they shall see meet Constitute and Appoint Guardians and Commissions not exceeding Three One of which Three shall

preside as Deputy and Chief Guardian during such Minority and shall have and Execute with the consent of the other Two all the powers of a Governour in all publick Affairs and Concerns of the said province.

22. THAT—as often as any day of the month mentoned in any Article of this Charter shall fall on the First day of the Week commonly called the Lord's day the Business appointed for that day shall be differred till the next day unless in Case of Emergency.

23. THAT—no act Law or Ordinance whatsoever shall at any time hereafter be made or done by the Governour of this Province his heirs or Assigns or by the ffreemen in the Provincial Council or the General Assembly to Alter Change or Diminish the dorm or Effect of this Charter or any part or Clause thereof or contrary to the true Intent and meaning thereof without the Consent of the Governour his heirs or Assigns and six parts of seven of the said ffreemen in Provincial Councll and General Assembly.

24. AND LASTLY THAT I the said William Penn for myself my heirs and Assigns have Solemnly declared granted and confirmed and do hereby solemnly declare grant and confirm that neither I my heirs nor Assigns shall procure or do anything or things w hereby the liberties in this Charter contained and expressed shall be Infringed or broken And if anything be procured by any person or persons contrary to these premises it shall be held of no force or Effect. IN WITNESS whereof I the said William Penn have unto this present Charter of Liberties Set my hand and Broad Seal this ffive and Twentieth day of the Second Month vulgarly called April in the year of our Lord One Thousand Six Hundred Eighty and Two.

WM, PENN.

Signed sealed and delivered by the within named William Penn as his Act and Deed in the presence of

CHRISTOPHER TAYLOR
CHARLES LLOYD
WILLIAM GIBSON
RICHARD DAVIES
N. MOORE
THO. RUDYARD
HARB. SPRINGETT
JAMES CLAYPOOLE
FRANS PLUMSTED
THOMAS BARKER
PHILIP FORD
EDWARD PRITCHARD
ANDREW SOWLE

SAMUEL SEWALL **10**

The Selling of Joseph, 1700

The Selling of Joseph *represents the first known abolitionist tract in Massachusetts. It emerged in 1700 as Judge Samuel Sewall engaged in a bitter dispute with another Massachusetts man, John Saffin, over the selling of a slave named Adam. In spite of rhetoric in this essay that would be condemned as racist in the twenty-first century, Sewall argues that liberty is not something to be bought and sold regardless of race. Slavery would remain legal in all the British colonies up to the Revolutionary War. As slavery established itself across the colonies, Sewall and others began to see the idea of human beings traded with less concern than farm animals as abhorrent. Liberty, as defined by absence of captivity, was considered as precious as life by Sewall in this essay. Judge Sewall, however, does not rely on English law to make his arguments in this essay; but, rather, using soaring Christian imagery, he invokes these principles to condemn the buying and selling of human beings and to counter Biblical arguments supporting slavery.*

Forasmuch as Liberty *is in real value next unto* Life: *None ought to part with it themselves, or deprive others of it, but upon most mature Consideration.*

The Numerousness of Slaves at this day in the Province, and the Uneasiness of them under their Slavery, hath put many upon thinking whether the Foundation of it be firmly and well laid; so as to sustain the Vast Weight that is built upon it. It is most certain that all Men, as they are the Sons of Adam, are Coheirs; and have equal Right unto Liberty, and all other outward Comforts of Life. *God hath given the Earth* [with all its Commodities] *unto the Sons of Adam, Psal 115.16. And hath made of One Blood, all Nations of Men, for to dwell on all the face of the Earth, and hath determined the Times before appointed, and the bounds of their habitation: That they should seek the Lord. Forasmuch then as we are the Offspring of GOD &c. Act 17.26, 27, 29.* Now although the Title given by the last ADAM, doth infinitely better Mens Estates, respecting GOD and themselves; and grants them a most beneficial and inviolable Lease under the Broad Seal of Heaven, who were before only Tenants at Will: Yet through the Indulgence of GOD to our First Parents after the Fall, the outward Estate of all and every of their Children, remains the same, as to one another. So that Originally, and Naturally, there is no such thing as Slavery. *Joseph* was rightfully no more a Slave to his Brethren, than they were to him: and they had no more Authority to *Sell* him, than they had to *Slay* him. And if *they* had nothing to do to Sell him; the Ishmaelites bargaining with them, and paying down Twenty pieces of Silver, could not make a Title. Neither could *Potiphar* have any better Interest in him than the *Ishmaelites* had, Gen. 37, 20, 27, 28. For he that shall in this case plead Alteration of Property, seems to have forfeited

Samuel Sewall, *The Selling of Joseph; A Memorial.* Boston: Bartholomew Green and John Allen, 1700.

a great part of his own claim to Humanity. There is no proportion between Twenty Pieces of Silver, and LIBERTY. The Commodity it self is the Claimer. If *Arabian* Gold be imported in any quantities, most are afraid to meddle with it, though they might have it at easy rates; lest if it should have been wrongfully taken from the Owners, it should kindle a fire to the Consumption of their whole estate.'Tis pity there should be more Caution used in buying a Horse, or a little lifeless dust; than there is in purchasing Men and Women: Whenas they are the Offspring of GOD, and their Liberty is,

> .... *Auro pretiosior Omni [More precious than gold].*

And seeing GOD hath said, *He that stealeth a Man and Selleth him, or if he be found in his hand, he shall surely be put to Death.* Exod. 12.16. This Law being of Everlasting Equity, wherein Man Stealing is ranked amongst the most atrocious of Capital Crimes: What louder Cry can there be made of the Celebrated Warning, *Caveat Emptor* [Buyer Beware]!

And all things considered, it would conduce more to the Welfare of the Province, to have White Servants for a Term of Years, than to have Slaves for Life. Few can endure to hear of a Negro's being made free; and indeed they can seldom use their freedom well; yet their continual aspiring after their forbidden Liberty, renders them Unwilling Servants. And there is such a disparity in their Conditions, Colour & Hair, that they can never embody with us, and grow up into orderly Families, to the Peopling of the Land: but still remain in our Body Politick as a kind of extravasat Blood. As many Negro men as there are among us, so many empty places there are in our Train Bands, and the places taken up of Men that might make Husbands for our Daughters. And the Sons and Daughters of *New England* would become more like *Jacob*, and *Rachel*, if this Slavery were thrust quite out of doors. Moreover it is too well known what Temptations Masters are under, to connive at the Fornification of their Slaves; lest they should be obliged to find them Wives, or pay their Fines. It seems to be practically pleaded that they might be Lawless; 'tis thought much of, that the Law should have Satisfaction for their Thefts, and other Immoralities; by which means, *Holiness to the Lord*, is more rarely engraven upon this sort of Servitude. It is likewise most lamentable to think, how in taking Negros out of *Africa*, and selling of them here, That which GOD has joined together men to boldly rend asunder; Men from their Country, Husbands from their Wives, Parents from their Children. How horrible is the Uncleanness, Mortality, if not Murder, that the Ships are guilty of that bring great Crowds of these miserable Men, and Women. Methinks, when we are bemoaning the barbarous Usage of our Friends and Kinsfolk in *Africa*: it might not be unseasonable to enquire wheter we are not culpable in forcing the *Africans* to become Slaves amongst our selves. And it may be a question whether all the Benefit received by Negro Slaves, will balance the Accompt of Cash laid out upon them; and for the Redemption of our own enslaved Friends out of *Africa*. Besides all the Persons and Estates that have perished there.

Obj. 1. *These Blackamores are of the Posterity of* Cham, *and therefore are under the Curse of Slavery.* Gen. 9.25, 26, 27.

Answ. Of all Offices, one would not begg this; *viz.* Uncall'd for, to be an Executioner fo the Vindictive Wrath of God; the extent and duration of which is to us uncertain.

If this ever was a Commission; How do we know but that it is long since out of date? Many have found it to their Cost, that a Prophetical Denunciation of Judgment against a Person or People, would not warrant them to inflict that evil. If it would, *Hazael* might justify himself in all he did against his Master, and the *Israelites*, from 2 *Kings* 8.10, 12.

But it is possible that by cursory reading, this Text may have been mistaken. For *Canaan* is the Person Cursed three times over, without the mentioning of *Cham*. Good Expositors suppose the Curse entailed on him, and that this Prophesie was accomplished in the Extirpation of the *Canaanites*, and in the Servitude of the *Gibeonites, Vide Pareum*. Whereas the Balckmores are not descended of *Canaan*, but of *Cush*. Psal. 68.31. *Princes shall come our to Egypt* [Mizraim] *Ethiopia* [Cush] *shall soon stretch out her hands unto God*. Under which Names, all *Aftrica* may be comprehended; and their Promised Conversion ought to be prayed for. Jer. 13,23. *Can the Ethiopian change his skin?* This shows that Black Men are the Posterity of *Cush*: who time out of mind have been distinguished by their Colour. And for want of the true, Ovid assigns a fabulous cause of it.

> Sanguine tum credunt in corpora cumma vacato
> Æthiopum populous nigrum traxisse coleorm.

Metomorph. lib.2. [Men believe that at that time the African nations acquired their black colour, after their blood had been summoned to the surface of their bodies. Metamorphoses Book 2, (by Ovid)].

Obj. 2. *The* Nigers *are brought out of a pagan country, into places where the Gospel is Preached.*

Answ. Evil must not be done, that good may come of it. The extraordinary and comprehensive Benefit accruing to the Church of God, and to Joseph personally, did not rectify his brethrens Sale of him.

Obj. 3. *The* Africans *have Wars one with another: Our Ships bring lawful Captives taken in those Wars.*

Answ. For ought is known, their Wars are much such as were between *Jacob's* Sons and their brother *Joseph*. If they be between Town and Town; Provincial, or National: Every War is upon one side Unjust. An Unlawful War can't make lawful Captives. And by Receiving, we are in danger to promote, and partake in their Barbarous Cruelties. I am sure, if some Gentlemen should go down to the *Brewsters* to take the Air and Fish: And a stronger party from *Hull* should Surprise them, and Sell them for Slaves to a Ship outward bound: they would think themselves unjustly dealt with; both by Sellers and Buyers. And yet 'tis to be feared, we have no other kind of Title to our Nigers. *Therefore all things whatsoever ye would that men should do to you, do ye even so to them: for this is the Law and the Prophets.* Matt. 7.12.

Obj. 4 Abraham *had servants bought with his Money, and born in his House.*

Answ. Until the Circumstances of Abraham's purchase be recorded, no Argument can be drawn from it. In the mean time, Charity obliges us to conclude, that He knew it was lawful and good.

It is Observable that the *Israelites* were strictly forbidden the buying, or selling one another for Slaves. Levit. 25.39, 46. Jer.34.8.....22. And GOD gaged His Blessing in lieu of any loss they might conceipt they suffered thereby. *Deut.* 15.18. And since the partition Wall is broken down, inordinate Self love should likewise be demolished. GOD expects that Christians should be of a more Ingenuous and benign frame of spirit. Christians should carry it to all the World, as the *Israelites* were to carry it one towards another. And for men obstinately to persist in holding their Neighbours and Brethren under the Rigor of perpetual Bondage, seems to be no proper way of gaining Assurance that God has given them Spiritual Freedom. Our Blessed Saviour has altered the Measures of the Ancient Love-Song, and set it to a most Excellent New Tune, which all ought to be ambitious of Learning. *Matt.* 5, 43, 44. *John* 13,34. These *Ethiopians*, as black as they are; seeing they are the Sons and Daughters of the First *Adam*, the Brethren and Sisters of the Last ADAM, and the Offspring of GOD; They ought to be treated with a Respect agreeable.

Servitus perfecta voluntaria, inter Christianum & Christiainum, ex parte servi patientis sæpe est licita quia est necessaria; sed ex parte domini agentis, & procurando & exercendo, vix potest esse licita; quia non convenit regulæ illi generali: Quæcunque volueritis ut faciant vobis homines, ita & vos facite eis. Matt. 7.12.

Perfecta servitus pænæ, non potest jure locum habere, nisi ex delicto gravi quod ultimum supplicium aliquo modo meretur; quia Libertas ex naturali æstimatione proximo accedit ad vitam ipsam, & eidem a multis præferri solet.

[Perfectly voluntary slavery, between Christian and Christian, is often licit on the part of the slave suffering it, because it is necessary; but on the part of the owner who takes the initiative both in obtaining the slave and exercising his right, force may be licit, because it does not conform to that general rule: "Do to men what you would have them do to you" (Matthew 7:12). Perfect slavery cannot by right take the place of punishment, unless it be as a consequence of some grave misdemeanor which in some way deserves the death penalty, for Freedom is the closest thing to life itself in a natural estimation, and is often preferred by many to it.].

Ames. Cas. Consc. Lib. 5

Cap. 23 Thes. 2, 3

BOSTON of the Massachusets

Printed by *Bartholomew Green, and John Allen*, June 24th, 1700.

JOHN PETER ZENGER **11**

Liberty of the Press, 1733

In the early years of the 1700s, New York City became the site of one of the most sensational trials of the colonial era. John Peter Zenger, a German immigrant and editor of The New York Weekly Journal, *had become embroiled in a bitter*

http://www.law.umkc.edu/faculty/projects/ftrials/zenger/journalissues3.html

war of words with the colonial governor of New York, William Cosby, over the governor's misuse of the colony's courts and misappropriation of funds. Cosby responded to the criticisms of his administration by having Zenger arrested on the charge of seditious libel (a criminal charge in colonial America rather than a civil matter) in November 1734. While in jail, Zenger continued to publish the Journal. After his trial started eight months later, Zenger's lawyers defended him by stating that no crime had been committed since everything Zenger had written was the truth. Jurors, in a surprise move, agreed with the argument that a man must not be arrested for telling the truth and acquitted Zenger. This trial became one of the cornerstones of freedom of the press as it became clear that a free society must protect the right of individuals to tell the truth about the world around them. This letter in a November 1733 issue of The New York Weekly Journal *argues that the liberty of all Englishmen depends on a free press exposing the actions of corrupt ministers, even if it means that an official becomes an object of satire. Without a free press, Zenger believed, the nation would eventually be lost to despotism.*

The liberty of the press is a subject of the greatest importance, and in which every individual is as much concerned as he is in any other part of liberty: Therefore it will not be improper to communicate to the public the sentiments of a late excellent writer upon this point. Such is the elegance and perspicuity of his writings, such the inimitable force of his reasoning, that it will be difficult to say anything new that he has not said, or not to say that much worse which he has said.

There are two sorts of monarchies, an absolute and a limited one. In the first, the liberty of the press can never be maintained, it is inconsistent with it; for what absolute monarch would suffer any subject to animadvert on his actions when it is in his power to declare the crime and to nominate the punishment? This would make it very dangerous to exercise such a liberty. Besides the object against which those pens must be directed is their sovereign, the sole supreme magistrate; for there being no law in those monarchies but the will of the prince, it makes it necessary for his ministers to consult his pleasure before anything, can be undertaken: He is therefore properly chargeable with the grievances of his subjects, and what the minister there acts being in obedience to the prince, he ought not to incur the hatred of the people; for it would be hard to impute that to him for a crime which is the fruit of his allegiance, and for refusing which he might incur the penalties of treason. Besides, in an absolute monarchy, the will of the prince being the law, a liberty of the press to complain of grievances would be complaining against the law and the constitution, to which they have submitted or have been obliged to submit; and therefore, in one sense, may be said to deserve punishment; so that under an absolute monarchy, I say, such a liberty is inconsistent with the constitution, having no proper subject to politics on which it might be exercised, and if exercised would incur a certain penalty.

But in a limited monarchy, as England is, our laws are known, fixed, and established. They are the straight rule and sure guide to direct the king, the ministers, and other his subjects: And therefore an offense against the laws is such an offense against the constitution as ought to receive a proper adequate punishment; the several constituents of the government, the ministry, and all subordinate magistrates, having their certain, known, and limited sphere in which they move; one part may certainly err, misbehave, and become criminal, without involving the rest or any of them in the crime or punishment.

But some of these may be criminal, yet above punishment, which surely cannot be denied, since most reigns have furnished us with too many instances of powerful and wicked ministers, some of whom by their power have absolutely escaped punishment, and the rest, who met their fate, are likewise instances of this power as much to the purpose; for it was manifest in them that their power had long protected them, their crimes having, often long preceded their much desired and deserved punishment and reward.

That might overcomes right, or which is the same thing, that might preserves and defends men from punishment, is a proverb established and confirmed by time and experience, the surest discoverers of truth and certainty. It is this therefore which makes the liberty of the press in a limited monarchy and in all its colonies and plantations proper, convenient, and necessary, or indeed it is rather incorporated and interwoven with our very constitution; for if such an overgrown criminal, or an impudent monster in iniquity, cannot immediately be come at by ordinary Justice, let him yet receive the lash of satire, let the glaring truths of his ill administration, if possible, awaken his conscience, and if he has no conscience, rouse his fear by showing him his deserts, sting him with the dread of punishment, cover him with shame, and render his actions odious to all honest minds. These methods may in time, and by watching and exposing his actions, make him at least more cautious, and perhaps at last bring down the great haughty and secure criminal within the reach and grasp of ordinary justice. This advantage therefore of exposing the exorbitant crimes of wicked ministers under a limited monarchy makes the liberty of the press not only consistent with, but a necessary part of, the constitution itself.

It is indeed urged that the liberty of the press ought to be restrained because not only the actions of evil ministers may be exposed, but the character of good ones traduced. Admit it in the strongest light that calumny and lies would prevail and blast the character of a great and good minister; yet that is a less evil than the advantages we reap from the liberty of the press, as it is a curb, a bridle, a terror, a shame, and restraint to evil ministers; and it may be the only punishment, especially for a time. But when did calumnies and lies ever destroy the character of one good minister? Their benign influences are known, tasted, and felt by everybody: Or if their characters have been clouded for a time, yet they have generally shined forth in greater luster: Truth will always prevail over falsehood.

The facts exposed are not to be believed because said or published; but it draws people's attention, directs their view, and fixes the eye in a proper position that everyone may judge for himself whether those facts are true or not People will recollect, enquire and search, before they condemn; and therefore very few good ministers can be hurt by falsehood, but many wicked ones by seasonable truth: But however the mischief that a few may possibly, but improbably, suffer by the freedom of the press is not to be put in competition with the danger which the KING and the people may suffer by a shameful, cowardly silence under the tyranny of an insolent, rapacious, infamous minister.

BENJAMIN FRANKLIN **12**

Plan of Union, 1754

In the summer of 1754, delegates from the colonies met at Albany, New York, to discuss the threat of war between Great Britain and France. The French and Indian War would erupt two years later. In the event of such a war, the French would, as in previous wars, stage attacks on the Atlantic colonies from French-controlled Canada. The Albany Congress hoped to establish a plan of defense from any French invasion, uniting all of the colonies into this single defensive purpose. A Pennsylvania delegate, Benjamin Franklin, suggested completely reorganizing the government of the colonies into one unit. His proposal was spelled out in the Plan of Union, which was unanimously adopted by the Albany Congress. King George III, his ministers, and the colonial assemblies rejected the plan, fearing it would give too much power either to the king or the colonies. This was the first attempt to unite the colonies, in this case, for the purpose of security.

It is proposed that humble application be made for an act of Parliament of Great Britain, by virtue of which one general government may be formed in America, including all the said colonies, within and under which government each colony may retain its present constitution, except in the particulars wherein a change may be directed by the said act, as hereafter follows.

1. That the said general government be administered by a President-General, to be appointed and supported by the crown; and a Grand Council, to be chosen by the representatives of the people of the several Colonies met in their respective assemblies.

2. That within—months after the passing such act, the House of Representatives that happen to be sitting within that time, or that shall especially for that purpose convened, may and shall choose members for the Grand Council, in the following proportion, that is to say,

Massachusetts Bay	7
New Hampshire	2
Connecticut	5
Rhode Island	2
New York	4
New Jersey	3
Pennsylvania	6
Maryland	4
Virginia	7
North Carolina	4
South Carolina	4
	48

Benjamin Franklin, "Plan of Union," *The Papers of Benjamin Franklin*, Vol. 5, Leonard W. Labaree, et al., eds. (New Haven, CT: Yale University Press, 1962): 387–393.

3. —who shall meet for the first time at the city of Philadelphia, being called by the President-General as soon as conveniently may be after his appointment.

4. That there shall be a new election of the members of the Grand Council every three years; and, on the death or resignation of any member, his place should be supplied by a new choice at the next sitting of the Assembly of the Colony he represented.

5. That after the first three years, when the proportion of money arising out of each Colony to the general treasury can be known, the number of members to be chosen for each Colony shall, from time to time, in all ensuing elections, be regulated by that proportion, yet so as that the number to be chosen by any one Province be not more than seven, nor less than two.

6. That the Grand Council shall meet once in every year, and oftener if occasion require, at such time and place as they shall adjourn to at the last preceding meeting, or as they shall be called to meet at by the President-General on any emergency; he having first obtained in writing the consent of seven of the members to such call, and sent duly and timely notice to the whole.

7. That the Grand Council have power to choose their speaker; and shall neither be dissolved, prorogued, nor continued sitting longer than six weeks at one time, without their own consent or the special command of the crown.

8. That the members of the Grand Council shall be allowed for their service ten shillings sterling per diem, during their session and journey to and from the place of meeting; twenty miles to be reckoned a day's journey.

9. That the assent of the President-General be requisite to all acts of the Grand Council, and that it be his office and duty to cause them to be carried into execution.

10. That the President-General, with the advice of the Grand Council, hold or direct all Indian treaties, in which the general interest of the Colonies may be concerned; and make peace or declare war with Indian nations.

11. That they make such laws as they judge necessary for regulating all Indian trade.

12. That they make all purchases from Indians, for the crown, of lands not now within the bounds of particular Colonies, or that shall not be within their bounds when some of them are reduced to more convenient dimensions.

13. That they make new settlements on such purchases, by granting lands in the King's name, reserving a quitrent to the crown for the use of the general treasury.

14. That they make laws for regulating and governing such new settlements, till the crown shall think fit to form them into particular governments.

15. That they raise and pay soldiers and build forts for the defence of any of the Colonies, and equip vessels of force to guard the coasts and protect the trade on the ocean, lakes, or great rivers; but they shall not impress men in any Colony, without the consent of the Legislature.

16. That for these purposes they have power to make laws, and lay and levy such general duties, imposts, or taxes, as to them shall appear most equal and just (considering the ability and other circumstances of the inhabitants in the several Colonies), and such as may be collected with the least inconvenience to the people; rather discouraging luxury, than loading industry with unnecessary burdens.

17. That they may appoint a General Treasurer and Particular Treasurer in each government when necessary; and, from time to time, may order the sums in the treasuries of each government into the general treasury; or draw on them for special payments, as they find most convenient.

18. Yet no money to issue but by joint orders of the President-General and Grand Council; except where sums have been appropriated to particular purposes, and the President-General is previously empowered by an act to draw such sums.

19. That the general accounts shall be yearly settled and reported to the several Assemblies.

20. That a quorum of the Grand Council, empowered to act with the President-General, do consist of twenty-five members; among whom there shall be one or more from a majority of the Colonies.

21. That the laws made by them for the purposes aforesaid shall not be repugnant, but, as near as may be, agreeable to the laws of England, and shall be transmitted to the King in Council for approbation, as soon as may be after their passing; and if not disapproved within three years after presentation, to remain in force.

22. That, in case of the death of the President-General, the Speaker of the Grand Council for the time being shall succeed, and be vested with the same powers and authorities, to continue till the King's pleasure be known.

23. That all military commission officers, whether for land or sea service, to act under this general constitution, shall be nominated by the President-General; but the approbation of the Grand Council is to be obtained, before they receive their commissions. And all civil officers are to be nominated by the Grand Council, and to receive the President-General's approbation before they officiate.

24. But, in case of vacancy by death or removal of any officer, civil or military, under this constitution, the Governor of the Province in which such vacancy happens may appoint, till the pleasure of the President-General and Grand Council can be known.

25. That the particular military as well as civil establishments in each Colony remain in their present state, the general constitution notwithstanding; and that on sudden emergencies any Colony may defend itself, and lay the accounts of expense thence arising before the President-General and General Council, who may allow and order payment of the same, as far as they judge such accounts just and reasonable.

13

Petition of the Virginia House of Burgesses to the House of Commons, 1764

After the French and Indian War ended in 1763, the British government faced crushing debts. In order to pay off these wartime debts, the British started increasing the efficiency of their import duty collections and raised taxes. One of these taxes, the Stamp Act, would tax all printed materials and would tax the colonists directly, something that had never happened before. In addition, the colonies had no vote in Parliament to even register a protest. The Stamp Act aroused intense anger in the American colonies and sparked massive demonstrations, boycotts, and petitions against the tax. In December 1764, the Virginia House of Burgesses, the representative assembly, passed this resolution condemning the act and asking Parliament to repeal the legislation. The resolution asserts the rights of Virginians as English subjects, in particular to representation in government before taxation. Parliament would eventually repeal the Stamp Act. But further attempts by the British to tighten their control over the colonies and the clash with the colonists over their rights only alienated the Americans and led to the American Revolution by 1775.

To the Honourable the Knights, Citizens, and Burgesses of Great Britain in Parliament assembled:

The Remonstrance of the Council and Burgesses of Virginia. It appearing by the printed votes of the House of Commons of Great Britain in Parliament assembled that in a committee of the whole House, the 17th day of March last, it was resolved that towards defending, protecting, and securing the British colonies and plantations in America, it may be proper to charge certain stamp duties in the said colonies and plantations; and it being apprehended that the same subject, which was then declined, may be resumed and further pursued in a succeeding session, the Council and Burgesses of Virginia, met in General Assembly, judge it their indispensable duty, in a respectful manner but with decent firmness, to remonstrate against such a measure, that at least a cession of those rights, which in their opinion must be infringed by that procedure, may not be inferred from their silence, at so important a crisis.

They conceive it is essential to British liberty that laws imposing taxes on the people ought not to be made without the consent of representatives chosen by themselves; who, at the same time that they are acquainted with the circumstances of their constituents, sustain a proportion of the burden laid on them. This privilege, inherent in the persons who discovered and settled these regions, could not be renounced or forfeited by their removal hither, not as vagabonds or fugitives, but licensed and encouraged by their prince and animated with a laudable desire of enlarging the British dominion, and extending its commerce. On the contrary, it was secured to them and their descendants, with all other rights and immunities of British subjects, by a royal charter, which hath been invariably recognized and confirmed by his Majesty and his predecessors in their commissions to the several governors, granting a power, and prescribing a forum of legislation; according to which, laws for the administration of justice, and for the welfare and good government of the colony, have been hitherto enacted by the Governor, Council, and General Assembly, and to them requisitions and applications for supplies have been directed by the Crown. As an instance of the opinion which former sovereigns entertained of these rights and privileges, we beg leave to refer to three acts of the General Assembly passed in the 32d year of the reign of King Charles II (one of which is entitled An Act for raising a Public Revenue for the better Support of the Government of his Majesty's Colony of Virginia, imposing several duties for that purpose) which they thought absolutely necessary, were prepared in England, and sent over by their then governor, the Lord Culpepper, to be passed by the General Assembly, with a full power to give the royal assent thereto; and which were accordingly passed, after several amendments were made to them here. Thus tender was his Majesty of the rights of his American subjects; and the remonstrants do not discern by what distinction they can be deprived of that sacred birthright and most valuable inheritance by their fellow subjects, nor with what propriety they can be taxed or affected in their estates by the Parliament, wherein they are not, and indeed cannot, constitutionally be represented. and if it were proper for the Parliament to impose taxes on the colonies at all, which the remonstrants take leave to think would be inconsistent with the fundamental principles of the constitution, the exercise of that power at this time would be ruinous to Virginia, who exerted herself in the late war, it is feared, beyond her strength, insomuch that to redeem the money granted for that exigence her people are taxed for several years to come; this with the large expenses incurred for defending the frontiers against the restless Indians, who have infested her as much since the peace as before, is so grievous that an increase of the burden will be intolerable; especially as the people are very greatly distressed already from the scarcity of circulating cash amongst them, and from the little value of their staple at the British markets.

And it is presumed that adding to that load which the colony now labours under will not be more oppressive to her people than destructive of the interests of Great Britain; for the plantation trade, confined as it is to the mother country, hath been a principal means of multiplying and enriching her inhabitants; and if not too much discouraged, may prove an inexhaustible source of treasure to the nation. For satisfaction in this point, let the present state of the British fleets and trade be compared with what they were before the settlement of the colonies; and let it be considered that whilst property in land may be acquired on very easy terms, in the vast uncultivated territory of North America, the colonists will be mostly, if not wholly, employed in agriculture; whereby the exportation of their commodities of Great Britain, and the consumption of their manufactures supplied from thence, will be daily increasing. But this most desirable connection between Great Britain and her colonies, supported by such a happy intercourse of reciprocal benefits as is continually advancing the prosperity of both, must be interrupted, if the people of the latter, reduced to extreme poverty, should be compelled to manufacture those articles they have been hitherto furnished with from the former.

From these considerations it is hoped that the honourable House of Commons will not prosecute a measure which those who may suffer under it cannot but look upon as fitter for exiles driven from their native country, after ignominiously forfeiting her favours and protection, than for the prosperity of Britons who have at all times been forward to demonstrate all due reverence to the mother kingdom, and are so instrumental in promoting her glory and felicity; and that British patriots will never consent to the exercise of anticonstitutional power, which even in this remote corner may be dangerous in its example to the interior parts of the British Empire, and will certainly be detrimental to its commerce.

JOHN DICKINSON   **14**

Letters from a Farmer in Pennsylvania, III, 1767

The Letters from a Farmer in Pennsylvania *was a series of essays appearing in Pennsylvania newspapers in 1767 and 1768 decrying the new autocratic direction that Parliament seemed to be taking with the colonies, particularly with the Stamp Act, the Quartering Act, and the repression of the New York legislature for protesting the Quartering Act. These essays argue that when a government takes a questionable action, the people have not only the right to object, but should object. The author, John Dickinson, a Philadelphia attorney, did not argue for independence in regards to recent British abuses. He instead argued that governments may occasionally make mistakes, but those mistakes need not destroy the freedoms of the people and can be reversed. The colonists had many options, in his opinion, including later boycotts against Great Britain. He urged cautious action by the colonists to preserve their natural liberties.*

My dear Countrymen,

I rejoice to find that my two former letters to you have been generally received with so much favor by such of you, whose sentiments I have had an opportunity of knowing. Could you look into my heart you would instantly perceive a zealous attachment to your interests, and a lively resentment of every insult and injury offered to you, to be the motives that have engaged me to address you.

I am no further concerned in anything affecting *America*, than any one of you; and when liberty leaves it, I can quit it much more conveniently

John Dickinson, "Letters from a Farmer in Pennsylvania," *Empire and Nation*, Forrest McDonald, ed. (Englewood Cliffs, NJ: Prentice Hall, 1962): 15–18.

than most of you: But while Divine Providence, that gave me existence in a land of freedom, permits my head to think, my lips to speak, and my hand to move, I shall so highly and gratefully value the blessing received as to take care that my silence and inactivity shall not give my implied assent to any act, degrading my brethren and myself from the birthright, wherewith heaven itself "*hath made us free.* "

Sorry I am to learn that there are some few persons who shake their heads with solemn motion, and pretend to wonder, what can be the meaning of these letters. "*Great Britain,* " they say, "is too powerful to contend with; she is determined to oppress us; it is in vain to speak of right on one side, when there is power on the other; when we are strong enough to resist we shall attempt it; but now we are not strong enough, and therefore we had better be quiet; it signifies nothing to convince us that our rights are invaded when we cannot defend them; and if we should get into riots and tumults about the late act, it will only draw down heavier displeasure upon us."

What can such men design? What do their grave observations amount to, but this—"that these colonies, totally regardless of their liberties, should commit them, with humble resignation, to *chance, time,* and the tender mercies of *ministers.* "

Are these men ignorant that usurpations, which might have been successfully opposed at first, acquire strength by continuance, and thus become irresistible? Do they condemn the conduct of these colonies, concerning the *Stamp Act* ? Or have they forgot its successful issue? Should the colonies at that time, instead of acting as they did, have trusted for relief to the fortuitous events of futurity? If it is needless "to speak of rights" now, it was as needless then. If the behavior of the colonies was prudent and glorious then, and successful too; it will be equally prudent and glorious to act in the same manner now, if our rights *are* equally invaded, and may be as successful. Therefore it becomes necessary to inquire whether "our rights are invaded." To talk of "defending" them, as if they could be no otherwise "defended" than by arms, is as much out of the way, as if a man having a choice of several roads to reach his journey's end, should prefer the worst, for no other reason, but because it *is* the worst.

As to "riots and tumults," the gentlemen who are so apprehensive of them, are much mistaken, if they think that grievances cannot be redressed without such assistance.

I will now tell the gentlemen, what is "the meaning of these letters." The meaning of them is, to convince the people of these colonies that they are at this moment exposed to the most imminent dangers; and to persuade them immediately, vigorously, and unanimously, to exert themselves in the most firm, but most peaceable manner, for obtaining relief.

The cause of *liberty* is a cause of too much dignity to be sullied by turbulence and tumult. It ought to be maintained in a manner suitable to her nature. Those who engage in it, should breathe a sedate, yet fervent spirit, animating them to actions of prudence, justice, modesty, bravery, humanity and magnanimity.

To such a wonderful degree were the ancient *Spartans*, as brave and free a people as ever existed, inspired by this happy temperature of soul, that rejecting even in their battles the use of trumpets and other instruments for exciting heat and rage, they marched up to scenes of havoc, and horror, with the sound of flutes, to the tunes of which their steps kept pace—"exhibiting," as *Plutarch* says, "at once a terrible and delightful fight, and proceeding with a deliberate valor, full of hope and good assurance, as if some divinity had sensibly assisted them."

I hope, my dear countrymen, that you will, in every colony, be upon your guard against those who may at any time endeavor to stir you up, under pretenses of patriotism, to any measures disrespectful to our Sovereign, and our mother country. Hot, rash, disorderly proceedings, injure the reputation of the people as to wisdom, valor, and virtue, without procuring them the least benefit. I pray GOD that he may be pleased to inspire you and your posterity, to the latest ages, with a spirit of which I have an idea, that I find a difficulty to express. To express it in the best manner I can, I mean a spirit that shall so guide you that it will be impossible to determine whether an *American's* character is most distinguishable for his loyalty to his Sovereign, his duty to his mother country, his love of freedom, or his affection for his native soil.

Every government at some time or other falls into wrong measures. These may proceed from mistake or passion. But every such measure does not dissolve the obligation between the governors and the governed. The mistake may be corrected; the passion may subside. It is the duty of the governed to endeavor to rectify the mistake, and to appease the passion. They have not at first any other right, than to represent their grievances, and to pray for redress, unless an emergency is so pressing as not to allow time for receiving an answer to their applications, which rarely happens. If their applications are disregarded, then that kind of *opposition* becomes justifiable which can be made without breaking the laws or disturbing the public peace. This conflicts in the *prevention of the oppressors reaping advantage from their oppressions*, and not in their punishment. For experience may teach them what reason did not; and harsh methods cannot be proper until milder ones have failed.

If at length it becomes undoubted that an inveterate resolution is formed to annihilate the liberties of the governed, the *English* history affords frequent examples of resistance by force. What particular circumstances will in any future case justify such resistance can never be ascertained till they happen. Perhaps it may be allowable to say generally, that it never can be justifiable until the people are fully convinced that any further submission will be destructive to their happiness.

When the appeal is made to the sword, highly probable is it, that the punishment will exceed the offense; and the calamities attending on war outweigh those preceding it. These considerations of justice and prudence, will always have great influence with good and wise men.

To these reflections on this subject, it remains to be added, and ought for ever to be remembered, that resistance, in the case of colonies against their mother country, is extremely different from the resistance of a people against their prince. A nation may change their king, or race of kings, and, retaining their ancient form of government, be gainers by changing. Thus *Great Britain*, under the illustrious house of *Brunswick*, a house that seems to flourish for the happiness of mankind, has found a felicity unknown in the reigns of the *Stuarts*. But if once *we* are separated from our mother country, what new form of government shall we adopt, or where shall we find another *Britain* to supply our loss? Torn from the body, to which we are united by religion, liberty, laws, affections, relation, language and commerce, we must bleed at every vein.

In truth—the prosperity of these provinces is founded in their dependence on *Great Britain;* and when she returns to her "old good humor, and her old good nature," as Lord *Clarendon* expresses it, I hope they will always think it their duty and interest, as it most certainly will be, to promote her welfare by all the means in their power.

We cannot act with too much caution in our disputes. Anger produces anger; and differences, that might be accommodated by kind and respectful behavior, may, by imprudence, be enlarged to an incurable rage. In quarrels between countries, as well as in those between individuals, when they have risen to a certain height, the first cause of dissension is no longer remembered, the minds of the parties being wholly engaged in recollecting and resenting the mutual expressions of their dislike. When feuds have reached that fatal point, all considerations of reason and equity vanish; and a blind fury governs, or rather confounds all things. A people no longer regards their interest, but the gratification of their wrath. The sway of the *Cleons and Clodiuses*, the designing and detectable flatterers of the *prevailing passion*, becomes confirmed. Wise and good men in vain oppose the storm, and may think themselves fortunate, if, in attempting to preserve their ungrateful fellow citizens, they do not ruin themselves. Their *prudence* will be called *baseness;* their *moderation* will be called guilt; and if their virtue does not lead them to destruction, as that of many other great and excellent persons has done, they may survive to receive from their expiring country the mournful glory of her acknowledgment, that their counsels, if regarded, would have saved her.

The constitutional modes of obtaining relief are those which I wish to see pursued on the present occasion; that is, by petitions of our assemblies, or where they are not permitted to meet, of the people, to the powers that can afford us relief.

We have an excellent prince [King George III], in whose good dispositions toward us we may confide. We have a generous, sensible and humane nation, to whom we may apply. They may be deceived. They may, by artful men, be provoked to anger against us. I cannot believe they will be cruel and unjust; or that their anger will be implacable. Let us behave like dutiful children who have received unmerited blows from a beloved parent. Let us complain to our parent; but let our complaints speak at the same time the language of affliction and veneration.

If, however, it shall happen, by an unfortunate course of affairs, that our applications to his Majesty and the parliament for redress, prove ineffectual, let us then take *another step*, by withholding from *Great Britain* all the advantages she has been used to receive from us. Then let us try, if our ingenuity, industry, and frugality, will not give weight to our remonstrances. Let us all be united with one spirit, in one cause. Let us invent—let us work—let us save—let us, continually, keep up our claim, and incessantly repeat our complaints — But, above all, let us implore the protection of that infinitely good and gracious being, "by whom kings reign, and princes decree justice."

Nil desperandum.

Nothing is to be despaired of.

A Farmer

BENJAMIN FRANKLIN **15**

Rules by Which a Great Empire May be Reduced to a Small One, 1773

Benjamin Franklin often used satire to make a larger point. His wit won him great adulation among the American people. In 1773, while he served as a colonial agent in London, he tried in vain to convince the British government to change its positions on taxation and the rights of the colonies in hopes of repairing the damaged relations between Great Britain and the American colonies. In this September 11, 1773, article, "Rules by Which a Great Empire May be Reduced to a Small One," Franklin argues that the hard-line stance against the colonies would neither solve the financial crisis of the United Kingdom nor undercut the growing opposition to British policies in the colonies, but instead these policies in the end would only herald the destruction of the British Empire. He issued the article anonymously in a newspaper, signing it only "Q. E. D.," Latin for "which was demonstrated," a phrase often used in philosophical debates. The article had no impact on British policy, but it became a powerful statement on the rights of the colonists to equality under the law and as citizens of the British Empire.

September 11, 1773

For the Public Advertiser.

RULES *by which a* GREAT EMPIRE *may be reduced to a* SMALL ONE. [Presented privately to a *late Minister* (a reference to Lord Hillsborough, British prime minister from 1768 to 1770), when he entered upon his Administration; and now first published.]

Franklin, "Rules by Which a Great Empire May Be Reduced to a Small One," *The Papers of Benjamin Franklin*, Vol. 20, William B. Willcox, ed. (New Haven, CT: Yale University Press, 1976): 414–418.

An ancient Sage valued himself upon this, that tho' he could not fiddle, he knew how to make a *great City* of a *little one*. The Science that I, a modern Simpleton, am about to communicate is the very reverse.

I address myself to all Ministers who have the Management of extensive Dominions, which from their very Greatness are become troublesome to govern, because the Multiplicity of their Affairs leaves no Time for *fiddling*.

I In the first Place, Gentlemen, you are to consider, that a great Empire, like a great Cake, is most easily diminished at the Edges. Turn your Attention therefore first to your remotest Provinces; that as you get rid of them, the next may follow in Order.

II That the Possibility of this Separation may always exist, take special Care the Provinces are never incorporated with the Mother Country, that they do not enjoy the same common Rights, the same Privileges in Commerce, and that they are governed by *severer* Laws, all of *your enacting*, without allowing them any Share in the Choice of the Legislators. By carefully making and preserving such Distinctions, you will (to keep my Simile of the Cake) act like a wise Gingerbread Baker, who, to facilitate a Division, cuts his Dough half through in those Places, where, when bak'd, he would have it *broken to Pieces*.

III These remote Provinces have perhaps been acquired, purchas'd, or conquer'd, at the *sole Expence* of the Settlers or their Ancestors, without the Aid of the Mother Country. If this should happen to increase her *Strength* by their growing Numbers ready to join in her Wars, her *Commerce* by their growing Demand for her Manufactures, or her *Naval Power* by greater Employment for her Ships and Seamen, they may probably suppose some Merit in this, and that it entitles them to some Favour; you are therefore to *forget it all*, or resent it as if they had done you Injury. If they happen to be zealous Whigs, Friends of Liberty, nurtur'd in Revolution Principles, *remember all that* to their Prejudice, and contrive to punish it: For such Principles, after a Revolution is thoroughly established, are of *no more Use*, they are even *odious* and *abominable*.

IV However peaceably your Colonies have submitted to your Government, shewn their Affection to your Interest, and patiently borne their Grievances, you are to *suppose* them always inclined to revolt, and treat them accordingly. Quarter Troops among the, who by their Insolence may *provoke* the rising of Mobs, and by their Bullets and Bayonets *suppress* them. By this Means, like the Husband who uses his Wife ill *from Suspicion*, you may in Time convert your *Suspicions* into *Realities*.

V Remote Provinces must have *Governors*, and *Judges*, to represent the Royal Person, and execute every where the delegated Parts of his Office and Authority. You Ministers know, that much of the Strength of Government depends on the *Opinion* of the People; and much of that Opinion on the Choice of Rulers placed immediately over them. If you send them wise and good Men for Governors, who study the Interest of the Colonists, and advance their Prosperity, they will think their King wise and good, and that he wishes the Welfare of his Subjects. If you send the learned and upright Men for judges, they will think him a Lover of Justice. This may attach your Provinces more to his Government. You are therefore to be careful who you recommend for those Offices. If you can find Prodigals who have ruined their Fortunes, broken Gamesters or Stock-Jobbers, these may do well as *Governors*; for they will probably be rapacious, and provoke the People by their Extortions. Wrangling Proctors and petty fogging Lawyers too are not amiss, for they will be for ever disputing and quarrelling with their little Parliaments, if withal they should be ignorant, wrong-headed and insolent, so much the better. Attorneys Clerks and Newgate Solicitors will do for *Chief-Justices*, especially if they hold their Places *during your Pleasure*; And all will contribute to impress those ideas of your Government that are proper for a People *you would wish to renounce it.*

VI To confirm these Impressions, and strike them deeper, whenever the Injured come to the Capital with Complaints of Mal-administration, Oppression, or Injustice, punish such Suitors with long Delay, enormous Expence, and a final Judgment in Favour of the Oppressor. This will have an admirable Effect every Way. The Trouble of future Complaints will be prevented, and Governors and Judges will be encouraged to farther Acts of Oppression and Injustice; and thence the People may become more disaffected, *and at length desperate.*

VII When such Governors have crammed their Coffers, and made themselves so odious to the People that they can no longer remain among them with Safety to their Persons, recall and *reward* them with Pensions. You may make them *Baronets* too, if that respectable Order should not think fit to resent it. All will contribute to encourage new Governors in the same Practices, and make the supreme Government *detestable.*

VIII If when you are engaged in War, your Colonies should vie in liberal Aids of Men and Money against the common Enemy, upon your simple Requisition, and give far beyond their Abilities, reflect, that a Penny taken from them by your Power is more honourable to you than a Pound presented by their Benevolence. Despise therefore their voluntary Grants, and resolve to harrass them with novel Taxes. They will probably complain to your Parliaments that they are taxed by a Body in which they have no Representative, and that this is contrary to common Right. They will petition for Redress. Let the Parliaments flout their Claims, reject their Petitions, refuse even to suffer the reading of them, and treat the Petitioners with the utmost Contempt. Nothing can have a better Effect, in producing the Alienation proposed; for though many can forgive Injuries, *none ever forgave Contempt.*

IX In laying these Taxes, never regard the heavy Burthens those remote People already undergo, in defending their own Frontiers, supporting their own provincial Governments, making new Roads, building Bridges, Churches and other public Edifices, which in old Countries have been done to your Hands by your Ancestors, but which occasion constant Calls and Demands on the Purses of a new People. Forget the *Restraints* you lay on their Trade for *your own* Benefit, and the Advantage a *Monopoly* of this Trade gives your exacting Merchants. Think nothing of the Wealth those Merchants and your Manufacturers acquire by the Colony Commerce; their encreased Ability thereby to pay Taxes at home; their accumulating, in the Price of their Commodities, most of those Taxes, and so levying them from their consuming Customers: All this, and the Employment and Support of thousands of your Poor by the Colonists, you are *intirely to forget*, But remember to make your arbitrary Tax more grievous to your Provinces, by public Declarations importing that your Power of taxing them has *no limits*, so that when you take from them without their Consent a Shilling in the Pound, you have a clear Right to the other nineteen. This will probably weaken every Idea of *Security in their Property*, and convince them that under such a Government *they have nothing they can call their own*; which can scarce fail of producing *the happiest Consequences*!

X Possibly indeed some of them might still comfort themselves, and say, "Though we have no Property, we have yet *something* left that is valuable; we have constitutional *Liberty* both of Person and of Conscience. This King, these Lords, and these Commons, who it seems are too remote from us to know us and feel for us, cannot take from us our *Habeas Corpus* Right, or our Right of Trial *by a Jury of our Neighbours* : They cannot deprive us of the Exercise of our Religion, alter our ecclesiastical Constitutions, and compel us to be Papists if they please, or Mahometans." To annihilate this Comfort, begin by Laws to perplex their Commerce with infinite Regulations impossible to be remembered and observed; ordain Seizures of their Property for every Failure; take away the Trial of such Property by Jury, and give it to arbitrary Judges of your own appointing, and of the lowest Characters in the Country, whose Salaries and Emoluments are to arise out of the Duties or Condemnations, and whose Appointments are *during Pleasure*. Then let there be a formal Declaration of both Houses, that Opposition to your Edicts is *Treason*, and that Persons suspected of Treason in the Provinces may, according to some obsolete Law, be seized and sent to the Metropolis of the Empire for Trial; and pass an Act that those there charged with certain other Offences shall be sent away in Chains from their Friends and Country to be tried in the same Manner for Felony. Then erect a new Court of Inquisition among them, accompanied by an armed Force, with Instructions to transport all such suspected Persons, to be ruined by the Expence if they bring over Evidences to prove their Innocence, or be found guilty and hanged if they can't afford it. And lest the People should think you cannot possibly go any farther, pass another solemn declaratory Act, that "King, Lords, and Commons had, hath, and of Right ought to have, full Power and Authority to make Statutes of sufficient Force and Validity to bind the unrepresented Provinces IN ALL CASES WHATSOEVER." This will include *Spiritual* with temporal; and taken together, must operate wonderfully to your Purpose, by convincing them, that they are at present under a Power something like that spoken of in the Scriptures, which can not only *kill their Bodies*, but *damn their Souls* to all Eternity, by compelling them, if it pleases, *to worship the Devil*.

XI To make your Taxes more odious, and more likely to procure Resistance, send from the Capital a Board of Officers to superintend the Collection, composed of the most *indiscreet*, *ill-bred*, and *insolent* you can find. Let these have large Salaries out of the extorted Revenue, and live in open grating Luxury upon the Sweat and Blood of the Industrious, whom they are to worry continually with groundless and expensive Prosecutions before the above-mentioned arbitrary Revenue-Judges, all *at the Cost of the Party prosecuted* tho' acquitted, because *the King is to pay no Costs*. Let these Men *by your Order* be exempted from all the common Taxes and Burthens of the Province, though they and their Property are protected by its Laws. If any Revenue Officers are *suspected* of the least Tenderness for the People, discard them. If others are justly complained of, protect and reward them. If any of the Under-officers behave so as to provoke the People to drub them, promote those to better Offices: This will encourage others to procure for themselves such profitable Drubbings, by multiplying and enlarging such Provocations, *and all with work towards the End you aim at.*

XII Another Way to make your Tax odious, is to misapply the Produce of it. If it was originally appropriated for the *Defence* of the Provinces and the better Support of Government, and the Administration of Justice where it may be *necessary*, then apply none of it to that *Defence*, but bestow it where it is *not necessary*, in augmented Salaries or Pensions to every Governor who has distinguished himself by his Enmity to the People, and by calumniating them to their Sovereign. This will make them pay it more unwillingly, and be more apt to quarrel with those that collect it, and those that imposed it, who will quarrel again with them, and shall contribute to your *main Purpose* of making them *weary of your Government.*

XIII If the People of any Province have been accustomed to support their own Governors and Judges to Satisfaction, you are to apprehend that such Governors and Judges may be thereby influenced to treat the People kindly, and to do them Justice. This is another Reason for applying Part of that Revenue in larger Salaries to such Governors and Judges, given, as their Commissions are, *during your Pleasure* only, forbidding them to take any Salaries from their Provinces; that thus the People may no longer hope any Kindness from their Governors, or (in Crown Cases) any Justice from their Judges. And as the Money thus mis-applied in one Province is extorted from all, probably *all will resent the Misapplication.*

XIV If the Parliaments of your Provinces should dare to claim Rights or complain of your Administration, order them to be harass'd with repeated *Dissolutions.* If the same Men are continually return'd by new Elections, adjourn their Meetings to some Country Village where they cannot be accommodated, and there keep them *during Pleasure*; for this, you know, is your PREROGATIVE; and an excellent one it is, as you may manage it, to promote Discontents among the People, diminish their Respect, and *increase their Disaffection.*

XV Convert the brave honest Officers of your Navy into pimping Tide-waiters and Colony Officers of the Customs. Let those who in Time of War fought gallantly in Defence of the Commerce of their Countrymen, in Peace be taught to prey upon it. Let them learn to be corrupted by great and real Smugglers; but (to shew their Diligence) scour with armed Boats every Bay, Harbour, River, Creek, Cove or Nook throughout the Coast of your Colonies, stop and detain every Coaster, every Woodboat, every Fisherman, tumble their Cargoes, and even their Ballast, inside out and upside down; and if a Penn'orth of Pins is found un-entered, let the Whole be seized and confiscated. Thus shall the Trade of your Colonists suffer more from their Friends in Time of Peace, than it did from their Enemies in War. Then let these Boats Crews land upon every Farm in their Way, rob the Orchards, steal the Pigs and Poultry, and insult the Inhabitants. If the injured and exasperated Farmers, unable to procure other Justice, should attack the Agressors, drub them and burn their Boats, you are to call this *High Treason* and *Rebellion*, order Fleets and Armies into their Country, and threaten to carry all the Offenders three thousand Miles to be hang'd, drawn and quartered. *O! this will work admirably!*

XVI If you are told of Discontents in your Colonies, never believe that they are general, or that you have given Occasion for them; therefore do not think of applying any Remedy, or of changing any offensive Measure. Redress no Grievance, lest they should be encouraged to demand the Redress of some other Grievance. Grant no Request that is just and reasonable, lest they should make another that is unreasonable. Take all your Informations of the State of the Colonies from your Governors and Officers in Enmity with them. Encourage and reward these *Leasing-makers*; secrete their lying Accusations lest they should be confuted; but act upon them as the clearest Evidence, and believe nothing you hear from the Friends of the People. Suppose all *their* Complaints to be invented and promoted by a few factious Demagogues, whom if you could catch and hang, all would be quiet. Catch and hang a few of them accordingly; and the *Blood of the Martyrs* shall *work Miracles* in favour of your Purpose.

XVII If you see *rival Nations* rejoicing at the Prospect of your Disunion with your Provinces, and endeavouring to promote it: If they translate, publish and applaud all the Complaints of your discontented Colonists, at the same Time privately stimulating you to severer Measures; let not that *alarm* or offend you. Why should it? since you all mean *the same Thing*.

XVIII If any Colony should at their own Charge erect a Fortress to secure their Port against the Fleets of a foreign Enemy, get your Governor to betray that Fortress into your Hands. Never think of paying what it cost the Country, for that would *look*, at least, like some Regard for Justice; but turn it into a Citadel to awe the Inhabitants and curb their Commerce. If they should have lodged in such Fortress the very Arms they bought and used to aid you in your Conquests, seize them all, 'twill provoke like *Ingratitude* added to *Robbery*. One admirable Effect of these Operations will be, to discourage every other Colony from erecting such Defences, and so their and your Enemies may more easily invade them, to the great Disgrace of your Government, and of course *the Furtherance of your Project*.

XIX Send Armies into their Country under Pretence of protecting the Inhabitants; but instead of garrisoning the Forts on their Frontiers with those Troops, to prevent Incursions, demolish those Forts, and order the Troops into the Heart of the Country, that the Savages may be encouraged to attack the Frontiers, and that the Troops may be protected by the Inhabitants: This will seem to proceed from your Ill will or your Ignorance, and contribute farther to produce and strengthen an Opinion among them, *that you are no longer fit to govern them*.

XX Lastly, Invest the General of your Army in the Provinces with great and unconstitutional Powers, and free him from the Controul of even your own Civil Governors. Let him have Troops enow under his Command, with all the Fortresses in his Possession; and who knows but (like some provincial Generals in the Roman Empire, and encouraged by the universal Discontent you have produced) he may take it into his Head to set up for himself. If he should, and you have carefully practised these few *excellent Rules* of mine, take my Word for it, all the Provinces will immediately join him, and you will that Day (if you have not done it sooner) get rid of the Trouble of governing them, and all the *Plagues* attending their *Commerce* and Connection from thenceforth and for ever.

Q. E. D.

PHILLIS WHEATLEY **16**

Letter Against Slavery, 1774

Phillis Wheatley, among the earliest of African-American poets in the United States, wrote extensively on her experiences as a slave in the years leading to the American Revolution. In this letter to Rev. Samson Occom, a Christian convert from the Mohegan nation, Wheatley describes how her own desire for freedom was just as strong and legitimate as the enslaved Israelites in the Bible. Further, in an argument to be echoed by abolitionists in the future, Wheatley contends that liberty and justice mean nothing without freedom, especially the freedom to control an individual's own life. The letter was written on February 11, 1774, and reprinted in the Connecticut Gazette *on March 11.*

Reverend and honoured Sir,

I have this day received your obliging kind epistle, and am greatly satisfied with your reasons respecting the negroes, and think highly reasonable what you offer in vindication of their natural rights: Those that invade them cannot be insensible that the divine light is chasing away the thick darkness which broods over the land of Africa; and the chaos which has reigned so long, is converting into beautiful order, and reveals more and more clearly the glorious dispensation of civil and religious liberty, which are so inseparably united, that there is little or no enjoyment of one without the other: Otherwise, perhaps, the Israelites had been less solicitous for their freedom from Egyptian slavery; I do not say they would have been contented without it, by no means; for in every human breast God has implanted a principle, which we call Love of Freedom; it is impatient of oppression, and pants for deliverance; and by the leave of our modern Egyptians I will assert, that the same principle lives in us. God grant deliverance in his own way and time, and get him honour upon all those whose avarice impels them to countenance and help forward the calamities of their fellow creatures. This I desire not for their hurt, but to convince them of the strange absurdity of their conduct, whose words and actions are so diametrically opposite. How well the cry for liberty, and the reverse disposition for the exercise of oppressive power over others agree—I humbly think it does not require the penetration of a philosopher to determine.

17

The Declaration of American Rights, Continental Congress, 1774

As tensions grew between Great Britain and the American colonies, colonial leaders decided to meet to discuss their grievances with Parliament and King George III. The Boston Massacre had left five Boston residents dead in 1770, inflaming colonial tensions. The British continued to raid homes, ports, warehouses, and businesses under the suspicion that some taxes had not been paid on goods. In 1773, Parliament passed the Tea Act to bail out a major import–export company, the East India Co., by giving it a virtual monopoly on the tea trade. Disgusted by the show of such special privilege, a small group in Boston boarded British ships in December 1773 and threw the tea into the harbor in protest. In response to the Boston Tea Party, Parliament passed the Coercive Acts to punish the whole city of Boston until the shippers had been reimbursed for the thousands of dollars in damage. Boston refused, and its port was closed in response. Parliament added insult to injury with the Quebec Act in 1774 which extended an autocratic, Roman Catholic-dominated government over the Ohio Valley, which was coveted by colonial speculators who envisioned Protestant, representative governments for the region.

Colonial leaders met in Philadelphia, Pennsylvania, as the first Continental Congress in September 1774. This resolution, passed on October 14, the Declaration of American Rights, averred the principles of the colonists. In the declaration, the delegates clamor for their rights as English subjects and demand a system of free government within the British system. The delegates were not yet ready to declare independence but remained fully aware of what lay at stake. Echoing the words of philosopher John Locke, the delegates declared that they had the rights of life, liberty, and property. In addition, the delegates proclaimed their rights to due process of law and the right to representative government. This resolution, along with many others, went unheeded by Parliament.

Whereas, since the close of the last war, the British parliament, claiming a power, of right, to bind the people of America by statutes in all cases whatsoever, hath, in some acts, expressly imposed taxes on them, and in others, under various presences, but in fact for the purpose of raising a revenue, hath imposed rates and duties payable in these colonies, established a board of commissioners, with unconstitutional powers, and extended the jurisdiction of courts of admiralty, not only for

Richard D. Brown, ed., "Declarations and Resolves of the First Continental Congress," Major Problems in the Era of the American Revolution, 1760-1791, 2nd ed. (Boston: Houghton Mifflin, 2000): 152–154.

collecting the said duties, but for the trial of causes merely arising within the body of a county:

And whereas, in consequence of other statutes, judges, who before held only estates at will in their offices, have been made dependant on the crown alone for their salaries, and standing armies kept in times of peace: And whereas it has lately been resolved in parliament, that by force of a statute, made in the thirty-fifth year of the reign of King Henry the Eighth, colonists may be transported to England, and tried there upon accusations for treasons and misprisions, or concealments of treasons committed in the colonies, and by a late statute, such trials have been directed in cases therein mentioned:

And whereas, in the last session of parliament, three statutes were made; one entitled, "An act to discontinue, in such manner and for such time as are therein mentioned, the landing and discharging, lading, or shipping of goods, wares and merchandise, at the town, and within the harbour of Boston, in the province of Massachusetts-Bay in New England;" another entitled, "An act for the better regulating the government of the province of Massachusetts-Bay in New England;" and another entitled, "An act for the impartial administration of justice, in the cases of persons questioned for any act done by them in the execution of the law, or for the suppression of riots and tumults, in the province of the Massachusetts-Bay in New England;" and another statute was then made, "for making more effectual provision for the government of the province of Quebec, etc." All which statutes are impolitic, unjust, and cruel, as well as unconstitutional, and most dangerous and destructive of American rights:

And whereas, assemblies have been frequently dissolved, contrary to the rights of the people, when they attempted to deliberate on grievances; and their dutiful, humble, loyal, and reasonable petitions to the crown for redress, have been repeatedly treated with contempt, by his Majesty's ministers of state:

The good people of the several colonies of New-Hampshire, Massachusetts-Bay, Rhode Island and Providence Plantations, Connecticut, New-York, New-Jersey, Pennsylvania, Newcastle, Kent, and Sussex on Delaware, Maryland, Virginia, North-Carolina and South-Carolina, justly alarmed at these arbitrary proceedings of parliament and administration, have severally elected, constituted, and appointed deputies to meet, and sit in general Congress, in the city of Philadelphia, in order to obtain such establishment, as that their religion, laws, and liberties, may not be subverted: Whereupon the deputies so appointed being now assembled, in a full and free representation of these colonies, taking into their most serious consideration, the best means of attaining the ends aforesaid, do, in the first place, as Englishmen, their ancestors in like cases have usually done, for asserting and vindicating their rights and liberties, DECLARE,

That the inhabitants of the English colonies in North-America, by the immutable laws of nature, the principles of the English constitution, and the several charters or compacts, have the following RIGHTS:

Resolved, N.C.D. 1. That they are entitled to life, liberty and property: and they have never ceded to any foreign power whatever, a right to dispose of either without their consent.

Resolved, N.C.D. 2. That our ancestors, who first settled these colonies, were at the time of their emigration from the mother country, entitled to all the rights, liberties, and immunities of free and natural- born subjects, within the realm of England.

Resolved, N.C.D. 3. That by such emigration they by no means forfeited, surrendered, or lost any of those rights, but that they were, and their descendants now are, entitled to the exercise and enjoyment of all such of them, as their local and other circumstances enable them to exercise and enjoy.

Resolved, 4. That the foundation of English liberty, and of all free government, is a right in the people to participate in their legislative council: and as the English colonists are not represented, and from their local and other circumstances, cannot properly be represented in the British parliament, they are entitled to a free and exclusive power of legislation in their several provincial legislatures, where their right of representation can alone be preserved, in all cases of taxation and internal polity, subject only to the negative of their sovereign, in such manner as has been heretofore used and accustomed: But, from the necessity of the case, and a regard to the mutual interest of both countries, we cheerfully consent to the operation of such acts of the British parliament, as are bona fide, restrained to the regulation of our external commerce, for the purpose of securing the commercial advantages of the whole empire to the mother country, and the commercial benefits of its respective members; excluding every idea of taxation internal or external, for raising a revenue on the subjects, in America, without their consent.

Resolved, N.C.D. 5. That the respective colonies are entitled to the common law of England, and more especially to the great and inestimable privilege of being tried by their peers of the vicinage, according to the course of that law.

Resolved, N.C.D. 6. That they are entitled to the benefit of such of the English statutes, as existed at the time of their colonization; and which they have, by experience, respectively found to be applicable to their several local and other circumstances.

Resolved, N.C.D. 7. That these, his Majesty's colonies, are likewise entitled to all the immunities and privileges granted and confirmed to them by royal charters, or secured by their several codes of provincial laws.

Resolved, N.C.D. 8. That they have a right peaceably to assemble, consider of their grievances, and petition the king; and that all prosecutions, prohibitory proclamations, and commitments for the same, are illegal.

Resolved, N.C.D. 9. That the keeping a standing army in these colonies, in times of peace, without the consent of the legislature of that colony, in which such army is kept, is against law.

Resolved, N.C.D. 10. It is indispensably necessary to good government, and rendered essential by the English constitution, that the constituent branches of the legislature be independent of each other; that, therefore, the exercise of legislative power in several colonies, by a council appointed, during pleasure, by the crown, is unconstitutional, dangerous and destructive to the freedom of American legislation.

All and each of which the aforesaid deputies, in behalf of themselves, and their constituents, do claim, demand, and insist on, as their indubitable rights and liberties, which cannot be legally taken from them, altered or abridged by any power whatever, without their own consent, by their representatives in their several provincial legislature.

In the course of our inquiry, we find many infringements and violations of the foregoing rights, which, from an ardent desire, that harmony and mutual intercourse of affection and interest may be restored, we pass over for the present, and proceed to state such acts and measures as have been adopted since the last war, which demonstrate a system formed to enslave America.

Resolved, N.C.D. That the following acts of parliament are infringements and violations of the rights of the colonists; and that the repeal of them is essentially necessary, in order to restore harmony between Great Britain and the American colonies, viz.

The several acts of Geo. III. ch. 15, and ch. 34.-5 Geo. III. ch.25.-6 Geo. ch. 52.-7 Geo.III. ch. 41 and ch. 46.-8 Geo. III. ch. 22. which impose duties for the purpose of raising a revenue in America, extend the power of the admiralty courts beyond their ancient limits, deprive the American subject of trial by jury, authorize the judges certificate to indemnify the prosecutor from damages, that he might otherwise be liable to, requiring oppressive security from a claimant of ships and goods seized, before he shall be allowed to defend his property, and are subversive of American rights.

Also 12 Geo. III. ch. 24, intituled, "An act for the better securing his majesty's dockyards, magazines, ships, ammunition, and stores," which declares a new offence in America, and deprives the American subject of a constitutional trial by jury of the vicinage, by authorizing the trial of any person, charged with the committing any offence described in the said act, out of the realm, to be indicted and tried for the same in any shire or county within the realm.

Also the three acts passed in the last session of parliament, for stopping the port and blocking up the harbour of Boston, for altering the charter and government of Massachusetts-Bay, and that which is entitled, "An act for the better administration of justice, etc."

Also the act passed in the same session for establishing the Roman Catholic religion, in the province of Quebec, abolishing the equitable system of English laws, and erecting a tyranny there, to the great danger (from so total a dissimilarity of religion, law and government) of the neighboring British colonies, by the assistance of whose blood and treasure the said country was conquered from France.

Also the act passed in the same session, for the better providing suitable quarters for officers and soldiers in his majesty's service, in North-America.

Also, that the keeping a standing army in several of these colonies, in time of peace, without the consent of the legislature of that colony, in which such army is kept, is against law.

To these grievous acts and measures, Americans cannot submit, but in hopes their fellow subjects in Great Britain will, on a revision of them, restore us to that state, in which both countries found happiness and prosperity, we have for the present, only resolved to pursue the following peaceable measures: 1. To enter into a non-importation, non-consumption, and non-exportation agreement or association. 2. To prepare an address to the people of Great-Britain, and a memorial to the inhabitants of British America: and 3. To prepare a loyal address to his majesty, agreeable to resolutions already entered into.

18

Articles of Association, Continental Congress, 1774

The delegates were becoming increasingly concerned about the treatment of the colonists—British citizens—by Parliament. The delegates agreed that they must defend their rights and passed a number of resolutions to that effect. Among the other resolutions passed by the first Continental Congress were the Articles of Association, on October 20, 1774. This resolution listed the grievances of the colonists, including the Quebec Act and the Coercive Acts. The delegates, while still professing their loyalty to the British government, announced that a boycott of British products would begin in protest of British actions against the colonies. The Continental Congress instructed local communities to form committees to enforce the boycotts. The resolution also announced that the colonists would also stop selling to Britain, non-exportation in 1775, unless the British gave into colonial demands. Parliament refused to yield, and the two were set on a collision course to the Revolutionary War.

We, his majesty's most loyal subjects, the delegates of the several colonies of New-Hampshire, Massachusetts-Bay, Rhode-Island, Connecticut, New-York, New-Jersey, Pennsylvania, the three lower counties of New-Castle, Kent and Sussex, on Delaware, Maryland, Virginia, North-Carolina, and South-Carolina, deputed to represent them in a continental Congress, held in the city of Philadelphia, on the 5th day of September, 1774, avowing our allegiance to his majesty, our affection and regard for our fellow-subjects in Great-Britain and elsewhere, affected with the deepest anxiety, and most alarming apprehensions, at those grievances and distresses, with which his Majesty's American subjects are oppressed; and having taken under our most serious deliberation, the state of the whole continent, find, that the present unhappy situation of our affairs is occasioned by a ruinous system of colony administration, adopted by the British ministry about the year 1763, evidently calculated for inslaving these colonies, and, with them, the British Empire. In prosecution of which system, various acts of parliament have been passed, for raising a revenue in America, for depriving the American subjects, in many instances, of the constitutional trial by jury, exposing their lives to danger, by directing a new and illegal trial beyond the seas, for crimes alleged to have been committed in America: and in prosecution of the same system, several late, cruel, and oppressive acts have been passed, respecting the town of Boston and the Massachusetts-Bay, and also an act for extending the province of Quebec, so as to border on the western frontiers of these colonies, establishing an arbitrary government therein, and discouraging the settlement of British subjects in that wide extended country; thus, by the influence of civil principles and ancient prejudices, to dispose the inhabitants to act with hostility against the free Protestant colonies, whenever a wicked ministry shall chuse so to direct them.

To obtain redress of these grievances, which threaten destruction to the lives, liberty, and property of his majesty's subjects, in North America, we are of opinion, that a non-importation, non-consumption, and non-exportation agreement, faithfully adhered to, will prove the most speedy, effectual, and peaceable measure: and, therefore, we do, for ourselves, and the inhabitants of the several colonies, whom we represent, firmly agree and associate, under the sacred ties of virtue, honour and love of our country, as follows:

1. That from and after the first day of December next, we will not import, into British America, from Great-Britain or Ireland, any goods, wares, or merchandise whatsoever, or from any other place, any such goods, wares, or merchandise, as shall have been exported from Great-Britain or Ireland; nor will we, after that day, import any East-India tea from any part of the world; nor any molasses, syrups, paneles, coffee, or pimento, from the British plantations or from Dominica; nor wines from Madeira, or the Western Islands; nor foreign indigo.

2. We will neither import nor purchase, any slave imported after the first day of December next; after which time, we will wholly discontinue the slave trade, and will neither be concerned in it ourselves, nor will we hire our vessels, nor sell our commodities or manufactures to those who are concerned in it.

3. As a non-consumption agreement, strictly adhered to, will be an effectual security for the observation of the non-importation, we, as above, solemnly agree and associate, that from this day, we will not purchase or use any tea, imported on account of the East-India company, or any on which a duty hath been or shall be paid; and from and after the first day of March next, we will not purchase or use any East-India tea whatever; nor will we, nor shall any person for or under us, purchase or use any of those goods, wares, or merchandise, we have agreed not to import, which we shall know, or have cause to suspect, were imported after the first day of December, except such as come under the rules and directions of the tenth article hereafter mentioned.

4. The earnest desire we have, not to injure our fellow-subjects in Great-Britain, Ireland, or the West-Indies, induces us to suspend a non-exportation, until the tenth day of September, 1775; at which time, if the said acts and parts of acts of the British parliament herein after mentioned, ate not repealed, we will not, directly or indirectly, export any merchandise or commodity whatsoever to Great-Britain, Ireland, or the West-Indies, except rice to Europe.

5. Such as are merchants, and use the British and Irish trade, will give orders, as soon as possible, to their factors, agents and correspondents, in Great-Britain and Ireland, not to ship any goods to them, on any pretence whatsoever, as they cannot be received in

America; and if any merchant, residing in Great-Britain or Ireland, shall directly or indirectly ship any goods, wares or merchandize, for America, in order to break the said non-importation agreement, or in any manner contravene the same, on such unworthy conduct being well attested, it ought to be made public; and, on the same being so done, we will not, from thenceforth, have any commercial connexion with such merchant.

6. That such as are owners of vessels will give positive orders to their captains, or masters, not to receive on board their vessels any goods prohibited by the said non-importation agreement, on pain of immediate dismission from their service.

7. We will use our utmost endeavours to improve the breed of sheep, and increase their number to the greatest extent; and to that end, we will kill them as seldom as may be, especially those of the most profitable kind; nor will we export any to the West-Indies or elsewhere; and those of us, who are or may become overstocked with, or can conveniently spare any sheep, will dispose of them to our neighbours, especially to the poorer sort, on moderate terms.

8. We will, in our several stations, encourage frugality, economy, and industry, and promote agriculture, arts and the manufactures of this country, especially that of wool; and will discountenance and discourage every species of extravagance and dissipation, especially all horse-racing, and all kinds of games, cock fighting, exhibitions of shews, plays, and other expensive diversions and entertainments; and on the death of any relation or friend, none of us, or any of our families will go into any further mourning-dress, than a black crepe or ribbon on the arm or hat, for gentlemen, and a black ribbon and necklace for ladies, and we will discontinue the giving of gloves and scarves at funerals.

9. Such as are venders of goods or merchandize will not take advantage of the scarcity of goods, that may be occasioned by this association, but will sell the same at the rates we have been respectively accustomed to do, for twelve months last past. —And if any vender of goods or merchandise shall sell such goods on higher terms, or shall, in any manner, or by any device whatsoever violate or depart from this agreement, no person ought, nor will any of us deal with any such person, or his or her factor or agent, at any time thereafter, for any commodity whatever.

10. In case any merchant, trader, or other person, shall import any goods or merchandize, after the first day of December, and before the first day of February next, the same ought forthwith, at the election of the owner, to be either re-shipped or delivered up to the committee of the country or town, wherein they shall be imported, to be stored at the risque of the importer, until the non-importation agreement shall cease, or be sold under the direction of the committee aforesaid; and in the last-mentioned case, the owner or owners of such goods shall be reimbursed out of the sales, the first cost and charges, the profit, if any, to be applied towards relieving and employing such poor inhabitants of the town of Boston, as are immediate sufferers by the Boston port-bill; and a particular account of all goods so returned, stored, or sold, to be inserted in the public papers; and if any goods or merchandizes shall be imported after the said first day of February, the same ought forthwith to be sent back again, without breaking any of the packages thereof.

11. That a committee be chosen in every county, city, and town, by those who are qualified to vote for representatives in the legislature, whose business it shall be

attentively to observe the conduct of all persons touching this association; and when it shall be made to appear, to the satisfaction of a majority of any such committee, that any person within the limits of their appointment has violated this association, that such majority do forthwith cause the truth of the case to be published in the gazette; to the end, that all such foes to the rights of British-America may be publicly known, and universally contemned as the enemies of American liberty; and thenceforth we respectively will break off all dealings with him or her.

12. That the committee of correspondence, in the respective colonies, do frequently inspect the entries of their custom-houses, and inform each other, from time to time, of the true state thereof, and of every other material circumstance that may occur relative to this association.

13. That all manufactures of this country be sold at reasonable prices, so that no undue advantage be taken of a future scarcity of goods.

14. And we do further agree and resolve, that we will have no trade, commerce, dealings or intercourse whatsoever, with any colony or province, in North-America, which shall not accede to, or which shall hereafter violate this association, but will hold them as unworthy of the rights of freemen, and as inimical to the liberties of their country.

And we do solemnly bind ourselves and our constituents, under the ties aforesaid, to adhere to this association, until such parts of the several acts of parliament passed since the close of the last war, as impose or continue duties on tea, wine, molasses, syrups paneles, coffee, sugar, pimento, indigo, foreign paper, glass, and painters' colours, imported into America, and extend the powers of the admiralty courts beyond their ancient limits, deprive the American subject of trial by jury, authorize the judge's certificate to indemnify the prosecutor from damages, that he might otherwise be liable to from a trial by his peers, require oppressive security from a claimant of ships or goods seized, before he shall be allowed to defend his property, are repealed. —And until that part of the act of the 12 G. 3. ch. 24, entitled "An act for the better securing his majesty's dock-yards magazines, ships, ammunition, and stores," by which any persons charged with committing any of the offences therein described, in America, may be tried in any shire or county within the realm, is repealed—and until the four acts, passed the last session of parliament, viz. that for stopping the port and blocking up the harbour of Boston—that for altering the charter and government of the Massachusetts-Bay—and that which is entitled "An act for the better administration of justice, &c."—and that "for extending the limits of Quebec, &c." are repealed. And we recommend it to the provincial conventions, and to the committees in the respective colonies, to establish such farther regulations as they may think proper, for carrying into execution this association.

The foregoing association being determined upon by the Congress, was ordered to be subscribed by the several members thereof; and thereupon, we have hereunto set our respective names accordingly.

IN CONGRESS, PHILADELPHIA, October 20, 1774.

Signed, PEYTON RANDOLPH, President.

New Hampshire

- Jn°. Sullivan
- Nath^el. Folsom

Massachusetts Bay

- Thomas Cushing
- Saml. Adams
- John Adams
- Robt. Treat Paine

Rhode Island

- Step. Hopkins
- Sam: Ward

Connecticut

- Elipht Dyer
- Roger Sherman
- Silas Deane

New York

- Isaac Low
- John Alsop
- John Jay
- Ja^s. Duane
- Phil. Livingston
- W^m. Floyd
- Henry Wisner
- S: Boerum

New Jersey

- J. Kinsey
- Wil: Livingston
- Step^n. Crane
- Rich^d. Smith
- John De Hart

Pennsylvania

- Jos. Galloway
- John Dickinson
- Cha Humphreys
- Thomas Mifflin
- E. Biddle

- John Morton
- Geo: Ross

The Lower Counties New Castle

- Cæsar Rodney
- Tho. M: Kean
- Geo: Read

Maryland

- Mat Tilghman"
- Thˢ. Johnson Junʳ.
- Wᵐ. Paca
- Samuel Chase

PATRICK HENRY **19**

Give Me Liberty or Give Me Death, 1775

Patrick Henry delivered this stirring address in the Virginia House of Burgesses on March 23, 1775. In this speech, Henry laid out the options the colonists now had: increasing oppression by the British or a war for their liberties as human beings. Henry declared that there was no choice between submission and freedom—that he would rather fight and risk his own death than live in chains. He darkly warned the other colonists that they would have to make the same decision soon. Less than a month later, fighting erupted between Massachusetts minutemen and British army troops at Lexington and Concord.

No man thinks more highly than I do of the patriotism, as well as abilities, of the very worthy gentlemen who have just addressed the House. But different men often see the same subject in different lights; and, therefore, I hope it will not be thought disrespectful to those gentlemen if, entertaining as I do opinions of a character very opposite to theirs, I shall speak forth my sentiments freely and without reserve. This is no time for ceremony. The question before the House is one of awful moment to this country. For my own part, I consider it as nothing less than a question of freedom or slavery; and in proportion to the magnitude of the subject ought to be the freedom of the debate. It is only in this way that we can hope to arrive at the truth, and fulfill the great responsibility which we hold to God and our country. Should I keep back

http://www.yale.edu/lawweb/avalon/patrick.htm

my opinions at such a time, through fear of giving offense, I should consider myself as guilty of treason towards my country, and of an act of disloyalty toward the Majesty of Heaven, which I revere above all earthly kings.

Mr. President, it is natural to man to indulge in the illusions of hope. We are apt to shut our eyes against a painful truth, and listen to the song of that siren till she transforms us into beasts. Is this the part of wise men, engaged in a great and arduous struggle for liberty? Are we disposed to be of the numbers of those who, having eyes, see not, and, having ears, hear not, the things which so nearly concern their temporal salvation? For my part, whatever anguish of spirit it may cost, I am willing to know the whole truth, to know the worst, and to provide for it.

I have but one lamp by which my feet are guided, and that is the lamp of experience. I know of no way of judging of the future but by the past. And judging by the past, I wish to know what there has been in the conduct of the British ministry for the last ten years to justify those hopes with which gentlemen have been pleased to solace themselves and the House. Is it that insidious smile with which our petition has been lately received?

Trust it not, sir; it will prove a snare to your feet. Suffer not yourselves to be betrayed with a kiss. Ask yourselves how this gracious reception of our petition comports with those warlike preparations which cover our waters and darken our land. Are fleets and armies necessary to a work of love and reconciliation? Have we shown ourselves so unwilling to be reconciled that force must be called in to win back our love? Let us not deceive ourselves, sir. These are the implements of war and subjugation; the last arguments to which kings resort. I ask gentlemen, sir, what means this martial array, if its purpose be not to force us to submission? Can gentlemen assign any other possible motive for it? Has Great Britain any enemy, in this quarter of the world, to call for all this accumulation of navies and armies? No, sir, she has none. They are meant for us: they can be meant for no other. They are sent over to bind and rivet upon us those chains which the British ministry have been so long forging. And what have we to oppose to them? Shall we try argument? Sir, we have been trying that for the last ten years. Have we anything new to offer upon the subject? Nothing. We have held the subject up in every light of which it is capable; but it has been all in vain. Shall we resort to entreaty and humble supplication? What terms shall we find which have not been already exhausted? Let us not, I beseech you, sir, deceive ourselves. Sir, we have done everything that could be done to avert the storm which is now coming on. We have petitioned; we have remonstrated; we have supplicated; we have prostrated ourselves before the throne, and have implored its interposition to arrest the tyrannical hands of the ministry and Parliament. Our petitions have been slighted; our remonstrances have produced additional violence and insult; our supplications have been disregarded; and we have been spurned, with contempt, from the foot of the throne! In vain, after these things, may we indulge the fond hope of peace and reconciliation.

There is no longer any room for hope. If we wish to be free——if we mean to preserve inviolate those inestimable privileges for which we have been so long contending——if we mean not basely to abandon the noble struggle in which we have been so long engaged, and which we have pledged ourselves never to abandon until the glorious object of our contest shall be obtained——we must fight! I repeat it, sir, we must fight! An appeal to arms and to the God of hosts is all that is left us!

They tell us, sir, that we are weak; unable to cope with so formidable an adversary. But when shall we be stronger? Will it be the next week, or the next year? Will it be when we are totally disarmed, and when a British guard shall be stationed in every house? Shall we gather strength but irresolution and inaction? Shall we acquire the means of effectual resistance by lying supinely on our backs and hugging the delusive phantom of hope, until our enemies shall have bound us hand and foot? Sir, we are not weak if we make a proper use of those means which the God of nature hath placed in our power. The millions of people, armed in the holy cause of liberty, and in such a country as that which we possess, are invincible by any force which our enemy can send against us. Besides, sir, we shall not fight our battles alone. There is a just God who presides over the destinies of nations, and who will raise up friends to fight our battles for us. The battle, sir, is not to the strong alone; it is to the vigilant, the active, the brave. Besides, sir, we have no election. If we were base enough to desire it, it is now too late to retire from the contest. There is no retreat but in submission and slavery! Our chains are forged! Their clanking may be heard on the plains of Boston! The war is inevitable—and let it come! I repeat it, sir, let it come.

It is in vain, sir, to extenuate the matter. Gentlemen may cry, Peace, Peace—but there is no peace. The war is actually begun! The next gale that sweeps from the north will bring to our ears the clash of resounding arms! Our brethren are already in the field! Why stand we here idle? What is it that gentlemen wish? What would they have? Is life so dear, or peace so sweet, as to be purchased at the price of chains and slavery? Forbid it, Almighty God! I know not what course others may take; but as for me, give me liberty or give me death!

20

Declaration of Causes and Necessity of Taking Up Arms, Continental Congress, 1775

By July 1775, the colonies and Great Britain were at war with each other. The battles of Lexington and Concord on April 19, 1775, were the first shots of a war that would have long-reaching consequences. Armies were gathering on both sides, and skirmishes were erupting across the Atlantic seaboard. The Continental Congress now began acting more as a national government, directing the resistance to Great Britain. Delegates still hesitated to declare independence, but sentiment was moving steadily in that direction. Nevertheless, the delegates believed that they needed to make a statement explaining why they took up arms against Great Britain. This statement, "A Declaration by the Representatives of the United Colonies of North-America, Now Met in Congress at Philadelphia,

Setting Forth the Causes and Necessity of Their Taking Up Arms," ratified on July 6, 1775, written largely by John Dickinson of Pennsylvania, declares that the colonies believed they must take up arms after King George III declared the colonies in a state of rebellion. The statement reviews the battles at Lexington and Concord and addresses the fact that the colonies were established for religious and civil liberty, rights that the colonists would vigorously defend, or as the Continental Congress declared, submit to slavery.

If it was possible for men, who exercise their reason, to believe, that the Divine Author of our existence intended a part of the human race to hold an absolute property in, and an unbounded power over others, marked out by his infinite goodness and wisdom, as the objects of a legal domination never rightfully resistible, however severe and oppressive, the Inhabitants of these Colonies might at least require from the Parliament of Great Britain some evidence, that this dreadful authority over them, has been granted to that body. But a reverence for our great Creator, principles of humanity, and the dictates of common sense, must convince all those who reflect upon the subject, that government was instituted to promote the welfare of mankind, and ought to be administered for the attainment of that end. The legislature of Great Britain, however, stimulated by an inordinate passion for a power, not only unjustifiable, but which they know to be peculiarly reprobated by the very constitution of that kingdom, and desperate of success in any mode of contest, where regard should be had to truth, law, or right, have at length, deserting those, attempted to effect their cruel and impolitic purpose of enslaving these Colonies by violence, and have thereby rendered it necessary for us to close with their last appeal from Reason to Arms.—Yet, however blinded that assembly may be, by their intemperate rage for unlimited domination, so to slight justice and the opinion of mankind, we esteem ourselves bound, by obligations of respect to the rest of the world, to make known the justice of our cause.

Our forefathers, inhabitants of the island of Great Britain, left their native land, to seek on these shores a residence for civil and religious freedom. At the expence of their blood, at the hazard of their fortunes, without the least charge to the country from which they removed, by unceasing labor, and an unconquerable spirit, they effected settlements in the distant and inhospitable wilds of America, then filled with numerous and warlike nations of barbarians. Societies or governments, vested with perfect legislatures, were formed under charters from the crown, and an harmonious intercourse was established between the colonies and the kingdom from which they derived their origin. The mutual benefits of this union became in a short time so extraordinary, as to excite astonishment. It is universally confessed, that the amazing increase of the wealth, strength, and navigation of the realm, arose from this source; and the minister, who so wisely and successfully directed the measures of Great Britain in the late war, publicly declared, that these colonies enabled her to triumph over her enemies.—Towards the conclusion of that war, it pleased our sovereign to make a change in his counsels.—From that fatal moment, the affairs of the British empire began to fall into confusion, and gradually sliding from the summit of glorious prosperity, to which they had been advanced by the virtues and abilities of one man, are at length distracted by the convulsions, that now shake it to its deepest foundations. The new ministry finding the brave foes of Britain, though frequently defeated, yet still contending, took up the unfortunate idea of granting them a hasty peace, and of then subduing her faithful friends.

These devoted colonies were judged to be in such a state, as to present victories without bloodshed, and all the easy emoluments of statuteable plunder.—The uninterrupted tenor of their peaceable and respectful behaviour from the beginning of colonization, their dutiful, zealous, and useful services during the war, though so recently and amply acknowledged in the most honorable manner by his majesty, by the late king, and by Parliament, could not save them from the meditated innovations.—Parliament was influenced to adopt the pernicious project, and assuming a new power over them, have, in the course of eleven years, given such decisive specimens of the spirit and consequences attending this power, as to leave no doubt concerning the effects of acquiescence under it. They have undertaken to give and grant our money without our consent, though we have ever exercised an exclusive right to dispose of our own property; statutes have been passed for extending the jurisdiction of courts of Admiralty and Vice-Admiralty beyond their ancient limits; for depriving us of the accustomed and inestimable privilege of trial by jury, in cases affecting both life and property; for suspending the legislature of one of the colonies; for interdicting all commerce to the capital of another; and for altering fundamentally the form of government established by charter, and secured by acts of its own legislature solemnly confirmed by the crown; for exempting the "murderers" of colonists from legal trial, and in effect, from punishment; for erecting in a neighboring province, acquired by the joint arms of Great Britain and America, a despotism dangerous to our very existence; and for quartering soldiers upon the colonists in time of profound peace. It has also been resolved in parliament, that colonists charged with committing certain offences, shall be transported to England to be tried.

But why should we enumerate our injuries in detail? By one statute it is declared, that parliament can "of right make laws to bind us IN ALL CASES WHATSOEVER." What is to defend us against so enormous, so unlimited a power? Not a single man of those who assume it, is chosen by us; or is subject to our controul or influence; but, on the contrary, they are all of them exempt from the operation of such laws, and an American revenue, if not diverted from the ostensible purposes for which it is raised, would actually lighten their own burdens in proportion as they increase ours. We saw the misery to which such despotism would reduce us. We for ten years incessantly and ineffectually besieged the Throne as supplicants; we reasoned, we remonstrated with parliament, in the most mild and decent language. But Administration, sensible that we should regard these oppressive measures as freemen ought to do, sent over fleets and armies to enforce them. The indignation of the Americans was roused, it is true; but it was the indignation of a virtuous, loyal, and affectionate people. A Congress of Delegates from the United Colonies was assembled at Philadelphia, on the fifth day of last September. We resolved again to offer an humble and dutiful petition to the King, and also addressed our fellow-subjects of Great Britain. We have pursued every temperate, every respectful measure: we have even proceeded to break off our commercial intercourse with our fellow-subjects, as the last peaceable admonition, that our attachment to no nation upon earth should supplant our attachment to liberty.—This, we flattered ourselves, was the ultimate step of the controversy: But subsequent events have shewn, how vain was this hope of finding moderation in our enemies.

Several threatening expressions against the colonies were inserted in his Majesty's speech; our petition, though we were told it was a decent one, and that his Majesty had been pleased to receive it graciously, and to promise laying it before his Parliament, was huddled into both houses amongst a bundle of American papers, and there neglected. The Lords and Commons in their address, in the month of February, said, that "a rebellion at that time actually existed within the province of Massachusetts bay; and that those concerned in it, had been countenanced and encouraged by unlawful combinations and engagements, entered into by his Majesty's subjects in several of the other colonies; and therefore they besought his Majesty, that he would take the most effectual measures to enforce due obedience to the laws and authority of the supreme legislature."—Soon after, the commercial intercourse of whole colonies, with foreign countries, and with each other, was cut off by an act of Parliament; by another, several of them were entirely prohibited from the fisheries in the seas near their coasts, on which they always depended for their sustenance; and large re-inforcements of ships and troops were immediately sent over to General Gage.

Fruitless were all the entreaties, arguments, and eloquence of an illustrious band of the most distinguished Peers, and Commoners, who nobly and strenuously asserted the justice of our cause, to stay, or even to mitigate the heedless fury with which these accumulated and unexampled outrages were hurried on. —Equally fruitless was the interference of the city of London, of Bristol, and many other respectable towns in our favour. Parliament adopted an insidious manoeuvre calculated to divide us, to establish a perpetual auction of taxations where colony should bid against colony, all of them uninformed what ransom would redeem their lives; and thus to extort from us, at the point of the bayonet, the unknown sums that should be sufficient to gratify, if possible to gratify, ministerial rapacity, with the miserable indulgence left to us of raising, in our own mode, the prescribed tribute. What terms more rigid and humiliating could have been dictated by remorseless victors to conquered enemies? In our circumstances to accept them, would be to deserve them.

Soon after the intelligence of these proceedings arrived on this continent [Governor of Massachusetts Thomas] General Gage, who in the course of the last year had taken possession of the town of Boston, in the province of Massachusetts Bay, and still occupied it as a garrison, on the 19th day of April, sent out from that place a large detachment of his army, who made an unprovoked assault on the inhabitants of the said province, at the town of Lexington, as appears by the affidavits of a great number of persons, some of whom were officers and soldiers of that detachment, murdered eight of the inhabitants, and wounded many others. From thence the troops proceeded in warlike array to the town of Concord, where they set upon another party of the inhabitants of the same province, killing several and wounding more, until compelled to retreat by the country people suddenly assembled to repel this cruel aggression. Hostilities, thus commenced by the British troops, have been since prosecuted by them without regard to faith or reputation.—The inhabitants of Boston being confined within that town by the General their Governor, and having, in order to procure their dismission, entered into a treaty with him, it was stipulated that the said inhabitants having deposited their arms with their own magistrates, should have liberty to depart, taking with them their other effects. They accordingly delivered up their arms, but in open violation of honor, in defiance of the obligation of treaties, which even savage nations esteemed sacred, the Governor ordered the arms deposited as aforesaid, that they might be preserved for their owners, to be seized by a body of soldiers; detained the greatest part of the inhabitants in the town, and compelled the few who were permitted to retire, to leave their most valuable effects behind.

By this perfidy wives are separated from their husbands, children from their parents, the aged and the sick from their relations and friends, who wish to attend and comfort them; and those who have been used to live in plenty and even elegance, are reduced to deplorable distress.

The General, further emulating his ministerial masters, by a proclamation bearing date on the 12th day of June, after venting the grossest falsehoods and calumnies against the good people of these colonies, proceeds to "declare them all, either by name or description, to be rebels and traitors, to supersede the course of the common law, and instead thereof to publish and order the use and exercise of the law martial."—His troops have butchered our countrymen, have wantonly burnt Charles-Town, besides a considerable number of houses in other places; our ships and vessels are seized; the necessary supplies of provisions are intercepted, and he is exerting his utmost power to spread destruction and devastation around him.

We have received certain intelligence that General Carleton, the Governor of Canada, is instigating the people of that province and the Indians to fall upon us; and we have but too much reason to apprehend, that schemes have been formed to excite domestic enemies against us. In brief, a part of these colonies now feels, and all of them are sure of feeling, as far as the vengance of administration can inflict them, the complicated calamities of fire, sword, and famine.—We are reduced to the alternative of chusing an unconditional submission to the tyranny of irritated ministers, or resistance by force.—The latter is our choice.—We have counted the cost of this contest, and find nothing so dreadful as voluntary slavery.—Honor, justice, and humanity, forbid us tamely to surrender that freedom which we received from our gallant ancestors, and which our innocent posterity have a right to receive from us. We cannot endure the infamy and guilt of resigning succeeding generations to that wretchedness which inevitably awaits them, if we basely entail hereditary bondage upon them.

Our cause is just. Our union is perfect. Our internal resources are great, and, if necessary, foreign assistance is undoubtedly attainable.—We gratefully acknowledge, as signal instances of the Divine favour towards us, that his Providence would not permit us to be called into this severe controversy, until we were grown up to our present strength, had been previously exercised in warlike operation, and possessed of the means of defending ourselves.—With hearts fortified with these animating reflections, we most solemnly, before God and the world, declare, that, exerting the utmost energy of those powers, which our beneficent Creator hath graciously bestowed upon us, the arms we have been compelled by our enemies to assume, we will, in defiance of every hazard, with unabating firmness and perseverance, employ for the presevation of our liberties; being with our [one] mind resolved to dye Free-men rather than live Slaves.

Lest this declaration should disquiet the minds of our friends and fellow-subjects in any part of the empire, we assure them that we mean not to dissolve that Union which has so long and so happily subsisted between us, and which we sincerely wish to see restored.—Necessity has not yet driven us into that desperate measure, or induced us to excite any other nation to war against them.—We have not raised armies with ambitious designs of separating from Great Britain, and establishing independent states. We fight not for glory or for conquest. We exhibit to mankind the remarkable spectacle of a people attacked by unprovoked enemies, without any imputation or even suspicion of offence. They boast of their privileges and civilization, and yet proffer no milder conditions than servitude or death.

In our own native land, in defence of the freedom that is our birth-right, and which we ever enjoyed till the late violation of it—for the protection of our property, acquired solely by the honest industry of our fore-fathers and ourselves, against violence actually offered, we have taken up arms. We shall lay them down when hostilities shall cease on the part of the aggressors, and all danger of their being renewed shall be removed, and not before.

With an humble confidence in the mercies of the supreme and impartial Judge and Ruler of the universe, we most devoutly implore his divine goodness to protect us happily through this great conflict, to dispose our adversaries to reconciliation on reasonable terms, and thereby to relieve the empire from the calamities of civil war.

21

The Olive Branch Petition, Continental Congress, 1775

As the Continental Congress continued to move to a war footing against England, John Dickinson penned this second of two major essays to emerge from this assembly. The Olive Branch Petition is an effort to offer a peaceful solution to the war before it spread any further. The statement reiterates the position of the colonies in taking up arms in their defense. But it also emphasizes the loyalty of the colonies and desire to remain under British rule. This attitude of reconciliation would fade quickly, however.

July 8, 1775

To the King's Most Excellent Majesty.

MOST GRACIOUS SOVEREIGN: We, your Majesty's faithful subjects of the Colonies of New-Hampshire, Massachusetts-Bay, Rhode-Island, New-Jersey, Pennsylvania, the Counties of Newcastle, Kent, and Sussex, on Delaware, Maryland, Virginia, North Carolina, and South Carolina, in behalf of ourselves and the inhabitants of these Colonies, who have deputed us to represent them in General Congress, entreat your Majesty's gracious attention to this our humble petition.

http://ahp.gatech.edu/olive_branch_1775.html

The union between our Mother Country and these Colonies, and the energy of mild and just Government, produce benefits so remarkably important, and afforded such an assurance of their permanency and increase, that the wonder and envy of other nations were excited, while they beheld Great Britain rising to a power the most extra-ordinary the world had ever known.

Her rivals, observing that there was no probability of this happy connexion being broken by civil dissensions, and apprehending its future effects if left any longer undisturbed, resolved to prevent her receiving such continual and formidable accessions of wealth and strength, by checking the growth of those settlements from which they were to be derived.

In the prosecution of this attempt, events so unfavourable to the design took place, that every friend to the interests of Great Britain and these Colonies, entertained pleasing and reasonable expectations of seeing an additional force and exertion immediately given to the operations of the union hitherto experienced, by an enlargement of the dominions of the Crown, and the removal of ancient and warlike enemies to a greater distance.

At the conclusion, therefore, of the late war, the most glorious and advantageous that ever had been carried on by British arms, your loyal Colonists having contributed to its success by such repeated and strenuous exertions as frequently procured them the distinguished approbation of your Majesty, of the late King, and of Parliament, doubted not but that they should be permitted, with the rest of the Empire, to share in the blessings of peace, and the emoluments of victory and conquest.

While these recent and honourable acknowledgements of their merits remained on record in the Journals and acts of that august Legislature, the Parliament, undefaced by the imputation or even the suspicion of any offence, they were alarmed by a new system of statutes and regulations adopted for the administration of the Colonies, that filled their minds with the most painful fears and jealousies; and, to their inexpressible astonishment, perceived the danger of a foreign quarrel quickly succeeded by domestick danger, in their judgment of a more dreadful kind.

Nor were these anxieties alleviated by any tendency in this system to promote the welfare of their Mother Country. For though its effects were more immediately felt by them, yet its influence appeared to be injurious to the commerce and prosperity of Great Britain.

We shall decline the ungrateful task of describing the irksome variety of artifices practised by many of your Majesty's Ministers, the delusive pretences, fruitless terrours, and unavailing severities, that have, from time to time, been dealt out by them, in their attempts to execute this impolitick plan, or of tracing through a series of years past the progress of the unhappy differences between Great Britain and these Colonies, that have flowed from this fatal source.

Your Majesty's Ministers, persevering in their measures, and proceeding to open hostilities for enforcing them, have compelled us to arm in our own defence, and have engaged us in a controversy so peculiarly abhorrent to the affections of your still faithful Colonists, that when we consider whom we must oppose in this contest, and if it continues, what may be the consequences, our own particular misfortunes are accounted by us only as parts of our distress.

Knowing to what violent resentments and incurable animosities civil discords are apt to exasperate and inflame the contending parties, we think ourselves required by indispensable obligations to Almighty God, to your Majesty, to our fellow-subjects, and to ourselves, immediately to use all the means in our power, not incompatible with our safety, for stopping the further effusion of blood, and for averting the impending calamities that threaten the British Empire.

Thus called upon to address your Majesty on affairs of such moment to America, and probably to all your Dominions, we are earnestly desirous of performing this office with the utmost deference for your Majesty; and we therefore pray, that your Majesty's royal magnanimity and benevolence may make the most favourable constructions of our expressions on so uncommon an occasion. Could we represent in their full force the sentiments that agitate the minds of us your dutiful subjects, we are persuaded your Majesty would ascribe any seeming deviation from reverence in our language, and even in our conduct, not to any reprehensible intention, but to the impossibility of reconciling the usual appearance of respect with a just attention to our own preservation against those artful and cruel enemies who abuse your royal confidence and authority, for the purpose of effecting our destruction.

Attached to your Majesty's person, family, and Government, with all devotion that principle and affection can inspire; connected with Great Britain by the strongest ties that can unite societies, and deploring every event that tends in any degree to weaken them, we solemnly assure your Majesty, that we not only most ardently desire the former harmony between her and these Colonies may be restored, but that a concord may be established between them upon so firm a basis as to perpetuate its blessings, uninterrupted by any future dissensions, to succeeding generations in both countries, and to transmit your Majesty's name to posterity, adorned with that signal and lasting glory that has attended the memory of those illustrious personages, whose virtues and abilities have extricated states from dangerous convulsions, and by securing the happiness to others, have erected the most noble and durable monuments to their own fame.

We beg further leave to assure your Majesty, that notwithstanding the sufferings of your loyal Colonists during the course of this present controversy, our breasts retain too tender a regard for the kingdom from which we derive our origin, to request such a reconciliation as might, in any manner, be inconsistent with her dignity or welfare. These, related as we are to her, honour and duty, as well as inclination, induce us to support and advance; and the apprehensions that now oppress our hearts with unspeakable grief, being once removed, your Majesty will find our faithful subject on this Continent ready and willing at all times, as they have ever been with their lives and fortunes, to assert and maintain the rights and interests of your Majesty, and of our Mother Country.

We therefore beseech your Majesty, that your royal authority and influence may be graciously interposed to procure us relief from our afflicting fears and jealousies, occasioned by the system before-mentioned, and to settle peace through every part of our Dominions, with all humility submitting to your Majesty's wise consideration, whether it may not be expedient, for facilitating those important purposes, that your Majesty be pleased to direct some mode, by which the united applications of your faithful Colonists to the Throne, in pursuance of their common counsels, may be improved into a happy and permanent reconciliation; and that, in the mean time, measures may be taken for preventing the further destruction of the lives of your Majesty's subjects; and that such statutes as more immediately distress any of your Majesty's Colonies may be repealed.

For such arrangements as your Majesty's wisdom can form for collecting the united sense of your American people, we are convinced your Majesty would receive such satisfactory proofs of the disposition of the Colonists towards their Sovereign and Parent State, that the wished for opportunity would soon be restored to them, of evincing the sincerity of their professions, by every testimony of devotion becoming the most dutiful subjects, and the most affectionate Colonists.

That your Majesty may enjoy long and prosperous reign, and that your descendants may govern your Dominions with honour to themselves and happiness to their subjects, is our sincere prayer.

JOHN HANCOCK,

JOHN LANGDON,

THOMAS CUSHING, New-Hampshire

SAMUEL ADAMS,

JOHN ADAMS,

ROBERT TREAT PAINE, Massachusetts

STEPHEN HOPKINS,

SAMUEL WARD,

ELIPHALET DYER, Rhode-Island

ROGER SHERMAN,

SILAS DEANE, Connecticut

PHILIP LIVINGSTON,

JAMES DUANE,

JOHN ALSOP,

FRANCIS LEWIS,

JOHN JAY,

ROBERT LIVINGSTON, JR.,

LEWIS MORRIS,

WILLIAM FLOYD,

HENRY WISNER, New-York

WILLIAM LIVINGSTON,

JOHN DE HART,

RICHARD SMITH, New-Jersey

JOHN DICKINSON,

BENJAMIN FRANKLIN,

GEORGE ROSS,

JAMES WILSON,

CHARLES HUMPHREYS,

EDWARD BIDDLE, Pennsylvania

CAESAR RODNEY,
THOMAS McKEAN,
GEORGE READ, Delaware Counties
MATTHEW TILGHMAN,
THOMAS JOHNSON, JR.,
WILLIAM PACA,
SAMUEL CHASE,
THOMAS STONE, Maryland
PATRICK HENRY, JR.,
RICHARD HENRY LEE,
EDMUND PENDLETON,
BENJAMIN HARRISON,
THOMAS JEFFERSON, Virginia
WILLIAM HOOPER,
JOSEPH HEWES, North-Carolina
HENRY MIDDLETON,
THOMAS LYNCH,
CHRISTOPHER GADSDEN,
JOHN RUTLEDGE,
EDWARD RUTLEDGE, South-Carolina

THOMAS PAINE **22**

Common Sense, 1776

Thomas Paine, born in England and an immigrant to the colonies, became the most celebrated pamphleteer of the American Revolution. In the early months of the war, many Americans remained unsure of whether to declare independence. Paine, in a compelling argument demonstrated that the colonies had nothing more to gain by reconciling with Great Britain. He attacked the very idea of a monarchy, boldly declaring that as free men, the colonists had a right to select a government of the best men of their choosing. Paine echoed the sentiments of many colonists as he wrote, "When republican virtues fail, slavery ensues." The work became an instant bestseller, selling an astonishing 150,000 copies in three months after its first publication in January 1776.

http://usinfo.state.gov/usa/infousa/facts/loa/commse.htm

Of Monarchy and Hereditary Succession

MANKIND being originally equals in the order of creation, the equality could only be destroyed by some subsequent circumstance: the distinctions of rich and poor may in a great measure be accounted for, and that without having recourse to the harsh ill-sounding names of oppression and avarice. Oppression is often the CONSEQUENCE, but seldom or never the MEANS of riches; and tho' avarice will preserve a man from being necessitously poor, it generally makes him too timorous to be wealthy.

But there is another and great distinction for which no truly natural or religious reason can be assigned, and that is the distinction of men into KINGS and SUBJECTS. Male and female are the distinctions of nature, good and bad the distinctions of Heaven; but how a race of men came into the world so exalted above the rest, and distinguished like some new species, is worth inquiring into, and whether they are the means of happiness or of misery to mankind.

In the early ages of the world, according to the scripture chronology there were no kings; the consequence of which was, there were no wars; it is the pride of kings which throws mankind into confusion. Holland, without a king hath enjoyed more peace for this last century than any of the monarchical governments in Europe. Antiquity favours the same remark; for the quiet and rural lives of the first Patriarchs have a snappy something in them, which vanishes when we come to the history of Jewish royalty.

Government by kings was first introduced into the world by the Heathens, from whom the children of Israel copied the custom. It was the most prosperous invention the Devil ever set on foot for the promotion of idolatry. The Heathens paid divine honours to their deceased kings, and the Christian World hath improved on the plan by doing the same to their living ones. How impious is the title of sacred Majesty applied to a worm, who in the midst of his splendor is crumbling into dust!

As the exalting one man so greatly above the rest cannot be justified on the equal rights of nature, so neither can it be defended on the authority of scripture; for the will of the Almighty as declared by Gideon, and the prophet Samuel, expressly disapproves of government by Kings.

All anti-monarchical parts of scripture, have been very smoothly glossed over in monarchical governments, but they undoubtedly merit the attention of countries which have their governments yet to form. "Render unto Cesar the things which are Cesar's" is the scripture doctrine of courts, yet it is no support of monarchical government, for the Jews at that time were without a king, and in a state of vassalage to the Romans.

Near three thousand years passed away, from the Mosaic account of the creation, till the Jews under a national delusion requested a king. Till then their form of government (except in extraordinary cases where the Almighty interposed) was a kind of Republic, administered by a judge and the elders of the tribes. Kings they had none, and it was held sinful to acknowledge any being under that title but the Lord of Hosts. And when a man seriously reflects on the idolatrous homage which is paid to the persons of kings, he need not wonder that the Almighty, ever jealous of his honour, should disapprove a form of government which so impiously invades the prerogative of Heaven.

Monarchy is ranked in scripture as one of the sins of the Jews, for which a curse in reserve is denounced against them. The history of that transaction is worth attending to.

The children of Israel being oppressed by the Midianites, Gideon marched against them with a small army, and victory thro' the divine interposition decided in his favour. The Jews, elate with success, and attributing it to the generalship of Gideon, proposed making him a king, saying, "Rule thou over us, thou and thy son, and thy son's son." Here was temptation in its fullest extent; not a kingdom only, but an hereditary one; but Gideon in the piety of his soul replied, "I will not rule over you, neither shall my son rule over you. THE LORD SHALL RULE OVER YOU." Words need not be more explicit: Gideon doth not decline the honour, but denieth their right to give it; neither doth he compliment them with invented declarations of his thanks, but in the positive style of a prophet charges them with disaffection to their proper Sovereign, the King of Heaven.

About one hundred and thirty years after this, they fell again into the same error. The hankering which the Jews had for the idolatrous customs of the Heathens, is something exceedingly unaccountable; but so it was, that laying hold of the misconduct of Samuel's two sons, who were intrusted with some secular concerns, they came in an abrupt and clamorous manner to Samuel, saying, "Behold thou art old, and they sons walk not in thy ways, now make us a king to judge us like all the other nations." And here we cannot observe but that their motives were bad, viz. that they might be LIKE unto other nations, i.e. the Heathens, whereas their true glory lay in being as much UNLIKE them as possible. "But the thing displeased Samuel when they said, give us a King to judge us; and Samuel prayed unto the Lord, and the Lord said unto Samuel, hearken unto the voice of the people in all that they say unto thee, for they have not rejected thee, but they have rejected me, THAT I SHOULD NOT REIGN OVER THEM. According to all the works which they have done since the day that I brought them up out of Egypt even unto this day, wherewith they have forsaken me, and served other Gods: so do they also unto thee. Now therefore hearken unto their voice, howbeit, protest solemnly unto them and show them the manner of the King that shall reign over them," i.e. not of any particular King, but the general manner of the Kings of the earth whom Israel was so eagerly copying after. And notwithstanding the great distance of time and difference of manners, the character is still in fashion. "And Samuel told all the words of the Lord unto the people, that asked of him a King. And he said, This shall be the manner of the King that shall reign over you. He will take your sons and appoint them for himself for his chariots and to be his horsemen, and some shall run before his chariots" (this description agrees with the present mode of impressing men) "and he will appoint him captains over thousands and captains over fifties, will set them to ear his ground and to reap his harvest, and to make his instruments of war, and instruments of his chariots, And he will take your daughters to be confectionaries, and to be cooks, and to be bakers" (this describes the expense and luxury as well as the oppression of Kings) "and he will take your fields and your vineyards, and your olive yards, even the best of them, and give them to his servants. And he will take the tenth of your seed, and of your vineyards, and give them to his officers and to his servants" (by which we see that bribery, corruption, and favouritism, are the standing vices of Kings) "and he will take the tenth of your men servants, and your maid servants, and your goodliest young men, and your asses, and put them to his work: and he will take the tenth of your sheep, and ye shall be his servants, and ye shall cry out in that day because of your king which ye shell have chosen, AND THE LORD WILL NOT HEAR YOU IN THAT DAY." This accounts for the continuation of Monarchy; neither do the characters of the few good kings which have lived since, either sanctify the title, or blot out the sinfulness of the origin; the high encomium of David takes no notice of him OFFICIALLY AS A KING, but only as a MAN after God's own heart. "Nevertheless the people refused to obey the voice of Samuel, and they said, Nay, but we will have a king over us, that we may be like all the nations, and that our king may judge us, and go out before us and fight our battles." Samuel continued to reason with them but to no purpose; he set before them their ingratitude, but all would not avail; and seeing them fully bent on their folly, he cried out, "I will call unto the Lord, and he shall send thunder and rain" (which was then a punishment, being in the time of wheat harvest) "that ye may perceive and see that your wickedness is great which ye have done in the sight of the Lord, IN ASKING YOU A KING. So Samuel called unto the Lord, and the Lord sent thunder and rain that day, and all the people greatly feared the Lord and Samuel. And all the people said unto Samuel, Pray for thy servants unto the Lord thy God that we die not, for WE HAVE ADDED UNTO OUR SINS THIS EVIL, TO ASK A KING." These portions of scripture are direct and positive. They admit of no equivocal construction. That the Almighty hath here entered his protest against monarchical government is true, or the scripture is false. And a man hath good reason to believe that there is as much of kingcraft as priestcraft in withholding the scripture from the public in popish countries. For monarchy in every instance is the popery of government.

To the evil of monarchy we have added that of hereditary succession; and as the first is a degradation and lessening of ourselves, so the second, claimed as a matter of right, is an insult and imposition on posterity. For all men being originally equals, no one by birth could have a right to set up his own family in perpetual preference to all others for ever, and tho' himself might deserve some decent degree of honours of his contemporaries, yet his descendants might be far too unworthy to inherit them. One of the strongest natural proofs of the folly of hereditary right in Kings, is that nature disapproves it, otherwise she would not so frequently turn it into ridicule, by giving mankind an ASS FOR A LION.

Secondly, as no man at first could possess any other public honors than were bestowed upon him, so the givers of those honors could have no power to give away the right of posterity, and though they might say "We choose you for our head," they could not without manifest injustice to their children say "that your children and your children's children shall reign over ours forever." Because such an unwise, unjust, unnatural compact might (perhaps) in the next succession put them under the government of a rogue or a fool. Most wise men in their private sentiments have ever treated hereditary right with contempt; yet it is one of those evils which when once established is not easily removed: many submit from fear, others from superstition, and the more powerful part shares with the king the plunder of the rest.

This is supposing the present race of kings in the world to have had an honorable origin: whereas it is more than probable, that, could we take off the dark covering of antiquity and trace them to their first rise, we should find the first of them nothing better than the principal ruffian of some restless gang, whose savage manners of pre-eminence in subtilty obtained him the title of chief among plunderers; and who by increasing in power and extending his depredations, overawed the quiet and defenseless to purchase their safety by frequent contributions. Yet his electors could have no idea of giving hereditary right to his descendants, because such a perpetual exclusion of themselves was incompatible with the free and restrained principles they professed to live by. Wherefore, hereditary succession in the early ages of monarchy could not take place as a matter of claim, but as something casual or complemental; but as few or no records were extant in those days, the traditionary history stuff'd with fables, it was very easy, after the lapse of a few generations, to trump up some superstitious tale conveniently timed, Mahomet-like, to cram hereditary right down the throats of the vulgar. Perhaps the disorders which threatened, or seemed to threaten, on the decease of a leader and the choice of a new one (for elections among ruffians could not be very orderly) induced many at first to favour hereditary pretensions; by which means it happened, as it hath happened since, that what at first was submitted to as a convenience was afterwards claimed as a right.

England since the conquest hath known some few good monarchs, but groaned beneath a much larger number of bad ones: yet no man in his senses can say that their claim under William the Conqueror is a very honourable one. A French bastard landing with an armed Banditti and establishing himself king of England against the consent of the natives, is in plain terms a very paltry rascally original. It certainly hath no divinity in it. However it is needless to spend much time in exposing the folly of hereditary right; if there are any so weak as to believe it, let them promiscuously worship the Ass and the Lion, and welcome. I shall neither copy their humility, nor disturb their devotion.

Yet I should be glad to ask how they suppose kings came at first? The question admits but of three answers, viz. either by lot, by election, or by usurpation. If the first king was taken by lot, it establishes a precedent for the next, which excludes hereditary succession. Saul was by lot, yet the succession was not hereditary, neither does it appear from that transaction that there was any intention it ever should. If the first king of any country was by election, that likewise establishes a precedent for the next; for to say, that the right of all future generations is taken away, by the act of the first electors, in their choice not only of a king but of a family of kings for ever, hath no parallel in or out of scripture but the doctrine of original sin, which supposes the free will of all men lost in Adam; and from such comparison, and it will admit of no other, hereditary succession can derive no glory. for as in Adam all sinned, and as in the first electors all men obeyed; as in the one all mankind were subjected to Satan, and in the other to sovereignty; as our innocence was lost in the first, and our authority in the last; and as both disable us from re-assuming some former state and privilege, it unanswerably follows that original sin and hereditary succession are parallels. Dishonourable rank! inglorious connection! yet the most subtle sophist cannot produce a juster simile.

As to usurpation, no man will be so hardy as to defend it; and that William the Conqueror was an usurper is a fact not to be contradicted. The plain truth is, that the antiquity of English monarchy will not bear looking into.

But it is not so much the absurdity as the evil of hereditary succession which concerns mankind. Did it ensure a race of good and wise men it would have the seal of divine authority, but as it opens a door to the FOOLISH, the WICKED, and the IMPROPER, it hath in it the nature of oppression. Men who look upon themselves born to reign, and others to obey, soon grow insolent. Selected from the rest of mankind, their minds are early poisoned by importance; and the world they act in differs so materially from the world at large, that they have but little opportunity of knowing its true interests, and when they succeed in the government are frequently the most ignorant and unfit of any throughout the dominions.

Another evil which attends hereditary succession is, that the throne is subject to be possessed by a minor at any age; all which time the regency acting under the cover of a king have every opportunity and inducement to betray their trust. The same national misfortune happens when a king worn out with age and infirmity enters the last stage of human weakness. In both these cases the public becomes a prey to every miscreant who can tamper successfully with the follies either of age or infancy.

The most plausible plea which hath ever been offered in favor of hereditary succession is, that it preserves a nation from civil wars; and were this true, it would be weighty; whereas it is the most bare-faced falsity ever imposed upon mankind. The whole history of England disowns the fact. Thirty kings and two minors have reigned in that distracted kingdom since the conquest, in which time there has been (including the revolution) no less than eight civil wars and nineteen Rebellions. Wherefore instead of making for peace, it makes against it, and destroys the very foundation it seems to stand upon.

The contest for monarchy and succession, between the houses of York and Lancaster, laid England in a scene of blood for many years. Twelve pitched battles besides skirmishes and sieges were fought between Henry and Edward. Twice was Henry prisoner to Edward, who in his turn was prisoner to Henry. And so uncertain is the fate of war and the temper of a nation, when nothing but personal matters are the ground of a quarrel, that Henry was taken in triumph from a prison to a palace, and Edward obliged to fly from a palace to a foreign land; yet, as sudden transitions of temper are seldom lasting, Henry in his turn was driven from the throne, and Edward re-called to succeed him. The parliament always following the strongest side.

This contest began in the reign of Henry the Sixth, and was not entirely extinguished till Henry the Seventh, in whom the families were united. Including a period of 67 years, viz. from 1422 to 1489.

In short, monarchy and succession have laid (not this or that kingdom only) but the world in blood and ashes. 'Tis a form of government which the word of God bears testimony against, and blood will attend it.

If we enquire into the business of a King, we shall find that in some countries they may have none; and after sauntering away their lives without pleasure to themselves or advantage to the nation, withdraw from the scene, and leave their successors to tread the same idle round. In absolute monarchies the whole weight of business civil and military lies on the King; the children of Israel in their request for a king urged this plea, "that he may judge us, and go out before us and fight our battles." But in countries where he is neither a Judge nor a General, as in England, a man would be puzzled to know what IS his business.

The nearer any government approaches to a Republic, the less business there is for a King. It is somewhat difficult to find a proper name for the government of England. Sir William Meredith calls it a Republic; but in its present state it is unworthy of the name, because the corrupt influence of the Crown, by having all the places in its disposal, hath so effectually swallowed up the power, and eaten out the virtue of the House of Commons (the Republican part in the constitution) that the government of England is nearly as monarchical as that of France or Spain. Men fall out with names without understanding them. For 'tis the Republican and not the Monarchical part of the Constitution of England which Englishmen glory in, viz. the liberty of choosing an House of Commons from out of their own body—and it is easy to see that when Republican virtues fail, slavery ensues. Why is the constitution of England sickly, but because monarchy hath poisoned the Republic; the Crown hath engrossed the Commons.

In England a King hath little more to do than to make war and giveaway places; which, in plain terms, is to empoverish the nation and set it together by the ears. A pretty business indeed for a man to be allowed eight hundred thousand sterling a year for, and worshipped into the bargain! Of more worth is one honest man to society, and in the sight of God, than all the crowned ruffians that ever lived.

Thoughts on the Present State of American Affairs

ON the following pages I offer nothing more than simple facts, plain arguments, and common sense: and have no other preliminaries to settle with the reader, than that he will divest himself of prejudice and prepossession, and suffer his reason and his feelings to determine for themselves that he will put on, or rather that he will not put off, the true character of a man, and generously enlarge his views beyond the present day.

Volumes have been written on the subject of the struggle between England and America. Men of all ranks have embarked in the controversy, from different motives, and with various designs; but all have been ineffectual, and the period of debate is closed. Arms as the last resource decide the contest; the appeal was the choice of the King, and the Continent has accepted the challenge.

It hath been reported of the late Mr. [Thomas] Pelham (who tho' an able minister was not without his faults) that on his being attacked in the House of Commons on the score that his measures were only of a temporary kind, replied, "THEY WILL LAST MY TIME." Should a thought so fatal and unmanly possess the Colonies in the present contest, the name of ancestors will be remembered by future generations with detestation.

The Sun never shined on a cause of greater worth. 'Tis not the affair of a City, a County, a Province, or a Kingdom; but of a Continent—of at least one-eighth part of the habitable Globe. 'Tis not the concern of a day, a year, or an age; posterity are virtually involved in the contest, and will be more or less affected even to the end of time, by the proceedings now. Now is the seed-time of Continental union, faith and honour. The least fracture now will be like a name engraved with the point of a pin on the tender rind of a young oak; the wound would enlarge with the tree, and posterity read in it full grown characters.

By referring the matter from argument to arms, a new era for politics is struck—a new method of thinking hath arisen. All plans, proposals, &c. prior to the nineteenth of April, i.e. to the commencement of hostilities, are like the almanacks of the last year; which tho' proper then, are superceded and useless now. Whatever was advanced by the advocates on either side of the question then, terminated in one and the same point, viz. a union with Great Britain; the only difference between the parties was the method of effecting it; the one proposing force, the other friendship; but it hath so far happened that the first hath failed, and the second hath withdrawn her influence.

As much hath been said of the advantages of reconciliation, which, like an agreeable dream, hath passed away and left us as we were, it is but right that we should examine the contrary side of the argument, and enquire into some of the many material injuries which these Colonies sustain, and always will sustain, by being connected with and dependant on Great Britain. To examine that connection and dependance, on the principles of nature and common sense, to see what we have to trust to, if separated, and what we are to expect, if dependant.

I have heard it asserted by some, that as America has flourished under her former connection with Great Britain, the same connection is necessary towards her future happiness, and will always have the same effect. Nothing can be more fallacious than this kind of argument. We may as well assert that because a child has thrived upon milk, that it is never to have meat, or that the first twenty years of our lives is to become a precedent for the next twenty. But even this is admitting more than is true; for I answer roundly that America would have flourished as much, and probably much more, had no European power taken any notice of her. The commerce by which she hath enriched herself are the necessaries of life, and will always have a market while eating is the custom of Europe.

But she has protected us, say some. That she hath engrossed us is true, and defended the Continent at our expense as well as her own, is admitted; and she would have defended Turkey from the same motive, viz.—for the sake of trade and dominion.

Alas! we have been long led away by ancient prejudices and made large sacrifices to superstition. We have boasted the protection of Great Britain, without considering, that her motive was INTEREST not ATTACHMENT; and that she did not protect us from OUR ENEMIES on OUR ACCOUNT; but from HER ENEMIES on HER OWN ACCOUNT, from those who had no quarrel with us on any OTHER ACCOUNT, and who will always be our enemies on the SAME ACCOUNT. Let Britain waive her pretensions to the Continent, or the Continent throw off the dependance, and we should be at peace with France and Spain, were they at war with Britain. The miseries of Hanover last war ought to warn us against connections.

It hath lately been asserted in parliament, that the Colonies have no relation to each other but through the Parent Country, i.e. that Pennsylvania and the Jerseys and so on for the rest, are sister Colonies by the way of England; this is certainly a very roundabout way of proving relationship, but it is the nearest and only true way of proving enmity (or enemyship, if I may so call it.) France and Spain never were, nor perhaps ever will be, our enemies as AMERICANS, but as our being the SUBJECTS OF GREAT BRITAIN.

But Britain is the parent country, say some. Then the more shame upon her conduct. Even brutes do not devour their young, nor savages make war upon their families. Wherefore, the assertion, if true, turns to her reproach; but it happens not to be true, or only partly so, and the phrase PARENT OR MOTHER COUNTRY hath been jesuitically adopted by the King and his parasites, with a low papistical design of gaining an unfair bias on the credulous weakness of our minds. Europe, and not England, is the parent country of America. This new World hath been the asylum for the persecuted lovers of civil and religious liberty from EVERY PART of Europe. Hither have they fled, not from the tender embraces of the mother, but from the cruelty of the monster; and it is so far true of England, that the same tyranny which drove the first emigrants from home, pursues their descendants still.

In this extensive quarter of the globe, we forget the narrow limits of three hundred and sixty miles (the extent of England) and carry our friendship on a larger scale; we claim brotherhood with every European Christian, and triumph in the generosity of the sentiment.

It is pleasant to observe by what regular gradations we surmount the force of local prejudices, as we enlarge our acquaintance with the World. A man born in any town in England divided into parishes, will naturally associate most with his fellow parishioners (because their interests in many cases will be common) and distinguish him by the name of NEIGHBOR; if he meet him but a few miles from home, he drops the narrow idea of a street, and salutes him by the name of TOWNSMAN; if he travel out of the county and meet him in any other, he forgets the minor divisions of street and town, and calls him COUNTRYMAN, i.e. COUNTYMAN; but if in their foreign excursions they should associate in France, or any other part of EUROPE, their local remembrance would be enlarged into that of ENGLISH-MEN. And by a just parity of reasoning, all Europeans meeting in America, or any other quarter of the globe, are COUNTRYMEN; for England, Holland, Germany, or Sweden, when compared with the whole, stand in the same places on the larger scale, which the divisions of street, town, and county do on the smaller ones; Distinctions too limited for Continental minds. Not one third of the inhabitants, even of this province, [Pennsylvania], are of English descent. Wherefore, I reprobate the phrase of Parent or Mother Country applied to England only, as being false, selfish, narrow and ungenerous.

But, admitting that we were all of English descent, what does it amount to? Nothing. Britain, being now an open enemy, extinguishes every other name and title: and to say that reconciliation is our duty, is truly farcical. The first king of England, of the present line (William the Conqueror) was a Frenchman, and half the peers of England are descendants from the same country; wherefore, by the same method of reasoning, England ought to be governed by France.

Much hath been said of the united strength of Britain and the Colonies, that in conjunction they might bid defiance to the world. But this is mere presumption; the fate of war is uncertain, neither do the expressions mean anything; for this continent would never suffer itself to be drained of inhabitants, to support the British arms in either Asia, Africa, or Europe.

Besides, what have we to do with setting the world at defiance? Our plan is commerce, and that, well attended to, will secure us the peace and friendship of all Europe; because it is the interest of all Europe to have America a free port. Her trade will always be a protection, and her barrenness of gold and silver secure her from invaders.

I challenge the warmest advocate for reconciliation to show a single advantage that this continent can reap by being connected with Great Britain. I repeat the challenge; not a single advantage is derived. Our corn will fetch its price in any market in Europe, and our imported goods must be paid for buy them where we will.

But the injuries and disadvantages which we sustain by that connection, are without number; and our duty to mankind at large, as well as to ourselves, instruct us to renounce the alliance: because, any submission to, or dependance on, Great Britain, tends directly to involve this Continent in European wars and quarrels, and set us at variance with nations who would otherwise seek our friendship, and against whom we have neither anger nor complaint. As Europe is our market for trade, we ought to form no partial connection with any part of it. It is the true interest of America to steer clear of European contentions, which she never can do, while, by her dependance on Britain, she is made the makeweight in the scale of British politics.

Europe is too thickly planted with Kingdoms to be long at peace, and whenever a war breaks out between England and any foreign power, the trade of America goes to ruin, BECAUSE OF HER CONNECTION WITH BRITAIN. The next war may not turn out like the last, and should it not, the advocates for reconciliation now will be wishing for separation then, because neutrality in that case would be a safer convoy than a man of war. Every thing that is right or reasonable pleads for separation. The blood of the slain, the weeping voice of nature cries, 'TIS TIME TO PART. Even the distance at which the Almighty hath placed England and America is a strong and natural proof that the authority of the one over the other, was never the design of Heaven. The time likewise at which the Continent was discovered, adds weight to the argument, and the manner in which it was peopled, encreases the force of it. The Reformation was preceded by the discovery of America: As if the Almighty graciously meant to open a sanctuary to the persecuted in future years, when home should afford neither friendship nor safety.

The authority of Great Britain over this continent, is a form of government, which sooner or later must have an end: And a serious mind can draw no true pleasure by looking forward, under the painful and positive conviction that what he calls "the present constitution" is merely temporary. As parents, we can have no joy, knowing that this government is not sufficiently lasting to ensure any thing which we may bequeath to posterity: And by a plain method of argument, as we are running the next generation into debt, we ought to do the work of it, otherwise we use them meanly and pitifully. In order to discover the line of our duty rightly, we should take our children in our hand, and fix our station a few years farther into life; that eminence will present a prospect which a few present fears and prejudices conceal from our sight.

Though I would carefully avoid giving unnecessary offence, yet I am inclined to believe, that all those who espouse the doctrine of reconciliation, may be included within the following descriptions.

Interested men, who are not to be trusted, weak men who CANNOT see, prejudiced men who will not see, and a certain set of moderate men who think better of the European world than it deserves; and this last class, by an ill-judged deliberation, will be the cause of more calamities to this Continent than all the other three.

It is the good fortune of many to live distant from the scene of present sorrow; the evil is not sufficiently brought to their doors to make them feel the precariousness with which all American property is possessed. But let our imaginations transport us a few moments to Boston; that seat of wretchedness will teach us wisdom, and instruct us for ever to renounce a power in whom we can have no trust. The inhabitants of that unfortunate city who but a few months ago were in ease and affluence, have now no other alternative than to stay and starve, or turn out to beg. Endangered by the fire of their friends if they continue within the city and plundered by the soldiery if they leave it, in their present situation they are prisoners without the hope of redemption, and in a general attack for their relief they would be exposed to the fury of both armies.

Men of passive tempers look somewhat lightly over the offences of Great Britain, and, still hoping for the best, are apt to call out, "Come, come, we shall be friends again for all this." But examine the passions and feelings of mankind: bring the doctrine of reconciliation to the touchstone of nature, and then tell me whether you can hereafter love, honour, and faithfully serve the power that hath carried fire and sword into your land? If you cannot do all these, then are you only deceiving yourselves, and by your delay bringing ruin upon posterity. Your future connection with Britain, whom you can neither love nor honour, will be forced and unnatural, and being formed only on the plan of present convenience, will in a little time fall into a relapse more wretched than the first. But if you say, you can still pass the violations over, then I ask, hath your house been burnt? Hath your property been destroyed before your face? Are your wife and children destitute of a bed to lie on, or bread to live on? Have you lost a parent or a child by their hands, and yourself the ruined and wretched survivor? If you have not, then are you not a judge of those who have. But if you have, and can still shake hands with the murderers, then are you unworthy the name of husband, father, friend or lover, and whatever may be your rank or title in life, you have the heart of a coward, and the spirit of a sycophant.

ABIGAIL ADAMS **23**

Remember the Ladies, 1776

In this famous letter to her husband, John Adams, Abigail Adams speaks out for the rights of women. Though only a short portion of the letter, this is one of the earliest affirmations in the United States of the need for equality for women. For Mrs. Adams, freedom denied to some would eventually mean freedom denied to all. Without equality, the nation would wither under the social strains caused by the resentment that inequality fostered.

I wish you would ever write me a letter half as long as I write you, and tell me, if you may, where your fleet are gone; what sort of defense Virginia can make against our common enemy; whether it is so situated as to make an able defense. Are not the gentry lords, and the common people vassals? Are they not like the uncivilized vassals Britain represents us to be? I hope their riflemen, who have shown themselves very savage and even blood-thirsty, are not a specimen of the generality of the people. I am willing to allow the colony great merit for having produced a Washington—but they have been shamefully duped by a Dunmore.

http://www.masshist.org/adams/manuscripts_1.cfm

I have sometimes been ready to think that the passion for liberty cannot be equally strong in the breasts of those who have been accustomed to deprive their fellow-creatures of theirs. Of this I am certain, that it is not founded upon that generous and Christian principle of doing to others as we would that others should do unto us.

Do not you want to see Boston? I am fearful of the small-pox, or I should have been in before this time. I got Mr. Crane to go to our house and see what state it was in. I find it has been occupied by one of the doctors of a regiment; very dirty, but no other damage has been done to it. The few things which were left in it are all gone. I look upon it as a new acquisition of property—a property which one month ago I did not value at a single shilling, and would with pleasure have seen it in flames.

The town in general is left in a better state than we expected; more owing to a precipitate flight than any regard to the inhabitants; though some individuals discovered a sense of honor and justice, and have left the rent of the houses in which they were, for the owners, and the furniture unhurt, or, if damaged, sufficient to make it good. Others have committed abominable ravages. The mansion house of your President is safe, and the furniture unhurt while the house and furniture of the Solicitor General have fallen a prey to their own merciless party. Surely the very fiends feel a reverential awe for virtue and patriotism, whilst they detest the parricide and traitor.

I feel very differently at the approach of spring from what I did a month ago. We knew not then whether we could plant or sow with safety, whether where we had tilled we could reap the fruits of our own industry, whether we could rest in our own cottages or whether we should be driven from the seacoast to seek shelter in the wilderness but now we feel a temporary peace, and the poor fugitives are returning to their deserted habitations.

Though we felicitate ourselves, we sympathize with those who are trembling lest the lot of Boston should be theirs. But they cannot be in similar circumstances unless pusillanimity and cowardice should take possession of them. They have time and warning given them to see the evil and shun it.

I long to hear that you have declared an independency. And, by the way, in the new code of laws which I suppose it will be necessary for you to make, I desire you would remember the ladies and be more generous and favorable to them than your ancestors. Do not put such unlimited power into the hands of the husbands. Remember, all men would be tyrants if they could. If particular care and attention is not paid to the ladies, we are determined to foment a rebellion, and will not hold ourselves bound by any laws in which we have no voice or representation.

That your sex are naturally tyrannical is a truth so thoroughly established as to admit of no dispute; but such of you as wish to be happy willingly give up the harsh title of master for the more tender and endearing one of friend. Why, then, not put it out of the power of the vicious and the lawless to use us with cruelty and indignity with impunity? Men of sense in all ages abhor those customs which treat us only as the vassals of your sex; regard us then as beings placed by Providence under your protection, and in imitation of the Supreme Being make use of that power only for our happiness. April 5.

I want to hear much oftener from you than I do. March 8th was the last date of any that I have yet had. You inquire of me whether I am making saltpetre. I have not yet attempted it, but after soap-making believe I shall make the experiment. I find as much as I can do to manufacture clothing for my family, which would else be naked. I know of but one person in this part of the town who has made any. That is Mr. Tertius Bass, as he is called, who has got very near a hundred-weight which has been found to be very good. I have heard of some others in the other parishes. Mr. Reed, of Weymouth, has been applied to, to go to Andover to the mills which are now at work, and he has gone.

I have lately seen a small manuscript describing the proportions of the various sorts of powder fit for cannon, small arms, and pistols. If it would be of any service your way I will get it transcribed and send it to you. Every one your friends sends regards, and all the little ones. Adieu.

RICHARD HENRY LEE **24**

Resolution for Declaration of Independence, 1776

As the Revolutionary War expanded across the continent, the Continental Congress began to act as a national government as it fought British forces. By summer 1776, the delegates concluded that independence must be declared as the injuries inflicted on the colonies by the British were now too egregious to reconcile. This was an important parliamentary move to cement American freedom. This resolution, proposed by Virginia delegate Richard Henry Lee on June 7, was approved by Congress on July 2, 1776. Two days later, the assembly would approve a much more powerful statement—the Declaration of Independence.

June 7, 1776

Resolved, That these United Colonies are, and of right ought to be, free and independent States; that they are absolved from all allegiance to the British Crown, and that all political connection between them and the State of Great Britain is and ought to be totally dissolved.

That it is expedient forthwith to take the most effectual measures for forming foreign Alliances.

That a plan of confederation be prepared and transmitted to the respective Colonies for their consideration and approbation.

http://www.yale.edu/lawweb/avalon/lee.htm;
http://www.ourdocuments.gov/doc.php?flash=true&doc=1

25

Virginia Declaration of Rights, 1776

By the summer of 1776, Virginia was divided into two warring camps, with both the royal governor and the independence-minded members of the dissolved House of Burgesses acting as the legitimate government. George Mason penned this declaration, approved unanimously by the Virginia Convention of Delegates on June 12, 1776. It proclaimed the principles for which Virginia would fight for in the American Revolution. The most important among those listed was the idea of the equality of all men, opposing special privileges for a select group of individuals, the right of free elections for communities to decide their own fates, and the freedom of conscience. Several sections of the Virginia Declaration of Rights would become the basis for the Bill of Rights in 1789.

I That all men are by nature equally free and independent, and have certain inherent rights, of which, when they enter into a state of society, they cannot, by any compact, deprive or divest their posterity; namely, the enjoyment of life and liberty, with the means of acquiring and possessing property, and pursuing and obtaining happiness and safety.

II That all power is vested in, and consequently derived from, the people; that magistrates are their trustees and servants, and at all times amenable to them.

III That government is, or ought to be, instituted for the common benefit, protection, and security of the people, nation or community; of all the various modes and forms of government that is best, which is capable of producing the greatest degree of happiness and safety and is most effectually secured against the danger of maladministration; and that, whenever any government shall be found inadequate or contrary to these purposes, a majority of the community hath an indubitable, unalienable, and indefeasible right to reform, alter or abolish it, in such manner as shall be judged most conducive to the public weal.

IV That no man, or set of men, are entitled to exclusive or separate emoluments or privileges from the community, but in consideration of public services; which, not being descendible, neither ought the offices of magistrate, legislator, or judge be hereditary.

V That the legislative and executive powers of the state should be separate and distinct from the judicative; and, that the members of the two first may be restrained from oppression by feeling and participating the burthens of the people, they should, at fixed periods, be reduced to a private station, return into that body from which they were originally taken, and the vacancies be supplied by frequent, certain, and regular elections in which all, or any part of the former members, to be again eligible, or ineligible, as the laws shall direct.

VI That elections of members to serve as representatives of the people in assembly ought to be free; and that all men, having sufficient evidence of permanent common interest with, and attachment to, the community have the right of suffrage and cannot be taxed or deprived of their property for public uses without their own consent or that of their representatives so elected, nor bound by any law to which they have not, in like manner, assented, for the public good.

VII That all power of suspending laws, or the execution of laws, by any authority without consent of the representatives of the people is injurious to their rights and ought not to be exercised.

VIII That in all capital or criminal prosecutions a man hath a right to demand the cause and nature of his accusation to be confronted with the accusers and witnesses, to call for evidence in his favor, and to a speedy trial by an impartial jury of his vicinage, without whose unanimous consent he cannot be found guilty, nor can he be compelled to give evidence against himself; that no man be deprived of his liberty except by the law of the land or the judgement of his peers.

IX That excessive bail ought not to be required, nor excessive fines imposed; nor cruel and unusual punishments inflicted.

X That general warrants, whereby any officer or messenger may be commanded to search suspected places without evidence of a fact committed, or to seize any person or persons not named, or whose offense is not particularly described and supported by evidence, are grievous and oppressive and ought not to be granted.

XI That in controversies respecting property and in suits between man and man, the ancient trial by jury is preferable to any other and ought to be held sacred.

XII That the freedom of the press is one of the greatest bulwarks of liberty and can never be restrained but by despotic governments.

XIII That a well regulated militia, composed of the body of the people, trained to arms, is the proper, natural, and safe defense of a free state; that standing armies, in time of peace, should be avoided as dangerous to liberty; and that, in all cases, the military should be under strict subordination to, and be governed by, the civil power.

XIV That the people have a right to uniform government; and therefore, that no government separate from, or independent of, the government of Virginia, ought to be erected or established within the limits thereof.

XV That no free government, or the blessings of liberty, can be preserved to any people but by a firm adherence to justice, moderation, temperance, frugality, and virtue and by frequent recurrence to fundamental principles.

XVI That religion, or the duty which we owe to our Creator and the manner of discharging it, can be directed by reason and conviction, not by force or violence; and therefore, all men are equally entitled to the free exercise of religion, according to the dictates of conscience; and that it is the mutual duty of all to practice Christian forbearance, love, and charity towards each other.

THOMAS JEFFERSON ET AL. **26**

Declaration of Independence, 1776

As the Continental Congress considered independence, it was decided that a state-ment to the world explaining this action was in order. Thomas Jefferson led a com-mittee that included Benjamin Franklin and John Adams to draft the document, although the wording is overwhelmingly the work of Jefferson. After submitting a draft to Congress, the delegates added and omitted several phrases. The final draft was approved and signed on July 4, 1776.

The first part of the Declaration of Independence defines the proper role of government, in the eyes of the colonists. This role was to defend the rights of the citizens. The second section lists how King George III of Great Britain had failed in those respects. This document became the ideological heart of the American Revolution, although it had no legal power. That a government should be empow-ered by the consent of the governed and that the most basic rights of human beings, including equality, became the ideal for free nations everywhere to aspire.

IN CONGRESS, JULY 4, 1776

The unanimous Declaration of the thirteen United States of America

When in the Course of human events it becomes necessary for one people to dissolve the political bands which have connected them with another and to assume among the powers of the earth, the separate and equal station to which the Laws of Nature and of Nature's God entitle them, a decent respect to the opinions of mankind requires that they should declare the causes which impel them to the separation.

We hold these truths to be self-evident, that all men are created equal, that they are endowed by their Creator with certain unalienable Rights, that among these are Life, Liberty and the pursuit of Happiness.—That to secure these rights, Governments are instituted among Men, deriving their just powers from the consent of the governed,—That whenever any Form of Government becomes destructive of these ends, it is the Right of the People to alter or to abolish it, and to institute new Government, laying its foundation on such principles and organizing its powers in such form, as to them shall seem most likely to effect their Safety and Happiness. Prudence, indeed, will dictate that Governments long established should not be changed for light and transient causes; and accordingly all experience hath shewn that mankind are more disposed to suffer, while evils are sufferable than to right them-selves by abolishing the forms to which they are accustomed. But when a long train of

Thomas Jefferson, "Declaration of Independence," *The Life and Selected Writings of Thomas Jefferson*, Adrienne Koch and William Peden, eds. (New York: Modern Library, 1993): 287–289; http://www.ourdocuments.gov/doc.php?flash=true&doc=2

abuses and usurpations, pursuing invariably the same Object evinces a design to reduce them under absolute Despotism, it is their right, it is their duty, to throw off such Government, and to provide new Guards for their future security.—Such has been the patient sufferance of these Colonies; and such is now the necessity which constrains them to alter their former Systems of Government. The history of the present King of Great Britain is a history of repeated injuries and usurpations, all having in direct object the establishment of an absolute Tyranny over these States. To prove this, let Facts be submitted to a candid world.

He has refused his Assent to Laws, the most wholesome and necessary for the public good.

He has forbidden his Governors to pass Laws of immediate and pressing importance, unless suspended in their operation till his Assent should be obtained; and when so suspended, he has utterly neglected to attend to them.

He has refused to pass other Laws for the accommodation of large districts of people, unless those people would relinquish the right of Representation in the Legislature, a right inestimable to them and formidable to tyrants only.

He has called together legislative bodies at places unusual, uncomfortable, and distant from the depository of their Public Records, for the sole purpose of fatiguing them into compliance with his measures.

He has dissolved Representative Houses repeatedly, for opposing with manly firmness his invasions on the rights of the people.

He has refused for a long time, after such dissolutions, to cause others to be elected; whereby the Legislative Powers, incapable of Annihilation, have returned to the People at large for their exercise; the State remaining in the mean time exposed to all the dangers of invasion from without, and convulsions within.

He has endeavoured to prevent the population of these States; for that purpose obstructing the Laws for Naturalization of Foreigners; refusing to pass others to encourage their migrations hither, and raising the conditions of new Appropriations of Lands.

He has obstructed the Administration of Justice by refusing his Assent to Laws for establishing Judiciary Powers.

He has made Judges dependent on his Will alone for the tenure of their offices, and the amount and payment of their salaries.

He has erected a multitude of New Offices, and sent hither swarms of Officers to harrass our people and eat out their substance.

He has kept among us, in times of peace, Standing Armies without the Consent of our legislatures.

He has affected to render the Military independent of and superior to the Civil Power.

He has combined with others to subject us to a jurisdiction foreign to our constitution, and unacknowledged by our laws; giving his Assent to their Acts of pretended Legislation:

For quartering large bodies of armed troops among us:

For protecting them, by a mock Trial from punishment for any Murders which they should commit on the Inhabitants of these States:

For cutting off our Trade with all parts of the world:

For imposing Taxes on us without our Consent:

For depriving us in many cases, of the benefits of Trial by Jury:

For transporting us beyond Seas to be tried for pretended offences:

For abolishing the free System of English Laws in a neighbouring Province, establishing therein an Arbitrary government, and enlarging its Boundaries so as to render it at once an example and fit instrument for introducing the same absolute rule into these Colonies

For taking away our Charters, abolishing our most valuable Laws and altering fundamentally the Forms of our Governments:

For suspending our own Legislatures, and declaring themselves invested with power to legislate for us in all cases whatsoever.

He has abdicated Government here, by declaring us out of his Protection and waging War against us.

He has plundered our seas, ravaged our Coasts burnt our towns, and destroyed the lives of our people.

He is at this time transporting large Armies of foreign Mercenaries to compleat the works of death, desolation, and tyranny, already begun with circumstances of Cruelty & Perfidy scarcely paralleled in the most barbarous ages, and totally unworthy the Head of a civilized nation.

He has constrained our fellow Citizens taken Captive on the high Seas to bear Arms against their Country, to become the executioners of their friends and Brethren, or to fall themselves by their Hands.

He has excited domestic insurrections amongst us, and has endeavoured to bring on the inhabitants of our frontiers, the merciless Indian Savages whose known rule of warfare, is an undistinguished destruction of all ages, sexes and conditions.

In every stage of these Oppressions We have Petitioned for Redress in the most humble terms: Our repeated Petitions have been answered only by repeated injury. A Prince, whose character is thus marked by every act which may define a Tyrant, is unfit to be the ruler of a free people.

Nor have We been wanting in attentions to our British brethren. We have warned them from time to time of attempts by their legislature to extend an unwarrantable jurisdiction over us. We have reminded them of the circumstances of our emigration and settlement here. We have appealed to their native justice and magnanimity, and we have conjured them by the ties of our common kindred. to disavow these usurpations, which would inevitably interrupt our connections and correspondence. They too have been deaf to the voice of justice and of consanguinity. We must, therefore, acquiesce in the necessity, which denounces our Separation, and hold them, as we hold the rest of mankind, Enemies in War, in Peace Friends.

WE, THEREFORE, the Representatives of the UNITED STATES OF AMERICA, in General Congress, Assembled, appealing to the Supreme Judge of the world for the rectitude of our intentions, do, in the Name, and by Authority of the good People of these Colonies, solemnly publish and declare, That these United Colonies are, and of Right ought to be FREE AND INDEPENDENT STATES; that they are Absolved from all Allegiance to the British Crown, and that all political connection between them and the State of Great Britain, is and ought to be totally dissolved; and that as Free and Independent States, they have full Power to levy War, conclude Peace contract Alliances, establish Commerce, and to do all other Acts and Things which Independent States may of right do.—And for the support of this Declaration, with a firm reliance on the protection of Divine Providence, we mutually pledge to each other our Lives, our Fortunes and our sacred Honor.

John Hancock

New Hampshire:
Josiah Bartlett, William Whipple, Matthew Thornton

Massachusetts:
John Hancock, Samuel Adams, John Adams, Robert Treat Paine, Elbridge Gerry

Rhode Island:
Stephen Hopkins, William Ellery

Connecticut:
Roger Sherman, Samuel Huntington, William Williams, Oliver Wolcott

New York:
William Floyd, Philip Livingston, Francis Lewis, Lewis Morris

New Jersey:
Richard Stockton, John Witherspoon, Francis Hopkinson, John Hart, Abraham Clark

Pennsylvania:

Robert Morris, Benjamin Rush, Benjamin Franklin, John Morton, George Clymer, James Smith, George Taylor, James Wilson, George Ross

Delaware:

Caesar Rodney, George Read, Thomas McKean

Maryland:

Samuel Chase, William Paca, Thomas Stone, Charles Carroll of Carrollton

Virginia:

George Wythe, Richard Henry Lee, Thomas Jefferson, Benjamin Harrison, Thomas Nelson, Jr., Francis Lightfoot Lee, Carter Braxton

North Carolina:

William Hooper, Joseph Hewes, John Penn

South Carolina:

Edward Rutledge, Thomas Heyward, Jr., Thomas Lynch, Jr., Arthur Middleton

Georgia:

Button Gwinnett, Lyman Hall, George Walton

THOMAS PAINE **27**

The Crisis, 1776

Thomas Paine's famous series, The Crisis, *included thirteen tracts, written from December 23, 1776, to April 19, 1783. These articles often addressed British generals and political leaders, mocking them as he tried to bolster the spirits of Americans during the Revolutionary War. As Paine writes this first essay, the Continental Army is in danger of collapse as it was forced to retreat from New York to Pennsylvania—but written three days before the stunning victory at Trenton, New Jersey. Paine asserts that no matter how desperate the situation, the British assault on freedom could not be ignored or delayed for a more opportune time. Freedom, the right of communities and individuals to govern themselves, was worth fighting for. But, as Paine states, "Tyranny, like hell, is not easily conquered."*

Thomas Paine, *The Crisis* (Albany, NY: Charles R. & George Webster, 1792): 1–20.

THESE are the times that try men's souls: The summer soldier and the sunshine patriot will, in this crisis, shrink from the service of their country but he that stands by it NOW, deserves the love and thanks of man and woman. Tyranny, like hell, is not easily conquered; yet we have this consolation with us, that the harder the conflict, the more glorious the triumph. What we obtain too cheap, we esteem too lightly: —'Tis dearness only that gives every thing its value. Heaven knows how to put a proper price upon its goods; and it would be strange indeed if so celestial an article as FREEDOM should not be highly rated. Britain, with an army to enforce her tyranny, has declared that she has a right (not only to TAX) but "to BIND us in ALL CASES WHATSO-EVER" and if being bound in that manner, is not slavery, then is there not such a thing as slavery upon earth. Even the expression is impious, for so unlimited a power can belong only to God.

Whether the Independence of the Continent was declared too soon, or delayed too long, I will not now enter into as an argument; my own simple opinion is, that had it been eight months earlier, it would have been much better. We did not make a proper use of last winter, neither could we, while we were in a dependent state. However, the fault, if it were one, was all our own (note); we have none to blame but ourselves. But no great deal is lost yet. All that [British Gen. William] Howe has been doing for this month past, is rather a ravage than a conquest, which the spirit of the Jerseys, a year ago, would have quickly repulsed, and which time and a little resolution will soon recover.

I have as little superstition in me as any man living, but my secret opinion has ever been, and still is, that God Almighty will not give up a people to military destruction, or leave them unsupportedly to perish, who have so earnestly and so repeatedly sought to avoid the calamities of war, by every decent method which wisdom could invent. Neither have I so much of the infidel in me, as to suppose that He has relinquished the government of the world, and given us up to the care of devils; and as I do not, I cannot see on what grounds the king of Britain can look up to heaven for help against us: a common murderer, a highwayman, or a house-breaker, has as good a pretence as he.

'Tis surprising to see how rapidly a panic will sometimes run through a country. All nations and ages have been subject to them; Britain has trembled like an ague at the report of a French fleet of flat-bottomed boats; and in the fourteenth [fifteenth] century the whole English army, after ravaging the kingdom of France, was driven back like men petrified with fear; and this brave exploit was performed by a few broken forces collected and headed by a woman, Joan of Arc. Would that heaven might inspire some Jersey maid to spirit up her countrymen, and save her fair fellow sufferers from ravage and ravishment! Yet panics, in some cases, have their uses; they produce as much good as hurt. Their duration is always short; the mind soon grows through them, and acquires a firmer habit than before. But their peculiar advantage is, that they are the touchstones of sincerity and hypocrisy, and bring things and men to light, which might otherwise have lain forever undiscovered. In fact, they have the same effect on secret traitors, which an imaginary apparition would have upon a private murderer. They sift out the hidden thoughts of man, and hold them up in public to the world. Many a disguised Tory has lately shown his head, that shall penitentially solemnize with curses the day on which Howe arrived upon the Delaware.

As I was with the troops at Fort Lee, and marched with them to the edge of Pennsylvania, I am well acquainted with many circumstances, which those, who lived at a distance, know but little or nothing of. Our situation there was exceedingly cramped, the place being a narrow neck of land between the North River and the Hackensack. Our force was inconsiderable, being not one-fourth so great as Howe could bring against us. We had no army at hand to have relieved the garrison, had we shut ourselves up and stood on our defence. Our ammunition, light artillery, and the best part of our stores, had been removed, on the apprehension that Howe would endeavor to penetrate the Jerseys, in which case Fort Lee could be of no use to us; for it must occur to every thinking man, whether in the army or not, that these kind of field forts are only for temporary purposes, and last in use no longer than the enemy directs his force against the particular object which such forts are raised to defend. Such was our situation and condition at Fort Lee on the morning of the 20th of November, when an officer arrived with information that the enemy with 200 boats had landed about seven miles above; Major General [Nathaniel] Green, who commanded the garrison, immediately ordered them under arms, and sent express to General Washington, at the town of Hackensack, distant by the way of the ferry six miles. Our first object was to secure the bridge over the Hackensack, which laid up the river between the enemy and us, about six miles from us, and three from them. General Washington arrived in about three-quarters of an hour, and marched at the head of the troops towards the bridge, which place I expected we should have a brush for; however, they did not choose to dispute it with us, and the greatest part of our troops went over the bridge, the rest over the ferry, except some which passed at a mill on a small creek, between the bridge and the ferry, and made their way through some marshy grounds up to the town of Hackensack, and there passed the river. We brought off as much baggage as the wagons could contain, the rest was lost. The simple object was to bring off the garrison, and march them on till they could be strengthened by the Jersey or Pennsylvania militia, so as to be enabled to make a stand. We staid four days at Newark, collected our out-posts with some of the Jersey militia, and marched out twice to meet the enemy, on being informed that they were advancing, though our numbers were greatly inferior to theirs. Howe, in my little opinion, committed a great error in generalship in not throwing a body of forces off from Staten Island through Amboy, by which means he might have seized all our stores at Brunswick, and intercepted our march into Pennsylvania; But if we believe the power of hell to be limited, we must likewise believe that their agents are under some providential control.

I shall not now attempt to give all the particulars of our retreat to the Delaware; suffice it for the present to say, that both officers and men, though greatly harassed and fatigued, frequently without rest, covering, or provision, the inevitable consequences of a long retreat, bore it with a manly and martial spirit. All their wishes centred in one, which was, that the country would turn out and help them to drive the enemy back. [French satirist] Voltaire has remarked that King William never appeared to full advantage but in difficulties and in action; the same remark may be made on General Washington, for the character fits him. There is a natural firmness in some minds which cannot be unlocked by trifles, but which, when unlocked, discovers a cabinet of fortitude; and I reckon it among those kind of public blessings, which we do not immediately see, that God hath blessed him with uninterrupted health, and given him a mind that can even flourish upon care.

I shall conclude this paper with some miscellaneous remarks on the state of our affairs; and shall begin with asking the following question, Why is it that the enemy have left the New England provinces, and made these middle ones the seat of war? The answer is easy: New England is not infested with Tories, and we are. I have been tender in raising the cry against these men, and used numberless arguments to show them their danger, but it will not do to sacrifice a world either to their folly or their baseness. The period is now arrived, in which either they or we must change our sentiments, or one or both must fall. And what is a Tory? Good God! What is he? I should not be afraid to go with a hundred Whigs against a thousand Tories, were they to attempt to get into arms. Every Tory is a coward; for servile, slavish, self-interested fear is the foundation of Toryism; and a man under such influence, though he may be cruel, never can be brave.

But, before the line of irrecoverable separation be drawn between us, let us reason the matter together: Your conduct is an invitation to the enemy, yet not one in a thousand of you has heart enough to join him. Howe is as much deceived by you as the American cause is injured by you. He expects you will all take up arms, and flock to his standard, with muskets on your shoulders. Your opinions are of no use to him, unless you support him personally, for 'tis soldiers, and not Tories, that he wants.

I once felt all that kind of anger, which a man ought to feel, against the mean principles that are held by the Tories: a noted one, who kept a tavern at Amboy, was standing at his door, with as pretty a child in his hand, about eight or nine years old, as I ever saw, and after speaking his mind as freely as he thought was prudent, finished with this unfatherly expression, "Well! give me peace in my day." Not a man lives on the continent but fully believes that a separation must some time or other finally take place, and a generous parent should have said, "If there must be trouble, let it be in my day, that my child may have peace;" and this single reflection, well applied, is sufficient to awaken every man to duty. Not a place upon earth might be so happy as America. Her situation is remote from all the wrangling world, and she has nothing to do but to trade with them. A man can distinguish himself between temper and principle, and I am as confident, as I am that God governs the world, that America will never be happy till she gets clear of foreign dominion. Wars, without ceasing, will break out till that period arrives, and the continent must in the end be conqueror; for though the flame of liberty may sometimes cease to shine, the coal can never expire.

America did not, nor does not want force; but she wanted a proper application of that force. Wisdom is not the purchase of a day, and it is no wonder that we should err at the first setting off. From an excess of tenderness, we were unwilling to raise an army, and trusted our cause to the temporary defence of a well-meaning militia. A summer's experience has now taught us better; yet with those troops, while they were collected, we were able to set bounds to the progress of the enemy, and, thank God! they are again assembling. I always considered militia as the best troops in the world for a sudden exertion, but they will not do for a long campaign. Howe, it is probable, will make an attempt on this city [Philadelphia]; should he fail on this side the Delaware, he is ruined. If he succeeds, our cause is not ruined. He stakes all on his side against a part on ours; admitting he succeeds, the consequence will be, that armies from both ends of the continent will march to assist their suffering friends in the middle states; for he cannot go everywhere, it is impossible. I consider Howe as the greatest enemy the Tories have; he is bringing a war into their country, which, had it not been for him and partly for themselves, they had been clear of. Should he now be expelled, I wish with all the devotion of a Christian, that the names of Whig and Tory may never more be mentioned; but should the Tories give him encouragement to come, or assistance if he come, I as sincerely wish that our next year's arms may expel them from the continent, and the Congress appropriate their possessions to the relief of those who have suffered in well-doing. A single successful battle next year will settle the whole. America could carry on a two years' war by the confiscation of the property of disaffected persons, and be made happy by their expulsion. Say not that this is revenge, call it rather the soft resentment of a suffering people, who, having no object in view but the good of all, have staked their own all upon a seemingly doubtful event. Yet it is folly to argue against determined hardness; eloquence may strike the ear, and the language of sorrow draw forth the tear of compassion, but nothing can reach the heart that is steeled with prejudice.

Quitting this class of men, I turn with the warm ardor of a friend to those who have nobly stood, and are yet determined to stand the matter out: I call not upon a few, but upon all: not on this state or that state, but on every state: up and help us; lay your shoulders to the wheel; better have too much force than too little, when so great an object is at stake. Let it be told to the future world, that in the depth of winter, when nothing but hope and virtue could survive, that the city and the country, alarmed at one common danger, came forth to meet and to repulse it. Say not that thousands are gone, turn out your tens of thousands; throw not the burden of the day upon Providence, but "show your faith by your works," that God may bless you. It matters not where you live, or what rank of life you hold, the evil or the blessing will reach you all. The far and the near, the home counties and the back, the rich and the poor, will suffer or rejoice alike. The heart that feels not now is dead; the blood of his children will curse his cowardice, who shrinks back at a time when a little might have saved the whole, and made them happy. I love the man that can smile in trouble, that can gather strength from distress, and grow brave by reflection. 'Tis the business of little minds to shrink; but he whose heart is firm, and whose conscience approves his conduct, will pursue his principles unto death. My own line of reasoning is to myself as straight and clear as a ray of light. Not all the treasures of the world, so far as I believe, could have induced me to support an offensive war, for I think it murder; but if a thief breaks into my house, burns and destroys my property, and kills or threatens to kill me, or those that are in it, and to "bind me in all cases whatsoever" to his absolute will, am I to suffer it? What signifies it to me, whether he who does it is a king or a common man; my countryman or not my countryman; whether it be done by an individual villain, or an army of them? If we reason to the root of things we shall find no difference; neither can any just cause be assigned why we should punish in the one case and pardon in the other. Let them call me rebel and welcome, I feel no concern from it; but I should suffer the misery of devils, were I to make a whore of my soul by swearing allegiance to one whose character is that of a sottish, stupid, stubborn, worthless, brutish man. I conceive likewise a horrid idea in receiving mercy from a being, who at the last day shall be shrieking to the rocks and mountains to cover him, and fleeing with terror from the orphan, the widow, and the slain of America.

There are cases which cannot be overdone by language, and this is one. There are persons, too, who see not the full extent of the evil which threatens them; they solace themselves with hopes that the enemy, if he succeed, will be merciful. It is the madness of folly, to expect mercy from those who have refused to do justice; and even mercy, where conquest is the object, is only a trick of war; the cunning of the fox is as murderous as the violence of the wolf, and we ought to guard equally against both. Howe's first object is, partly by threats and partly by promises, to terrify or seduce the people to deliver up their arms and receive mercy. The ministry recommended the same plan to Gage, and this is what the tories call making their peace, "a peace which passeth all understanding" indeed! A peace which would be the immediate forerunner of a worse ruin than any we have yet thought of. Ye men of Pennsylvania, do reason upon these things! Were the back counties to give up their arms, they would fall an easy prey to the Indians, who are all armed: this perhaps is what some Tories would not be sorry for. Were the home counties to deliver up their arms, they would be exposed to the resentment of the back counties who would then have it in their power to chastise their defection at pleasure. And were any one state to give up its arms, that state must be garrisoned by all Howe's army of Britons and Hessians to preserve it from the anger of the rest. Mutual fear is the principal link in the chain of mutual love, and woe be to that state that breaks the compact. Howe is mercifully inviting you to barbarous destruction, and men must be either rogues or fools that will not see it. I dwell not upon the vapors of imagination; I bring reason to your ears, and, in language as plain as A, B, C, hold up truth to your eyes.

I thank God, that I fear not. I see no real cause for fear. I know our situation well, and can see the way out of it. While our army was collected, Howe dared not risk a battle; and it is no credit to him that he decamped from the White Plains, and waited a mean opportunity to ravage the defenceless Jerseys; but it is great credit to us, that, with a handful of men, we sustained an orderly retreat for near an hundred miles, brought off our ammunition, all our field pieces, the greatest part of our stores, and had four rivers to pass. None can say that our retreat was precipitate, for we were near three weeks in performing it, that the country might have time to come in. Twice we marched back to meet the enemy, and remained out till dark. The sign of fear was not seen in our camp, and had not some of the cowardly and disaffected inhabitants spread false alarms through the country, the Jerseys had never been ravaged. Once more we are again collected and collecting; our new army at both ends of the continent is recruiting fast, and we shall be able to open the next campaign with sixty thousand men, well armed and clothed. This is our situation, and who will may know it. By perseverance and fortitude we have the prospect of a glorious issue; by cowardice and submission, the sad choice of a variety of evils—a ravaged country— a depopulated city—habitations without safety, and slavery without hope—our homes turned into barracks and bawdy-houses for Hessians, and a future race to provide for, whose fathers we shall doubt of. Look on this picture and weep over it! and if there yet remains one thoughtless wretch who believes it not, let him suffer it unlamented.

December 23, 1776

Note: (The present winter is worth an age, if rightly employed; but, if lost or neglected, the whole continent will partake of the evil; and there is no punishment that man does not deserve, be he who, or what, or where he will, that may be the means of sacrificing a season so precious and useful.)

28

Constitution of Vermont, 1777

Vermont was caught in the middle of a land dispute between New York and New Hampshire, unable to break free. With the outbreak of the American Revolution, Vermonters took it upon themselves to solve the issue by creating a state for themselves. The Vermont Constitution of 1777 recounts the history of this struggle between the two states and the reasons for declaring their statehood. As other states began experimenting with their own constitutions, Vermont drafted a document guaranteeing unprecedented freedom to its citizens. This constitution made Vermont the first state to ban slavery. It also declared the right of self-defense, free speech, the right to a jury trial, and free religion (although only professed Protestants could hold state offices). The state even had officials who would review the actions of the government periodically to ensure that the constitution had been faithfully executed. Many of these rights would be echoed in the drafting of the Bill of Rights.

WHEREAS, all government ought to be instituted and supported, for the security and protection of the community, as such, and to enable the individuals who compose it, to enjoy their natural rights, and the other blessings which the Author of existence has bestowed upon man; and whenever those great ends of government are not obtained, the people have a right, by common consent, to change it, and take such measures as to them may appear necessary to promote their safety and happiness.

And whereas, the inhabitants of this State have (in consideration of protection only) heretofore acknowledged allegiance to the King of Great Britain, and the said King has not only withdrawn that protection, but commenced, and still continues to carry on, with unabated vengeance, a most cruel and unjust war against them; employing therein, not only the troops of Great Britain, but foreign mercenaries, savages and slaves, for the avowed purpose of reducing them to a total and abject submission to the despotic domination of the British parliament, with many other acts of tyranny, (more fully set forth in the declaration of Congress) whereby all allegiance and fealty to the said King and his successors, are dissolved and at an end; and all power and authority derived from him, ceased in the American Colonies.

And whereas, the territory which now comprehends the State of *Vermont*, did antecedently, of right, belong to the government of *New-Hampshire*; and the former Governor thereof, viz. his Excellency *Benning Wentworth*, Esq., granted many charters of lands and corporations, within this State, to the present inhabitants and others. And whereas, the late Lieutenant Governor *Colden*, of *New York*, with others, did, in violation of the tenth command, covet those very lands; and by a false representation made to the court of Great Britain, (in the year 1764, that for the convenience of trade and administration of justice, the inhabitants were desirous of being annexed to that government,) obtained jurisdiction of those very identical lands, *ex-parte*; which ever was, and is, disagreeable to the inhabitants. And whereas, the legislature of *New-York*, ever have, and still continue to disown the good people of this State, in their landed property, which will appear in the complaints hereafter inserted, and in the 36th section of their present constitution, in which is established the grants of land made by that government.

They have refused to make regents of our lands to the original proprietors and occupants, unless at the exorbitant rate of 2300 dollars fees for each township; and did enhance the quit-rent, three fold, and demanded an immediate delivery of the title derived before, from *New-Hampshire*.

The judges of their supreme court have made a solemn declaration that the charters, conveyances, &c. of the lands included in the before described premises, were utterly null and void, on which said title was founded: in consequence of which declaration, writs of possession have been by them issued, and the sheriff of the county of Albany sent, at the head of six or seven hundred men, to enforce the execution thereof. They have passed an act, annexing a penalty thereto, of thirty pounds fine and six months imprisonment, on any person who should refuse assisting the sheriff, after being requested, for the purpose of executing writs of possession.

The Governors, *Dunmore, Tryon* and *Colden*, have made re-grants of several tracts of land, included in the premises, to certain favorite land jobbers in the government of *New-York*, in direct violation of his Britannic majesty's express prohibition, in the Year 1767.

They have issued proclamations, wherein they have offered large slims of money, for the purpose of apprehending those very persons who have dared boldly, and publicly, to appear in defence of their just rights.

They did pass twelve acts of outlawry, on the 9th day of March, A. D. 1774, impowering the respective judges of their supreme court, to award execution of death against those inhabitants in said district, that they should judge to be offenders, without trial.

They have, and still continue, an unjust claim to those lands, which greatly retards emigration into, and the settlement of, this State.

They have hired foreign troops, emigrants from *Scotland*, at two different times, and armed them, to drive us out of possession.

They have sent the savages on our frontiers, to distress us.

They have proceeded to erect the counties of Cumberland and Glocester, and establish courts of justice there, after they were discountenanced by the authority of Great Britain.

The free convention of the State of *New-York* at *Harlem*, in the year 1776, unanimously voted, "That all quit-rents, formerly due to the King of Great Britain, are now due and owing to this Convention. Or such future government as shall be hereafter established in this State."

In the several stages of the aforesaid oppressions, we have petitioned his Britannic majesty, in the most humble manner, for redress? and have, at very great expense, received several reports in our favor; and, in other instances, wherein we have petitioned the late legislative authority of New-York, those petitions have been treated with neglect. And whereas, the local situation of this State, from *New-York*, at the extreme part, is upward of four hundred and fifty miles from the seat of that government, which renders it extreme difficult to continue under the jurisdiction of said State.

Therefore, it is absolutely necessary, for the welfare and safety of the inhabitants of this State, that it should be, henceforth, a free and independent State; and that a just, permanent, and proper form of government, should exist in it, derived from, and founded on, the authority of the people only, agreeable to the direction of the honorable American Congress.

We the representatives of the freemen of Vermont, in General Convention met, for the express purpose of forming such a government, confessing the goodness of the Great Governor of the universe, (who alone, knows to what degree of earthly happiness, mankind may attain, by perfecting the arts of government,) in permitting the people of this State, by common consent, and without violence, deliberately to form for themselves, such just rules as they shall think best for governing their future society; and being fully convinced that it is our indispensable duty, to establish such original principles of government, as will best promote the general happiness of the people of this State, and their posterity, and provide for future improvements, without partiality for, or prejudice against, any particular class, sect, or denomination of men whatever,-do, by virtue of authority vested in us, by our constituents, ordain, declare, and establish, the following declaration of rights, and frame of government, to be the CONSTITUTION of this COMMONWEALTH, and to remain in force therein, forever, unaltered, except in such articles, as shall, hereafter, on experience, be found to require improvement, and which shall, by the same authority of the people, fairly delegated, as this frame of government directs, be amended or improved, for the more effectual obtaining and securing the great end and design of all government, herein before mentioned.

CHAPTER I

A DECLARATION OF THE RIGHTS OF THE INHABITANTS OF THE STATE OF VERMONT

I THAT all men are born equally free and independent, and have certain natural, inherent and unalienable rights, amongst which are the enjoying and defending life and liberty; acquiring, possessing and protecting property, and pursuing and obtaining happiness and safety. Therefore, no male person, born in this country, or brought from over sea, ought to be holden by law, to serve any person, as a servant, slave or apprentice, after he arrives to the age of twenty-one Years, nor female, in like manner, after she arrives to the age of eighteen years, unless they are bound by their own consent, after they arrive to such age, or bound by law, for the payment of debts, damages, fines, costs, or the like.

II That private property ought to be subservient to public uses, when necessity requires it; nevertheless, whenever any particular man's property is taken for the use of the public, the owner ought to receive an equivalent in money.

III That all men have a natural and unalienable right to worship ALMIGHTY GOD, according to the dictates of their own consciences and understanding, regulated by the word of GOD; and that no man ought, or of right can be compelled to attend any religious worship, or erect, or support any place of worship, or maintain any minister, contrary to the dictates of his conscience; nor can any man who professes the protestant religion, be justly deprived or abridged of any civil right, as a citizen, on account of his religious sentiment, or peculiar mode of religious worship, and that no authority can, or ought to be vested in, or assumed by, any power whatsoever, that shall, in any case, interfere with, or in any manner controul, the rights of conscience, in the free exercise of religious worship: nevertheless, every sect or denomination of people ought to observe the Sabbath, or the Lord's day, and keep up, and support, some sort of religious worship, which to them shall seem most agreeable to the revealed will of GOD.

IV That the people of this State have the sole, exclusive and inherent right of governing and regulating the internal police of the same.

V That all power being originally inherent in, and consequently, derived from, the people; therefore, all officers of government, whether legislative or executive, are their trustees and servants. and at all times accountable to them.

VI That government is, or ought to be, instituted for the common benefit, protection, and security of the people, nation or community; and not for the particular emolument or advantage of any single man, family or set of men, who are a part only of that community; and that the community hath an indubitable, unalienable and indefeasible right to reform, alter, or abolish, government, in such manner as shall be, by that community, judged most conducive to the public weal.

VII That those who are employed in the legislative and executive business of the State, may be restrained from oppression, the people have a right, at such periods as they may think proper, to reduce their public officers to a private station, and supply the vacancies by certain and regular elections.

VIII That all elections ought to be free; and that all freemen. having a sufficient, evident, common interest with, and attachment to the community, have a right to elect officers, or be elected into office.

IX That every member of society hath a right to be protected in the enjoyment of life, liberty and property, and therefore, is bound to contribute his proportion towards the expense of that protection, and yield his personal service, when necessary, or an equivalent thereto; but no part of a man's property can be justly taken from him, or applied to public uses, without his own consent, or that of his legal representatives; nor can any man who is conscientiously scrupulous of bearing arms, be justly compelled thereto, if he will pay such equivalent; nor are the people bound by any law but such as they have, in like manner, assented to, for their common good.

X That, in all prosecutions for criminal offences, a man hath a right to be heard, by himself and his counsel—to demand the cause and nature of his accusation—to be confronted with the witnesses—to call for evidence in his favor, and a speedy public trial, by an impartial jury of the country; without the unanimous consent of which jury, he cannot be found guilty; nor can he be compelled to give evidence against himself; nor can any man be justly deprived of his liberty, except by the laws of the land or the judgment of his peers.

XI That the people have a right to hold themselves, their houses, papers and possessions free from search or seizure; and therefore warrants without oaths or affirmations first made, affording a sufficient foundation for them, and whereby any officer or messenger may be commanded or required to search suspected places, or to seize any person or persons, his, her or their property, not particularly described, are contrary to that right, and ought not to be granted.

XII That no warrant or writ to attach the person or estate. of any freeholder within this State, shall be issued in civil action, without the person or persons, who may request such warrant or attachment, first make oath, or affirm, before the authority who may be requested to issue the same, that he, or they, are in danger of losing his, her or their debts.

XIII That, in controversies respecting property, and in suits between man and man, the parties have a right to a trial by jury; which ought to be held sacred.

XIV That the people have a right to freedom of speech, and of writing and publishing their sentiments; therefore, the freedom of the press ought not be restrained.

XV That the people have a right to bear arms for the defence of themselves and the State; and, as standing armies, in the time of peace, are dangerous to liberty, they ought not to be kept up; and that the military should be kept under strict subordination to, and governed by, the civil power.

XVI That frequent recurrence to fundamental principles, and a firm adherence to justice, moderation, temperance, industry and frugality, are absolutely necessary to preserve the blessings of liberty, and keep government free. The people ought, therefore, to pay particular attention to these points, in the choice of officers and representatives, and have a right to exact a due and constant regard to them, from their legislators and magistrates, in the making and executing such laws as are necessary for the good government of the State.

XVII That all people have a natural and inherent right to emigrate from one State to another, that will receive them, or to form a new State in vacant countries, or in such countries as they can purchase whenever they think that thereby they can promote their own happiness.

XVIII That the people have a right to assemble together, to consult for their common good—to instruct their representatives, and to apply to the legislature for redress of grievances, by address, petition or remonstrance.

XIX That no person shall be liable to be transported out of this State for trial, for any offence committed within this State.

CHAPTER II

PLAN OR FRAME OF GOVERNMENT

SECTION I THE COMMONWEALTH or STATE of VERMONT, shall be governed, hereafter, by a Governor, Deputy Governor, Council, and an Assembly of the Representatives of the Freemen of the same, in manner and form following.

SECTION II The supreme legislative power shall be vested in a House of Representatives of the Freemen or Commonwealth or State of *Vermont*.

SECTION III The supreme executive power shall be vested in a Governor and Council.

SECTION IV Courts of justice shall be established in every county in this State.

SECTION V The freemen of this Commonwealth, and their sons, shall be trained and armed for its defence, under such regulations, restrictions and exceptions, as the general assembly shall, by law, direct; preserving always to the people, the right of choosing their colonels of militia, and all commissioned officers under that rank, in such manner, and as often, as by the said laws shall be directed.

SECTION VI Every man of the full age of twenty-one years, having resided in this State for the space of one whole year, next before the election of representatives, and who is of a quiet and peaceable behaviour, and will take the following oath (or affirmation) shall be entitled to all the privileges of a freeman of this State.

I_____solemnly swear, by the ever living God, (or affirm, in the presence of Almighty God,) that whenever I am called to give any vote or suffrage, touching any matter that concerns the State of Vermont, I will do it so, as in arty conscience, I shall judge will roost conduce to the best good of the same, as established by the constitution, without fear or favor of any man.

SECTION VII The House of Representatives of the Freemen of this State, shall consist of persons most noted for wisdom and virtue, to be chosen by the freemen of every town in this State, respectively. And no foreigner shall be chosen, unless he has resided in the town for which he shall be elected, one year immediately before said election.

SECTION VIII The members of the House of Representatives, shall be chosen annually, by ballot, by the freemen of this State, on the first Tuesday of September, forever, (except this present year) and shall meet on the second Thursday of the succeeding October, and shall be stiled the General Asembly of the Representatives of the Freemen of *Vermont*; and shall have power to choose their Speaker, Secretary of the State, their Clerk, and other necessary officers of the house- sit on their own adjournments-prepare bills and enact them into laws-judge of the elections and qualifications of their own members-they may expel a member, but not a second time for the same cause-They may administer oaths (or affirmations) on examination of witnesses-redress grievances-impeach State criminals-grant charters of incorporation-constitute towns, boroughs, cities and counties, and shall have all other powers necessary for the legislature of a free State; but they shall have no power to add to, alter, abolish, or infringe any part of this constitution. And for this present year, the members of the General Assembly shall be chosen on the first Tuesday of March next, and shall meet at the meeting-house, in *Windsor*, on the second Thursday of March next.

SECTION IX A quorum of the house of representatives shall consist of two-thirds of the whole number of members elected; and having met and chosen their speaker, shall, each of them, before they proceed to business, take and subscribe, as well the oath of fidelity and allegiance herein after directed, as the following oath or affirmation, viz.

"I _____ do solemnly swear, by the ever living God, (or, I do solemnly affirm in the presence of Almighty God) that as a member of this assembly, I will not propose or assent to any bill, vote, or resolution, which shall appear to me injurious to the people; nor do or consent to any act or thing whatever, that shall have a tendency to lessen or abridge their rights and privileges, as declared in the Constitution of this State; but will, in all things' conduct myself as a faithful, honest representative and guardian of the people, according to the best of my judgment and abilities."

And each member, before he takes his seat, shall make and subscribe the following declaration, viz.

"I _____ do believe in one God, the Creator and Governor of the Diverse, the rewarder of the good and punisher of the wicked. And I do acknowledge the scriptures of the old and new testament to be given by divine inspiration, and own and profess the protestant religion."

And no further or other religious test shall ever, hereafter, be required of any civil officer or magistrate in this State.

SECTION X Delegates to represent this State in Congress shall be chosen, by ballot, by the future General Assembly, at their first meeting, and annually, forever afterward, as long as such representation shall be necessary. Any Delegate may be superseded, at any time. by the General Asembly appointing another in his stead. No man shall sit in Congress longer than two years successively, nor be capable of re election for three years afterwards; and no person who holds any office in the gift of the Congress, shall, thereafter, be elected to represent this State in Congress.

SECTION XI If any town or towns shall neglect or refuse to elect and send representatives to the General Assembly, two thirds of the members of the towns, that do elect and send representatives, (provided they be a majority of the inhabited towns of the whole State) when met, shall have all the powers of the General Assembly, as fully and amply, as if the whole were present.

SECTION XII The doors of the house in which the representatives of the Greene of this State, shall sit, in General Assembly, shall be and remain open for the admission of all persons, who behave decently, except only, when the welfare of this State may require the doors to be shut.

SECTION XIII The votes and proceedings of the General Assembly shall be printed, weekly, during their sitting, with the yeas and nays, on any question, vote or resolution, where one-third of the members require it; (except when the votes are taken by ballot) and when the yeas and nays are so taken, every member shall have a right to insert the reasons of his votes upon the minutes, if he desire it.

SECTION XIV To the end that laws, before they are enacted, may be more maturely considered, and the inconveniency of hasty determination as much as possible prevented, all bills of public nature, shall be first laid before the Governor and Council, for their perusal and proposals of amendment, and shall be printed for the consideration of the people, before they are read in General Assembly, for the last time of debate and amendment; except temporary acts, which, after being laid before the Governor and Council, may (in case of sudden necessity) be passed into laws; and no other shall be passed into laws, until the next session of assembly. And for the more perfect satisfaction of the public, the reasons and motives for making such laws, shall be fully and clearly expressed and set forth in their preambles.

SECTION XV The style of the laws of this State shall be,—"Be it enacted, and it is hereby enacted, by the Representatives of the Freemen of the State of Vermont, in General Assembly met, and by the authority of the same."

SECTION XVI In order that the Freemen of this State might enjoy the benefit of election, as equally as may be, each town within this State, that consists, or may consist, of eighty taxable inhabitants, within one septenary or seven years, next after the establishing this constitution, may hold elections therein, and choose each, two representatives; and each other inhabited town in this State may, in like manner, choose each, one representative, to represent them in General Assembly, during the said septenary or seven years; and after that, each inhabited town may, in like manner, hold such election, and choose each, one representative, forever thereafter.

SECTION XVII The Supreme Executive Council of this State, shall consist of a Governor, Lieutenant-Governor, and twelve persons, chosen in the following manner, viz. The Freemen of each town, shall, on the day of election for choosing representatives to attend the General Assembly, bring in their votes—for Governor, with his name fairly written, to the constable, who shall seal them up, and write on them, votes for the Governor, and deliver them to the representative chosen to attend the General Assembly; and, at the opening of the General Assembly, there shall be a committee appointed out of the Council and Assembly, who, after being duly sworn to the faithful discharge of their trust, shall proceed to receive, sort, and count, the votes for the Governor, and declare the person who has the major part of the votes, to be Governor, for the year ensuing. And if there be no choice made, then the Council and General Assembly, by their joint ballot. shall make choice of a Governor.

The Lieutenant Governor and Treasurer, shall be chosen in the manner above directed; and each freeman shall give in twelve votes for twelve councillors, in the same manner; and the twelve highest in nomination shall serve for the ensuing year as Councillors.

The Council that shall act in the recess of this Convention, shall supply the place of a Council for the next General Assembly, until the new Council be declared chosen. The Council shall meet annually, at the same time and place with the General Assembly; and every member of the Council shall be a Justice of the Peace for the whole State, by virtue of his office.

SECTION XVIII The Governor, and in his absence, the Lieutenant or Deputy Governor, with the Council—seven of whom shall be a quorum—shall have power to appoint and commissionate all officers, (except those who are appointed by the General Assembly,) agreeable to this frame of government, and the laws that may be made hereafter; and shall supply every vacancy in any office, occasioned by death, resignation, removal or disqualification, until the office can be filled, in the time and manner directed by law or this constitution. They are to correspond with other States, and transact business with officers of government, civil and military; and to prepare such business as may appear to them necessary to lay before the General Assembly. They shall sit as judges to hear and determine on impeachments, taking to their assistance, for advice only, the justices of the supreme court; and shall have power to grant pardons, and remit fines, in all cases whatsoever, except cases of impeachment, and in cases of treason and murder-shall have power to grant reprieves, but not to pardon, until the end of the next session of the Assembly: but there shall be no remission or mitigation of punishment, on impeachments, except by act of legislation. They are also, to take care that the laws be faithfully executed. They are to expedite the execution of such measures as may be resolved upon by General Assembly; and they may draw upon the Treasurer for such sums as may be appropriated by the House: they may also lay embargoes, or prohibit the exportation of any commodity for any time, not exceeding thirty days, in the recess of the House only: they may grant such licenses as shall be directed by law, and shall have power to call together the General Assembly, when necessary, before the day to which they shall stand adjourned. The Governor shall be commander-in-chief of the forces of the State; but shall not command in person, except advised thereto by the Council, and then, only as long as they shall approve thereof. The Governor and Council shall have a Secretary, and keep fair books of their proceedings, wherein any Councillor may enter his dissent, with his reasons to support it.

SECTION XIX All commissions shall be in the name of the freemen of the State of Vermont, sealed with the State seal, signed by the Governor, and in his absence, the Lieutenant Governor, and attested by the Secretary; which seal shall be kept by the Council.

SECTION XX Every officer of State, whether judicial or executive, shall be liable to be impeached by the General Assembly, either when in office, or after his resignation, or removal for mar-administration All impeachments shall be before the Governor or Lieutenant Governor and Council, who shall hear and determine the same.

SECTION XXI The supreme court, and the several courts of common pleas of this State shall, besides the powers usually exercised by such courts, have the powers of a court of chancery, so far as relates to perpetuating testimony, obtaining evidence from places not within this State, and the care of persons and estates of those who are *non compotes mentis*, and such other powers as may be found necessary by future General Assemblies, not inconsistent with this constitution.

SECTION XXII Trials shall be by jury; and it is recommended to the legislature of this State to provide by law, against every corruption or partiality in the choice, and return, or appointment, of juries.

SECTION XXIII All courts shall be open, and justice shall be impartially administered, without corruption or unnecessary delay; all their officers shall be paid an adequate, but moderate, compensation for their services; and if any officer shall take greater or other fees than the laws allow him, either directly or indirectly, it shall ever after disqualify him from holding any office in this State.

SECTION XXIV All prosecution shall commence in the name and by the authority of the freemen of the State of *Vermont*, and all indictments shall conclude with these words, "against the peace and dignity of the same." The style of all process hereafter, in this State, shall be,-The State of *Vermont*.

SECTION XXV The person of a debtor, where there is not a strong presumption of fraud, shall not be continued in prison, after delivering up, *bone fide*, all his estate, real and personal, for the use of his creditors, in such manner as shall be hereafter regulated by law. All prisoners shall be bailable by sufficient securities, unless for capital offences, when the proof is evident or presumption great.

SECTION XXVI Excessive bail shall not be exacted for bailable offences: and all fines shall be moderate.

SECTION XXVII That the General Assembly, when legally formed, shall appoint times and places for county elections, and at such times and places, the freemen in each county respectively, shall have the liberty of choosing the judges of inferior court of common pleas, sheriffs, justices of the peace, and judges of probates, commissioned by the Governor and Council, during good behavior, removable by the General Assembly upon proof of mal-administration.

SECTION XXVIII That no person, shall be capable of holding any civil office, in this State, except he has acquired, and maintains a good moral character.

SECTION XXIX All elections, whether by the people or in General Assembly, shall be by ballot, free and voluntary: and any elector who shall receive any gift or reward for his vote, In meat, drink, monies or otherwise' shall forfeit his right to elect at that time, and suffer such other penalty as future laws shall direct. And any person who shall, directly or indirectly, give, promise, or bestow, any such rewards to be elected, shall, thereby, be rendered incapable to serve for the ensuing year.

SECTION XXX All fines, license money, fees and forfeitures, shall be paid, according to the direction hereafter to be made by the General Assembly.

SECTION XXXI All deeds and conveyances of land shall be recorded in the town clerk's office, in their respective towns.

SECTION XXXII The printing presses shall-be free to every person who undertakes to examine the proceedings of the legislature or any part of government.

SECTION XXXIII As every freeman, to preserve his independence (if without a sufficient estate) ought to have some profession, calling, trade or farm, whereby he may honestly subsist, there can be no necessity for, nor use in, establishing offices of profit, the usual effects of which are dependence and servility, unbecoming freemen, in the possessors or expectants; faction, contention, corruption and disorder among people. But if any man is called into public service, to the prejudice of his private affairs, he has a right to a reasonable compensation; and whenever an office, through increase of fees, or otherwise, becomes so profitable as to occasion many to apply for it the profits ought to be lessened by the legislature.

SECTION XXXIV The future legislature of this State, shall regulate entails, in such manner as to prevent perpetuities.

SECTION XXXV To deter more effectually from the commission of crimes, by continued visible punishment of long duration, and to make sanguinary punishments less necessary; houses ought to be provided for punishing, by hard labor, those who shall be convicted of crimes not capital; wherein the criminal shall be employed for the benefit of the public, or for reparation of injuries done to private persons; and all persons, at proper times, shall be admitted to see the prisoners at their labor.

SECTION XXXVI Every officer, whether judicial, executive or military, in authority under this State. shall take the following oath or affirmation of allegiance, and general oath of office, before he enter on the execution of his office.

THE OATH OR AFFIRMATION OF ALLEGIANCE

"I _____ do solemnly swear by the ever living God, (or affirm in presence of Almighty God,) that I will be true and faithful to the State of *Vermont*; and that I will not, directly or indirectly do any act or thing, prejudicial or injurious, to the constitution or government thereof, as established by Convention."

THE OATH OR AFFIRMATION OF OFFICE

"I _____ do solemnly swear by the ever living God, (or affirm in presence of Almighty God) that I will faithfully execute the office of for the of; and will do equal right and justice to all men, to the best of my judgment and abilities, according to law."

SECTION XXXVII No public tax, custom or contribution shall be imposed upon, or paid by, the people of this State, except by a law for that purpose; and before any law be made for raising it, the purpose for which any tax is to be raised ought to appear clear to the legislature to be of more service to the community than the money would be, if not collected; which being well observed, taxes can never be burthens.

SECTION XXXVIII Every foreigner of good character, who comes to settle in this State, having first taken an oath or affirmation of allegiance to the same, may purchase, or by other just means acquire, hold, and transfer, land or other real estate; and after one years residence, shall be deemed a free denizen thereof, and intitled to all the rights of a natural born subject of this State; except that he shall not be capable of being elected a representative, until after two years residence.

SECTION XXXIX That the inhabitants of this State, shall have liberty to hunt and fowl, in seasonable times, on the lands they hold, and on other lands (not enclosed;) and, in like manner, to fish in all beatable and other waters, not private property, under proper regulations, to be hereafter made and provided by the General Assembly.

SECTION XL A school or schools shall be established in each town, by the legislature, for the convenient instruction of youth, with such salaries to the masters, paid by each town; making proper use of school lands in each town, thereby to enable them to instruct youth at low prices. One grammar school in each county, and one university in this State, ought to be established by direction of the General Assembly.

SECTION XLI Laws for the encouragement of virtue and prevention of vice and immorality, shall be made and constantly kept in force; and provision shall be made for their due execution; and all religious societies or bodies of men, that have or may be hereafter united and incorporated, for the advancement of religion and learning, or for other pious and charitable purposes, shall be encouraged and protected in the enjoyment of the privileges, immunities and estates which they, in justice, ought to enjoy, under such regulations; as the General Assembly of this State shall direct.

SECTION XLII All field and staff officers, and commissioned officers of the army, and all general officers of the militia, shall be chosen by the General Assembly.

SECTION XLIII The declaration of rights is hereby declared to be part of the Constitution of this State, and ought never to be violated, on any presence whatsoever.

SECTION XLIV In order that the freedom of this Commonwealth may be preserved inviolate, forever, there shall be chosen, by ballot, by the freemen of this State, on the last Wednesday in March, in the year one thousand seven hundred and eighty-five, and on the last Wednesday in March, in every seven years thereafter, thirteen persons, who shall be chosen in the same manner the council is chosen—except they shall not be out of the Council or General Assembly—to be called the Council of Censors; who shall meet together, on the first Wednesday of June next ensuing their election; the majority of whom shall be a quorum in every case, except as to calling a Convention, in which two-thirds of the whole number elected shall agree; mod whose duty it shall be to enquire whether the constitution has been preserved inviolate, in every part; and whether the legislative and executive branches of government have performed their duty as guardians of the people; or assumed to themselves, or exercised, other or greater powers, than they are entitled to by the constitution. They are also to enquire whether the public taxes have been justly laid and collected, in all parts of this Commonwealth—in what manner the public monies have been disposed of, and whether the laws have been duly executed. For these purposes they shall have power to send for persons, papers and records; they shall have authority to pass public censures—to order impeachments, and to recommend to the legislature the repealing such laws as appear to them to have been enacted contrary to the principles of the constitution. These powers they shall continue to have, for and during the space of one year from the day of their election, and no longer. The said Council of Censors shall also have power to call a Convention, to meet within two years after their sitting, if there appears to them an absolute necessity of amending any article of this constitution which may be defective—explaining such as may be thought not clearly expressed, and of adding such as are necessary for the preservation of the rights and happiness of the people; but the articles to be amended, and the amendments proposed, and such articles as are proposed to be added or abolished, shall be promulgated at least six months before the day appointed for the election of such convention, for the previous consideration of the people, that they may have an opportunity of instructing their delegates on the subject.

29

The Articles of Confederation and Perpetual Union, Continental Congress, 1777

The Articles of Confederation served as America's first national constitution. The Continental Congress approved the articles in 1777 and sent the document to the states for approval, requiring the consent of all thirteen states for ratification. Because of this, the Articles of Confederation did not go into effect until March 1781 when Maryland finally gave its approval. The structure of the national government was much different than the present form under the 1787 Constitution. Congress, in effect, was the national government. But Congress had very few powers in which to conduct business, which many Americans at the time preferred to a strong government that could strip away the freedoms of the people. The Congress lacked much power to act, but the Articles of Confederation contained no bill of rights or guarantees of specific freedoms, save for the freedom of speech to be preserved on the floor of Congress. With such little power to act, the government under the Articles of Confederation could not meet the difficult demands on an independent nation in the 1780s.

To all to whom these Presents shall come, we the undersigned Delegates of the States affixed to our Names, send greeting.

Whereas the Delegates of the United States of America, in Congress assembled, did, on the 15th day of November, in the Year of Our Lord One thousand Seven Hundred and Seventy seven, and in the Second Year of the Independence of America, agree to certain articles of Confederation and perpetual Union between the States of New-hampshire, Massachusetts-bay, Rhode-island and Providence Plantations, Connecticut, New York, New Jersey Pennsylvania, Delaware, Maryland, Virginia, North-Carolina, South-Carolina, and Georgia in the words following, viz. "Articles of Confederation and perpetual Union between the states of New-hampshire, Massachusetts-bay, Rhode-island and Providence Plantations, Connecticut, New-York, New-Jersey, Pennsylvania, Delaware, Maryland, Virginia, North-Carolina, South-Carolina and Georgia".

Article I

The Stile of this confederacy shall be "The United States of America."

Article II

Each state retains its sovereignty, freedom, and independence, and every Power, Jurisdiction and right, which is not by this confederation expressly delegated to the United States, in Congress assembled.

Article III

The said states hereby severally enter into a firm league of friendship with each other, for their common defence, the security of their Liberties, and their mutual and general welfare, binding themselves to assist each other, against all force offered to, or attacks made upon them, or any of them, on account of religion, sovereignty, trade, or any other pretence whatever.

Article IV

The better to secure and perpetuate mutual friendship and intercourse among the people of the different states in this union, the free inhabitants of each of these states, paupers, vagabonds and fugitives from justice excepted, shall be entitled to all privileges and immunities of free citizens in the several states; and the people of each state shall have free ingress and regress to and from any other state, and shall enjoy therein all the privileges of trade and commerce, subject to the same duties impositions and restrictions as the inhabitants thereof respectively, provided that such restriction shall not extend so far as to prevent the removal of property imported into any state, to any other state, of which the Owner is an inhabitant; provided also that no imposition, duties or restriction shall be laid by any state, on the property of the united states, or either of them. If any Person guilty of, or charged with treason, felony,—or other high misdemeanor in any state, shall flee from Justice, and be found in any of the united states, he shall, upon demand of the Governor or executive power, of the state from which he fled, be delivered up and removed to the state having jurisdiction of his offence. Full faith and credit shall be given in each of these states to the records, acts and judicial proceedings of the courts and magistrates of every other state.

Article V

For the more convenient management of the general interests of the united states, delegates shall be annually appointed in such manner as the legislature of each state shall direct, to meet in Congress on the first Monday in November, in every year, with a power reserved to each state, to recal its delegates, or any of them, at any time within the year, and to send others in their stead, for the remainder of the Year.

No state shall be represented in Congress by less than two, nor by more than seven Members; and no person shall be capable of being a delegate for more than three years in any term of six years; nor shall any person, being a delegate, be capable of holding any office under the united states, for which he, or another for his benefit receives any salary, fees or emolument of any kind.

Each state shall maintain its own delegates in a meeting of the states, and while they act as members of the committee of the states. In determining questions in the united states in Congress assembled, each state shall have one vote.

Freedom of speech and debate in Congress shall not be impeached or questioned in any Court, or place out of Congress, and the members of congress shall be protected in their persons from arrests and imprisonments, during the time of their going to and from, and attendance on congress, except for treason, felony, or breach of the peace.

Article VI

No state, without the Consent of the united states in congress assembled, shall send any embassy to, or receive any embassy from, or enter into any conference agreement, alliance or treaty with any King prince or state; nor shall any person holding any office of profit or trust under the united states, or any of them, accept of any present, emolument, office or title of any kind whatever from any king, prince or foreign state; nor shall the united states in congress assembled, or any of them, grant any title of nobility.

No two or more states shall enter into any treaty, confederation or alliance whatever between them, without the consent of the united states in congress assembled, specifying accurately the purposes for which the same is to be entered into, and how long it shall continue.

No state shall lay any imposts or duties, which may interfere with any stipulations in treaties, entered into by the united states in congress assembled, with any king, prince or state, in pursuance of any treaties already proposed by congress, to the courts of France and Spain.

No vessels of war shall be kept up in time of peace by any state, except such number only, as shall be deemed necessary by the united states in congress assembled, for the defence of such state, or its trade; nor shall any body of forces be kept up by any state, in time of peace, except such number only, as in the judgment of the united states, in congress assembled, shall be deemed requisite to garrison the forts necessary for the defence of such state; but every state shall always keep up a well regulated and disciplined militia, sufficiently armed and accoutered, and shall provide and constantly have ready for use, in public stores, a due number of field pieces and tents, and a proper quantity of arms, ammunition and camp equipage. No state shall engage in any war without the consent of the united states in congress assembled, unless such state be actually invaded by enemies, or shall have received certain advice of a resolution being formed by some nation of Indians to invade such state, and the danger is so imminent as not to admit of a delay till the united states in congress assembled can be consulted: nor shall any state grant commissions to any ships or vessels of war, nor letters of marque or reprisal, except it be after a declaration of war by the united states in congress assembled, and then only against the kingdom or state and the subjects thereof, against which war has been so declared, and under such regulations as shall be established by the united states in congress assembled, unless such state be infested by pirates, in which case vessels of war may be fitted out for that occasion, and kept so long as the danger shall continue, or until the united states in congress assembled, shall determine otherwise.

Article VII

When land-forces are raised by any state for the common defence, all officers of or under the rank of colonel, shall be appointed by the legislature of each state respectively, by whom such forces shall be raised, or in such manner as such state shall direct, and all vacancies shall be filled up by the State which first made the appointment.

Article VIII

All charges of war, and all other expences that shall be incurred for the common defence or general welfare, and allowed by the united states in congress assembled, shall be defrayed out of a common treasury, which shall be supplied by the several states in proportion to the value of all land within each state, granted to or surveyed for any Person, as such land and the buildings and improvements thereon shall be estimated according to such mode as the united states in congress assembled, shall from time to time direct and appoint.

The taxes for paying that proportion shall be laid and levied by the authority and direction of the legislatures of the several states within the time agreed upon by the united states in congress assembled.

Article IX

The united states in congress assembled, shall have the sole and exclusive right and power of determining on peace and war, except in the cases mentioned in the sixth article—of sending and receiving ambassadors—entering into treaties and alliances, provided that no treaty of commerce shall be made whereby the legislative power of the respective states shall be restrained from imposing such imposts and duties on foreigners as their own people are subjected to, or from prohibiting the exportation or importation of any species of goods or commodities, whatsoever—of establishing rules for deciding in all cases, what captures on land or water shall be legal, and in what manner prizes taken by land or naval forces in the service of the united states shall be divided or appropriated—of granting letters of marque and reprisal in times of peace—appointing courts for the trial of piracies and felonies committed on the high seas and establishing courts for receiving and determining finally appeals in all cases of captures, provided that no member of congress shall be appointed a judge of any of the said courts.

The united states in congress assembled shall also be the last resort on appeal in all disputes and differences now subsisting or that hereafter may arise between two or more states concerning boundary, jurisdiction or any other cause whatever; which authority shall always be exercised in the manner following. Whenever the legislative or executive authority or lawful agent of any state in controversy with another shall present a petition to congress stating the matter in question and praying for a hearing, notice thereof shall be given by order of congress to the legislative or executive authority of the other state in controversy, and a day assigned for the appearance of the parties by their lawful agents, who shall then be directed to appoint by joint consent, commissioners or judges to constitute a court for hearing and determining the matter in question: but if they cannot agree, congress shall name three persons out of each of the united states, and from the list of such persons each party shall alternately strike out one, the petitioners beginning, until the number shall be reduced to thirteen; and from that number not less than seven, nor more than nine names as congress shall direct, shall in the presence of congress be drawn out by lot, and the persons whose names shall be so drawn or any five of them, shall be commissioners or judges, to hear and finally determine the controversy, so always as a major part of the judges who shall hear the cause shall agree in the determination: and if either party shall neglect to attend at the day appointed, without showing reasons, which congress shall judge sufficient, or being present shall refuse to strike, the congress shall proceed to nominate three persons out of each state, and the secretary of congress shall strike in behalf of such party absent or refusing; and the judgment and sentence of the court to be appointed, in the manner before prescribed, shall be final and conclusive; and if any of the parties shall refuse to submit to the authority of such court, or to appear or defend their claim or cause, the court shall nevertheless proceed to pronounce sentence, or judgment, which shall in like manner be final and decisive, the judgment or sentence and other proceedings being in either case transmitted to congress, and lodged among the acts of congress for the security of the parties concerned: provided that every commissioner, before he sits in judgment, shall take an oath to be administered by one of the judges of the supreme or superior court of the state, where the cause shall be tried, "well and truly to hear and determine the matter in question, according to the best of his judgment, without favour, affection or hope of reward:" provided also, that no state shall be deprived of territory for the benefit of the united states.

All controversies concerning the private right of soil claimed under different grants of two or more states, whose jurisdictions as they may respect such lands, and the states which passed such grants are adjusted, the said grants or either of them being at the same time claimed to have originated antecedent to such settlement of jurisdiction, shall on the petition of either party to the congress of the united states, be finally determined as near as may be in the same manner as is before prescribed for deciding disputes respecting territorial jurisdiction between different states.

The united states in congress assembled shall also have the sole and exclusive right and power of regulating the alloy and value of coin struck by their own authority, or by that of the respective states—fixing the standard of weights and measures throughout the united states—regulating the trade and managing all affairs with the Indians, not members of any of the states, provided that the legislative right of any state within its own limits be not infringed or violated—establishing or regulating post offices from one state to another, throughout all the united states, and exacting such postage on the papers passing thro' the same as may be requisite to defray the expences of the said office—appointing all officers of the land forces, in the service of the united states, excepting regimental officers—appointing all the officers of the naval forces, and commissioning all officers whatever in the service of the united states—making rules for the government and regulation of the said land and naval forces, and directing their operations.

The united states in congress assembled shall have authority to appoint a committee, to sit in the recess of congress, to be denominated "A Committee of the States," and to consist of one delegate from each state; and to appoint such other committees and civil officers as may be necessary for managing the general affairs of the united states under their direction—to appoint one of their number to preside, provided that no person be allowed to serve in the office of president more than one year in any term of three years; to ascertain the necessary sums of money to be raised for the service of the united states, and to appropriate and apply the same for defraying the public expences to borrow money, or emit bills on the credit of the united states, transmitting every half year to the respective states an account of the sums of money so borrowed or emitted,—to build and equip a navy—to agree upon the number of land forces, and to make requisitions from each state for its quota, in proportion to the number of white inhabitants in such state; which requisition shall be binding, and thereupon the legislature of each state shall appoint the regimental officers, raise the men and cloth, arm and equip them in a soldier like manner, at the expence of the united states; and the officers and men so cloathed, armed and quipped shall march to the place appointed, and within the time agreed on by the united states in congress assembled: But if the united states in congress assembled shall, on consideration of circumstances judge proper that any state should not raise men, or should raise a smaller number than its quota, and that any other state should raise a greater number of men than the quota thereof, such extra number shall be raised, officered, cloathed, armed and equipped in the same manner as the quota of such state, unless the legislature of such state shall judge that such extra number cannot be safely spared out of the same, in which case they shall raise officer, cloath, arm and equip as many of such extra number as they judge can be safely spared. And the officers and men so cloathed, armed and equipped, shall march to the place appointed, and within the time agreed on by the united states in congress assembled.

The united states in congress assembled shall never engage in a war, nor grant letters of marque and reprisal in time of peace, nor enter into any treaties or alliances, nor coin money, nor regulate the value thereof, nor ascertain the sums and expences necessary for the defence and welfare of the united states, or any of them, nor emit bills, nor borrow money on the credit of the united states, nor appropriate money, nor agree upon the number of vessels of war, to be built or purchased, or the number of land or sea forces to be raised, nor appoint a commander in chief of the army or navy, unless nine states assent to the same: nor shall a question on any other point, except for adjourning from day to day be determined, unless by the votes of a majority of the united states in congress assembled.

The congress of the united states shall have power to adjourn to any time within the year, and to any place within the united states, so that no period of adjournment be for a longer duration than the space of six Months, and shall publish the Journal of their proceedings monthly, except such parts thereof relating to treaties, alliances or military operations, as in their judgment require secrecy; and the yeas and nays of the delegates of each state on any question shall be entered on the Journal, when it is desired by any delegate; and the delegates of a state, or any of them, at his or their request shall be furnished with a transcript of the said Journal, except such parts as are above excepted, to lay before the legislatures of the several states.

Article X

The committee of the states, or any nine of them, shall be authorized to execute, in the recess of congress, such of the powers of congress as the united states in congress assembled, by the consent of nine states, shall from time to time think expedient to vest them with; provided that no power be delegated to the said committee, for the exercise of which, by the articles of confederation, the voice of nine states in the congress of the united states assembled is requisite.

Article XI

Canada acceding to this confederation, and joining in the measures of the united states, shall be admitted into, and entitled to all the advantages of this union: but no other colony shall be admitted into the same, unless such admission be agreed to by nine states.

Article XII

All bills of credit emitted, monies borrowed and debts contracted by, or under the authority of congress, before the assembling of the united states, in pursuance of the present confederation, shall be deemed and considered as a charge against the united states, for payment and satisfaction whereof the said united states, and the public faith are hereby solemnly pledged.

Article XIII

Every state shall abide by the determinations of the united states in congress assembled, on all questions which by this confederation are submitted to them. And the Articles of this confederation shall be inviolably observed by every state, and the union shall be perpetual; nor shall any alteration at any time hereafter be made in any of them; unless such alteration be agreed to in a congress of the united states, and be afterwards confirmed by the legislatures of every state.

And Whereas it hath pleased the Great Governor of the World to incline the hearts of the legislatures we respectively represent in congress, to approve of, and to authorize us to ratify the said articles of confederation and perpetual union. Know Ye that we the undersigned delegates, by virtue of the power and authority to us given for that purpose, do by these presents, in the name and in behalf of our respective constituents, fully and entirely ratify and confirm each and every of the said articles of confederation and perpetual union, and all and singular the matters and things therein contained: And we do further solemnly plight and engage the faith of our respective constituents, that they shall abide by the determinations of the united states in congress assembled, on all questions, which by the said confederation are submitted to them. And that the articles thereof shall be inviolably observed by the states we respectively represent, and that the union shall be perpetual.

In Witness whereof we have hereunto set our hands in Congress. Done at Philadelphia in the state of Pennsylvania the ninth day of July in the Year of our Lord one Thousand seven Hundred and Seventy-eight, and in the third year of the independence of America.

On the part of & behalf of the State of New Hampshire:

Josiah Bartlett
John Wentworth. Junr; August 8th, 1778

On the part and behalf of the State of Rhode-Island and Providence Plantations:

William Ellery
Henry Marchant
John Collins

On the part and behalf of the State of New York:

Jas Duane
Fra: Lewis
Wm Duer
Gouvr Morris

On the part and behalf of the State of Pennsylvania:

Robert Morris
Daniel Roberdeau
Jon. Bayard Smith
William Clingar
Joseph Reed; 22d July, 1778

On the part and behalf of the State of Maryland:

John Hanson; March 1, 1781
Daniel Carroll, do.

On the part and behalf of the State of North Carolina:

John Penn; July 21st, 1778
Corns Harnett
Jno Williams

On the part and behalf of the State of Georgia:

Jno Walton; 24th July, 1778
Edwd Telfair
Edwd Langworthy

On the part of & behalf of the State of Massachusetts Bay:

John Hancock
Samuel Adams
Elbridge Gerry
Francis Dana
James Lovell
Samuel Holten

On the part and behalf of the State of Connecticut:

Roger Sherman
Samuel Huntington
Oliver Wolcott
Titus Hosmer
Andrew Adams

On the Part and in Behalf of the State of New Jersey, November 26th, 1778:

Jno Witherspoon
Nathl Scudder

On the part and behalf of the State of Delaware:

Thos McKean; Febr 22d, 1779
John Dickinson; May 5th, 1779
Nicholas Van Dyke

On the part and behalf of the State of Virginia:

Richard Henry Lee
John Banister
Thomas Adams
Jno Harvie
Francis Lightfoot Lee

On the part and behalf of the State of South Carolina:

Henry Laurens
William Henry Drayton
Jno Mathews
Richd Hutson
Thos Heyward, junr.

30

Massachusetts Bill of Rights, 1780

As new state constitutions began replacing colonial charters, many states went to great lengths to define the freedoms of their citizens and to craft governments designed to protect these freedoms at all costs. In 1780, Massachusetts presented this document as a guarantee of the rights of the citizens of the state. The thirty rights listed below reflected the sentiments expressed in the Declaration of Independence as they became codified into law in Massachusetts. These rights included freedom of the press, the right of legislators to debate freely without fear of arrest, and the right to due process of law. But reflecting its Puritan roots, Massachusetts continued to limit religious freedom to Protestants and mandate donations to churches, an issue that would linger into the 1800s. Above all, the Massachusetts Bill of Rights declared that all men were born free and equal, an idea that citizens strove to defend and in a later court case was used to declare slavery unconstitutional in Massachusetts.

PART THE FIRST

A DECLARATION OF THE RIGHTS OF THE INHABITANTS OF THE COMMONWEALTH OF MASSACHUSETTS

ARTICLE I All men are born free and equal, and have certain natural, essential, and unalienable rights; among which may be reckoned the right of enjoying and

Richard D. Brown, ed., "Massachusetts Declaration of Rights," *Major Problems in the Era of the American Revolution, 1760–1791*, 2nd ed. (Boston: Houghton Mifflin, 2000): 314–315.

defending their lives and liberties; that of acquiring, possessing, and protecting property; in fine, that of seeking and obtaining their safety and happiness.

II It is the right as well as the duty of all men in society, publicly, and at stated seasons, to worship the SUPREME BEING, the great Creator and Preserver of the universe. And no subject shall be hurt, molested, or restrained, in his person, liberty, or estate, for worshipping GOD in the manner and season most agreeable to the dictates of his own conscience; or for his religious profession of sentiments; provided he doth not disturb the public peace, or obstruct others in their religious worship.

III *[As the happiness of a people, and the good order and preservation of civil government, essentially depend upon piety, religion, and morality; and as these cannot be generally diffused through a community but by the restitution of the public worship of GOD, and of public instructions in piety, religion, and morality: Therefore, to promote their happiness, and to secure the good order and preservation of their government, the people of this commonwealth have a right to invest their legislature with power to authorize and require, and the legislature shall, from time to time, authorize and require, the several towns, parishes, precincts, and other bodies politic, or religious societies, to make suitable provision, at their own expense, for the institution of the public worship of God, and for the support and maintenance of public Protestant teachers of piety, religion, and morality. in all cases where such provision shall not be made voluntarily.

And the people of this commonwealth have also a right to, and do, invest their legislature with authority to enjoin upon all the subjects an attendance upon the instructions of the public teachers aforesaid, at stated times and seasons, if there be any on whose instructions they can conscientiously and conveniently attend.

Provided, notwithstanding, that the several towns, parishes, precincts, and other bodies politic, or religious societies, shall, at all times, have the exclusive right of electing their public teachers, and of contracting with them for their support and maintenance. And all moneys paid by the subject to the support of public worship, and of the public teachers aforesaid, shall, if he require it, be uniformly applied to the support of the public teacher or teachers of his own religious sect or denomination, provided there be any on whose instructions he attends; otherwise, it may be paid towards the support, of the teacher or teachers of the parish or precinct in which the said moneys are raised. And every denomination of Christians, demeaning themselves peaceably, and as good subjects of the commonwealth, shall be equally under the protection of the law: and no subordination of any one sect or denomination to another shall ever be established by law.]

IV The people of this commonwealth have the sole and exclusive right of governing themselves, as a free, sovereign, and independent state; and do, and forever hereafter shall; exercise and enjoy every power, jurisdiction, and right, which is not, or may not hereafter by them expressly delegated to the United States of America, in Congress assembled.

V All power residing originally in the people, and being derived from them, the several magistrates and officers of government, vested with authority, whether

*Amendment, Art. XI, substituted for this.

legislative, executive, or judicial, are their substitutes and agents, and are at all times accountable to them.

VI No man, nor corporation, or association of men, have any other title to obtain advantages, or particular and exclusive privileges, distinct from those of the community, than what arises from the consideration of services rendered to the public; and this title being in nature neither hereditary, nor transmissible to children, or descendants, or relations by blood, the idea of a man born a magistrate, law giver, or judge, is absurd and unnatural.

VII Government is instituted for the common good; for the protection, safety, prosperity, and happiness of the people; and not for the profit, honor, or private interest of any one man, family, or class of men: Therefore the people alone have all incontestible unalienable, and indefeasible right to institute government; and to reform, alter, or totally change the same, when their protection, safety, prosperity, and happiness require it.

VIII In order to prevent those who are vested with authority from becoming oppressors, the people have a right, at such periods and in such manner as they shall establish by their frame of government, to cause their public officers to return to private life; and to fill up vacant places by certain and regular elections and appointments.

IX All elections ought to be free; and all the inhabitants of this commonwealth, having such qualifications as they shall establish by their frame of government, have an equal right to elect officers, and to be elected, for public employments.

X Each individual of the society has a right to be protected by it in the enjoyment of his life, liberty, and property, according to standing laws. He is obliged, consequently, to contribute his share to the expense of this protection; to give his personal service, or an equivalent, when necessary: but no part of the property of any individual can, with justice, be taken from him, or applied to public uses, without his own consent, or that of the representative body of the people. In fine, the people of this commonwealth are not controllable by any other laws than those to which their constitutional representative body have given their consent. And whenever the public exigencies require that the property of any individual should be appropriated to public uses, he shall receive a reasonable compensation therefor.

XI Every subject of the commonwealth ought to find a certain remedy, by having recourse to the laws, for all injuries or wrongs which he may receive in his person, property, or character. He ought to obtain right and justice freely, and without being obliged to purchase it; completely, and without any denial; promptly, and without delay; conformably to the laws.

XII No subject shall be held to answer for any crimes or offence, until the same is fully and plainly, substantially, and formally, described to him; or be compelled to accuse, or furnish evidence against himself. And every subject shall have a right to produce all proofs that may be favorable to him; to meet the witnesses against him face to face, and to be fully heard in his defence by himself, or his counsel at his election. And no subject shall be arrested, imprisoned, despoiled, or deprived of his property, immunities, or privileges, put, out, of the protection of the law, exiled, or deprived of his life, liberty, or estate, but by the judgment of his peers, or the law of the land.

And the legislature shall not make any law that shall subject any person to a capital or infamous punishment, excepting for the government of the army and navy, without trial by jury.

XIII In criminal prosecutions, the verification of facts, in the vicinity where they happen, is one of the greatest securities of the life, liberty, and property of the citizen.

XIV Every subject has a right to be secure from all unreasonable searches, and seizures, of his person, his houses, his papers, and all his possessions. All warrants, therefore, are contrary to this right, if the cause or foundation of them be not previously supported by oath or affirmation, and if the order in the warrant to a civil officer, to make search in suspected places, or to arrest one or more suspected persons, or to seize their property, be not accompanied with a special designation of the persons or objects of search, arrest, or seizure; and no warrant ought to be issued but in cases, and with the formalities prescribed by the laws.

XV In all controversies concerning property, and in all suits between two or more persons, except in cases in which it has heretofore been otherways used and practised, the parties have a right to a trial by jury; and this method of procedure shall be held sacred, unless, in causes arising on the high seas, and such as relate to mariners' wages, the legislature shall hereafter find it necessary to alter it.

XVI The liberty of the press is essential to the security of freedom in a state it ought not, therefore, to be restricted in this commonwealth.

XVII The people have a right to keep and to bear arms for the common defence. And as, in time of peace, armies are dangerous to liberty, they ought not to be maintained without the consent of the legislature; and the military power shall always be held in an exact subordination to the civil authority, and be governed by it.

XVIII A frequent recurrence to the fundamental principles of the constitution, and a constant. adherence to those of piety, justice, moderation, temperance, industry, and frugality, are absolutely necessary to preserve the advantages of liberty, and to maintain a free government. The people ought, consequently, to have a particular attention to all those principles, in the choice of their officers and representatives: and the have a right to require of their lawgivers and magistrates an exact and constant observance of them, in the formation and execution of the laws necessary for the good administration of the commonwealth.

XIX The people have a right, in an orderly and peaceable manner, to assemble to consult upon the common good; give instructions to their representatives, and to request of the legislature body, by the way of addresses, petitions, or remonstrances, redress of the wrongs done them, and of the grievances they suffer.

XX The power of suspending the laws, or the execution of the laws, ought never to be exercised but by the legislature, or by authority derived from it, to be exercised in such particular cases only as the legislature shall expressly provide for.

XXI The freedom of deliberation, speech, and debate, in either house of the legislature, is so essential to the rights of the people, that it cannot be the foundation of any accusation or prosecution, action or complaint, in any other court or place whatsoever.

XXII The legislature ought frequently to assemble for the redress of grievances, for correcting, strengthening, and confirming the laws, and for making new laws, as the common good may require.

XXIII No subsidy, charge, tax, impost, or duties ought to be established, fixed, laid, or levied, under any pretext whatsoever, without the consent of the people or their representatives in the legislature.

XXIV Laws made to punish for actions done before the existence of such laws, and which have not been declared crimes by preceding laws, are unjust, oppressive, and inconsistent with the fundamental principles of a free government.

XXV No subject ought, in any case, or in any time, to be declared guilty of treason or felony by the legislature.

XXVI No magistrate or court of law shall demand excessive bail or sureties, impose excessive fines, or inflict cruel or unusual punishments.

XXVII In time of peace, no soldier ought to be quartered in any house without the consent of the owner; and in time of war, such quarters ought not to be made but by the civil magistrate, in a manner ordained by the legislature.

XXVIII No person can in any case be subject to law-martial, or to any penalties or pains, by virtue of that law, except those employed in the army or navy, and except the militia in actual service, but by authority of the legislature.

XXIX It is essential to the preservation of the rights of every individual, his life, liberty, property, and character, that there be an impartial interpretation of the laws, and administration of justice. It is the right of every citizen to be tried by judges as free, impartial, and independent as the lot of humanity will admit. It is, therefore, not only the best policy, but for the security of the rights of the people, and of every citizen, that the judges of the supreme judicial court should hold their offices as long as they behave themselves well; and that they should have honorable salaries ascertained and established by standing laws.

XXX In the government of this commonwealth, the legislative department shall never exercise the executive and judicial powers, or either of them: the executive shall never exercise the legislative and judicial powers, or either of them: the judicial shall never exercise the legislative and executive powers, or either of them: to the end it may be a government of laws and not of men.

31

An Act for the Gradual Abolition of Slavery, Pennsylvania General Assembly, 1780

As the American Revolution continued, a number of states began to reconsider slavery. So often the colonists had complained that the British had attempted to reduce them to slavery and the declaration of the equality of all men convinced many that such a glaring hypocrisy must be rectified. Vermont had already abolished slavery in 1777, and on March 1, 1780, Pennsylvania followed suit. This act proposed a system of gradual emancipation, whereby every slave child born after 1780 would be freed at age 28. Other northern states followed a similar system of gradual emancipation while the southern states only increased their slave populations. The Pennsylvania General Assembly tied this issue closely to the cause of the Revolutionary War, believing that not only should the free population be freed from the tyranny of Great Britain, but that slaves should also share this taste of freedom. Consistent with the writing style usually employed at the time, the letter "s" is substituted with "f" while not affecting its pronunciation. With a sophisticated tone, the legislators state that skin color should not become an issue of human rights. Since all human beings were created by God, the assembly argued, men should only increase their affection and generosity toward each other. To live in peace and dignity is perhaps the most important of freedoms.

SECTION 1. WHEN we contemplate our abhorrence of that condition to which the arms and tyranny of Great Britain were exerted to reduce us; when we look back on the variety of dangers to which we have been expofed, and how miraculously our wants in many inftances have been fupplied, and our deliverances wrought, when even hope and human fortitude have become unequal to the conflict; we are unavoidably led to a ferious and grateful fence of the manifold bleffings which we have undeservedly received from the hand of that Being from whom every good and perfect gift cometh. Impreffed with there ideas, we conceive that it is our duty, and we rejoice that it is in our power to extend a portion of that freedom to others, which hath been extended to us; and a releafe from that state of thraldom to which we ourfelves were tyrannically doomed, and from which we have now every profpect of being delivered. It is not for us to enquire why, in the creation of mankind, the inhabitants of the feveral parts of the earth were diftinguifhed by a difference in feature or complexion. It is fufficient to know that all are the work of an Almighty Hand. We find in the distribution of the human fpecies, that the moft fertile as well as the moft barren parts of the earth are inhabited by men of complexions different from ours, and from each other; from whence we may reasonably, as well as religiously, infer, that He who placed them in their various situations, hath extended equally his care and protection to all, and that it becometh not us to counteract his mercies. We efteem it a peculiar bleffing granted to us, that we are enabled this day to add one more ftep to univerfal civilization, by removing as much as poffible the forrows of thofe who have lived in undeferved bondage, and from which, by the assumed authority of the kings of Great Britain, no effectual, legal relief could be obtained. Weaned by a long courfe of experience from thofe narrower prejudices and partialities we had imbibed, we find our hearts enlarged with kindness and benevolence towards men of all conditions and nations; and we conceive ourfelves at this particular period extraordinarily called upon, by the bleffings which we have received, to manifeft the fincerity of our profeffion, and to give a Substantial proof of our gratitude.

SECT. 2. And whereas the condition of thofe perfons who have heretofore been denominated Negro and Mulatto flaves, has been attended with circumftances which not only deprived them of the common bleffings that they were by nature entitled to, but has caft them into the deepeft afflictions, by an unnatural feparation and fale of hufband and wife from each other and from their children; an injury, the greatnefs of which can only be conceived by fuppofing that we were in the fame unhappy cafe. In juftice therefore to perfons So unhappily circumftanced, and who, having no profpect before them whereon they may reft their forrows and their hopes, have no reasonable inducement to render their fervice to fociety, which they otherwise might; and also in grateful commemoration of our own happy deliverance from that ftate of unconditional fubmiffion to which we were doomed by the tyranny of Britain.

SECT. 3. Be it enacted, and it is hereby enacted, by the reprefentatives of the freeman of the commonwealth of Pennfylvania, in general affembly met, and by the authority of the fame, That all perfons, as well Negroes and Mulattoes as others, who fhall be born within this ftate from and after the paffing of this act, fhall not be deemed and confidered as fervants for life, or flaves; and that all fervitude for life, or flavery of children, in confequence of the flavery of their mothers, in the cafe of all children born within this ftate, from and after the paffing of this act as aforefaid, fhall be, and hereby is utterly taken away, extinguifhed and for ever abolifhed.

SECT. 4. Provided always, and be it further enacted by the authority aforefaid, That every Negro and Mulatto child born within this ftate after the paffing of this act as aforefaid (who would, in cafe this act had not been made, have been born a fervent for years, or life, or a flave) fhall be deemed to be and fhall be by virtue of this act the fervant of fuch perfon or his or her affigns, who would in fuch cafe have been entitled to the fervice of fuch child, until fuch child fhall attain unto the age of twenty eight years, in the manner and on the conditions whereon fervants bound by indenture for four years are or may be retained and holder; and fhall be liable to like correction and punifhment, and entitled to like relief in cafe he or fhe be evilly treated by his or her mafter or miftrefs, and to like freedom dues and other privileges as fervants bound by indenture for four years are or may be entitled, unlefs the perfon to whom the fervice of any fuch child fhall belong fhall abandon his or her claim to the fame; in which cafe the overfeers of the poor of the city, township or diftrict refpectively, where fuch child fhall be So abandoned, fhall by indenture bind out every child fo abandoned, as an apprentice for a time not exceeding the age herein before limited for the fervice of fuch children.

SECT. 5. And be it further enacted by the authority aforefaid, That every person, who is or fhall be the owner of any Negro or Mulatto flave or fervant for life or till the age of thirty one years, now within this ftate, or his lawful attorney, fhall on or before the faid firft day of November next deliver or calm to be delivered in writing to the clerk of the peace of the county, or to the clerk of the court of record of the city of Philadelphia, in which he or fhe fhall respectively inhabit, the name and furname and occupation or profeffion of fuch owner, and the name of the county and townfhip, diftrict or ward wherein he or fhe refideth; and alfo the name and names of any fuch flave and flaves, and fervant and fervants for life or till the age of thirty one years, together with their ages and fexes feverally and refpectively fet forth and annexed, by fuch perfon owned or ftatedly employed and then being within this ftate, in order to afcertain and diftinguifh the flaves and fervants for life, and till the age of thirty one years, within this ftate, who fhall be fuch on the faid firft day of November next, from all other perfons; which particulars fhall by faid clerk of the feffions asked clerk of the faid city court be entered in books to be provided for that purpofe by the faid clerks; and that no Negro or Mulatto, now within this ftate, fhall from and after the faid firft day of November, be deemed a flave or fervant for life, or till the age of thirty one years, unlefs his or her name fhall be entered as aforefaid on fuch record, except fuch Negro and Mulatto flaves and fervants as are herein after excepted; the faid clerk to be entitled to a fee of two dollars for each flave or fervant fo entered as aforefaid from the treafurer of the county, to be allowed to him in his accounts.

SECT. 6. Provided always, That any perfon, in whom the ownerfhip or right to the fervice of any Negro or Mulatto fhall be vefted at the paffing of this act, other than fuch as are herein before excepted, his or her heirs, executors, adminiftrators and affigns, and all and every of them feverally fhall be liable to the overfeers of the poor of the city, townfhip or diftrict to which any fuch Negro or Mulatto fhall become chargeable, for fuch neceffary expence, with cofts of fuit thereon, as fuch overfeers may be put to, through the neglect of the owner, mafter or miftrefs of fuch Negro or Mulatto; notwithftanding the name and other defcriptions of fuch Negro or Mulatto fhall not be entered and recorded as aforefaid; unlefs his or her mafter or owner fhall before fuch flave or fervant attain his or her twenty eighth year execute and record in the proper county a deed or inftrument, fecuring to fuch flave or or fervant his or her freedom.

SECT. 7. And be it further enacted by the authority aforefaid, That the offences and crimes of Negroes and Mulattoes, as well flaves and fervants as freemen, fhall be enquired of, adjudged, corrected and punifhed in like manner as the offences and crimes of the other inhabitants of this ftate are and fhall be enquired of, adjudged, corrected and punifhed, and not otherwife; except that a flave fhall not be admitted to bear witnefs againft a freeman.

SECT. 8. And be it further enacted by the authority aforefaid, That in all cafes wherein fentence of death fhall be pronounced againft a flave, the jury before whom he or fhe fhall be tried, fhall appraife and declare the value of fuch flave; and in cafe fuch fentence be executed, the court fhall make an order on the ftate treasurer, payable to the owner for the fame and for the cofts of profecution; but cafe of remiffion or mitigation, for the cofts only.

SECT. 9. And be it further enacted by the authority aforefaid, That the reward for taking up runaway and abfconding Negro and Mulatto flaves and fervants, and the penalties for enticing away, dealing with, or harbouring, concealing or employing Negro and Mulatto flaves and fervants, fhall be the fame, and fhall be recovered in like manner as in cafe of fervants bound for four years.

SECT. 10. And be it further enacted by the authority aforefaid, That no man or woman of any nation or colour, except the Negroes or Mulattoes who fhall be regiftered as aforefaid, fhall at any time hereafter be deemed, adjudged, or holden within the territories of this commonwealth as flaves or fervants for life, but as free men and free women; except the domestic flaves attending upon delegates in congrefs from the other American ftates, foreign minifters and confuls, and perfons paffing through or fojourning in this ftate, and not becoming refident therein; and feamen employed in fhips not belonging to any inhabitant of this ftate, nor employed in any fhip owned by any fuch inhabitant. Provided fuch domeftic flaves be not aliened or fold to any inhabitants nor (except in the cafe of members of congrefs, foreign minifters and confuls) retained in this ftate longer than fix months.

SECT. 11. Provided always; And be it further enacted by the authority aforefaid, That this act or any thing in it contained fhall not give any relief or fhelter to any abfconding or runaway Negro or Mulatto flave or fervant, who has absented himfelf or fhall absent himfelf from his or her owner, mafter or miftrefs refiding in any other ftate or country, but fuch owner, mafter or miftrefs fhall have like right and aid to demand, claim and take away his flave or fervant, as he might have had in cafe this act had not been made: And that all Negro and Mulatto flaves now owned and heretofore refident in this ftate, who have abfented themfelves, or been clandeftinely carried away, or who may be employed abroad as feamen and have not returned or been brought back to their owners, mafters or miftreffes, before the paffing of this act, may within five years be regiftered as effectually as is ordered by this act concerning thofe who are now within the ftate, on producing fuch flave before any two juftices of the peace, and fatisfying the faid juftices by due proof of the former refidence, abfconding, taking away, or abfence of fuch flaves as aforefaid; who thereupon fhall direct and order the said flave to be entered on the record as aforefaid.

SECT. 12. And whereas attempts maybe made to evade this act, by introducing into this ftate Negroes and Mulatoes bound by covenant to ferve for long and unreafonable terms of years, if the fame be not prevented:

SECT. 13. Be it therefore enacted by the authority aforefaid, That no covenant of perfonal fervitude or apprenticefhip whatfoever fhall be valid or binding on a Negro or Mulatto for a longer time than feven years, unlefs fuch fervant or apprentice were at the commencement of fuch fervitude or apprenticefhip under the age of twenty one years; in which cafe fuch Negro or Mulatto may be holden as a fervant or apprentice refpectively, according to the covenant, as the cafe fhall be, until he or fhe fhall attain the age of twenty eight years, but no longer.

SECT. 14. And be it further enacted by the authority aforefaid, That an act of affembly of die province of Pennfylvania, paffed in the year one thousand Seven hundred and five, intitled, "an Act for the trial of Negroes;" and another act of affembly of the faid province, paffed in the year one thousand feven hundred and twenty five, intitled, "An Act for the better regulating of Negroes in this province;" and another act of affembly of the faid province, paffed in the year one thousand feven hundred and fixty one, intitled, .. An Act for laying a duty on Negro and Mulatto flaves imported into this province;" and also another act of affembly of the faid province, paffed in the year one thousand feven hundred and feventy three, inititled, "An Act making perpetual an Act laying a duty on Negro and Mulatto flaves imported into this province, and for laying an additional duty faid flaves," fhall be and are hereby repealed, annulled and made void.

JOHN BAYARD, SPEAKER

Enabled into a law at Philadelphia, on Wednefday, the firft day of March, A.D. 1780 Thomas Paine, clerk of the general affembly.

JAMES MADISON **32**

Memorial and Remonstrance Against Religious Assessments, 1785

The question of an official church in the states festered as an issue in the years following the American Revolution. Most nations and most American states required tithing to an official church. In 1785, a bill was proposed in the Virginia General Assembly titled, "A Bill establishing a provision for Teachers of the Christian Religion," essentially requiring taxpayer support of churches and church-supported religion teachers. James Madison decried the bill as an affront to religious liberty in this statement, "A Memorial and Remonstrance Against Religious Assessments." He stated that each individual must have the opportunity to explore religious issues for themselves, not to have answers dictated to them by the state. The question of infidelity, he wrote, must be decided by God. Madison warned that mixing church and state inevitably would lead to the corruption of both.

To the Honorable the General Assembly of the Commonwealth of Virginia A Memorial and Remonstrance Against Religious Assessments

We the subscribers, citizens of the said Commonwealth, having taken into serious consideration, a Bill printed by order of the last Session of General Assembly, entitled "A Bill establishing a provision for Teachers of the Christian Religion," and conceiving that the same if finally armed with the sanctions of a law, will be a dangerous abuse of power, are bound as faithful members of a free State to remonstrate against it, and to declare the reasons by which we are determined. We remonstrate against the said Bill,

James Madison, "Memorial and Remonstrance against Religious Assessment," *Major Problems in American Constitutional History, II* (Lexington, MA: D.C. Heath, 1992): 463–467; http://religiousfreedom.lib.virginia.edu/sacred/madison_m&r_1785.html

1. Because we hold it for a fundamental and undeniable truth, "that religion or the duty which we owe to our Creator and the manner of discharging it, can be directed only by reason and conviction, not by force or violence." The Religion then of every man must be left to the conviction and conscience of every man; and it is the right of every man to exercise it as these may dictate. This right is in its nature an unalienable right. It is unalienable, because the opinions of men, depending only on the evidence contemplated by their own minds cannot follow the dictates of other men: It is unalienable also, because what is here a right towards men, is a duty towards the Creator. It is the duty of every man to render to the Creator such homage and such only as he believes to be acceptable to him. This duty is precedent, both in order of time and in degree of obligation, to the claims of Civil Society. Before any man can be considerd as a member of Civil Society, he must be considered as a subject of the Governour of the Universe: And if a member of Civil Society, do it with a saving of his allegiance to the Universal Sovereign. We maintain therefore that in matters of Religion, no man's right is abridged by the institution of Civil Society and that Religion is wholly exempt from its cognizance. True it is, that no other rule exists, by which any question which may divide a Society, can be ultimately determined, but the will of the majority; but it is also true that the majority may trespass on the rights of the minority.

2. Because Religion be exempt from the authority of the Society at large, still less can it be subject to that of the Legislative Body. The latter are but the creatures and vicegerents of the former. Their jurisdiction is both derivative and limited: it is limited with regard to the co-ordinate departments, more necessarily is it limited with regard to the constituents. The preservation of a free Government requires not merely, that the metes and bounds which separate each department of power be invariably maintained; but more especially that neither of them be suffered to overleap the great Barrier which defends the rights of the people. The Rulers who are guilty of such an encroachment, exceed the commission from which they derive their authority, and are Tyrants. The People who submit to it are governed by laws made neither by themselves nor by an authority derived from them, and are slaves.

3. Because it is proper to take alarm at the first experiment on our liberties. We hold this prudent jealousy to be the first duty of Citizens, and one of the noblest characteristics of the late Revolution. The free men of America did not wait till usurped power had strengthened itself by exercise, and entagled the question in precedents. They saw all the consequences in the principle, and they avoided the consequences by denying the principle. We revere this lesson too much soon to forget it. Who does not see that the same authority which can establish Christianity, in exclusion of all other Religions, may establish with the same ease any particular sect of Christians, in exclusion of all other Sects? that the same authority which can force a citizen to contribute three pence only of his property for the support of any one establishment, may force him to conform to any other establishment in all cases whatsoever?

4. Because the Bill violates the equality which ought to be the basis of every law, and which is more indispensible, in proportion as the validity or expediency of any law is more liable to be impeached. If "all men are by nature equally free and independent," all men are to be considered as entering into Society on equal conditions; as relinquishing no more, and therefore retaining no less, one than another, of their natural rights. Above all are they to be considered as retaining an "equal title to the free exercise of Religion according to the dictates of Conscience." Whilst we assert for ourselves a freedom to embrace, to profess and to observe the Religion which we believe to be of divine origin, we cannot deny an equal freedom to those whose minds have not yet yielded to the evidence which has convinced us. If this freedom be abused, it is an offence against God, not against man: To God, therefore, not to man, must an account of it be rendered. As the Bill violates equality by subjecting some to peculiar burdens, so it violates the same principle, by granting to others peculiar exemptions. Are the quakers and Menonists the only sects who think a compulsive support of their Religions unnecessary and unwarrantable? can their piety alone be entrusted with the care of public worship? Ought their Religions to be endowed above all others with extraordinary privileges by which proselytes may be enticed from all others? We think too favorably of the justice and good sense of these demoninations to believe that they either covet pre-eminences over their fellow citizens or that they will be seduced by them from the common opposition to the measure.

5. Because the Bill implies either that the Civil Magistrate is a competent Judge of Religious Truth; or that he may employ Religion as an engine of Civil policy. The first is an arrogant pretension falsified by the contradictory opinions of Rulers in all ages, and throughout the world: the second an unhallowed perversion of the means of salvation.

6. Because the establishment proposed by the Bill is not requisite for the support of the Christian Religion. To say that it is, is a contradiction to the Christian Religion itself, for every page of it disavows a dependence on the powers of this world: it is a contradiction to fact; for it is known that this Religion both existed and flourished, not only without the support of human laws, but in spite of every opposition from them, and not only during the period of miraculous aid, but long after it had been left to its own evidence and the ordinary care of Providence. Nay, it is a contradiction in terms; for a Religion not invented by human policy, must have pre-existed and been supported, before it was established by human policy. It is moreover to weaken in those who profess this Religion a pious confidence in its innate excellence and the patronage of its Author; and to foster in those who still reject it, a suspicion that its friends are too conscious of its fallacies to trust it to its own merits.

7. Because experience witnesseth that eccelsiastical establishments, instead of maintaining the purity and efficacy of Religion, have had a contrary operation. During almost fifteen centuries has the legal establishment of Christianity been on trial. What have been its fruits? More or less in all places, pride and indolence in the Clergy, ignorance and servility in the laity, in both, superstition, bigotry and persecution. Enquire of the Teachers of Christianity for the ages in which it appeared in its greatest lustre; those of every sect, point to the ages prior to its incorporation with Civil policy. Propose a restoration of this primitive State in which its Teachers depended on the voluntary rewards of their flocks, many of them predict its downfall. On which Side ought their testimony to have greatest weight, when for or when against their interest?

8. Because the establishment in question is not necessary for the support of Civil Government. If it be urged as necessary for the support of Civil Government only as it is a means of supporting Religion, and it be not necessary for the latter purpose, it cannot be necessary for the former. If Religion be not within the cognizance of Civil Government how can its legal establishment be necessary to Civil Government? What influence in fact have ecclesiastical establishments had on Civil Society? In some instances they have been seen to erect a spiritual tyranny on the ruins of the Civil authority; in many instances they have been seen upholding the thrones of political tyranny: in no instance have they been seen the guardians of the liberties of the people. Rulers who wished to subvert the public liberty, may have found an established Clergy convenient auxiliaries. A just Government instituted to secure & perpetuate it needs them not. Such a Government will be best supported by protecting every Citizen in the enjoyment of his Religion with the same equal hand which protects his person and his property; by neither invading the equal rights of any Sect, nor suffering any Sect to invade those of another.

9. Because the proposed establishment is a departure from the generous policy, which, offering an Asylum to the persecuted and oppressed of every Nation and Religion, promised a lustre to our country, and an accession to the number of its citizens. What a melancholy mark is the Bill of sudden degeneracy? Instead of holding forth an Asylum to the persecuted, it is itself a signal of persecution. It degrades from the equal rank of Citizens all those whose opinions in Religion do not bend to those of the Legislative authority. Distant as it may be in its present form from the Inquisition, it differs from it only in degree. The one is the first step, the other the last in the career of intolerance. The maganimous sufferer under this cruel scourge in foreign Regions, must view the Bill as a Beacon on our Coast, warning him to seek some other haven, where liberty and philanthrophy in their due extent, may offer a more certain respose from his Troubles.

10. Because it will have a like tendency to banish our Citizens. The allurements presented by other situations are every day thinning their number. To superadd a fresh motive to emigration by revoking the liberty which they now enjoy, would be the same species of folly which has dishonoured and depopulated flourishing kingdoms.

11. Because it will destroy that moderation and harmony which the forbearance of our laws to intermeddle with Religion has produced among its several sects. Torrents of blood have been split in the old world, by vain attempts of the secular arm, to extinguish Religious disscord, by proscribing all difference in Religious opinion. Time has at length revealed the true remedy. Every relaxation of narrow and rigorous policy, wherever it has been tried, has been found to assuage the disease. The American Theatre has exhibited proofs that equal and compleat liberty, if it does not wholly eradicate it, sufficiently destroys its malignant influence on the health and prosperity of the State. If with the salutary effects of this system under our own eyes, we begin to contract the bounds of Religious freedom, we know no name that will too severely reproach our folly. At least let warning be taken at the first fruits of the threatened innovation. The very appearance of the Bill has transformed "that Christian forbearance, love and chairty," which of late mutually prevailed, into animosities and jeolousies, which may not soon be appeased. What mischiefs may not be dreaded, should this enemy to the public quiet be armed with the force of a law?

12. Because the policy of the Bill is adverse to the diffusion of the light of Christianity. The first wish of those who enjoy this precious gift ought to be that it may be imparted to the whole race of mankind. Compare the number of those who have as yet received it with the number still remaining under the dominion of false Religions; and how small is the former! Does the policy of the Bill tend to lessen the disproportion? No; it at once discourages those who are strangers to the light of revelation from coming into the Region of it; and countenances by example the nations who continue in darkness, in shutting out those who might convey it to them. Instead of Levelling as far as possible, every obstacle to the victorious progress of Truth, the Bill with an ignoble and unchristian timidity would circumscribe it with a wall of defence against the encroachments of error.

13. Because attempts to enforce by legal sanctions, acts obnoxious to go great a proportion of Citizens, tend to enervate the laws in general, and to slacken the bands of Society. If it be difficult to execute any law which is not generally deemed necessary or salutary, what must be the case, where it is deemed invalid and dangerous? And what may be the effect of so striking an example of impotency in the Government, on its general authority?

14. Because a measure of such singular magnitude and delicacy ought not to be imposed, without the clearest evidence that it is called for by a majority of citizens, and no satisfactory method is yet proposed by which the voice of the majority in this case may be determined, or its influence secured. The people of the respective counties are indeed requested to signify their opinion respecting the adoption of the Bill to the next Session of Assembly. But the representatives or of the Counties will be that of the people. Our hope is that neither of the former will, after due consideration, espouse the dangerous principle of the Bill. Should the event disappoint us, it will still leave us in full confidence, that a fair appeal to the latter will reverse the sentence against our liberties.

15. Because finally, "the equal right of every citizen to the free exercise of his Religion according to the dictates of conscience" is held by the same tenure with all our other rights. If we recur to its origin, it is equally the gift of nature; if we weigh its importance, it cannot be less dear to us; if we consult the "Declaration of those rights which pertain to the good people of Vriginia, as the basis and foundation of Government," it is enumerated with equal solemnity, or rather studied emphasis. Either the, we must say, that the Will of the Legislature is the only measure of their authority; and that in the plenitude of this authority, they may sweep away all our fundamental rights; or, that they are bound to leave this particular right untouched and sacred: Either we must say, that they may controul the freedom of the press, may abolish the Trial by Jury, may swallow up the Executive and Judiciary Powers of the State; nay that they may despoil us of our very right of suffrage, and erect themselves into an independent and hereditary Assembly or, we must say, that they have no authority to enact into the law the Bill under consideration.

We the Subscribers say, that the General Assembly of this Commonwealth have no such authority: And that no effort may be omitted on our part against so dangerous an usurpation, we oppose to it, this remonstrance; earnestly praying, as we are in duty bound, that the Supreme Lawgiver of the Universe, by illuminating those to whom it is addressed, may on the one hand, turn their Councils from every act which would affront his holy prerogative, or violate the trust committed to them: and on the other, guide them into every measure which may be worthy of his [blessing, may re]dound to their own praise, and may establish more firmly the liberties, the prosperity and the happiness of the Commonwealth.

THOMAS JEFFERSON **33**

Virginia Act for Establishing Religious Freedom, 1786

Thomas Jefferson had proposed this bill in 1779. After the General Assembly rejected the assessment bill for religious teachers in 1785, assemblymen worked to pass the Virginia Act For Establishing Religious Freedom in early 1786. Jefferson declared that all men had been created with free minds and it would be affront to God to impose a church on an individual or restrict their search for spiritual truths. Through this bill, Virginia would end taxpayer support of churches and allow each individual to practice their religion as they saw fit. "Our civil rights have no dependence on our religious opinions," wrote Jefferson. An individual cannot practice freedom if they are not allowed to follow their conscience, and differences of religion made no difference to Jefferson on the liberties an individual should have since all men must be equal. Jefferson would later list this bill as one of the proudest achievements of his life.

Well aware that Almighty God hath created the mind free; that all attempts to influence it by temporal punishments or burdens, or by civil incapacitations, tend only to beget habits of hypocrisy and meanness, and are a departure from the plan of the Holy Author of our religion, who being Lord both of body and mind, yet chose not to propagate it by coercions on either, as was in his Almighty power to do; that the impious presumption of legislators and rulers, civil as well as ecclesiastical, who, being themselves but fallible and uninspired men, have assumed dominion over the faith of others, setting up their own opinions and modes of thinking as the only true and infallible, and as such endeavoring to impose them on others,

Thomas Jefferson, "An Act for Establishing Religious Freedom," *Life and Selected Writings of Thomas Jefferson*, 289–291.

hath established and maintained false religions over the greatest part of the world, and through all time; that to compel a man to furnish contributions of money for the propagation of opinions which he disbelieves, is sinful and tyrannical; that even the forcing him to support this or that teacher of his own religious persuasion, is depriving him of the comfortable liberty of giving his contributions to the particular pastor whose morals he would make his pattern, and whose powers he feels most persuasive to righteousness, and is withdrawing from the ministry those temporal rewards, which proceeding from an approbation of their personal conduct, are an additional incitement to earnest and unremitting labors for the instruction of mankind; that our civil rights have no dependence on our religious opinions, more than our opinions in physics or geometry; that, therefore, the proscribing any citizen as unworthy the public confidence by laying upon him an incapacity of being called to the offices of trust and emolument, unless he profess or renounce this or that religious opinion, is depriving him injuriously of those privileges and advantages to which in common with his fellow citizens he has a natural right; that it tends also to corrupt the principles of that very religion it is meant to encourage, by bribing, with a monopoly of worldly honors and emoluments, those who will externally profess and conform to it; that though indeed these are criminal who do not withstand such temptation, yet neither are those innocent who lay the bait in their way; that to suffer the civil magistrate to intrude his powers into the field of opinion and to restrain the profession or propagation of principles, on the supposition of their ill tendency, is a dangerous fallacy, which at once destroys all religious liberty, because he being of course judge of that tendency, will make his opinions the rule of judgment, and approve or condemn the sentiments of others only as they shall square with or differ from his own; that it is time enough for the rightful purposes of civil government, for its officers to interfere when principles break out into overt acts against peace and good order; and finally, that truth is great and will prevail if left to herself, that she is the proper and sufficient antagonist to error, and has nothing to fear from the conflict, unless by human interposition disarmed of her natural weapons, free argument and debate, errors ceasing to be dangerous when it is permitted freely to contradict them.

Be it therefore enacted by the General Assembly, That no man shall be compelled to frequent or support any religious worship, place, or ministry whatsoever, nor shall be enforced, restrained, molested, or burdened in his body or goods, nor shall otherwise suffer on account of his religious opinions or belief; but that all men shall be free to profess, and by argument to maintain, their opinions in matters of religion, and that the same shall in nowise diminish, enlarge, or affect their civil capacities.

And though we well know this Assembly, elected by the people for the ordinary purposes of legislation only, have no powers equal to our own and that therefore to declare this act irrevocable would be of no effect in law, yet we are free to declare, and do declare, that the rights hereby asserted are of the natural rights of mankind, and that if any act shall be hereafter passed to repeal the present or to narrow its operation, such act will be an infringement of natural right.

34

Constitution of the United States, 1787

The Constitution is the heart of American civil liberties. Drafted at the Constitutional Convention in Philadelphia in 1787 and ratified in 1788, it has stood for two hundred years as the blueprint for American government and American political discourse. In 218 years, it has only been amended twenty-seven times and only seventeen times since 1791 and is the oldest constitution still in use in the world. The Constitution replaced the cumbersome Articles of Confederation with a framework that spells out the duties of the government and the powers of the three branches of the federal government. James Madison, the Father of the Constitution, said of this document, "Every word decides a question between power and liberty." The Constitution was designed to be strong enough to protect the nation but also durable enough to defend the liberties of the people. For what have become three of the most important words in America is for whom the framers dedicated the Constitution, "We the People."

We the People of the United States, in Order to form a more perfect Union, establish Justice, insure domestic Tranquility, provide for the common defence, promote the general Welfare, and secure the Blessings of Liberty to ourselves and our Posterity, do ordain and establish this Constitution for the United States of America.

Article I

Section 1. All legislative Powers herein granted shall be vested in a Congress of the United States, which shall consist of a Senate and House of Representatives.

Section 2. The House of Representatives shall be composed of Members chosen every second Year by the People of the several States, and the Electors in each State shall have the Qualifications requisite for Electors of the most numerous Branch of the State Legislature.

No Person shall be a Representative who shall not have attained to the Age of twenty five Years, and been seven Years a Citizen of the United States, and who shall not, when elected, be an Inhabitant of that State in which he shall be chosen.

Representatives and direct Taxes shall be apportioned among the several States which may be included within this Union, according to their respective Numbers, which shall be determined by adding to the whole Number of free Persons, including those bound to Service for a Term of Years, and excluding Indians not taxed, three fifths of all other Persons. [Section repealed in 1913.] The actual Enumeration shall

http://www.ourdocuments.gov/doc.php?flash=true&doc=9; http://usinfo.state.gov/usa/infousa/facts/democrac/6.htm; http://www.ourdocuments.gov/doc.php?flash=true&doc=13

be made within three Years after the first Meeting of the Congress of the United States, and within every subsequent Term of ten Years, in such Manner as they shall by Law direct. The number of Representatives shall not exceed one for every thirty Thousand, but each State shall have at Least one Representative; and until such enumeration shall be made, the State of New Hampshire shall be entitled to chuse three, Massachusetts eight, Rhode-Island and Providence Plantations one, Connecticut five, New-York six, New Jersey four, Pennsylvania eight, Delaware one, Maryland six, Virginia ten, North Carolina five, South Carolina five, and Georgia three.

When vacancies happen in the Representation from any State, the Executive Authority thereof shall issue Writs of Election to fill such Vacancies.

The House of Representatives shall chuse their Speaker and other Officers; and shall have the sole Power of Impeachment.

Section 3. The Senate of the United States shall be composed of two Senators from each State, chosen by the Legislature thereof [section repealed in 1913], for six Years; and each Senator shall have one Vote.

Immediately after they shall be assembled in Consequence of the first Election, they shall be divided as equally as may be into three Classes. The Seats of the Senators of the first Class shall be vacated at the Expiration of the second Year, of the second Class at the Expiration of the fourth Year, and of the third Class at the Expiration of the sixth Year, so that one third may be chosen every second Year; and if Vacancies happen by Resignation, or otherwise, during the Recess of the Legislature of any State, the Executive thereof may make temporary Appointments until the next Meeting of the Legislature, which shall then fill such Vacancies. [Section modified in 1913.]

No Person shall be a Senator who shall not have attained to the Age of thirty Years, and been nine Years a Citizen of the United States, and who shall not, when elected, be an Inhabitant of that State for which he shall be chosen.

The Vice President of the United States shall be President of the Senate, but shall have no Vote, unless they be equally divided.

The Senate shall chuse their other Officers, and also a President pro tempore, in the Absence of the Vice President, or when he shall exercise the Office of President of the United States.

The Senate shall have the sole Power to try all Impeachments. When sitting for that Purpose, they shall be on Oath or Affirmation. When the President of the United States is tried, the Chief Justice shall preside: And no Person shall be convicted without the Concurrence of two thirds of the Members present.

Judgment in Cases of Impeachment shall not extend further than to removal from Office, and disqualification to hold and enjoy any Office of honor, Trust or Profit under the United States: but the Party convicted shall nevertheless be liable and subject to Indictment, Trial, Judgment and Punishment, according to Law.

Section 4. The Times, Places and Manner of holding Elections for Senators and Representatives, shall be prescribed in each State by the Legislature thereof; but the Congress may at any time by Law make or alter such Regulations, except as to the Places of chusing Senators.

The Congress shall assemble at least once in every Year, and such Meeting shall be on the first Monday in December, unless they shall by Law appoint a different Day. [Section modified in 1933.]

Section 5. Each House shall be the Judge of the Elections, Returns and Qualifications of its own Members, and a Majority of each shall constitute a Quorum to do Business, but a smaller Number may adjourn from day to day, and may be authorized to compel the Attendance of absent Members, in such Manner, and under such Penalties as each House may provide.

Each House may determine the Rules of its Proceedings, punish its Members for disorderly Behaviour, and, with the Concurrence of two thirds, expel a Member.

Each House shall keep a Journal of its Proceedings, and from time to time publish the same, excepting such Parts as may in their Judgment require Secrecy; and the Yeas and Nays of the Members of either House on any question shall, at the Desire of one fifth of those Present, be entered on the Journal.

Neither House, during the Session of Congress, shall, without the Consent of the other, adjourn for more than three days, nor to any other Place than that in which the two Houses shall be sitting.

Section 6. The Senators and Representatives shall receive a Compensation for their Services, to be ascertained by law, and paid out of the Treasury of the United States. They shall in all Cases, except Treason, Felony and Breach of the Peace, be privileged from Arrest during their Attendance at the Session of their respective Houses, and in going to and returning from the same; and for any Speech or Debate in either House, they shall not be questioned in any other Place.

No Senator or Representative shall, during the Time for which he was elected, be appointed to any civil Office under the Authority of the United States, which shall have been created, or the Emoluments whereof shall have been encreased during such time; and no Person holding any Office under the United States, shall be a Member of either House during his Continuance in Office.

Section 7. All Bills for raising Revenue shall originate in the House of Representatives; but the Senate may propose or concur with Amendments as on other Bills.

Every Bill which shall have passed the House of Representatives and the Senate, shall, before it becomes a Law, be presented to the President of the United States; If he approve he shall sign it, but if not he shall return it, with his Objections to that House in which it shall have originated, who shall enter the Objections at large on their Journal, and proceed to reconsider it. If after such Reconsideration two thirds of that House shall agree to pass the Bill, it shall be sent, together with the Objections, to the other House, by which it shall likewise be reconsidered, and if approved by two thirds of that House, it shall become a Law. But in all such Cases the Votes of both Houses shall be determined by Yeas and Nays, and the Names of the Persons voting for and against the Bill shall be entered on the Journal of each House respectively. If any Bill shall not be returned by the President within ten Days (Sundays excepted) after it shall have been presented to him, the Same shall be a Law, in like Manner as if he had signed it, unless the Congress by their Adjournment prevent its Return, in which Case it shall not be a Law.

Every Order, Resolution, or Vote to which the Concurrence of the Senate and House of Representatives may be necessary (except on a question of Adjournment) shall be presented to the President of the United States, and before the Same shall take Effect, shall be approved by him, or being disapproved by him, shall be repassed by two thirds of the Senate and House of Representatives, according to the Rules and Limitations prescribed in the Case of a Bill.

Section 8. The Congress shall have Power To lay and collect Taxes, Duties, Imposts and Excises, to pay the Debts and provide for the common Defence and general Welfare of the United States; but all Duties, Imposts and Excises shall be uniform throughout the United States

To borrow Money on the credit of the United States;

To regulate Commerce with foreign Nations, and among the several States, and with the Indian Tribes;

To establish an uniform Rule of Naturalization, and uniform Laws on the subject of Bankruptcies throughout the United States;

To coin Money, regulate the Value thereof, and of foreign Coin, and fix the Standard of Weights and Measures;

To provide for the Punishment of counterfeiting the Securities and current Coin of the United States;

To establish Post Offices and post Roads;

To promote the Progress of Science and useful Arts, by securing for limited Times to Authors and Inventors the exclusive Right to their respective Writings and Discoveries;

To constitute Tribunals inferior to the supreme Court;

To define and punish Piracies and Felonies committed on the high Seas, and Offenses against the Law of Nations;

To declare War, grant Letters of Marque and Reprisal, and make Rules concerning Captures on land and Water;

To raise and support Armies, but no Appropriation of Money to that Use shall be for a longer Term than two Years;

To provide and maintain a Navy;

To make Rules for the Government and Regulation of the land and naval Forces;

To provide for calling forth the Militia to execute the Laws of the Union, suppress Insurrections and repel Invasions;

To provide for organizing, arming, and disciplining, the Militia, and for governing such Part of them as may be employed in the Service of the United States, reserving to the States respectively, the Appointment of the Officers, and the Authority of training the Militia according to the discipline prescribed by Congress;

To exercise exclusive Legislation in all Cases whatsoever, over such District (not exceeding ten Miles square) as may, by Cession of particular States, and the Acceptance of Congress, become the Seat of the Government of the United States, and to exercise like Authority over all Places purchased by the Consent of the Legislature of the State in which the Same shall be, for the Erection of Forts, Magazines, Arsenals, dock-Yards and other needful Buildings;—And

To make all Laws which shall be necessary and proper for carrying into Execution the foregoing Powers, and all other Powers vested by this Constitution in the Government of the United States, or in any Department or Officer thereof.

Section 9. The Migration or Importation of such Persons as any of the States now existing shall think proper to admit, shall not be prohibited by the Congress prior to the Year one thousand eight hundred and eight, but a Tax or duty may be imposed on such Importation, not exceeding ten dollars for each Person.

The Privilege of the Writ of Habeas Corpus shall not be suspended, unless when in Cases of Rebellion or Invasion the public Safety may require it.

No Bill of Attainder or ex post facto Law shall be passed.

No Capitation, or other direct, Tax shall be laid, unless in Proportion to the Census or Enumeration herein before directed to be taken.[Section modified in 1913.]

No Tax or Duty shall be laid on Articles exported from any State.

No Preference shall be given by any Regulation of Commerce or Revenue to the Ports of one State over those of another: nor shall Vessels bound to, or from, one State, be obliged to enter, clear, or pay Duties in another.

No Money shall be drawn from the Treasury, but in Consequence of Appropriations made by Law; and a regular Statement and Account of the Receipts and Expenditures of all public Money shall be published from time to time.

No Title of Nobility shall be granted by the United States: And no Person holding any Office of Profit or Trust under them, shall, without the Consent of the Congress, accept of any present, Emolument, Office, or Title, of any kind whatever, from any King, Prince, or foreign State.

Section 10. No State shall enter into any Treaty, Alliance, or Confederation; grant Letters of Marque and Reprisal; coin Money; emit Bills of Credit; make any Thing but gold and silver Coin a Tender in Payment of Debts; pass any Bill of Attainder, ex post facto Law, or Law impairing the Obligation of Contracts, or grant any Title of Nobility; No State shall, without the Consent of the Congress, lay any Imposts or Duties on Imports or Exports, except what may be absolutely necessary for executing it's inspection Laws: and the net Produce of all Duties and Imposts, laid by any State on Imports or Exports, shall be for the Use of the Treasury of the United States; and all such Laws shall be subject to the Revision and Controul of the Congress.

No State shall, without the Consent of Congress, lay any Duty of Tonnage, keep Troops, or Ships of War in time of Peace, enter into any Agreement or Compact with another State, or with a foreign Power, or engage in War, unless actually invaded, or in such imminent Danger as will not admit of delay.

Article II

Section 1. The executive Power shall be vested in a President of the United States of America. He shall hold his Office during the Term of four Years, and, together with the Vice President, chosen for the same Term, be elected, as follows.

Each State shall appoint, in such Manner as the Legislature thereof may direct, a Number of Electors, equal to the whole Number of Senators and Representatives to which the State may be entitled in the Congress: but no Senator or Representative, or Person holding an Office of Trust or Profit under the United States, shall be appointed an Elector.

The Electors shall meet in their respective States, and vote by Ballot for two Persons, of whom one at least shall not be an Inhabitant of the same State with themselves. And they shall make a List of all the Persons voted for, and of the Number of Votes for each; which List they shall sign and certify, and transmit sealed to the Seat of the Government of the United States, directed to the President of the Senate. The President of the Senate shall, in the Presence of the Senate and House of Representatives, open all the Certificates, and the Votes shall then be counted. The

Person having the greatest Number of Votes shall be the President, if such Number be a Majority of the whole Number of Electors appointed; and if there be more than one who have such Majority, and have an equal Number of Votes, then the House of Representatives shall immediately chuse by Ballot one of them for President; and if no Person have a Majority, then from the five highest on the List the said House shall in like Manner chuse the President. But in chusing the President, the Votes shall be taken by States, the Representation from each State having one Vote; A quorum for this Purpose shall consist of a Member or Members from two thirds of the States, and a Majority of all the States shall be necessary to a Choice. In every Case, after the Choice of the President, the Person having the greatest Number of Votes of the Electors shall be the Vice President. But if there should remain two or more who have equal Votes, the Senate shall chuse from them by Ballot the Vice President. [Section modified 1804.]

The Congress may determine the Time of chusing the Electors, and the Day on which they shall give their Votes; which Day shall be the same throughout the United States.

No Person except a natural born Citizen, or a Citizen of the United States, at the time of the Adoption of this Constitution, shall be eligible to the Office of President; neither shall any person be eligible to that Office who shall not have attained to the Age of thirty five Years, and been fourteen Years a Resident within the United States.

In Case of the Removal of the President from Office, or of his Death, Resignation, or Inability to discharge the Powers and Duties of the said Office, the Same shall devolve on the Vice President, and the Congress may be Law provide for the Case of Removal, Death, Resignation or Inability, both of the President and Vice President, declaring what Officer shall then act as President, and such Officer shall act accordingly, until the Disability be removed, or a President shall be elected. [Section modified 1967.]

The President shall, at stated Times, receive for his Services, a Compensation, which shall neither be increased nor diminished during the Period for which he shall have been elected, and he shall not receive within that Period any other Emolument from the United States, or any of them.

Before he enter on the Execution of his Office, he shall take the following Oath or Affirmation:—"I do solemnly swear (or affirm) that I will faithfully execute the Office of President of the United States, and will to the best of my Ability, preserve, protect and defend the Constitution of the United States."

Section 2. The President shall be Commander in Chief of the Army and Navy of the United States, and of the Militia of the several States, when called into the actual Service of the United States; he may require the Opinion, in writing, of the principal Officer in each of the executive Departments, upon any Subject relating to the Duties of their respective Offices, and he shall have Power to grant Reprieves and Pardons for Offenses against the United States, except in Cases of Impeachment.

He shall have Power, by and with the Advice and Consent of the Senate, to make Treaties, provided two thirds of the Senators present concur; and he shall nominate, and by and with the Advice and Consent of the Senate, shall appoint Ambassadors, other public Ministers and Consuls, Judges of the supreme Court, and all other Officers of the United States, whose Appointments are not herein otherwise provided for, and which shall be established by Law: but the Congress may by law vest the

Appointment of such inferior Officers, as they think proper, in the President alone, in the Courts of Law, or in the Heads of Departments.

The President shall have Power to fill up all Vacancies that may happen during the Recess of the Senate, by granting Commissions which shall expire at the End of their next Session.

Section 3. He shall from time to time give to the Congress Information of the State of the Union, and recommend to their Consideration such Measures as he shall judge necessary and expedient; he may, on extraordinary Occasions, convene both Houses, or either of them and in Case of Disagreement between them with Respect to the Time of Adjournment, he may adjourn them to such Time as he shall think proper; he shall receive Ambassadors and other public Ministers; he shall take Care that the Laws be faithfully executed, and shall Commission all the Officers of the United States.

Section 4. The President, Vice President and all civil Officers of the United States, shall be removed from Office on Impeachment for, and Conviction of, Treason, Bribery, or other high Crimes and Misdemeanors.

Article III

Section 1. The judicial Power of the United States, shall be vested in one supreme Court, and in such inferior Courts as the Congress may from time to time ordain and establish. The Judges, both of the supreme and inferior Courts, shall hold their Officer during good Behaviour, and shall at stated Times, receive for their Services, a Compensation, which shall not be diminished during their Continuance in Office.

Section 2. The judicial Power shall extend to all Cases, in Law and Equity, arising under this Constitution, the Laws of the United States, and Treaties made, or which shall be made, under their Authority,—to all Cases affecting Ambassadors, other public Ministers and Consuls;—to all Cases of admiralty and maritime Jurisdiction,—to Controversies to which the United States shall be a Party;—to Controversies between two or more States,—between a State and Citizens of another State; between Citizens of different States,—between Citizens of the same State claiming Lands under Grants of different States, and between a State or the Citizens thereof, and foreign States, Citizens or Subjects. [Sections modified in 1798.]

In all Cases affecting Ambassadors, other public Ministers and Consuls, and those in which a State shall be Party, the supreme Court shall have original Jurisdiction. In all the other Cases before mentioned, the supreme Court shall have appellate Jurisdiction, both as to Law and Fact, with such Exceptions, and under such Regulations as the Congress shall make.

The Trial of all Crimes, except in Cases of Impeachment; shall be by Jury, and such Trial shall be held in the State where the said Crimes shall have been committed but when not committed within any State, the Trial shall be at such Place or Places as the Congress may by Law have directed.

Section 3. Treason against the United States, shall consist only in levying War against them, or in adhering to their Enemies, giving them Aid and Comfort. No Person shall be convicted of Treason unless on the Testimony of two Witnesses to the same overt Act, or on Confession in open Court.

The Congress shall have Power to declare the Punishment of Treason, but no Attainder of Treason shall work Corruption of Blood, or Forfeiture except during the Life of the Person attainted.

Article IV

Section 1. Full Faith and Credit shall be given in each State to the public Acts, Records, and judicial Proceedings of every other State; And the Congress may by general Laws prescribe the Manner in which such Acts, Records and Proceedings shall be proved, and the Effect thereof.

Section 2. The Citizens of each State shall be entitled to all Privileges and Immunities of Citizens in the several States.

A Person charged in any State with Treason, Felony, or other Crime, who shall flee from Justice, and be found in another State, shall on Demand of the executive Authority of the State from which he fled, be delivered up, to be removed to the State having Jurisdiction of the Crime.

No Person held to Service or Labour in one State, under the Laws thereof, escaping into another, shall, in Consequence of any Law or Regulation therein, be discharged from such Service or Labour, but shall be delivered up on Claim of the party to whom such Service or Labour may be due. [Section repealed in 1865.]

Section 3. New States may be admitted by the Congress into this Union; but no new State shall be formed or erected within the Jurisdiction of any other State; nor any State be formed by the Junction of two or more States, or Parts of States, without the Consent of the Legislatures of the States concerned as well as of the Congress.

The Congress shall have rower to dispose of and make all needful Rules and Regulations respecting the Territory or other Property belonging to the United States; and nothing in this Constitution shall be construed as to Prejudice any Claims of the United States, or of any particular State.

Section 4. The United States shall guarantee to every State in this Union a Republican Form of Government, and shall protect each of them against Invasion; and on Application of the Legislature, or of the Executive (when the Legislature cannot be convened) against domestic Violence.

Article V

The Congress, whenever two thirds of both houses shall deem it necessary, shall propose Amendments to this Constitution, or, on the Application of the Legislatures of two thirds of the several States, shall call a Convention for proposing Amendments, which in either Case, shall be valid to all Intents and Purposes, as Part of this Constitution, when ratified by the Legislatures of three fourths of the several States, or by Conventions in three fourths thereof, as the one or the other Mode of Ratification may be proposed by the Congress; Provided that no Amendment which may be made prior to the Year One thousand eight hundred and eight shall in any Manner affect the first and fourth Clauses in the Ninth Section of the first Article; and that no State, without its Consent, shall be deprived of its equal Suffrage in the Senate.

Article VI

All Debts contracted and Engagements entered into, before the Adoption of this Constitution, shall be as valid against the United States under this Constitution, as under the Confederation.

   This Constitution, and the Laws of the United States which shall be made in Pursuance thereof; and all Treaties made, or which shall be made, under the Authority of the United States, shall be the supreme Law of the Land; and the Judges in every State shall be bound thereby, any Thing in the Constitution or Laws of any State to the Contrary notwithstanding.

   The Senators and Representatives before mentioned, and the Members of the several State Legislatures, and all executive and judicial Officers, both of the United States and of the several States, shall be bound by Oath or Affirmation, to support this Constitution; but no religious Test shall ever be required as a Qualification to any Office or public Trust under the United States.

Article VII

The Ratification of the Conventions of nine States, shall be sufficient for the Establishment of this Constitution between the States so ratifying the Same.

   Done in Convention by the Unanimous Consent of the States present the Seventeenth Day of September in the Year of our Lord one thousand seven hundred and Eighty seven and of the Independence of the United States of America the Twelfth In Witness whereof We have hereunto subscribed our Names, G.° Washington— Presd.t and deputy from Virginia

New Hampshire	John Langdon
	Nicholas Gilman
Massachusetts	Nathaniel Gorham
	Rufus King
Connecticut	Wm. Saml. Johnson
	Roger Sherman
New York	Alexander Hamilton
New Jersey	Wil: Livingston
	David Brearley
	Wm. Paterson
	Jona: Dayton
Pennsylvania	B Franklin
	Thomas Mifflin
	Robt Morris
	Geo. Clymer
	Thos. FitzSimons
	Jared Ingersoll
	James Wilson
	Gouv Morris

Delaware	Geo: Read
	Gunning Bedford jun
	John Dickinson
	Richard Bassett
	Jaco: Broom
Maryland	James McHenry
	Dan of St. Thos. Jenifer
	Danl Carroll
Virginia	John Blair
	James Madison Jr.
North Carolina	Wm. Blount
	Richd. Dobbs Spaight
	Hu Williamson
South Carolina	J. Rutledge
	Charles Cotesworth Pinckney
	Charles Pinckney
	Pierce Butler
Georgia	William Few
	Abr Baldwin

Attest—William Jackson, Secretary

[Articles of Amendment, the first ten, the Bill of Rights, were ratified December 15, 1791.]

Article I

Congress shall make no law respecting an establishment of religion, or prohibiting the free exercise thereof; or abridging the freedom of speech, or of the press, or the right of the people peaceably to assemble, and to petition the Government for a redress of grievances.

Article II

A well regulated Militia, being necessary to the security of a free State, the right of the people to keep and bear Arms, shall not be infringed.

Article III

No Soldier shall, in time of peace be quartered in any house, without the consent of the Owner, nor in time of war, but in a manner to be prescribed by law.

Article IV

The right of the people to be secure in their persons, houses, papers, and effects, against unreasonable searches and seizures, shall not be violated, and no Warrants shall issue, but upon probable cause, supported by Oath or affirmation, and particularly describing the place to be searched, and the persons or things to be seized.

Article V

No person shall be held to answer for a capital, or otherwise infamous crime, unless on a presentment or indictment of a Grand Jury, except in cases arising in the land or naval forces, or in the Militia, when in actual service in time of War or public danger; nor shall any person be subject for the same offence to be twice put in jeopardy of life or limb, nor shall be compelled in any criminal case to be a witness against himself, nor be deprived of life, liberty, or property, without due process of law; nor shall private property be taken for public use, without just compensation.

Article VI

In all criminal prosecutions, the accused shall enjoy the right to a speedy and public trial, by an impartial jury of the State and district wherein the crime shall have been committed; which district shall have been previously ascertained by law, and to be informed of the nature and cause of the accusation; to be confronted with the witnesses against him; to have compulsory process for obtaining witnesses in his favor, and to have the assistance of counsel for his defence.

Article VII

In Suits at common law, where the value in controversy shall exceed twenty dollars, the right of trial by jury shall be preserved, and no fact tried by a jury shall be otherwise re-examined in any Court of the United States, than according to the rules of the common law.

Article VIII

Excessive bail shall not be required, nor excessive fines imposed, nor cruel and unusual punishments inflicted.

Article IX

The enumeration in the Constitution of certain rights shall not be construed to deny or disparage others retained by the people.

Article X

The powers not delegated to the United States by the Constitution, nor prohibited by it to the States, are reserved to the States respectively, or to the people.

Article XI

The Judicial power of the United States shall not be construed to extend to any suit in law or equity, commenced or prosecuted against one of the United States by Citizens of another State, or by Citizens or Subjects of any Foreign State.
Ratified January 8, 1798.

Article XII

The Electors shall meet in their respective states, and vote by ballot for President and Vice-President, one of whom, at least, shall not be an inhabitant of the same state with themselves; they shall name in their ballots the person voted for as President, and in distinct ballots the person voted for as Vice-President, and they shall make distinct lists of all persons voted for as President, and of all persons voted for as Vice-President, and of the number of votes for each, which lists they shall sign and certify, and transmit sealed to the seat of the government of the United States, directed to the President of the Senate;—The President of the Senate shall, in the presence of the Senate and House of Representatives, open all the certificates and the votes shall then be counted;—The person having the greatest number of votes for President, shall be the President, if such number be a majority of the whole number of Electors appointed; and if no person have such majority, then from the persons having the highest numbers not exceeding three on the list of those voted for as President, the House of Representatives shall choose immediately, by ballot, the President. But in choosing the President, the votes shall be taken by states, the representation from each state having one vote; a quorum for this purpose shall consist of a member or members from two-thirds of the states, and a majority of all the states shall be necessary to a choice. And if the House of Representatives shall not choose a President whenever the right of choice shall devolve upon them, before the fourth day of March next following, then the Vice-President shall act as President, as in the case of the death or other constitutional disability of the President [Modified in 1933]. The person having the greatest number of votes as Vice-President, shall be the Vice-President, if such number be a majority of the whole number of Electors appointed, and if no person have a majority, then from the two highest numbers on the list, the Senate shall choose the Vice-President; a quorum for the purpose shall consist of two-thirds of the whole number of Senators, and a majority of the whole number shall be necessary to a choice. But no person constitutionally ineligible to the office of President shall be eligible to that of Vice-President of the United States.
Ratified June 15, 1804.

Article XIII

Section 1. Neither slavery nor involuntary servitude, except as a punishment for crime whereof the party shall have been duly convicted, shall exist within the United States, or any place subject to their jurisdiction.

Section 2. Congress shall have power to enforce these article by appropriate legislation.
Ratified December 6, 1865.

Article XIV

Section 1. All persons born or naturalized in the United States and subject to the jurisdiction thereof, are citizens of the United States and of the State wherein they reside. No State shall make or enforce any law which shall abridge the privileges or immunities of citizens of the United States; nor shall any State deprive any person of life, liberty, or property, without due process of law; nor deny to any person within its jurisdiction the equal protection of the laws.

Section 2. Representatives shall be apportioned among the several States according to their respective numbers, counting the whole number of persons in each State, excluding Indians not taxed. But when the right to vote at any election for the choice of electors for President and Vice President of the United States, Representatives in Congress, the Executive and Judicial officers of a State, or the members of the Legislature thereof, is denied to any of the male inhabitants of such State, being twenty-one years of age, and citizens of the United States, or in any way abridged, except for participation in rebellion, or other crime, the basis of representation therein shall be reduced in the proportion which the number of such male citizens shall bear to the whole number of male citizens twenty-one years of age in such State.

Section 3. No person shall be a Senator or Representative in Congress, or elector of President and Vice President, or hold any office, civil or military, under the United States, or under any State, who, having previously taken an oath, as a member of Congress, or as an officer of the United States, or as a member of any State legislature, or as an executive or judicial officer of any State, to support the Constitution of the United States, shall have engaged in insurrection or rebellion against the same, or given aid or comfort to the enemies thereof. But Congress may by a vote of two-thirds of each House, remove such disability.

Section 4. The validity of the public debt of the United States, authorized by law, including debts incurred for payment of pensions and bounties for services in suppressing insurrection or rebellion, shall not be questioned. But neither the United States nor any State shall assume or pay any debt or obligation incurred in aid of insurrection or rebellion against the United States, or any claim for the loss or emancipation of any slave; but all such debts, obligations and claims shall be held illegal and void.

Section 5. The Congress shall have power to enforce, by appropriate legislation, the provisions of this article.

Ratified July 9, 1868.

Article XV

Section 1. The right of citizens of the United States to vote shall not be denied or abridged by the United States or by any State on account of race, color, or previous condition of servitude.

Section 2. The Congress shall have power to enforce this article by appropriate legislation.

Ratified February 3, 1870.

Article XVI

The Congress shall have power to lay and collect taxes on incomes, from whatever source derived, without apportionment among the several States, and without regard to any census or enumeration.

Ratified February 3, 1913.

Article XVII

The Senate of the United States shall be composed of two senators from each State, elected by the people thereof, for six years; and each Senator shall have one vote. The electors in each State shall have the qualifications requisite for electors of the most numerous branch of the State legislature.

When vacancies happen in the representation of any State in the Senate, the executive authority of such State shall issue writs of election to fill such vacancies: *Provided*, That the legislature of any State may empower the executive thereof to make temporary appointments until the people fill the vacancies by election as the legislature may direct.

This amendment shall not be so construed as to affect the election or term of any Senator chosen before it becomes valid as part of the Constitution.

Ratified April 8, 1913.

Article XVIII

Section 1. After one year from the ratification of this article, the manufacture, sale, or transportation of intoxicating liquors within, the importation thereof into, or the exportation thereof from the United States and all territory subject to the jurisdiction thereof for beverage purposes is hereby prohibited.

Section 2. The Congress and the several States shall have concurrent power to enforce this article by appropriate legislation.

Section 3. This article shall be inoperative unless it shall have been ratified as an amendment to the Constitution by the legislatures of the several States, as provided in the Constitution, within seven years from the date of the submission hereof to the States by the Congress.

Ratified January 16, 1919. Repealed December 5, 1933.

Article XIX

The right of citizens of the United States to vote shall not be denied or abridged by the United States or by any States on account of sex.

Congress shall have power to enforce this article by appropriate legislation.

Ratified August 18, 1920.

Article XX

Section 1. The terms of the President and Vice President shall end at noon the 20th day of January, and the terms of Senators and Representatives at noon on the 3d day of January, of the years in which such terms would have ended if this article had not been ratified; and the terms of their successors shall then begin.

Section 2. The Congress shall assemble at least once in every year, and such meeting shall begin at noon on the 3d day of January, unless they shall by law appoint a different day.

Section 3. If, at the time fixed for the beginning of the term of the President, the President elect shall have died, the Vice President elect shall become President. If a

President shall not have been chosen before the time fixed for the beginning of his term, or if the President elect shall have failed to qualify, then the Vice President elect shall act as President until a President shall have qualified; and the Congress may by law provide for the case wherein neither a President elect nor a Vice-President elect shall have qualified, declaring who shall then act as President, or the manner in which one who is to act shall be selected, and such person shall act accordingly until a President or Vice President shall have qualified.

Section 4. The Congress may by law provide for the case of the death of any of the persons from whom the House of Representatives may choose a President whenever the right of choice shall have devolved upon them, and for the case of the death of any of the persons from whom the Senate may choose a Vice President whenever the right of choice shall have devolved upon them.

Section 5. Sections 1 and 2 shall take effect on the 15th day of October following the ratification of this article.

Section 6. This article shall be inoperative unless it shall have been ratified as an amendment to the Constitution by the legislatures of three-fourths of the several States within seven years from the date of its submission.

Ratified January 23, 1933.

Article XXI

Section 1. The eighteenth article of amendment to the Constitution of the United States is hereby repealed.

Section 2. The transportation or importation into any State, Territory, or possession of the United States for delivery or use therein of intoxicating liquors, in violation of the laws thereof, is hereby prohibited.

Section 3. The article shall be inoperative unless it shall have been ratified as an amendment to the Constitution by conventions in the several States, as provided in the Constitution, within seven years from the date of the submission hereof to the States by the Congress.

Ratified December 5, 1933.

Article XXII

Section 1. No person shall be elected to the office of the President more than twice, and no person who has held the office of President, or acted as President, for more than two years of a term to which some other person was elected President shall be elected to the office of the President more than once. But this Article shall not apply to any person holding the office of President when this Article was proposed by the Congress, and shall not prevent any person who may be holding the office of President, or acting as President, during the term within which this Article becomes operative from holding the office of President or acting as President during the remainder of such term.

Section 2. This article shall be inoperative unless it shall have been ratified as an amendment to the Constitution by the legislatures of three-fourths of the several States within seven years from the date of its submission to the States by the Congress.

Ratified February 27, 1951.

Article XXIII

Section 1. The District constituting the seat of government of the United States shall appoint in such manner as the Congress may direct:

A number of electors of President and Vice President equal to the whole number of Senators and Representatives in Congress to which the District would be entitled if it were a state, but in no event more than the least populous State; they shall be in addition to those appointed by the States, but they shall be considered, for the purposes of the election of President and Vice President, to be electors appointed by a State; and they shall meet in the District and perform such duties as provided by the twelfth article of amendment.

Section 2. The Congress shall have power to enforce this article by appropriate legislation.

Ratified March 29, 1961.

Article XXIV

Section 1. The right of citizens of the United States to vote in any primary or other election for President or Vice President, for electors for President or Vice President, or for Senator or Representative in Congress, shall not be denied or abridged by the United States or any State by reason of failure to pay any poll tax or other tax.

Section 2. The Congress shall have power to enforce this article by appropriate legislation.

Ratified January 23, 1964.

Article XXV

Section 1. In case of the removal of the President from office or of his death or resignation, the Vice President shall become President.

Section 2. Whenever there is a vacancy in the office of the Vice President, the President shall nominate a Vice President who shall take office upon confirmation by a majority vote of both Houses of Congress.

Section 3. Whenever the President transmits to the President pro tempore of the Senate and the Speaker of the House of Representatives his written declaration that he is unable to discharge the powers and duties of his office, and until he transmits to them a written declaration to the contrary, such powers and duties shall be discharged by the Vice President as Acting President.

Section 4. Whenever the Vice President and a majority of either the principal officers of the executive departments or of such other body as Congress may by law provide, transmit to the President pro tempore of the Senate and the Speaker of the House of Representatives their written declaration that the President is unable to discharge the powers and duties of his office, the Vice President shall immediately assume the powers and duties of the office as Acting President.

Thereafter, when the President transmits to the President pro tempore of the Senate and the Speaker of the House of Representatives his written declaration that no inability exists, he shall resume the powers and duties of his office unless the Vice

President and a majority of either the principal officers of the executive department or of such other body as Congress may by law provide, transmit within four days to the President pro tempore of the Senate and the Speaker of the House of Representatives their written declaration that the President is unable to discharge the powers and duties of his office. Thereupon Congress shall decide the issue, assembling within forty-eight hours for that purpose if not in session. If the Congress, within twenty-one days after receipt of the latter written declaration, or, if Congress is not in session, within twenty-one days after Congress is required to assemble, determines by two-thirds vote of both Houses that the President is unable to discharge the powers and duties of his office, the Vice President shall continue to discharge the same as Acting President; otherwise, the President shall resume the powers and duties of his office.

Ratified February 10, 1967.

Article XXVI

Section 1. The right of citizens of the United States, who are eighteen years of age or older, to vote shall not be denied or abridged by the United States or by any State on account of age.

Section 2. The Congress shall have power to enforce this article by appropriate legislation.

Ratified June 30, 1971.

Article XXVII

No law, varying the compensation for the services of the Senators and Representatives, shall take effect, until an election of Representatives shall have intervened.

Ratified May 7, 1992

MELANCTON SMITH   **35**

Letters from the Federal Farmer, II, 1787

Once the Constitution was signed by thirty-nine of the delegates at the Constitutional Convention in September 1787, a bitter debate immediately erupted over its ratification. One group, the Federalists, argued in favor of ratification through speeches, pamphlets, and essays distributed across the country. Those opposed to ratification, the anti-Federalists, similarly argued their position

Melancton Smith, "Letters to the Federal Farmer II," *The Anti-Federalist Papers and the Constitutional Convention Debates*, Ralph Ketcham, ed. (New York: Penguin, 1986): 264–269.

with as much passion and as many words against ratification, fearing the new Constitution would undermine their liberties. The Letters from the Federal Farmer *was a series of eighteen letters written in the Poughkeepsie County, Pennsylvania,* Country Journal *between November 1787 and January 1788. For many years, historians believed that Richard Henry Lee of Virginia had written these essays. Recent scholarship, however, suggests that outspoken anti-Federalist Melancton Smith of New York wrote the* Federal Farmer *essays. Smith wrote that the large scale of the new federal government made it impossible to adequately represent the people—the heart of a free government. Because of the size of the nation, the federal government could not execute its laws without either risking anarchy through neglect or becoming a despotic tyranny in a zeal to enforce them. Smith concluded that the best way to defend freedom was to keep the government close to the people.*

October 9, 1787

Dear Sir,

The essential parts of a free and good government are a full and equal representation of the people in the legislature, and the jury trial of the vicinage in the administration of justice—a full and equal representation, is that which possesses the same interests, feelings, opinions, and views the people themselves would were they all assembled—a fair representation, therefore, should be so regulated, that every order of men in the community, according to the common course of elections, can have a share in it—in order to allow professional men, merchants, traders, farmers, mechanics, etc. to bring a just proportion of their best informed men respectively into the legislature, the representation must be considerably numerous—We have about 200 state senators in the United States, and a less number than that of federal representatives cannot, clearly, be a full representation of this people, in the affairs of internal taxation and police, were there but one legislature for the whole union. The representation cannot be equal, or the situation of the people proper for one government only—if the extreme parts of the society cannot be represented as fully as the central—It is apparently impracticable that this should be the case in this extensive country—it would be impossible to collect a representation of the parts of the country five, six, and seven hundred miles from the seat of government.

Under one general government alone, there could be but one judiciary, one supreme and a proper number of inferior courts. I think it would be totally impracticable in this case to preserve a due administration of justice, and the real benefits of the jury trial of the vicinage,—there are now supreme courts in each state in the union; and a great number of county and other courts subordinate to each supreme court—most of these supreme and inferior courts are itinerant, and hold their sessions in different parts every year of their respective states, counties and districts—with all these moving courts, our citizens, from the vast extent of the country must travel very considerable distances from home to find the place where justice is administered. I am not for bringing justice so near to individuals as

to afford them any temptation to engage in law suits; though I think it one
of the greatest benefits in a good government, that each citizen should find
a court of justice within a reasonable distance, perhaps, within a day's travel
of his home; so that, without great inconveniences and enormous expences,
he may have the advantages of his witnesses and jury—it would be impracticable to derive these advantages from one judiciary—the one supreme court
at most could only set in the centre of the union, and move once a year into
the centre of the eastern and southern extremes of it—and, in this case,
each citizen, on an average, would travel 150 or 200 miles to find this
court—that, however, inferior courts might be properly placed in the different counties, and districts of the union, the appellate jurisdiction would be
intolerable and expensive.

If it were possible to consolidate the states, and preserve the features of
a free government, still it is evident that the middle states, the parts of the
union, about the seat of government, would enjoy great advantages, while
the remote states would experience the many inconveniences of remote
provinces. Wealth, offices, and the benefits of government would collect in
the centre: and the extreme states and their principal towns, become much
less important.

There are other considerations which tend to prove that the idea of one
consolidated whole, on free principles, is ill-founded—the laws of a free
government rest on the confidence of the people, and operate gently—and
never can extend their influence very far—if they are executed on free principles, about the centre, where the benefits of the government induce the
people to support it voluntarily; yet they must be executed on the principles
of fear and force in the extremes—This has been the case with every extensive republic of which we have any accurate account.

There are certain unalienable and fundamental rights, which in forming
the social compact, ought to be explicitly ascertained and fixed—a free and
enlightened people, in forming this compact, will not resign all their rights
to those who govern, and they will fix limits to their legislators and rulers,
which will soon be plainly seen by those who are governed, as well as by
those who govern: and the latter will know they cannot be passed unper-
ceived by the former, and without giving a general alarm—These rights
should be made the basis of every constitution: and if a people be so situated,
or have such different opinions that they cannot agree in ascertaining and
fixing them, it is a very strong argument against their attempting to form
one entire society, to live under one system of laws only.—I confess, I never
thought the people of these states differed essentially in these respects; they
having derived all these rights from one common source, the British systems;
and having in the formation of their state constitutions, discovered that their
ideas relative to these rights are very similar. However, it is now said that the
states differ so essentially in these respects, and even in the important article
of the trial by jury, that when assembled in convention, they can agree to no
words by which to establish that trial, or by which to ascertain and establish
many other of these rights, as fundamental articles in the social compact. If
so, we proceed to consolidate the states on no solid basis whatever.

But I do not pay much regard to the reasons given for not bottoming the new constitution on a better bill of rights. I still believe a complete federal bill of rights to be very practicable. Nevertheless I acknowledge the proceedings of the convention furnish my mind with many new and strong reasons, against a complete consolidation of the states. They tend to convince me, that it cannot be carried with propriety very far—that the convention have gone much farther in one respect than they found it practicable to go in another; that is, they propose to lodge in the general government very extensive powers—*powers* nearly, if not altogether, complete and unlimited, over the purse and the sword. But, in its organization, they furnish the strongest proof that the proper limbs, or parts of a government, to support and execute those powers on proper principles (or in which they can be safely lodged) cannot be formed. These powers must be lodged somewhere in every society; but then they should be lodged where the strength and guardians of the people are collected. They can be wielded, or safely used, in a free country only by an able executive and judiciary, a respectable senate, and a secure, full, and equal representation of the people. I think the principles I have premised or brought into view, are well founded—I think they will not be denied by any fair reasoner. It is in connection with these, and other solid principles, we are to examine the constitution. It is not a few democratic phrases, or a few well formed features, that will prove its merits; or a few small omissions that will produce its rejection among men of sense; they will enquire what are the essential powers in a community, and what are nominal ones; where and how the essential powers shall be lodged to secure government, and to secure true liberty.

In examining the proposed constitution carefully, we must clearly perceive an unnatural separation of these powers from the substantial representation of the people. The state governments will exist, with all their governors, senators, representatives, officers and expences; in these will be nineteen-twentieths of the representatives of the people; they will have a near connection, and their members an immediate intercourse with the people; and the probability is, that the state governments will possess the confidence of the people, and be considered generally as their immediate guardians.

The general government will consist of a new species of executive, a small senate, and a very small house of representatives. As many citizens will be more than three hundred miles from the seat of this government as will be nearer to it, its judges and officers cannot be very numerous, without making our governments very expensive. Thus will stand the state and the general governments, should the constitution be adopted without any alterations in their organization; but as to powers, the general government will possess all essential ones, at least on paper, and those of the states a mere shadow of power. And therefore, unless the people shall make some great exertions to restore to the state governments their powers in matters of internal police; as the powers to lay and collect, exclusively, internal taxes, to govern the militia, and to hold the decisions of their own judicial courts upon their own laws final, the balance cannot possibly continue long; but the state governments must be annihilated, or continue to exist for no purpose.

It is however to be observed, that many of the essential powers given the national government are not exclusively given; and the general government may have prudence enough to forbear the exercise of those which may still be exercised by the respective states. But this cannot justify the impropriety of giving powers, the exercise of which prudent men will not attempt, and imprudent men will, or probably can, exercise only in a manner destructive of free government. The general government, organized as it is, may be adequate to many valuable objects, and be able to carry its laws into execution on proper principles in several cases; but I think its wannest friends will not contend, that it can carry all the powers proposed to be lodged in it into effect, without calling to its aid a military force, which must very soon destroy all elective governments in the country, produce anarchy, or establish despotism. Though we cannot have now a complete idea of what will be the operations of the proposed system, we may, allowing things to have their common course, have a very tolerable one. The powers lodged in the general government, if exercised by it, must intimately effect the internal police of the states, as well as external concerns; and there is no reason to expect the numerous state governments, and their connections, will be very friendly to the execution of federal laws in those internal affairs, which hitherto have been under their own immediate management. There is more reason to believe, that the general government, far removed from the people, and none of its members elected oftener than once in two years, will be forgot or neglected, and its laws in many cases disregarded, unless a multitude of officers and military force be continually kept in view, and employed to enforce the execution of the laws, and to make the government feared and respected. No position can be truer than this, that in this country either neglected laws, or a military execution of them, must lead to a revolution, and to the destruction of freedom. Neglected laws must first lead to anarchy and confusion; and a military execution of laws is only a shorter way to the same point—despotic government.

Your's, &c.

The Federal Farmer.

JAMES MADISON **36**

The Federalist No. 10, 1787

The Federalist Papers *was a series of eighty-five essays written in New York in favor of ratification of the Constitution. This effort to persuade New York to approve the new document has since become a classic commentary on the different*

James Madison, "*Federalist* No. 10," *The Federalist Papers*, Clinton Rossieter, ed. (New York: Penguin, 1961): 77–84.

aspects of the Constitution. The Federalist essays were written by Alexander Hamilton, John Jay, James Madison, and sometimes in a combination of the three. Federalist No.10, written by Madison in the New York Daily Advertiser *on November 22, 1787, discussed the issue of political parties and factions. Many in the United States feared that such factions would lead to corruption and deep division in the nation. Madison answered these fears by stating that the new federal government would absorb any excesses of factionalism through the principles of free government. To gain a majority in an election, particularly in a diverse nation, meant reaching out to different interests. Differences of opinion are natural, Madison wrote, and were nothing to fear. It is a byproduct of a healthy body politic. The solution to the problem of freedom was quite simple to Madison—more freedom.*

The Utility of the Union as a Safeguard Against Domestic Faction and Insurrection (continued)

To the People of the State of New York:

AMONG the numerous advantages promised by a well constructed Union, none deserves to be more accurately developed than its tendency to break and control the violence of faction. The friend of popular governments never finds himself so much alarmed for their character and fate, as when he contemplates their propensity to this dangerous vice. He will not fail, therefore, to set a due value on any plan which, without violating the principles to which he is attached, provides a proper cure for it. The instability, injustice, and confusion introduced into the public councils, have, in truth, been the mortal diseases under which popular governments have everywhere perished; as they continue to be the favorite and fruitful topics from which the adversaries to liberty derive their most specious declamations. The valuable improvements made by the American constitutions on the popular models, both ancient and modern, cannot certainly be too much admired; but it would be an unwarrantable partiality, to contend that they have as effectually obviated the danger on this side, as was wished and expected. Complaints are everywhere heard from our most considerate and virtuous citizens, equally the friends of public and private faith, and of public and personal liberty, that our governments are too unstable, that the public good is disregarded in the conflicts of rival parties, and that measures are too often decided, not according to the rules of justice and the rights of the minor party, but by the superior force of an interested and overbearing majority. However anxiously we may wish that these complaints had no foundation, the evidence, of known facts will not permit us to deny that they are in some degree true. It will be found, indeed, on a candid review of our situation, that some of the distresses under which we labor have been erroneously charged on the operation of our governments; but it will be found, at the same time, that other causes will not alone account for many of our heaviest misfortunes; and, particularly, for that prevailing and increasing distrust of public engagements, and alarm for private rights, which are echoed from one end of the continent to the other. These must be chiefly, if not wholly, effects of the unsteadiness and injustice with which a factious spirit has tainted our public administrations.

By a faction, I understand a number of citizens, whether amounting to a majority or a minority of the whole, who are united and actuated by some common impulse of passion, or of interest, adversed to the rights of other citizens, or to the permanent and aggregate interests of the community.

There are two methods of curing the mischiefs of faction: the one, by removing its causes; the other, by controlling its effects.

There are again two methods of removing the causes of faction: the one, by destroying the liberty which is essential to its existence; the other, by giving to every citizen the same opinions, the same passions, and the same interests.

It could never be more truly said than of the first remedy, that it was worse than the disease. Liberty is to faction what air is to fire, an aliment without which it instantly expires. But it could not be less folly to abolish liberty, which is essential to political life, because it nourishes faction, than it would be to wish the annihilation of air, which is essential to animal life, because it imparts to fire its destructive agency.

The second expedient is as impracticable as the first would be unwise. As long as the reason of man continues fallible, and he is at liberty to exercise it, different opinions will be formed. As long as the connection subsists between his reason and his self-love, his opinions and his passions will have a reciprocal influence on each other; and the former will be objects to which the latter will attach themselves. The diversity in the faculties of men, from which the rights of property originate, is not less an insuperable obstacle to a uniformity of interests. The protection of these faculties is the first object of government. From the protection of different and unequal faculties of acquiring property, the possession of different degrees and kinds of property immediately results; and from the influence of these on the sentiments and views of the respective proprietors, ensues a division of the society into different interests and parties.

The latent causes of faction are thus sown in the nature of man; and we see them everywhere brought into different degrees of activity, according to the different circumstances of civil society. A zeal for different opinions concerning religion, concerning government, and many other points, as well of speculation as of practice; an attachment to different leaders ambitiously contending for pre-eminence and power; or to persons of other descriptions whose fortunes have been interesting to the human passions, have, in turn, divided mankind into parties, inflamed them with mutual animosity, and rendered them much more disposed to vex and oppress each other than to co-operate for their common good. So strong is this propensity of mankind to fall into mutual animosities, that where no substantial occasion presents itself, the most frivolous and fanciful distinctions have been sufficient to kindle their unfriendly passions and excite their most violent conflicts. But the most common and durable source of factions has been the various and unequal distribution of property. Those who hold and those who are without property have ever formed distinct interests in society. Those who are creditors, and those who are debtors, fall under a like discrimination. A landed interest, a manufacturing interest, a mercantile interest, a moneyed interest, with many lesser interests, grow up of necessity in civilized nations, and divide them into different classes, actuated by different sentiments and views. The regulation of these various and interfering interests forms the principal task of modern legislation, and involves the spirit of party and faction in the necessary and ordinary operations of the government.

No man is allowed to be a judge in his own cause, because his interest would certainly bias his judgment, and, not improbably, corrupt his integrity. With equal, nay with greater reason, a body of men are unfit to be both judges and parties at the same time; yet what are many of the most important acts of legislation, but so many judicial determinations, not indeed concerning the rights of single persons, but concerning the rights of large bodies of citizens? And what are the different classes of legislators but advocates and parties to the causes which they determine? Is a law proposed concerning private debts? It is a question to which the creditors are parties on one side and the debtors on the other. Justice ought to hold the balance between them. Yet the parties are, and must be, themselves the judges; and the most numerous party, or, in other words, the most powerful faction must be expected to prevail. Shall domestic manufactures be encouraged, and in what degree, by restrictions on foreign manufactures? are questions which would be differently decided by the landed and the manufacturing classes, and probably by neither with a sole regard to justice and the public good. The apportionment of taxes on the various descriptions of property is an act which seems to require the most exact impartiality; yet there is, perhaps, no legislative act in which greater opportunity and temptation are given to a predominant party to trample on the rules of justice. Every shilling with which they overburden the inferior number, is a shilling saved to their own pockets.

It is in vain to say that enlightened statesmen will be able to adjust these clashing interests, and render them all subservient to the public good. Enlightened statesmen will not always be at the helm. Nor, in many cases, can such an adjustment be made at all without taking into view indirect and remote considerations, which will rarely prevail over the immediate interest which one party may find in disregarding the rights of another or the good of the whole.

The inference to which we are brought is, that the *causes* of faction cannot be removed, and that relief is only to be sought in the means of controlling its *effects*.

If a faction consists of less than a majority, relief is supplied by the republican principle, which enables the majority to defeat its sinister views by regular vote. It may clog the administration, it may convulse the society; but it will be unable to execute and mask its violence under the forms of the Constitution. When a majority is included in a faction, the form of popular government, on the other hand, enables it to sacrifice to its ruling passion or interest both the public good and the rights of other citizens. To secure the public good and private rights against the danger of such a faction, and at the same time to preserve the spirit and the form of popular government, is then the great object to which our inquiries are directed. Let me add that it is the great desideratum by which this form of government can be rescued from the opprobrium under which it has so long labored, and be recommended to the esteem and adoption of mankind.

By what means is this object attainable? Evidently by one of two only. Either the existence of the same passion or interest in a majority at the same time must be prevented, or the majority, having such coexistent passion or interest, must be rendered, by their number and local situation, unable to concert and carry into effect schemes of oppression. If the impulse and the opportunity be suffered to coincide, we well know that neither moral nor religious motives can be relied on as an adequate control. They are not found to be such on the injustice and violence of individuals, and lose their efficacy in proportion to the number combined together, that is, in proportion as their efficacy becomes needful.

From this view of the subject it may be concluded that a pure democracy, by which I mean a society consisting of a small number of citizens, who assemble and administer the government in person, can admit of no cure for the mischiefs of faction. A common passion or interest will, in almost every case, be felt by a majority of the whole; a communication and concert result from the form of government itself; and there is nothing to check the inducements to sacrifice the weaker party or an obnoxious individual. Hence it is that such democracies have ever been spectacles of turbulence and contention; have ever been found incompatible with personal security or the rights of property; and have in general been as short in their lives as they have been violent in their deaths. Theoretic politicians, who have patronized this species of government, have erroneously supposed that by reducing mankind to a perfect equality in their political rights, they would, at the same time, be perfectly equalized and assimilated in their possessions, their opinions, and their passions.

A republic, by which I mean a government in which the scheme of representation takes place, opens a different prospect, and promises the cure for which we are seeking. Let us examine the points in which it varies from pure democracy, and we shall comprehend both the nature of the cure and the efficacy which it must derive from the Union.

The two great points of difference between a democracy and a republic are: first, the delegation of the government, in the latter, to a small number of citizens elected by the rest; secondly, the greater number of citizens, and greater sphere of country, over which the latter may be extended.

The effect of the first difference is, on the one hand, to refine and enlarge the public views, by passing them through the medium of a chosen body of citizens, whose wisdom may best discern the true interest of their country, and whose patriotism and love of justice will be least likely to sacrifice it to temporary or partial considerations. Under such a regulation, it may well happen that the public voice, pronounced by the representatives of the people, will be more consonant to the public good than if pronounced by the people themselves, convened for the purpose. On the other hand, the effect may be inverted. Men of factious tempers, of local prejudices, or of sinister designs, may, by intrigue, by corruption, or by other means, first obtain the suffrages, and then betray the interests, of the people. The question resulting is, whether small or extensive republics are more favorable to the election of proper guardians of the public weal; and it is clearly decided in favor of the latter by two obvious considerations:

In the first place, it is to be remarked that, however small the republic may be, the representatives must be raised to a certain number, in order to guard against the cabals of a few; and that, however large it may be, they must be limited to a certain number, in order to guard against the confusion of a multitude. Hence, the number of representatives in the two cases not being in proportion to that of the two constituents, and being proportionally greater in the small republic, it follows that, if the proportion of fit characters be not less in the large than in the small republic, the former will present a greater option, and consequently a greater probability of a fit choice.

In the next place, as each representative will be chosen by a greater number of citizens in the large than in the small republic, it will be more difficult for unworthy candidates to practice with success the vicious arts by which elections are too often carried; and the suffrages of the people being more free, will be more likely to centre in men who possess the most attractive merit and the most diffusive and established characters.

It must be confessed that in this, as in most other cases, there is a mean, on both sides of which inconveniences will be found to lie. By enlarging too much the number of electors, you render the representatives too little acquainted with all their local circumstances and lesser interests; as by reducing it too much, you render him unduly attached to these, and too little fit to comprehend and pursue great and national objects. The federal Constitution forms a happy combination in this respect; the great and aggregate interests being referred to the national, the local and particular to the State legislatures.

The other point of difference is, the greater number of citizens and extent of territory which may be brought within the compass of republican than of democratic government; and it is this circumstance principally which renders factious combinations less to be dreaded in the former than in the latter. The smaller the society, the fewer probably will be the distinct parties and interests composing it; the fewer the distinct parties and interests, the more frequently will a majority be found of the same party; and the smaller the number of individuals composing a majority, and the smaller the compass within which they are placed, the more easily will they concert and execute their plans of oppression. Extend the sphere, and you take in a greater variety of parties and interests; you make it less probable that a majority of the whole will have a common motive to invade the rights of other citizens; or if such a common motive exists, it will be more difficult for all who feel it to discover their own strength, and to act in unison with each other. Besides other impediments, it may be remarked that, where there is a consciousness of unjust or dishonorable purposes, communication is always checked by distrust in proportion to the number whose concurrence is necessary.

Hence, it clearly appears, that the same advantage which a republic has over a democracy, in controlling the effects of faction, is enjoyed by a large over a small republic,—is enjoyed by the Union over the States composing it. Does the advantage consist in the substitution of representatives whose enlightened views and virtuous sentiments render them superior to local prejudices and schemes of injustice? It will not be denied that the representation of the Union will be most likely to possess these requisite endowments. Does it consist in the greater security afforded by a greater variety of parties, against the event of any one party being able to outnumber and oppress the rest? In an equal degree does the increased variety of parties comprised within the Union, increase this security. Does it, in fine, consist in the greater obstacles opposed to the concert and accomplishment of the secret wishes of an unjust and interested majority? Here, again, the extent of the Union gives it the most palpable advantage.

The influence of factious leaders may kindle a flame within their particular States, but will be unable to spread a general conflagration through the other States. A religious sect may degenerate into a political faction in a part of the Confederacy; but the variety of sects dispersed over the entire face of it must secure the national councils against any danger from that source. A rage for paper money, for an abolition of debts, for an equal division of property, or for any other improper or wicked project, will be less apt to pervade the whole body of the Union than a particular member of it; in the same proportion as such a malady is more likely to taint a particular county or district, than an entire State.

In the extent and proper structure of the Union, therefore, we behold a republican remedy for the diseases most incident to republican government. And according to the degree of pleasure and pride we feel in being republicans, ought to be our zeal in cherishing the spirit and supporting the character of Federalists.

PUBLIUS

JAMES MADISON **37**

The Federalist No. 51, 1788

On February 6, 1788, Federalist *No. 51 appeared in the* New York Independent Journal. *Madison argues in this essay that the separation of powers will preserve civil liberties in the United States. The separation of powers preserved civil liberties since a small faction of the government could not operate without the consent of the other branches or the people. The Constitution's separation of powers of the federal government, instead of threatening civil liberties through a lack of oversight, created a government that had to preserve those rights in order to function and to survive at all.*

The Structure of the Government Must Furnish the Proper Checks and Balances Between the Different Departments

To the People of the State of New York:

TO WHAT expedient, then, shall we finally resort, for maintaining in practice the necessary partition of power among the several departments, as laid down in the Constitution? The only answer that can be given is, that as all these exterior provisions are found to be inadequate, the defect must be supplied, by so contriving the interior structure of the government as that its several constituent parts may, by their mutual relations, be the means of keeping each other in their proper places. Without presuming to undertake a full development of this important idea, I will hazard a few general observations, which may perhaps place it in a clearer light, and enable us to form a more correct judgment of the principles and structure of the government planned by the convention.

In order to lay a due foundation for that separate and distinct exercise of the different powers of government, which to a certain extent is admitted on all hands to be essential to the preservation of liberty, it is evident that each department should have a will of its own; and consequently should be so constituted that the members of each should have as little agency as possible in the appointment of the members of the

James Madison, *"Federalist* No. 51," *The Federalist Papers,* Clinton Rossieter, ed. (New York: Penguin, 1961): 320–325.

others. Were this principle rigorously adhered to, it would require that all the appointments for the supreme executive, legislative, and judiciary magistracies should be drawn from the same fountain of authority, the people, through channels having no communication whatever with one another. Perhaps such a plan of constructing the several departments would be less difficult in practice than it may in contemplation appear. Some difficulties, however, and some additional expense would attend the execution of it. Some deviations, therefore, from the principle must be admitted. In the constitution of the judiciary department in particular, it might be inexpedient to insist rigorously on the principle: first, because peculiar qualifications being essential in the members, the primary consideration ought to be to select that mode of choice which best secures these qualifications; secondly, because the permanent tenure by which the appointments are held in that department, must soon destroy all sense of dependence on the authority conferring them.

It is equally evident, that the members of each department should be as little dependent as possible on those of the others, for the emoluments annexed to their offices. Were the executive magistrate, or the judges, not independent of the legislature in this particular, their independence in every other would be merely nominal.

But the great security against a gradual concentration of the several powers in the same department, consists in giving to those who administer each department the necessary constitutional means and personal motives to resist encroachments of the others. The provision for defense must in this, as in all other cases, be made commensurate to the danger of attack. Ambition must be made to counteract ambition. The interest of the man must be connected with the constitutional rights of the place. It may be a reflection on human nature, that such devices should be necessary to control the abuses of government. But what is government itself, but the greatest of all reflections on human nature? If men were angels, no government would be necessary. If angels were to govern men, neither external nor internal controls on government would be necessary. In framing a government which is to be administered by men over men, the great difficulty lies in this: you must first enable the government to control the governed; and in the next place oblige it to control itself. A dependence on the people is, no doubt, the primary control on the government; but experience has taught mankind the necessity of auxiliary precautions.

This policy of supplying, by opposite and rival interests, the defect of better motives, might be traced through the whole system of human affairs, private as well as public. We see it particularly displayed in all the subordinate distributions of power, where the constant aim is to divide and arrange the several offices in such a manner as that each may be a check on the other—that the private interest of every individual may be a sentinel over the public rights. These inventions of prudence cannot be less requisite in the distribution of the supreme powers of the State.

But it is not possible to give to each department an equal power of self-defense. In republican government, the legislative authority necessarily predominates. The remedy for this inconveniency is to divide the legislature into different branches; and to render them, by different modes of election and different principles of action, as little connected with each other as the nature of their common functions and their common dependence on the society will admit. It may even be necessary to guard against dangerous encroachments by still further precautions. As the weight of the legislative authority requires that it should be thus divided, the weakness of the executive may require, on the other hand, that it should be fortified. An absolute negative on the legislature appears, at first view, to be the natural defense with which the executive magistrate should be armed. But perhaps it would be neither altogether safe nor alone sufficient. On ordinary occasions it might not be exerted with the requisite firmness, and on extraordinary occasions it might be perfidiously abused. May not this defect of an absolute negative be supplied by some qualified connection between this weaker department and the weaker branch of the stronger department, by which the latter may be led to support the constitutional rights of the former, without being too much detached from the rights of its own department?

If the principles on which these observations are founded be just, as I persuade myself they are, and they be applied as a criterion to the several State constitutions, and to the federal Constitution it will be found that if the latter does not perfectly correspond with them, the former are infinitely less able to bear such a test.

There are, moreover, two considerations particularly applicable to the federal system of America, which place that system in a very interesting point of view.

First. In a single republic, all the power surrendered by the people is submitted to the administration of a single government; and the usurpations are guarded against by a division of the government into distinct and separate departments. In the compound republic of America, the power surrendered by the people is first divided between two distinct governments, and then the portion allotted to each subdivided among distinct and separate departments. Hence a double security arises to the rights of the people. The different governments will control each other, at the same time that each will be controlled by itself.

Second. It is of great importance in a republic not only to guard the society against the oppression of its rulers, but to guard one part of the society against the injustice of the other part. Different interests necessarily exist in different classes of citizens. If a majority be united by a common interest, the rights of the minority will be insecure. There are but two methods of providing against this evil: the one by creating a will in the community independent of the majority—that is, of the society itself; the other, by comprehending in the society so many separate descriptions of citizens as will render an unjust combination of a majority of the whole very improbable, if not impracticable. The first method prevails in all governments possessing an hereditary or self-appointed authority. This, at best, is but a precarious security; because a power independent of the society may as well espouse the unjust views of the major, as the rightful interests of the minor party, and may possibly be turned against both parties. The second method will be exemplified in the federal republic of the United States. Whilst all authority in it will be derived from and dependent on the society, the society itself will be broken into so many parts, interests, and classes of citizens, that the rights of individuals, or of the minority, will be in little danger from interested combinations of the majority. In a free government the security for civil rights must be the same as that for religious rights. It consists in the one case in the multiplicity of interests, and in the other in the multiplicity of sects. The degree of security in both cases will depend on the number of interests and sects; and this may be presumed to depend on the extent of country and number of people comprehended under the same government. This view of the subject must particularly recommend a proper federal system to all the sincere and considerate friends of republican government, since it shows that in exact proportion as the territory of the Union may be formed into more circumscribed Confederacies, or States oppressive combinations of a majority will be facilitated: the best security, under the republican forms, for the rights of every class of citizens, will be diminished: and consequently the stability and independence of some member of the government, the only other security, must be proportionately increased. Justice is the end of government. It is the end of civil society. It ever has been and ever will be pursued until it be obtained, or until liberty be lost in the pursuit. In a society under the forms of which the stronger faction can readily unite and oppress the weaker, anarchy may as truly be said to reign as in a state of nature, where the weaker individual is not secured against the violence of the stronger; and as, in the latter state, even the stronger individuals are prompted, by the uncertainty of their condition, to submit to a government which may protect the weak as well as themselves; so, in the former state, will the more powerful factions or parties be gradually induced, by a like motive, to wish for a government which will protect all parties, the weaker as well as the more powerful. It can be little doubted that if the State of Rhode Island was separated from the Confederacy and left to itself, the insecurity of rights under the popular form of government within such narrow limits would be displayed by such reiterated oppressions of factious majorities that some power altogether independent of the people would soon be called for by the voice of the very factions whose misrule had proved the necessity of it. In the extended republic of the United States, and among the great variety of interests, parties, and sects which it embraces, a coalition of a majority of the whole society could seldom take place on any other principles than those of justice and the general good; whilst there being thus less danger to a minor from the will of a major party, there must be less pretext, also, to provide for the security of the former, by introducing into the government a will not dependent on the latter, or, in other words, a will independent of the society itself. It is no less certain than it is important, notwithstanding the contrary opinions which have been entertained, that the larger the society, provided it lie within a practical sphere, the more duly capable it will be of self-government. And happily for the *republican cause*, the practicable sphere may be carried to a very great extent, by a judicious modification and mixture of the *federal principle*.

PUBLIUS

ALEXANDER HAMILTON  **38**

The Federalist No. 84, 1788

Alexander Hamilton wrote the eighty-fourth Federalist *essay, appearing in* The New York Independent Journal *on July 16, July 26, and August 9, 1788. Hamilton, a New York resident himself, summarizes the arguments for and against ratification of the Constitution in this essay. He attempts to answer the*

Alexander Hamilton, "*Federalist No. 84,*" *The Federalist Papers*, Clinton Rossieter, ed. (New York: Penguin, 1961): 510–520.

most powerful argument against ratification, that the Constitution had no Bill of Rights. He argues that many provisions of the Constitution strictly spelled out the rights of the people and restrains the power of the federal government from infringing on those liberties. Hamilton and others argued that the Constitution itself was a Bill of Rights and a defense of free government and civil liberties against tyranny.

Certain General and Miscellaneous Objections to the Constitution Considered and Answered

To the People of the State of New York:

IN THE course of the foregoing review of the Constitution, I have taken notice of, and endeavored to answer most of the objections which have appeared against it. There, however, remain a few which either did not fall naturally under any particular head or were forgotten in their proper places. These shall now be discussed; but as the subject has been drawn into great length, I shall so far consult brevity as to comprise all my observations on these miscellaneous points in a single paper.

The most considerable of the remaining objections is that the plan of the convention contains no bill of rights. Among other answers given to this, it has been upon different occasions remarked that the constitutions of several of the States are in a similar predicament. I add that New York is of the number. And yet the opposers of the new system, in this State, who profess an unlimited admiration for its constitution, are among the most intemperate partisans of a bill of rights. To justify their zeal in this matter, they allege two things: one is that, though the constitution of New York has no bill of rights prefixed to it, yet it contains, in the body of it, various provisions in favor of particular privileges and rights, which, in substance amount to the same thing; the other is, that the Constitution adopts, in their full extent, the common and statute law of Great Britain, by which many other rights, not expressed in it, are equally secured.

To the first I answer, that the Constitution proposed by the convention contains, as well as the constitution of this State, a number of such provisions.

Independent of those which relate to the structure of the government, we find the following: Article 1, section 3, clause 7—"Judgment in cases of impeachment shall not extend further than to removal from office, and disqualification to hold and enjoy any office of honor, trust, or profit under the United States; but the party convicted shall, nevertheless, be liable and subject to indictment, trial, judgment, and punishment according to law." Section 9, of the same article, clause 2—"The privilege of the writ of habeas corpus shall not be suspended, unless when in cases of rebellion or invasion the public safety may require it." Clause 3—"No bill of attainder or ex-post-facto law shall be passed." Clause 7—"No title of nobility shall be granted by the United States; and no person holding any office of profit or trust under them, shall, without the consent of the Congress, accept of any present, emolument, office, or title of any kind whatever, from any king, prince, or foreign state." Article 3, section 2, clause 3—"The trial of all crimes, except in cases of impeachment, shall be by jury; and such trial shall be held in the State where the said crimes shall have been committed; but when not committed within any State, the trial shall be at such place or places as the Congress may by law have directed." Section 3, of the same article—"Treason against the United States shall consist only in levying war against them, or in adhering to their enemies, giving them aid and comfort. No person shall be convicted of treason, unless on the testimony of two witnesses to the same overt act, or on confession in open court." And clause 3, of the same section—"The Congress shall have power to declare the punishment of treason; but no attainder of treason shall work corruption of blood, or forfeiture, except during the life of the person attainted."

It may well be a question, whether these are not, upon the whole, of equal importance with any which are to be found in the constitution of this State. The establishment of the writ of *habeas corpus*, the prohibition of *ex post facto* laws, and of TITLES OF NOBILITY, *to which we have no corresponding provision in our Constitution*, are perhaps greater securities to liberty and republicanism than any it contains. The creation of crimes after the commission of the fact, or, in other words, the subjecting of men to punishment for things which, when they were done, were breaches of no law, and the practice of arbitrary imprisonments, have been, in all ages, the favorite and most formidable instruments of tyranny. The observations of the judicious Blackstone, in reference to the latter, are well worthy of recital: "To bereave a man of life, [says he] or by violence to confiscate his estate, without accusation or trial, would be so gross and notorious an act of despotism, as must at once convey the alarm of tyranny throughout the whole nation; but confinement of the person, by secretly hurrying him to jail, where his sufferings are unknown or forgotten, is a less public, a less striking, and therefore *a more dangerous engine* of arbitrary government." And as a remedy for this fatal evil he is everywhere peculiarly emphatical in his encomiums on the *habeas corpus* act, which in one place he calls "the BULWARK of the British Constitution."

Nothing need be said to illustrate the importance of the prohibition of titles of nobility. This may truly be denominated the corner-stone of republican government; for so long as they are excluded, there can never be serious danger that the government will be any other than that of the people.

To the second that is, to the pretended establishment of the common and state law by the Constitution, I answer, that they are expressly made subject "to such alterations and provisions as the legislature shall from time to time make concerning the same." They are therefore at any moment liable to repeal by the ordinary legislative power, and of course have no constitutional sanction. The only use of the declaration was to recognize the ancient law and to remove doubts which might have been occasioned by the Revolution. This consequently can be considered as no part of a declaration of rights, which under our constitutions must be intended as limitations of the power of the government itself.

It has been several times truly remarked that bills of rights are, in their origin, stipulations between kings and their subjects, abridgements of prerogative in favor of privilege, reservations of rights not surrendered to the prince. Such was MAGNA CHARTA, obtained by the barons, sword in hand, from King John. Such were the subsequent confirmations of that charter by succeeding princes. Such was the *Petition of Right* assented to by Charles I., in the beginning of his reign. Such, also, was the Declaration of Right presented by the Lords and Commons to the Prince of Orange in 1688, and afterwards thrown into the form of an act of parliament called the Bill of Rights. It is evident, therefore, that, according to their primitive signification, they have no application to constitutions professedly founded upon the power of the people, and executed by their immediate representatives and servants. Here, in strictness, the people surrender nothing; and as they retain every thing they have no need of particular reservations. "WE, THE PEOPLE of the United States, to secure the blessings of liberty to ourselves and our posterity, do *ordain* and *establish* this Constitution for the United States of America." Here is a better recognition of popular rights, than volumes of those aphorisms which make the principal figure in several of our State bills of rights, and which would sound much better in a treatise of ethics than in a constitution of government.

But a minute detail of particular rights is certainly far less applicable to a Constitution like that under consideration, which is merely intended to regulate the general political interests of the nation, than to a constitution which has the regulation of every species of personal and private concerns. If, therefore, the loud clamors against the plan of the convention, on this score, are well founded, no epithets of reprobation will be too strong for the constitution of this State. But the truth is, that both of them contain all which, in relation to their objects, is reasonably to be desired.

I go further, and affirm that bills of rights, in the sense and to the extent in which they are contended for, are not only unnecessary in the proposed Constitution, but would even be dangerous. They would contain various exceptions to powers not granted; and, on this very account, would afford a colorable pretext to claim more than were granted. For why declare that things shall not be done which there is no power to do? Why, for instance, should it be said that the liberty of the press shall not be restrained, when no power is given by which restrictions may be imposed? I will not contend that such a provision would confer a regulating power; but it is evident that it would furnish, to men disposed to usurp, a plausible pretense for claiming that power. They might urge with a semblance of reason, that the Constitution ought not to be charged with the absurdity of providing against the abuse of an authority which was not given, and that the provision against restraining the liberty of the press afforded a clear implication, that a power to prescribe proper regulations concerning it was intended to be vested in the national government. This may serve as a specimen of the numerous handles which would be given to the doctrine of constructive powers, by the indulgence of an injudicious zeal for bills of rights.

On the subject of the liberty of the press, as much as has been said, I cannot forbear adding a remark or two: in the first place, I observe, that there is not a syllable concerning it in the constitution of this State; in the next, I contend, that whatever has been said about it in that of any other State, amounts to nothing. What signifies a declaration, that "the liberty of the press shall be inviolably preserved"? What is the liberty of the press? Who can give it any definition which would not leave the utmost latitude for evasion? I hold it to be impracticable; and from this I infer, that its security, whatever fine declarations may be inserted in any constitution respecting it, must altogether depend on public opinion, and on the general spirit of the people and of the government. And here, after all, as is intimated upon another occasion, must we seek for the only solid basis of all our rights.

There remains but one other view of this matter to conclude the point. The truth is, after all the declamations we have heard, that the Constitution is itself, in every rational sense, and to every useful purpose, A BILL OF RIGHTS. The several bills of rights in Great Britain form its Constitution, and conversely the constitution of each State is its bill of rights. And the proposed Constitution, if adopted, will be the bill of rights of the Union. Is it one object of a bill of rights to declare and specify the political privileges of the citizens in the structure and administration of the government? This is done in the most ample and precise manner in the plan of the convention; comprehending various precautions for the public security, which are not to be found in any of the State constitutions. Is another object of a bill of rights to define certain immunities and modes of proceeding, which are relative to personal and private concerns? This we have seen has also been attended to, in a variety of cases, in the same plan. Adverting therefore to the substantial meaning of a bill of rights, it is absurd to allege that it is not to be found in the work of the convention. It may be said that it does not go far enough, though it will not be easy to make this appear; but it can with no propriety be contended that there is no such thing. It certainly must be immaterial what mode is observed as to the order of declaring the rights of the citizens, if they are to be found in any part of the instrument which establishes the government. And hence it must be apparent, that much of what has been said on this subject rests merely on verbal and nominal distinctions, entirely foreign from the substance of the thing.

Another objection which has been made, and which, from the frequency of its repetition, it is to be presumed is relied on, is of this nature: "It is improper [say the objectors] to confer such large powers, as are proposed, upon the national government, because the seat of that government must of necessity be too remote from many of the States to admit of a proper knowledge on the part of the constituent, of the conduct of the representative body." This argument, if it proves any thing, proves that there ought to be no general government whatever. For the powers which, it seems to be agreed on all hands, ought to be vested in the Union, cannot be safely intrusted to a body which is not under every requisite control. But there are satisfactory reasons to show that the objection is in reality not well founded. There is in most of the arguments which relate to distance a palpable illusion of the imagination. What are the sources of information by which the people in Montgomery County must regulate their judgment of the conduct of their representatives in the State legislature? Of personal observation they can have no benefit. This is confined to the citizens on the spot. They must therefore depend on the information of intelligent men, in whom they confide; and how must these men obtain their information? Evidently from the complexion of public measures, from the public prints, from correspondences with their representatives, and with other persons who reside at the place of their deliberations. This does not apply to Montgomery County only, but to all the counties at any considerable distance from the seat of government.

It is equally evident that the same sources of information would be open to the people in relation to the conduct of their representatives in the general government, and the impediments to a prompt communication which distance may be supposed to create, will be overbalanced by the effects of the vigilance of the State governments. The executive and legislative bodies of each State will be so many sentinels over the persons employed in every department of the national administration; and as it will be in their power to adopt and pursue a regular and effectual system of intelligence, they can never be at a loss to know the behavior of those who represent their constituents in the national councils, and can readily communicate the same knowledge to the people. Their disposition to apprise the community of whatever may prejudice its interests from another quarter, may be relied upon, if it were only from the rivalship of power. And we may conclude with the fullest assurance that the people, through that channel, will be better informed of the conduct of their national representatives, than they can be by any means they now possess of that of their State representatives.

It ought also to be remembered that the citizens who inhabit the country at and near the seat of government will, in all questions that affect the general liberty and prosperity, have the same interest with those who are at a distance, and that they will stand ready to sound the alarm when necessary, and to point out the actors in any pernicious project. The public papers will be expeditious messengers of intelligence to the most remote inhabitants of the Union.

Among the many curious objections which have appeared against the proposed Constitution, the most extraordinary and the least colorable is derived from the want of some provision respecting the debts due *to* the United States. This has been represented as a tacit relinquishment of those debts, and as a wicked contrivance to screen public defaulters. The newspapers have teemed with the most inflammatory railings on this head; yet there is nothing clearer than that the suggestion is entirely void of foundation, the offspring of extreme ignorance or extreme dishonesty. In addition to the remarks I have made upon the subject in another place, I shall only observe that as it is a plain dictate of common-sense, so it is also an established doctrine of political law, that *"States neither lose any of their rights, nor are discharged from any of their obligations, by a change in the form of their civil government."*

The last objection of any consequence, which I at present recollect, turns upon the article of expense. If it were even true, that the adoption of the proposed government would occasion a considerable increase of expense, it would be an objection that ought to have no weight against the plan.

The great bulk of the citizens of America are with reason convinced, that Union is the basis of their political happiness. Men of sense of all parties now, with few exceptions, agree that it cannot be preserved under the present system, nor without radical alterations; that new and extensive powers ought to be granted to the national head, and that these require a different organization of the federal government—a single body being an unsafe depositary of such ample authorities. In conceding all this, the question of expense must be given up; for it is impossible, with any degree of safety, to narrow the foundation upon which the system is to stand. The two branches of the legislature are, in the first instance, to consist of only sixty-five persons, which is the same number of which Congress, under the existing Confederation, may be composed. It is true that this number is intended to be increased; but this is to keep pace with the progress of the population and resources of the country. It is evident that a less number would, even in the first instance, have been unsafe, and that a continuance of the present number would, in a more advanced stage of population, be a very inadequate representation of the people.

Whence is the dreaded augmentation of expense to spring? One source indicated, is the multiplication of offices under the new government. Let us examine this a little.

It is evident that the principal departments of the administration under the present government, are the same which will be required under the new. There are now a Secretary of War, a Secretary of Foreign Affairs, a Secretary for Domestic Affairs, a Board of Treasury, consisting of three persons, a Treasurer, assistants, clerks, etc. These officers are indispensable under any system, and will suffice under the new as well as the old. As to ambassadors and other ministers and agents in foreign countries, the proposed Constitution can make no other difference than to render their characters, where they reside, more respectable, and their services more useful. As to persons to be employed in the collection of the revenues, it is unquestionably true that these will form a very considerable addition to the number of federal officers; but it will not follow that this will occasion an increase of public expense. It will be in most cases nothing more than an exchange of State for national officers. In the collection of all duties, for instance, the persons employed will be wholly of the latter description. The States individually will stand in no need of any for this purpose. What difference can it make in point of expense to pay officers of the customs appointed by the State or by the United States? There is no good reason to suppose that either the number or the salaries of the latter will be greater than those of the former.

Where then are we to seek for those additional articles of expense which are to swell the account to the enormous size that has been represented to us? The chief item which occurs to me respects the support of the judges of the United States. I do not add the President, because there is now a president of Congress, whose expenses may not be far, if any thing, short of those which will be incurred on account of the President of the United States. The support of the judges will clearly be an extra expense, but to what extent will depend on the particular plan which may be adopted in regard to this matter. But upon no reasonable plan can it amount to a sum which will be an object of material consequence.

Let us now see what there is to counterbalance any extra expense that may attend the establishment of the proposed government. The first thing which presents itself is that a great part of the business which now keeps Congress sitting through the year will be transacted by the President. Even the management of foreign negotiations will naturally devolve upon him, according to general principles concerted with the Senate, and subject to their final concurrence. Hence it is evident that a portion of the year will suffice for the session of both the Senate and the House of Representatives; we may suppose about a fourth for the latter and a third, or perhaps half, for the former. The extra business of treaties and appointments may give this extra occupation to the Senate. From this circumstance we may infer that, until the House of Representatives shall be increased greatly beyond its present number, there will be a considerable saving of expense from the difference between the constant session of the present and the temporary session of the future Congress.

But there is another circumstance of great importance in the view of economy. The business of the United States has hitherto occupied the State legislatures, as well as Congress. The latter has made requisitions which the former have had to provide for. Hence it has happened that the sessions of the State legislatures have been protracted greatly beyond what was necessary for the execution of the mere local business of the States. More than half their time has been frequently employed in matters which related to the United States. Now the members who compose the legislatures of the several States amount to two thousand and upwards, which number has hitherto performed what under the new system will be done in the first instance by sixty-five persons, and probably at no future period by above a fourth or fifth of that number. The Congress under the proposed government will do all the business of the United States themselves, without the intervention of the State legislatures, who thenceforth will have only to attend to the affairs of their particular States, and will not have to sit in any proportion as long as they have heretofore done. This difference in the time of the sessions of the State legislatures will be clear gain, and will alone form an article of saving, which may be regarded as an equivalent for any additional objects of expense that may be occasioned by the adoption of the new system.

The result from these observations is that the sources of additional expense from the establishment of the proposed Constitution are much fewer than may have been imagined; that they are counterbalanced by considerable objects of saving; and that while it is questionable on which side the scale will preponderate, it is certain that a government less expensive would be incompetent to the purposes of the Union.

PUBLIUS

GEORGE WASHINGTON **39**

Farewell Address, 1796

President George Washington delivered this farewell address to a small gathering in Philadelphia in 1796 to announce his intention to decline any third term in office and to offer words of wisdom for the nation in the future. Washington takes careful care to look to foreign relations, urging America to treat all nations with justice. In addition, he urges all Americans to renounce factionalism, a rising problem in the United States with the development of political parties and sectionalism. The president said that the nation must remember their commonalities, that everyone was an American. But most important, Washington added, was the love of liberty which he believed had already become an inseparable component of the national character. For years afterward, Americans used Washington's speech to help craft foreign and domestic policy decisions.

Friends and Fellow Citizens:

The period for a new election of a citizen to administer the executive government of the United States being not far distant, and the time actually arrived when your thoughts must be employed in designating the person who is to be clothed with that important trust, it appears to me proper, especially as it may conduce to a more distinct expression of the public voice, that I should now apprise you of the resolution I have formed, to decline being considered among the number of those out of whom a choice is to be made.

I beg you, at the same time, to do me the justice to be assured that this resolution has not been taken without a strict regard to all the considerations appertaining to the relation which binds a dutiful citizen to his country; and that in withdrawing the tender of service, which silence in my situation might imply, I am influenced by no diminution of zeal for your future interest, no deficiency of grateful respect for your past kindness, but am supported by a full conviction that the step is compatible with both.

The acceptance of, and continuance hitherto in, the office to which your suffrages have twice called me have been a uniform sacrifice of inclination to the opinion of duty and to a deference for what appeared to be your desire. I constantly hoped that it would have been much earlier in my power, consistently with motives which I was not at liberty to disregard, to return to that retirement from which I had been reluctantly drawn. The strength of my inclination to do this, previous to the last election, had even led to the preparation of an address to declare it to you; but mature reflection on the then perplexed and critical posture of our affairs with foreign nations, and the unanimous advice of persons entitled to my confidence, impelled me to abandon the idea.

I rejoice that the state of your concerns, external as well as internal, no longer renders the pursuit of inclination incompatible with the sentiment of duty or propriety, and am persuaded, whatever partiality may be retained for my services, that, in the present circumstances of our country, you will not disapprove my determination to retire.

The impressions with which I first undertook the arduous trust were explained on the proper occasion. In the discharge of this trust, I will only say that I have, with good intentions, contributed towards the organization and administration of the government the best exertions of which a very fallible judgment was capable. Not unconscious in the outset of the inferiority of my qualifications, experience in my own eyes, perhaps still more in the eyes of others, has strengthened the motives to diffidence of myself; and every day the increasing weight of years admonishes me more and more that the shade of retirement is as necessary to me as it will be welcome. Satisfied that if any circumstances have given peculiar value to my services, they were temporary, I have the consolation to believe that, while choice and prudence invite me to quit the political scene, patriotism does not forbid it.

In looking forward to the moment which is intended to terminate the career of my public life, my feelings do not permit me to suspend the deep acknowledgment of that debt of gratitude which I owe to my beloved country for the many honors it has conferred upon me; still more for the steadfast confidence with which it has supported me; and for the opportunities I have thence enjoyed of manifesting my inviolable attachment, by services faithful and persevering, though in usefulness unequal to my zeal. If benefits have resulted to our country from these services, let it always be remembered to your praise, and as an instructive example in our annals, that under circumstances in which the passions, agitated in every direction, were liable to mislead, amidst appearances sometimes dubious, vicissitudes of fortune often discouraging, in situations in which not unfrequently want of success has countenanced the spirit of criticism, the constancy of your support was the essential prop of the efforts, and a guarantee of the plans by which they were effected. Profoundly penetrated with this idea, I shall carry it with me to my grave, as a strong incitement to unceasing vows that heaven may continue to you the choicest tokens of its beneficence; that your union and brotherly affection may be perpetual; that the free Constitution, which is the work of your hands, may be sacredly maintained; that its administration in every department may be stamped with wisdom and virtue; that, in fine, the happiness of the people of these

States, under the auspices of liberty, may be made complete by so careful a preservation and so prudent a use of this blessing as will acquire to them the glory of recommending it to the applause, the affection, and adoption of every nation which is yet a stranger to it.

Here, perhaps, I ought to stop. But a solicitude for your welfare, which cannot end but with my life, and the apprehension of danger, natural to that solicitude, urge me, on an occasion like the present, to offer to your solemn contemplation, and to recommend to your frequent review, some sentiments which are the result of much reflection, of no inconsiderable observation, and which appear to me all-important to the permanency of your felicity as a people. These will be offered to you with the more freedom, as you can only see in them the disinterested warnings of a parting friend, who can possibly have no personal motive to bias his counsel. Nor can I forget, as an encouragement to it, your indulgent reception of my sentiments on a former and not dissimilar occasion.

Interwoven as is the love of liberty with every ligament of your hearts, no recommendation of mine is necessary to fortify or confirm the attachment.

The unity of government which constitutes you one people is also now dear to you. It is justly so, for it is a main pillar in the edifice of your real independence, the support of your tranquility at home, your peace abroad; of your safety; of your prosperity; of that very liberty which you so highly prize. But as it is easy to foresee that, from different causes and from different quarters, much pains will be taken, many artifices employed to weaken in your minds the conviction of this truth; as this is the point in your political fortress against which the batteries of internal and external enemies will be most constantly and actively (though often covertly and insidiously) directed, it is of infinite moment that you should properly estimate the immense value of your national union to your collective and individual happiness; that you should cherish a cordial, habitual, and immovable attachment to it; accustoming yourselves to think and speak of it as of the palladium of your political safety and prosperity; watching for its preservation with jealous anxiety; discountenancing whatever may suggest even a suspicion that it can in any event be abandoned; and indignantly frowning upon the first dawning of every attempt to alienate any portion of our country from the rest, or to enfeeble the sacred ties which now link together the various parts.

For this you have every inducement of sympathy and interest. Citizens, by birth or choice, of a common country, that country has a right to concentrate your affections. The name of American, which belongs to you in your national capacity, must always exalt the just pride of patriotism more than any appellation derived from local discriminations. With slight shades of difference, you have the same religion, manners, habits, and political principles. You have in a common cause fought and triumphed together. The independence and liberty you possess are the work of joint counsils, and joint efforts of common dangers, sufferings, and successes.

But these considerations, however powerfully they address themselves to your sensibility, are greatly outweighed by those which apply more immediately to your interest. Here every portion of our country finds the most commanding motives for carefully guarding and preserving the union of the whole.

The North, in an unrestrained intercourse with the South, protected by the equal laws of a common government, finds in the productions of the latter great additional resources of maritime and commercial enterprise and precious materials of manufacturing industry. The South, in the same intercourse, benefiting by the agency of the North, sees its agriculture grow and its commerce expand. Turning partly into its own channels the seamen of the North, it finds its particular navigation invigorated; and, while it contributes, in different ways, to nourish and increase the general mass of the national navigation, it looks forward to the protection of a maritime strength, to which itself is unequally adapted. The East, in a like intercourse with the West, already finds, and in the progressive improvement of interior communications by land and water, will more and more find a valuable vent for the commodities which it brings from abroad, or manufactures at home. The West derives from the East supplies requisite to its growth and comfort, and, what is perhaps of still greater consequence, it must of necessity owe the secure enjoyment of indispensable outlets for its own productions to the weight, influence, and the future maritime strength of the Atlantic side of the Union, directed by an indissoluble community of interest as one nation. Any other tenure by which the West can hold this essential advantage, whether derived from its own separate strength, or from an apostate and unnatural connection with any foreign power, must be intrinsically precarious.

While, then, every part of our country thus feels an immediate and particular interest in union, all the parts combined cannot fail to find in the united mass of means and efforts greater strength, greater resource, proportionably greater security from external danger, a less frequent interruption of their peace by foreign nations; and, what is of inestimable value, they must derive from union an exemption from those broils and wars between themselves, which so frequently afflict neighboring countries not tied together by the same governments, which their own rival ships alone would be sufficient to produce, but which opposite foreign alliances, attachments, and intrigues would stimulate and embitter. Hence, likewise, they will avoid the necessity of those overgrown military establishments which, under any form of government, are inauspicious to liberty, and which are to be regarded as particularly hostile to republican liberty. In this sense it is that your union ought to be considered as a main prop of your liberty, and that the love of the one ought to endear to you the preservation of the other.

These considerations speak a persuasive language to every reflecting and virtuous mind, and exhibit the continuance of the Union as a primary object of patriotic desire. Is there a doubt whether a common government can embrace so large a sphere? Let experience solve it. To listen to mere speculation in such a case were criminal. We are authorized to hope that a proper organization of the whole with the auxiliary agency of governments for the respective subdivisions, will afford a happy issue to the experiment. It is well worth a fair and full experiment. With such powerful and obvious motives to union, affecting all parts of our country, while experience shall not have demonstrated its impracticability, there will always be reason to distrust the patriotism of those who in any quarter may endeavor to weaken its bands.

In contemplating the causes which may disturb our Union, it occurs as matter of serious concern that any ground should have been furnished for characterizing parties by geographical discriminations, Northern and Southern, Atlantic and Western; whence designing men may endeavor to excite a belief that there is a real difference of local interests and views. One of the expedients of party to acquire influence within particular districts is to misrepresent the opinions and aims of other districts. You cannot shield yourselves too much against the jealousies and heartburnings which spring from these misrepresentations; they tend to render alien to each other those who ought to be bound together by fraternal affection. The inhabitants of our Western country have lately had a useful lesson on this head; they have seen, in the negotiation by the Executive, and in the unanimous ratification by the Senate, of the treaty with Spain, and in the universal satisfaction at that event, throughout the United States, a decisive proof how unfounded were the suspicions propagated among them of a policy in the General Government and in the Atlantic States unfriendly to their interests in regard to the Mississippi; they have been witnesses to the formation of two treaties, that with Great Britain, and that with Spain, which secure to them everything they could desire, in respect to our foreign relations, towards confirming their prosperity. Will it not be their wisdom to rely for the preservation of these advantages on the Union by which they were procured ? Will they not henceforth be deaf to those advisers, if such there are, who would sever them from their brethren and connect them with aliens?

To the efficacy and permanency of your Union, a government for the whole is indispensable. No alliance, however strict, between the parts can be an adequate substitute; they must inevitably experience the infractions and interruptions which all alliances in all times have experienced. Sensible of this momentous truth, you have improved upon your first essay, by the adoption of a constitution of government better calculated than your former for an intimate union, and for the efficacious management of your common concerns. This government, the offspring of our own choice, uninfluenced and unawed, adopted upon full investigation and mature deliberation, completely free in its principles, in the distribution of its powers, uniting security with energy, and containing within itself a provision for its own amendment, has a just claim to your confidence and your support. Respect for its authority, compliance with its laws, acquiescence in its measures, are duties enjoined by the fundamental maxims of true liberty. The basis of our political systems is the right of the people to make and to alter their constitutions of government. But the Constitution which at any time exists, until changed by an explicit and authentic act of the whole people, is sacredly obligatory upon all. The very idea of the power and the right of the people to establish government presupposes the duty of every individual to obey the established government.

All obstructions to the execution of the laws, all combinations and associations, under whatever plausible character, with the real design to direct, control, counteract, or awe the regular deliberation and action of the constituted authorities, are destructive of this fundamental principle, and of fatal tendency. They serve to organize faction, to give it an artificial and extraordinary force; to put, in the place of the delegated will of the nation the will of a party, often a small but artful and enterprising minority of the community; and, according to the alternate triumphs of different parties, to make the public administration the mirror of the ill-concerted and incongruous projects of faction, rather than the organ of consistent and wholesome plans digested by common counsils and modified by mutual interests.

However combinations or associations of the above description may now and then answer popular ends, they are likely, in the course of time and things, to become potent engines, by which cunning, ambitious, and unprincipled men will be enabled to subvert the power of the people and to usurp for themselves the reins of government, destroying afterwards the very engines which have lifted them to unjust dominion.

Towards the preservation of your government, and the permanency of your present happy state, it is requisite, not only that you steadily discountenance irregular oppositions to its acknowledged authority, but also that you resist with care the spirit of innovation upon its principles, however specious the pretexts. One method of assault may be to effect, in the forms of the Constitution, alterations which will impair the energy of the system, and thus to undermine what cannot be directly overthrown. In all the changes to which you may be invited, remember that time and habit are at least as necessary to fix the true character of governments as of other human institutions; that experience is the surest standard by which to test the real tendency of the existing constitution of a country; that facility in changes, upon the credit of mere hypothesis and opinion, exposes to perpetual change, from the endless variety of hypothesis and opinion; and remember, especially, that for the efficient management of your common interests, in a country so extensive as ours, a government of as much vigor as is consistent with the perfect security of liberty is indispensable. Liberty itself will find in such a government, with powers properly distributed and adjusted, its surest guardian. It is, indeed, little else than a name, where the government is too feeble to withstand the enterprises of faction, to confine each member of the society within the limits prescribed by the laws, and to maintain all in the secure and tranquil enjoyment of the rights of person and property.

I have already intimated to you the danger of parties in the State, with particular reference to the founding of them on geographical discriminations. Let me now take a more comprehensive view, and warn you in the most solemn manner against the baneful effects of the spirit of party generally.

This spirit, unfortunately, is inseparable from our nature, having its root in the strongest passions of the human mind. It exists under different shapes in all governments, more or less stifled, controlled, or repressed; but, in those of the popular form, it is seen in its greatest rankness, and is truly their worst enemy.

The alternate domination of one faction over another, sharpened by the spirit of revenge, natural to party dissension, which in different ages and countries has perpetrated the most horrid enormities, is itself a frightful despotism. But this leads at length to a more formal and permanent despotism. The disorders and miseries which result gradually incline the minds of men to seek security and repose in the absolute power of an individual; and sooner or later the chief of some prevailing faction, more able or more fortunate than his competitors, turns this disposition to the purposes of his own elevation, on the ruins of public liberty.

Without looking forward to an extremity of this kind (which nevertheless ought not to be entirely out of sight), the common and continual mischiefs of the spirit of party are sufficient to make it the interest and duty of a wise people to discourage and restrain it.

It serves always to distract the public councils and enfeeble the public administration. It agitates the community with ill-founded jealousies and false alarms, kindles the animosity of one part against another, foments occasionally riot and insurrection. It opens the door to foreign influence and corruption, which finds a facilitated access to the government itself through the channels of party passions. Thus the policy and the will of one country are subjected to the policy and will of another.

There is an opinion that parties in free countries are useful checks upon the administration of the government and serve to keep alive the spirit of liberty. This within certain limits is probably true; and in governments of a monarchical cast, patriotism may look with indulgence, if not with favor, upon the spirit of party. But in those of the popular character, in governments purely elective, it is a spirit not to be encouraged. From their natural tendency, it is certain there will always be enough of that spirit for every salutary purpose. And there being constant danger of excess, the effort ought to be by force of public opinion, to mitigate and assuage it. A fire not to be quenched, it demands a uniform vigilance to prevent its bursting into a flame, lest, instead of warming, it should consume.

It is important, likewise, that the habits of thinking in a free country should inspire caution in those entrusted with its administration, to confine themselves within their respective constitutional spheres, avoiding in the exercise of the powers of one department to encroach upon another. The spirit of encroachment tends to consolidate the powers of all the departments in one, and thus to create, whatever the form of government, a real despotism. A just estimate of that love of power, and proneness to abuse it, which predominates in the human heart, is sufficient to satisfy us of the truth of this position. The necessity of reciprocal checks in the exercise of political power, by dividing and distributing it into different depositaries, and consti- tuting each the guardian of the public weal against invasions by the others, has been evinced by experiments ancient and modern; some of them in our country and under our own eyes. To preserve them must be as necessary as to institute them. If, in the opinion of the people, the distribution or modification of the constitutional powers be in any particular wrong, let it be corrected by an amendment in the way which the Constitution designates. But let there be no change by usurpation; for though this, in one instance, may be the instrument of good, it is the customary weapon by which free governments are destroyed. The precedent must always greatly overbalance in permanent evil any partial or transient benefit, which the use can at any time yield.

Of all the dispositions and habits which lead to political prosperity, religion and morality are indispensable supports. In vain would that man claim the tribute of patriotism, who should labor to subvert these great pillars of human happiness, these firmest props of the duties of men and citizens. The mere politician, equally with the pious man, ought to respect and to cherish them. A volume could not trace all their connections with private and public felicity. Let it simply be asked: Where is the security for property, for reputation, for life, if the sense of religious obligation desert the oaths which are the instruments of investigation in courts of justice? And let us with caution indulge the supposition that morality can be maintained without reli- gion. Whatever may be conceded to the influence of refined education on minds of peculiar structure, reason and experience both forbid us to expect that national morality can prevail in exclusion of religious principle.

It is substantially true that virtue or morality is a necessary spring of popular gov- ernment. The rule, indeed, extends with more or less force to every species of free government. Who that is a sincere friend to it can look with indifference upon attempts to shake the foundation of the fabric?

Promote then, as an object of primary importance, institutions for the general diffusion of knowledge. In proportion as the structure of a government gives force to public opinion, it is essential that public opinion should be enlightened.

As a very important source of strength and security, cherish public credit. One method of preserving it is to use it as sparingly as possible, avoiding occasions of expense by cultivating peace, but remembering also that timely disbursements to prepare for danger frequently prevent much greater disbursements to repel it, avoiding likewise the accumulation of debt, not only by shunning occasions of expense, but by vigorous exertion in time of peace to discharge the debts which unavoidable wars may have occasioned, not ungenerously throwing upon posterity the burden which we ourselves ought to bear. The execution of these maxims belongs to your representatives, but it is necessary that public opinion should co-operate. To facilitate to them the performance of their duty, it is essential that you should practically bear in mind that towards the payment of debts there must be revenue; that to have revenue there must be taxes; that no taxes can be devised which are not more or less inconvenient and unpleasant; that the intrinsic embarrassment, inseparable from the selection of the proper objects (which is always a choice of difficulties), ought to be a decisive motive for a candid construction of the conduct of the government in making it, and for a spirit of acquiescence in the measures for obtaining revenue, which the public exigencies may at any time dictate.

Observe good faith and justice towards all nations; cultivate peace and harmony with all. Religion and morality enjoin this conduct; and can it be, that good policy does not equally enjoin it. It will be worthy of a free, enlightened, and at no distant period, a great nation, to give to mankind the magnanimous and too novel example of a people always guided by an exalted justice and benevolence. Who can doubt that, in the course of time and things, the fruits of such a plan would richly repay any temporary advantages which might be lost by a steady adherence to it? Can it be that Providence has not connected the permanent felicity of a nation with its virtue? The experiment, at least, is recommended by every sentiment which ennobles human nature. Alas! is it rendered impossible by its vices?

In the execution of such a plan, nothing is more essential than that permanent, inveterate antipathies against particular nations, and passionate attachments for others, should be excluded; and that, in place of them, just and amicable feelings towards all should be cultivated. The nation which indulges towards another a habitual hatred or a habitual fondness is in some degree a slave. It is a slave to its animosity or to its affection, either of which is sufficient to lead it astray from its duty and its interest. Antipathy in one nation against another disposes each more readily to offer insult and injury, to lay hold of slight causes of umbrage, and to be haughty and intractable, when accidental or trifling occasions of dispute occur. Hence, frequent collisions, obstinate, envenomed, and bloody contests. The nation, prompted by ill-will and resentment, sometimes impels to war the government, contrary to the best calculations of policy. The government sometimes participates in the national propensity, and adopts through passion what reason would reject; at other times it makes the animosity of the nation subservient to projects of hostility instigated by pride, ambition, and other sinister and pernicious motives. The peace often, sometimes perhaps the liberty, of nations, has been the victim.

So likewise, a passionate attachment of one nation for another produces a variety of evils. Sympathy for the favorite nation, facilitating the illusion of an imaginary common interest in cases where no real common interest exists, and infusing into one the enmities of the other, betrays the former into a participation in the quarrels and wars of the latter without adequate inducement or justification. It leads also to concessions to the favorite nation of privileges denied to others which is apt doubly to injure the nation making the concessions; by unnecessarily parting with what ought to have been retained, and by exciting jealousy, ill-will, and a disposition to retaliate, in the parties from whom equal privileges are withheld. And it gives to ambitious, corrupted, or deluded citizens (who devote themselves to the favorite nation), facility to betray or sacrifice the interests of their own country, without odium, sometimes even with popularity; gilding, with the appearances of a virtuous sense of obligation, a commendable deference for public opinion, or a laudable zeal for public good, the base or foolish compliances of ambition, corruption, or infatuation.

As avenues to foreign influence in innumerable ways, such attachments are particularly alarming to the truly enlightened and independent patriot. How many opportunities do they afford to tamper with domestic factions, to practice the arts of seduction, to mislead public opinion, to influence or awe the public councils 7 Such an attachment of a small or weak towards a great and powerful nation dooms the former to be the satellite of the latter.

Against the insidious wiles of foreign influence (I conjure you to believe me, fellow-citizens) the jealousy of a free people ought to be constantly awake, since history and experience prove that foreign influence is one of the most baneful foes of republican government. But that jealousy to be useful must be impartial; else it becomes the instrument of the very influence to be avoided, instead of a defense against it. Excessive partiality for one foreign nation and excessive dislike of another cause those whom they actuate to see danger only on one side, and serve to veil and even second the arts of influence on the other. Real patriots who may resist the intrigues of the favorite are liable to become suspected and odious, while its tools and dupes usurp the applause and confidence of the people, to surrender their interests.

The great rule of conduct for us in regard to foreign nations is in extending our commercial relations, to have with them as little political connection as possible. So far as we have already formed engagements, let them be fulfilled with perfect good faith. Here let us stop. Europe has a set of primary interests which to us have none; or a very remote relation. Hence she must be engaged in frequent controversies, the causes of which are essentially foreign to our concerns. Hence, therefore, it must be unwise in us to implicate ourselves by artificial ties in the ordinary vicissitudes of her politics, or the ordinary combinations and collisions of her friendships or enmities.

Our detached and distant situation invites and enables us to pursue a different course. If we remain one people under an efficient government. the period is not far off when we may defy material injury from external annoyance; when we may take such an attitude as will cause the neutrality we may at any time resolve upon to be scrupulously respected; when belligerent nations, under the impossibility of making acquisitions upon us, will not lightly hazard the giving us provocation; when we may choose peace or war, as our interest, guided by justice, shall counsel.

Why forego the advantages of so peculiar a situation? Why quit our own to stand upon foreign ground? Why, by interweaving our destiny with that of any part of Europe, entangle our peace and prosperity in the toils of European ambition, rivalship, interest, humor or caprice?

It is our true policy to steer clear of permanent alliances with any portion of the foreign world; so far, I mean, as we are now at liberty to do it; for let me not be understood as capable of patronizing infidelity to existing engagements. I hold the maxim no less applicable to public than to private affairs, that honesty is always the best policy. I repeat it, therefore, let those engagements be observed in their genuine sense. But, in my opinion, it is unnecessary and would be unwise to extend them.

Taking care always to keep ourselves by suitable establishments on a respectable defensive posture, we may safely trust to temporary alliances for extraordinary emergencies.

Harmony, liberal intercourse with all nations, are recommended by policy, humanity, and interest. But even our commercial policy should hold an equal and impartial hand; neither seeking nor granting exclusive favors or preferences; consulting the natural course of things; diffusing and diversifying by gentle means the streams of commerce, but forcing nothing; establishing (with powers so disposed, in order to give trade a stable course, to define the rights of our merchants, and to enable the government to support them) conventional rules of intercourse, the best that present circumstances and mutual opinion will permit, but temporary, and liable to be from time to time abandoned or varied, as experience and circumstances shall dictate; constantly keeping in view that it is folly in one nation to look for disinterested favors from another; that it must pay with a portion of its independence for whatever it may accept under that character; that, by such acceptance, it may place itself in the condition of having given equivalents for nominal favors, and yet of being reproached with ingratitude for not giving more. There can be no greater error than to expect or calculate upon real favors from nation to nation. It is an illusion, which experience must cure, which a just pride ought to discard.

In offering to you, my countrymen, these counsels of an old and affectionate friend, I dare not hope they will make the strong and lasting impression I could wish; that they will control the usual current of the passions, or prevent our nation from running the course which has hitherto marked the destiny of nations. But, if I may even flatter myself that they may be productive of some partial benefit, some occasional good; that they may now and then recur to moderate the fury of party spirit, to warn against the mischiefs of foreign intrigue, to guard against the impostures of pretended patriotism; this hope will be a full recompense for the solicitude for your welfare, by which they have been dictated.

How far in the discharge of my official duties I have been guided by the principles which have been delineated, the public records and other evidences of my conduct must witness to you and to the world. To myself, the assurance of my own conscience is, that I have at least believed myself to be guided by them.

In relation to the still subsisting war in Europe, my proclamation of the twenty-second of April, 1793, is the index of my plan. Sanctioned by your approving voice, and by that of your representatives in both houses of Congress, the spirit of that measure has continually governed me, uninfluenced by any attempts to deter or divert me from it.

After deliberate examination, with the aid of the best lights I could obtain, I was well satisfied that our country, under all the circumstances of the case, had a right to take, and was bound in duty and interest to take, a neutral position. Having taken it, I determined, as far as should depend upon me, to maintain it, with moderation, perseverance, and firmness.

The considerations which respect the right to hold this conduct, it is not necessary on this occasion to detail. I will only observe that, according to my understanding of the matter, that right, so far from being denied by any of the belligerent powers, has been virtually admitted by all.

The duty of holding a neutral conduct may be inferred, without anything more, from the obligation which justice and humanity impose on every nation, in cases in which it is free to act, to maintain inviolate the relations of peace and amity towards other nations.

The inducements of interest for observing that conduct will best be referred to your own reflections and experience. With me a predominant motive has been to endeavor to gain time to our country to settle and mature its yet recent institutions, and to progress without interruption to that degree of strength and consistency which is necessary to give it, humanly speaking, the command of its own fortunes.

Though, in reviewing the incidents of my administration, I am unconscious of intentional error, I am nevertheless too sensible of my defects not to think it probable that I may have committed many errors. Whatever they may be, I fervently beseech the Almighty to avert or mitigate the evils to which they may tend. I shall also carry with me the hope that my country will never cease to view them with indulgence; and that, after forty five years of my life dedicated to its service with an upright zeal, the faults of incompetent abilities will be consigned to oblivion, as myself must soon be to the mansions of rest.

Relying on its kindness in this as in other things, and actuated by that fervent love towards it, which is so natural to a man who views in it the native soil of himself and his progenitors for several generations, I anticipate with pleasing expectation that retreat in which I promise myself to realize, without alloy, the sweet enjoyment of partaking, in the midst of my fellow-citizens, the benign influence of good laws under a free government, the ever-favorite object of my heart, and the happy reward, as I trust, of our mutual cares, labors, and dangers.

United States 19th September, 1796

Geo. Washington

40

The Kentucky Resolution, Kentucky General Assembly, 1799

In 1798, as war with France threatened, Congress passed a series of acts known as the Alien and Sedition Acts. While supposedly passed to protect the nation from subversion during any potential war, critics, led by Thomas Jefferson and James Madison, condemned the acts as unconstitutional infringements on the people's rights and charged that the laws were aimed at silencing opposition to the government and undermining immigrant voting strength which mostly favored

Jefferson and his supporters. Ten Americans, including a sitting congressman, were convicted under the Sedition Act of criticizing the administration of President John Adams. A number of resolutions were passed by state legislatures in protest of the acts. These included the Kentucky Resolution, in which Kentuckians blasted the Alien and Sedition Acts and declared that to stay silent on this matter was itself criminal. Adams and his Federalist Party were swept out of power in the 1800 election, and the Alien and Sedition Acts were ultimately repealed.

Resolutions in General Assembly

THE representatives of the good people of this commonwealth in general assembly convened, having maturely considered the answers of sundry states in the Union, to their resolutions passed at the last session, respecting certain unconstitutional laws of Congress, commonly called the alien and sedition laws, would be faithless indeed to themselves, and to those they represent, were they silently to acquiesce in principles and doctrines attempted to be maintained in all those answers, that of Virginia only excepted. To again enter the field of argument, and attempt more fully or forcibly to expose the unconstitutionality of those obnoxious laws, would, it is apprehended be as unnecessary as unavailing.

We cannot however but lament, that in the discussion of those interesting subjects, by sundry of the legislatures of our sister states, unfounded suggestions, and uncandid insinuations, derogatory of the true character and principles of the good people of this commonwealth, have been substituted in place of fair reasoning and sound argument. Our opinions of those alarming measures of the general government, together with our reasons for those opinions, were detailed with decency and with temper, and submitted to the discussion and judgment of our fellow citizens throughout the Union. Whether the decency and temper have been observed in the answers of most of those states who have denied or attempted to obviate the great truths contained in those resolutions, we have now only to submit to a candid world. Faithful to the true principles of the federal union, unconscious of any designs to disturb the harmony of that Union, and anxious only to escape the fangs of despotism, the good people of this commonwealth are regardless of censure or calumniation.

Least however the silence of this commonwealth should be construed into an acquiescence in the doctrines and principles advanced and attempted to be maintained by the said answers, or least those of our fellow citizens throughout the Union, who so widely differ from us on those important subjects, should be deluded by the expectation, that we shall be deterred from what we conceive our duty; or shrink from the principles contained in those resolutions: therefore.

RESOLVED, That this commonwealth considers the federal union, upon the terms and for the purposes specified in the late compact, as conducive to the liberty and happiness of the several states: That it does now unequivocally declare its attachment to the Union, and to that compact, agreeable to its obvious and real intention, and will be among the last to seek its dissolution: That if those who administer the general government be permitted to transgress the limits fixed by that compact, by a total disregard to the special delegations of power therein contained, annihilation of the state governments, and the erection upon their ruins, of a general consolidated government, will be the inevitable consequence: That the principle and construction contended for by sundry of the state legislatures, that the general government is the exclusive judge of the extent of the powers delegated to it, stop nothing short of despotism; since the discretion of those who administer the government, and not the constitution, would be the measure of their powers: That the several states who formed that instrument, being sovereign and independent, have the unquestionable right to judge of its infraction; and that a nullification, by those sovereignties, of all unauthorized acts done under colour of that instrument, is the rightful remedy: That this commonwealth does upon the most deliberate reconsideration declare, that the said alien and sedition laws, are in their opinion, palpable violations of the said constitution; and however cheerfully it may be disposed to surrender its opinion to a majority of its sister states in matters of ordinary or doubtful policy; yet, in momentous regulations like the present, which so vitally wound the best rights of the citizen, it would consider a silent acquiesecence as highly criminal: That although this commonwealth as a party to the federal compact; will bow to the laws of the Union, yet it does at the same time declare, that it will not now, nor ever hereafter, cease to oppose in a constitutional manner, every attempt from what quarter soever offered, to violate that compact:

AND FINALLY, in order that no pretexts or arguments may be drawn from a supposed acquiescence on the part of this commonwealth in the constitutionality of those laws, and be thereby used as precedents for similar future violations of federal compact; this commonwealth does now enter against them, its SOLEMN PROTEST.

Approved December 3rd, 1799.

THOMAS JEFFERSON **41**

First Inaugural Address, 1801

The election of 1800 saw the first transfer of power on the national level of one party to another, from the Federalist Party of John Adams to the Republican Party of Thomas Jefferson (which would later evolve into the modern Democratic Party). In his inaugural address of March 4, 1801, Jefferson sought to quell the bitter partisanship and emphasize the most important aspect of freedom: the right to disagree with the government or another party and still be considered a loyal citizen, an idea that Americans had fought for during the Revolutionary War.

Thomas Jefferson, *Life and Selected Writings of Thomas Jefferson*, 297–301.

Friends and Fellow-Citizens:

CALLED upon to undertake the duties of the first executive office of our country, I avail myself of the presence of that portion of my fellow-citizens which is here assembled to express my grateful thanks for the favor with which they have been pleased to look toward me, to declare a sincere consciousness that the task is above my talents, and that I approach it with those anxious and awful presentiments which the greatness of the charge and the weakness of my powers so justly inspire. A rising nation, spread over a wide and fruitful land, traversing all the seas with the rich productions of their industry, engaged in commerce with nations who feel power and forget right, advancing rapidly to destinies beyond the reach of mortal eye—when I contemplate these transcendent objects, and see the honor, the happiness, and the hopes of this beloved country committed to the issue, and the auspices of this day, I shrink from the contemplation, and humble myself before the magnitude of the undertaking. Utterly, indeed, should I despair did not the presence of many whom I here see remind me that in the other high authorities provided by our Constitution I shall find resources of wisdom, of virtue, and of zeal on which to rely under all difficulties. To you, then, gentlemen, who are charged with the sovereign functions of legislation, and to those associated with you, I look with encouragement for that guidance and support which may enable us to steer with safety the vessel in which we are all embarked amidst the conflicting elements of a troubled world.

During the contest of opinion through which we have passed the animation of discussions and of exertions has sometimes worn an aspect which might impose on strangers unused to think freely and to speak and to write what they think; but this being now decided by the voice of the nation, announced according to the rules of the Constitution, all will, of course, arrange themselves under the will of the law, and unite in common efforts for the common good. All, too, will bear in mind this sacred principle, that though the will of the majority is in all cases to prevail, that will to be rightful must be reasonable; that the minority possess their equal rights, which equal law must protect, and to violate would be oppression. Let us, then, fellow-citizens, unite with one heart and one mind. Let us restore to social intercourse that harmony and affection without which liberty and even life itself are but dreary things. And let us reflect that, having banished from our land that religious intolerance under which mankind so long bled and suffered, we have yet gained little if we countenance a political intolerance as despotic, as wicked, and capable of as bitter and bloody persecutions. During the throes and convulsions of the ancient world, during the agonizing spasms of infuriated man, seeking through blood and slaughter his long-lost liberty, it was not wonderful that the agitation of the billows should reach even this distant and peaceful shore; that this should be more felt and feared by some and less by others, and should divide opinions as to measures of safety. But every difference of opinion is not a difference of principle. We have called by different names brethren of the same principle. We are all Republicans, we are all Federalists. If there be any among us who would wish to dissolve this Union or to change its republican form, let them stand undisturbed as monuments of the safety with which error of opinion may be tolerated where reason is left free to combat it. I know, indeed, that some honest men fear that a republican government can not be strong, that this Government is not strong enough; but would the honest patriot, in the full tide of successful experiment, abandon a government which has so far kept us free and firm on the theoretic and visionary fear that this Government, the world's best hope, may by possibility want energy to preserve itself? I trust not. I believe this, on the contrary, the strongest Government on earth. I believe it the only one where every man, at the call of the law, would fly to the standard of the law, and would meet invasions of the public order as his own personal concern. Sometimes it is said that man can not be trusted with the government of himself. Can he, then, be trusted with the government of others? Or have we found angels in the forms of kings to govern him? Let history answer this question.

Let us, then, with courage and confidence pursue our own Federal and Republican principles, our attachment to union and representative government. Kindly separated by nature and a wide ocean from the exterminating havoc of one quarter of the globe; too high-minded to endure the degradations of the others; possessing a chosen country, with room enough for our descendants to the thousandth and thousandth generation; entertaining a due sense of our equal right to the use of our own faculties, to the acquisitions of our own industry, to honor and confidence from our fellow-citizens, resulting not from birth, but from our actions and their sense of them; enlightened by a benign religion, professed, indeed, and practiced in various forms, yet all of them inculcating honesty, truth, temperance, gratitude, and the love of man; acknowledging and adoring an overruling Providence, which by all its dispensations proves that it delights in the happiness of man here and his greater happiness hereafter—with all these blessings, what more is necessary to make us a happy and a prosperous people? Still one thing more, fellow-citizens—a wise and frugal Government, which shall restrain men from injuring one another, shall leave them otherwise free to regulate their own pursuits of industry and improvement, and shall not take from the mouth of labor the bread it has earned. This is the sum of good government, and this is necessary to close the circle of our felicities.

About to enter, fellow-citizens, on the exercise of duties which comprehend everything dear and valuable to you, it is proper you should understand what I deem the essential principles of our Government, and consequently those which ought to shape its Administration. I will compress them within the narrowest compass they will bear, stating the general principle, but not all its limitations. Equal and exact justice to all men, of whatever state or persuasion, religious or political; peace, commerce, and honest friendship with all nations, entangling alliances with none; the support of the State governments in all their rights, as the most competent administrations for our domestic concerns and the surest bulwarks against antirepublican tendencies; the preservation of the General Government in its whole constitutional vigor, as the sheet anchor of our peace at home and safety abroad; a jealous care of the right of election by the people—a mild and safe corrective of abuses which are lopped by the sword of revolution where peaceable remedies are unprovided; absolute acquiescence in the decisions of the majority, the vital principle of republics, from which is no appeal but to force, the vital principle and immediate parent of despotism; a well disciplined militia, our best reliance in peace and for the first moments of war, till regulars may relieve them; the supremacy of the civil over the military authority; economy in the public expense, that labor may be lightly burthened; the honest payment of our debts and sacred preservation of the public faith; encouragement of agriculture, and of commerce as its handmaid; the diffusion of information and arraignment of all abuses at the bar of the public reason; freedom of religion; freedom of the press, and freedom of person under the protection of the habeas corpus, and trial by juries impartially selected. These principles form the bright constellation which has gone before us and guided our steps through an age of revolution and reformation. The wisdom of our sages and blood of our heroes have been devoted to their attainment. They should be the creed of our political faith, the text of civic instruction, the touchstone by which to try the services of those we trust; and should we wander from them in moments of error or of alarm, let us hasten to retrace our steps and to regain the road which alone leads to peace, liberty, and safety.

I repair, then, fellow-citizens, to the post you have assigned me. With experience enough in subordinate offices to have seen the difficulties of this the greatest of all, I have learnt to expect that it will rarely fall to the lot of imperfect man to retire from this station with the reputation and the favor which bring him into it. Without pretensions to that high confidence you reposed in our first and greatest revolutionary character, whose preeminent services had entitled him to the first place in his country's love and destined for him the fairest page in the volume of faithful history, I ask so much confidence only as may give firmness and effect to the legal administration of your affairs. I shall often go wrong through defect of judgment. When right, I shall often be thought wrong by those whose positions will not command a view of the whole ground. I ask your indulgence for my own errors, which will never be intentional, and your support against the errors of others, who may condemn what they would not if seen in all its parts. The approbation implied by your suffrage is a great consolation to me for the past, and my future solicitude will be to retain the good opinion of those who have bestowed it in advance, to conciliate that of others by doing them all the good in my power, and to be instrumental to the happiness and freedom of all.

Relying, then, on the patronage of your good will, I advance with obedience to the work, ready to retire from it whenever you become sensible how much better choice it is in your power to make. And may that Infinite Power which rules the destinies of the universe lead our councils to what is best, and give them a favorable issue for your peace and prosperity.

THOMAS JEFFERSON **42**

Letter to the Danbury Baptist Association, 1802

This famous letter to Nehemiah Dodge and the Danbury Baptist Association written on January 1, 1802, has become famous for Jefferson's description of what he saw as the proper role between church and state. He describes the first amendment as acting as a "wall of separation" between the two, allowing individuals to practice their faiths as they see fit, unmolested by any government

Thomas Jefferson, *Life and Selected Writings of Thomas Jefferson*, 307.

interference or directives or prohibitions. The phrase "wall of separation" in the years since evolved into the phrase "separation of church and state." This short letter became an important component of the debate over church-state issues as the states still struggled with the issue of taxpayer support of churches and state-sanctioned churches.

To: Messrs. Nehemiah Dodge and Others, a Committee of the Danbury Baptist Association, in the State of Connecticut

Gentlemen:

The affectionate sentiments of esteem and approbation which you are so good as to express towards me, on behalf of the Danbury Baptist Association, give me the highest satisfaction. My duties dictate a faithful and zealous pursuit of the interests of my constituents, and in proportion as they are persuaded of my fidelity to those duties, the discharge of them becomes more and more pleasing.

Believing with you that religion is a matter which lies solely between man and his God, that he owes account to none other for his faith or his worship, that the legislative powers of government reach actions only, and not opinions, I contemplate with sovereign reverence that act of the whole American people which declared that their legislature should "make no law respecting an establishment of religion, or prohibiting the free exercise thereof," thus building a wall of separation between church and State. Adhering to this expression of the supreme will of the nation in behalf of the rights of conscience, I shall see with sincere satisfaction the progress of those sentiments which tend to restore to man all his natural rights, convinced he has no natural right in opposition to his social duties.

I reciprocate your kind prayers for the protection and blessing of the common Father and Creator of man, and tender you for yourselves and your religious association, assurances of my high respect and esteem.

Thomas Jefferson

DANIEL WEBSTER **43**

The Bunker Hill Speech, 1825

Daniel Webster became one of the most renowned orators of the early nineteenth century. This speech, The Bunker Hill Speech, delivered on June 17, 1825, was delivered as part of the dedication of a monument to the Americans who fought at the Battle of Bunker Hill fifty years earlier. In this address, Webster lauds the heroism and patriotism of the veterans present. He goes further to discuss the meaning of American freedom. Free men had a duty to preserve that freedom

http://www.dartmouth.edu/~dwebster/speeches/bunker-hill.html

through hard work and dedication to the interests of the nation. Defending free government from tyrannical powers abroad was a concern for a very young and still vulnerable republic. Because Americans had demonstrated this determination to defend freedom, Webster observed, free government had become an inseparable part of the American character.

This uncounted multitude before me and around me proves the feeling which the occasion has excited. These thousands of human faces, glowing with sympathy and joy, and from the impulses of a common gratitude turned reverently to heaven in this spacious temple of the firmament, proclaim that the day, the place, and the purpose of our assembling have made a deep impression on our hearts.

If, indeed, there be any thing in local association fit to affect the mind of man, we need not strive to repress the emotions which agitate us here. We are among the sepulchres of our fathers. We are on ground, distinguished, by their valor, their constancy, and the shedding of their blood. We are here, not to fix an uncertain date in our annals, nor to draw into notice an obscure and unknown spot. If our humble purpose had never been conceived, if we ourselves had never been born, the 17th of June, 1775 would have been a day on which all subsequent history would have poured its light, and the eminence where we stand a point of attraction to the eyes of successive generations. But we are Americans. We live in what may be called the early age of this great continent; and we know that our posterity, through all time, are here to enjoy and suffer the allotments of humanity. We see before us a probably train of great events; we know that our own fortunes have been happily cast; and it is natural, therefore, that we should be moved by the contemplation of occurrences which have guided our destiny before many of us were born, and settled the condition in which we should pass that portion of our existence which God allows to men on earth.

We do not read even of the discovery of this continent, without feeling something of a personal interest in the event; without being reminded how much it has affected our own fortunes and our own existence. It would be still more unnatural for us, therefore, than for others. to contemplate with unaffected minds that interesting, I may say that most touching and pathetic scene, when the great discovery of America stood on the deck of his shattered bark, the shades of night falling on the sea, yet no man sleeping; tossed on the billows of an unknown ocean, yet the stronger billows of alternate hope and despair tossing his own troubled thoughts; extending forward his harassed frame, straining westward his anxious and eager eyes, till Heaven at last granted him a moment of rapture and ecstacy, in blessing his vision with the sight of the unknown world.

Nearer to our times, more closely connected with our fates, and therfore still more interesting to our feelings and affections, is the settlement of our own country by colonists from England. We cherish every memorial of these worthy ancestors; we celebrate their patience and fortitude; we admire their daring enterprise; we teach our children to venerate their piety; and we are justly proud of being descended from men who have set the world an example of founding civil institutions on the great and united principles of human freedom and human knowledge. To us, their children, the story of their labors and sufferings can never be without its interest. We shall not stand unmoved on the shores of Plymouth, while the sea continues to wash it; nor will our brethren in another early and ancient Colony forget the place of its first establishment, till their river shall cease to flow by it. No vigor of youth, no maturity of manhood, will lead the nation to forget the spots where its infancy was cradled and defended.

But the great event in the history of the continent, which we are now met here to commemorate, that prodigy of modern times, at once the wonder and the blessing of the world, is the American Revolution. In a day of extraordinary prosperity and happiness, of high national honor, distinction, and power, we are brought together, in this place, by our love of country, by our admiration of exalted character, by our gratitude for signal services and patriotic devotion...

VENERABLE MEN! you have come down to us from a former generation. Heaven has bounteously lengthened out your lives, that you might behold this joyous day. You are now where you stood fifty years ago, this very hour, with your brothers and your neighbors, shoulder to shoulder, in the strife for your country. Behold, how altered! The same heavens are indeed over your heads; the same oceans roll at your feet; but all else how changed! You hear now no roar of hostile cannon, you see no mixed volumes of smoke and flame rising from burning Charlestown. The ground strowed with the dead and the dying; the impetuous charge; the steady and successful repulse; the loud call to resistance; a thousand bosoms freely and fearlessly bared in an instant to whatever of terror there may be in war and death;—all these you have witnessed, but you witness them no more. All is peace. The heights of yonder metropolis, its towers and roofs, which you then saw filled with wives and children and countrymen in distress and terror, and looking with unutterable emotions for the issue of the combat, have presented you to-day with the sight of its whole happy population, come out to welcome and greet you with a universal jubilee. Yonder proud ships, by a felicity of position appropriately lying at the foot of this mount, and seemingly fondly to cling around it, are not means of annoyance to you, but your country's own means of distinction and defence. All is peace; and God has granted you this sight of your country's happiness, ere you slumber in the grave. He has allowed you to behold and to partake the reward of your patriotic toils; and he has allowed us, your sons and countrymen, to meet you here, and in the name of the present generation, in the name of your country, in the name of liberty, to thank you!...

The great wheel of political revolution began to move in America. Here its rotation was guarded, regular, and safe. Transferred to the other continent, from unfortunate but natural causes, it received an irregular and violent impulse; it whirled along with a fearful celerity; till at length, like the chariot-wheels in the races of antiquity, it took fire from the rapidity of its own motion, and blazed onward, spreading conflagration and terror around.

We learn from the result of this experiment how fortunate was our own condition, and how admirably the character of our people was calculated for setting the great example of popular governments. The possession of power did not turn the heads of the American people, for they had long been in the habit of exercising a great degree of self control. Although the paramount authority of the parent state existed over them, yet a large field of legislation had always been open to our Colonial assemblies. They were accustomed to representative bodies and the forms of free government; they understood the doctrine of the division of power among different branches, and the necessity of checks on each. The character of our countrymen, moreover, was sober, moral, and religious; and there was, little in the change to shock their feelings of justice and humanity, or even to disturb an honest prejudice.

We had no domestic throne to overturn, no privileged orders to cast down, no violent changes of property to encounter. In the American Revolution, no man sought or wished for more than to defend and enjoy his own. None hoped for plunder or for spoil. Rapacity was unknown to it; the axe was not among the instruments of its accomplishment; and we all know that it could not have lived a single day under any well-founded imputation of possessing a tendency adverse to the Christian religion.

It need not surprise us, that, under circumstances less auspicious, political revolutions elsewhere, even when well intended, have terminated differently. It is, indeed, a great achievement, it is the masterwork of the world, to establish a government entirely popular on lasting foundations; nor is it easy, indeed to introduce the popular principle at all into governments to which it has been altogether a stranger. It cannot be doubted, however, that Europe has come out of the contest, in which she has been so long engaged, with greatly superior knowledge, and, in many respects, a highly improved condition. Whatever benefit has been acquired is likely to be retained, for it consists mainly in the acquisition of more enlightened ideas. And although kingdoms and provinces may be wrested from the hands that hold them, in the same manner they were obtained; although ordinary and vulgar power may, in human affairs, be lost as it has been won; yet it is the glorious prerogative of the empire of knowledge, that what it gains it never loses. On the contrary, it increases by the multiple of its own power; all its ends become means; all its attainments, helps to new conquests. Its whole abundant harvest is but so much seed of wheat, and nothing has limited, and nothing can limit, the amount of ultimate product.

Under the influence of this rapidly increasing knowledge, the people have begun, in all forms of government, to think, and to reason, on affairs of state. Regarding government as an institution for the public good, they demand a knowledge of its operations, and a participation in its exercise. A call for the representative system, wherever it is not enjoyed, and where there is already intelligence enough to estimate its value, is perseveringly made. Where men may speak out, they demand it; where the bayonet is at their throates, they pray for it...

And, now, let us indulge an honest exultation in the conviction of the benefit which the example of our country has produced, and is likely to produce, on human freedom and human happiness. Let us endeavor to comprehend in all its magnitude, and to feel in all its importance, the part assigned to us in the great drama of human affairs. We are placed at the head of the system of representative and popular governments. Thus far our example shows that such governments are compatible, not only with respectability and power, but with repose, with peace, with security of personal rights, with good laws, and a just administration.

We are not propagandists. Wherever other systems are preferred, either as being thought better in themselves, or as better suited to existing conditions, we leave the preference to be enjoyed. Our history hitherto proves, however, that the popular form is practicable, and that with wisddome and knowledge men may govern themselves; and the duty incumbent on us it, to preserve the consistency of this cheering world. If, in our case, the representative system ultimately fail, popular governments must be pronounced impossible. No combination of circumstances more favorable to the experiement can ever be expected to occur. The last hopes of mankind, therefore, rest with us; and if it should be proclaimed, that our example had become an argument against the experiment, the knell of popular liberty would be sounded throughout the earth.

These are excitements to duty; but they are not suggestions of doubt. Our history and our condition, all that is gone before us and all that surrounds us, authorize the belief, that popular governments, though subject to occasional variations, in form perhaps not always for the better, may yet, in their general character, be as durable and permanent as other systems. We know, indeed, that in our country any other is impossible. The *principle* of free government adheres to American soil. It is bedded in it, immovable as its mountains.

And let the sacred obligation which have devolved on this generation, and on us, sink deep into our hearts. Those who established our liberty and our government are daily dropping from among us. The great trust now descends to new hands. Let us apply ourselves to that which is presented to us, as our appropriate object. We can win no laurels in a war for independence. Earlier and worthier hands have gathered them all. Nor are there places for us by the side of Solon [of fifth-century BC Athens], and Alfred [the Great, ninth century king of England], and other founders of states. Our fathers have filled them. But there remains to us a great duty of defence and preservation, and there is opened to us, also, a noble pursuit, to which the spirit of the times strongly invites us. Our proper business is improvement. Let our age be the age of improvement. In a day of peace, let us advance the arts of peace and the works of peace. Let us develop the resources of our land, call forth its powers, build up its institutions, promote all its great interests, and see whether we also, in our day and generation, may not perform something worthy to be remembered. Let us cultivate a true spirit of union and harmony. In pursuing the great objects which our condition points out to us, let us act under a settled conviction, and an habitual feeling, that these twenty-four States are one country. Let our conception be enlarged to the circle of our duties. Let us extend our ideas over the whole of the vast field in which we are called to act. Let our object be, OUR COUNTRY, OUR WHOLE COUNTRY, AND NOTHING BUT OUR COUNTRY. And, by the blessing of God, may that country itself become a vast and splendid monument, not of oppression and terror, but of Wisdom, of Peace, and of Liberty, upon which the world may gaze with admiration for ever!!

44

Declaration of Sentiments, American Anti-Slavery Society, 1833

By 1833, the United States had already weathered a number of crises pitting the free states against the slave states. Abolitionists became increasingly furious at the power of slave interests and decided to organize to combat the institution. In

American Anti-Slavery Society, "Declaration of Sentiments," *Against Slavery: An Abolitionist Reader*, Mason Lawrence, ed. (New York: Putnam Penguin, 2000): 119–122.

1833, the American Anti-Slavery Society was formed for that purpose. By 1838, the society had 250,000 members. William Lloyd Garrison, whose fiery aboli-tionist newspaper, The Liberator, *won praise and scorn across the nation, led the society and the drafting of this declaration. The Declaration of Sentiments argued against slavery in moral, legal, and biblical terms. Lloyd and others argued that slavery was condemned by the Bible, at the same time that a number of southern preachers attempted to use the Bible to justify slavery. The American Anti-Slavery Society declared that the heart of who they were as Americans and as Christians demanded the end of slavery and, at the very least, the acknowl-edgement of the very humanity of the slaves.*

We have met together for the achievement of an enterprise, without which that of our fathers is incomplete; and which, for its magnitude, solemnity, and probable results upon the destiny of the world, as far transcends theirs as moral truth does physical force. In purity of motive, in earnestness of zeal, in decision of purpose, in intrepidity of action, in steadfastness of faith, in sincerity of spirit, we would not be inferior to them....

Their grievances, great as they were, were trifling in comparison with the wrongs and sufferings of those for whom we plead. Our fathers were never slaves—never bought and sold like cattle—never shut out from the light of knowledge and religion—never subjected to the lash of brutal taskmasters.

But those, for whose emancipation we are striving—constituting at the present time at least one-sixth part of our countrymen—are recognized by law, and treated by their fellow-beings, as brute beasts; are plundered daily of the fruits of their toil with-out redress; really enjoy no constitutional nor legal protection from licentious and murderous outrages upon their persons; and are ruthlessly torn asunder—the tender babe from the arms of its frantic mother—the heartbroken wife from her weeping husband—at the caprice or pleasure of irresponsible tyrants. For the crime of having a dark complexion, they suffer the pangs of hunger, the infliction of stripes, the ignominy of brutal servitude. They are kept in heathenish darkness by laws expressly enacted to make their instruction a criminal offence.

These are the prominent circumstances in the condition of more than two mil-lion people, the proof of which may be found in thousands of indisputable facts, and in the laws of the slave-holding States.

Hence we maintain—that, in view of the civil and religious privileges of this nation, the guilt of its oppression is unequalled by any other on the face of the earth; and, therefore, that it is bound to repent instantly, to undo the heavy burdens, and to let the oppressed go free...

It is piracy to buy or steal a native African, and subject him to servitude. Surely, the sin is as great to enslave an American as an African.

Therefore we believe and affirm—that there is no difference, in principle, between the African slave trade and American slavery:

That every American citizen, who detains a human being in involuntary bondage as his property, is, according to Scripture, (Ex. xxi, 16,) a manstealer.

That the slaves ought instantly to be set free, and brought under the protection of law:

That if they had lived from the time of Pharaoh down to the present period, and had been entailed through successive generations, their right to be free could never have been alienated, but their claims would have constantly risen in solemnity:

That all those laws which are now in force, admitting the right of slavery, are therefore, before God, utterly null and void; being an audacious usurpation of the Divine prerogative, a daring infringement on the law of nature, a base overthrow of the very foundations of the social compact, a complete extinction of all the relations, endearments and obligations of mankind, and a presumptuous transgression of all the holy commandments; and that therefore they ought instantly to be abrogated.

We further believe and affirm—that all persons of color, who possess the qualifications which are demanded of others, ought to be admitted forthwith to the enjoyment of the same privileges, and the exercise of the same prerogatives, as others; and that the paths of preferment, of wealth and of intelligence, should be opened as widely to them as to persons of a white complexion.

We maintain that no compensation should be given to the planters emancipating their slaves:

Because it would be a surrender of the great fundamental principle, that man cannot hold property in man:

Because slavery is a crime, and therefore is not an article to be sold:

Because the holders of slaves are not the just proprietors of what they claim; freeing the slave is not depriving them of property, but restoring it to its rightful owner; it is not wronging the master, but righting the slave—restoring him to himself:

Because immediate and general emancipation would only destroy nominal, not real property; it would not amputate a limb or break a bone of the slaves, but by infusing motives into their breasts, would make them doubly valuable to the masters as free laborers; and

Because, if compensation is to be given at all, it should be given to the outraged and guiltless slaves, and not to those who have plundered and abused them.

We regard as delusive, cruel and dangerous, any scheme of expatriation which pretends to aid, either directly or indirectly, in the emancipation of the slaves, or to be a substitute for the immediate and total abolition of slavery.

We fully and unanimously recognize the sovereignty of each State, to legislate exclusively on the subject of the slavery which is tolerated within its limits; we concede that Congress, under the present national compact, has no right to interfere with any of the slave States, in relation to this momentous subject:

But we maintain that Congress has a right, and is solemnly bound, to suppress the domestic slave trade between the several States, and to abolish slavery in those portions of our territory which the Constitution has placed under its exclusive jurisdiction.

We also maintain that there are, at the present time, the highest obligations resting upon the people of the free States to remove slavery by moral and political action, as prescribed in the Constitution of the United States. They are now living under a pledge of their tremendous physical force, to fasten the galling fetters of tyranny upon the limbs of millions in the Southern States; they are liable to be called at any moment to suppress a general insurrection of the slaves; they authorize the slave owner to vote for three-fifths of his slaves as property, and thus enable him to perpetuate his oppression; they support a standing army at the South for its protection; and they seize the slave, who has escaped into their territories, and send him back to be tortured by an enraged master or a brutal driver. This relation to slavery is criminal, and full of danger: It must be broken up.

These are our views and principles—these our designs and measures. With entire confidence in the overruling justice of God, we plant ourselves upon the Declaration of our Independence and the truths of Divine Revelation, as upon the Everlasting Rock.

WILLIAM ELLERY CHANNING **45**

Rights, 1835

William Ellery Channing became a popular Unitarian theologian in New England in the early years of the nineteenth century, writing on a wide variety of topics. His works influenced such later writers at Ralph Waldo Emerson and Henry Wadsworth Longfellow. This essay is the second chapter of Channing's abolitionist treatise, Slavery, *written in 1835, just as the abolitionist movement was starting to gain speed across the United States. In this reading, Channing defines what the rights of human beings are and what the proper role of government should be. He argues that everyone has right by virtue of their humanity, particularly the right to make their own decisions about their lives. Slavery, Channing argues, robs the individual of that liberty. And what is right— freedom—must be the supreme law of any nation. He sought to slowly end slavery through peaceful means, not with a sudden jolt of war as such abolitionists as William Lloyd Garrison and John Brown intoned. This became a popular work among abolitionists but did little to stop the growth of slavery in the American South in the years before the Civil War.*

I now proceed to the second division of the subject. I am to show, that man has sacred Rights, the gifts of God, and inseparable from human nature, which are violated by slavery. Some important principles, which belong to this head, were necessarily anticipated under the preceding; but they need a fuller exposition. The whole subject of Rights needs to be reconsidered. Speculations and reasonings about it have lately been given to the public, not only false, but dangerous to freedom, and there is a strong tendency to injurious views. Rights are made to depend on circumstances, so that pretences may easily be made or created for violating them successively, till none shall remain. Human rights have been represented as so modified and circumscribed by men's entrance into the social state, that only the shadows of them are left. They have been spoken of as absorbed in the public good; so that a man may be innocently enslaved, if the public good shall so require. To meet fully all these errors, for such

William Ellery Channing, "Rights," *Against Slavery: An Abolitionist Reader,* Mason Lawrence, ed. (New York: Putnam Penguin, 2000): 181–183; Channing, *The Works of William Ellery Channing,* 2nd ed. (Boston: James Munroe and Co., 1843): 31–50.

I hold them, a larger work than the present is required. The nature of man, his relations to the state, the limits of civil government, the elements of the public good, and the degree to which the individual must be surrendered to this good, these are the topics which the present subject involves. I cannot enter into them particularly, but shall lay down what seem to me the great and true principles in regard to them. I shall show, that man has rights from his very nature, not the gifts of society, but of God; that they are not surrendered on entering the social state; that they must not be taken away under the plea of public good; that the Individual is never to be sacrificed to the Community; that the idea of Rights is to prevail above all the interests of the state.

Man has rights by nature. The disposition of some to deride abstract rights, as if all rights were uncertain, mutable, and conceded by society, shows a lamentable ignorance of human nature. Whoever understands this must see in it an immovable foundation of rights. These are gifts of the Creator, bound up indissolubly with our moral constitution. In the order of things, they precede society, lie at its foundation, constitute man's capacity for it, and are the great objects of social institutions. The consciousness of rights is not a creation of human art, a conventional sentiment, but essential to and inseparable from the human soul.

Man's rights belong to him as a Moral Being, as capable of perceiving moral distinctions, as a subject of moral obligation. As soon as he becomes conscious of Duty, a kindred consciousness springs up, that he has a Right to do what the sense of duty enjoins, and that no foreign will or power can obstruct his moral action without crime. He feels, that the sense of duty was given to him as a Law, that it makes him responsible for himself, that to exercise, unfold, and obey it is the end of his being, and that he has a right to exercise and obey it without hindrance or opposition. A consciousness of dignity, however obscure, belongs also to this divine principle; and, though he may want words to do justice to his thoughts, he feels that he has that within him which makes him essentially equal to all around him.

The sense of duty is the fountain of human rights. In other words, the same inward principle, which teaches the former, bears witness to the latter. Duties and Rights must stand or fall together. It has been too common to oppose them to one another; but they are indissolubly joined together. That same inward principle, which teaches a man what he is bound to do to others, teaches equally, and at the same instant, what others are bound to do to him. That same voice, which forbids him to injure a single fellow-creature, forbids every fellow-creature to do him harm. His conscience, in revealing the moral law, does not reveal a law for himself only, but speaks as a Universal Legislator. He has an intuitive conviction, that the obligations of this divine code press on others as truly as on himself. That principle, which teaches him that he sustains the relation of brotherhood to all human beings, teaches him that this relation is reciprocal, that it gives indestructible claims, as well as imposes solemn duties, and that what he owes to the members of this vast family, they owe to him in return. Thus the moral nature involves rights. These enter into its very essence. They are taught by the very voice which enjoins duty. Accordingly there is no deeper principle in human nature, than the consciousness of rights. So profound, so ineradicable is this sentiment, that the oppressions of ages have nowhere wholly stifled it.

Having shown the foundation of human rights in human nature, it may be asked what they are. Perhaps they do not admit very accurate definition, any more than human duties; for the Spiritual cannot be weighed and measured like the Material. Perhaps a minute criticism may find fault with the most guarded exposition of them; but they may easily be stated in language which the unsophisticated mind will recognise as the truth. Volumes could not do justice to them; and yet, perhaps they may be comprehended in one sentence. They may all be comprised in the right, which belongs to every rational being, to exercise his powers for the promotion of his own and others' Happiness and Virtue. These are the great purposes of his existence. For these his powers were given, and to these he is bound to devote them. He is bound to make himself and others better and happier, according to his ability. His ability for this work is a sacred trust from God, the greatest of all trusts. He must answer for the waste or abuse of it. He consequently suffers an unspeakable wrong, when stripped of it by others, or forbidden to employ it for the ends for which it is given; when the powers, which God has given for such generous uses, are impaired or destroyed by others, or the means for their action and growth are forcibly withheld. As every human being is bound to employ his faculties for his own and others' good, there is an obligation on each to leave all free for the accomplishment of this end; and whoever respects this obligation, whoever uses his own, without invading others' powers, or obstructing others' duties, has a sacred, indefeasible right to be unassailed, unobstructed, unharmed by all with whom he may be connected. Here is the grand, all-comprehending right of human nature. Every man should revere it, should assert it for himself and for all, and should bear solemn testimony against every infraction of it, by whomsoever made or endured. Having considered the great fundamental right of human nature, particular rights may easily be deduced. Every man has a right to exercise and invigorate his intellect or the power of knowledge, for knowledge is the essential condition of successful effort for every good; and whoever obstructs or quenches the intellectual life in another, inflicts a grievous and irreparable wrong. Every man has a right to inquire into his duty, and to conform himself to what he learns of it. Every man has a right to use the means, given by God and sanctioned by virtue, for bettering his condition. He has a right to be respected according to his moral worth; a right to be regarded as a member of the community to which he belongs, and to be protected by impartial laws; and a right to be exempted from coercion, stripes, and punishment, as long as he respects the rights of others. He has a right to an equivalent for his labor. He has a right to sustain domestic relations, to discharge their duties, and to enjoy the happiness which flows from fidelity in these and other domestic relations. Such are a few of human rights; and if so, what a grievous wrong is slavery!

Perhaps nothing has done more to impair the sense of the reality and sacredness of human rights, and to sanction oppression, than loose ideas as to the change made in man's natural rights by his entrance into civil society. It is commonly said, that men part with a portion of these by becoming a community, a body politic; that government consists of powers surrendered by the individual; and it is said, "If certain rights and powers may be surrendered, why not others? why not all? what limit is to be set? The good of the community, to which a part is given up, may demand the whole; and in this good, all private rights are merged." This is the logic of despotism. We are grieved that it finds its way into republics, and that it sets down the great principles of freedom as abstractions and metaphysical theories, good enough for the cloister, but too refined for practical and real life.

Human rights, however, are not to be so reasoned away. They belong, as we have seen, to man as a moral being, and nothing can divest him of them but the destruction of his nature. They are not to be given up to society as a prey. On the contrary, the great end of civil society is to secure them. The great end of government is to repress ALL WRONG. Its highest function is to protect the weak against the powerful, so that the obscurest human being may enjoy his rights in peace. Strange that an institution, built on the idea of Rights, should be used to unsettle this idea, to confuse our moral perceptions, to sanctify wrongs as means of general good! It is said, that, in forming civil society, the individual surrenders a part of his rights. It would be more proper to say, that he adopts new modes of securing them. He consents, for example, to desist from self-defence, that he and all may be more effectually defended by the public force. He consents to submit his cause to an umpire or tribunal, that justice may be more impartially awarded, and that he and all may more certainly receive their due. He consents to part with a portion of his property in taxation, that his own and others' property may be the more secure. He submits to certain restraints, that he and others may enjoy more enduring freedom. He expects an equivalent for what he relinquishes, and insists on it as his right. He is wronged by partial laws, which compel him to contribute to the state beyond his proportion, his ability, and the measure of benefits which he receives. How absurd is it to suppose, that, by consenting to be protected by the state, and by yielding it the means, he surrenders the very rights which were the objects of his accession to the social compact!

The authority of the state to impose laws on its members I cheerfully allow; but this has limits, which are found to be more and more narrow in proportion to the progress of moral science. The state is equally restrained with individuals by the Moral Law. For example, it may not, must not, on any account, put an innocent man to death, or require of him a dishonorable or criminal service. It may demand allegiance, but only on the ground of the protection it affords. It may levy taxes, but only because it takes all property and all interests under its shield. It may pass laws, but only impartial ones, framed for the whole, and not for the few. It must not seize, by a special act, the property of the humblest individual, without making him an equivalent. It must regard every man, over whom it extends its authority, as a vital part of itself, as entitled to its care and to its provisions for liberty and happiness. If, in an emergency, its safety, which is the interest of each and all, may demand the imposition of peculiar restraints on one or many, it is bound to limit these restrictions to the precise point which its safety prescribes, to remove the necessity of them as far and as fast as possible, to compensate by peculiar protection such as it deprives of the ordinary means of protecting themselves, and, in general, to respect and provide for liberty in the very acts which for a time restrain it. The idea of Rights should be fundamental and supreme in civil institutions. Government becomes a nuisance and scourge, in proportion as it sacrifices these to the many or the few. Government, I repeat it, is equally bound with the individual by the Moral Law. The ideas of Justice and Rectitude, of what is due to man from his fellow-creatures, of the claims of every moral being, are far deeper and more primitive than Civil Polity. Government, far from originating them, owes to them its strength. Right is older than human law. Law ought to be its voice. It should be built on, and should correspond to, the principle of justice in the human breast, and its weakness is owing to nothing more than to its clashing with our indestructible moral convictions.

That government is most perfect, in which Policy is most entirely subjected to Justice, or in which the supreme and constant aim is to secure the rights of every human being. This is the beautiful idea of a free government, and no government is free but in proportion as it realizes this. Liberty must not be confounded with popular institutions. A representative government may be as despotic as an absolute monarchy. In as far as it tramples on the rights, whether of many or one, it is a despotism. The sovereign power, whether wielded by a single hand or several hands, by a king or a congress, which spoils one human being of the immunities and privileges bestowed on him by God, is so far a tyranny. The great argument in favor of representative institutions is, that a people's rights are safest in their own hands, and should never be surrendered to an irresponsible power. Rights, Rights, lie at the foundation of a popular government; and when this betrays them, the wrong is more aggravated than when they are crushed by despotism.

Still the question will be asked, "Is not the General Good the supreme Law of the state?—Are not all restraints on the individual just, which this demands? When the rights of the individual clash with this, must they not yield? Do they not, indeed, cease to be rights? Must not every thing give place to the General Good?" I have started this question in various forms, because I deem it worthy of particular examination. Public and private morality, the freedom and safety of our national institutions, are greatly concerned in settling the claims of the "General Good." In monarchies, the Divine Right of kings swallowed up all others. In republics, the General Good threatens the same evil. It is a shelter for the abuses and usurpations of government, for the profligacies of statesmen, for the vices of parties, for the wrongs of slavery. In considering this subject, I take the hazard of repeating principles already laid down; but this will be justified by the importance of reaching and determining the truth. Is the General Good, then, the supreme law, to which every thing must bow? This question may be settled at once by proposing another. Suppose the public good to require, that a number of the members of a state, no matter how few, should perjure themselves, or should disclaim their faith in God and virtue. Would their right to follow conscience and God be annulled? Would they be bound to sin? Suppose a conqueror to menace a state with ruin, unless its members should insult their parents, and stain themselves with crimes at which nature revolts. Must the public good prevail over purity and our holiest affections? Do we not all feel that there are higher goods than even the safety of the state? that there is a higher law than that of mightiest empires? that the idea of Rectitude is deeper in human nature than that of private or public interest? and that this is to bear sway over all private and public acts?

The supreme law of a state is not its safety, its power, its prosperity, its affluence, the flourishing state of agriculture, commerce, and the arts. These objects, constituting what is commonly called the Public Good, are indeed proposed, and ought to be proposed, in the constitution and administration of states. But there is a higher law, even Virtue, Rectitude, the voice of Conscience, the Will of God. Justice is a greater good than property, not greater in degree, but in kind. Universal benevolence is infinitely superior to prosperity. Religion, the love of God, is worth incomparably more than all his outward gifts. A community, to secure or aggrandize itself, must never forsake the Right, the Holy, the Just.

Moral Good, Rectitude in all its branches, is the Supreme Good; by which I do not intend, that it is the surest means to the security and prosperity of the state. Such, indeed, it is, but this is too low a view. It must not be looked upon as a Means, an Instrument. It is the Supreme End, and states are bound to subject to it all their legislation, be the apparent loss of prosperity ever so great. National wealth is not the End. It derives all its worth from national virtue. If accumulated by rapacity, conquest, or any degrading means, or if concentrated in the hands of the few, whom it strengthens to crush the many, it is a curse. National wealth is a blessing, only when it springs from and represents the intelligence and virtue of the community; when it is a fruit and expression of good habits, of respect for the rights of all, of impartial and beneficent legislation; when it gives impulse to the higher faculties, and occasion and incitement to justice and beneficence. No greater calamity can befall a people than to prosper by crime. No success can the compensation for the wound inflicted on a nation's mind by renouncing Right as its Supreme Law.

Let a people exalt Prosperity above Rectitude, and a more dangerous end cannot be proposed. Public Prosperity, General Good, regarded by itself, or apart from the moral law, is something vague, unsettled, and uncertain, and will infallibly be so construed by the selfish and grasping as to secure their own aggrandizement. It may be made to wear a thousand forms, according to men's interests and passions. This is illustrated by every day's history. Not a party springs up, which does not sanctify all its projects for monopolizing power by the plea of General Good. Not a measure, however ruinous, can be proposed, which cannot be shown to favor one or another national interest. The truth is, that, in the uncertainty of human affairs, an uncertainty growing out of the infinite and very subtle causes which are acting on communities, the consequences of no measure can be foretold with certainty. The best concerted schemes of policy often fail; whilst a rash and profligate administration may, by unexpected concurrences of events, seem to advance a nation's glory. In regard to the means of national prosperity, the wisest are weak judges. For example, the present rapid growth of this country, carrying, as it does, vast multitudes beyond the institutions of religion and education, may be working ruin, whilst the people exult in it as a pledge of greatness. We are too short-sighted to find our law in outward interests. To states, as to individuals, Rectitude is the Supreme Law. It was never designed that the public good, as disjoined from this, as distinct from justice and reverence for all rights, should be comprehended and made our end. Statesmen work in the dark, until the idea of Right towers above expediency or wealth. Woe to that people which would found its prosperity in wrong! It is time that the low maxims of policy, which have ruled for ages, should fall. It is time that public interest should no longer hallow injustice, and fortify government in making the weak their prey.

In this discussion, I have used the phrase, Public or General Good, in its common acceptation, as signifying the safety and prosperity of a state. Why can it not be used in a larger sense? Why can it not be made to comprehend inward and moral, as well as outward good? And why cannot the former be understood to be incomparably the most important element of the public weal? Then, indeed, I should assent to the proposition, that the General Good is the Supreme Law. So construed, it would support the great truths which I have maintained. It would condemn the infliction of wrong on the humblest individual, as a national calamity. It would plead with us to extend to every individual the means of improving his character and lot.

If the remarks under this head be just, it will follow, that the good of the Individual is more important than the outward prosperity of the State. The former is not vague and unsettled, like the latter, and it belongs to a higher order of interests. It consists in the free exertion and expansion of the individual's powers, especially of his higher faculties; in the energy of his intellect, conscience, and good affections; in sound judgment; in the acquisition of truth; in laboring honestly for himself and his family; in loving his Creator, and subjecting his own will to the Divine; in loving his fellow creatures, and making cheerful sacrifices to their happiness; in friendship; in sensibility to the beautiful, whether in nature or art; in loyalty to his principles; in moral courage; in self-respect; in understanding and asserting his rights; and in the Christian hope of immortality. Such is the good of the Individual; a more sacred, exalted, enduring interest, than any accessions of wealth or power to the State. Let it not be sacrificed to these. He should find, in his connexion with the community, aids to the accomplishment of these purposes of his being, and not be chained and subdued by it to the inferior interests of any fellow- creature.

In all ages the Individual has, in one form or another, been trodden in the dust. In monarchies and aristocracies, he has been sacrificed to One or to the Few; who, regarding government as an heirloom in their families, and thinking of the people as made only to live and die for their glory, have not dreamed that the sovereign power was designed to shield every man, without exception, from wrong. In the ancient Republics, the Glory of the State, especially Conquest, was the end to which the individual was expected to offer himself a victim, and in promoting which, no cruelty was to be declined, no human right revered. He was merged in a great whole, called the Commonwealth, to which his whole nature was to be immolated. It was the glory of the American people, that, in their Declaration of Independence, they took the ground of the indestructible rights of every human being. They declared all men to be essentially equal, and each born to be free. They did not, like the Greek or Roman, assert for themselves a liberty, which they burned to wrest from other states. They spoke in the name of humanity, as the representatives of the rights of the feeblest, as well as mightiest of their race. They published universal, everlasting principles, which are to work out the deliverance of every human being. Such was their glory. Let not the idea of Rights be erased from their children's minds by false ideas of public good. Let not the sacredness of Individual Man be forgotten in the feverish pursuit of property. It is more important that the Individual should respect himself, and be respected by others, than that the wealth of both worlds should be accumulated on our shores. National wealth is not the end of society. It may exist where large classes are depressed and wronged. It may undermine a nation's spirit, institutions, and independence. It can have no value and no sure foundation, until the supremacy of the Rights of the Individual is the first article of a nation's faith, and until reverence for them becomes the spirit of public men.

Perhaps it will be replied to all which has now been said, that there is an argument from experience, which invalidates the doctrines of this section. It may be said, that human rights, notwithstanding what has been said of their sacredness, do and must yield to the exigencies of real life; that there is often a stern necessity in human affairs to which they bow. I may be asked, whether, in the history of nations, circumstances do not occur, in which the rigor of the principles now laid down must be relaxed; whether, in seasons of imminent peril to the state, private rights must not give way. I may be asked, whether the establishment of martial law and a dictator has not sometimes been justified and demanded by public danger; and whether, of course, the rights and liberties of the individual are not held at the discretion of the state. I admit, in reply, that extreme cases may occur, in which the exercise of rights and freedom may be suspended; but suspended only for their ultimate and permanent security. At such times, when the frantic fury of the many, or the usurpations of the few, interrupt the administration of law, and menace property and life, society, threatened with ruin, puts forth instinctively spasmodic efforts for its own preservation. It flies to an irresponsible dictator for its protection. But in these cases, the great idea of Rights predominates amidst their apparent subversion. A power above all laws is conferred, only that the empire of law may be restored. Despotic restraints are imposed, only that liberty may be rescued from ruin. All rights are involved in the safety of the state; and hence, in the cases referred to, the safety of the state becomes the supreme law. The individual is bound for a time to forego his freedom, for the salvation of institutions, without which liberty is but a name. To argue from such sacrifices, that he may be permanently made a slave, is as great an insult to reason as to humanity. It may be added, that sacrifices, which may be demanded for the safety, are not due from the individual to the prosperity of the state. The great end of civil society is to secure rights, not accumulate wealth; and to merge the former in the latter is to turn political union into degradation and a scourge. The community is bound to take the rights of each and all under its guardianship. It must substantiate its claim to universal obedience by redeeming its pledge of universal protection. It must immolate no man to the prosperity of the rest. Its laws should be made for all, its tribunals opened to all. It cannot without guilt abandon any of its members to private oppression, to irresponsible power.

We have thus established the reality and sacredness of human rights; and that slavery is an infraction of these, is too plain to need any labored proof. Slavery violates, not one, but all; and violates them, not incidentally, but necessarily, systematically, from its very nature. In starting with the assumption, that the slave is property, it sweeps away every defence of human rights, and lays them in the dust. Were it necessary, I might enumerate them, and show how all fall before this terrible usurpation; but a few remarks will suffice. Slavery strips man of the fundamental right to inquire into, consult, and seek his own happiness. His powers belong to another, and for another they must be used. He must form no plans, engage in no enterprises, for bettering his condition. Whatever be his capacities, however equal to great improvements of his lot, he is chained for life, by another's will, to the same unvaried toil. He is forbidden to do, for himself or others, the work for which God stamped him with his own image, and endowed him with his own best gifts.—Again, the slave is stripped of the right to acquire property. Being himself owned, his earnings belong to another. He can possess nothing but by favor. That right, on which the development of men's powers so much depends, the right to make accumulations, to gain exclusive possessions by honest industry, is withheld. "The slave can acquire nothing," says one of the slave codes, "but what must belong to his master;" and however this definition, which moves the indignation of the free, may be mitigated by favor, the spirit of it enters into the very essence of slavery.—Again, the slave is stripped of his right to his wife and children. They belong to another, and may be torn from him, one and all, at any moment, at his master's pleasure.—Again, the slave is stripped of the right to the culture of his rational powers. He is in some cases deprived by law of instruction, which is placed within his reach by the improvements of society and the philanthropy of the age. He is not allowed to toil, that his children may enjoy a better education than himself. The most sacred right of human nature, that of developing his best faculties, is denied. Even should it be granted, it would be conceded as a favor, and might at any moment be withheld by the capricious will of another.—Again, the slave is deprived of the right of self-defence. No injury from a white man is he suffered to repel, nor can he seek redress from the laws of his country. If accumulated insult and wrong provoke him to the slightest retaliation, this effort for self-protection, allowed and commended to others, is a crime, for which he must pay a fearful penalty.—Again, the slave is stripped of the right to be exempted from all harm, except for wrong-doing. He is subjected to the lash by those, whom he has never consented to serve, and whose claim to him as property we have seen to be a usurpation; and this power of punishment, which, if justly claimed, should be exercised with a fearful care, is often delegated to men in whose hands there is a moral certainty of its abuse.

I will add but one more example of the violation of human rights by slavery. The slave virtually suffers the wrong of robbery, though with utter unconsciousness on the part of those who inflict it. It may, indeed, be generally thought, that, as he is suffered to own nothing, he cannot fall, at least, under this kind of violence. But it is not true that he owns nothing. Whatever he may be denied by man, he holds from nature the most valuable property, and that from which all other is derived, I mean his strength. His labor is his own, by the gift of that God, who nerved his arm, and gave him intelligence and conscience to direct the use of it to his own and others' happiness. No possession is so precious as a man's force of body and mind. The exertion of this in labor is the great foundation and source of property in outward things. The worth of articles of traffic is measured by the labor expended in their production. To the great mass of men, in all countries, their strength or labor is their whole fortune. To seize on this would be to rob them of their all. In truth, no robbery is so great, as that to which the slave is habitually subjected. To take by force a man's whole estate, the fruit of years of toil, would, by universal consent, be denounced as a great wrong; but what is this, compared with seizing the man himself, and appropriating to our use the limbs, faculties, strength, and labor, by which all property is won and held fast? The right of property in outward things is as nothing, compared with our right to ourselves. Were the slave-holder stripped of his fortune, he would count the violence slight, compared with what he would suffer, were his person seized and devoted as a chattel to another's use. Let it not be said, that the slave receives an equivalent, that he is fed and clothed, and is not, therefore, robbed. Suppose another to wrest from us a valued possession, and to pay us his own price. Should we not think ourselves robbed? Would not the laws pronounce the invader a robber? Is it consistent with the right of property, that a man should determine the equivalent for what he takes from his neighbour? Especially is it to be hoped, that the equivalent due to the laborer will be scrupulously weighed, when he himself is held as property, and all his earnings are declared to be his master's. So great an infraction of human right is slavery!

In reply to these remarks, it may be said, that the theory and practice of slavery differ; that the rights of the slave are not as wantonly sported with as the claims of the master might lead us to infer; that some of his possessions are sacred; that not a few slave-holders refuse to divorce husband and wife, to sever parent and child; and that, in many cases, the power of punishment is used so reluctantly, as to encourage insolence and insubordination. All this I have no disposition to deny. Indeed, it must be so. It is not in human nature to wink wholly out of sight the rights of a fellow-creature. Degrade him as we may, we cannot altogether forget his claims. In every slave-country, there are, undoubtedly, masters, who desire and purpose to respect these, to the full extent which the nature of the relation will allow. Still, human rights are denied. They lie wholly at another's mercy; and we must have studied history in vain, if we need be told that they will be continually the prey of this absolute power.— The evils, involved in and flowing from the denial and infraction of the rights of the slave, will form the subject of a subsequent chapter.

46

Texas Declaration of Independence, 1836

The Declaration of Independence of 1776 became a model for oppressed people struggling for freedom. Its style and sentiment has been copied on many occasions. On March 2, 1836, delegates at Washington-on-the-Brazos, Texas, drafted this statement to declare their independence from Mexico. Mexico, in the midst of its own internal convulsions, watched numerous provinces fall into rebellion. Texas, dominated by Americans, believed that independence and preferably annexation to the Untied States afterward, was the best course available. The Texas settlers listed as among their most important rights the freedom of religion, the right to a jury trial, the right to self-determination, and the right to self-improvement through education. The Texas Revolution would rage another six weeks until the Mexican Army succumbed to the ragtag Texas troops. Texas would become an independent republic until its annexation to the United States in 1845.

The Unanimous Declaration of Independence made by the Delegates of the People of Texas in General Convention at the town of Washington on the 2nd day of March 1836

When a government has ceased to protect the lives, liberty and property of the people, from whom its legitimate powers are derived, and for the advancement of whose happiness it was instituted, and so far from being a guarantee for the enjoyment of those inestimable and inalienable rights, becomes an instrument in the hands of evil rulers for their oppression.

When the Federal Republican Constitution of their country, which they have sworn to support, no longer has a substantial existence, and the whole nature of their government has been forcibly changed, without their consent, from a restricted

Telegraph and Texas Register, March 12, 1836.

federative republic, composed of sovereign states, to a consolidated central military despotism, in which every interest is disregarded but that of the army and the priesthood, both the eternal enemies of civil liberty, the everready minions of power, and the usual instruments of tyrants.

When, long after the spirit of the constitution has departed, moderation is at length so far lost by those in power, that even the semblance of freedom is removed, and the forms themselves of the constitution discontinued, and so far from their petitions and remonstrances being regarded, the agents who bear them are thrown into dungeons, and mercenary armies sent forth to force a new government upon them at the point of the bayonet.

When, in consequence of such acts of malfeasance and abdication on the part of the government, anarchy prevails, and civil society is dissolved into its original elements. In such a crisis, the first law of nature, the right of self-preservation, the inherent and inalienable rights of the people to appeal to first principles, and take their political affairs into their own hands in extreme cases, enjoins it as a right towards themselves, and a sacred obligation to their posterity, to abolish such government, and create another in its stead, calculated to rescue them from impending dangers, and to secure their future welfare and happiness.

Nations, as well as individuals, are amenable for their acts to the public opinion of mankind. A statement of a part of our grievances is therefore submitted to an impartial world, in justification of the hazardous but unavoidable step now taken, of severing our political connection with the Mexican people, and assuming an independent attitude among the nations of the earth.

The Mexican government, by its colonization laws, invited and induced the Anglo-American population of Texas to colonize its wilderness under the pledged faith of a written constitution, that they should continue to enjoy that constitutional liberty and republican government to which they had been habituated in the land of their birth, the United States of America.

In this expectation they have been cruelly disappointed, inasmuch as the Mexican nation has acquiesced in the late changes made in the government by General Antonio Lopez de Santa Anna, who having overturned the constitution of his country, now offers us the cruel alternative, either to abandon our homes, acquired by so many privations, or submit to the most intolerable of all tyranny, the combined despotism of the sword and the priesthood.

It has sacrificed our welfare to the state of Coahuila, by which our interests have been continually depressed through a jealous and partial course of legislation, carried on at a far distant seat of government, by a hostile majority, in an unknown tongue, and this too, notwithstanding we have petitioned in the humblest terms for the establishment of a separate state government, and have, in accordance with the provisions of the national constitution, presented to the general Congress a republican constitution, which was, without just cause, contemptuously rejected.

It incarcerated in a dungeon, for a long time, one of our citizens, for no other cause but a zealous endeavor to procure the acceptance of our constitution, and the establishment of a state government.

It has failed and refused to secure, on a firm basis, the right of trial by jury, that palladium of civil liberty, and only safe guarantee for the life, liberty, and property of the citizen.

It has failed to establish any public system of education, although possessed of almost boundless resources (the public domain), and although it is an axiom in political science, that unless a people are educated and enlightened, it is idle to expect the continuance of civil liberty, or the capacity for self government.

It has suffered the military commandants, stationed among us, to exercise arbitrary acts of oppression and tyrany, thus trampling upon the most sacred rights of the citizens, and rendering the military superior to the civil power.

It has dissolved, by force of arms, the state Congress of Coahuila and Texas, and obliged our representatives to fly for their lives from the seat of government, thus depriving us of the fundamental political right of representation.

It has demanded the surrender of a number of our citizens, and ordered military detachments to seize and carry them into the Interior for trial, in contempt of the civil authorities, and in defiance of the laws and the constitution.

It has made piratical attacks upon our commerce, by commissioning foreign desperadoes, and authorizing them to seize our vessels, and convey the property of our citizens to far distant ports for confiscation.

It denies us the right of worshipping the Almighty according to the dictates of our own conscience, by the support of a national religion, calculated to promote the temporal interest of its human functionaries, rather than the glory of the true and living God.

It has demanded us to deliver up our arms, which are essential to our defence, the rightful property of freemen, and formidable only to tyrannical governments.

It has invaded our country both by sea and by land, with intent to lay waste our territory, and drive us from our homes; and has now a large mercenary army advancing, to carry on against us a war of extermination.

It has, through its emissaries, incited the merciless savage, with the tomahawk and scalping knife, to massacre the inhabitants of our defenseless frontiers.

It hath been, during the whole time of our connection with it, the contemptible sport and victim of successive military revolutions, and hath continually exhibited every characteristic of a weak, corrupt, and tyranical government.

These, and other grievances, were patiently borne by the people of Texas, untill they reached that point at which forbearance ceases to be a virtue. We then took up arms in defence of the national constitution. We appealed to our Mexican brethren for assistance. Our appeal has been made in vain. Though months have elapsed, no sympathetic response has yet been heard from the Interior. We are, therefore, forced to the melancholy conclusion, that the Mexican people have acquiesced in the destruction of their liberty, and the substitution therfor of a military government; that they are unfit to be free, and incapable of self government.

The necessity of self-preservation, therefore, now decrees our eternal political separation.

We, therefore, the delegates with plenary powers of the people of Texas, in solemn convention assembled, appealing to a candid world for the necessities of our condition, do hereby resolve and declare, that our political connection with the Mexican nation has forever ended, and that the people of Texas do now constitute a free, Sovereign, and independent republic, and are fully invested with all the rights and attributes which properly belong to independent nations; and, conscious of the rectitude of our intentions, we fearlessly and confidently commit the issue to the decision of the Supreme arbiter of the destinies of nations.

Richard Ellis, President of the Convention and Delegate from Red River.

Charles B. Stewart	Tho. Barnett	John S. D. Byrom
Francis Ruis	J. Antonio Navarro	Jesse B. Badgett
Wm D. Lacy	William Menifee	Jn. Fisher
Matthew Caldwell	William Motley	Lorenzo de Zavala
Stephen H. Everett	George W. Smyth	Elijah Stapp
Claiborne West	Wm. B. Scates	M. B. Menard
A. B. Hardin	J. W. Burton	Thos. J. Gazley
R. M. Coleman	Sterling C. Robertson	James Collinsworth
Edwin Waller	Asa Brigham	Geo. C. Childress
Bailey Hardeman	Rob. Potter	Thomas Jefferson Rusk
Chas. S. Taylor	John S. Roberts	Robert Hamilton
Collin McKinney	Albert H. Latimer	James Power
Sam Houston	David Thomas	Edwd. Conrad
Martin Palmer	Edwin O. Legrand	Stephen W. Blount
Jms. Gaines	Wm. Clark, Jr.	Sydney O. Pennington
Wm. Carrol Crawford	Jno. Turner	Benj. Briggs Goodrich
G. W. Barnett	James G. Swisher	Jesse Grimes
S. Rhoads Fisher	John W. Moore	John W. Bower
Saml. A. Maverick (from Bejar)	J. B. Woods	Sam P. Carson
A. Briscoe		H. S. Kimble, Secretary

47

The Declaration of Sentiments, Seneca Falls Convention, 1848

The Seneca Falls Convention, held July 19–20, 1848, in Seneca Falls, New York, has been considered the beginning of the modern women's rights movement. The Declaration of Sentiments was modeled on the Declaration of Independence, structured with the same rhetoric. In a sense, this was a declaration of independence by

Elizabeth Cady Stanton, *A History of Woman Suffrage*, vol. 1 (Rochester, NY: Fowler and Wells, 1889), 70–71; Hall, ed. "Declaration of Sentiments," *Major Problems in American Constitutional History*, I, 526–529.

the women of the convention, demanding their own equality in both legal and social terms. The delegates stated that men and women were created equal and only society had placed them in unequal positions. The Declaration of Sentiments was signed by Elizabeth Cady Stanton, Lucretia Mott, Frederick Douglass, and others. Seventy-two years would pass, however, before women in the United States would gain the right to vote nationwide.

When, in the course of human events, it becomes necessary for one portion of the family of man to assume among the people of the earth a position different from that which they have hitherto occupied, but one to which the laws of nature and of nature's God entitle them, a decent respect to the opinions of mankind requires that they should declare the causes that impel them to such a course.

We hold these truths to be self-evident: that all men and women are created equal; that they are endowed by their Creator with certain inalienable rights: that among these are life, liberty, and the pursuit of happiness; that to secure these rights governments are instituted, deriving their just powers from the consent of the governed. Whenever any form of government becomes destructive of these ends, it is the right of those who suffer from it to refuse allegiance to it, and to insist upon the institution of a new government, laying its foundation on such principles, and organizing its powers in such form, as to them shall seem most likely to effect their safety and happiness. Prudence, indeed, will dictate that governments long established should not be changed for light and transient causes; and accordingly, all experience hath shown that mankind are more disposed to suffer. while evils are sufferable, than to right themselves by abolishing the forms to which they were accustomed. But when a long train of abuses and usurpations, pursuing invariably the same object, evinces a design to reduce them under absolute despotism, it is their duty to throw off such government, and to provide new guards for their future security. Such has been the patient sufferance of the women under this government, and such is now the necessity which constrains them to demand the equal station to which they are entitled. The history of mankind is a history of repeated injuries and usurpations on the part of man toward woman, having in direct object the establishment of an absolute tyranny over her. To prove this, let facts be submitted to a candid world.

The history of mankind is a history of repeated injuries and usurpations on the part of man toward woman, having in direct object the establishment of an absolute tyrranny over her. To prove this, let facts be submitted to a candid world.

He has never permitted her to exercise her inalienable right to the elective franchise.

He has compelled her to submit to laws, in the formation of which she had no voice.

He has withheld from her rights which are given to the most ignorant and degraded men—both natives and foreigners.

Having deprived her of this first right of a citizen, the elective franchise, thereby leaving her without representation in the halls of legislation, he has oppressed her on all sides.

He has made her, if married, in the eye of the law, civilly dead.

He has taken from her all right in property, even to the wages she earns.

He has made her, morally, an irresponsible being, as she can commit many crimes with impunity, provided they be done in the presence of her husband. In the covenant of marriage, she is compelled to promise obedience to her husband, he becoming, to all intents and purposes, her master—the law giving him power to deprive her of her liberty, and to administer chastisement.

He has so framed the laws of divorce, as to what shall be the proper causes of divorce; and in case of separation, to whom the guardianship of the children shall be given; as to be wholly regardless of the happiness of women—the law, in all cases, going upon a false supposition of the supremacy of man, and giving all power into his hands.

After depriving her of all rights as a married woman, if single, and the owner of property, he has taxed her to support a government which recognizes her only when her property can be made profitable to it.

He has monopolized nearly all the profitable employments, and from those she is permitted to follow, she receives but a scanty remuneration. He closes against her all the avenues to wealth and distinction which he considers most honorable to himself. As a teacher of theology, medicine, or law, she is not known.

He has denied her the facilities for obtaining a thorough education, all colleges being closed against her.

He allows her in Church, as well as State, but a subordinate position, claiming Apostolic authority for her exclusion from the ministry, and, with some exceptions, from any public participation in the affairs of the Church.

He has created a false public sentiment by giving to the world a different code of morals for men and women, by which moral delinquencies which exclude women from society, are not only tolerated, but deemed of little account in man.

He has usurped the prerogative of Jehovah himself, claiming it as his right to assign for her a sphere of action, when that belongs to her conscience and to her God.

He has endeavored, in every way that he could, to destroy her confidence in her own powers, to lessen her self-respect, and to make her willing to lead a dependent and abject life.

Now, in view of this entire disfranchisement of one-half the people of this country, their social and religious degradation—in view of the unjust laws above mentioned, and because women do feel themselves aggrieved, oppressed, and fraudulently deprived of their most sacred rights, we insist that they have immediate admission to all the rights and privileges which belong to them as citizens of the United States.

Barker, Caroline	Barker, Eunice	Barker, William G.
Bonnel, Rachel D. (Mitchell)	Bunker, Joel D.	Burroughs, William
Capron, E.W.	Chamberlain, Jacob	Conklin, Elizabeth
Conklin, Mary	Culvert, P.A.	Davis, Cynthia
Dell, Thomas	Dell, William S.	Doty, Elias J.
Doty, Susan R.	Douglass, Frederick	Drake, Julia Ann
Eaton, Harriet Cady	Foote, Elisha	Foote, Eunice Newton
Frink, Mary Ann	Fuller, Cynthia	Gibbs, Experience
Gilbert, Mary	Gild, Lydia	Hallowell, Sarah
Hallowell, Mary H.	Hatley, Henry	Hioffman, Sarah

Hoskins, Charles L.	Hunt, Jane C.	Hunt, Richard P.
Jenkins, Margaret	Jones, John	Jones, Lucy
King, Phebe	Latham, Hannah J	Latham, Lovina
Leslie, Elizabeth	Martin, Eliza	Martin, Nary
Mathews, Delia	Mathews, Dorothy	Mathews, Jacob
McClintock, Elizabeth W.	McClintock, Mary	McClintock, Mary Ann
McClintock, Thomas	Metcalf, Jonathan	Milliken, Nathan J.
Mirror, Nary S.	Mosher, Pheobe	Mosher, Sarah A.
Mott, James	Mott, Lucretia	Mount, Lydia
Paine, Catharine G.	Palmer, Rhoda	Phillips, Saron
Pitcher, Sally	Plant, Hannah	Porter, Ann Post, Amy
Pryor, George W.	Pryor, Margaret	Quinn, Susan
Race, Rebecca	Ridley, Martha	Schooley, Azaliah
Schooley, Margaret	Scott, Deborah	Segur, Antoinette E.
Seymour, Henry	Seymour, Henry W.	Seymour, Malvina
Shaw, Catharine	Shear, Stephen	Sisson, Sarah
Smallbridge, Robert	Smith, Elizabeth D.	Smith, Sarah
Spalding, David	Spalding, Lucy	Stanton, Elizabeth Cady
Stebbins, Catharine	Taylor, Sophrouia	Tewksbury, Betsey
Tiliman, Samuel D.	Underhill, Edward F.	Underhill, Martha
Vail, Mary E.	Van Tassel, Isaac	Whitney, Sarah
Wilbur, Maria E.	Williams, Justin	Woods, Sarah R.
Woodward, Charlotte	Woodworth, S.E.	Wright, Martha C.

Daniel Webster **48**

The Seventh of March Speech, 1850

By 1850, the nation was tearing itself apart over the issue of slavery. The South, with a rising slave population, felt increasingly isolated and threatened as the abolitionist movement gained strength in the North. The venerable orator, Sen. Daniel Webster, Whig-Massachusetts, took to the Senate floor on March 7, 1850, to plead for the continuation of the union in this famous address. At stake was the 1850 Compromise, a desperate attempt to keep North and South

Congressional Globe, 31st Congress, 1st Session (1850), 476–484.

together. Webster took a different view, much to the anger of abolitionists. He knew the destruction that a civil war would bring, but spoke to the principle of the right to have different opinions and still live in peace, attempting to reassure the South. Peace was his goal. The Union would survive for another decade until it exploded into civil war in 1861. Webster's view was ultimately rejected as the course of the war demanded that slavery must end for a free, united nation to continue. In Senate speeches, speakers are to address the chairman of the body, referred to as the President of the Senate.

Mr. President,—I wish to speak to-day, not as a Massachusetts man, nor as a Northern man, but as an American, and a member of the Senate of the United States. It is fortunate that there is a Senate of the United States; a body not yet moved from its propriety, not lost to a just sense of its own dignity and its own high responsibilities, and a body to which the country looks, with confidence, for wise, moderate, patriotic, and healing counsels. It is not to be denied that we live in the midst of strong agitations, and are surrounded by very considerable dangers to our institutions and our government. The imprisoned winds are let loose. The East, the North, and the stormy South combine to throw the whole sea into commotion, to toss its billows to the skies, and disclose its profoundest depths. I do not affect to regard myself, Mr. President, as holding, or as fit to hold, the helm in this combat with the political elements; but I have a duty to perform, and I mean to perform it with fidelity, not without a sense of existing dangers, but not without hope. I have a part to act, not for my own security or safety, for I am looking out for no fragment upon which to float away from the wreck, if wreck there must be, but for the good of the whole, and the preservation of all; and there is that which will keep me to my duty during this struggle, whether the sun and the stars shall appear, or shall not appear for many days. I speak to-day for the preservation of the Union. "Hear me for my cause." I speak to-day, out of a solicitous and anxious heart for the restoration to the country of that quiet and harmonious harmony which make the blessings of this Union so rich, and so dear to us all. These are the topics I propose to myself to discuss; these are the motives, and the sole motives, that influence me in the wish to communicate my opinions to the Senate and the country; and if I can do any thing, however little, for the promotion of these ends, I shall have accomplished all that I expect...

Now, Sir, upon the general nature and influence of slavery there exists a wide difference of opinion between the northern portion of this country and the southern. It is said on the one side, that, although not the subject of any injunction or direct prohibition in the New Testament, slavery is a wrong; that it is founded merely in the right of the strongest; and that is an oppression, like unjust wars, like all those conflicts by which a powerful nation subjects a weaker to its will; and that, in its nature, whatever may be said of it in the modifications which have taken place, it is not according to the meek spirit of the Gospel. It is not "kindly affectioned"; it does not "seek another's, and not its own"; it does not "let the oppressed go free". These are the sentiments that are cherished, and of late with greatly augmented force, among the people of the Northern States. They have taken hold of the religious sentiment of that part of the country, as they have, more or less, taken hold of the religious feeling of a considerable portion of mankind. The South, upon the other side, having been accustomed to this relation between two races all their lives, from their birth, having been taught, in general, to treat the subjects of this bondage with care and kindness, and I believe, in general, feeling great kindness for them, have not taken the view of the subject which I have mentioned. There are thousands of religious men, with consciences as tender as any of their brethren at the North, who do not see the unlawfulness of slavery; and there are more thousands, perhaps, that whatsoever they may think of it in its origin, and as a matter depending upon natural right, yet take things as they are, and, finding slavery to be an established relation of the society in which they live, can see no way in which, let their opinions on the abstract question be what they may, it is in the power of the present generation to relieve themselves from this relation. And candor obliges me to say, that I believe they are just as conscientious, many of them, and the religious people, all of them, as they are at the North who hold different opinions.

The honorable Senator from South Carolina [John C. Calhoun] the other day alluded to the seperation of that great religious community, the Methodist Episcopal Church. That separation was brought about by differences of opinion upon this particular subject of slavery. I felt great concern, as that dispute went on, about the result. I was in hopes that the difference of opinion might be adjusted, because I looked upon that religious denomination as one of the great props of religion and morals throughout the whole country, from Maine to Georgia, and westward to our utmost boundary. The result was against my wishes and against my hopes. I have read all their proceedings and all their arguments; but I have never yet been able to come to the conclusion that there was any real ground for that separation; in other words, that any good could be produced by that separation. I must say I think there was some want of candor or charity. Sir, when a question of this kind seizes on the religious sentiments of mankind, and comes to be discussed in religious assemblies of the clergy and laity, there is always to be expected, or always to be feared, a great degree of excitement. It is in the nature of man, manifested in his whole history, that religious disputes are apt to become warm in proportion to the strength of the convictions which men entertain of the magnitude of the questions at issue. In all such disputes, there will sometimes be found men with whome every thing is absolute; absolutely wrong, or absolutely right. They see the right clearly; they think others ought so to see it, and they are disposed to establish a broad line of distinction between what is right and what is wrong. They are not seldom willing to establish that line upon their own convictions of truth or justice; and are ready to mark and guard it by placing along it a series of dogmas, as lines of boundary on the earth's surface are marked by posts and stones. There are men who, with clear perception, as they think, of their own duty, do not see how too eager a pursuit of one duty may involve them in the violation of others, or how too warm an embracement of one truth may lead to a disregard of other truths equally important. As I heard it stated strongly, not many days ago, these persons are disposed to mount upon some particular duty, as upon a war-horse, and to drive furiously on and upon and over all other duties that may stand in the way. There are men who, in reference to disputes of that sort, are of the opinion that human duties may be ascertained with the exactness of mathematics. They deal with morals as with mathematics; and they think what is right may be distinguished from what is wrong with the precision of an algebraic equation. They have, therefore, none too much charity towards others who differ from them. They are apt, too, to think that nothing is good but what is perfect, and that there are no compromises or modifications to be made in consideration of difference of opinion or in deference to other men's judgment. If their perspicacious vision enables them to detect a spot on the face of the sun, they think that a good reason why the sun should be struck down fro heaven. They prefer the chance of running into utter darkness to living in heavenly light, if that heavenly light be not absolutely without any imperfection. There are impatient men; too impatient always to give heed to the admonition of St. Paul, that we are not to "do evil that good may come"; too impatient to wait for the slow progress of moral causes in the improvement of mankind . . .

Mr. President, in the excited times in which we live, there is found to exist a state of crimination and recrimination between the North and South. There are lists of grievances produced by each; and those grievances, real or supposed, alienate the minds of one portion of the country from the other, exasperate the feelings, and subdue the sense of fraternal affection, patriotic love, and mutual regard. I shall bestow a little attention, Sir, upon these various grievances existing on the one side and on the other. I begin with complaints of the South. I will not answer, further than I have, the general statements of the honorable Senator from South Carolina [Calhoun], that the North has prospered at the expense of the South in consequence of the manner of administering this government, in the collecting of its revenues, and so forth. These are disputed topics, and I have no inclination to enter into them. But I will allude to the other complaints of the South, and especially to one which has in my opinion just foundation; and that is, that there has been found at the North, among individuals and among legislators, a disinclination to perform fully their constitutional duties in regard to the return of persons bound to service who have escaped into the free States. In that respect, the South, in my judgment, is right, and the North is wrong. Every member of every Northern legislature is bound by oath, like every other officer in the country, to support the Constitution of the United States; and the article of the Constitution which says to these States that they shall deliver up fugitives from service is as binding in honor and conscience as any other article. No man fulfills his duty in any legislature who sets himself to find excuses, evasions, escapes from this constitutional obligation. I have always thought that the Constitution addressed itself to the legislatures of the States or to the States themselves. It says that those persons escaping to other States "shall be delivered up," and I confess I have always been of the opinion that it was an injunction upon the States themselves. When it is said that a person escaping into another State, and coming therefore within the jurisdiction of that State, shall be delivered up, it seems to me the import of the clause is, that the State itself, in obedience to the Constitution, shall cause him to be delivered up. That is my judgment. I have always entertained that opinion, and I entertain it now. But when the subject, some years ago, was before the Supreme Court of the United States, the majority of the judges held that the power to cause fugitives from service to be delivered up was a power to be exercised under the authority of this government. I do not know, on the whole, that it may not have been a fortunate decision. My habit is to respect the result of judicial deliberations and the solemnity of judicial decisions. As it now stands, the business of seeing that these fugitives are delivered up resides in the power of Congress and the national judicature, and my friend at the head of the Judiciary Committee [James M. Mason] has a bill on the subject now before the Senate, which, with some amendments tot, I propose to support, with all its provisions, to the fullest extent. And I desire to call the attention of all sober-minded men at the North, of all conscientious men, of all men who are not carried away by some fanatical idea or some false impression, to their constitutional obligations. I put it to all the sober and sound minds at the North as a question of morals and a question of conscience. What right have they, in their legislative capacity or any other capacity, to endeavor to get round this Constitution, or to embarass the free exercise of the rights secured by the Constitution to the persons whose slaves escape from them? None at all; none at all. Neither in the forum of conscience, nor before the face of the Constitution, are they, in my opinion, justified in such an attempt. Of course it is a matter for their consideration. They probably, in the excitement of the times, have not stopped to consider of this. They have followed what seemed to be the current of thought and of motives, as the occasion arose, and they have neglected to investigate fully the real question, and to consider their constitutional obligations; which, I am sure, if they did consider, they would fulfil with alacrity. I repeat, therefore, Sir, that here is a well-founded ground of complaint against the North, which ought to be removed, which it is now in the power of the different departments of this government to remove; which calls for the enactment of proper laws authorizing the judicature of this government, in the several States, to do all that is necessary for the recapture of fugitive slaves and for their restoration to those who claim them. Wherever I go, and whenever I speak on the subject, and when I speak here I desire to speak to the whole North, I say that the South has been injured in this respect, and has a right to complain; and the North has been too careless of what I think the Constitution peremptorily and emphatically enjoins upon her as a duty...

Then, Sir, there are the Abolition societies, of which I am unwilling to speak, but in regard to which I have very clear notions and opinions. I do not think them useful. I think their operations for the last twenty years have produced nothing good or valuable. At the same time, I believe thousands of their members to be honest and good men, perfectly well-meaning men. They have excited feelings; they think they must do something for the cause of liberty; and, in their sphere of action, they do not see what else they can do than to contribute to an Abolition press, or an Abolition society, or to pay an Abolition lecturer. I do not mean to impute gross motives even to the leaders of these societies, but I am not blind to the consequences of their proceedings. I cannot but see what mischiefs their interference with the South has produced. And is it not plain to every man? Let any gentleman who entertains doubts on this point recur to the debates in the Virginia House of Delegates in 1832, and he will see with what freedom a proposition made by Mr. [Thomas] Jefferson Randolph for the gradual abolition of slavery was discussed in that body. Every one spoke of slavery as he thought; very ignominious and disparaging names and epithets were applied to it. The debates in the House of Delegates on that occasion, I believe, were all published. They were read by every colored man who could read, and to those who could not read, those debates were read by others. At that time Virginia was not unwilling or unafraid to discuss this question, and to let that part of her population know as much of the discussion as they could learn. That was in 1832. As has been said by the honorable member from South Carolina [Calhoun], these Abolition societies commenced their course of action in 1835. It is said, I do not know how true it may be, that they sent incendiary publications into the slave States; at any rate, they attempted to arouse, and did arouse, a very strong feeling; in other words, they created great agitation in the North against Southern slavery. Well, what was the result?

The bonds of the slave were bound more firmly than before, their rivets were more strongly fastened. Public opinion, which in Virginia had begun to be exhibited against slavery, and was opening out for the discussion of the question, drew back and shut itself up in its castle. I wish to know whether any body in Virginia can now talk openly as Mr. Randoph, Governor [James] McDowell, and others talked in 1832 and sent their remarks to the press? We all know the fact, and we all know the cause; and every thing that these agitating people have done has been, not to enlarge, but to restrain, not to set free, but to bind faster the slave population of the South...

Mr. President, I should much prefer to have heard from every member on this floor declarations of opinion that this Union could never be dissolved, than the declaration of opinion by any body, that, in any case, under the pressure of any circumstances, such a dissolution was possible. I hear with distress and anguish the word "secession," especially when it falls from the lips of those who are patriotic, and known to the country, and known all over the world, for their political services. Secession! Peaceable secession! Sir, your eyes and mine are never destined to see that miracle. The dismemberment of this vast country without convulsion! The breaking up of the fountains of the great deep without ruffling the surface! Who is so foolish, I beg every body's pardon, as to expect to see any such thing? Sir, he who sees these States, now revolving in harmony around a common centre, and expects to see them quit their places and fly off without convulsion, may look the next hour to see heavenly bodies rush from their spheres, and jostle against each other in the realms of space, without causing the wreck of the universe. There can be no such thing as peaceable secession. Peaceable secession is an utter impossibility. Is the great Constitution under which we live, covering this whole country, is it to be thawed and melted away by secession, as the snows on the mountain melt under the influence of a vernal sun, disappear almost unobserved, and run off? No, Sir! No, Sir! I will not state what might produce the disruption of the Union; but, Sir, I see as plainly as I see the sun in heaven what that disruption itself must produce; I see that it must produce war, and such a war as I will not describe, *in its twofold character*.

Peaceable secession! Peaceable secession! The concurrent agreement of all the members of this great republic to seperate! A voluntary separation, with alimony on one side and on the other. Why, what would be the result? Where is the line to be drawn? What States are to seceded? What is to remain American? What am I toe? An American no longer? Am I to become a sectional man, a local man, a separatist, with no country in common with the gentlemen who sit around me here, or who fill the other house of Congress? Heaven forbid! Where is the flag of the republic to remain? Where is the eagle still to tower? or is he to cower, and shrink, and fall to the ground? Why, Sir, our ancestors, our fathers and our grandfathers, those of them that are yet living amongst us with prolonged lives, would rebuke and reproach us; and our children and our grandchildren would cry out shame upon us, if we of this generation should dishonor these ensigns of the power of the government and the harmony of that Union which is every day felt among us with so much joy and gratitude. What is to become of the army? What is to become of the navy? What is to become of the public lands? How is each of the thirty States to defend itself? I know, although the idea has not been stated distinctly, there is to be, or it is supposed possible that there will be, a Southern Confederacy. I do not mean, when I allude to this statement, that any one seriously contemplates such a state of things. I do not mean to say that it is true, but I have heard it suggested elsewhere, that the idea has been entertained, that, after the dissolution of this Union, a Southern Confederacy might be formed. I am sorry, Sir, that it has ever been thought of, talked of, or dreamed of, in the wildest flights of human imagination. But the idea, so far as it exists, must be of a separation, assigning the slave States to one side and the free States to the other. Sir, I may express myself too strongly, perhaps, but there are impossibilities in the natural as well as in the physical world, and I hold the idea of a separation of these States, those that are free to form one government, and those that are slave-holding to form another, as such an impossibility. We could not separate the States by any such line, if we were to draw it. We could not sit down here to-day and draw a line of seperation that would satisfy any five men in the country. There are natural causes that would keep and tie us together, and there are social and domestic relations which we could not break if we would, and which we should not if we could.

Sir, nobody can look over the face of this country at the present moment, nobody can see where its population is the most dense and growing, without being ready to admit, and compelled to admit, that ere long the strength of America will be in the Valley of the Mississippi. Well, now, Sir, I beg to inquire what the wildest enthusiast has to say about the possibility of cutting that river in two, and leaving free States at its source and on its branches, and slave States down near its mouth, each forming a separate government? Pray, Sir, let me say to the people of this country, that these things are worthy of their pondering and of their consideration. Here, Sir, are five millions of freemen in the free States north of the river of Ohio. Can any body suppose that this population can be severed, by a line that divides them fro the territory of a foreign and alien government, down somewhere, the Lord knows where, upon the lower banks of the Mississippi? What would become of Missouri? Will she join the *arrondissement* of the slave States? Shall the man from the Yellow Stone and the Platte be conncected, in the new republic, with the man who lives on the southern extremity of the Cape of Florida? Sir, I am ashamed to pursue this line of remark. I dislike it, I have an utter disgust for it. I would rather hear of natural blasts and mildews, war, pestilence, and famine, than to hear gentlemen talk of secession. To break up this great government! to dismember this glorious country! to astonish Europe with an act of folly such as Europe for two centuries has never beheld in any government or any people! No, Sir! no, Sir! There will be no secession! Gentlemen are not serious when they talk of secession...

And now, Mr. President, I draw these observations to a close. I have spoken freely, and I meant to do so. I have sought to make no display. I have sought to enliven the occasion by no animated discussion, nor have I attempted any train of elaborate argument. I have wished only to speak my sentiments, fully and at length, being desirous, once and for all, to let the Senate know, and to let the country know, the opinions and sentiments which I entertain on all these subjects. These opinions are not likely to be suddenly changed. If there be any future service that I can render to the country, consistently with these sentiments and opinions, I shall cheerfully render it. If there be not, I shall still be glad to have had an opportunity to disburden myself from the bottom of my heart, and to make known every political sentiment that therein exists.

And now, Mr. President, instead of speaking of the possibility or utility of secession, instead of dwelling in those caverns of darkness, instead of groping with those ideas so full of all that is horrid and horrible, let us come out into the light of day; let us enjoy the fresh air of Liberty and Union; let us cherish those hopes which belong to us; let us devote ourselves to those great objects that are fit for our consideration and action; let us raise our conceptions to the magnitude and the importance of the duties that devolve upon us; let our comprehension be as broad as the country for which we act, our asperations as high as its certain destiny; let us not be pigmies in a case that calls for men. Never did there devolve on any generation of men higher trusts than now devolve upon us, for the preservation of this Constitution and the harmony and peace of all who are destined to live under it. Let us make our generation one of the strongest and brightest links in that golden chain which is destined, I fondly believe, to grapple the people of all the States to this Constitution for ages to come. We have a great, popular, constitutional government, guarded by law and by judicature, and defended by the affections of the whole people. No monarchical throne presses these States together, no iron chain of military power encircles them; they live and stand under a government popular in its form, representative in its character, founded upon principles of equality, and so constructed, we hope, as to last for ever. In all its history it has been beneficent; it has trodden down no man's liberty; it has crushed no State. Its daily respiration is liberty and patriotism; its yet youthful veins are full of enterprise, courage, and honorable love of glory and renown. Large before, the country has noe, by recent events, become vastly larger. This republic now extends, with a vast breadth, across the whole continent. The two great seas of the world wash the one and the other shore. We realize, on a mighty scale, the beautiful description of the ornamental border of the buckler of Achilles:—

"Now, the broad shield completed, the artist crowned
With his last hand, and poured the ocean round;
In living silver seemed the waves to roll,
And beat the bucklers verge, and bound the whole."

SOJOURNER TRUTH **49**

Ain't I a Woman?, 1851

Sojourner Truth was born into slavery in New York around 1797 and escaped to freedom in 1826. Although uneducated, she became a famed evangelist, abolitionist, and women's rights advocate, delivering thundering speeches to crowds across the United States. This speech was delivered in 1851 to a women's rights convention in Akron, Ohio. In this address, she connects the struggle for freedom for the slaves and the quest for women's equality and dismisses the religious arguments against both. Sojourner Truth argued in this brief statement that freedom and equality were not complex legal issues but simply matters of what is right and what

Anti-Slavery Standard, May 2, 1863.

is wrong. She emphasized that everyone had the power to make equality a reality. This version of Truth's address was published in the Anti-Slavery Standard *on May 2, 1863, by fellow Akron delegate Frances Gage. This version was markedly different and far less eloquent than the alternate version, but it was more widely distributed and accepted as the standard for many years afterward.*

Well, children, where there is so much racket there must be something out of kilter. I think that 'twixt the negroes of the South and the women at the North, all talking about rights, the white men will be in a fix pretty soon. But what's all this here talking about? That man over there says that women need to be helped into carriages, and lifted over ditches, and to have the best place everywhere. Nobody ever helps me into carriages, or over mud-puddles, or gives me any best place! And ain't I a woman? Look at me! Look at my arm! I have ploughed and planted, and gathered into barns, and no man could head me! And ain't I a woman? I could work as much and eat as much as a man—when I could get it—and bear the lash as well! And ain't I a woman? I have borne thirteen children, and seen most all sold off to slavery, and when I cried out with my mother's grief, none but Jesus heard me! And ain't I a woman?

Then they talk about this thing in the head; what's this they call it? [member of audience whispers, "intellect"] That's it, honey. What's that got to do with women's rights or negroes' rights? If my cup won't hold but a pint, and yours holds a quart, wouldn't you be mean not to let me have my little half measure full?

Then that little man in black there, he says women can't have as much rights as men, 'cause Christ wasn't a woman! Where did your Christ come from? Where did your Christ come from? From God and a woman! Man had nothing to do with Him.

If the first woman God ever made was strong enough to turn the world upside down all alone, these women together ought to be able to turn it back, and get it right side up again! And now they is asking to do it, the men better let them.

Obliged to you for hearing me, and now old Sojourner ain't got nothing more to say.

SOJOURNER TRUTH **50**

Ain't I a Woman? (Alternate Version), 1851

This following alternate version is one of two versions of Sojourner Truth's famous address. It was first published on June 21, 1851, in the Anti-Slavery Bugle. *In recent years, more historians have accepted this version, as the* Bugle's *editor, Marcus Robinson, is known to have worked closely with Truth. Since this speech took place decades before sound recording technology existed, the exact words spoken on that day in 1851 may be a source of controversy for some time.*

Anti-Slavery Bugle, June 21, 1851.

I want to say a few words about this matter. I am a woman's rights. I have as much muscle as any man, and can do as much work as any man. I have plowed and reaped and husked and chopped and mowed, and can any man do more than that? I have heard much about the sexes being equal. I can carry as much as any man, and can eat as much too, if I can get it. I am as strong as any man that is now.

As for intellect, all I can say is, if a woman have a pint, and a man a quart—why can't she have her little pint full? You need not be afraid to give us our rights for fear we will take too much,—for we can't take more than our pint'll hold.

The poor men seems to be all in confusion, and don't know what to do. Why children, if you have woman's rights, give it to her and you will feel better. You will have your own rights, and they won't be so much trouble.

I can't read, but I can hear. I have heard the bible and have learned that Eve caused man to sin. Well, if woman upset the world, do give her a chance to set it right side up again. The Lady has spoken about Jesus, how he never spurned woman from him, and she was right. When Lazarus died, Mary and Martha came to him with faith and love and besought him to raise their brother. And Jesus wept and Lazarus came forth. And how came Jesus into the world? Through God who created him and the woman who bore him. Man, where was your part?

But the women are coming up blessed be God and a few of the men are coming up with them. But man is in a tight place, the poor slave is on him, woman is coming on him, he is surely between a hawk and a buzzard.

FREDERICK DOUGLASS **51**

What to the Slave Is the Fourth of July?, 1852

On July 5, 1852, Frederick Douglass delivered one of the most stirring abolitionist speeches in American history before the Rochester Ladies Anti-Slavery Society in Rochester, New York. This powerful address demonstrated the stark contrasts between white America and African-Americans living in slavery. For those living in freedom, the Fourth of July was a day to celebrate freedom; for those toiling under the chains of slavery, it only served to remind them of the birthright which they had been denied. Himself a former slave, Douglass mesmerized audiences with his graphic depictions of the institution and won him fame and admiration among abolitionists. Douglass emphasizes in this speech that in spite of the promise of freedom that the United States had built by this time, the system of slavery had left him as a non-American and reminded his audience that freedom would corrode in an atmosphere of slavery and

Frederick Douglass, "What to the Slave Is the Fourth of July?" *Against Slavery: An Abolitionist Reader*, Mason Lawrence, ed. (New York: Putnam Penguin, 2000): 39–45.

subjugation. Freedom for Douglass meant that he and other African-Americans must have the basic right to determine their own fates and not be considered anyone's property.

Mr. President, Friends and Fellow Citizens: He who could address this audience without a quailing sensation, has stronger nerves than I have. I do not remember ever to have appeared as a speaker before any assembly more shrinkingly, nor with greater distrust of my ability, than I do this day. A feeling has crept over me, quite unfavorable to the exercise of my limited powers of speech. The task before me is one which requires much previous thought and study for its proper performance. I know that apologies of this sort are generally considered flat and unmeaning. I trust, however, that mine will not be so considered. Should I seem at ease, my appearance would much misrepresent me. The little experience I have had in addressing public meetings, in country school houses, avails me nothing on the present occasion.

The papers and placards say, that I am to deliver a 4th [of] July oration. This certainly sounds large, and out of the common way, for it is true that I have often had the privilege to speak in this beautiful Hall, and to address many who now honor me with their presence. But neither their familiar faces, nor the perfect gage I think I have of Corinthian Hall, seems to free me from embarrassment.

The fact is, ladies and gentlemen, the distance between this platform and the slave plantation, from which I escaped, is considerable—and the difficulties to be overcome in getting from the latter to the former, are by no means slight. That I am here to-day is, to me, a matter of astonishment as well as of gratitude. You will not, therefore, be surprised, if in what I have to say, I evince no elaborate preparation, nor grace my speech with any high sounding exordium. With little experience and with less learning, I have been able to throw my thoughts hastily and imperfectly together; and trusting to your patient and generous indulgence, I will proceed to lay them before you.

This, for the purpose of this celebration, is the 4th of July. It is the birthday of your National Independence, and of your political freedom. This, to you, is what the Passover was to the emancipated people of God. It carries your minds back to the day, and to the act of your great deliverance; and to the signs, and to the wonders, associated with that act, and that day. This celebration also marks the beginning of another year of your national life; and reminds you that the Republic of America is now 76 years old. I am glad, fellow-citizens, that your nation is so young. Seventy-six years, though a good old age for a man, is but a mere speck in the life of a nation. Three score years and ten is the allotted time for individual men; but nations number their years by thousands. According to this fact, you are, even now, only in the beginning of your national career, still lingering in the period of childhood. I repeat, I am glad this is so. There is hope in the thought, and hope is much needed, under the dark clouds which lower above the horizon. The eye of the reformer is met with angry flashes, portending disastrous times; but his heart may well beat lighter at the thought that America is young, and that she is still in the impressible stage of her existence. May he not hope that high lessons of wisdom, of justice and of truth, will yet give direction to her destiny? Were the nation older, the patriot's heart might be sadder, and the reformer's brow heavier. Its future might be shrouded in gloom, and the hope of its prophets go out in sorrow. There is consolation in the thought that America is young. Great streams are not easily turned from channels, worn deep in the course of ages. They may sometimes rise in quiet and stately majesty, and inundate the land, refreshing and fertilizing the earth with their mysterious properties. They may also rise in wrath and fury, and bear away, on their angry waves, the accumulated wealth of years of toil and hardship. They, however, gradually flow back to the same old channel, and flow on as serenely as ever. But, while the river may not be turned aside, it may dry up, and leave nothing behind but the withered branch, and the unsightly rock, to howl in the abyss-sweeping wind, the sad tale of departed glory. As with rivers so with nations.

Fellow-citizens, I shall not presume to dwell at length on the associations that cluster about this day. The simple story of it is that, 76 years ago, the people of this country were British subjects. The style and title of your "sovereign people" (in which you now glory) was not then born. You were under the British Crown . Your fathers esteemed the English Government as the home government; and England as the fatherland. This home government, you know, although a considerable distance from your home, did, in the exercise of its parental prerogatives, impose upon its colonial children, such restraints, burdens and limitations, as, in its mature judgement, it deemed wise, right and proper.

But, your fathers, who had not adopted the fashionable idea of this day, of the infallibility of government, and the absolute character of its acts, presumed to differ from the home government in respect to the wisdom and the justice of some of those burdens and restraints. They went so far in their excitement as to pronounce the measures of government unjust, unreasonable, and oppressive, and altogether such as ought not to be quietly submitted to. I scarcely need say, fellow-citizens, that my opinion of those measures fully accords with that of your fathers. Such a declaration of agreement on my part would not be worth much to anybody. It would, certainly, prove nothing, as to what part I might have taken, had I lived during the great controversy of 1776. To say now that America was right, and England wrong, is exceedingly easy. Everybody can say it; the dastard, not less than the noble brave, can flippantly discant on the tyranny of England towards the American Colonies. It is fashionable to do so; but there was a time when to pronounce against England, and in favor of the cause of the colonies, tried men's souls. They who did so were accounted in their day, plotters of mischief, agitators and rebels, dangerous men. To side with the right, against the wrong, with the weak against the strong, and with the oppressed against the oppressor! Here lies the merit, and the one which, of all others, seems unfashionable in our day. The cause of liberty may be stabbed by the men who glory in the deeds of your fathers. But, to proceed.

Feeling themselves harshly and unjustly treated by the home government, your fathers, like men of honesty, and men of spirit, earnestly sought redress. They petitioned and remonstrated; they did so in a decorous, respectful, and loyal manner. Their conduct was wholly unexceptionable. This, however, did not answer the purpose. They saw themselves treated with sovereign indifference, coldness and scorn. Yet they persevered. They were not the men to look back.

As the sheet anchor takes a firmer hold, when the ship is tossed by the storm, so did the cause of your fathers grow stronger, as it breasted the chilling blasts of kingly displeasure. The greatest and best of British statesmen admitted its justice, and the loftiest eloquence of the British Senate came to its support. But, with that blindness which seems to be the unvarying characteristic of tyrants, since Pharaoh and his hosts were drowned in the Red Sea, the British Government persisted in the exactions complained of.

The madness of this course, we believe, is admitted now, even by England; but we fear the lesson is wholly lost on our present rulers.

Oppression makes a wise man mad. Your fathers were wise men, and if they did not go mad, they became restive under this treatment. They felt themselves the victims of grievous wrongs, wholly incurable in their colonial capacity. With brave men there is always a remedy for oppression. Just here, the idea of a total separation of the colonies from the crown was born! It was a startling idea, much more so, than we, at this distance of time, regard it. The timid and the prudent (as has been intimated) of that day, were, of course, shocked and alarmed by it.

Such people lived then, had lived before, and will, probably, ever have a place on this planet; and their course, in respect to any great change, (no matter how great the good to be attained, or the wrong to be redressed by it), may be calculated with as much precision as can be the course of the stars. They hate all changes, but silver, gold and copper change! Of this sort of change they are always strongly in favor.

These people were called tories in the days of your fathers; and the appellation, probably, conveyed the same idea that is meant by a more modern, though a somewhat less euphonious term, which we often find in our papers, applied to some of our old politicians.

Their opposition to the then dangerous thought was earnest and powerful; but, amid all their terror and affrighted vociferations against it, the alarming and revolutionary idea moved on, and the country with it.

On the 2nd of July, 1776, the old Continental Congress, to the dismay of the lovers of ease, and the worshipers of property, clothed that dreadful idea with all the authority of national sanction. They did so in the form of a resolution; and as we seldom hit upon resolutions, drawn up in our day, whose transparency is at all equal to this, it may refresh your minds and help my story if I read it.

"Resolved, That these united colonies are, and of right, ought to be free and Independent States; that they are absolved from all allegiance to the British Crown; and that all political connection between them and the State of Great Britain is, and ought to be, dissolved."

Citizens, your fathers made good that resolution. They succeeded; and to-day you reap the fruits of their success. The freedom gained is yours; and you, therefore, may properly celebrate this anniversary. The 4th of July is the first great fact in your nation's history—the very ring-bolt in the chain of your yet undeveloped destiny.

Pride and patriotism, not less than gratitude, prompt you to celebrate and to hold it in perpetual remembrance. I have said that the Declaration of Independence is the ring-bolt to the chain of your nation's destiny; so, indeed, I regard it. The principles contained in that instrument are saving principles. Stand by those principles, be true to them on all occasions, in all places, against all foes, and at whatever cost.

From the round top of your ship of state, dark and threatening clouds may be seen. Heavy billows, like mountains in the distance, disclose to the leeward huge forms of flinty rocks! That bolt drawn, that chain broken, and all is lost. Cling to this day—cling to it, and to its principles, with the grasp of a storm-tossed mariner to a spar at midnight.

The coming into being of a nation, in any circumstances, is an interesting event. But, besides general considerations, there were peculiar circumstances which make the advent of this republic an event of special attractiveness.

The whole scene, as I look back to it, was simple, dignified and sublime.

The population of the country, at the time, stood at the insignificant number of three millions. The country was poor in the munitions of war. The population was weak and scattered, and the country a wilderness unsubdued. There were then no means of concert and combination, such as exist now. Neither steam nor lightning had then been reduced to order and discipline. From the Potomac to the Delaware was a journey of many days. Under these, and innumerable other disadvantages, your fathers declared for liberty and independence and triumphed.

Fellow Citizens, I am not wanting in respect for the fathers of this republic. The signers of the Declaration of Independence were brave men. They were great men too—great enough to give fame to a great age. It does not often happen to a nation to raise, at one time, such a number of truly great men. The point from which I am compelled to view them is not, certainly, the most favorable; and yet I cannot contemplate their great deeds with less than admiration. They were statesmen, patriots and heroes, and for the good they did, and the principles they contended for, I will unite with you to honor their memory.

They loved their country better than their own private interests; and, though this is not the highest form of human excellence, all will concede that it is a rare virtue, and that when it is exhibited, it ought to command respect. He who will, intelligently, lay down his life for his country, is a man whom it is not in human nature to despise. Your fathers staked their lives, their fortunes, and their sacred honor, on the cause of their country. In their admiration of liberty, they lost sight of all other interests.

They were peace men; but they preferred revolution to peaceful submission to bondage. They were quiet men; but they did not shrink from agitating against oppression. They showed forbearance; but that they knew its limits. They believed in order; but not in the order of tyranny. With them, nothing was "settled" that was not right. With them, justice, liberty and humanity were "final;" not slavery and oppression. You may well cherish the memory of such men. They were great in their day and generation. Their solid manhood stands out the more as we contrast it with these degenerate times.

How circumspect, exact and proportionate were all their movements! How unlike the politicians of an hour! Their statesmanship looked beyond the passing moment, and stretched away in strength into the distant future. They seized upon eternal principles, and set a glorious example in their defence. Mark them!

Fully appreciating the hardship to be encountered, firmly believing in the right of their cause, honorably inviting the scrutiny of an on-looking world, reverently appealing to heaven to attest their sincerity, soundly comprehending the solemn responsibility they were about to assume, wisely measuring the terrible odds against them, your fathers, the fathers of this republic, did, most deliberately, under the inspiration of a glorious patriotism, and with a sublime faith in the great principles of justice and freedom, lay deep the corner-stone of the national superstructure, which has risen and still rises in grandeur around you.

Of this fundamental work, this day is the anniversary. Our eyes are met with demonstrations of joyous enthusiasm. Banners and pennants wave exultingly on the breeze. The din of business, too, is hushed. Even Mammon seems to have quitted his grasp on this day. The ear-piercing fife and the stirring drum unite their accents with the ascending peal of a thousand church bells. Prayers are made, hymns are sung, and sermons are preached in honor of this day; while the quick martial tramp of a great and multitudinous nation, echoed back by all the hills, valleys and mountains of a vast continent, bespeak the occasion one of thrilling and universal interests nation's jubilee.

Friends and citizens, I need not enter further into the causes which led to this anniversary. Many of you understand them better than I do. You could instruct me in regard to them. That is a branch of knowledge in which you feel, perhaps, a much deeper interest than your speaker. The causes which led to the separation of the colonies from the British crown have never lacked for a tongue. They have all been taught in your common schools, narrated at your firesides, unfolded from your pulpits, and thundered from your legislative halls, and are as familiar to you as household words. They form the staple of your national poetry and eloquence.

I remember, also, that, as a people, Americans are remarkably familiar with all facts which make in their own favor. This is esteemed by some as a national trait— perhaps a national weakness. It is a fact, that whatever makes for the wealth or for the reputation of Americans, and can be had cheaply will be found by Americans. I shall not be charged with slandering Americans, if I say I think the American side of any question may be safely left in American hands.

I leave, therefore, the great deeds of your fathers to other gentlemen whose claim to have been regularly descended will be less likely to be disputed than mine!

THE PRESENT

My business, if I have any here to-day, is with the present. The accepted time with God and his cause is the ever-living now.

> "Trust no future, however pleasant,
> Let the dead past bury its dead;
> Act, act in the living present,
> Heart within, and God overhead."

We have to do with the past only as we can make it useful to the present and to the future. To all inspiring motives, to noble deeds which can be gained from the past, we are welcome. But now is the time, the important time. Your fathers have lived, died, and have done their work, and have done much of it well. You live and must die, and you must do your work. You have no right to enjoy a child's share in the labor of your fathers, unless your children are to be blest by your labors. You have no right to wear out and waste the hard-earned fame of your fathers to cover your indolence. Sydney Smith tells us that men seldom eulogize the wisdom and virtues of their fathers, but to excuse some folly or wickedness of their own. This truth is not a doubtful one. There are illustrations of it near and remote, ancient and modern. It was fashionable, hundreds of years ago, for the children of Jacob to boast, we have "Abraham to our father," when they had long lost Abraham's faith and spirit. That people contented themselves under the shadow of Abraham's great name, while they repudiated the deeds which made his name great. Need I remind you that a similar thing is being done all over this country to-day? Need I tell you that the Jews are not the only people who built the tombs of the prophets, and garnished the sepulchres of the righteous? Washington could not die till he had broken the chains of his slaves. Yet his monument is built up by the price of human blood, and the traders in the bodies and souls of men, shout—"We have Washington to our father." Alas! that it should be so; yet so it is.

> "The evil that men do, lives after them,
> The good is oft' interred with their bones."

Fellow-citizens, pardon me, allow me to ask, why am I called upon to speak here to-day? What have I, or those I represent, to do with your national independence? Are the great principles of political freedom and of natural justice, embodied in that Declaration of Independence, extended to us? and am I, therefore, called upon to bring our humble offering to the national altar, and to confess the benefits and express devout gratitude for the blessings resulting from your independence to us?

Would to God, both for your sakes and ours, that an affirmative answer could be truthfully returned to these questions! Then would my task be light, and my burden easy and delightful. For who is there so cold, that a nation's sympathy could not warm him? Who so obdurate and dead to the claims of gratitude, that would not thankfully acknowledge such priceless benefits? Who so stolid and selfish, that would not give his voice to swell the hallelujahs of a nation's jubilee, when the chains of servitude had been torn from his limbs? I am not that man. In a case like that, the dumb might eloquently speak, and the "lame man leap as an hart."

But, such is not the state of the case. I say it with a sad sense of the disparity between us. I am not included within the pale of this glorious anniversary! Your high independence only reveals the immeasurable distance between us. The blessings in which you, this day, rejoice, are not enjoyed in common. The rich inheritance of justice, liberty, prosperity and independence, bequeathed by your fathers, is shared by you, not by me. The sunlight that brought life and healing to you, has brought stripes and death to me. This Fourth [of] July is yours, not mine. You may rejoice, I must mourn. To drag a man in fetters into the grand illuminated temple of liberty, and call upon him to join you in joyous anthems, were inhuman mockery and sacrilegious irony. Do you mean, citizens, to mock me, by asking me to speak to-day? If so, there is a parallel to your conduct. And let me warn you that it is dangerous to copy the example of a nation whose crimes, lowering up to heaven, were thrown down by the breath of the Almighty, burying that nation in irrecoverable ruin! I can to-day take up the plaintive lament of a peeled and woe-smitten people!

"By the rivers of Babylon, there we sat down. Yea! We wept when we remembered Zion. We hanged our harps upon the willows in the midst thereof. For there, they that carried us away captive, required of us a song; and they who wasted us required of us mirth, saying, Sing us one of the songs of Zion. How can we sing the Lord's song in a strange land? If I forget thee, O Jerusalem, let my right hand forget her cunning. If I do not remember thee, let my tongue cleave to the roof of my mouth."

Fellow-citizens; above your national, tumultous joy, I hear the mournful wail of millions! whose chains, heavy and grievous yesterday, are, to-day, rendered more intolerable by the jubilee shouts that reach them. If I do forget, if I do not faithfully remember those bleeding children of sorrow this day, "may my right hand forget her cunning, and may my tongue cleave to the roof of my mouth!" To forget them, to pass lightly over their wrongs, and to chime in with the popular theme, would be treason most scandalous and shocking, and would make me a reproach before God and the world. My subject, then fellow-citizens, is AMERICAN SLAVERY. I shall see, this day, and its popular characteristics, from the slave's point of view. Standing, there, identified with the American bondman, making his wrongs mine, I do not hesitate to declare, with all my soul, that the character and conduct of this nation never looked blacker to me than on this 4th of July! Whether we turn to the declarations of the past, or to the professions of the present, the conduct of the nation seems equally hideous and revolting. America is false to the past, false to the present, and solemnly binds herself to be false to the future. Standing with God and the crushed and bleeding slave on this occasion, I will, in the name of humanity which is outraged, in the name of liberty which is fettered, in the name of the constitution and the Bible, which are disregarded and trampled upon, dare to call in question and to denounce, with all the emphasis I can command, everything that serves to perpetuate slavery-the great sin and shame of America! "I will not equivocate; I will not excuse;" I will use the severest language I can command; and yet not one word shall escape me that any man, whose judgement is not blinded by prejudice, or who is not at heart a slaveholder, shall not confess to be right and just.

But I fancy I hear some one of my audience say, it is just in this circumstance that you and your brother abolitionists fail to make a favorable impression on the public mind. Would you argue more, and denounce less, would you persuade more, and rebuke less, your cause would be much more likely to succeed. But, I submit, where all is plain there is nothing to be argued. What point in the anti-slavery creed would you have me argue? On what branch of the subject do the people of this country need light? Must I undertake to prove that the slave is a man? That point is conceded already. Nobody doubts it. The slaveholders themselves acknowledge it in the enactment of laws for their government. They acknowledge it when they punish disobedience on the part of the slave. There are seventy-two crimes in the State of Virginia, which, if committed by a black man, (no matter how ignorant he be), subject him to the punishment of death; while only two of the same crimes will subject a white man to the like punishment. What is this but the acknowledgement that the slave is a moral, intellectual and responsible being? The manhood of the slave is conceded. It is admitted in the fact that Southern statute books are covered with enactments forbidding, under severe fines and penalties, the teaching of the slave to read or to write. When you can point to any such laws, in reference to the beasts of the field, then I may consent to argue the manhood of the slave. When the dogs in your streets, when the fowls of the air, when the cattle on your hills, when the fish of the sea, and the reptiles that crawl, shall be unable to distinguish the slave from a brute, there will I argue with you that the slave is a man!

For the present, it is enough to affirm the equal manhood of the negro race. Is it not astonishing that, while we are ploughing, planting and reaping, using all kinds of mechanical tools, erecting houses, constructing bridges, building ships, working in metals of brass, iron, copper, silver and gold; that, while we are reading, writing and cyphering, acting as clerks, merchants and secretaries, having among us lawyers, doctors, ministers, poets, authors, editors, orators and teachers; that, while we are engaged in all manner of enterprises common to other men, digging gold in California, capturing the whale in the Pacific, feeding sheep and cattle on the hillside, living, moving, acting, thinking, planning, living in families as husbands, wives and children, and, above all, confessing and worshipping the Christian's God, and looking hopefully for life and immortality beyond the grave, we are called upon to prove that we are men!

Would you have me argue that man is entitled to liberty? That he is the rightful owner of his own body? You have already declared it. Must I argue the wrongfulness of slavery? Is that a question for Republicans? Is it to be settled by the rules of logic and argumentation, as a matter beset with great difficulty, involving a doubtful application of the principle of justice, hard to be understood? How should I look to-day, in the presence of Americans, dividing, and subdividing a discourse, to show that men have a natural right to freedom? speaking of it relatively, and positively, negatively, and affirmatively. To do so, would be to make myself ridiculous, and lo offer an insult to your understanding. There is not a man beneath the canopy of heaven, that does not know that slavery is wrong for him.

What, am I to argue that it is wrong to make men brutes, to rob them of their liberty, to work them without wages, to keep them ignorant of their relations to their fellow men, to beat them with sticks, to flay their flesh with the lash, to load their limbs with irons, to hunt them with dogs, to sell them at auction, to sunder their families, to knock out their teeth, to burn their flesh, to starve them into obedience and submission to their masters? Must I argue that a system thus marked with blood, and stained with pollution, is wrong? No! I will not. I have better employments for my time and strength, than such arguments would imply.

What, then, remains to be argued? Is it that slavery is not divine; that God did not establish it; that our doctors of divinity are mistaken? There is blasphemy in the thought. That which is inhuman, cannot be divine! Who can reason on such a proposition? They that can, may; I cannot. The time for such argument is past.

At a time like this, scorching irony, not convincing argument, is needed. O! had I the ability, and could I reach the nation's ear, I would, to-day, pour out a fiery stream of biting ridicule, blasting reproach, withering sarcasm, and stern rebuke. For it is not light that is needed, but fire; it is not the gentle shower, but thunder. We need the storm, the whirlwind, and the earthquake. The feeling of the nation must be quickened; the conscience of the nation must be roused; the propriety of the nation must be startled; the hypocrisy of the nation must be exposed; and its crimes against God and man must be proclaimed and denounced.

What, to the American slave, is your 4th of July? I answer: a day that reveals to him, more than all other days in the year, the gross injustice and cruelty to which he is the constant victim. To him, your celebration is a sham; your boasted liberty, an unholy license; your national greatness, swelling vanity; your sounds of rejoicing are empty and heartless; your denunciations of tyrants, brass fronted impudence; your shouts of liberty and equality, hollow mockery; your prayers and hymns, your sermons and thanksgivings, with all your religious parade, and solemnity, are, to him, mere bombast, fraud, deception, impiety, and hypocrisy—a thin veil to cover up crimes which would disgrace a nation of savages. There is not a nation on the earth guilty of practices, more shocking and bloody, than are the people of these United States, at this very hour.

Go where you may, search where you will, roam through all the monarchies and despotisms of the old world, travel through South America, search out every abuse, and when you have found the last, lay your facts by the side of the everyday practices of this nation, and you will say with me, that, for revolting barbarity and shameless hypocrisy, America reigns without a rival.

INTERNAL SLAVE TRADE

Take the American slave-trade, which, we are told by the papers, is especially prosperous just now. Ex-Senator [of Missouri, Thomas Hart] Benton tells us that the price of men was never higher than now. He mentions the fact to show that slavery is in no danger. This trade is one of the peculiarities of American institutions. It is carried on in all the large towns and cities in one-half of this confederacy; and millions are pocketed every year, by dealers in this horrid traffic. In several states, this trade is a chief source of wealth. It is called (in contradistinction to the foreign slave-trade) "the internal slave trade." It is, probably, called so, too, in order to divert from it the horror with which the foreign slave-trade is contemplated. That trade has long since been denounced by this government, as piracy. It has been denounced with burning words, from the high places of the nation, as an execrable traffic. To arrest it, to put an end to it, this nation keeps a squadron, at immense cost, on the coast of Africa. Everywhere, in this country, it is safe to speak of this foreign slave-trade, as a most inhuman traffic, opposed alike to the laws of God and of man. The duty to extirpate and destroy it, is admitted even by our DOCTORS OF DIVINITY. In order to put an end to it, some of these last have consented that their colored brethren (nominally free) should leave this country, and establish themselves on the western coast of Africa! It is, however, a notable fact that, while so much execration is poured out by Americans upon those engaged in the foreign slave-trade, the men engaged in the slave-trade between the states pass without condemnation, and their business is deemed honorable.

Behold the practical operation of this internal slave-trade, the American slave-trade, sustained by American politics and American religion. Here you will see men and women reared like swine for the market. You know what is a swine-drover? I will show you a man-drover. They inhabit all our Southern States. They perambulate the country, and crowd the highways of the nation, with droves of human stock. You will see one of these human flesh-jobbers, armed with pistol, whip and bowie-knife, driving a company of a hundred men, women, and children, from the Potomac to the slave market at New Orleans. These wretched people are to be sold singly, or in lots, to suit purchasers. They are food for the cotton-field, and the deadly sugar-mill. Mark the sad procession, as it moves wearily along, and the inhuman wretch who drives them. Hear his savage yells and his blood-chilling oaths, as he hurries on his affrighted captives! There, see the old man, with locks thinned and gray. Cast one glance, if you please, upon that young mother, whose shoulders are bare to the scorching sun, her briny tears falling on the brow of the babe in her arms. See, too, that girl of thirteen, weeping, yes! Weeping, as she thinks of the mother from whom she has been torn! The drove moves tardily. Heat and sorrow have nearly consumed their strength; suddenly you hear a quick snap, like the discharge of a rifle; the fetters clank, and the chain rattles simultaneously; your ears are saluted with a scream, that seems to have torn its way to the centre of your soul! The crack you heard, was the sound of the slave-whip; the scream you heard, was from the woman you saw with the babe. Her speed had faltered under the weight of her child and her chains! That gash on her shoulder tells her to move on. Follow this drove to New Orleans. Attend the auction; see men examined like horses; see the forms of women rudely and brutally exposed to the shocking gaze of American slave-buyers. See this drove sold and separated forever; and never forget the deep, sad sobs that arose from that scattered multitude. Tell me citizens, WHERE, under the sun, you can witness a spectacle more fiendish and shocking. Yet this is but a glance at the American slave-trade, as it exists, at this moment, in the ruling part of the United States.

I was born amid such sights and scenes. To me the American slave-trade is a terrible reality. When a child, my soul was often pierced with a sense of its horrors. I lived on Philpot Street, Fell's Point, Baltimore, and have watched from the wharves, the slave ships in the Basin, anchored from the shore, with their cargoes of human flesh, waiting for favorable winds to waft them down the Chesapeake. There was, at that time, a grand slave mart kept at the head of Pratt Street, by Austin Woldfolk. His agents were sent into every town and county in Maryland, announcing their arrival, through the papers, and on flaming "hand-bills," headed CASH FOR NEGROES. These men were generally well dressed men, and very captivating in their manners. Ever ready to drink, to treat, and to gamble. The fate of many a slave has depended upon the turn of a single card; and many a child has been snatched from the arms of its mother by bargains arranged in a state of brutal drunkenness.

The flesh-mongers gather up their victims by dozens, and drive them, chained, to the general depot at Baltimore. When a sufficient number have been collected here, a ship is chartered, for the purpose of conveying the forlorn crew to Mobile, or to New Orleans. From the slave prison to the ship, they are usually driven in the darkness of night; for since the antislavery agitation, a certain caution is observed.

In the deep still darkness of midnight, I have been often aroused by the dead heavy footsteps, and the piteous cries of the chained gangs that passed our door. The anguish of my boyish heart was intense; and I was often consoled, when speaking to my mistress in the morning, to hear her say that the custom was very wicked; that she hated to hear the rattle of the chains, and the heart-rending cries. I was glad to find one who sympathised with me in my horror.

Fellow-citizens, this murderous traffic is, to-day, in active operation in this boasted republic. In the solitude of my spirit, I see clouds of dust raised on the highways of the South; I see the bleeding footsteps; I hear the doleful wail of fettered humanity, on the way to the slave-markets, where the victims are to be sold like horses, sheep, and swine, knocked off to the highest bidder. There I see the tenderest ties ruthlessly broken, to gratify the lust, caprice and rapacity of the buyers and sellers of men. My soul sickens at the sight.

> Is this the land your Fathers loved,
> The freedom which they toiled to win?
> Is this the earth whereon they moved?
> Are these the graves they slumber in?"

But a still more inhuman, disgraceful, and scandalous state of things remains to be presented.

By an act of the American Congress, not yet two years old, slavery has been nationalized in its most horrible and revolting form. By that act, Mason & Dixon's line has been obliterated; New York has become as Virginia; and the power to hold, hunt, and sell men, women, and children as slaves remains no longer a mere state institution, but is now an institution of the whole United States. The power is co-extensive with the star-spangled banner and American Christianity. Where these go, may also go the merciless slave-hunter. Where these are, man is not sacred. He is a bird for the sportsman's gun. By that most foul and fiendish of all human decrees, the liberty and person of every man are put in peril. Your broad republican domain is hunting ground for men. Not for thieves and robbers, enemies of society, merely, but for men guilty of no crime. Your lawmakers have commanded all good citizens to engage in this hellish sport. Your President, your Secretary of State, your lords, nobles, and ecclesiastics, enforce, as a duty you owe to your free and glorious country, and to your God, that you do this accursed thing. Not fewer than forty Americans have, within the past two years, been hunted down and, without a moment's warning, hurried away in chains, and consigned to slavery and excruciating torture. Some of these have had wives and children, dependent on them for bread; but of this, no account was made. The right of the hunter to his prey stands superior to the right of marriage, and to all rights in this republic, the rights of God included! For black men there are neither law, justice, humanity, not religion. The Fugitive Slave Law makes MERCY TO THEM, A CRIME; and bribes the judge who tries them. An American JUDGE GETS TEN DOLLARS FOR EVERY VICTIM HE CONSIGNS to slavery, and five, when he fails to do so. The oath of any two villains is sufficient, under this hell-black enactment, to send the most pious and exemplary black man into the remorseless jaws of slavery! His own testimony is nothing. He can bring no witnesses for himself. The minister of American justice is bound by the law to hear but one side; and that side, is the side of the oppressor. Let this damning fact be perpetually told. Let it be thundered around the world, that, in tyrant-killing, king-hating, people-loving, democratic, Christian America, the seats of justice are filled with judges, who hold their offices under an open and palpable bribe, and are bound, in deciding in the case of a man's liberty, hear only his accusers!

In glaring violation of justice, in shameless disregard of the forms of administering law, in cunning arrangement to entrap the defenceless, and in diabolical intent, this Fugitive Slave Law stands alone in the annals of tyrannical legislation. I doubt if there be another nation on the globe, having the brass and the baseness to put such a law on the statute-book. If any man in this assembly thinks differently from me in this matter, and feels able to disprove my statements, I will gladly confront him at any suitable time and place he may select.

RELIGIOUS LIBERTY

I take this law to be one of the grossest infringements of Christian Liberty, and, if the churches and ministers of our country were not stupidly blind, or most wickedly indifferent, they, too, would so regard it.

At the very moment that they are thanking God for the enjoyment of civil and religious liberty, and for the right to worship God according to the dictates of their own consciences, they are utterly silent in respect to a law which robs religion of its chief significance, and makes it utterly worthless to a world lying in wickedness. Did this law concern the "mint, anise and cumin"—abridge the right to sing psalms, to partake of the sacrament, or to engage in any of the ceremonies of religion, it would be smitten by the thunder of a thousand pulpits. A general shout would go up from the church, demanding repeal, repeal, instant repeal! And it would go hard with that politician who presumed to solicit the votes of the people without inscribing this motto on his banner. Further, if this demand were not complied with, another Scotland would be added to the history of religious liberty, and the stern old Covenanters would be thrown into the shade. A John Knox would be seen at every church door, and heard from every pulpit, and Fillmore would have no more quarter than was shown by Knox, to the beautiful, but treacherous queen Mary of Scotland. The fact that the church of our country, (with fractional exceptions), does not esteem "the Fugitive Slave Law" as a declaration of war against religious liberty, implies that that church regards religion simply as a form of worship, an empty ceremony, and not a vital principle, requiring active benevolence, justice, love and good will towards man. It esteems sacrifice above mercy; psalm-singing above right doing; solemn meetings above practical righteousness. A worship that can be conducted by persons who refuse to give shelter to the houseless, to give bread to the hungry, clothing to the naked, and who enjoin obedience to a law forbidding these acts of mercy, is a curse, not a blessing to mankind. The Bible addresses all such persons as "scribes, pharisees, hypocrites, who pay tithe of mint, anise, and cummin, and have omitted the weightier matters of the law, judgement, mercy and faith."

THE CHURCH RESPONSIBLE

But the church of this country is not only indifferent to the wrongs of the slave, it actually takes sides with the oppressors. It has made itself the bulwark of American slavery, and the shield of American slave-hunters. Many of its most eloquent Divines. who stand as the very lights of the church, have shamelessly given the sanction of religion and the Bible to the whole slave system. They have taught that man may, properly, be a slave; that the relation of master and slave is ordained of God; that to send back an escaped bondman to his master is clearly the duty of all the followers of the Lord Jesus Christ; and this horrible blasphemy is palmed off upon the world for Christianity.

For my part, I would say, welcome infidelity! welcome atheism! welcome anything! in preference to the gospel, as preached by those Divines! They convert the very name of religion into an engine of tyranny, and barbarous cruelty, and serve to confirm more infidels, in this age, than all the infidel writings of Thomas Paine, Voltaire, and Bolingbroke, put together, have done! These ministers make religion a cold and flinty-hearted thing, having neither principles of right action, nor bowels of compassion. They strip the love of God of its beauty, and leave the throne of religion a huge, horrible, repulsive form. It is a religion for oppressors, tyrants, man-stealers, and thugs. It is not that "pure and undefiled religion" which is from above, and which is "first pure, then peaceable, easy to be entreated, full of mercy and good fruits, without partiality, and without hypocrisy." But a religion which favors the rich against the poor; which exalts the proud above the humble; which divides mankind into two classes, tyrants and slaves; which says to the man in chains, stay there; and to the oppressor, oppress on; it is a religion which may be professed and enjoyed by all the robbers and enslavers of mankind; it makes God a respecter of persons, denies his fatherhood of the race, and tramples in the dust the great truth of the brotherhood of man. All this we affirm to be true of the popular church, and the popular worship of our land and nation—a religion, a church, and a worship which, on the authority of inspired wisdom, we pronounce to be an abomination in the sight of God. In the language of Isaiah, the American church might be well addressed, "Bring no more vain ablations; incense is an abomination unto me: the new moons and Sabbaths, the calling of assemblies, I cannot away with; it is iniquity, even the solemn meeting. Your new moons and your appointed feasts my soul hateth. They are a trouble to me; I am weary to bear them; and when ye spread forth your hands I will hide mine eyes from you. Yea! When ye make many prayers, I will not hear. YOUR HANDS ARE FULL OF BLOOD; cease to do evil, learn to do well; seek judgement; relieve the oppressed; judge for the fatherless; plead for the widow."

The American church is guilty, when viewed in connection with what it is doing to uphold slavery; but it is superlatively guilty when viewed in connection with its ability to abolish slavery. The sin of which it is guilty is one of omission as well as of commission. Albert Barnes but uttered what the common sense of every man at all observant of the actual state of the case will receive as truth, when he declared that "There is no power out of the church that could sustain slavery an hour, if it were not sustained in it."

Let the religious press, the pulpit, the Sunday school, the conference meeting, the great ecclesiastical, missionary, Bible and tract associations of the land array their immense powers against slavery and slave-holding; and the whole system of crime and blood would be scattered to the winds; and that they do not do this involves them in the most awful responsibility of which the mind can conceive.

In prosecuting the anti-slavery enterprise, we have been asked to spare the church, to spare the ministry; but how, we ask, could such a thing be done? We are met on the threshold of our efforts for the redemption of the slave, by the church and ministry of the country, in battle arrayed against us; and we are compelled to fight or flee. From what quarter, I beg to know, has proceeded a fire so deadly upon our ranks, during the last two years, as from the Northern pulpit? As the champions of oppressors, the chosen men of American theology have appeared—men, honored for their so-called piety, and their real learning. The LORDS of Buffalo, the SPRINGS of New York, the LATHROPS of Auburn, the COXES and SPENCERS of Brooklyn, the GANNETS and SHARPS of Boston, the DEWEYS of Washington, and other great religious lights of the land, have, in utter denial of the authority of Him, by whom they professed to he called to the ministry, deliberately taught us, against the example of the Hebrews and against the remonstrance of the Apostles, they teach "that we ought to obey man's law before the law of God."

My spirit wearies of such blasphemy; and how such men can be supported, as the "standing types and representatives of Jesus Christ," is a mystery which I leave others to penetrate. In speaking of the American church, however, let it be distinctly understood that I mean the great mass of the religious organizations of our land. There are exceptions, and I thank God that there are. Noble men may be found, scattered all over these Northern States, of whom Henry Ward Beecher of Brooklyn, Samuel J.

May of Syracuse, and my esteemed friend on the platform [Rev. R. R. Raymond], are shining examples; and let me say further, that upon these men lies the duty to inspire our ranks with high religious faith and zeal, and to cheer us on in the great mission of the slave's redemption from his chains.

RELIGION IN ENGLAND AND RELIGION IN AMERICA

One is struck with the difference between the attitude of the American church towards the anti-slavery movement, and that occupied by the churches in England towards a similar movement in that country. There, the church, true to its mission of ameliorating, elevating, and improving the condition of mankind, came forward promptly, bound up the wounds of the West Indian slave, and restored him to his liberty. There, the question of emancipation was a high[ly] religious question. It was demanded, in the name of humanity, and according to the law of the living God. The Sharps, the Clarksons, the Wilberforces, the Buxtons, and Burchells and the Knibbs, were alike famous for their piety, and for their philanthropy. The anti-slavery movement there was not an anti-church movement, for the reason that the church took its full share in prosecuting that movement: and the anti-slavery movement in this country will cease to be an anti-church movement, when the church of this country shall assume a favorable, instead of a hostile position towards that movement. Americans! Your republican politics, not less than your republican religion, are flagrantly inconsistent. You boast of your love of liberty, your superior civilization, and your pure Christianity, while the whole political power of the nation (as embodied in the two great political parties), is solemnly pledged to support and perpetuate the enslavement of three millions of your countrymen. You hurl your anathemas at the crowned headed tyrants of Russia and Austria, and pride yourselves on your Democratic institutions, while you yourselves consent to be the mere tools and bodyguards of the tyrants of Virginia and Carolina. You invite to your shores fugitives of oppression from abroad, honor them with banquets, greet them with ovations, cheer them, toast them, salute them, protect them, and pour out your money to them like water; but the fugitives from your own land you advertise, hunt, arrest, shoot and kill. You glory in your refinement and your universal education; yet you maintain a system as barbarous and dreadful as ever stained the character of a nation—a system begun in avarice, supported in pride, and perpetuated in cruelty. You shed tears over fallen Hungary, and make the sad story of her wrongs the theme of your poets, statesmen and orators, till your gallant sons are ready to fly to arms to vindicate her cause against her oppressors; but, in regard to the ten thousand wrongs of the American slave, you would enforce the strictest silence, and would hail him as an enemy of the nation who dares to make those wrongs the subject of public discourse! You are all on fire at the mention of liberty for France or for Ireland; but are as cold as an iceberg at the thought of liberty for the enslaved of America. You discourse eloquently on the dignity of labor; yet, you sustain a system which, in its very essence, casts a stigma upon labor. You can bare your bosom to the storm of British artillery to throw off a threepenny tax on tea; and yet wring the last hard-earned farthing from the grasp of the black laborers of your country. You profess to believe "that, of one blood, God made all nations of men to dwell on the face of all the earth," and hath commanded all men, everywhere to love one another; yet you notoriously hate, (and glory in your hatred), all men whose skins are not colored like your own. You declare, before the world, and are understood by the world to declare, that you "hold these truths to be self evident, that all men are created equal; and are endowed by their Creator with certain inalienable rights; and that, among these are, life, liberty, and the pursuit of happiness;" and yet, you hold securely, in a bondage which, according to your own Thomas Jefferson, "is worse than ages of that which your fathers rose in rebellion to oppose," a seventh part of the inhabitants of your country.

Fellow-citizens! I will not enlarge further on your national inconsistencies. The existence of slavery in this country brands your republicanism as a sham, your humanity as a base pretence, and your Christianity as a lie. It destroys your moral power abroad; it corrupts your politicians at home. It saps the foundation of religion; it makes your name a hissing, and a by word to a mocking earth. It is the antagonistic force in your government, the only thing that seriously disturbs and endangers your Union. It fetters your progress; it is the enemy of improvement, the deadly foe of education; it fosters pride; it breeds insolence; it promotes vice; it shelters crime; it is a curse to the earth that supports it; and yet, you cling to it, as if it were the sheet anchor of all your hopes. Oh! Be warned! Be warned! A horrible reptile is coiled up in your nation's bosom; the venomous creature is nursing at the tender breast of your youthful republic; for the love of God, tear away, and fling from you the hideous monster, and let the weight of twenty millions crush and destroy it forever!

THE CONSTITUTION

But it is answered in reply to all this, that precisely what I have now denounced is, in fact, guaranteed and sanctioned by the Constitution of the United States; that the right to hold and to hunt slaves is a part of that Constitution framed by the illustrious Fathers of this Republic.

Then, I dare to affirm, notwithstanding all I have said before, your fathers stooped, basely stooped

"To palter with us in a double sense:
And keep the word of promise to the ear,
But break it to the heart."

And instead of being the honest men I have before declared them to be, they were the veriest imposters that ever practised on mankind. This is the inevitable conclusion, and from it there is no escape. But I differ from those who charge this baseness on the framers of the Constitution of the United States. It is a slander upon their memory, at least, so I believe. There is not time now to argue the constitutional question at length—nor have I the ability to discuss it as it ought to be discussed. The subject has been handled with masterly power by Lysander Spooner, Esq., by William Goodell, by Samuel E. Sewall, Esq., and last, though not least, by Gerritt Smith, Esq. These gentlemen have, as I think, fully and clearly vindicated the Constitution from any design to support slavery for an hour.

Fellow-citizens! there is no matter in respect to which, the people of the North have allowed themselves to be so ruinously imposed upon, as that of the pro-slavery character of the Constitution. In that instrument I hold there is neither warrant, license, nor sanction of the hateful thing; but, interpreted as it ought to be interpreted, the Constitution is a GLORIOUS LIBERTY DOCUMENT. Read its preamble, consider its purposes. Is slavery among them? Is it at the gateway? or is it in the temple? It is neither. While I do not intend to argue this question on the present occasion, let me ask, if it be not somewhat singular that, if the Constitution were intended to be, by its framers and adopters, a slave-holding instrument, why neither slavery, slaveholding, nor slave can anywhere be found in it. What would be thought of an instrument, drawn up, legally drawn up, for the purpose of entitling the city of Rochester to a tract of land, in which no mention of land was made? Now, there are certain rules of interpretation, for the proper understanding of all legal instruments. These rules are well established. They are plain, common-sense rules, such as you and I, and all of us, can understand and apply, without having passed years in the study of law. I scout the idea that the question of the constitutionality or unconstitutionality of slavery is not a question for the people. I hold that every American citizen has a right to form an opinion of the constitution, and to propagate that opinion, and to use all honorable means to make his opinion the prevailing one. Without this right, the liberty of an American citizen would be as insecure as that of a Frenchman. Ex-Vice-President [George M.] Dallas tells us that the constitution is an object to which no American mind can be too attentive, and no American heart too devoted. He further says, the constitution, in its words, is plain and intelligible, and is meant for the home-bred, unsophisticated understandings of our fellow-citizens. Senator Berrien tell us that the Constitution is the fundamental law, that which controls all others. The charter of our liberties, which every citizen has a personal interest in understanding thoroughly. The testimony of Senator [Sidney] Breese, [Senator] Lewis Cass, and many others that might be named, who are everywhere esteemed as sound lawyers, so regard the constitution. I take it, therefore, that it is not presumption in a private citizen to form an opinion of that instrument.

Now, take the constitution according to its plain reading, and I defy the presentation of a single pro-slavery clause in it. On the other hand it will be found to contain principles and purposes, entirely hostile to the existence of slavery.

I have detained my audience entirely too long already. At some future period I will gladly avail myself of an opportunity to give this subject a full and fair discussion.

Allow me to say, in conclusion, notwithstanding the dark picture I have this day presented of the state of the nation, I do not despair of this country. There are forces in operation, which must inevitably work. The downfall of slavery. "The arm of the Lord is not shortened," and the doom of slavery is certain. I, therefore, leave off where I began, with hope. While drawing encouragement from the Declaration of Independence, the great principles it contains, and the genius of American Institutions, my spirit is also cheered by the obvious tendencies of the age. Nations do not now stand in the same relation to each other that they did ages ago. No nation can now shut itself up from the surrounding world, and trot round in the same old path of its fathers without interference. The time was when such could be done. Long established customs of hurtful character could formerly fence themselves in, and do their evil work with social impunity. Knowledge was then confined and enjoyed by the privileged few, and the multitude walked on in mental darkness. But a change has now come over the affairs of mankind. Walled cities and empires have become unfashionable. The arm of commerce has borne away the gates of the strong city. Intelligence is penetrating the darkest corners of the globe. It makes its pathway over and under the sea, as well as on the earth. Wind, steam, and lightning are its chartered agents. Oceans no longer divide, but link nations together. From Boston to London is now a holiday excursion. Space is comparatively annihilated. Thoughts expressed on one side of the Atlantic are, distinctly heard on the other. The far off and almost fabulous Pacific rolls in grandeur at our feet. The Celestial Empire, the mystery of ages, is being solved. The fiat of the Almighty, "Let there be Light," has not yet spent its force. No abuse, no outrage whether in taste, sport or avarice, can now hide itself from the all-pervading light. The iron shoe, and crippled foot of China must be seen, in contrast with nature. Africa must rise and put on her yet unwoven garment. "Ethiopia shall stretch out her hand unto God." In the fervent aspirations of William Lloyd Garrison, I say, and let every heart join in saying it:

> God speed the year of jubilee
> The wide world o'er!
> When from their galling chains set free,
> Th' oppress'd shall vilely bend the knee,
> And wear the yoke of tyranny
> Like brutes no more.
> That year will come, and freedom's reign,
> To man his plundered rights again
> Restore.
>
> God speed the day when human blood
> Shall cease to flow!
> In every clime be understood,
> The claims of human brotherhood,
> And each return for evil, good,
> Not blow for blow;
> That day will come all feuds to end
> And change into a faithful friend
> Each foe.
>
> God speed the hour, the glorious hour,
> When none on earth
> Shall exercise a lordly power,
> Nor in a tyrant's presence cower;
> But all to manhood's stature tower,
> By equal birth!
> THAT HOUR WILL, COME, to each, to all,
> And from his prison-house, the thrall
> Go forth.

Until that year, day, hour, arrive,
With head, and heart, and hand I'll strive,
To break the rod, and rend the gyve,
The spoiler of his prey deprive-
So witness Heaven!
And never from my chosen post,
Whate'er the peril or the cost,
Be driven.

ABRAHAM LINCOLN **52**

First Inaugural Address, 1861

As Abraham Lincoln took the oath of office as the sixteenth President of the United States on March 4, 1861, seven states had seceded from the Union. More threatened to follow and the nation was on the edge of civil war. Lincoln pleaded for peace, the continuation of the Union, and the preservation of the Constitution. This address was an appeal to the nation's sense of community, and the idea of all men uniting for the common defense of freedom, which the Constitution stood for.

Fellow-Citizens of the United States:

In compliance with a custom as old as the Government itself, I appear before you to address you briefly and to take in your presence the oath prescribed by the Constitution of the United States to be taken by the President "before he enters on the execution of this office." I do not consider it necessary at present for me to discuss those matters of administration about which there is no special anxiety or excitement. Apprehension seems to exist among the people of the Southern States that by the accession of a Republican Administration their property and their peace and personal security are to be endangered. There has never been any reasonable cause for such apprehension. Indeed, the most ample evidence to the contrary has all the while existed and been open to their inspection. It is found in nearly all the published speeches of him who now addresses you. I do but quote from one of those speeches when I declare that—I have no purpose, directly or indirectly, to interfere with the institution of slavery in the States where it exists. I believe I have no lawful right to do so, and I have no inclination to do so.

Those who nominated and elected me did so with full knowledge that I had made this and many similar declarations and had never recanted them; and more than this,

Abraham Lincoln, "First Inaugural Address," *Selected Writings of Abraham Lincoln*, Herbert Mitgang, ed. (New York: Bantam, 1992): 145–155.

they placed in the platform for my acceptance, and as a law to themselves and to me, the clear and emphatic resolution which I now read:

> *Resolved*, That the maintenance inviolate of the rights of the States, and especially the right of each State to order and control its own domestic institutions according to its own judgment exclusively, is essential to that balance of power on which the perfection and endurance of our political fabric depend; and we denounce the lawless invasion by armed force of the soil of any State or Territory, no matter under what pretext, as among the gravest of crimes.

I now reiterate these sentiments, and in doing so I only press upon the public attention the most conclusive evidence of which the case is susceptible that the property, peace, and security of no section are to be in any wise endangered by the now incoming Administration. I add, too, that all the protection which, consistently with the Constitution and the laws, can be given will be cheerfully given to all the States when lawfully demanded, for whatever cause—as cheerfully to one section as to another.

There is much controversy about the delivering up of fugitives from service or labor. The clause I now read is as plainly written in the Constitution as any other of its provisions:

> No person held to service or labor in one State, under the laws thereof, escaping into another, shall in consequence of any law or regulation therein be discharged from such service or labor, but shall be delivered up on claim of the party to whom such service or labor may be due.

It is scarcely questioned that this provision was intended by those who made it for the reclaiming of what we call fugitive slaves; and the intention of the lawgiver is the law. All members of Congress swear their support to the whole Constitution—to this provision as much as to any other. To the proposition, then, that slaves whose cases come within the terms of this clause "shall be delivered up" their oaths are unanimous. Now, if they would make the effort in good temper, could they not with nearly equal unanimity frame and pass a law by means of which to keep good that unanimous oath?

There is some difference of opinion whether this clause should be enforced by national or by State authority, but surely that difference is not a very material one. If the slave is to be surrendered, it can be of but little consequence to him or to others by which authority it is done. And should anyone in any case be content that his oath shall go unkept on a merely unsubstantial controversy as to *how* it shall be kept?

Again: In any law upon this subject ought not all the safeguards of liberty known in civilized and humane jurisprudence to be introduced, so that a free man be not in any case surrendered as a slave? And might it not be well at the same time to provide by law for the enforcement of that clause in the Constitution which guarantees that "the citizens of each State shall be entitled to all privileges and immunities of citizens in the several States"?

I take the official oath to-day with no mental reservations and with no purpose to construe the Constitution or laws by any hypercritical rules; and while I do not choose now to specify particular acts of Congress as proper to be enforced, I do suggest that it will be much safer for all, both in official and private stations, to conform to and abide by all those acts which stand unrepealed than to violate any of them trusting to find impunity in having them held to be unconstitutional.

It is seventy-two years since the first inauguration of a President under our National Constitution. During that period fifteen different and greatly distinguished citizens have in succession administered the executive branch of the Government. They have conducted it through many perils, and generally with great success. Yet, with all this scope for precedent, I now enter upon the same task for the brief constitutional term of four years under great and peculiar difficulty. A disruption of the Federal Union, heretofore only menaced, is now formidably attempted.

I hold, that in contemplation of universal law, and of the Constitution, the Union of these States is perpetual. Perpetuity is implied, if not expressed, in the fundamental law of all national governments. It is safe to assert that no government proper ever had a provision in its organic law for its own termination. Continue to execute all the express provisions of our National Constitution, and the Union will endure forever, it being impossible to destroy it except by some action not provided for in the instrument itself.

Again: If the United States be not a government proper, but an association of States in the nature of contract merely, can it, as a contract, be peaceably unmade by less than all the parties who made it? One party to a contract may violate it—break it, so to speak—but does it not require all to lawfully rescind it?

Descending from these general principles, we find the proposition that in legal contemplation the Union is perpetual confirmed by the history of the Union itself. The Union is much older than the Constitution. It was formed, in fact, by the Articles of Association in 1774. It was matured and continued by the Declaration of Independence in 1776. It was further matured, and the faith of all the then thirteen States expressly plighted and engaged that it should be perpetual, by the Articles of Confederation in 1778. And finally, in 1787, one of the declared objects for ordaining and establishing the Constitution was *"to form a more perfect Union."*

But if destruction of the Union by one or by a part only of the States be lawfully possible, the Union is *less* perfect than before the Constitution, having lost the vital element of perpetuity.

It follows from these views that no State upon its own mere motion can lawfully get out of the Union; that *resolves* and *ordinances* to that effect are legally void, and that acts of violence within any State or States against the authority of the United States are insurrectionary or revolutionary, according to circumstances.

I therefore consider that in view of the Constitution and the laws the Union is unbroken, and to the extent of my ability, I shall take care, as the Constitution itself expressly enjoins upon me, that the laws of the Union be faithfully executed in all the States. Doing this I deem to be only a simple duty on my part, and I shall perform it so far as practicable unless my rightful masters, the American people, shall withhold the requisite means or in some authoritative manner direct the contrary. I trust this will not be regarded as a menace, but only as the declared purpose of the Union that it *will* constitutionally defend and maintain itself.

In doing this there needs to be no bloodshed or violence, and there shall be none unless it be forced upon the national authority. The power confided to me will be used to hold, occupy, and possess the property and places belonging to the Government and to collect the duties and imposts; but beyond what may be necessary for these objects, there will be no invasion, no using of force against or among the people anywhere. Where hostility to the United States in any interior locality shall be so great and universal as to prevent competent resident citizens from holding the Federal offices, there will be no attempt to force obnoxious strangers among the people for that object. While the strict legal right may exist in the Government to enforce the exercise of these offices, the attempt to do so would be so irritating and so nearly impracticable withal that I deem it better to forego for the time the uses of such offices.

The mails, unless repelled, will continue to be furnished in all parts of the Union. So far as possible the people everywhere shall have that sense of perfect security which is most favorable to calm thought and reflection. The course here indicated will be followed unless current events and experience shall show a modification or change to be proper, and in every case and exigency my best discretion will be exercised, according to circumstances actually existing and with a view and a hope of a peaceful solution of the national troubles and the restoration of fraternal sympathies and affections.

That there are persons in one section or another who seek to destroy the Union at all events and are glad of any pretext to do it I will neither affirm nor deny; but if there be such, I need address no word to them. To those, however, who really love the Union may I not speak?

Before entering upon so grave a matter as the destruction of our national fabric, with all its benefits, its memories, and its hopes, would it not be wise to ascertain precisely why we do it? Will you hazard so desperate a step while there is any possibility that any portion of the ills you fly from have no real existence? Will you, while the certain ills you fly to are greater than all the real ones you fly from, will you risk the commission of so fearful a mistake?

All profess to be content in the Union if all constitutional rights can be maintained. Is it true, then, that any right plainly written in the Constitution has been denied? I think not. Happily, the human mind is so constituted that no party can reach to the audacity of doing this. Think, if you can, of a single instance in which a plainly written provision of the Constitution has ever been denied. If by the mere force of numbers a majority should deprive a minority of any clearly written constitutional right, it might in a moral point of view justify revolution; certainly would if such right were a vital one. But such is not our case. All the vital rights of minorities and of individuals are so plainly assured to them by affirmations and negations, guaranties and prohibitions, in the Constitution that controversies never arise concerning them. But no organic law can ever be framed with a provision specifically applicable to every question which may occur in practical administration. No foresight can anticipate nor any document of reasonable length contain express provisions for all possible questions. Shall fugitives from labor be surrendered by national or by State authority? The Constitution does not expressly say. *May* Congress prohibit slavery in the Territories? The Constitution does not expressly say. *Must* Congress protect slavery in the Territories? The Constitution does not expressly say.

From questions of this class spring all our constitutional controversies, and we divide upon them into majorities and minorities. If the minority will not acquiesce, the majority must, or the Government must cease. There is no other alternative, for continuing the Government is acquiescence on one side or the other. If a minority in such case will secede rather than acquiesce, they make a precedent which in turn will divide and ruin them, for a minority of their own will secede from them whenever a majority refuses to be controlled by such minority. For instance, why may not any portion of a new confederacy a year or two hence arbitrarily secede again, precisely as portions of the present Union now claim to secede from it? All who cherish disunion sentiments are now being educated to the exact temper of doing this. Is there such perfect identity of interests among the States to compose a new union as to produce harmony only and prevent renewed secession?

Plainly the central idea of secession is the essence of anarchy. A majority held in restraint by constitutional checks and limitations, and always changing easily with deliberate changes of popular opinions and sentiments, is the only true sovereign of a free people. Whoever rejects it does of necessity fly to anarchy or to despotism. Unanimity is impossible. The rule of a minority, as a permanent arrangement, is wholly inadmissible; so that, rejecting the majority principle, anarchy or despotism in some form is all that is left.

I do not forget the position assumed by some that constitutional questions are to be decided by the Supreme Court, nor do I deny that such decisions must be binding in any case upon the parties to a suit as to the object of that suit, while they are also entitled to very high respect and consideration in all parallel cases by all other departments of the Government. And while it is obviously possible that such decision may be erroneous in any given case, still the evil effect following it, being limited to that particular case, with the chance that it may be overruled and never become a precedent for other cases, can better be borne than could the evils of a different practice. At the same time, the candid citizen must confess that if the policy of the Government upon vital questions affecting the whole people is to be irrevocably fixed by decisions of the Supreme Court, the instant they are made in ordinary litigation between parties in personal actions the people will have ceased to be their own rulers, having to that extent practically resigned their Government into the hands of that eminent tribunal. Nor is there in this view any assault upon the court or the judges. It is a duty from which they may not shrink to decide cases properly brought before them, and it is no fault of theirs if others seek to turn their decisions to political purposes.

One section of our country believes slavery is *right* and ought to be extended, while the other believes it is *wrong* and ought not to be extended. This is the only substantial dispute. The fugitive-slave clause of the Constitution and the law for the suppression of the foreign slave trade are each as well enforced, perhaps, as any law can ever be in a community where the moral sense of the people imperfectly supports the law itself. The great body of the people abide by the dry legal obligation in both cases, and a few break over in each. This, I think, can not be perfectly cured, and it would be worse in both cases *after* the separation of the sections than before. The foreign slave trade, now imperfectly suppressed, would be ultimately revived without restriction in one section, while fugitive slaves, now only partially surrendered, would not be surrendered at all by the other.

Physically speaking, we can not separate. We can not remove our respective sections from each other nor build an impassable wall between them. A husband and wife may be divorced and go out of the presence and beyond the reach of each other, but the different parts of our country can not do this. They can not but remain face to face, and intercourse, either amicable or hostile, must continue between them. Is it possible, then, to make that intercourse more advantageous or more satisfactory *after* separation than *before?* Can aliens make treaties easier than friends can make laws? Can treaties be more faithfully enforced between aliens than laws can among friends? Suppose you go to war, you can not fight always; and when, after much loss on both sides and no gain on either, you cease fighting, the identical old questions, as to terms of intercourse, are again upon you.

This country, with its institutions, belongs to the people who inhabit it. Whenever they shall grow weary of the existing Government, they can exercise their *constitutional* right of amending it or their *revolutionary* right to dismember or overthrow it. I can not be ignorant of the fact that many worthy and patriotic citizens are desirous of having the National Constitution amended. While I make no recommendation of amendments, I fully recognize the rightful authority of the people over the whole subject, to be exercised in either of the modes prescribed in the instrument itself; and I should, under existing circumstances, favor rather than oppose a fair opportunity being afforded the people to act upon it.

I will venture to add that to me the convention mode seems preferable, in that it allows amendments to originate with the people themselves, instead of only permitting them to take or reject propositions originated by others, not especially chosen for the purpose, and which might not be precisely such as they would wish to either accept or refuse. I understand a proposed amendment to the Constitution—which amendment, however, I have not seen—has passed Congress, to the effect that the Federal Government shall never interfere with the domestic institutions of the States, including that of persons held to service. To avoid misconstruction of what I have said, I depart from my purpose not to speak of particular amendments so far as to say that, holding such a provision to now be implied constitutional law, I have no objection to its being made express and irrevocable.

The Chief Magistrate derives all his authority from the people, and they have referred none upon him to fix terms for the separation of the States. The people themselves can do this if also they choose, but the Executive as such has nothing to do with it. His duty is to administer the present Government as it came to his hands and to transmit it unimpaired by him to his successor.

Why should there not be a patient confidence in the ultimate justice of the people? Is there any better or equal hope in the world? In our present differences, is either party without faith of being in the right? If the Almighty Ruler of Nations, with His eternal truth and justice, be on your side of the North, or on yours of the South, that truth and that justice will surely prevail by the judgment of this great tribunal of the American people.

By the frame of the Government under which we live this same people have wisely given their public servants but little power for mischief, and have with equal wisdom provided for the return of that little to their own hands at very short intervals. While the people retain their virtue and vigilance no Administration by any extreme of wickedness or folly can very seriously injure the Government in the short space of four years.

My countrymen, one and all, think calmly and *well* upon this whole subject. Nothing valuable can be lost by taking time. If there be an object to *hurry* any of you in hot haste to a step which you would never take *deliberately*, that object will be frustrated by taking time; but no good object can be frustrated by it. Such of you as are now dissatisfied still have the old Constitution unimpaired, and, on the sensitive point, the laws of your own framing under it; while the new Administration will have no immediate power, if it would, to change either. If it were admitted that you who are dissatisfied hold the right side in the dispute, there still is no single good reason for precipitate action. Intelligence, patriotism, Christianity, and a firm reliance on Him who has never yet forsaken this favored land are still competent to adjust in the best way all our present difficulty.

In *your* hands, my dissatisfied fellow-countrymen, and not in *mine*, is the momentous issue of civil war. The Government will not assail *you*. You can have no conflict without being yourselves the aggressors. *You* have no oath registered in heaven to destroy the Government, while I shall have the most solemn one to "preserve, protect, and defend it." I am loath to close. We are not enemies, but friends. We must not be enemies. Though passion may have strained it must not break our bonds of affection. The mystic chords of memory, stretching from every battlefield and patriot grave to every living heart and hearthstone all over this broad land, will yet swell the chorus of the Union, when again touched, as surely they will be, by the better angels of our nature.

ABRAHAM LINCOLN **53**

The Emancipation Proclamation, 1863

As the Civil War wore on, many abolitionists pressed President Abraham Lincoln to make the freeing of the slaves a war aim. Concerned about the four slave states still in the Union and the attitudes of northern white soldiers, Lincoln hesitated initially. After the Battle of Antietam, the repulse the Confederate attack on Maryland encouraged Lincoln to proceed with emancipation. On September 22, 1862, he sent a warning to the Confederacy to cease its hostilities against the Union government within one hundred days or all slaves in areas under Confederate control would be declared free and liberated once under Union control. The South ignored Lincoln's demands in the Preliminary Emancipation Proclamation, and on January 1, 1863, Lincoln issued the Emancipation Proclamation, freeing those slaves. With the stroke of a pen, Lincoln changed the focus of the war and paved the way for the freedom of roughly one out of every four slaves still in bondage. This statement became the ultimate declaration of freedom—the right to live a life without oppression.

Abraham Lincoln, "Emancipation Proclamation," *Selected Writings of Abraham Lincoln*, 261–263; "Emancipation Proclamation," http://www.ourdocuments.gov/doc.php?flash=true&doc=34

A PROCLAMATION

Whereas on the 22nd day of September, A.D. 1862, a proclamation was issued by the President of the United States, containing, among other things, the following, to wit:

"That on the 1st day of January, A.D. 1863, all persons held as slaves within any State or designated part of a State the people whereof shall then be in rebellion against the United States shall be then, thenceforward, and forever free; and the executive government of the United States, including the military and naval authority thereof, will recognize and maintain the freedom of such persons and will do no act or acts to repress such persons, or any of them, in any efforts they may make for their actual freedom."

"That the executive will on the 1st day of January aforesaid, by proclamation, designate the States and parts of States, if any, in which the people thereof, respectively, shall then be in rebellion against the United States; and the fact that any State or the people thereof shall on that day be in good faith represented in the Congress of the United States by members chosen thereto at elections wherein a majority of the qualified voters of such States shall have participated shall, in the absence of strong countervailing testimony, be deemed conclusive evidence that such State and the people thereof are not then in rebellion against the United States."

Now, therefore, I, Abraham Lincoln, President of the United States, by virtue of the power in me vested as Commander-In-Chief of the Army and Navy of the United States in time of actual armed rebellion against the authority and government of the United States, and as a fit and necessary war measure for supressing said rebellion, do, on this 1st day of January, A.D. 1863, and in accordance with my purpose so to do, publicly proclaimed for the full period of one hundred days from the first day above mentioned, order and designate as the States and parts of States wherein the people thereof, respectively, are this day in rebellion against the United States the following, to wit:

Arkansas, Texas, Louisiana (except the parishes of St. Bernard, Plaquemines, Jefferson, St. John, St. Charles, St. James, Ascension, Assumption, Terrebone, Lafourche, St. Mary, St. Martin, and Orleans, including the city of New Orleans), Mississippi, Alabama, Florida, Georgia, South Carolina, North Carolina, and Virginia (except the forty-eight counties designated as West Virginia, and also the counties of Berkeley, Accomac, Northhampton, Elizabeth City, York, Princess Anne, and Norfolk, including the cities of Norfolk and Portsmouth), and which excepted parts are for the present left precisely as if this proclamation were not issued.

And by virtue of the power and for the purpose aforesaid, I do order and declare that all persons held as slaves within said designated States and parts of States are, and henceforward shall be, free; and that the Executive Government of the United States, including the military and naval authorities thereof, will recognize and maintain the freedom of said persons.

And I hereby enjoin upon the people so declared to be free to abstain from all violence, unless in necessary self-defence; and I recommend to them that, in all case when allowed, they labor faithfully for reasonable wages.

And I further declare and make known that such persons of suitable condition will be received into the armed service of the United States to garrison forts, positions, stations, and other places, and to man vessels of all sorts in said service.

And upon this act, sincerely believed to be an act of justice, warranted by the Constitution upon military necessity, I invoke the considerate judgment of mankind and the gracious favor of Almighty God.

ABRAHAM LINCOLN **54**

The Gettysburg Address, 1863

The Gettysburg Address has become one of the most famous statements on the dedication to freedom and the Civil War. Abraham Lincoln delivered this address on November 19, 1863, as part of a day-long dedication of the new national cemetery at Gettysburg, Pennsylvania. The battle just four months earlier had left thousands dead and would shift the course of the war in favor of the Union. But the war in 1863 seemed to have no end in sight. In this speech, Lincoln refocused the aim of the Union cause against the Confederacy. The men at Gettysburg and other battlefields across the land had died for freedom, and the living must continue that cause. Lincoln declared that democratic government, the right of the people to rule their government was a cause worth fighting for and a cause worth dying for. Lincoln himself would die less than two years later just as the Union clenched victory.

Fourscore and seven years ago our fathers brought forth on this continent a new nation, conceived in liberty and dedicated to the proposition that all men are created equal.

Now we are engaged in a great civil war, testing whether that nation, or any nation so conceived and so dedicated, can long endure. We are met on a great battle-field of that war. We have come to dedicate a portion of that field as a final resting-place for those who here gave their lives that that nation might live. It is altogether fitting and proper that we should do this. But, in a larger sense, we cannot dedicate—we cannot consecrate—we cannot hallow—this ground. The brave men, living and dead, who struggled here have consecrated it, far above our poor power to add or detract. The world will little note, nor long remember what we say here, but it can never forget what they did here. It is for us the living, rather, to be dedicated here to the unfinished work which they who fought here have thus far so nobly advanced. It is rather for us to be here dedicated to the great task remaining before us—that from these honored dead we take increased devotion to that cause for which they gave the

Abraham Lincoln, "Gettysburg Address," *Selected Writings of Abraham Lincoln*, 279–280; "Gettysburg Address," http://www.ourdocuments.gov/doc.php?flash=true&doc=36

last full measure of devotion—that we here highly resolve that these dead shall not have died in vain—that this nation, under God, shall have a new birth of freedom and that government of the people, by the people, for the people, shall not perish from the earth.

ZEBULON VANCE **55**

The Duties of Defeat, 1866

Zebulon Vance had been a strong Unionist while in Congress in the years before the Civil War but joined the Confederate Army when North Carolina seceded in May 1861. He served as governor of North Carolina from 1862 until the Confederacy collapsed in 1865, with his arrest and brief imprisonment by Union troops. At this address before the Dialectic and Philanthropic societies at the University of North Carolina on June 7, 1866, Vance appealed to the embittered population of former Confederates in his state to accept the new political reality. Though he praised the efforts of Confederate troops and the Reconstruction policies of President Andrew Johnson, he also extolled the idea that the South's survivors had a duty to rebuild a prosperous democratic nation. Vance explained that even the vanquished in America still had rights. As part of a democracy, the will of the majority must be accepted, but the minority still enjoys rights and still has a voice. Although many southerners were still hostile to the idea of emancipation or any rights for racial minorities (African-Americans in particular), the idea of rights for the political minority had a resonance in a region that had feared the political minority would be destroyed by the majority. Though the idea of civil rights for racial minorities would not become a reality in the South for another century, the principle that all individuals had a voice in a democracy would become an important force in the civil rights debate. Vance would again be elected governor of North Carolina in 1876.

Gentlemen of the Dialectic and Philanthropic Societies:

As the traveller, who, during his absence, has learned that a great fire has swept over his native city, welcomes with the keenest rapture the first glance of his own home, which he trembles at the thought of finding in the ashes of the general ruin, so should *we* rejoice, to behold our honored University surviving the wreck of so much that we loved and revered.—Though staggering under the blows of adversity, I am most happy to see for myself, this day, so goodly a display of her ancient life and energy. May she soon attain to that full measure of prosperity and usefulness, which has heretofore rendered her the pride and chiefest ornament of North Carolina!

Zebulon B. Vance, *The Duties of Defeat: An Address Delivered Before the Two Literary Societies of the University of North Carolina, June 7th, 1866.* Raleigh, NC: William B. Smith and Co., 1866.

Since the first keel of an European vessel grated upon the sands of the new world, and the first axe was lifted against the vast forest which covered it as with a crown of glory, the lines could not have fallen to the educated young men of our State in a more interesting or important era. We stand to-day amidst the stranded fragments and floating timbers of the greatest civil war in history. Astounded at the mighty results we are as yet unable to comprehend them. Indeed, the profound significance of their full philosophical import, can scarcely be gathered by this generation. For we are not yet at the end of the Revolution as is popularly supposed, but are only, as we trust, at the end of armed violence. The changes, which constituted the real objects of the Revolution, began with us, only when the last Confederate soldier, by laying down his arms, removed that last obstacle to their approach.

Revolutions are not now what they were. They partake in the manner of their accomplishment of the spirit of the age; and are hurried forward by the same impulses of science and discovery which have so accelerated the material affairs of the world. How suddenly all of our well settled theories in regard to the relative powers and duties of the States and the Federal Government, have been overthrown, and the whole system changed, it is astonishing to contemplate. The almost immediate emancipation of three million five hundred thousand slaves, without one moment's preparation, of either themselves or their masters, for the great change, is equally unprecedented, and brings us with breathless haste, face to face, with some of the most startling and dangerous questions of the age. But when we remember some of the chief strides of physical science in the past few years, our wonder will diminish. It was but thirty-six years ago that the first railroad was built, and the first steam engine mounted upon his iron track. Already there are in existence fifty-six thousand miles, threading and permeating the civilized world; more than enough, if stretched out in straight and parallel lines, to bind an iron girdle twice around the solid framework of the globe! That narrow highway of the lightning—now become the guide and friend of the engine,—if stretched by its side, would enable one to hurl his words around the entire earth, returning to him who spoke them almost ere they had sounded upon his own ear! By these and similar wondrous agencies, during the recent war, two stupendous *corps d'armée*, who were facing each other on the banks of the Potomac, would steal in their picket lines under cover of darkness, and, rushing away with all their trains and animals, and munitions of war, would, within a few short hours, be hurled against each other again in deadly strife on some distant field, half across the continent! Change, therefore, not only cometh upon us, but cometh with speed and with power.

Perhaps in modern annals there will scarcely be found a parallel to the complete ruin and impoverishment of the people of the Southern States. Absolute annihilation of a great community by armed violence is deemed scarcely possible in modern times, though instances are not wanting among the ancients, before a humane code of international law had interposed to protect the weak against the strong, and mitigate the horrors of war. The most wonderful example was that of Carthage.—Though her walls were twenty-seven miles in circumference, and she could keep five hundred elephants for the public amusements; though she could send three hundred thousand soldiers to the invasion of Greece, while Rome was engaged in a death struggle with a petty town only twelve miles distant from her walls; though the waters of every sea were white with her sails and the shores of every known land were visited by her merchants, or planted with her colonies; yet the iron hand of her rival smote her so utterly into the dust that there is not a *vestige left!* Not a monument is standing; no literature, no relic of her laws, her language or her blood remains. The very site of this great city is of the doubtful knowledge of the antiquary. Such barbarous inflictions of a barbarous age we have indeed escaped, but changes greater than the dreams of the wildest, and ruin, social and political, fearfully deep, has been our hapless lot.—A glance at these things, for the purpose of attempting to deduce the outline of the changed duties which devolve upon us, will suffice to-day.

What with the value of our slaves, the injury inflicted upon real property, the destruction of personal, the depreciation or annihilation of all manner of stocks and securities, together with the sums expended in the maintenance of the war, make our material losses alone, all told, in the estimation of the most prudent, equal to five thousand million dollars! And of that highest and noblest property of a State—her citizens—full two hundred and fifty thousand of our bravest and best have perished by the casualties of war alone! The filling up of this fearful outline, with the revolting minutiæ of individual suffering, or the estimation of the moral losses we have incurred, is a task I have neither heart nor time for attempting. The whole scene reminds one of the portraiture of Rome, drawn by one of the panegyrists, when addressing the Emperor Theodosius:—"Thou, Rome, that having once suffered by the madness of Cinna, and of the cruel Marius raging from banishment, and of Sylla that won his wreath of prosperity from thy disasters, and of Cæsar compassionate to the dead, didst shudder at every blast of the trumpet filled by the breath of civil commotion.—Thou, that beside the wreck of thy soldiery perishing on either side, didst bewail amongst thy spectacles of domestic woe, the luminaries of thy Senate extinguished, the heads of thy consuls fixed upon a halberd, weeping for ages over thy slaughtered Catos, thy headless Ciceros and unburied Pompeys;—to whom the party madness of thy own children had wrought in every age heavier woe than the Carthaginians thundering at thy gates, or the Gaul admitted within thy walls; on whom Emathia more fatal than the day of Allia—Collina more dismal than Cannæ—had inflicted such deep memorials of wounds that, from bitter experience of thy own valor no enemy was to thee so formidable as thyself." Would that, with the spirit of prophecy, I could add the remainder of the quotation: "Now first in thy long annals, thou didst rest from a civil war in such a peace, that righteously and with maternal tenderness, thou mightest claim for it the honors of a civic triumph!"

Upon our own beloved State a full share of these common calamities has fallen. Nor does it relieve them of their crushing weight to remember the deep hostility of her people to the policy which inaugurated them. Quiet, conservative, law-abiding, as her people have ever been,—though jealous of their rights and honor, and ready at any moment to perish for them,—yet slow to violate compacts, they have never ceased to prefer exhausting all civil remedies for the redress of public grievances rather than evoke the terrible and uncertain arbitrament of revolution. Steady in the exercise of this resolution, she was forced, the very last, into a conflict which she was the very first in maintaining. The sufferings of our people have, indeed, been fearfully commensurate with their honesty and their courage. With her homesteads burned to ashes, with fields desolated, with thousands of her noblest and bravest children sleeping in beds of slaughter; innumerable orphans, widows, and helpless persons, reduced to beggary and deprived of their natural protectors; her corporations bankrupt and her own credit gone; her public charities overthrown, her educational fund utterly lost, her land filled from end to end with her maimed and mutilated soldiers; denied all representation in the public councils, her heart-broken and wretched people are not only oppressed with the weight of their own indebtedness, but are crushed into the very dust by taxation for the mighty debt incurred as the cost of their own subjugation! The very race of beasts of burthen,—by which alone we could extort bread from the half-tilled earth,—was, at the close of hostilities, almost destroyed; leaving us destitute of even the means of labor! Such a picture of suffering would seem sufficient to sate a generous enemy, and should move the deepest depths in the bosoms of her loving sons. Truly might they, as during the ever memorable year 1865 they beheld "all this wealth and glory turn'd to dust and tears," have fancied that they could hear:

"A cry of nations o'er her sunken halls,
A loud lament along the sweeping sea."

It was enough to cause her despairing children to re-echo the plaintive wail of the poet over fallen Venice:

"There is no hope for nations. Search the page
Of many thousand years,—the daily scene,
The flood and ebb of each recurring age,
The everlasting *to be* which *hath been*,
Hath taught us naught or little,—still we lean
On things that rot beneath our weight, and wear
Our strength away in wrestling with the air."

There was indeed a cry and a lament, through all her borders. From her Alpine heights to her tidal sands, from her plains and valleys and all her habitations, the wail went up. The dismal cypress, garlanded with funereal moss, became fit emblem of her woe; and her sombre pines, moaning in the breeze, sang requiems solemn, as for the dead. And though nature was still kindly, and invited us to forget our sorrow; though the sun still warmed and cherished the earth; though the early and the latter rains still descended according to the Promise, clothing the fields with verdure, and causing the tender herb to put forth; and though the mocking bird—sweetest of our warblers—embowered within the shadows of his leafy home, poured forth his glorious song, "every note that we loved awaking," yet no joyous response stirred our bosoms. It seemed, indeed, that despair had claimed us for her own. We felt that it was demanded of us to sing a song in a strange land, and we could but hang our harps upon the willows of our own native rivers—famous now with the rich memories of our children's blood—and weep when we remembered the pleasant places from which we had fallen. It was in truth a prospect to appal the stoutest hearted; and many of our aged and infirm, who had bravely borne all the sufferings of a four years war, have sunk down like the oak which, having withstood the storm, yet falls in the ensuing calm, and died, "rejoicing exceedingly and being glad that they could find the grave."

Such are the changes through which we have passed and are still passing. Such is the condition, physical and social, of your country at the moment when you are to enter upon the earnest duties of life. You will probably agree with me in thinking that the time is an important one, and that the duties before young men of education and patriotism differ widely from, and far exceed in weighty responsibility, those which have devolved on any of your predecessors.

It will not be improper to glance at some of the peculiar fields where your energies, as well as your kindly charities, may be most beneficially expended. The task of uplifting and regenerating our fallen country, indeed, belongs to us all; but it will devolve more especially upon you. Neither spent, nor broken down, by the fierce conflicts and deadly disappointments of the past, your fresh spirits are not only endowed with the vigor necessary to successful action, but they can more easily bend to the Procrustean bed of circumstances, which is spread for the repose of a conquered people,—wherein lies, now, and at all times, the true secret of statesmanship.

The work is not near so hopeless as it would seem at first, and it is noble and glorious beyond anything that ever fired the ambition of youth. Though the destruction is so wide-spread and through, it should be remembered that there is nothing which can exceed the recuperative powers of nature when aided by the industry of man. These gaping wounds in our country's bosom are to be healed, these enormous losses of our wealth are to be repaired, these wasted fields are to be restored to the glorious verdure of peaceful abundance—from the ashes of the homes which once sheltered us must arise the beams and rafters of homes still as beautiful and as happy. The blackened chimneys must no longer stand, grim and solitary, on the landscape, surrounded by rank and profitless weeds, the sorrowful mile-marks of the sweep of desolation as it marched, devouring our substance, but must be made to send up again, from mansion roofs, the cheerful columns of smoke which once bespoke plenty and repose, and to glow again with winter's blaze of domestic peace and sacred hospitality. All the bloody footprints of ruthless war must be erased by the hand of intelligent industry.

Looking despairingly at the condition of things, the country turns toward her young men, and calls to them to lead the way in preaching and practicing *hope*. You are required, above all things, to teach our people to look up from the crumbling ashes and prostrate columns of their present ruin, to the majestic proportions and surpassing grandeur of that temple which may yet be built by the hand which labors, the mind which conceives, and the great soul which faints not.

An officer leading his men into battle, himself going first and charging home upon the enemy, with the high and lofty daring of a hero, rallying his troops when they waver, cheering when they advance, applauding the brave and sustaining the fainthearted, bearing aloft the colors of his command, and struggling with all the strength and spirit of manhood, resolving to conquer or to perish, is esteemed one of the noblest exhibitions of which man is capable. We thrill and burn, as we read the glowing story, and exhaust the language of praise, in extolling his virtues. But not less glorious, not less worthy the commendations of his countrymen, is he who in an hour like this bravely submits to fate; and scorning alike the promptings of despair, and the unmanly refuge of expatriation, rushes to the rescue of his perishing country, inspires his fellow citizens with hope, cheers the disconsolate, arouses the sluggish, lifts up the helpless and the feeble, and by voice and example, in every possible way, urges forward all to the blessed and bloodless and crowning victories of peace. It is a noble thing to die for one's country: it is a higher and a nobler thing to *live for it*.

The best test of the best heroism *now*, is a cheerful and loyal submission to the powers and events established by our defeat, and a ready obedience to the Constitution and laws of our country. Being denied the immortal distinction of dying for your country, as did your fathers and your eldest brothers, you may yet rival their glory, by *living* for it, if you will live wisely, earnestly and well. The greatest campaign, for which soldiers ever buckled on armor, is now before you. The drum beats, and the bugle sounds to arms, to repel invading poverty and destitution, which have seized our strongholds and are waging war, cruel and ruthless, upon our women and children. The teeming earth is blockaded by the terrible lassitude of exhaustion, and we are required, through toil and tribulation, to retake, as by storm, that prosperity and happiness, which were once our own, and to plant our banners firmly upon their everlasting ramparts, amid the plaudits of a redeemed and regenerated people. The noblest soldier, *now*, is he that, with axe and plough, pitches his tent against the waste places of his fire-blasted home, and swears that from its ruins there shall arise another like unto it; and that from its barren fields, there shall come again the gladdening sheen of dew-gemmed meadows, in the rising, and the golden waves of ripening harvests, in the setting sun! This is a besieging of fate itself; a hand to hand struggle with the stern columns of calamity and despair. But the God of nature hath promised that it shall not fail, when courage, faith and industry sustain the assailant; and this victory won, without one drop of human blood, unstained by a single tear, imparting and receiving blessings on every hand, will be such as the wise and good of all the earth may applaud, and over which even the angels might unite in rejoicing. Now, from the earth, directly or indirectly, comes all the wealth of man, whether it be in flocks upon the hills, in palaces within the city, or in ships upon the sea. In this prolific and never failing source alone, must be laid the foundations of our regeneration, and the plow is the great instrument with which it is to be effected. The oldest born, the simplest and most beneficent of inventions, the father and king of all the implements of man, upon it depends all of agriculture, of manufactures, of commerce and of civilization. Remembering this, it will be your first and last great duty, whether as legislators or as private citizens, to encourage, foster and protect *labor upon the soil:* being assured when it prospers that all other desirable things shall be added.

During the course of the recent war it was often a subject of remark that each side was grievously deceived in its estimate of the other. And especially was it a favorite opinion at the North, that we of the South were not capable of sustaining for a protracted period the rigors of war. It was said that our climate, and more especially the system of slavery, had unmanned us, and sunk us into effeminacy, and rendered us totally unfit to grapple with the hardier and more robust races of the North.—How they were undeceived by four years of the most desperate strife against overwhelming numbers and resources, it is the province of history to tell. Nor need we fear to let *them* write that history; for a denial of the full and glorious import of our deeds would be a confession of their own shame and inferiority. It will be our duty now, in better ways, and under happier auspices, still further to undeceive them, by the vigor and energy with which we shall clear away the wreck of our fallen fortunes, adapt ourselves to circumstances under changed institutions and new systems of labor, and the rapidity with which we shall travel in those ways which lead to the rebuilding and adorning a State. Nor will it admit of a doubt that the same courage, constancy and skill, which led our slender battalions through so many pitched fields of glory, will, when directed into the peaceful channels of national prosperity and quickened by the sharp lessons of adversity, be sufficient to place the Southern States of the American Union side by side with the richest and the mightiest.

Deserving also of your earnest attention is that moral ruin—scarcely less extensive than the physical—which dogs the footsteps of revolution. No classes of our society have altogether escaped it, whilst in some its ravages have been fearful. The peculiar counteracting influences—those of schools and schoolmasters—the general poverty of the country has well nigh destroyed. The almost total loss of the very considerable fund set apart by the wisdom of our Legislators in happier times for the education of the poor children of the State, and the consequent abandonment of our system of Common Schools, are by no means to be reckoned among the least of our many misfortunes. To the thousands of children, whose parents were heretofore unable to educate them, are now added other thousands reduced to a worse condition by the results of the war.

Their situation forms a subject of the most serious magnitude, and imposes additional obligations upon all, who, like you, have been favored with the means and opportunity of education. But among all the sacred duties which will devolve on you as citizens and patriots, there are some more sacred still than others; and one of these is the looking after, and caring for, the orphans of those who perished in your defence and mine. Numbers of them are destitute not only of the means of education, but of subsistence itself. Without friends or protectors, they will wander into ways of wickedness and ruin. It has already been my painful fortune, to witness an instance of such an one brought into the courts of justice, charged with crimes committed under the influence of want, and in the absence of a father's teachings. But that father was sleeping far away in a rude soldier's grave in the wilderness of the Chickahominy, and his orphan boy, without a parent, a protector, or a friend in the world, lone and homeless, had wandered among strangers and been tempted into crime. I visited him in prison, where without a coat, without shoes or hat, and his few remaining garments displaying his pale and delicate frame, he told me his simple and piteous story. His tender years and helpless condition appealed so strongly to the court that the penalties of the law were not inflicted on him. A kind gentleman came forward, agreed to give him a home and became bound for his better behavior: and being admonished to go and sin no more, he was led away. But my heart bled within me, when I remembered that he was only one of thousands whose fortune was equally hard, and that he had thus lost home, and father, and an honest life, *for you and for me!* Oh! my friends, may God do so to you, and more also, if you ever turn your backs upon an orphan child of one who perished in your defence! Their blood was shed, whether wisely or unwisely, in your behalf; let it appeal to you for their naked and helpless children, from the fields of slaughter where they spilled it, and woe be unto you, if it appeals in vain! "The Lord deal kindly with you, as ye have dealt with the dead."

Nor do our duties to these brave men cease with their children. There is a debt which neither test oaths nor Congressional amendments have forbidden us to pay. We owe to the dead what it is possible to do for their remains and their memories, and no charge of faithlessness to our own obligations, it seems to me, should stand between us and its discharge.

> "Their bones are scattered far and wide,
> By mount, by stream and sea,"

and it is not for the purpose of eulogizing the *cause*, for which they perished, (for that is already in the hands of history,) that we would gather them up for decent sepulture, and perpetuate their memories by tablets of stone. It is simply to testify our love for our own blood, and our grateful admiration of the virtue and patriotism, and unavailing courage, which laid them low. From that fatal wall of Gettysburg to the banks of the Rio Grande, two thousand miles of travel are marked by the Golgothas of our kindred. In nameless valleys, on rugged mountains, in wild and solitary swamps, the noblest, and the bravest, and the highest of Southern manhood—children of the Cavalier and the Huguenot—sleep in shallow and unknown graves, or moulder upon the soil like the beasts that perish.—The lawgiver and the plowman, the poet and the cart boy, the accomplished scholar and the rude father of the hamlet, rest side by side awaiting the final trump, and many a mother that bore him knows not of his lowly bed, nor can cast one flower upon the grave of her lost boy. And yet the nations listened to the roar of that boy's musket, and watched, with heart aglow and blood on fire, as he strove to erect the "arch of empire" through the belching flames and glittering bayonets of many a battlemented height! Lustre and glory—everything but success—he shed abundantly upon his country.

> "The silent pillar, lone and gray,
> Claims kindred with his sacred clay;
> The meanest rill, the mightiest river,
> Rolls mingling with his fame forever."

When the civilized world has rung with the praises of these men, and even the generous of their foes have not withheld the homage ever due to valor and to virtue, certainly we may be pardoned for seeking to do this poor honor to our own.

> "If I, a Northern wanderer, weep for thee,
> What should thy sons do?"

The very least that we can do, is to bring their remains home and bury them with decency and in silence. No monuments of victory are for us, no national jubilee can we celebrate, no songs of triumph can our maidens sing, or garlands of glory weave; there is no welcoming of returning conquerors, nor erecting of triumphal arches for us to console us for our great suffering. We are all alone with our great defeat and that heavy sorrow, which, "never flitting, still is sitting, still is sitting," in our households; and all that we have left for our comfort is the sad, yet tender light which plays around the memory of those who died to make it otherwise! The poor honors we show to them are as much shown to ourselves, and still more to humanity.—Respect to the memory of the worthy dead is older than civilization. In all ages, and among all nations and peoples, from those "who dwell within the gates of the rising sun," to those who behold his mightier light give place to the dreamy dominions of the evening star, it has been usual to revere those who died for their country, and to celebrate their virtues with the highest funeral honors.

Our noble country-women, abounding in that tenderness which ever cleaves to misfortune, have undertaken this pious duty. But you must help them, the whole people of the South must help; and small, indeed, will be the hopes we may claim of the living if, by refusing you show yourselves insensible to the virtues of the dead. I hope yet to see the honored dust of every Southern soldier reverently gathered up, and placed where gentle hands can show, by beautifying and adorning his quiet home, that we love him all the same, and bless him all the more, though he died in vain. And in due time, I doubt not, monuments of marble and granite will tell the stranger how North Carolina cherishes the memory of her illustrious children.

> "Tread lightly,—'tis a soldier's grave,
> This lonely, mossy mound,—
> And yet, to hearts like mine and thine,
> It should be holy ground.
> Tread lightly,—for this man bequeathed,
> Ere laid below this sod,
> His ashes to his native land,
> His gallant soul to God!"

The time is not far distant, when as citizens, I trust, you will be permitted to take a part in the government of your country. The path of the statesman for the past decade has been beset with peculiar difficulties; nor is it likely that the surroundings of the present period will prove less embarrassing to any public man honestly seeking his country's good. The lessons of experience would make us all wise, if they were not forgotten. In taking whatever positions your talents or inclinations may cause to be assigned you, my most solemn injunction would be to burn into your memories, for-ever, the teachings of the terrible experience of the past five years. The great problem we have just worked out is full of mighty meaning, its theorem is demonstrated in characters of "fraternal blood," and all its corollaries teem with changes of power and the downfall of systems. Let it ever be before your eyes, and learn of it, among other wise things, that the yielding to blind passions and personal resentments, when the happiness of thousands is entrusted to your *judgment*, is a *crime* for which God will hold you accountable. The subjection of every passion and prejudice in the breast, to the cooler sway of judgment and reason, when the common welfare is concerned, is the first victory to be won in a political career. Without it, you can win no other in which your country can rejoice. The philosophy of politics exhibits many instructive phenomena, which you should carefully study. The federative system of separate and quasi-independent States, which composed the American Union, embraced many peculiar features in relation to the science of government, little known or practiced by other nations. Years ago, M. Guizot pronounced it the most difficult and complex in the world; an opinion which the infinite disagreements of our own statesmen, in regard to its power and limitations, have amply justified. Its structure, originally, was not unlike the planetary system; as each State was assigned, by its authors, an orbit in which to move around the General Government as a grand centre. The dangers, against which its founders seemed most anxious to provide, were to arise from the imperfect balancing of the centrifugal and centripetal forces, a predominance of either being esteemed fatal. Should the former prevail, the Government would be destroyed by the flying off of the States, or the dismemberment of its parts. This would be secession.—Should the latter predominate, there would be an end of the system, by the crushing out and merging of all the parts in the Central Government. This would be consolidation. It was believed that the Constitution (the law of gravitation) had so wisely distributed its forces that each would act, in accordance with the original design, without destroying the other. But these fond hopes were doomed to a terrible disappointment. Whether it be that, as history teaches, there has been a constant tendency to centralization among all governments which had maintained and thrown off the feudal system; or that no written constitution can stand the strain of civil war; or simply that men, in times of great excitement, cannot preserve judgment to discern the right from the wrong, or integrity enough to keep intact an official oath, it is needless on the present occasion to inquire. The recent attempt, on the part of a minority of the States, to withdraw from the system, was successfully resisted by the majority, in the name and by the authority of the Central Government. In order to effect this, powers were claimed and exercised by the latter, as the contest proceeded, higher and more extraordinary than the wildest consolidationist ever dreamed of asserting before. This destroyed, in letter and spirit, the original compact, utterly and absolutely; and so disturbed the whole system that, in the very nature of things, it is impossible for it to oscillate into place again. The predominance of the centripetal power is complete, and the results established, logically, are that the States cannot withdraw, that they are subject to coercion, not only as to their external relations, but as to their internal policy, their domestic laws, and everything else whatsoever pertaining to sovereignty. It *does not* logically follow, however, not even by the logic of revolutions, that, having neither the legal nor the physical power to withdraw, they are yet out of the Union. That were, indeed, a moral and a physical impossibility. The very flower of the prerogative of the States is, therefore, swept away by the decision of this tribunal which is the last resort of kings, and to which a conquered people can interpose no demurrer.

Such is now the actual state of things, unfortunate as we may regard it, and contrary as it may seem to all of our ideas of the true purposes of the government. But it is *our* country still, and if it cannot be governed as *we* wish it, it must yet be governed some other way; and it is still our duty to labor for its prosperity and glory, with ardor and sincerity. I earnestly urge upon you the strictest conformity of your conduct to the situation; to what the government actually is, not what you may think it ought to be. It is our bounden duty as honest men to give our new formed institutions a full and fair trial—especially the new system of labor—and if they prove better than the old, let us forget our sufferings and be thankful. And let us not doubt, if the occasion should ever come, that, for the sake of her own theory, Massachusetts will cheerfully submit to the same degradation which North Carolina has borne.

In the discussion and progress of political questions, you will mostly find that there are practically three divisions of the people, though there generally appear but two. Two of these occupy the extremest opposite positions, whilst the third, usually denominated conservative, stands between. This class generally exceeds either or both of the others in numbers, and in the character and worth of its leaders. Could it always rule, whilst there would certainly be less of progress, there would yet be less of civil commotion, and far more of true happiness. But strange to say, though in a majority, this class is seldom in power; for paradoxical as it may appear, the extremists are nearer to each other than to the intermediate class, and generally combine to overcome it. It is, moreover, a well known defect of popular governments, that they are prone to mistake the zeal and earnestness of the extremists for sound policy, which contributes further to their triumph. The cooler wisdom of the conservative statesman is generally appreciated after the mischief is done. Those bold and striking qualities, so apt to captivate the young and enthusiastic, in war and in politics, are mostly dangerous to good government. And yet mankind have been ever eager to be deceived by them. Even history, stern and dignified, lends itself, perhaps unconsciously, to the damaging delusion. Whilst page after page paints the glories of the hero who plunged his country into war, and brought desolation to the doors of his people, a few brief and passing lines suffice for the sagacious statesman who has honored his humanity by preventing slaughter. It is to some extent so, in the nature of things. The great deeds done are tangible and real; the great calamities *avoided* are only in the mind, and we cannot fully grasp them. Just as the sublime description of Dante's Inferno, with all the powers of the most vivid imagination, fails to inspire an idea of torture half equal to that which we feel by holding the finger for one moment in the blaze of a candle.—But if history could be differently written, and were it possible to set against what this great man has done, charged with the misery which he inflicted, that which another greater and better man has *not done*, credited with the suffering which he has *spared* his people, how different would be the verdict of posterity! and how naked would many a popular hero appear! Alas, alas! why will civilization permit its true heroes to sleep in forgotten graves, while marble and bronze celebrate the virtues of those whose greatness consisted in their power to inflict wretchedness?

There is no more valuable lesson to be learned from the troubled and conflicting scenes of the recent past, than the obvious value of self-respecting consistency to the character of a public man. And this, not in the narrow and popular sense of that much abused term, as meaning an unchanging adherence to one opinion or set of opinions. The dullest intellect and the meanest spirit can not only do that, but is most apt to do it; whilst wise men see the necessity of changing as often as the ever-varying phases of the case may render it indispensable; as a good general changes front so often as it is required in order to face the enemy. But all public men should propose certain great truths or principles as their objects to be attained—never to be abandoned except upon the clearest convictions of their falsity—and though the means, by which those principles should be preserved, may be varied to suit expediency, through good and evil report the great objects should be conscientiously adhered to.—This is consistency. You will find it not only the best policy for the truth's sake, but to inspire confidence. For without truth there can be no confidence, and without confidence governments cannot, any more than armies, be led to victory. A blunder, honestly confessed, is already half atoned; persisted in wilfully, it perpetuates ruin and becomes a crime. Nor is it excusable to attempt the extenuation of one blunder, by confessing to another; or to refuse to your confederates in error the same mercy which has been extended to you. It is a mean plea, and one of a meaner culprit, which tries to evade the halter for the first crime, by owning that he infinitely more deserved a hanging for the second: and a politician, who cannot forgive as he is forgiven, is both a bad statesman and a bad man. Faith, honestly kept, even in the worst of causes, can never fail to inspire respect in the breast of a generous foe, which not even the bitterness of a civil war can destroy. In this connection, I would recommend to your earnest consideration, the masterly delineation of the character of Shaftesbury by Macaulay, as instructively portraying a set of men who swarm in times of revolution, and are justly regarded as greatly aggravating the public misfortunes.

With regard to current political events and speculations of the future, of which we are permitted to be only quiet, though deeply interested spectators, I do not, altogether, share the general alarm that pervades the Southern mind. The taunts, the gibes, the sneers and the vulgar triumphs of ignoble spirits, which so annoy and mortify, were to be expected. Their brief day will soon pass. They were born of the license of victory, and will endure no longer than the excitements of the occasion serve to render good men ungenerous. Happily it is not in the nature of man always to hate; and the reign of the bad passions is short-lived. It is hardly possible that hatred will long continue between two communities brought into daily, familiar intercourse, when the subjects of contention have been removed, and when mutual interests and common associations invite to good will. "The disposition of man is so kindly and good," says M. Guizot, in his History of Civilization, "that it is almost impossible for a number of individuals to be placed for any length of time in a social situation, without giving birth to a certain moral tie between them; sentiments of protection, of benevolence, of affection spring up naturally." As the passions cool, reason must return, and with reason comes justice, whose inseparable companion is fraternity. If it were not so, there would be no end of strife. Could we calmly and impartially consider now the depth and fierceness of the passions which so lately raged in the hearts of all, it would doubtless appear that the embers of bitterness, though still burning, were yet flickering day by day to their extinction, with a rapidity for which we should fervently thank God. The reaction to this great stretch of human passion is sure to come; it will come soon, and, like everything; else American, it will come with *power.* Magnanimity, the greatest of national as of private virtues, will once more reign, and will soon shame the Northern manhood from assailing a brave people who no longer resist. They have already a shining example in their Chief Magistrate of the Republic, worthy of all honor and emulation. In contemplating his official action toward those who were so lately his extremest enemies, and observing how he has magnanimously sunk what must have been the feelings of the *man* in those of the patriot and the statesman, and how his keen intellect has appreciated the true situation of affairs, disappointing none so much as those who undervalued him, we are at once reminded of that splendid burst of eloquence uttered by Cicero on the occasion of returning the thanks of the Senate to Cæsar for the pardon and restoration of his enemy, Marcellus. Though fulsome and extravagant—a fault both of the orator and his age—it yet contains so fine a tribute to a great virtue that I cannot refrain from quoting a portion of it. Addressing Cæsar, he said: "You have conquered nations brutally barbarous, immensely numerous, boundlessly extended, and furnished with everything that can make war successful. Yet all these, their own nature and the nature of things made it possible to conquer. For no strength is so great as to be absolutely invincible, and no power so formidable as to be proof against superior force and courage. But the man who subdues passion, stifles resentments, tempers victory, and not only rears the noble, wise and virtuous foe when prostrate, but heightens his former dignity, is a man not to be ranked with the greatest mortals, but resembles a god!" Well might our Christian religion teach us the sublime duty of mercy to the fallen foe, when even the splendid imagery of the greatest of ancient orators, in the midst of the highest types of heathen civilization, could find no nobler attribute with which to invest his deities!

What a genuine stroke of statesmanship this noble clemency of President [Andrew] Johnson was; and how warmly appreciated it has been, not only by its poor and afflicted recipients, but by the whole world! How soon was the terrible suspense and troubled anxiety, which filled all the land after the surrender of our armies, turned into blessing and praise! Through him, and such as he, we begin to see how it is possible to love our whole country once more. Through him it is—far more than test oaths and similar feeble contrivances—that the deep and sincere feeling pervades all the South to submit nobly to, and abide honestly by, all the results of the war. The true bonds to impose upon a conquered people are wrought in the magnanimity of the conquerors. The mightiest cables of iron ever forged in the mammoth furnaces of the land, though long enough and strong enough to link together, indissolubly, the countless fleets of the Republic, in the midst of the wildest tempest that ever strewed our shores with the wreck of stranded ships, are yet not so strong as the cords of lasting gratitude with which a generous people receive the magnanimous kindness of those late foes, with whom they have just measured strength in many a manly field; especially when those kindnesses reveal glimpses of an ancient and once glorious brotherhood! May God in his infinite mercy grant that these glimpses may ripen into full and everlasting realities, and that the spirit of reconciled brothers may again animate all the people of this mighty land, which has hitherto rendered it so renowned among the nations!

Respect must be the foundation of all national as well as all private friendships. And when the bitter pangs of the recent struggle are buried, as they must be, there will remain no reason why mutual respect should not prevail; unless, indeed, our conduct, in the hour of our humiliation, should furnish it. Here we have been in danger of the most cruel mistake. For grievously do we deceive ourselves, if we suppose that we inspire respect in the bosoms of our late enemies, in proportion as we voluntarily practice uncalled for self-abasement. We can but inspire disgust alone when we thus show them that their vast armies and great generals were, after all, only employed to subdue a race of mean-spirited dirt-eaters, from among whom the truly noble had been mercifully slain in the battle! The severest contempt of civilization is richly merited by a people who would cast obloquy upon the ashes of their own dead children; and as the best evidence of the truth and sincerity of their present obligations aver the utter falsity of their former ones! That a man must be necessarily telling truth to-day, because he was undoubtedly a liar only so late as yesterday! When we approach our conquerors with such evidences of loyalty, there is little wonder that we inspire contempt and suspicion. Surely the *fact* of our submission can be sufficiently complete and sincere, without making the manner thereof such as to forfeit the respect either of ourselves or our late foes.

Our great country, of the South, with its fertile soil, happy climate, and boundless resources, excites the highest admiration of the Northern people. The vigorous scope and conservative tendency of our statesmanship they have never failed to respect, and have even acknowledged that it has controlled, to a great degree, the policy of the

Government, in and from its organisation; thereby giving us credit for much of its power and glory. They cannot but remember that it was Southern farmer-statesmen of Mecklenburg, North Carolina, who sounded the key note of Independence in 1775, in that celebrated paper, in which, as pronounced by their own Adams, "the genuine sense of America at that moment was never so well expressed before nor since;" and by the side of which Tom. Paine's famous "Common Sense" tracts, according to the same author, were a "poor, ignorant, malicious, crapulous mass." They cannot forget that the other world-renowned declaration, that of 1776, was from the brain of a Southern statesman; and that it was the genius of a Southern general, who, in making good its bold assumptions, rendered himself the most illustrious of mankind. Nor yet can they forget that in two foreign wars the most signal glory shed upon our country's arms was by the skill and valor of Southern commanders, followed by Southern volunteers. And certainly they cannot overlook, even now, that fund of military genius, intrepid gallantry, heroic constancy under misfortune, and all the traits which mark a noble people, that we have so lately exhibited. I would as soon believe that there was no room for such things in the breasts of men as truth and honor, as that every soldier in the Army of the Potomac, from its General to the humblest private that followed its banners, did not, in his heart, respect and honor the lofty courage, consummate skill, and patient constancy of *that other army*, which, though vastly inferior in numbers and appointments, yet kept it four years on the short but bloody journey from the Potomac to the James, and piled *every inch* of its pathway with ghastly monuments of the slain! Let not the sneer of the supercilious, nor the taunt of the ungenerous, over our final defeat, deceive us in this matter, or cause us to abate one jot of our just claims to the high place in history which posterity will award us. That, which has so moved upon the sympathy and admiration of the world, has already excited, and will yet more excite, that of our Northern friends. And in due time if we faint not, we shall reap those fruits which the generous and the better feelings of men never fail to bear. Years hence when, as I trust, time and a juster policy shall have healed many an ugly wound, and quieted many an aching heart, the story of the great civil war will be read around a thousand firesides among the homes of the North, and as the glowing recital burns upon the ear, how that one-fourth of the people of the United States, without manufactures and almost without arms, without ships, arsenals or foundries, shut out from all the world by a sealed blockade, for four long and terrible years fought back and kept at bay the other three-fourths, who were aided by manumitted slaves, who had great navies, their own and the workshops of the world at their control, and whose slaughtered armies were filled up again and again, from the swarming populations of Europe; and how the ragged battalions of the South, under [Robert E.] Lee and [Thomas J. "Stonewall"] Jackson, and [Edward] Johnson, and [Robert] Hoke, and [William] Pender, and [Jubal] Early, struggled with the great armies of [George] McClellan and [Ulysses S.] Grant, and [William T.] Sherman, and [Philip] Sheridan, and [Don] Buell, until the world was full of their fame; a thousand fathers, burning with the unconfessed pride of country and of race, will say to their sons who wonder how all this could have been: "These were the countrymen of Washington and Jackson. These were Americans—none but American citizens could have done these things!"

And now what is said is said. Would that it were better said. The one great theme—our country and its sufferings—so fills my heart, as I presume it does all hearts, that I have spoken much of it. Your letter of invitation likewise implied that, though it was a literary occasion, a purely literary address was not expected. I trust that I may have assisted somewhat in pointing you to those paths of usefulness and honor, in treading which you may best serve your dear old Mother, rent and ruined as she is. Her eyes are turned now yearningly and with maternal pride, toward her educated sons, pleading that they will hold up her arms that her evil days may be few. May this honored and reviving University speedily, and from time to time, open again its gates and send forth to the work of the regeneration of their country as many high-souled and generous, brave and enthusiastic youths, as rushed through its portals to untimely graves during the years of our tribulation. I could not endure to live but for the comforting hope that compensating years of peace and happiness are yet in store for those who have struggled so manfully and endured so nobly. Having gone down into the very lowest depths of the fiery furnace of affliction, seven times heated by the cruel malice of civil war, I believe there will yet appear, walking with and comforting our mourning people, One, whose form is like unto that of the Son of God!

FREDERICK DOUGLASS **56**

An Appeal to Congress for Impartial Suffrage, 1867

By 1867, in spite of the end of the Civil War, violence against African-Americans and supporters of civil rights for freedmen was increasing at an appalling rate. As the conservative planters attempted to reassert themselves politically across the former Confederacy, they resisted calls for civil rights for African-Americans and the right of African-American men to vote. Supporters of enfranchisement and civil rights often argued that the best means of former slaves to protect their new freedom was through their power at the ballot box. Frederick Douglass, who had so passionately fought for an end to slavery before the Civil War called for full political rights for African-Americans in this 1867 essay printed in Atlantic Monthly. *For a man to be a man, Douglass argued he must have the same rights as everyone else or be little more than a slave again. To deny a fellow human being a basic human right was the moral equivalent of theft. He argued that the idea that some men had rights while others had none must be eradicated as surely as slavery had been eradicated, else risk generations of bitter recriminations. The fourteenth amendment guaranteeing civil rights for all citizens was ratified in 1868, while the fifteenth amendment and its guarantee of African-American male suffrage was ratified in 1870. But slowly, the rights African-Americans won after the Civil War would disappear in the South until the 1960s.*

Frederick Douglass, "An Appeal to Congress for Impartial Suffrage," *Atlantic Monthly* 19 (January 1867): 112–117.

A very limited statement of the argument for impartial suffrage, and for including the negro in the body politic, would require more space than can be reasonably asked here. It is supported by reasons as broad as the nature of man, and as numerous as the wants of society. Man is the only government-making animal in the world. His right to a participation in the production and operation of government is an inference from his nature, as direct and self-evident as is his right to acquire property or education. It is no less a crime against the manhood of a man, to declare that he shall not share in the making and directing of the government under which he lives, than to say that he shall not acquire property and education. The fundamental and unanswerable argument in favor of the enfranchisement of the negro is found in the undisputed fact of his manhood. He is a man, and by every fact and argument by which any man can sustain his right to vote, the negro can sustain his right equally. It is plain that, if the right belongs to any, it belongs to all. The doctrine that some men have no rights that others are bound to respect, is a doctrine which we must banish as we have banished slavery, from which it emanated. If black men have no rights in the eyes of white men, of course the whites can have none in the eyes of the blacks. The result is a war of races, and the annihilation of all proper human relations.

But suffrage for the negro, while easily sustained upon abstract principles, demands consideration upon what are recognized as the urgent necessities of the case. It is a measure of relief,—a shield to break the force of a blow already descending with violence, and render it harmless. The work of destruction has already been set in motion all over the South. Peace to the country has literally meant war to the loyal men of the South, white and black; and negro suffrage is the measure to arrest and put an end to that dreadful strife.

Something then, not by way of argument, (for that has been done by Charles Sumner, Thaddeus Stevens, Wendell Phillips, Gerrit Smith, and other able men) but rather of statement and appeal.

For better or for worse, (as in some of the old marriage ceremonies) the negroes are evidently a permanent part of the American population. They are too numerous and useful to be colonized, and too enduring and self-perpetuating to disappear by natural causes. Here they are, four millions of them, and, for weal or for woe, here they must remain. Their history is parallel to that of the country; but while the history of the latter has been cheerful and bright with blessings, theirs has been heavy and dark with agonies and curses. What O'Connell said of the history of Ireland may with greater truth be said of the negro's. It may be "traced like a wounded man through a crowd, by the blood." Yet the negroes have marvellously survived all the exterminating forces of slavery, and have emerged at the end of two hundred and fifty years of bondage, not morose, misanthropic, and revengeful, but cheerful, hopeful, and forgiving. They now stand before Congress and the country, not complaining of the past, but simply asking for a better future. The spectacle of these dusky millions thus imploring, not demanding, is touching; and if American statesmen could be moved by a simple appeal to the nobler elements of human nature, if they had not fallen, seemingly, into the incurable habit of weighing and measuring every proposition of reform by some standard of profit and loss, doing wrong from choice, and right only from necessity or some urgent demand of human selfishness, it would be enough to plead for the negroes on the score of past services and sufferings. But no such appeal shall be relied on here. Hardships, services, sufferings, and sacrifices are all waived. It is true that they came to the relief of the country at the hour of its extremest need. It is true that, in many of the rebellious States, they were almost the only reliable friends the nation had throughout the whole tremendous war. It is true that, notwithstanding their alleged ignorance, they were wiser than their masters, and knew enough to be loyal, while those masters only knew enough to be rebels and traitors. It is true that they fought side by side in the loyal cause with our gallant and patriotic white soldiers, and that, but for their help,—divided as the loyal States were,—the Rebels might have succeeded in breaking up the Union, thereby entailing border wars and troubles of unknown duration and incalculable calamity. All this and more is true of these loyal negroes. Many daring exploits will be told to their credit. Impartial history will paint them as men who deserved well of their country. It will tell how they forded and swam rivers, with what consummate address they evaded the sharp-eyed Rebel pickets, how they toiled in the darkness of night through the tangled marshes of briers and thorns, barefooted and weary, running the risk of losing their lives, to warn our generals of Rebel schemes to surprise and destroy our loyal army. It will tell how these poor people, whose rights we still despised, behaved to our wounded soldiers, when found cold, hungry, and bleeding on the deserted battle-field; how they assisted our escaping prisoners from [Confederate prisoner-of-war camps at] Andersonville, Belle Isle, Castle Thunder, and elsewhere, sharing with them their wretched crusts, and otherwise affording them aid and comfort; how they promptly responded to the trumpet call for their services, fighting against a foe that denied them the rights of civilized warfare, and for a government which was without the courage to assert those rights and avenge their violation in their behalf; with what gallantry they flung themselves upon Rebel fortifications, meeting death as fearlessly as any other troops in the service. But upon none of these things is reliance placed. These facts speak to the better dispositions of the human heart; but they seem of little weight with the opponents of impartial suffrage.

It is true that a strong plea for equal suffrage might be addressed to the national sense of honor. Something, too, might be said of national gratitude. A nation might well hesitate before the temptation to betray its allies. There is something immeasurably mean, to say nothing of the cruelty, in placing the loyal negroes of the South under the political power of their Rebel masters. To make peace with our enemies is all well enough; but to prefer our enemies and sacrifice our friends,—to exalt our enemies and cast down our friends,—to clothe our enemies, who sought the destruction of the government, with all political power, and leave our friends powerless in their hands,— is an act which need not be characterized here. We asked the negroes to espouse our cause, to be our friends, to fight for us, and against their masters; and now, after they have done all that we asked them to do,—helped us to conquer their masters, and thereby directed toward themselves the furious hate of the vanquished,—it is proposed in some quarters to turn them over to the political control of the common enemy of the government and of the negro. But of this let nothing be said in this place. Waiving humanity, national honor, the claims of gratitude, the precious satisfaction arising from deeds of charity and justice to the weak and defenceless,—the appeal for impartial suffrage addresses itself with great pertinency to the darkest, coldest, and flintiest side of the human heart, and would wring righteousness from the unfeeling calculations of human selfishness.

For in respect to this grand measure it is the good fortune of the negro that enlightened selfishness, not less than justice, fights on his side. National interest and national duty, if elsewhere separated, are firmly united here. The American people can, perhaps, afford to brave the censure of surrounding nations for the manifest injustice and meanness of excluding its faithful black soldiers from the ballot-box, but it cannot afford to allow the moral and mental energies of rapidly increasing millions to be consigned to hopeless degradation.

Strong as we are, we need the energy that slumbers in the black man's arm to make us stronger. We want no longer any heavy- footed, melancholy service from the negro. We want the cheerful activity of the quickened manhood of these sable millions. Nor can we afford to endure the moral blight which the existence of a degraded and hated class must necessarily inflict upon any people among whom such a class may exist. Exclude the negroes as a class from political rights,—teach them that the high and manly privilege of suffrage is to be enjoyed by white citizens only,—that they may bear the burdens of the state, but that they are to have no part in its direction or its honors,—and you at once deprive them of one of the main incentives to manly character and patriotic devotion to the interests of the government; in a word, you stamp them as a degraded caste,—you teach them to despise themselves, and all others to despise them. Men are so constituted that they largely derive their ideas of their abilities and their possibilities from the settled judgments of their fellow-men, and especially from such as they read in the institutions under which they live. If these bless them, they are blest indeed; but if these blast them, they are blasted indeed. Give the negro the elective franchise, and you give him at once a powerful motive for all noble exertion, and make him a man among men. A character is demanded of him, and here as elsewhere demand favors supply. It is nothing against this reasoning that all men who vote are not good men or good citizens. It is enough that the possession and exercise of the elective franchise is in itself an appeal to the nobler elements of manhood, and imposes education as essential to the safety of society.

To appreciate the full force of this argument, it must be observed, that disfranchisement in a republican government based upon the idea of human equality and universal suffrage, is a very different thing from disfranchisement in governments based upon the idea of the divine right of kings, or the entire subjugation of the masses. Masses of men can take care of themselves. Besides, the disabilities imposed upon all are necessarily without that bitter and stinging element of invidiousness which attaches to disfranchisement in a republic. What is common to all works no special sense of degradation to any. But in a country like ours, where men of all nations, kindred, and tongues are freely enfranchised, and allowed to vote, to say to the negro, You shall not vote, is to deal his manhood a staggering blow, and to burn into his soul a bitter and goading sense of wrong, or else work in him a stupid indifference to all the elements of a manly character. As a nation, we cannot afford to have amongst us either this indifference and stupidity, or that burning sense of wrong. These sable millions are too powerful to be allowed to remain either indifferent or discontented. Enfranchise them, and they become self-respecting and country-loving citizens. Disfranchise them, and the mark of Cain is set upon them less mercifully than upon the first murderer, for no man was to hurt him. But this mark of inferiority— all the more palpable because of a difference of color—not only dooms the negro to be a vagabond, but makes him the prey of insult and outrage everywhere. While nothing may be urged here as to the past services of the negro, it is quite within the line of this appeal to remind the nation of the possibility that a time may come when the services of the negro may be a second time required. History is said to repeat itself, and, if so, having wanted the negro once, we may want him again. Can that statesmanship be wise which would leave the negro good ground to hesitate, when the exigencies of the country required his prompt assistance? Can that be sound statesmanship which leaves millions of men in gloomy discontent, and possibly in a state of alienation in the day of national trouble? Was not the nation stronger when two hundred thousand sable soldiers were hurled against the Rebel fortifications, than it would have been without them? Arming the negro was an urgent military necessity three years ago,—are we sure that another quite as pressing may not await us? Casting aside all thought of justice and magnanimity, is it wise to impose upon the negro all the burdens involved in sustaining government against foes within and foes without, to make him equal sharer in all sacrifices for the public good, to tax him in peace and conscript him in war, and then coldly exclude him from the ballot-box?

Look across the sea. Is Ireland, in her present condition, fretful, discontented, compelled to support an establishment in which she does not believe, and which the vast majority of her people abhor, a source of power or of weakness to Great Britain? Is not Austria wise in removing all ground of complaint against her on the part of Hungary? And does not the Emperor of Russia act wisely, as well as generously, when he not only breaks up the bondage of the serf, but extends him all the advantages of Russian citizenship? Is the present movement in England in favor of manhood suffrage—for the purpose of bringing four millions of British subjects into full sympathy and co-operation with the British government—a wise and humane movement, or otherwise? Is the existence of a rebellious element in our borders—which New Orleans, Memphis, and Texas show to be only disarmed, but at heart as malignant as ever, only waiting for an opportunity to reassert itself with fire and sword—a reason for leaving four millions of the nation's truest friends with just cause of complaint against the Federal government? If the doctrine that taxation should go hand in hand with representation can be appealed to in behalf of recent traitors and rebels, may it not properly be asserted in behalf of a people who have ever been loyal and faithful to the government? The answers to these questions are too obvious to require statement. Disguise it as we may, we are still a divided nation. The Rebel States have still an anti-national policy. Massachusetts and South Carolina may draw tears from the eyes of our tender-hearted President by walking arm in arm into his Philadelphia Convention, but a citizen of Massachusetts is still an alien in the Palmetto State. There is that, all over the South, which frightens Yankee industry, capital, and skill from its borders. We have crushed the Rebellion, but not its hopes or its malign purposes. The South fought for perfect and permanent control over the Southern laborer. It was a war of the rich against the poor. They who waged it had no objection to the government, while they could use it as a means of confirming their power over the laborer. They fought the government, not because they hated the government as such, but because they found it, as they thought, in the way between them and their one grand purpose of rendering permanent and indestructible their authority and power over the Southern laborer. Though the battle is for the present lost, the hope of gaining this object still exists, and pervades the whole South with a feverish excitement. We have thus far only gained a Union without unity, marriage without love, victory without peace. The hope of gaining by politics what they lost by the sword, is the secret of all this Southern unrest; and that hope must be extinguished before national ideas and objects can take full possession of the Southern mind. There is but one safe and constitutional way to banish that mischievous hope from the South, and that is by lifting the laborer beyond the unfriendly political designs of his former master. Give the negro the elective franchise, and you at once destroy the purely sectional policy, and wheel the Southern States into line with national interests and national objects. The last and shrewdest turn of Southern politics is a recognition of the necessity of getting into Congress immediately, and at any price. The South will comply with any conditions but suffrage for the negro. It will swallow all the unconstitutional test oaths, repeal all the ordinances of Secession, repudiate the Rebel debt, promise to pay the debt incurred in conquering its people, pass all the constitutional amendments, if only it can have the negro left under its political control. The proposition is as modest as that made on the mountain: "All these things will I give unto thee if thou wilt fall down and worship me."

But why are the Southerners so willing to make these sacrifices? The answer plainly is, they see in this policy the only hope of saving something of their old sectional peculiarities and power. Once firmly seated in Congress, their alliance with Northern Democrats re-established, their States restored to their former position inside the Union, they can easily find means of keeping the Federal government entirely too busy with other important matters to pay much attention to the local affairs of the Southern States. Under the potent shield of State Rights, the game would be in their own hands. Does any sane man doubt for a moment that the men who followed Jefferson Davis through the late terrible Rebellion, often marching barefooted and hungry, naked and penniless, and who now only profess an enforced loyalty, would plunge this country into a foreign war to-day, if they could thereby gain their coveted independence, and their still more coveted mastery over the negroes? Plainly enough, the peace not less than the prosperity of this country is involved in the great measure of impartial suffrage. King Cotton is deposed, but only deposed, and is ready to-day to reassert all his ancient pretensions upon the first favorable opportunity. Foreign countries abound with his agents. They are able, vigilant, devoted. The young men of the South burn with the desire to regain what they call the lost cause; the women are noisily malignant towards the Federal government. In fact, all the elements of treason and rebellion are there under the thinnest disguise which necessity can impose.

What, then, is the work before Congress? It is to save the people of the South from themselves, and the nation from detriment on their account. Congress must supplant the evident sectional tendencies of the South by national dispositions and tendencies. It must cause national ideas and objects to take the lead and control the politics of those States. It must cease to recognize the old slave-masters as the only competent persons to rule the South. In a word, it must enfranchise the negro, and by means of the loyal negroes and the loyal white men of the South build up a national party there, and in time bridge the chasm between North and South, so that our country may have a common liberty and a common civilization. The new wine must be put into new bottles. The lamb may not be trusted with the wolf. Loyalty is hardly safe with traitors.

Statesmen of America! beware what you do. The ploughshare of rebellion has gone through the land beam-deep. The soil is in readiness, and the seed-time has come. Nations, not less than individuals, reap as they sow. The dreadful calamities of the past few years came not by accident, nor unbidden, from the ground. You shudder to-day at the harvest of blood sown in the spring-time of the Republic by your patriot fathers. The principle of slavery, which they tolerated under the erroneous impression that it would soon die out, became at last the dominant principle and power at the South. It early mastered the Constitution, became superior to the Union, and enthroned itself above the law.

Freedom of speech and of the press it slowly but successfully banished from the South, dictated its own code of honor and manners to the nation, brandished the bludgeon and the bowie-knife over Congressional debate, sapped the foundations of loyalty, dried up the springs of patriotism, blotted out the testimonies of the fathers against oppression, padlocked the pulpit, expelled liberty from its literature, invented nonsensical theories about master-races and slave-races of men, and in due season produced a Rebellion fierce, foul, and bloody.

This evil principle again seeks admission into our body politic. It comes now in shape of a denial of political rights to four million loyal colored people. The South does not now ask for slavery. It only asks for a large degraded caste, which shall have no political rights. This ends the case. Statesmen, beware what you do. The destiny of unborn and unnumbered generations is in your hands. Will you repeat the mistake of your fathers, who sinned ignorantly? or will you profit by the blood-bought wisdom all round you, and forever expel every vestige of the old abomination from our national borders? As you members of the Thirty-ninth Congress decide, will the country be peaceful, united, and happy, or troubled, divided, and miserable.

TERENCE POWDERLY **57**

Preamble and Declaration of Principles of the Knights of Labor of America, 1878

In the late 1860s and into the 1870s and 1880s, the United States saw a surge in industrial activity. A new manufacturing economy was taking root throughout the United States. The laborers who built these manufacturing empires saw few of the benefits, living with paltry wages and working under life-threatening conditions. Labor unions began to spread across the nation in pursuit of a better life for laborers. One of these unions, the Noble and Holy Order of the Knights of Labor, emerged in 1869 under the leadership of Uriah H. Stephens. Originally a secretive fraternal society, it had little influence in its early years. In 1878, Terence Powderly took control of the Knights of Labor and changed the organization's focus to securing humanitarian reforms for all workers. These reforms

"The Purposes and Program of the Knights of Labor, 1878," *Major Problems in the Gilded Age and Progressive Era*, Leon Fink, ed. (Lexington, MA: D.C. Heath and Co., 1993): 38–40.

included calls for eight-hour work days, the abolition of child labor, the abolition of contract labor, and equal pay for both men and women. Some of these proposals would not come to fruition for decades in the United States. The Knights of Labor believed that men and women must have the freedom and leverage to take control of their own lives and their own destinies. The statement below was distributed as a handbill to potential members of this union, which sought to make itself into a movement to transform the economy and transform American society.

TO THE PUBLIC:

The alarming development and aggressiveness of great capitalists and corporations, unless checked, will inevitably lead to the pauperization and hopeless degradation of the toiling masses.

It is imperative, if we desire to enjoy the full blessings of life, that a check be placed upon unjust accumulation, and the power for evil of aggregated wealth.

This much-desired object can be accomplished only by the united efforts of those who obey the divine injunction, "In the sweat of they face shalt thou eat bread."

Therefore we have formed the Order of Knights of Labor, for the purpose of organizing and directing the power of the industrial masses, not as a political party, for it is more—in it are crystallized sentiments and measures for the benefit of the whole people, but it should be borne in mind, when exercising the right of suffrage, that most of the objects herein set forth can only be obtained through legislation, and that it is the duty of all to assist in nominating and supporting with their votes only such candidates as will pledge their support to those measures, regardless of party. But no one shall, however, be compelled to vote with the majority, and calling upon all who believe in securing "the greatest good to the greatest number," to join and assist us, we declare to the world that are our aims are:

I To make individual and moral worth, not wealth, the true standard of individual and National greatness.

II To secure to the workers the full enjoyment of the wealth they create, sufficient leisure in which to develop their intellectual, moral, and social faculties: all of the benefits, recreation and pleasures of association; in a word, to enable them to share in the gains and honors of advancing civilization.

In order to secure these results, we demand at the hands of the State:

III The establishment of Bureaus of Labor Statistics, that we may arrive at a correct knowledge of the educational, moral and financial condition of the laboring masses.

IV That the public lands, the heritage of the people, be reserved for actual settlers; not another acre for railroads or speculators, and that all lands now held for speculative purposes be taxed to their full value.

V The abrogation of all laws that do not bear equally upon capital and labor, and the removal of unjust technicalities, delays and discriminations in the administration of justice.

VI The adoption of measures providing for the health and safety of those engaged in mining and manufacturing, building industries, and for indemnification to those engaged therein for injuries received through lack of necessary safeguards.

VII The recognition, by incorporation, of trades' unions, orders and such other associations as may be organized by the working masses to improve their condition and protect their rights.

VIII The enactment of laws to compel corporations to pay their employees weekly, in lawful money, for the labor of the preceding week, and giving mechanics and laborers a first lien upon the product of their labor to the extend of their full wages.

IX The abolition of the contract system on National, State and Municipal works.

X The enactment of laws providing for arbitration between employers and employed, and to enforce the decision of the arbitrators.

XI The prohibition by law of the employment of children under 15 years of age in workshops, mines and factories.

XII To prohibit the hiring out of convict labor.

XIII That a graduated income tax be levied.

And we demand at the hands of Congress:

XIV The establishment of a National monetary system, in which a circulating medium in necessary quantity shall issue direct to the people, without the intervention of banks; that all the National issue shall be full legal tender in payment of all debts, public and private; and that the Government shall not guarantee or recognize any private banks, or create any banking corporations.

XV That interest-bearing bonds, bills of credit or notes shall never be issued by the Government, but that, when need arises, the emergency shall be met by issue of legal tender, non-interest-bearing money.

XVI That the importation of foreign labor under contract be prohibited.

XVII That, in connection wit the post-office, the Government shall organize financial exchanges, safe deposits and facilities for deposit of the savings of the people in small sums.

XVIII That the Government shall obtain possession, by purchase, under the right of eminent domain, of all telegraphs, telephones and railroads, and that hereafter no charter or license be issued to any corporation for construction or operation of any means of transporting intelligence, passengers or freight.

And while making the foregoing demands upon the State and National Government, we will endeavor to associate our own labors.

XIX To establish co-operative institutions such as will tend to supersede the wage system, by the introduction of a co-operative industrial system.

XX To secure for both sexes equal pay for equal work.

XXI To shorten the hours of labor by a general refusal to work for more than eight hours.

XXII To persuade employers to agree to arbitrate all differences which may arise between them and their employees, in order that the bonds of sympathy between them may be strengthened and that strikes may be rendered unnecessary.

If you believe in organization, you are earnestly invited to join with us in securing these objects. All information on the subject of organization should be sent to the General Secretary-Treasurer of the Order, who will have an Organizer visit you and assist in furthering the good work.

CHIEF JOSEPH OF NEZ PERCE **58**

Address in Washington, DC, 1879

After the Civil War, the United States government became determined to place the remaining Native American tribes of the Great Plains onto reservations, stripping them of their cultures and their homes in the process. This sparked numerous wars with tribes across the region as they resisted this decision.

Among the outspoken critics of the federal government's reservation policy for Native Americans, Chief Joseph (or Hin-mah-too-yah-lat-kekht in the Nez Perce language) succeeded his father to become chief of the Wallowa band of the Nez Perce in 1873. In 1877, the federal government ordered his tribe to abandon their homes in Oregon for reservations in Idaho. Chief Joseph instead led his tribe on a daring 1,500- mile voyage in hopes of reaching the perceived safety of Canada to escape federal authorities and the United States Army attempting to force them onto the reservations. Thirty miles short of the border, the Nez Perce were captured and forced onto reservations in the Indian Territory (present-day Oklahoma) where many would die. In 1879, Chief Joseph traveled to Washington, DC, to speak for the rights of the Nez Perce and other Native Americans. Regardless of how different Native Americans were or how different they lived from white Americans, Chief Joseph argued, Native Americans were still entitled to the same rights to live as they pleased. To travel freely, to trade freely, to live in a place freely were the basic rights of all human beings. Freedom and equality could not be confined to a particular race or lifestyle, in Chief Joseph's view. He also added that for justice to prevail, the promises of governments and politicians must be upheld through their actions. The federal

government, however, would continue to attempt to dismantle the tribes and their
cultures and would not recognize the rights of Native Americans to govern their
own affairs or acknowledge their rights for many years.

At last I was granted permission to come to Washington and bring my friend Yellow Bull and our interpreter with me. I am glad I came. I have shaken hands with a good many friends, but there are some things I want to know which no one seems able to explain. I cannot understand how the Government sends a man out to fight us, as it did General [Nelson Appleton] Miles, and then breaks his word. Such a government has something wrong about it. I cannot understand why so many chiefs are allowed to talk so many different ways, and promise so many different things. I have seen the Great Father Chief [President Rutherford B. Hayes]; the Next Great Chief [Secretary of the Interior]; the Commissioner Chief; the Law Chief; and many other law chiefs [Congressmen] and they all say they are my friends, and that I shall have justice, but while all their mouths talk right I do not understand why nothing is done for my people. I have heard talk and talk but nothing is done. Good words do not last long unless they amount to something. Words do not pay for my dead people. They do not pay for my country now overrun by white men. They do not protect my father's grave. They do not pay for my horses and cattle. Good words do not give me back my children. Good words will not make good the promise of your war chief, General Miles. Good words will not give my people a home where they can live in peace and take care of themselves. I am tired of talk that comes to nothing. It makes my heart sick when I remember all the good words and all the broken promises. There has been too much talking by men who had no right to talk. Too many misinterpretations have been made; too many misunderstandings have come up between the white men and the Indians. If the white man wants to live in peace with the Indian he can live in peace. There need be no trouble. Treat all men alike. Give them the same laws. Give them all an even chance to live and grow. All men were made by the same Great Spirit Chief. They are all brothers. The earth is the mother of all people, and all people should have equal rights upon it. You might as well expect all rivers to run backward as that any man who was born a free man should be contented penned up and denied liberty to go where he pleases. If you tie a horse to a stake, do you expect he will grow fat? If you pen an Indian up on a small spot of earth and compel him to stay there, he will not be contented nor will he grow and prosper. I have asked some of the Great White Chiefs where they get their authority to say to the Indian that he shall stay in one place, while he sees white men going where they please. They cannot tell me.

I only ask of the Government to be treated as all other men are treated. If I cannot go to my own home, let me have a home in a country where my people will not die so fast. I would like to go to Bitter Root Valley. There my people would be happy; where they are now they are dying. Three have died since I left my camp to come to Washington.

When I think of our condition, my heart is heavy. I see men of my own race treated as outlaws and driven from country to country, or shot down like animals.

I know that my race must change. We cannot hold our own with the white men as we are. We only ask an even chance to live as other men live. We ask to be recognized as men. We ask that the same law shall work alike on all men. If an Indian breaks the law, punish him by the law. If a white man breaks the law, punish him also.

Let me be a free man, free to travel, free to stop, free to work, free to trade where I choose, free to choose my own teachers, free to follow the religion of my fathers, free to talk, think and act for myself—and I will obey every law or submit to the penalty.

Whenever the white man treats the Indian as they treat each other then we shall have no more wars. We shall be all alike—brothers of one father and mother, with one sky above us and one country around us and one government for all. Then the Great Spirit Chief who rules above will smile upon this land and send rain to wash out the bloody spots made by brothers' hands upon the face of the earth. For this time the Indian race is waiting and praying. I hope no more groans of wounded men and women will ever go to the ear of the Great Spirit Chief above, and that all people may be one people.

Hin-mah-too-yah-lat-kekht has spoken for his people.

FREDERICK DOUGLASS **59**

The Color Line, 1881

By 1881, abolitionist and civil rights activist Frederick Douglass watched with disappointment as the successes of Reconstruction for African-Americans began to be eroded by a new wave of prejudice and legal oppression. In this article, Douglass denounces the argument that race hatred was a natural condition and instead declared that a true spirit of greatness in the individual could overcome it. African-Americans remained oppressed not because of stereotypes but because of the desire to have power over others, he claimed. For any free society and any population, the basic dignities of human beings must be upheld. All in all, freedom for Douglass and other minorities in the United States meant the freedom of a man to be a man and be treated as one, not an object of scorn without cause but an individual worthy of respect.

Few evils are less accessible to the force of reason, or more tenacious of life and power, than a long-standing prejudice. It is a moral disorder, which creates the conditions necessary to its own existence, and fortifies itself by refusing all contradiction. It paints a hateful picture according to its own diseased imagination, and distorts the features of the fancied original to suit the portrait. As those who believe in the visibility of ghosts can easily see them, so it is always easy to see repulsive qualities in those we despise and hate.

Prejudice of race has at some time in their history afflicted all nations. "I am more holy than thou" is the boast of races, as well as that of the Pharisee. Long after the Norman invasion and the decline of Norman power, long after the sturdy Saxon had shaken off the dust of his humiliation and was grandly asserting his great qualities

Frederick Douglass, "The Color Line," *North American Review* 132 (June 1881): 567–577; www.lib.uvirginia.edu/etext/ETC.html

in all directions, the descendants of the invaders continued to regard their Saxon brothers as made of coarser clay than themselves, and were not well pleased when one of the former subject race came between the sun and their nobility. Having seen the Saxon a menial, a hostler, and a common drudge, oppressed and dejected for centuries, it was easy to invest him with all sorts of odious peculiarities, and to deny him all manly predicates. Though eight hundred years have passed away since Norman power entered England, and the Saxon has for centuries been giving his learning, his literature, his language, and his laws to the world more successfully than any other people on the globe, men in that country still boast their Norman origin and Norman perfections. This superstition of former greatness serves to fill out the shriveled sides of a meaningless race-pride which holds over after its power has vanished. With a very different lesson from the one this paper is designed to impress, the great Daniel Webster once told the people of Massachusetts (whose prejudices in the particular instance referred to were right) that they "had conquered the sea, and had conquered the land," but that "it remained for them to conquer their prejudices." At one time we are told that the people in some of the towns of Yorkshire cherished a prejudice so strong and violent against strangers and foreigners that one who ventured to pass through their streets would be pelted with stones.

Of all the races and varieties of men which have suffered from this feeling, the colored people of this country have endured most. They can resort to no disguises which will enable them to escape its deadly aim. They carry in front the evidence which marks them for persecution. They stand at the extreme point of difference from the Caucasian race, and their African origin can be instantly recognized, though they may be several removes from the typical African race. They may remonstrate like Shylock—"Hath not a Jew eyes? hath not a Jew hands, organs, dimensions, senses, affections, passions? fed with the same food, hurt with the same weapons, subject to the same diseases, healed by the same means, warmed and cooled by the same summer and winter, as a Christian is?"—but such eloquence is unavailing. They are negroes—and that is enough, in the eye of this unreasoning prejudice, to justify indignity and violence. In nearly every department of American life they are confronted by this insidious influence. It fills the air. It meets them at the workshop and factory, when they apply for work. It meets them at the church, at the hotel, at the ballot-box, and worst of all, it meets them in the jury-box. Without crime or offense against law or gospel, the colored man is the Jean Valjean of American society. He has escaped from the galleys, and hence all presumptions are against him. The workshop denies him work, and the inn denies him shelter; the ballot-box a fair vote, and the jury-box a fair trial. He has ceased to be the slave of society. He may not now be bought and sold like a beast in the market, but he is the trammeled victim of a prejudice, well calculated to repress his manly ambition, paralyze his energies, and make him a dejected and spiritless man, if not a sullen enemy to society, fit to prey upon life and property and to make trouble generally.

When this evil spirit is judge, jury, and prosecutor, nothing less than overwhelming evidence is sufficient to overcome the force of unfavorable presumptions.

Everything against the person with the hated color is promptly taken for granted; while everything in his favor is received with suspicion and doubt.

A boy of this color is found in his bed tied, mutilated, and bleeding, when forthwith all ordinary experience is set aside, and he is presumed to have been guilty of the outrage upon himself; weeks and months he is kept on trial for the offense, and every effort is made to entangle the poor fellow in the confused meshes of expert testimony (the least trustworthy of all evidence). This same spirit, which promptly assumes everything against us, just as readily denies or explains away everything in our favor. We are not, as a race, even permitted to appropriate the virtues and achievements of our individual representatives. Manliness, capacity, learning, laudable ambition, heroic service, by any of our number, are easily placed to the credit of the superior race. One drop of Teutonic blood is enough to account for all good and great qualities occasionally coupled with a colored skin; and on the other hand, one drop of negro blood, though in the veins of a man of Teutonic whiteness, is enough of which to predicate all offensive and ignoble qualities. In presence of this spirit, if a crime is committed, and the criminal is not positively known, a suspicious-looking colored man is sure to have been seen in the neighborhood. If an unarmed colored man is shot down and dies in his tracks, a jury, under the influence of this spirit, does not hesitate to find the murdered man the real criminal, and the murderer innocent.

Now let us examine this subject a little more closely. It is claimed that this wonder-working prejudice—this moral magic that can change virtue into vice, and innocence to crime; which makes the dead man the murderer, and holds the living homicide harmless—is a natural, instinctive, and invincible attribute of the white race, and one that cannot be eradicated; that even evolution itself cannot carry us beyond or above it. Alas for this poor suffering world (for four-fifths of mankind are colored), if this claim be true! In that case men are forever doomed to injustice, oppression, hate, and strife; and the religious sentiment of the world, with its grand idea of human brotherhood, its "peace on earth and good-will to men," and its golden rule, must be voted a dream, a delusion, and a snare.

But is this color prejudice the natural and inevitable thing it claims to be? If it is so, then it is utterly idle to write against it, preach, pray, or legislate against it, or pass constitutional amendments against it. Nature will have her course, and one might as well preach and pray to a horse against running, to a fish against swimming, or to a bird against flying. Fortunately, however, there is good ground for calling in question this high pretension of a vulgar and wicked prepossession.

If I could talk with all my white fellow-countrymen on this subject, I would say to them, in the language of Scripture: "Come and let us reason together." Now, without being too elementary and formal, it may be stated here that there are at least seven points which candid men will be likely to admit, but which, if admitted, will prove fatal to the popular thought and practice of the times.

First. If what we call prejudice against color be natural, *i.e.*, a part of human nature itself, it follows that it must be co-extensive with human nature, and will and must manifest itself whenever and wherever the two races are brought into contact. It would not vary with either latitude, longitude, or altitude; but like fire and gunpowder, whenever brought together, there would be an explosion of contempt, aversion, and hatred.

Secondly. If it can be shown that there is anywhere on the globe any considerable country where the contact of the African and Caucasian is not distinguished by this explosion of race-wrath, there is reason to doubt that the prejudice is an ineradicable part of human nature.

Thirdly. If this so-called natural, instinctive prejudice can be satisfactorily accounted for by facts and considerations wholly apart from the color features of the respective races, thus placing it among the things subject to human volition and control, we may venture to deny the claim set up for it in the name of human nature.

Fourthly. If any considerable number of white people have overcome this prejudice in themselves, have cast it out as an unworthy sentiment, and have survived the operation, the fact shows that this prejudice is not at any rate a vital part of human nature, and may be eliminated from the race without harm.

Fifthly. If this prejudice shall, after all, prove to be, in its essence and in its natural manifestation, simply a prejudice against condition, and not against race or color, and that it disappears when this or that condition is absent, then the argument drawn from the nature of the Caucasian race falls to the ground.

Sixthly. If prejudice of race and color is only natural in the sense that ignorance, superstition, bigotry, and vice are natural, then it has no better defense than they, and should be despised and put away from human relations as an enemy to the peace, good order, and happiness of human society.

Seventhly. If, still further, this averson to the negro arises out of the fact that he is as we see him, poor, spiritless, ignorant, and degraded, then whatever is humane, noble, and superior, in the mind of the superior and more fortunate race, will desire that all arbitrary barriers against his manhood, intelligence, and elevation shall be removed, and a fair chance in the race of life be given him.

The first of these propositions does not require discussion. It commends itself to the understanding at once. Natural qualities are common and universal, and do not change essentially on the mountain or in the valley. I come therefore to the second point—the existence of countries where this malignant prejudice, as we know it in America, does not prevail; where character, not color, is the passport to consideration; where the right of the black man to be a man, and a man among men, is not questioned; where he may, without offense, even presume to be a gentleman. That there are such countries in the world there is ample evidence. Intelligent and observing travelers, having no theory to support, men whose testimony would be received without question in respect of any other matter, and should not be questioned in this, tell us that they find no color prejudice in Europe, except among Americans who reside there. In England and on the Continent, the colored man is no more an object of hate than any other person. He mingles with the multitude unquestioned, without offense given or received. During the two years which the writer spent abroad, though he was much in society, and was sometimes in the company of lords and ladies, he does not remember one word, look, or gesture that indicated the slightest aversion to him on account of color. His experience was not in this respect exceptional or singular. Messrs. Remond, Ward, Garnet, Brown, Pennington, Crummell, and Bruce, all of them colored, and some of them black, bear the same testimony. If what these gentleman say (and it can be corroborated by a thousand witnesses) is true there is no prejudice against color in England, save as it is carried there by Americans—carried there as a moral disease from an infected country. It is American, not European; local, not general; limited, not universal, and must be ascribed to artificial conditions, and not to any fixed and universal law of nature.

The third point is: Can this prejudice against color, as it is called, be accounted for by circumstances outside and independent of race or color? If it can be thus explained, an incubus may be removed from the breasts of both the white and the black people of this country, as well as from that large intermediate population which has sprung up between these alleged irreconcilable extremes. It will help us to see that it is not necessary that the Ethiopian shall change his skin, nor needful that the white man shall change the essential elements of his nature, in order that mutual respect and consideration may exist between the two races.

Now it is easy to explain the conditions outside of race or color from which may spring feelings akin to those which we call prejudice. A man without the ability or the disposition to pay a just debt does not feel at ease in the presence of his creditor. He does not want to meet him on the street, or in the market-place. Such meeting makes him uncomfortable. He would rather find fault with the bill than pay the debt, and the creditor himself will soon develop in the eyes of the debtor qualities not altogether to his taste.

Some one has well said, we may easily forgive those who injure us, but it is hard to forgive those whom we injure. The greatest injury this side of death, which one human being can inflict on another, is to enslave him, to blot out his personality, degrade his manhood, and sink him to the condition of a beast of burden; and just this has been done here during more than two centuries. No other people under heaven, of whatever type or endowments, could have been so enslaved without falling into contempt and scorn on the part of those enslaving them. Their slavery would itself stamp them with odious features, and give their oppressors arguments in favor of oppression. Besides the long years of wrong and injury inflicted upon the colored race in this country, and the effect of these wrongs upon that race, morally, intellectually, and physically, corrupting their morals, darkening their minds, and twisting their bodies and limbs out of all approach to symmetry, there has been a mountain of gold—uncounted millions of dollars—resting upon them with crushing weight. During all the years of their bondage, the slave master had a direct interest in discrediting the personality of those he held as property. Every man who had a thousand dollars so invested had a thousand reasons for painting the black man as fit only for slavery. Having made him the companion of horses and mules, he naturally sought to justify himself by assuming that the negro was not much better than a mule. The holders of twenty hundred million dollars' worth of property in human chattels procured the means of influencing press, pulpit, and politician, and through these instrumentalities they belittled our virtues and magnified our vices, and have made us odious in the eyes of the world. Slavery had the power at one time to make and unmake Presidents, to construe the law, dictate the policy, set the fashion in national manners and customs, interpret the Bible, and control the church; and, naturally enough, the old masters set themselves up as much too high as they set the manhood of the negro too low. Out of the depths of slavery has come this prejudice and this color line. It is broad enough and black enough to explain all the malign influences which assail the newly emancipated millions to-day. In reply to this argument it will perhaps be said that the negro has no slavery now to contend with, and that having been free during the last sixteen years, he ought by this time to have contradicted the degrading qualities which slavery formerly ascribed to him. All very true as to the letter, but utterly false as to the spirit. Slavery is indeed gone, but its shadow still lingers over the country and poisons more or less the moral atmosphere of all sections of the republic. The money motive for assailing the negro which slavery represented is indeed absent, but love of power and dominion, strengthened by two centuries of irresponsible power, still remains.

Having now shown how slavery created and sustained this prejudice against race and color, and the powerful motive for its creation, the other four points made against it need not be discussed in detail and at length, but may only be referred to in a general way.

If what is called the instinctive aversion of the white race for the colored, when analyzed, is seen to be the same as that which men feel or have felt toward other objects wholly apart from color; if it should be the same as that sometimes exhibited by the haughty and rich to the humble and poor, the same as the Brahmin feels toward the lower caste, the same as the Norman felt toward the Saxon, the same as that cherished by the Turk against Christians, the same as Christians have felt toward the Jews, the same as that which murders a Christian in Wallachia, calls him a "dog" in Constantinople, oppresses and persecutes a Jew in Berlin, hunts down a socialist in St. Petersburg, drives a Hebrew from an hotel at Saratoga, that scorns the Irishman in London, the same as Catholics once felt for Protestants, the same as that which insults, abuses, and kills the Chinaman on the Pacific slope—then may we well enough affirm that this prejudice really has nothing whatever to do with race or color, and that it has its motive and mainspring in some other source with which the mere facts of color and race have nothing to do.

After all, some very well informed and very well meaning people will read what I have now said, and what seems to me so just and reasonable, and will still insist that the color of the negro has something to do with the feeling entertained toward him; that the white man naturally shudders at the thought of contact with one who is black—that the impulse is one which he can neither resist nor control. Let us see if this conclusion is a sound one. An argument is unsound when it proves too little or too much, or when it proves nothing. If color is an offense, it is so, entirely apart from the manhood it envelops. There must be something in color of itself to kindle rage and inflame hate, and render the white man generally uncomfortable. If the white man were really so constituted that color were, in itself, a torment to him, this grand old earth of ours would be no place for him. Colored objects confront him here at every point of the compass. If he should shrink and shudder every time he sees anything dark, he would have little time for anything else. He would require a colorless world to live in—a world where flowers, fields, and floods should all be of snowy whiteness; where rivers, lakes, and oceans should all be white; where all the men, and women, and children should be white; where all the fish of the sea, all the birds of the air, all the "cattle upon a thousand hills," should be white; where the heavens above and the earth beneath should be white, and where day and night should not be divided by light and darkness, but the world should be one eternal scene of light. In such a white world, the entrance of a black man would be hailed with joy by the inhabitants. Anybody or anything would be welcome that would break the oppressive and tormenting monotony of the all-prevailing white.

In the abstract, there is no prejudice against color. No man shrinks from another because he is clothed in a suit of black, nor offended with his boots because they are black. We are told by those who have resided there that a white man in Africa comes to think that ebony is about the proper color for man. Good old Thomas Whitson— a noble old Quaker—a man of rather odd appearance—used to say that even he would be handsome if he could change public opinion.

Aside from the curious contrast to himself, the white child feels nothing on the first sight of a colored man. Curiosity is the only feeling. The office of color in the color line is a very plain and subordinate one. It simply advertises the objects of oppression, insult, and persecution. It is not the maddening liquor, but the black letters on the sign telling the world where it may be had. It is not the hated Quaker, but the broad brim and the plain coat. It is not the hateful Cain, but the mark by which he is known. The color is innocent enough, but things with which it is coupled make it hated. Slavery, ignorance, stupidity, servility, poverty, dependence, are undesirable conditions. When these shall cease to be coupled with color, there will be no color line drawn. It may help in this direction to observe a few of the inconsistencies of the color-line feeling, for it is neither uniform in its operations nor consistent in its principles. Its contradictions in the latter respect would be amusing if the feeling itself were not so deserving of unqualified abhorrence. Our Californian brothers, of Hibernian descent, hate the Chinaman, and kill him, and when asked why they do so, their answer is that a Chinaman is so industrious he will do all the work, and can live by wages upon which other people would starve. When the same people and others are asked why they hate the colored people, the answer is that they are indolent and wasteful, and cannot take care of themselves. Statesmen of the South will tell you that the negro is too ignorant and stupid properly to exercise the elective franchise, and yet his greatest offense is that he acts with the only party intelligent enough in the eyes of the nation to legislate for the country. In one breath they tell us that the negro is so weak in intellect, and so destitute of manhood, that he is but the echo of designing white men, and yet in another they will virtually tell you that the negro is so clear in his moral perceptions, so firm in purpose, so steadfast in his convictions, that he cannot be persuaded by arguments or intimidated by threats, and that nothing but the shot-gun can restrain him from voting for the men and measures he approves. They shrink back in horror from contact with the negro as a man and a gentleman, but like him very well as a barber, waiter, coachman, or cook. As a slave, he could ride anywhere, side by side with his white master, but as a freeman, he must be thrust into the smoking-car. As a slave, he could go into the first cabin; as a freeman, he was not allowed abaft the wheel. Formerly it was said he was incapable of learning, and at the same time it was a crime against the State for any man to teach him to read. To-day he is said to be originally and permanently inferior to the white race, and yet wild apprehensions are expressed lest six millions of this inferior race will somehow or other manage to rule over thirty-five millions of the superior race. If inconsistency can prove the hollowness of anything, certainly the emptiness of this pretense that color has any terrors is easily shown. The trouble is that most men, and especially mean men, want to have something under them. The rich man would have the poor man, the white would have the black, the Irish would have the negro, and the negro must have a dog, if he can get nothing higher in the scale of intelligence to dominate. This feeling is one of the vanities which enlightenment will dispel. A good but simple-minded Abolitionist said to me that he was not ashamed to walk with me down Broadway arm-in-arm, in open daylight, and evidently thought he was saying something that must be very pleasing to my self-importance, but it occurred to me, at the moment, this man does not dream of any reason why I might be ashamed to walk arm-in-arm with him through Broadway in open daylight. Riding in a stage-coach from Concord, New Hampshire, to Vergennes, Vermont, many years ago, I found myself on very pleasant terms with all the passengers through the night, but the morning light came to me as it comes to the stars; I was as Dr. Beecher says he was at the first fire he witnessed, when a bucket of cold water was poured down his back—"the fire was not put out, but he was." The fact is, the higher the colored man rises in the scale of society, the less prejudice does he meet.

The writer has met and mingled freely with the leading great men of his time,—at home and abroad, in public halls and private houses, on the platform and at the fireside,—and can remember no instance when among such men has he been made to feel himself an object of aversion. Men who are really great are too great to be small. This was gloriously true of the late Abraham Lincoln, William H. Seward, Salmon P. Chase, Henry Wilson, John P. Hale, Lewis Tappan, Edmund Quincy, Joshua R. Giddings, Gerrit Smith, and Charles Sumner, and many others among the dead. Good taste will not permit me now to speak of the living, except to say that the number of those who rise superior to prejudice is great and increasing. Let those who wish to see what is to be the future of America, as relates to races and race relations, attend, as I have attended, during the administration of President Hayes, the grand diplomatic receptions at the executive mansion, and see there, as I have seen, in its splendid east room, the wealth, culture, refinement, and beauty of the nation assembled, and with it the eminent representatives of other nations,—the swarthy Turk with his "fez," the Englishman shining with gold, the German, the Frenchman, the Spaniard, the Japanese, the Chinaman, the Caucasian, the Mongolian, the Sandwich Islander, and the negro,—all moving about freely, each respecting the rights and dignity of the other, and neither receiving nor giving offense.

"Then let us pray that come it may,
As come it will for a' that,
That sense and worth, o'er a' the earth,
May bear the gree, and a' that;
"That man to man, the world o'er,
Shall brothers be, for a' that."

FREDERICK DOUGLASS.

60

The Ocala Demands, 1890

The post-Civil War years were difficult for the American farmer. Crop prices collapsed, leading to widespread bankruptcies. In addition, railroads, warehouses, and retailers routinely gave favored rates to their preferred customers at the expense of the average farmer. This frustration boiled over into a number of popular movements in the 1870s, 1880s, and 1890s. At a convention in Ocala, Nebraska, in

John D. Hicks, *The Populist Revolt, A History of the Farmers' Alliance and the People's Party* (Minneapolis: University of Minnesota Press, 1931): 430–431.

December 1890, a group of farmers came together to form the Populist Party, a party dedicated to preserving the economic interests of the American farmer and restoring what the farmers saw as economic justice. This platform approved by the delegates, the Ocala Demands, centers on the idea of restoring the economic balance and sense of equality that farmers believed was slipping away from them. The farmers feared that a class system of special privileges for the wealthy was danger of emerging and destroying the American idea of fairness.

1. We demand the abolition of national banks.
2. We demand that the government shall establish sub-treasuries or depositories in the several states, which shall loan money direct to the people at a low rate of interest, not to exceed two per cent per annum, on non-perishable farm products, and also upon real estate, with proper limitations upon the quantity of land and amount of money.
3. We demand that the amount of the circulating medium be speedily increased to not less than $50 per capita.
4. We demand that Congress shall pass such laws as will effectually prevent the dealing in futures of all agricultural and mechanical productions; providing a stringent system of procedure in trials that will secure the prompt conviction, and imposing such penalties as shall secure the most perfect compliance with the law.
5. We condemn the silver bill recently passed by Congress, and demand in lieu thereof the free and unlimited coinage of silver.
6. We demand the passage of laws prohibiting alien ownership of land, and that Congress take prompt action to devise some plan to obtain all lands now owned by aliens and foreign syndicates; and that all lands now held by railroads and other corporations in excess of such as is actually used and needed by them be reclaimed by the government and held for actual settlers only.
7. Believing in the doctrine of equal rights to all and special privileges to none, we demand—
8. That our national legislation shall be so framed in the future as not to build up one industry at the expense of another.
9. We further demand a removal of the existing heavy tariff tax from the necessities of life, that the poor of our land must have.
10. We further demand a just and equitable system of graduated tax on incomes.
11. We believe that the money of the county should be kept as much as possible in the hands of the people, and hence we demand that all national and state revenues shall be limited to the necessary expenses of the government economically and honestly administered.
12. We demand the most rigid, honest and just state and national government control and supervision of the means of public communication and transportation, and if this control and supervision does not remove the abuse now existing, we demand the government ownership of such means of communication and transportation.
13. We demand that the Congress of the United States submit an amendment to the Constitution providing for the election of United States Senators by direct vote of the people of each state.

Booker T. Washington **61**

The Atlanta Compromise, 1895

Booker T. Washington, the noted educator, spoke at the Atlanta Cotton States and International Exposition on September 18, 1895. Here he delivered one of the most praised and condemned speeches of his career. In this address, he described the poor condition of African-American education and business and declared that the African-American community should take more time to develop itself before pushing for equality. He believed that in time, an economically and educationally self-sufficient African-American community would be able to pull itself up to a level of equality. Equality would come in time, Washington believed. The Atlanta Compromise was bitterly condemned by many in the African-American community as a surrender to the rising forces of bigotry in American politics and became the focus of a bitter debate over the proper course of progress for civil rights.

Mr. President and Gentlemen of the Board of Directors and Citizens:

One-third of the population of the South is of the Negro race. No enterprise seeking the material, civil, or moral welfare of this section can disregard this element of our population and reach the highest success. I but convey to you, Mr. President and Directors, the sentiment of the masses of my race when I say that in no way have the value and manhood of the American Negro been more fittingly and generously recognized than by the managers of this magnificent Exposition at every stage of its progress. It is a recognition that will do more to cement the friendship of the two races than any occurrence since the dawn of our freedom.

Not only this, but the opportunity here afforded will awaken among us a new era of industrial progress. Ignorant and inexperienced, it is not strange that in the first years of our new life we began at the top instead of at the bottom; that a seat in Congress or the state legislature was more sought than real estate or industrial skill; that the political convention or stump speaking had more attractions than starting a dairy farm or truck garden.

A ship lost at sea for many days suddenly sighted a friendly vessel. From the mast of the unfortunate vessel was seen a signal, "Water, water; we die of thirst!" The answer from the friendly vessel at once came back, "Cast down your bucket where you are." A second time the signal, "Water, water; send us water!" ran up from the distressed vessel, and was answered, "Cast down your bucket where you are." And a third and fourth signal for water was answered, "Cast down your bucket where you are." The captain of the distressed vessel, at last heeding the injunction, cast down his

Booker T. Washington, *The Booker T. Washington Papers*, Vol. 3, Louis R. Harlan, ed. (Urbana: University of Illinois Press, 1974), 583–587.

bucket, and it came up full of fresh, sparkling water from the mouth of the Amazon River.

To those of my race who depend on bettering their condition in a foreign land or who underestimate the importance of cultivating friendly relations with the Southern white man, who is their next-door neighbor, I would say: "Cast down your bucket where you are"—cast it down in making friends in every manly way of the people of all races by whom we are surrounded.

Cast it down in agriculture, mechanics, in commerce, in domestic service, and in the professions. And in this connection it is well to bear in mind that whatever other sins the South may be called to bear, when it comes to business, pure and simple, it is in the South that the Negro is given a man's chance in the commercial world, and in nothing is this Exposition more eloquent than in emphasizing this chance. Our greatest danger is that in the great leap from slavery to freedom we may overlook the fact that the masses of us are to live by the productions of our hands, and fail to keep in mind that we shall prosper in proportion as we learn to dignify and glorify common labor, and put brains and skill into the common occupations of life; shall prosper in proportion as we learn to draw the line between the superficial and the substantial, the ornamental gewgaws of life and the useful. No race can prosper till it learns that there is as much dignity in tilling a field as in writing a poem. It is at the bottom of life we must begin, and not at the top. Nor should we permit our grievances to overshadow our opportunities.

To those of the white race who look to the incoming of those of foreign birth and strange tongue and habits for the prosperity of the South, were I permitted I would repeat what I say to my own race, "Cast down your bucket where you are." Cast it down among the eight millions of Negroes whose habits you know, whose fidelity and love you have tested in days when to have proved treacherous meant the ruin of your firesides. Cast down your bucket among these people who have, without strikes and labor wars, tilled your fields, cleared your forests, builded your railroads and cities, and brought forth treasures from the bowels of the earth, and helped make possible this magnificent representation of the progress of the South. Casting down your bucket among my people, helping and encouraging them as you are doing on these grounds, and to education of head, hand, and heart, you will find that they will buy your surplus land, make blossom the waste places in your fields, and run your factories. While doing this, you can be sure in the future, as in the past, that you and your families will be surrounded by the most patient, faithful, law-abiding, and unresentful people that the world has seen. As we have proved our loyalty to you in the past, in nursing your children, watching by the sick-bed of your mothers and fathers, and often following them with tear-dimmed eyes to their graves, so in the future, in our humble way, we shall stand by you with a devotion that no foreigner can approach, ready to lay down our lives, if need be, in defense of yours, interlacing our industrial, commercial, civil, and religious life with yours in a way that shall make the interests of both races one. In all things that are purely social, we can be as separate as the fingers, yet one as the hand in all things essential to mutual progress.

There is no defense or security for any of us except in the highest intelligence and development of all. If anywhere there are efforts tending to curtail the fullest growth of the Negro, let these efforts be turned into stimulating, encouraging, and making him the most useful and intelligent citizen. Effort or means so invested will pay a thousand percent interest. These efforts will be twice blessed—blessing him that gives and him that takes.

There is no escape through law of man or God from the inevitable:

The laws of changeless justice bind
Oppressor with oppressed;
And close as sin and suffering joined
We march to fate abreast.

Nearly sixteen millions of hands will aid you in pulling the load upward, or they will pull against you the load downward. We shall constitute one-third and more of the ignorance and crime of the South, or one-third its intelligence and progress; we shall contribute one-third to the business and industrial prosperity of the South, or we shall prove a veritable body of death, stagnating, depressing, retarding every effort to advance the body politic.

Gentlemen of the Exposition, as we present to you our humble effort at an exhibition of our progress, you must not expect overmuch. Starting thirty years ago with ownership here and there in a few quilts and pumpkins and chickens (gathered from miscellaneous sources), remember the path that has led from these to the inventions and production of agricultural implements, buggies, steam-engines, newspapers, books, statuary, carving, paintings, the management of drug stores and banks, has not been trodden without contact with thorns and thistles.

While we take pride in what we exhibit as a result of our independent efforts, we do not for a moment forget that our part in this exhibition would fall far short of your expectations but for the constant help that has come to our educational life, not only from the southern states, but especially from northern philanthropists, who have made their gifts a constant stream of blessing and encouragement.

The wisest among my race understand that the agitation of questions of social equality is the extremist folly, and that progress in the enjoyment of all the privileges that will come to us must be the result of severe and constant struggle rather than of artificial forcing. No race that has anything to contribute to the markets of the world is long in any degree ostracized. It is important and right that all privileges of the law be ours, but it is vastly more important that we be prepared for the exercise of these privileges. The opportunity to earn a dollar in a factory just now is worth infinitely more than the opportunity to spend a dollar in an opera-house.

In conclusion, may I repeat that nothing in thirty years has given us more hope and encouragement, and drawn us so near to you of the white race, as this opportunity offered by the Exposition; and here bending, as it were, over the altar that represents the results of the struggles of your race and mine, both starting practically empty-handed three decades ago, I pledge that in your effort to work out the great and intricate problem which God has laid at the doors of the South, you shall have at all times the patient, sympathetic help of my race; only let this be constantly in mind, that, while from representations in these buildings of the product of field, of forest, of mine, of factory, letters, and art, much good will come, yet far above and beyond material benefits will be that higher good, that, let us pray God, will come, in a blotting out of sectional differences and racial animosities and suspicions, in a determination to administer absolute justice, in a willing obedience among all classes to the mandates of law.

This, coupled with our material prosperity, will bring into our beloved South a new heaven and a new earth.

THEODORE ROOSEVELT **62**

Inaugural Address, 1905

Theodore Roosevelt became the youngest president in American history at age 42 when President William McKinley succumbed to an assassin's bullets in 1901. Roosevelt won a full term as president by a resounding margin in 1904. At his inaugural address on March 4, 1905, Roosevelt addressed the issue of the United States as a world power. He had long since developed an interest in expanding American power and prestige overseas. Roosevelt believed that the best way to guarantee its prestige and freedom was by seeking "the peace of justice" in its international relations. Similarly, Roosevelt stated, it should seek that peace at home as well.

My fellow-citizens, no people on earth have more cause to be thankful than ours, and this is said reverently, in no spirit of boastfulness in our own strength, but with gratitude to the Giver of Good who has blessed us with the conditions which have enabled us to achieve so large a measure of well-being and of happiness. To us as a people it has been granted to lay the foundations of our national life in a new continent. We are the heirs of the ages, and yet we have had to pay few of the penalties which in old countries are exacted by the dead hand of a bygone civilization. We have not been obliged to fight for our existence against any alien race; and yet our life has called for the vigor and effort without which the manlier and hardier virtues wither away. Under such conditions it would be our own fault if we failed; and the success which we have had in the past, the success which we confidently believe the future will bring, should cause in us no feeling of vainglory, but rather a deep and abiding realization of all which life has offered us; a full acknowledgment of the responsibility which is ours; and a fixed determination to show that under a free government a mighty people can thrive best, alike as regards the things of the body and the things of the soul.

Much has been given us, and much will rightfully be expected from us. We have duties to others and duties to ourselves; and we can shirk neither. We have become a great nation, forced by the fact of its greatness into relations with the other nations of the earth, and we must behave as beseems a people with such responsibilities. Toward all other nations, large and small, our attitude must be one of cordial and sincere friendship. We must show not only in our words, but in our deeds, that we are earnestly desirous of securing their good will by acting toward them in a spirit of just and generous recognition of all their rights. But justice and generosity in a nation, as in an individual, count most when shown not by the weak but by the strong. While ever careful to refrain from wrongdoing others, we must be no less insistent that we are not wronged ourselves. We wish peace, but we wish the peace of justice, the peace of righteousness. We wish it because we think it is right and not because we are afraid. No weak nation that acts manfully and justly should ever have cause to fear us, and no strong power should ever be able to single us out as a subject for insolent aggression.

Our relations with the other powers of the world are important; but still more important are our relations among ourselves. Such growth in wealth, in population, and in power as this nation has seen during the century and a quarter of its national life is inevitably accompanied by a like growth in the problems which are ever before every nation that rises to greatness. Power invariably means both responsibility and danger. Our forefathers faced certain perils which we have outgrown. We now face other perils, the very existence of which it was impossible that they should foresee. Modern life is both complex and intense, and the tremendous changes wrought by the extraordinary industrial development of the last half century are felt in every fiber of our social and political being. Never before have men tried so vast and formidable an experiment as that of administering the affairs of a continent under the forms of a Democratic republic. The conditions which have told for our marvelous material well-being, which have developed to a very high degree our energy, self-reliance, and individual initiative, have also brought the care and anxiety inseparable from the accumulation of great wealth in industrial centers. Upon the success of our experiment much depends, not only as regards our own welfare, but as regards the welfare of mankind. If we fail, the cause of free self-government throughout the world will rock to its foundations, and therefore our responsibility is heavy, to ourselves, to the world as it is to-day, and to the generations yet unborn. There is no good reason why we should fear the future, but there is every reason why we should face it seriously, neither hiding from ourselves the gravity of the problems before us nor fearing to approach these problems with the unbending, unflinching purpose to solve them aright.

Yet, after all, though the problems are new, though the tasks set before us differ from the tasks set before our fathers who founded and preserved this Republic, the spirit in which these tasks must be undertaken and these problems faced, if our duty is to be well done, remains essentially unchanged. We know that self-government is difficult. We know that no people needs such high traits of character as that people which seeks to govern its affairs aright through the freely expressed will of the freemen who compose it. But we have faith that we shall not prove false to the memories of the men of the mighty past. They did their work, they left us the splendid heritage we now enjoy. We in our turn have an assured confidence that we shall be able to leave this heritage unwasted and enlarged to our children and our children's children. To do so we must show, not merely in great crises, but in the everyday affairs of life, the qualities of practical intelligence, of courage, of hardihood, and endurance, and above all the power of devotion to a lofty ideal, which made great the men who founded this Republic in the days of Washington, which made great the men who preserved this Republic in the days of Abraham Lincoln.

W. E. B. DuBois   **63**

Harpers Ferry Address to the Niagara Conference, 1906

The 1895 Atlanta Compromise speech by Booker T. Washington created a firestorm of debate in the African-American community. In response to the call to "cast down your bucket where you are," W. E. B. DuBois and others created the Niagara Movement in Niagara Falls, Ontario, Canada, to counter Washington's ideas on civil rights. At the second annual meeting of the Niagara Conference in August 1906, DuBois delivered this address on the principles of his movement. Meeting at Harpers Ferry, West Virginia, site of the 1859 raid on the federal arsenal by radical abolitionist John Brown, DuBois thought it fitting to reflect on that incident. Just as Brown hoped to free enslaved African-Americans, DuBois hoped to prevent the re-enslavement of African-Americans through segregation laws and disfranchisement laws. DuBois believed that the principles of the Niagara Movement were plain enough: respect the dignity and equality of all men and above all preserve the "right to rise." By 1909, the movement would coalesce into the National Association for the Advancement of Colored People, the oldest civil rights organization in the United States by the twenty-first century.

The men of the Niagara Movement coming from the toil of the year's hard work and pausing a moment from the earning of their daily bread turn toward the nation and ask again, in the name of ten million, the privilege of a hearing.

In the past year the work of the Negro-hater has flourished in the land. Step by step the defenders of the rights of American citizens have retreated. The work of stealing the black man's ballot has progressed and the fifty and more representatives of stolen votes still sit in the nation's capital. Discrimination in travel and public accommodation has so spread that some of our weaker brethren are actually afraid to thunder against color discrimination as such and are simply whispering for ordinary decencies. Against this the Niagara Movement eternally protests. We will not be satisfied to take one jot or little less than our full manhood rights!

We claim for ourselves every single right that belongs to a freeborn American, political, civil and social; and until we get these rights we will never cease to protest and assail the ears of America! The battle we wage is not for ourselves alone but for all true Americans. It is a fight for ideals, lest this, our common fatherland, false to its founding, become in truth, the land of the thief and the home of the slave, a byword and a hissing among the nations for its sounding pretensions and pitiful accomplishments.

Never before in the modern age has a great and civilized folk threatened to adopt so cowardly a creed in the treatment of its fellow citizens born and bred on its soil. Stripped of verbiage and subterfuge and in its naked nastiness, the new American creed says: "Fear to let black men even try to rise lest they become the equals of the white." And this is the land that professes to follow Jesus Christ! The blasphemy of such a course is only matched by its cowardice.

In detail, our demands are clear and unequivocal. First, we would vote; with the right to vote goes everything: freedom, manhood, the honor of your wives, the chastity of your daughters, the right to work, and the chance to rise, and let no man listen to those who deny this.

We want full manhood suffrage, and we want it now, henceforth and forever!

Second. We want discrimination in public accommodation to cease. Separation in railway and street cars, based simply on race and color, is un-American, undemocratic, and silly.

Third. We claim the right of freemen to walk, talk, and be with them that wish to be with us. No man has a right to choose another man's friends, and to attempt to do so is an impudent interference with the most fundamental human privilege.

Fourth. We want the laws enforced against rich as well as poor; against capitalist as well as laborer; against white as well as black. We are not more lawless than the white race: We are more often arrested, convicted and mobbed. We want Congress to take charge of Congressional elections. We want the Fourteenth Amendment carried out to the letter and every state disfranchised in Congress which attempts to disfranchise its rightful voters. We want the Fifteenth Amendment enforced and no state allowed to base its franchise simply on color.

The failure of the Republican Party in Congress at the session just closed to redeem its pledge ... to suffrage conditions in the South seems a plain, deliberate, and premeditated breach of promise, and stamps that Party as guilty of obtaining votes under false pretense.

Fifth. We want our children educated. The school system in the country districts of the South is a disgrace, and in few towns and cities are the Negro schools what they ought to be. We want the national government to step in and wipe out illiteracy in the South. Either the United States will destroy ignorance, or ignorance will destroy the United States.

And when we call for education we mean real education. We believe in work. We ourselves are workers, but work is not necessarily education. Education is the development of power and ideal. We want our children trained as intelligent human beings should be, and we will fight for all time against any proposal to educate black boys and girls simply as servants and underlings, or simply for the use of other people. They have a right to know, to think, to aspire.

These are some of the chief things which we want. How shall we get them? By voting where we may vote, by persistent, unceasing agitation, by hammering at the truth, by sacrifice and work.

We do not believe in violence, neither in the despised violence of the raid nor the lauded violence of the soldier, nor the barbarous of the mob, but we do believe in John Brown, in that incarnate spirit of justice, that hatred of a lie, that willingness to sacrifice money, reputation, and life itself on the altar of right. And here on the scene of John Brown's martyrdom, we reconsecrate ourselves, our honor, our property to the final emancipation of the race which John Brown died to make free.

Our enemies, triumphant for the present, are fighting the stars in their courses. Justice and humanity must prevail. We live to tell these dark brothers of ours— scattered in counsel, wavering, and weak—that no bribe of money or notoriety, no promise of wealth or fame, is worth the surrender of a people's manhood or the loss of a man's self-respect. We refuse to surrender the leadership of this race to cowards and trucklers. We are men; we will be treated as men. On this rock we have planted our banners. We will never give up, though the trump of doom finds us still fighting.

And we shall win! The past promised it. The present foretells it. Thank God for John Brown. Thank God for [abolitionist William Lloyd] Garrison and [Frederick] Douglass, [Sen. Charles] Sumner and [abolitionst Wendell] Phillips, Nat Turner and Robert Gould Shaw, and all the hallowed dead who died for freedom. Thank God for all those today, few though their voices be, who have not forgotten the divine brotherhood of all men, white and black, rich and poor, fortunate and unfortunate.

We appeal to the young men and women of this nation, to those whose nostrils are not yet befouled by greed and snobbery and racial narrowness: Stand up for the right, prove yourselves worthy of your heritage and, whether born North or South, dare to treat men as men. Cannot the nation that has absorbed ten-million foreigners into its political life without catastrophe absorb ten-million Negro Americans into that same political life at less cost than their unjust and illegal exclusion will involve?

Courage, brothers! The battle for humanity is not lost or losing. All across the skies sit signs of promise! The Slav is rising in his might, the yellow millions are tasting liberty, the black Africans are writhing toward the light, and everywhere the laborer, with ballot in his hand, is voting open the gates of opportunity and peace.

The morning breaks over blood-stained hills. We must not falter, we may not shrink.

Above are the everlasting stars.

WOODROW WILSON   **64**

Inaugural Address, 1913

As Woodrow Wilson took the oath of office on March 4, 1913, to begin the first of his two terms, the United States faced a mounting debate on social policies. The United States had reached an unprecedented standard of living, but at a price. At the beginning of the twentieth century, few laws existed to protect workplace safety, the safety of foods and medicines, or the wages and hours of laborers. Child labor was a lingering issue. Many progressives demanded government protection for society's downtrodden and laborers, but many conservatives argued that such regulations were improper. Wilson won the 1912 election promising a "New Freedom," promising to ratify the demands of the progressives, frustrated by years of delays, court defeats, and parliamentary maneuvers. Wilson depicted the issue in this speech as a matter of morality. He believed that human lives should not be destroyed for economic gain, that the most fundamental right of all was at stake for the working poor of America—the right to life.

http://www.bartleby.com/124/pres44.html

THERE has been a change of government. It began two years ago, when the House of Representatives became Democratic by a decisive majority. It has now been completed. The Senate about to assemble will also be Democratic. The offices of President and Vice-President have been put into the hands of Democrats. What does the change mean? That is the question that is uppermost in our minds to-day. That is the question I am going to try to answer, in order, if I may, to interpret the occasion.

It means much more than the mere success of a party. The success of a party means little except when the Nation is using that party for a large and definite purpose. No one can mistake the purpose for which the Nation now seeks to use the Democratic Party. It seeks to use it to interpret a change in its own plans and point of view. Some old things with which we had grown familiar, and which had begun to creep into the very habit of our thought and of our lives, have altered their aspect as we have latterly looked critically upon them, with fresh, awakened eyes; have dropped their disguises and shown themselves alien and sinister. Some new things, as we look frankly upon them, willing to comprehend their real character, have come to assume the aspect of things long believed in and familiar, stuff of our own convictions. We have been refreshed by a new insight into our own life.

We see that in many things that life is very great. It is incomparably great in its material aspects, in its body of wealth, in the diversity and sweep of its energy, in the industries which have been conceived and built up by the genius of individual men and the limitless enterprise of groups of men. It is great, also, very great, in its moral force. Nowhere else in the world have noble men and women exhibited in more striking forms the beauty and the energy of sympathy and helpfulness and counsel in their efforts to rectify wrong, alleviate suffering, and set the weak in the way of strength and hope. We have built up, moreover, a great system of government, which has stood through a long age as in many respects a model for those who seek to set liberty upon foundations that will endure against fortuitous change, against storm and accident. Our life contains every great thing, and contains it in rich abundance.

But the evil has come with the good, and much fine gold has been corroded. With riches has come inexcusable waste. We have squandered a great part of what we might have used, and have not stopped to conserve the exceeding bounty of nature, without which our genius for enterprise would have been worthless and impotent, scorning to be careful, shamefully prodigal as well as admirably efficient. We have been proud of our industrial achievements, but we have not hitherto stopped thoughtfully enough to count the human cost, the cost of lives snuffed out, of energies overtaxed and broken, the fearful physical and spiritual cost to the men and women and children upon whom the dead weight and burden of it all has fallen pitilessly the years through. The groans and agony of it all had not yet reached our ears, the solemn, moving undertone of our life, coming up out of the mines and factories, and out of every home where the struggle had its intimate and familiar seat. With the great Government went many deep secret things which we too long delayed to look into and scrutinize with candid, fearless eyes. The great Government we loved has too often been made use of for private and selfish purposes, and those who used it had forgotten the people.

At last a vision has been vouchsafed us of our life as a whole. We see the bad with the good, the debased and decadent with the sound and vital. With this vision we approach new affairs. Our duty is to cleanse, to reconsider, to restore, to correct the evil without impairing the good, to purify and humanize every process of our common life without weakening or sentimentalizing it. There has been something crude and heartless and unfeeling in our haste to succeed and be great. Our thought has been "Let every man look out for himself, let every generation look out for itself," while we reared giant machinery which made it impossible that any but those who stood at the levers of control should have a chance to look out for themselves. We had not forgotten our morals. We remembered well enough that we had set up a policy which was meant to serve the humblest as well as the most powerful, with an eye single to the standards of justice and fair play, and remembered it with pride. But we were very heedless and in a hurry to be great.

We have come now to the sober second thought. The scales of heedlessness have fallen from our eyes. We have made up our minds to square every process of our national life again with the standards we so proudly set up at the beginning and have always carried at our hearts. Our work is a work of restoration.

We have itemized with some degree of particularity the things that ought to be altered and here are some of the chief items: A tariff which cuts us off from our proper part in the commerce of the world, violates the just principles of taxation, and makes the Government a facile instrument in the hand of private interests; a banking and currency system based upon the necessity of the Government to sell its bonds fifty years ago and perfectly adapted to concentrating cash and restricting credits; an industrial system which, take it on all its sides, financial as well as administrative, holds capital in leading strings, restricts the liberties and limits the opportunities of labor, and exploits without renewing or conserving the natural resources of the country; a body of agricultural activities never yet given the efficiency of great business undertakings or served as it should be through the instrumentality of science taken directly to the farm, or afforded the facilities of credit best suited to its practical needs; watercourses undeveloped, waste places unreclaimed, forests untended, fast disappearing without plan or prospect of renewal, unregarded waste heaps at every mine. We have studied as perhaps no other nation has the most effective means of production, but we have not studied cost or economy as we should either as organizers of industry, as statesmen, or as individuals.

Nor have we studied and perfected the means by which government may be put at the service of humanity, in safeguarding the health of the Nation, the health of its men and its women and its children, as well as their rights in the struggle for existence. This is no sentimental duty. The firm basis of government is justice, not pity. These are matters of justice. There can be no equality or opportunity, the first essential of justice in the body politic, if men and women and children be not shielded in their lives, their very vitality, from the consequences of great industrial and social processes which they can not alter, control, or singly cope with. Society must see to it that it does not itself crush or weaken or damage its own constituent parts. The first duty of law is to keep sound the society it serves. Sanitary laws, pure food laws, and laws determining conditions of labor which individuals are powerless to determine for themselves are intimate parts of the very business of justice and legal efficiency.

These are some of the things we ought to do, and not leave the others undone, the old-fashioned, never-to-be-neglected, fundamental safeguarding of property and of individual right. This is the high enterprise of the new day: To lift everything that concerns our life as a Nation to the light that shines from the hearthfire of every man's conscience and vision of the right. It is inconceivable that we should do this as partisans; it is inconceivable we should do it in ignorance of the facts as they are or in blind haste. We shall restore, not destroy. We shall deal with our economic system as it is and as it may be modified, not as it might be if we had a clean sheet of paper to write upon; and step by step we shall make it what it should be, in the spirit of those who question their own wisdom and seek counsel and knowledge, not shallow self-satisfaction or the excitement of excursions whither they can not tell. Justice, and only justice, shall always be our motto.

And yet it will be no cool process of mere science. The Nation has been deeply stirred, stirred by a solemn passion, stirred by the knowledge of wrong, of ideals lost, of government too often debauched and made an instrument of evil. The feelings with which we face this new age of right and opportunity sweep across our heart-strings like some air out of God's own presence, where justice and mercy are reconciled and the judge and the brother are one. We know our task to be no mere task of politics but a task which shall search us through and through, whether we be able to understand our time and the need of our people, whether we be indeed their spokesmen and interpreters, whether we have the pure heart to comprehend and the rectified will to choose our high course of action.

This is not a day of triumph; it is a day of dedication. Here muster, not the forces of party, but the forces of humanity. Men's hearts wait upon us; men's lives hang in the balance; men's hopes call upon us to say what we will do. Who shall live up to the great trust? Who dares fail to try? I summon all honest men, all patriotic, all forward-looking men, to my side. God helping me, I will not fail them, if they will but counsel and sustain me!

ANNA HOWARD SHAW   **65**

Fundamental Principles of a Republic, 1915

Anna Shaw had become part of a new generation of women's suffrage activists in the late 1800s. By the beginning of the twentieth century, suffragists were slowly winning the franchise for women in states and territories across the United States. In this address in Albany, New York, on June 21, 1915, she addresses the issue once again. For Shaw, if the United States were to be a republic, it could not deny basic rights to such a significant portion of the population. The nation had a clear choice, Shaw told the crowd, that the United States could either stand as a republic or an aristocracy. But to differentiate itself from the warring nations of Germany and Austria-Hungary, it should cling to the ideals of a republic.

When I came into your hall tonight, I thought of the last time I was in your city. Twenty-one years ago I came here with Susan B. Anthony, and we came for exactly the same purpose as that for which we are here tonight. Boys have been born since that time and have become voters, and the women are still trying to persuade American men to believe in the fundamental principles of democracy.

I never quite feel as if it was a fair field to argue this question with men, because in doing it you have to assume that a man who professes to believe in a republican form of government does not believe in a republican form of government, for the only thing that women's enfranchisement means at all is that a government which claims to be a republic should be a republic, and not an aristocracy...

Now one of two things is true: Either a republic is a desirable form of government, or else it is not. If it is, then we should have it, if it is not, then we ought not to pretend that we have it. We ought, at least, to be true to our ideals, and the men of New York have, for the first time in their lives, the rare opportunity, on the second day of next November, of making this state truly a part of a republic.

If women's suffrage is wrong, it is a great wrong; if it is right, it is a profound and fundamental principle, and we all know—if we know what a republic is—that it is the fundamental principle upon which a republic must rise. Let us see where we are as a people; how we act here and what we think we are.

The difficulty with the men of this country is that they are so consistent in their inconsistency that they are not aware of having been inconsistent; because their consistency has been so continuous, and their inconsistency so consecutive, that it has never been broken, from the beginning of our nation's life to the present time.

If we trace our history back, we will find that from the very dawn of our existence as a people, men have been imbued with a spirit and a vision more lofty than they have been able to live. They have been led by visions of the sublimest truth, both in regard to religion and in regard to government that ever inspired the souls of men from the time the Puritans left the Old World to come to this country, led by the Divine ideal which is the sublimest and supremest ideal in religious freedom which men have ever known: The theory that a man has a right to worship God according to the dictates of his own conscience, without the intervention of any other man or any other group of men. And it was this theory, this vision of the right of the human soul, which led men first to the shores of this country.

Now, nobody can deny that [these were] sincere, honest and earnest men. No one can deny that the Puritans were men of profound conviction, and yet these men, who gave up everything in behalf of an ideal, hardly established their communities in this new country before they began to practice exactly the same sort of persecutions on other men which had been practiced upon them. They settled in their communities on the New England shores, and when they formed their compacts by which they governed their local societies, they permitted no man to have a voice in their affairs unless he was a member of the church, and not a member of any church, but a member of the particular church which dominated the particular community in which he happened to be. In Massachusetts they drove the Baptists down to Rhode Island; in Connecticut they drove the Presbyterians over to New Jersey; they burned the Quakers in Massachusetts and ducked the witches, and no colony, either Catholic or Protestant, allowed a Jew to have a voice. And so a man must worship God according to the conscience of the particular community in which he was located.

[Even though] they called that religious freedom, they were not able to live the ideal of religious liberty, and from that time to this, the men of this government have been following along the same line of inconsistency, while they, too, have been following a vision of equal grandeur and power.

Never in the history of the world did it dawn upon the human mind as it dawned upon your ancestors, what it would mean for men to be free. They got the vision of a government in which the people would be the supreme power, and so inspired by this vision, men wrote such documents as were sent from Massachusetts legislature, from the New York legislature and from the Pennsylvania group over to the Parliament of Great Britain, which rang with the profoundest measures of freedom and justice. They did not equivocate in a single word when they wrote the Declaration of Independence; no one can dream that these men had not got the sublimest ideal of democracy which had ever dawned upon the souls of men.

But as soon as the war was over and our government was formed, instead of asking the question, who shall be the governing force in this great new republic, when they brought those thirteen little territories together, they began to eliminate instead of include the men who should be the great governing forces. And they said, who shall have the voice in this great new republic, and you would have supposed that such men as fought the Revolutionary War would have been able to answer that every man who has fought, every one who has given up all he has and all he has been able to accumulate, shall be free, yet it never entered their minds. These excellent ancestors of yours had not been away from the Old World long enough to realize that a man is of more value than his purse, so they said every man who has an estate in the government shall have a voice. They [asked] what shall that estate be? And they answered that a man who had property valued at two hundred and fifty dollars will be able to cast a vote, and so they sang about "the land of the free and the home of the brave." And they wrote into their Constitution, "All males who pay taxes on $250 shall cast a vote," and they called themselves a republic, and we call ourselves a republic [too]...

We might call ourselves angels, but that wouldn't make us angels. You have got to be an angel before you are an angel, and you have got to be a republic before you are a republic.

Now what did we do? Before the word "male" in the local compacts they wrote the word "church member;" after that they rubbed out "church member" and they wrote in the word "tax-payer."

Then there arose a great Democrat, Thomas Jefferson, who looked down into the day when you and I are living and saw that the rapidly accumulated wealth in the hands of a few men would endanger the liberties of the people, and he knew what you and I know, that no power under heaven or among men is known in a republic by which men can defend their liberties except by the power of the ballot, and so the Democratic party took another step in the evolution of a republic out of a monarchy, and they rubbed out the word "tax-payer" and wrote in the word "white," and then the Democrats thought the millennium had come, and they sang "the land of the free and the home of the brave" as lustily as the Republicans had sung it before them, and they spoke of the divine right of motherhood with the same thrill in their voices and at the same time they were selling mother's babies by the pound on the auction block and forcing mothers apart from their babies.

Another arose who said a man is not a good citizen because he is white, he is a good citizen because he is a man, and the Republican party took out that progressive evolutionary eraser and rubbed out the word "white" from before the word "male" and could not think of another word to put in there—they were all in, black and white, rich and poor, wise and otherwise, drunk and sober; not a man left out to be put in, and so the Republicans could not write anything before the word "male," and they had to let that little word "male" stay alone by itself.

And God said in the beginning "It is not good for man to stand alone," Genesis 2:18. That is why we are here tonight, and that is all that women's suffrage means; just to repeat again and again that first declaration of the Divine, "It is not good for man to stand alone," and so the women of this state are asking that the word "male" shall be stricken out of the Constitution altogether, and that the Constitution stand as it ought to have stood in the beginning, and as it must before this state is any part of a republic.

Now what is a republic? Take your dictionary, encyclopedia, lexicon, or anything else you like, and look up the definition and you will find that a republic is a form of government in which the laws are enacted by representatives elected by the people. Now when did the people of New York ever elect their representatives? Never in the world. The men of New York have, and I grant you that men are people—admirable people, as far as they go—but they only go half-way. There is still another half of the people who have not elected representatives, and you never read a definition of a republic in which half of the people elect representatives to govern the whole of the people. That is an aristocracy and that is just what we are. We have been many kinds of aristocracies. We have been a hierarchy of church members, then an aristocracy of wealth, then an oligarchy of sex.

There are two old theories which are dying today. Dying hard, but dying. One of them is dying on the plains of Flanders and the Mountains of Galicia and Austria and that is the theory of the divine right of kings. The other is dying here in the states of New York and Massachusetts and New Jersey and Pennsylvania and that is the divine right of sex. Neither of them has a foundation in reason, or justice or common sense.

Whenever a republic prescribes the qualifications as apply equally to all the citizens of the republic, so that when the republic says in order to vote, a citizen must be twenty-one years of age, it applies to all alike, there is no discrimination against any race or sex. When the government says that a citizen must be a native-born citizen or a naturalized citizen, that applies to all; we are either born or naturalized, somehow or other we are here. Whenever the government says that a citizen, in order to vote, must be a resident of a community a certain length of time, and of the state a certain length of time, and of the nation a certain length of time, that applies to all equally. There is no discrimination.

But when the government says not only that you must be twenty-one years of age, a resident of the community and a native born or naturalized, those are qualifications, but when it says that an elector must be a male, that is not a qualification for citizenship; that is an insurmountable barrier between half of the people and the other half, and no government which erects an insurmountable barrier between one half of the citizens and their rights as citizens can call itself a republic!

Men know the inconsistencies themselves; they realize it in one way while they do not realize it in another, because you never heard a man make a political speech when he did not speak of this country as a whole as though the thing existed which does not exist and that is that the people were equally free, because you hear them declare over and over again on the Fourth of July, "under God, the people rule." They know it is not true but they say it with a great hurrah, and then they repeat over and over again that clause from the Declaration of Independence, "governments derive their just powers from the consent of the governed," and then they see how they can prevent half of us from giving our consent to anything, and then they give it to us on the Fourth of July in two languages, so if [it] is not true in one, it will be in the other, "*vox populi, vox Dei.*" "The voice of the people is the voice of God," and the orator forgets that in the people's voice there is a soprano as well as a bass. If the voice of the people is the voice of God, how are we ever going to know what God's voice is when we are content to listen to a bass solo? Now if it is true that the voice of the people is the voice of God, we will never know what the Deity's voice in government is until the bass and soprano are mingled together, the result of which will be the divine harmony!

Men are so sentimental. We used to believe that women were the sentimental sex, but they cannot hold a tallow candle compared with the arc light of the men. I think the average man recognizes that he has no more right to anything at the hands of the government than has every other man. He has no right at all to anything to which every other man has not an equal right with himself. He says why have I a right to certain things in the government; why have I a right to life and liberty; why have I a right to this or this? Does he say because I am a man? Not at all, because I am human, and being human, I have a right to everything which belongs to humanity, and every right which any other human being has, I have. And then he says of his neighbor and my neighbor, he also is human, therefore every right which belongs to me as a human being, belongs to him as a human being, and I have no right to anything under the government to which he is not equally entitled.

And then up comes a woman, and then they say, now she's a woman; she is not quite human, but she is my wife, or my sister, or my daughter, or an aunt, or my cousin. She is not quite human, she is only related to a human, and being related to a human, a human will take care of her. So we have had that care-taking human being to look after us, and they have not recognized that women too are equally human with men.

What are the arguments which our good "Anti-" friends give us? We know that lately they have stopped to argue and call suffragists all sorts of creatures. . . .[They say] suffragists are feminists, and when I ask what that is, no one is able to tell me...Then they cry that we are socialists, and anarchists. Just how a human can be both at the same time, I really do not know. If I know what socialism means it means absolute government, and anarchism means no government at all. So we are feminists, socialists, anarchists and Mormons or spinsters! Now that is about the list, I have not heard the last speech.

Now, as a matter of fact, as a unit we are nothing, as individuals we are like all other individuals. We have our theories, our beliefs, but as suffragists we have but one belief, but one principle, but one theory and that is the right of a human being to have a voice in the government under which he or she lives. On that we agree, if on nothing else. Whether we agree or not on religion or politics, we are not concerned.

A clergyman asked me the other day, "By the way, what church does your official board belong to?" I said, "I don t know."

He said, "Don't you know what religion your official board believes?" I said, "Really it never occurred to me, but I will hunt them up and see, they are not elected to my board because they believe in any particular church. We had no concern either as to what we believe as religionists or as to what we believe as women in regard to theories of government, except that one fundamental theory in the right of democracy. We do not believe in this fad or the other, but whenever any question is to be settled in any community, then the people of that community shall settle that question, the women-people equally with the men-people." That is all there is to it.

[When] it comes to arguing our case, [anti-suffragists] bring up all sorts of arguments, and the beauty of it is, they always answer all their own arguments!...

I was followed up last year by a young married woman from New Jersey. She left her husband and home for three months to tell the women that their place was at home, and that they could not leave home long enough to go to the ballot box, and she brought all her arguments out in pairs and backed them up by statistics.

She started by proving that it was no use to give the women the ballot because if they did have it they would not use it, and she had statistics to prove it. If we would not use it, then I really cannot see the harm of giving it to us, we would not hurt anybody with it and what an easy way for you men to get rid of us. No more suffrage meetings, never any nagging you again, no one could blame you for anything that went wrong with the town; if it did not run right, all you would have to say is, you have the power, why don't you go ahead and clean up.

Then the young lady, unfortunately for her first argument, proved, by statistics, of which she had many, the awful results which happened where women did have the ballot[—]how deeply women get interested in politics, because women are hysterical, and we cannot think of anything else, we just forget our families, cease to care for our children, cease to love our husbands, and just go to the polls and vote and keep on voting for ten hours a day, 365 days in the year, and never let up! If we ever get to the polls once, you will never get us home. So that the women will not vote at all, *and* they will not do anything but vote Now these are two very strong anti-suffrage arguments, and they can prove them, by figures.

Then they will tell you that if women are permitted to vote, it will be a great expense and no use because wives will vote just as their husbands do; even if we have no husbands, that would not affect the result because we would vote just as our husbands would vote if we had one. How I wish the anti-suffragists could make the men believe that; if they could make men believe that the women would vote just as they wanted them to, do you think we would ever have to make another speech or hold another meeting? We would have to vote whether we wanted to or not.

And then the very one who will tell you that women will vote just as their husbands do will tell you in five minutes that they will not vote as their husbands will, and then warn you of the discord in the homes, and the divorce. Why, they have discovered that in Colorado, there are more divorces now than there were before women began to vote, but they have forgotten to tell you that there are four times as many people in Colorado today as there were when women began to vote, and that may have some effect.

Then they will tell you all the trouble that happens in the home. A gentleman told me that in California—and when he was talking I had a wonderful thing pass through my mind, because he said he and his wife had lived together for twenty years and never had a difference in opinion in the whole twenty years, and he was afraid if women began to vote that his wife would vote differently from him and then that beautiful harmony which they had had for twenty years would be broken, and all the time he was talking I could not help wondering which was the idiot—because I knew that no intelligent human beings could live together for twenty years and not have differences of opinion. All the time he was talking, I looked at that splendid type of manhood and thought, how would a man feel being tagged up by a little woman for twenty years saying, "me too, me too." I would not want to live in a house with a human being for twenty hours who agreed with everything I said. The stagnation of a frog pond would be hilarious compared to that. What a reflection is that on men. Great big overgrown babies! Cannot be disputed without having a row! In fact my theory of the whole matter is exactly opposite, because instead of believing that men and women will quarrel, I think just the opposite thing will happen. I think just about six weeks before election, a sort of honeymoon will start and it will continue until they will think they are again hanging over the gate, all in order to get each other's votes. When men want each other's votes they do not go up and knock them down; they are very solicitous of each other, [especially] if they are thirsty or need a smoke!

The husband and wife who are quarreling after the vote are quarreling now. I remember hearing Rev. Dr. Abbott speak before the anti-suffrage meeting in Brooklyn, and he stated that if women were permitted to vote we could not have so much time for charity and philanthropy, and I would like to say: "Thank God, there will not be so much need of charity and philanthropy!" The end and aim of the suffrage movement is not to furnish an opportunity for excellent old ladies to be charitable. There are two words that we ought to be able to get along without, and they are "charity" and "philanthropy." They are not needed in a republic. If we put in the word "opportunity" instead, that is what republics stand for. Our doctrine is not to extend the length of our bread lines or the size of our soup kitchens; what we need is the opportunity for people to buy their own bread and eat their own soup!

We will either vote as our husbands vote, or we will not vote as our husbands vote. We either have time to vote, or we don't have time to vote. We will either not vote at all, or we will vote all the time. It reminds me of the story of the old Irish woman who had twin boys, and they were so much alike that the neighbors could not tell them apart, and the mother always seemed to be able to tell them apart, so one of the neighbors said, "Now Mrs. Mahoney, you have two of the finest twin boys I ever saw in all my life, but how do you know them apart." "Oh," she says, "That's easy enough, anyone could tell them apart. When I want to know which is which I just put my finger in Patsey's mouth, and, if he bites, it is Mikey!"

Now what does it matter whether the women will vote as their husbands do or will not vote; whether they have time or have not, or [even] whether they will vote for prohibition or not? What has that to do with the fundamental question of democracy, no one has yet discovered. But they cannot argue on that; they cannot argue on the fundamental basis of our existence so that they have to get off on all these side tracks to get anything approaching an argument.

And so our good friends go on with one thing after another, and they say if women should vote they will have to sit on the jury, and they ask whether we will like to see a woman sitting on a jury. I have seen some juries that ought to be sat on, and I have seen some women that would be glad to sit on anything! When a woman stands up all day behind a counter, or when she stands all day doing a-washing, she is glad enough to sit; and when she stands for seventy-five cents, she would like to sit for two dollars a day. But don't you think we need some women on juries in this country? You read your paper, and you read that one day last week, or the week before, or the week before a little girl went out to school and never came back; another little girl was sent on an errand and never came back; another little girl was left in charge of a little sister, and her mother went out to work, and when she returned the little girl was not there, and you read it over and over again, and the horror of it strikes you. You read that in these United States, five thousand young girls go out and never come back, don't you think that the men and women, the vampires of our country who fatten and grow rich on the ignorance and innocence of children, would rather face Satan himself than a jury of mothers?

When I was speaking in North Dakota from an automobile in front of a great crowd, a man who had been sitting in front of a store whittling a stick called out: "If women get the vote, will they go over to Germany and fight the Germans?" I said, "Why no. Why should we women fight men? But if Germany should send an army of women over here, then we would show you what we would do. We would go down and meet them and say, "Come on, let's go up to the opera house and talk this matter over!" It might grow wearisome, but it would not be death.

Would it not be better if the heads of the governments in Europe had talked things over? What might have happened to the world if a dozen men had gotten together in Europe and settled the awful controversy which is today decimating the nations of Europe?

When I turned away from that place up in North Dakota, that man in the crowd called out again, just as we were leaving and said, "Well, what does a woman know about war anyway?"

I had read my paper that morning, and I knew what the awful headline was. I saw a gentleman standing in the crowd with a paper in his pocket, and I said, will that gentleman hold the paper up, and he held it up, and the headline read, "250,000 Men Killed Since the War Began."

I said you ask me what a woman knows about war?

No woman can read that line and comprehend the awful horror; no woman knows the significance of 250,000 dead men, but you tell me that one man lay dead, and I might be able to tell you something of its awful meaning to one woman. I would know that years before, a woman whose heart beat in unison with her love and her desire for motherhood walked day by day with her face to an open grave, with courage, which no man has ever surpassed, and if she did not fill that grave, if she lived, and if there was laid in her arms a tiny little bit of helpless humanity, I would know that there went out from her soul such a cry of thankfulness as none save a mother could know. And then I would know, what men have not yet learned, that women are human; that they have human hopes and human passions, aspirations and desires as men have, and I would know that that mother who had laid aside all those hopes and aspirations of herself, but never for one moment did she lay them aside for her boy, and if, after years had passed by, she forgot her nights of sleeplessness and her days of fatiguing toil in her care of her growing boy, and when, at last, he became a man, and she stood looking up into his eyes and beheld him, bone of her bone and flesh of her flesh, for out of her woman's life she had carved twenty beautiful years that went into the making of a man, and there he stands, the most wonderful thing in all the world, for in all the universe of God, there is nothing more sublimely wonderful than a strong limbed, clean hearted, keen brained, aggressive young man, standing as he does on the border line of life, ready to reach out and grapple with its problems. Oh, how wonderful he is, and he is hers. She gave her life for him, and, in an hour, this country calls him out, and, in an hour, he lies dead; that wonderful, wonderful thing lies dead, and sitting by his side, that mother looking into the dark years to come knows that when her son died her life's hope died with him, and in the face of that wretched motherhood, what man dare ask what a woman knows of war? And that is not all. Read your papers, you cannot read it because it is not printable; you cannot tell it because it is not speakable, you cannot even think it because it is not thinkable, the horrible crimes perpetrated against women by the blood-drunken men of the war.

You read your paper again and the second headline reads, "It Costs Twenty Millions of Dollars a Day." For what? To buy the material to slaughter the splendid results of civilization of the centuries. Men whom it has taken centuries to build up and make into great scientific forces of brain, the flower of the manhood of the great nations of Europe, and we spend twenty millions of dollars a day to blot out all the results of civilization of hundreds and hundreds of years. And what do we do? We lay a mortgage on every unborn child for a hundred and more years to come. Mortgage his brain, his brawn, every pulse of his heart in order to pay the debt, to buy the material to slaughter the men of our country.

Read what they are doing. They are calling out every man, every young man, every virile man from seventeen to forty-five or fifty years-old to be food for the cannon. The crime of crimes of the war is the crime against the unborn children that we take from them what every child has a right to, that is a virile father, and we rob women of fit mates to become the fathers of their children. In the face of these crimes against women and against children, and in the face of the fact that women are driven out of the home, shall men ask if women shall fight, if they are permitted to vote?

No, we women do not want the ballot in order that we may fight, but we do want the ballot in order that we may help men to keep from fighting, whether it is in war or in peace; whether it is in the home or in the state, just as the home is not without the man, so the state is not without the woman, and you can no more build up homes without men than you can build up the state without women. We are needed everywhere where human life is. We are needed everywhere where human problems are [needed] to be solved. Men and women must go through this world together from the cradle to the grave; it is God's way, and it is the fundamental principle of a republican form of government.

WOODROW WILSON **66**

War Address, 1917

Since 1914, Europe had been embroiled in the most horrific war yet fought, World War I. The war would eventually cost some 15 million people their lives. The United States managed to stay neutral in the early years of the war, but German submarine attacks on civilian merchant ships and American merchant ships sailing into the war zone had become too much for President Wilson and the United States. On April 2, 1917, he appeared before Congress to ask for a declaration of war. Wilson avowed that the war would be fought for the freedom of all nations to live without fear of attack, that democracy and self-determination should rule the world rather than dictators and the force of arms. Congress would pass the war declaration. By the time the fighting ended on November 11, 1918, approximately 112,000 American soldiers would be dead.

Gentlemen of the Congress:

I have called the Congress into extraordinary session because there are serious, very serious choices of policy to be made, and made immediately, which it was neither right nor constitutionally permissible that I should assume the responsibility of making.

On the third of February last I officially laid before you the extraordinary announcement of the Imperial German Government that on and after the first day of February it was its purpose to put aside all restraints of law or of humanity and use its submarines to sink every vessel that sought to approach either the ports of Great Britain and Ireland or the western coasts of Europe or any of the ports controlled by the enemies of Germany within the Mediterranean. That had seemed to be the object of the German submarine warfare earlier in the war, but since April of last year the Imperial Government had somewhat restrained the commanders of its undersea craft in conformity with its promise then given to us that passenger boats should not be sunk and that due warning would be given to all other vessels which its submarines might seek to destroy, when no resistance was offered or escape attempted, and care taken that their crews were given at least a fair chance to save their lives in their open boats. The precautions taken were meager and haphazard enough, as was proved in distressing instance after instance in the progress of the cruel and unmanly business, but a certain degree of restraint was observed. The new policy has swept every restriction aside. Vessels of every kind, whatever their flag, their character, their cargo, their destination, their errand, have been ruthlessly sent to the bottom without warning and without thought of help or mercy for those on board, the vessels of friendly neutrals along with those of belligerents. Even hospital ships and ships carrying relief to the sorely bereaved and stricken people of Belgium, though the latter were provided with safe conduct through the proscribed areas by the German

Government itself and were distinguished by unmistakable marks of identity, have been sunk with the same reckless lack of compassion or of principle...

I was for a little while unable to believe that such things would in fact be done by any government that had hitherto subscribed to humane practices of civilized nations. International law had its origin in the attempt to set up some law which would be respected and observed upon the seas, where no nation had right of dominion and where lay the free highways of the world. By painful stage after stage has that law been built up, with meager enough results, indeed, after all was accomplished that could be accomplished, but always with a clear view, at least, of what the heart and conscience of mankind demanded. This minimum of right the German Government has swept aside, under the plea of retaliation and necessity and because it had no weapons which it could use at sea except these which it is impossible to employ as it is employing them without throwing to the wind all scruples of humanity or of respect for the understandings that were supposed to underlie the intercourse of the world. I am not now thinking of the loss of property involved, immense and serious as that is, but only of the wanton and wholesale destruction of the lives of non-combatants, men, women, and children, engaged in pursuits which have always, even in the darkest periods of modern history, been deemed innocent and legitimate. Property can be paid for; the lives of peaceful and innocent people cannot be. The present German submarine warfare against commerce is a warfare against mankind.

It is a war against all nations. American ships have been sunk, American lives taken, in ways which it has stirred us very deeply to learn of, but the ships and people of other neutral and friendly nations have been sunk and overwhelmed in the waters in the same way. There has been no discrimination. The challenge is to all mankind. Each nation must decide for itself how it will meet it. The choice we make for ourselves must be made with a moderation of counsel and a temperateness of judgment befitting our character and our motives as a nation. We must put excited feeling away. Our motive will not be revenge or the victorious assertion of the physical might of the nation, but only the vindication of right, of human right, of which we are only a single champion.

When I addressed the Congress on the twenty-sixth of February last I thought that it would suffice to assert our neutral rights with arms, our right to use the seas against unlawful interference, our right to keep our people safe against unlawful violence. But armed neutrality, it now appears, is impracticable. Because submarines are in effect outlaws when used as the German submarines have been used against merchant shipping, it is impossible to defend ships against their attacks as the law of nations has assumed that merchantmen would defend themselves against privateers or cruisers, visible craft giving chase upon the open sea. It is common prudence in such circumstances, grim necessity indeed, to endeavor to destroy them before they have shown their own intention. They must be dealt with upon sight, if dealt with at all. The German Government denies the right of neutrals to use arms at all within the areas of the sea which it has proscribed, even in the defense of rights which no modern publicist has ever before questioned their right to defend. The intimation is conveyed that the armed guards which we have placed on our merchant ships will be treated as beyond the pale of law and subject to be dealt with as pirates would be. Armed neutrality is ineffectual enough at best; in such circumstances and in the face of such pretensions it is worse than ineffectual; it is likely only to produce what it was meant to prevent; it is practically certain to draw us into the war without either the rights or the effectiveness of belligerents. There is one choice we cannot make, we are incapable of making; we will not choose the path of submission and suffer the most sacred rights of our nation and our people to be ignored or violated. The wrongs against which we now array ourselves are no common wrongs; they cut to the very roots of human life.

With a profound sense of the solemn and even tragical character of the step I am taking and of the grave responsibilities which it involves, but in unhesitating obedi- ence to what I deem my constitutional duty, I advise that the Congress declare the recent course of the Imperial German Government to be in fact nothing less than war against the Government and people of the United States; that it formally accept the status of belligerent which has thus been thrust upon it; and that it take immediate steps not only to put the country in a more thorough state of defense, but also to exert all its power and employ all its resources to bring the Government of the German Empire to terms and end the war.

What this will involve is clear. It will involve the utmost practicable cooperation in counsel and action with the governments now at war with Germany, and, as inci- dent to that, the extension to those governments of the most liberal financial credits, in order that our resources may so far as possible be added to theirs. It will involve the organization and mobilization of all the material resources of the country to supply the materials of war and serve the incidental needs of the nation in the most abundant and yet the most economical and efficient way possible. It will involve the immediate full equipment of the navy in all respects but particularly in supplying it with the best means of dealing with the enemy's submarines. It will involve the immediate addition to the armed forces of the United States already provided for by law in case of war of at least five hundred thousand men, who should, in my opinion, be chosen upon the principle of universal liability to service, and also the authorization of subsequent additional increments of equal force so soon as they may be needed and can be han- dled in training. It will involve also, of course, the granting of adequate credits to the Government, sustained, I hope, so far as they can equitably be sustained by the pres- ent generation, by well-conceived taxation.

I say sustained so far as may be equitable by taxation because it seems to me that it would be most unwise to base the credits which will now be necessary entirely on money borrowed. It is our duty, I most respectfully urge, to protect our people so far as we may against the very serious hardships and evils which would be likely to arise out of the inflation which would be produced by vast loans....

While we do these things, these deeply momentous things, let us be very clear, and make very clear to all the world, what our motives and our objects are. My own thought has not been driven from its habitual and normal course by the unhappy events of the last two months, and I do not believe that the thought of the nation has been altered or clouded by them. I have exactly the same things in mind now that I had in mind when I addressed the Senate on the twenty-second of January last; the same that I had in mind when I addressed the Congress on the third of February and on the twenty-sixth of February. Our object now, as then, is to vindicate the principles of peace and justice in the life of the world as against selfish and autocratic power, and to set up among the really free and self-governed peoples of the world such a concert of purpose and of action as will henceforth ensure the observance of those principles.

Neutrality is no longer feasible or desirable where the peace of the world is involved and the freedom of its peoples, and the menace to that peace and freedom lies in the existence of autocratic governments, backed by organized force which is controlled wholly by their will, not by the will of their people. We have seen the last of neutrality in such circumstances. We are at the beginning of an age in which it will be insisted that the same standards of conduct and of responsibility for wrong done shall be observed among nations and their governments that are observed among the individual citizens of civilized states.

We have no quarrel with the German people. We have no feeling towards them but one of sympathy and friendship. It was not upon their impulse that their government acted in entering this war. It was not with their previous knowledge or approval. It was a war determined upon as wars used to be determined upon in the old, unhappy days when peoples were nowhere consulted by their rulers and wars were provoked and waged in the interest of dynasties or of little groups of ambitious men who were accustomed to use their fellow-men as pawns and tools.

Self-governed nations do not fill their neighbor states with spies or set the course of intrigue to bring about some critical posture of affairs which will give them an opportunity to strike and make conquest. Such designs can be successfully worked out only under cover and where no one has the right to ask questions. Cunningly contrived plans of deception or aggression, carried, it may be, from generation to generation, can be worked out and kept from the light only within the privacy of courts or behind the carefully guarded confidences of a narrow and privileged class. They are happily impossible where public opinion commands and insists upon full information concerning all the nation's affairs.

A steadfast concern for peace can never be maintained except by a partnership of democratic nations. No autocratic government could be trusted to keep faith within it or observe its covenants. It must be a league of honor, a partnership of opinion. Intrigue would eat its vitals away; the plottings of inner circles who could plan what they would and render account to no one would be a corruption seated at its very heart. Only free peoples can hold their purpose and their honor steady to a common end and prefer the interests of mankind to any narrow interest of their own.

Does not every American feel that assurance has been added to our hope for the future peace of the world by the wonderful and heartening things that have been happening within the last few weeks in Russia? Russia was known by those who knew her best to have been always in fact democratic at heart in all the vital habits of her thought, in all the intimate relationships of her people that spoke their natural instinct, their habitual attitude towards life. The autocracy that crowned the summit of her political structure, long as it had stood and terrible as was the reality of its power, was not in fact Russian in origin, character, or purpose; and now it has been shaken off and the great, generous Russian people have been added, in all their naive majesty and might, to the forces that are fighting for freedom in the world, for justice, and for peace. Here is a fit partner for a league of honor.

One of the things that has served to convince us that the Prussian autocracy was not and could never be our friend is that from the very outset of the present war it has filled our unsuspecting communities, and even our offices of government, with spies and set criminal intrigues everywhere afoot against our national unity of counsel, our peace within and without, our industries and our commerce. Indeed, it is now evident that its spies were here even before the war began; and it is unhappily not a matter of conjecture but a fact proved in our courts of justice that the intrigues which have more than once come perilously near to disturbing the peace and dislocating the industries of the country have been carried on at the instigation, with the support, and even under the personal direction of official agents of the Imperial Government accredited to the Government of the United States.

Even in checking these things and trying to extirpate them we have sought to put the most generous interpretation possible upon them.... But they have played their part in serving to convince us at last that government entertains no real friendship for us, and means to act against our peace and security at its convenience. That it means to stir up enemies against us at our very doors the intercepted note to the German Minister at Mexico City is eloquent evidence....

We are now about to accept the gauge of battle with this natural foe to liberty and shall, if necessary, spend the whole force of the nation to check and nullify its pretensions and its power. We are glad, now that we see the facts with no veil of false pretense about them, to fight thus for the ultimate peace of the world and for the liberation of its peoples, the German peoples included; for the rights of nations, great and small, and the privilege of men everywhere to choose their way of life and of obedience. The world must be made safe for democracy. Its peace must be planted upon the tested foundations of political liberty. We have no selfish ends to serve. We desire no conquest, no dominion. We seek no indemnities for ourselves, no material compensation for the sacrifices we shall freely make. We are but one of the champions of the rights of mankind. We shall be satisfied when those rights have been made as secure as the faith and the freedom of nations can make them.

Just because we fight without rancor and without selfish object, seeking nothing for ourselves but what we shall wish to share with all free peoples, we shall, I feel confident, conduct our operations as belligerents without passion and ourselves observe with proud punctilio the principles of right and of fair play we profess to be fighting for.

I have said nothing of the government allied with the Imperial Government of Germany because they have not made war upon us or challenged us to defend our right and our honor. The Austria-Hungarian Government has actually engaged in warfare against citizens of the United States on the seas, and I take the liberty, for the present at least, of postponing a discussion of our relations with the authorities at Vienna. We enter this war only where we are clearly forced into it because there are no other means of defending our rights.

We are, let me say again, the sincere friends of the German people, and shall desire nothing so much as the early reestablishment of intimate relations of mutual advantage between us.

We shall, happily, still have an opportunity to prove that friendship in our daily attitude and actions toward the millions of men and women of German birth and native sympathy who live among us and share our life, and we shall be proud to prove it towards all who are in fact loyal to their neighbors and to the Government in the hour of test. They are, most of them, as true and loyal Americans as if they had never known any other fealty or allegiance. They will be prompt to stand with us in rebuking and restraining the few who may be of a different mind and purpose. If there should be disloyalty, it will be dealt with a firm hand of stern repression; but, if it lifts its head at all, it will lift it only here and there and without countenance except from a lawless and malignant few.

It is a distressing and oppressive duty, Gentlemen of the Congress, which I have performed in thus addressing you. There are, it may be, many months of fiery trial and sacrifice ahead of us. It is a fearful thing to lead this great peaceful people into war, into the most terrible and disastrous of all wars, civilization itself seeming to be in the balance. But the right is more precious than peace, and we shall fight for the things which we have always carried nearest our hearts—for democracy, for the right of those who submit to authority to have a voice in their own governments, for the rights and liberties of small nations, for a universal dominion of right by such a concert of free peoples as shall bring peace and safety to all nations and make the world itself at last free.

To such a task we can dedicate our lives and our fortunes, everything that we are and everything that we have, with the pride of those who know that the day has come when America is privileged to spend her blood and her might for the principles that gave her birth and happiness and the peace which she has treasured.

God helping her, she can do no other.

ROBERT LAFOLLETTE **67**

Freedom of Speech in Wartime, 1917

During World War I, fears of sabotage and spying created an atmosphere of near-paranoia for some Americans. Anything less than total, enthusiastic support for the war effort was considered unacceptable and possibly treasonous. In response to these fears, Congress passed the Espionage Act and Sedition Act in 1917 and 1918 which essentially outlawed any criticism of the war. In response to these acts, the arrests of dozens of people under these acts, and a number of other incidents that had erupted across the country, Sen. Robert LaFollette of Wisconsin took to the floor of the U.S. Senate on October 6, 1917, to defend the freedom of speech in wartime. He stated that what was at stake with the freedom of speech was nothing less than the right of the people to control their government, that without free speech there could be no democracy.

Mr. President:

I rise to a question of personal privilege. I have no intention of taking the time of the Senate with a review of the events which led to our entrance into the war except in so far as they bear upon the question of personal privilege to which I am addressing myself. Six Members of the Senate and fifty Members of the House voted against the declaration of war. Immediately there was let lose upon those Senators and Representatives a flood of invective and abuse from newspapers and individuals who had been clamoring for war, unequaled, I believe in the history of civilized society.

Prior to the declaration of war every man who had ventured to oppose our entrance into it had been condemned as a coward or worse, and even the President had by no means been immune from these attacks.

Since the declaration of war the triumphant war press has pursued those Senators and Representatives who voted against war with malicious falsehood and recklessly libelous attacks, going to the extreme limit of charging them with treason against their country.

This campaign of libel and character assassination directed against the Members of Congress who opposed our entrance into the war has been continued down to the present hour, and I have upon my desk newspaper clippings, some of them libels upon me alone, some directed as well against other Senators who voted in opposition to the declaration of war. One of these newspaper reports most widely circulated represents a Federal judge in the state of Texas as saying, in a charge to a grand jury—I read the article as it appeared in the newspaper and the headline with which it is introduced:

DISTRICT JUDGE WOULD LIKE TO TAKE SHOT AT TRAITORS IN CONGRESS
(A.P.) HOUSTON, TEXAS, OCT. 1, Judge Waller T. Burns, of the United States district court, in charging a Federal grand jury at the beginning of the October term today, after calling by name Senators Stone of Missouri, Hardwick of Georgia, Vardaman of Mississippi, Gronna of North Dakota, Gore of Oklahoma, and LaFollette of Wisconsin, said: "If I had a wish, I would wish that you men had jurisdiction to return bills of indictment against these men. They ought to be tried promptly and fairly, and I believe this court could administer the law fairly; but I have a conviction, as strong as life, that this country should stand them up against an adobe wall tomorrow and give them what they deserve. If any man deserves death, it is a traitor. I wish that I could pay for the ammunition. I would like to attend the execution, and if I were in the firing squad I would not want to be the marksman who had the blank shell." ...

If this newspaper clipping were a single or exceptional instance of lawless defamation, I should not trouble the Senate with a reference to it. But, Mr. President, it is not.

In this mass of newspaper clippings which I have here upon my desk, and which I shall not trouble the Senate to read unless it is desired. I find other Senators, as well as myself, accused of the highest crimes of which any man can be guilty—t reason and disloyalty—and, sir, accused not only with no evidence to support the accusation, but without the suggestion that such evidence anywhere exists. It is not claimed that Senators who opposed the declaration of war have since that time acted with any concerted purpose either regarding war measures or any others. They have voted according to their individual opinions, have often been opposed to each other on bills which have come before the Senate since the declaration of war, and, according to my recollection, have never all voted together since that time upon any single proposition upon which the Senate has been divided.

I am aware, Mr. President, that in pursuance of this campaign of vilification and attempted intimidation, requests from various individuals and certain organizations have been submitted to the Senate for my expulsion from this body, and that such requests have been referred to and considered by one of the committees of the Senate.

If I alone had been made the victim of these attacks, I should not take one moment of the Senate's time for their consideration, and I believe that other Senators who have been unjustly and unfairly assailed, as I have been, hold the same attitude upon this that I do. Neither the clamor of the mob nor the voice of power will ever turn me by the breadth of a hair from the course I mark out for myself, guided by such knowledge as I can obtain and controlled and directed by a solemn conviction of right and duty.

But, sir, it is not alone Members of Congress that the war party in this country has sought to intimidate. The mandate seems to have gone forth to the sovereign people of this country that they must be silent while those things are being done by their Government which most vitally concern their well-being, their happiness, and their lives. Today and for weeks past honest and law-abiding citizens of this country are being terrorized and outraged in their rights by those sworn to uphold the laws and protect the rights of the people. I have in my possession numerous affidavits establishing the fact that people are being unlawfully arrested, thrown into jail, held incommunicado for days, only to be eventually discharged without ever having been taken into court, because they have committed no crime. Private residences are being invaded, loyal citizens of undoubted integrity and probity arrested, cross-examined, and the most sacred constitutional rights guaranteed to every American citizen are being violated.

It appears to be the purpose of those conducting this campaign to throw the country into a state of terror, to coerce public opinion, to stifle criticism, and suppress discussion of the great issues involved in this war.

I think all men recognize that in time of war the citizen must surrender some rights for the common good which he is entitled to enjoy in time of peace. But sir, the right to control their own Government according to constitutional forms is not one of the rights that the citizens of this country are called upon to surrender in time of war.

Rather in time of war the citizen must be more alert to the preservation of his right to control his Government. He must be most watchful of the encroachment of the military upon the civil power. He must beware of those precedents in support of arbitrary action by administration officials which, excused on the plea of necessity in war time, become the fixed rule when the necessity has passed and normal conditions have been restored.

More than all, the citizen and his representative in Congress in time of war must maintain his right of free speech. More than in times of peace it is necessary that the channels for free public discussion of governmental policies shall be open and unclogged. I believe, Mr. President, that I am now touching upon the most important question in this country today—and that is the right of the citizens of this country and their representatives in Congress to discuss in an orderly way frankly and publicly and without fear, from the platform and through the press, every important phase of this war; its causes, and manner in which it should be conducted, and the terms upon which peace should be made. The belief which is becoming widespread in this land that this most fundamental right is being denied to the citizens of this country is a fact, the tremendous significance of which those in authority have not yet begun to appreciate. I am contending, Mr. President, for the great fundamental right of the sovereign people of this country to make their voice heard and have that voice heeded upon the great questions arising out of this war, including not only how the war shall be prosecuted but the conditions upon which it may be terminated with a due regard for the rights and the honor of this Nation and the interests of humanity.

I am contending for this right because the exercise of it is necessary to the welfare, to the existence, of this Government, to the successful conduct of this war, and to a peace which shall be enduring for the best interest of this country.

Suppose success attends the attempt to stifle all discussion of the issues of this war, all discussions of the terms upon which it should be concluded, all discussion of the objects and purposes to be accomplished by it, and concede the demand of the war-mad press and war extremists that they monopolize the right of public utterance upon these questions unchallenged, what think you would be the consequences to this country not only during the war but after the war?

It is no answer to say that when the war is over the citizen may once more resume his rights and feel some security in his liberty and his person. As I have already tried to point out, now is precisely the time when the country needs the counsel of all its citizens. In time of war even more than in time of peace, whether citizens happen to agree with the ruling administration or not, these precious fundamental personal rights—free speech, free press, and right of assemblage so explicitly and emphatically guaranteed by the Constitution should be maintained inviolable. There is no rebellion in the land, no martial law, no courts are closed, no legal processes suspended, and there is no threat even of invasion.

But more than this, if every preparation for war can be made the excuse for destroying free speech and a free press and the right of the people to assemble together for peaceful discussion, then we may well despair of ever again finding ourselves for a long period in a state of peace. The destruction of rights now occurring will be pointed to then as precedents for a still further invasion of the rights of the citizen.

Mr. President, our Government, above all others, is founded on the right of the people freely to discuss all matters pertaining to their Government, in war not less than in peace. It is true, sir, that Members of the House of Representatives are elected for two years, the President for four years, and the Members of the Senate for six years, and during their temporary official terms these officers constitute what is called the Government. But back of them always is the controlling sovereign power of the people, and when the people can make their will known, the faithful officer will obey that will. Though the right of the people to express their will by ballot is suspended during the term of office of the elected official, nevertheless the duty of the official to obey the popular will continue throughout his entire term of office. How can that popular will express itself between elections except by meetings, by speeches, by publications, by petitions, and by addresses to the representatives of the people? Any man who seeks to set a limit upon those rights, whether in war or peace, aims a blow at the most vital part of our Government. And then as the time for election approaches and the official is called to account for his stewardship—not a day, not a week, not a month, before the election, but a year or more before it, if the people choose—they must have the right to the freest possible discussion of every question upon which their representative has acted, of the merits of every measure he has supported or opposed, of every vote he has cast and every speech that he has made. And before this great fundamental right every other must, if necessary, give way, for in no other manner can representative government be preserved.

WILLIAM TYLER PAGE **68**

The American's Creed, 1917

William Tyler Page, the clerk for the U. S. House of Representatives wrote this short piece in 1917 as part of a nationwide contest to find the best statement that reflected the political faith of the nation. To Page, it was simply loving freedom and defending it when threatened. The House of Representatives adopted this creed on April 3, 1918, as a rallying point for a nation at war.

I believe in the United States of America as a government of the people, by the people, for the people; whose just powers are derived from the consent of the governed, a democracy in a republic, a sovereign Nation of many sovereign States; a perfect union, one and inseparable; established upon those principles of freedom, equality, justice, and humanity for which American patriots sacrificed their lives and fortunes.

I therefore believe it is my duty to my country to love it, to support its Constitution, to obey its laws to respect its flag, and to defend it against all enemies.

WOODROW WILSON **69**

Fourteen Points, 1918

On January 8, 1918, while World War I consumed Europe and millions of lives, President Woodrow Wilson proposed a dramatic new direction for the nations of the world. In this speech, Wilson outlines the Fourteen Points, a guide for building a lasting peace in a new, democratic world. Wilson fervently believed that the world should take the tragedy of the Great War and use it to start a new covenant among all of the nations where each country lived in peace and equality, not under domination or the threat of war. For Wilson, the principles of liberty and democracy that had made the United States a free nation could life the world to a new age of freedom, peace, and understanding. But a world embittered by years of war and loss remained skeptical of his proposals.

It will be our wish and purpose that the processes of peace, when they are begun, shall be absolutely open and that they shall involve and permit henceforth no secret understandings of any kind. The day of conquest and aggrandizement is gone by; so is also the day of secret covenants entered into in the interest of particular governments and likely at some unlooked-for moment to upset the peace of the world. It is this happy fact, now clear to the view of every public man whose thoughts do not still linger in an age that is dead and gone, which makes it possible for every nation whose purposes are consistent with justice and the peace of the world to avow now or at any other time the objects it has in view.

We entered this war because violations of right had occurred which touched us to the quick and made the life of our own people impossible unless they were corrected and the world secured once for all against their recurrence. What we demand in this war, therefore, is nothing peculiar to ourselves. It is that the world be made fit and safe to live in; and particularly that it be made safe for every peace-loving nation which, like our own, wishes to live its own life, determine its own institutions, be assured of justice and fair dealing by the other peoples of the world as against force and selfish aggression. All the peoples of the world are in effect partners in this interest, and for our own part we see very clearly that unless justice be done to others it will not be done to us. The programme of the world's peace, therefore, is our programme; and that programme, the only possible programme, as we see it, is this:

I Open covenants of peace, openly arrived at, after which there shall be no private international understandings of any kind but diplomacy shall proceed always frankly and in the public view.

II Absolute freedom of navigation upon the seas, outside territorial waters, alike in peace and in war, except as the seas may be closed in whole or in part by international action for the enforcement of international covenants.

III The removal, so far as possible, of all economic barriers and the establishment of an equality of trade conditions among all the nations consenting to the peace and associating themselves for its maintenance.

IV Adequate guarantees given and taken that national armaments will be reduced to the lowest point consistent with domestic safety.

V A free, open-minded, and absolutely impartial adjustment of all colonial claims, based upon a strict observance of the principle that in determining all such questions of sovereignty the interests of the populations concerned must have equal weight with the equitable claims of the government whose title is to be determined.

VI The evacuation of all Russian territory and such a settlement of all questions affecting Russia as will secure the best and freest cooperation of the other nations of the world in obtaining for her an unhampered and unembarrassed opportunity for the independent determination of her own political development and national policy and assure her of a sincere welcome into the society of free nations under institutions of her own choosing; and, more than a welcome, assistance also of every kind that she may need and may herself desire. The treatment accorded Russia by her sister nations in the months to come will be the acid test of their good will, of their comprehension of her needs as distinguished from their own interests, and of their intelligent and unselfish sympathy.

VII Belgium, the whole world will agree, must be evacuated and restored, without any attempt to limit the sovereignty which she enjoys in common with all other free nations. No other single act will serve as this will serve to restore confidence among the nations in the laws which they have themselves set and determined for the government of their relations with one another. Without this healing act the whole structure and validity of international law is forever impaired.

VIII All French territory should be freed and the invaded portions restored, and the wrong done to France by Prussia in 1871 in the matter of Alsace-Lorraine, which has unsettled the peace of the world for nearly fifty years, should be righted, in order that peace may once more be made secure in the interest of all.

IX A readjustment of the frontiers of Italy should be effected along clearly recognizable lines of nationality.

X The peoples of Austria-Hungary, whose place among the nations we wish to see safeguarded and assured, should be accorded the freest opportunity of autonomous development.

XI Rumania, Serbia, and Montenegro should be evacuated; occupied territories restored; Serbia accorded free and secure access to the sea; and the relations of the several Balkan states to one another determined by friendly counsel along historically established lines of allegiance and nationality; and international guarantees of the political and economic independence and territorial integrity of the several Balkan states should be entered into.

XII The Turkish portions of the present Ottoman Empire should be assured a secure sovereignty, but the other nationalities which are now under Turkish rule should be assured an undoubted security of life and an absolutely unmolested opportunity of autonomous development, and the Dardanelles should be permanently opened as a free passage to the ships and commerce of all nations under international guarantees.

XIII An independent Polish state should be erected which should include the territories inhabited by indisputably Polish populations, which should be assured a free and secure access to the sea, and whose political and economic independence and territorial integrity should be guaranteed by international covenant.

XIV A general association of nations must be formed under specific covenants for the purpose of affording mutual guarantees of political independence and territorial integrity to great and small states alike.

In regard to these essential rectifications of wrong and assertions of right we feel ourselves to be intimate partners of all the governments and peoples associated together against the Imperialists. We cannot be separated in interest or divided in purpose. We stand together until the end.

For such arrangements and covenants we are willing to fight and to continue to fight until they are achieved; but only because we wish the right to prevail and desire a just and stable peace such as can be secured only by removing the chief provocations to war, which this programme does not remove. We have no jealousy of German greatness, and there is nothing in this programme that impairs it. We grudge her no achievement or distinction of learning or of pacific enterprise such as have made her record very bright and very enviable. We do not wish to injure her or to block in any way her legitimate influence or power. We do not wish to fight her either with arms or with hostile arrangements of trade if she is willing to associate herself with us and the other peace-loving nations of the world in covenants of justice and law and fair dealing. We wish her only to accept a place of equality among the peoples of the world,—the new world in which we now live,—instead of a place of mastery.

Neither do we presume to suggest to her any alteration or modification of her institutions. But it is necessary, we must frankly say, and necessary as a preliminary to any intelligent dealings with her on our part, that we should know whom her spokesmen speak for when they speak to us, whether for the Reichstag majority or for the military party and the men whose creed is imperial domination.

We have spoken now, surely, in terms too concrete to admit of any further doubt or question. An evident principle runs through the whole program I have outlined. It is the principle of justice to all peoples and nationalities, and their right to live on equal terms of liberty and safety with one another, whether they be strong or weak. Unless this principle be made its foundation no part of the structure of international justice can stand. The people of the United States could act upon no other principle; and to the vindication of this principle they are ready to devote their lives, their honor, and everything that they possess. The moral climax of this the culminating and final war for human liberty has come, and they are ready to put their own strength, their own highest purpose, their own integrity and devotion to the test.

WOODROW WILSON # 70

Defense of the League of Nations, 1919

Woodrow Wilson saw his dream of the League of Nations faltering in 1919 and went on a nationwide tour to build up support in the Senate for passage of the treaty which would lead the United States into the League. This effort brought him to Pueblo, Colorado, on September 26, 1919, to deliver this address. In what many historians consider his most impassioned speech ever, Wilson urged the crowd to let the deaths of the American troops in France to have some meaning— to give the next generation a chance to enjoy peace. Wilson insisted that the League of Nations was instrument to preserve liberty and the peace of the world, to take the future and the lives of millions from petty dictators and give them back to the people. The very right of everyone on Earth to existence, free from the threat of harm, was at the heart of Wilson's dream. Shortly after he gave this speech, the strain of this new campaign led Wilson to suffer a debilitating stroke, from which he would never fully recover. The treaty went down to defeat, and the United States never joined the League of Nations.

Mr. Chairman and Fellow Countrymen:

It is with a great deal of genuine pleasure that I find myself in Pueblo... I have crossed the continent this time of the homogeneity of this great people to whom we belong. They come from many stocks, but they are all of one kind. They come from many origins, but they are all shot through with the same principles, and desire the same righteous and honest things. I have received a more inspiring impression this time of the public opinion of the United States than it was ever my privilege to receive before.

But there have been unpleasant impressions as well as pleasant impressions, my fellow citizens, as I have crossed the continent. I have perceived more and more that men have been busy creating an absolutely false impression of what the treaty of peace and the Covenant of the League of Nations contain and mean. Therefore, in order to clear away the mists, in order to remove the impressions, in order to check the falsehoods that have clustered around this great subject, I want to tell you a few very simple things about the treaty and the Covenant.

Do not think of this treaty of peace as merely a settlement with Germany. It is that. It is a very severe settlement with Germany, but there is not anything in it that she did not earn... It is not merely a settlement with Germany; it is a readjustment of those great injustices which underlie the whole structure of European and Asiatic society. This is only the first of several treaties. They are all constructed upon the same plan. The Austrian treaty follows the same lines. The treaty with Hungary follows the same lines. The treaty with Bulgaria follows the same lines. The treaty with Turkey, when it is formulated, will follow the same lines. What are those lines? They are based upon the purpose to see that every government dealt with in this great settlement is put in the hands of the people, and taken out of the hands of coteries and of sovereigns who had no right to rule over the people. It is a people's treaty, that accomplishes by a great sweep of practical justice the liberation of men who never could have liberated themselves, and the power of the most powerful nations has been devoted not to their aggrandizement but to the liberation of people whom they could have put under their control if they had chosen to do so...

At the front of this great treaty is put the Covenant of the League of Nations. It will also be at the front of the Austrian treaty and the Hungarian treaty and the Bulgarian treaty and the treaty with Turkey. Every one of them will contain the Covenant of the League of Nations, because you cannot work any of them without the Covenant of the League of Nations. Unless you get the united, concerted purpose and power of the great Governments of the world behind this settlement, it will fall down like a house of cards. There is only one power to put behind the liberation of mankind, and that is the power of mankind. It is the power of the united moral forces of the world, and in the Covenant of the League of Nations the moral forces of the world are mobilized. For what purpose? Reflect, my fellow citizens, that the membership of this great League is going to include all the great fighting nations of the world, as well as the weak ones. It is not for the present going to include Germany, but for the time being Germany is not a great fighting country. All the nations that have power that can be mobilized are going to be members of this League, including the United States. And what do they unite for? They enter into a solemn promise to one another that they will never use their power against one another for aggression; that they never will impair the territorial integrity of a neighbor; that they never will interfere with the political independence of a neighbor; that they will abide by the principle that great populations are entitled to determine their own destiny, and that they will not interfere with that destiny; and that no matter what differences arise amongst them, they will never resort to war without first having done one or other of two things——either submitted the matter of controversy to arbitration, in which case they agree to abide by the result without question, or submitted it to the consideration of the council of the League of Nations, laying before that council all the documents, all the facts, agreeing that the council can publish the documents and the facts to the whole world, agreeing that there shall be six months allowed for the mature consideration of those facts by the council, and agreeing that at the expiration of the six months, even if they are not then ready to accept the advice of the council with regard to the settlement of the dispute, they will still not go to war for another three months. In other words, they consent, no matter what happens, to submit every matter of difference between them to the judgment of mankind, and just so certainly as they do that, my fellow citizens, war will be in the far background, war will be pushed out of that foreground of terror in which it has kept the world for generation after generation, and men will know that there will be a calm time of deliberate counsel. The most dangerous thing for a bad cause is to expose it to the opinion of the world. The most certain way that you can prove that a man is mistaken is by letting all his neighbors know what he thinks, by letting all his neighbors discuss what he thinks, and if he is in the wrong you will notice that he will stay at home, he will not walk on the street. He will be afraid of the eyes of his neighbors. He will be afraid of their judgment of his character. He will know that his cause is lost unless he can sustain it by the arguments of right and of justice. The same law that applies to individuals applies to nations.

But, you say, "We have heard that we might be at a disadvantage in the League of Nations." Well, whoever told you that either was deliberately falsifying or he had not read the Covenant of the League of Nations. When you come to the heart of the Covenant, my fellow citizens, you will find it in Article X, and I am very much interested to know that the other things have been blown away like bubbles. There is nothing in the other contentions with regard to the League of Nations, but there is something in Article X that you ought to realize and ought to accept or reject. Article X is the heart of the whole matter. What is Article X? I never am certain that I can from memory give a literal repetition of its language, but I am sure that I can give an exact interpretation of its meaning. Article X provides that every member of the League covenants to respect and preserve the territorial integrity and existing political independence of every other member of the League as against external aggression. Following Article X is Article XI, which makes it the right of any member of the League at any time to call attention to anything, anywhere, that is likely to disturb the peace of the world or the good understanding between nations upon which the peace of the world depends. I want to give you an illustration of what that would mean.

You have heard a great deal—something that was true and a great deal that was false—about that provision of the treaty which hands over to Japan the rights which Germany enjoyed in the Province of Shantung in China. In the first place, Germany did not enjoy any rights there that other nations had not already claimed. For my part, my judgment, my moral judgment, is against the whole set of concessions. They were all of them unjust to China, they ought never to have been exacted, they were all exacted by duress, from a great body of thoughtful and ancient and helpless people. There never was any right in any of them. Thank God, America never asked for any, never dreamed of asking for any. But when Germany got this concession in 1898, the Government of the United States made no protest whatever. That was not because the Government of the United States was not in the hands of high-minded and conscientious men. It was. William McKinley was President and John Hay was Secretary of State—as safe hands to leave the honor of the United States in as any that you can cite. They made no protest because the state of international law at that time was that it was none of their business unless they could show that the interests of the United States were affected, and the only thing that they could show with regard to the interests of the United States was that Germany might close the doors of Shantung Province against the trade of the United States. They, therefore, demanded, and obtained, promises that we could continue to sell merchandise in Shantung. Immediately following that concession to Germany, there was a concession to Russia of the same sort, of Port Arthur, and Port Arthur was handed over subsequently to Japan. Now, read Articles X and XI. You will see that international law is revolutionized by putting morals into it. Article X says that no member of the League, and that includes all these nations that have demanded these things unjustly of China, shall impair the territorial integrity or the political independence of any other member of the League. China is going to be a member of the League. Article XI says that any member of the League can call attention to anything that is likely to disturb the peace of the world or the good understanding between nations, and China is, for the first time in the history of mankind, afforded a standing before the jury of the world. I, for my part, have a profound sympathy for China, and I am proud to have taken part in an arrangement which promises the protection of the world to the rights of China. The whole atmosphere of the world is changed by a thing like that, my fellow citizens. The whole international practice of the world is revolutionized.

Article X strikes at the taproot of war. Article X is a statement that the very things that have always been sought in imperialistic wars are henceforth forgone by every ambitious nation in the world. I would have felt very lonely, my fellow countrymen, and I would have felt very much disturbed if, sitting at the peace table in Paris, I had supposed that I was expounding my own ideas. Whether you believe it or not, I know the relative size of my own ideas; I know how they stand related in bulk and proportion to the moral judgments of my fellow countrymen, and proposed nothing whatever at the peace table at Paris that I had not sufficiently certain knowledge embodied the moral judgment of the citizens of the United States. What of our pledges to the men that lie dead in France? We said that they went over there not to prove the prowess of America or her readiness for another war, but to see to it that there never was such a war again. It always seems to make it difficult for me to say anything, my fellow citizens, when I think of my clients in this case. My clients are the children; my clients are the next generation. They do not know what promises and bonds I undertook when I ordered the armies of the United States to the soil of France, but I know, and I intend to redeem my pledges to the children; they shall not be sent upon a similar errand.

Again and again, my fellow citizens, mothers who lost their sons in France have come to me and, taking my hand, have shed tears upon it not only, but they have added, "God bless you, Mr. President!" Why, my fellow citizens, should they pray God to bless me? I advised the Congress of the United States to create the situation that led to the death of their sons. I ordered their sons overseas. I consented to their sons being put in the most difficult parts of the battle line, where death was certain, as in the impenetrable difficulties of the forest of Argonne. Why should they weep upon my hand and call down the blessings of God upon me? Because they believe that their boys died for something that vastly transcends any of the immediate and palpable objects of the war. They believe, and they rightly believe, that their sons saved the liberty of the world. They believe that wrapped up with the liberty of the world is the continuous protection of that liberty by the concerted powers of all civilized people. They believe that this sacrifice was made in order that other sons should not be called upon for a similar gift—the gift of life, the gift of all that died—and if we did not see this thing through, if we fulfilled the dearest present wish of Germany, and now dissociated ourselves from those alongside whom we fought in the war, would not something of the halo go away from the gun over the mantelpiece, or the sword? Would not the old uniform lose something of its significance? These men were crusaders. They were not going forth to prove the might of the United States. They were going forth to prove the might of justice and right, and all the world accepted them as crusaders, and their transcendent achievement has made all the world believe in America as it believes in no other nation organized in the modern world.

There seems to me to stand between us and the rejection or qualification of this treaty the serried ranks of those boys in khaki, not only these boys who came home, but those dear ghosts that still deploy upon the fields of France.

My friends, on last Decoration Day, I went to a beautiful hillside near Paris where was located the cemetery of Suresnes, a cemetery given over to the burial of the American dead. Behind me on the slopes was rank upon rank of living American soldiers, and lying before me upon the levels of the plain was rank upon rank of departed American soldiers. Right by the side of the stand where I spoke there was a little group of French women who had adopted those graves, had made themselves mothers of those dear ghosts by putting flowers every day upon those graves, taking them as their own sons, their own beloved, because they had died in the same cause—France was free and the world was free because America had come! I wish some men in public life who are now opposing the settlement for which these men died could visit such a spot as that. I wish that the thought that comes out of those graves could penetrate their consciousness. I wish that they could feel the moral obligation that rests upon us not to go back on those boys, but to see the thing through, to see it through to the end and make good their redemption of the world. For nothing less depends upon this decision, nothing less than the liberation and salvation of the world.

You will say, "Is the League an absolute guarantee against war?" No; I do not know any absolute guarantee against the errors of human judgment or the violence of human passion, but I tell you this: With a cooling space of nine months for human passion, not much of it will keep hot.

I had a couple of friends who were in the habit of losing their tempers, and when they lost their tempers they were in the habit of using very unparliamentary language. Some of their friends induced them to make a promise that they never would swear inside the town limits. When the impulse next came upon them, they took a streetcar to go out of town to swear, and by the time they got out of town, they did not want to swear. They came back convinced that they were just what they were, a couple of unspeakable fools, and the habit of getting angry and of swearing suffered great inroads upon it by that experience.

Now, illustrating the great by the small, that is true of the passions of nations. It is true of the passions of men however you combine them. Give them space to cool off. I ask you this: If it is not an absolute insurance against war, do you want no insurance at all? Do you want nothing? Do you want not only no probability that war will not recur, but the probability that it will recur? The arrangements of justice do not stand of themselves, my fellow citizens. The arrangements of this treaty are just, but they need the support of the combined power of the great nations of the world. And they will have that support. Now that the mists of this great question have cleared away, I believe that men will see the truth, eye to eye and face to face. There is one thing that the American people always rise to and extend their hand to, and that is the truth of justice, and of liberty, and of peace. We have accepted that truth and we are going to be led by it, and it is going to lead us, and through us the world, out into pastures of quietness and peace such as the world never dreamed of before.

OLIVER WENDELL HOLMES **71**

Dissenting Opinion, *Gitlow v. New York*, 1925

The Gitlow v. New York case stemmed from the arrest of Benjamin Gitlow, a Socialist, for distributing a pamphlet titled, The Left-Wing Manifesto, *which called for the overthrow of the United States government. Gitlow, convicted under New York's criminal anarchy law, challenged his conviction by arguing it violated his freedom of speech. In a 7-2 decision in June 1925, the Supreme Court upheld the conviction, using the "Clear and Present Danger" test that stipulated that speech could be censored or punished if it posed an immediate threat to public safety.*

The idea of "clear and present danger" was authored by Supreme Court Justice Oliver Wendell Holmes in the 1919 Schenck v. U.S. *case, but he denied Gitlow's statements were a danger to the public. In this dissent, Holmes argues not only should the right to express oneself be upheld as an essential element of a free society, but he touches on another idea: freedom of thought. He argues that all ideas are a challenge of some sort, but not all ideas will prompt individuals to act unless they can convince another that action is necessary. And all ideas should have a chance to be heard. Holmes was appointed to the United States Supreme Court in 1902 and served for thirty years. In that time, he became considered one of the most eloquent and respected of justices. He authored numerous majority opinions and dissenting opinions on cases involving civil liberties throughout his Supreme Court career.*

Mr. Justice HOLMES (dissenting).

Mr. Justice [LOUIS] BRANDEIS and I are of opinion that this judgment should be reversed. The general principle of free speech, it seems to me, must be taken to be included in the Fourteenth Amendment, in view of the scope that has been given to the word 'liberty' as there used, although perhaps it may be accepted with a somewhat larger latitude of interpretation than is allowed to Congress by the sweeping language that governs or ought to govern the laws of the United States. If I am right then I think that the criterion sanctioned by the full Court in Schenck v. United States, 249 U.S. 47, 52 , 39 S. Ct. 247, 249 (63 L. Ed. 470), applies:

> "The question in every case is whether the words used are used in such circumstances and are of such a nature as to create a clear and present danger that they will bring about the substantive evils [268 U.S. 652, 673] evils that [the State] has a right to prevent."

It is true that in my opinion this criterion was departed from in Abrams v. United States, 250 U.S. 616, 40 S. Ct. 17, but the convictions that I expressed in that case are too deep for it to be possible for me as yet to believe that it and Schaefer v. United States, 251 U.S 466, 40 S. Ct. 259, have settled the law. If what I think the correct test is applied it is manifest that there was no present danger of an attempt to overthrow the government by force on the part of the admittedly small minority who shared the defendant's views. It is said that this manifesto was more than a theory, that it was an incitement. Every idea is an incitement. It offers itself for belief and if believed it is acted on unless some other belief outweighs it or some failure of energy stifles the movement at its birth. The only difference between the expression of an opinion and an incitement in the narrower sense is the speaker's enthusiasm for the result. Eloquence may set fire to reason. But whatever may be thought of the redundant discourse before us it had no chance of starting a present conflagration. If in the long run the beliefs expressed in proletarian dictatorship are destined to be accepted by the dominant forces of the community, the only meaning of free speech is that they should be given their chance and have their way.

If the publication of this document had been laid as an attempt to induce an uprising against government at once and not at some indefinite time in the future it would have presented a different question. The object would have been one with which the law might deal, subject to the doubt whether there was any danger that the publication could produce any result, or in other words, whether it was not futile and too remote from possible consequences. But the indictment alleges the publication and nothing more.

FRANKLIN D. ROOSEVELT **72**

Practical Explanations and Practical Policies, 1934

As president, Franklin D. Roosevelt would regularly deliver addresses to the nation on radio in what became known as his "fireside chats." He used these occasions to explain new programs designed to alleviate the poverty and unemployment caused by the Great Depression. In this June 28, 1934, address, Roosevelt uses the occasion to respond to critics who stated that his work relief programs and regulatory programs undermined American freedoms. He responded by stating that practical solutions to the pressing problems of human need did not threaten freedom but rather fulfilled the promise of freedom, breaking the chains of privation.

It has been several months since I have talked with you concerning the problems of government. Since January, those of us in whom you have vested responsibility have been engaged in the fulfillment of plans and policies which had been widely discussed in previous months. It seemed to us our duty not only to make the right path clear but also to tread that path.

As we review the achievements of this session of the Seventy-third Congress, it is made increasingly clear that its task was essentially that of completing and fortifying the work it had begun in March, 1933. That was no easy task, but the Congress was equal to it. It has been well said that while there were a few exceptions, this Congress displayed a greater freedom from mere partisanship than any other peace-time Congress since the Administration of President Washington himself. The session was distinguished by the extent and variety of legislation enacted and by the intelligence and good will of debate upon these measures.

I mention only a few of the major enactments. It provided for the readjustment of the debt burden through the corporate and municipal bankruptcy acts and the farm relief act. It lent a hand to industry by encouraging loans to solvent industries unable to secure adequate help from banking institutions. It strengthened the integrity of finance through the regulation of securities exchanges. It provided a rational method of increasing our volume of foreign trade through reciprocal trading agreements. It strengthened our naval forces to conform with the intentions and permission of existing treaty rights. It made further advances towards peace in industry through the labor adjustment act. It supplemented our agricultural policy through measures widely demanded by farmers themselves and intended to avert price destroying surpluses. It strengthened the hand of the Federal Government in its attempts to suppress gangster crime. It took definite steps towards a national housing program through an act which I signed today designed to encourage private capital in the rebuilding of the homes of the Nation. It created a permanent Federal body for the just regulation of all forms of communication, including the telephone, the telegraph and the radio.

Russel D. Bahite and David W. Levy, eds., *FDR's Fireside Chats* (New York: Penguin Books, 1992): 46–52

Finally, and I believe most important, it reorganized, simplified and made more fair and just our monetary system, setting up standards and policies adequate to meet the necessities of modern economic life, doing justice to both gold and silver as the metal bases behind the currency of the United States. In the consistent development of our previous efforts toward the saving and safeguarding of our national life, I have continued to recognize three related steps. The first was relief, because the primary concern of any Government dominated by the humane ideals of democracy is the simple principle that in a land of vast resources no one should be permitted to starve. Relief was and continues to be our first consideration. It calls for large expenditures and will continue in modified form to do so for a long time to come. We may as well recognize that fact. It comes from the paralysis that arose as the after-effect of that unfortunate decade characterized by a mad chase for unearned riches and an unwillingness of leaders in almost every walk of life to look beyond their own schemes and speculations. In our administration of relief we follow two principles: First, that direct giving shall, wherever possible, be supplemented by provision for useful and remunerative work and, second, that where families in their existing surroundings will in all human probability never find an opportunity for full self-maintenance, happiness and enjoyment, we will try to give them a new chance in new surroundings.

The second step was recovery, and it is sufficient for me to ask each and every one of you to compare the situation in agriculture and in industry today with what it was fifteen months ago.

At the same time we have recognized the necessity of reform and reconstruction—reform because much of our trouble today and in the past few years has been due to a lack of understanding of the elementary principles of justice and fairness by those in whom leadership in business and finance was placed—reconstruction because new conditions in our economic life as well as old but neglected conditions had to be corrected. Substantial gains well known to all of you have justified our course. I could cite statistics to you as unanswerable measures of our national progress—statistics to show the gain in the average weekly pay envelope of workers in the great majority of industries—statistics to show hundreds of thousands reemployed in private industries and other hundreds of thousands given new employment through the expansion of direct and indirect government assistance of many kinds, although, of course, there are those exceptions in professional pursuits whose economic improvement, of necessity, will be delayed. I also could cite statistics to show the great rise in the value of farm products—statistics to prove the demand for consumers' goods, ranging all the way from food and clothing to automobiles and of late to prove the rise in the demand for durable goods—statistics to cover the great increase in bank deposits and to show the scores of thousands of homes and of farms which have been saved from foreclosure.

But the simplest way for each of you to judge recovery lies in the plain facts of your own individual situation. Are you better off than you were last year? Are your debts less burdensome? Is your bank account more secure? Are your working conditions better? Is your faith in your own individual future more firmly grounded?

Also, let me put to you another simple question: Have you as an individual paid too high a price for these gains? Plausible self-seekers and theoretical die-hards will tell you of the loss of individual liberty. Answer this question also out of the facts of your own life. Have you lost any of your rights or liberty or constitutional freedom of action and choice? Turn to the Bill of Rights of the Constitution, which I have solemnly sworn to maintain and under which your freedom rests secure. Read each provision of that Bill of Rights and ask yourself whether you personally have suffered the impairment of a single jot of these great assurances. I have no question in my mind as to what your answer will be. The record is written in the experiences of your own personal lives.

In other words, it is not the overwhelming majority of the farmers or manufacturers or workers who deny the substantial gains of the past year. The most vociferous of the doubting Thomases may be divided roughly into two groups: First, those who seek special political privilege and, second, those who seek special financial privilege. About a year ago I used as an illustration the 90% of the cotton manufacturers of the United States who wanted to do the right thing by their employees and by the public but were prevented from doing so by the 10% who undercut them by unfair practices and un-American standards. It is well for us to remember that humanity is a long way from being perfect and that a selfish minority in every walk of life— farming, business, finance and even Government service itself—will always continue to think of themselves first and their fellow-being second.

In the working out of a great national program which seeks the primary good of the greater number, it is true that the toes of some people are being stepped on and are going to be stepped on. But these toes belong to the comparative few who seek to retain or to gain position or riches or both by some short cut which is harmful to the greater good. In the execution of the powers conferred on it by Congress, the Administration needs and will tirelessly seek the best ability that the country affords. Public service offers better rewards in the opportunity for service than ever before in our history—not great salaries, but enough to live on. In the building of this service there are coming to us men and women with ability and courage from every part of the Union. The days of the seeking of mere party advantage through the misuse of public power are drawing to a close. We are increasingly demanding and getting devotion to the public service on the part of every member of the Administration, high and low.

The program of the past year is definitely in operation and that operation month by month is being made to fit into the web of old and new conditions. This process of evolution is well illustrated by the constant changes in detailed organization and method going on in the National Recovery Administration. With every passing month we are making strides in the orderly handling of the relationship between employees and employers. Conditions differ, of course, in almost every part of the country and in almost every industry. Temporary methods of adjustment are being replaced by more permanent machinery and, I am glad to say, by a growing recognition on the part of employers and employees of the desirability of maintaining fair relationships all around.

So also, while almost everybody has recognized the tremendous strides in the elimination of child labor, in the payment of not less than fair minimum wages and in the shortening of hours, we are still feeling our way in solving problems which relate to self-government in industry, especially where such self-government tends to eliminate the fair operation of competition.

In this same process of evolution we are keeping before us the objectives of protecting on the one hand industry against chiselers within its own ranks, and on the other hand the consumer through the maintenance of reasonable competition for the prevention of the unfair sky-rocketing of retail prices.

But, in addition to this our immediate task, we must still look to the larger future. I have pointed out to the Congress that we are seeking to find the way once more to well-known, long-established but to some degree forgotten ideals and values. We seek the security of the men, women and children of the Nation.

That security involves added means of providing better homes for the people of the Nation. That is the first principle of our future program.

The second is to plan the use of land and water resources of this country to the end that the means of livelihood of our citizens may be more adequate to meet their daily needs. And, finally, the third principle is to use the agencies of government to assist in the establishment of means to provide sound and adequate protection against the vicissitudes of modern life—in other words, social insurance.

Later in the year I hope to talk with you more fully about these plans. A few timid people, who fear progress, will try to give you new and strange names for what we are doing. Sometimes they will call it "Fascism", sometimes "Communism", sometimes "Regimentation", sometimes "Socialism". But, in so doing, they are trying to make very complex and theoretical something that is really very simple and very practical.

I believe in practical explanations and in practical policies. I believe that what we are doing today is a necessary fulfillment of what Americans have always been doing—a fulfillment of old and tested American ideals.

Let me give you a simple illustration:

While I am away from Washington this summer, a long needed renovation of and addition to our White House office building is to be started. The architects have planned a few new rooms built into the present all too small one-story structure. We are going to include in this addition and in this renovation modern electric wiring and modern plumbing and modern means of keeping the offices cool in the hot Washington summers. But the structural lines of the old Executive Office Building will remain. The artistic lines of the White House buildings were the creation of master builders when our Republic was young. The simplicity and the strength of the structure remain in the face of every modern test. But within this magnificent pattern, the necessities of modern government business require constant reorganization and rebuilding.

If I were to listen to the arguments of some prophets of calamity who are talking these days, I should hesitate to make these alterations. I should fear that while I am away for a few weeks the architects might build some strange new Gothic tower or a factory building or perhaps a replica of the Kremlin or of the Potsdam Palace. But I have no such fears. The architects and builders are men of common sense and of artistic American tastes. They know that the principles of harmony and of necessity itself require that the building of the new structure shall blend with the essential lines of the old. It is this combination of the old and the new that marks orderly peaceful progress—not only in building buildings but in building government itself.

Our new structure is a part of and a fulfillment of the old.

All that we do seeks to fulfill the historic traditions of the American people. Other nations may sacrifice democracy for the transitory stimulation of old and discredited autocracies. We are restoring confidence and well-being under the rule of the people themselves. We remain, as John Marshall said a century ago, "emphatically and truly, a government of the people. "Our government" in form and in substance . . . emanates from them. Its powers are granted by them, and are to be exercised directly on them, and for their benefits."

Before I close, I want to tell you of the interest and pleasure with which I look forward to the trip on which I hope to start in a few days. It is a good thing for everyone who can possibly do so to get away at least once a year for a change of scene. I do not want to get into the position of not being able to see the forest because of the thickness of the trees.

I hope to visit our fellow Americans in Puerto Rico, in the Virgin Islands, in the Canal Zone and in Hawaii. And, incidentally, it will give me an opportunity to exchange a friendly word of greeting to the Presidents of our sister Republics: Haiti, Colombia and Panama.

After four weeks on board ship, I plan to land at a port in our Pacific northwest, and then will come the best part of the whole trip, for I am hoping to inspect a number of our new great national projects on the Columbia, Missouri and Mississippi Rivers, to see some of our national parks and, incidentally, to learn much of actual conditions during the trip across the continent back to Washington.

While I was in France during the War our boys used to call the United States "God's country". Let us make it and keep it "God's country".

JOHN L. LEWIS # 73

Labor and the Nation, 1937

John L. Lewis was a powerful figure in the American labor movement for decades. He served as president of the United Mine Workers of America from 1920 to 1960. In 1936, Lewis and other labor leaders split from the American Federation of Labor into the Committee of Industrial Organization in hopes of unionizing workers in the automotive manufacturing and steel industry. Hundreds of thousands of workers rushed to join the new United Auto Workers Union and United Steel Workers unions to secure what they saw as their rightful share of the profits their work created. For the CIO, this was just the beginning.

In this address to the new Committee of Industrial Organization in Washington, DC, on September 3, 1937, Lewis defended the labor movement and challenged the charges of labor critics that unions were communistic, un-American, or undemocratic. Lewis contended that the CIO simply wanted justice—the right for workers to be treated as equals with their employers by negotiating as a united front (collective bargaining), better wages, and to not be assaulted by strikebreakers hired by their employers to break the momentum of union members. For Lewis and other labor leaders, freedom and justice were simple issues for the American worker: the right to ask for something better and the right to believe that their work would be rewarded. The CIO reunited with the American Federation of Labor as the AFL-CIO in 1955.

Out of the agony and travail of economic America the Committee for Industrial Organization was born. To millions of Americans exploited without stint by corporate industry and socially debased beyond the understanding of the fortunate, its coming was as welcomed as the dawn to the night watcher. To a lesser group of

Americans, infinitely more fortunately situated, blessed with larger quantities of the world's goods and insolent in their assumption of privilege, its coming was heralded as a harbinger of ill, sinister of purpose, of unclean methods and non-virtuous objectives. But the Committee for Industrial Organizations is here. It is now henceforth a definite instrumentality, destined greatly to influence the lives of our people and the internal and external course of the republic.

This is true only because the purposes and objectives of the Committee for Industrial Organization find economic, social, political and moral justification in the hearts of the millions who are its members and the millions more who support it. The organization and constant onward sweep of this movement exemplifies the resentment of the many toward the selfishness, greed and the neglect of the few.

The workers of the nation were tired of waiting for corporate industry to right their economic wrongs, to alleviate their social agony and to grant them their political rights. Despairing of fair treatment, they resolved to do something for themselves. They, therefore, have organized a new labor movement, conceived within the principles of the national bill of rights and committed to the proposition that the workers are free to assemble in their own forums, voice their own grievances, declare their own hopes and contract on even terms with modern industry for the sale of their only material possession—their labor.

The Committee for Industrial Organization has a numerical enrollment of 3,718,000 members. It has 32 affiliated national and international unions. Of this number 11 unions account for 2,765,000 members. This group is organized in the textile, auto, garment, lumber, rubber, electrical manufacturing, power, steel, coal and transport industries. The remaining membership exists in the maritime, oil production and refining, ship building, leather, chemical, retail, meat packing, vegetable canning, metalliferous mining, miscellaneous manufacturing, agricultural labor, and service and miscellaneous industries. Some 200,000 workers are organized into 507 chartered local unions not yet attached to a national industrial union.

This record bespeaks progress. It is a development without precedent in our own country. Some of this work was accomplished with the enlightened cooperation or the tolerant acquiescence of employers who recognized that a new labor movement was being forged and who were not disposed, in any event, to flout the law of the land. On the other hand, much of this progress was made in the face of violent and deadly opposition which reached its climax in the slaughter of workers paralleling the massacres of Ludlow [Colorado] and Homestead [Pennsylvania].

In the steel industry the corporations generally have accepted collective bargaining and negotiated wage agreements with the Committee for Industrial Organization. Eighty-five per cent of the industry is thus under contract and a peaceful relationship exits between the management and the workers. Written wage contracts have been negotiated with 399 steel companies covering 510,000 men. One thousand thirty-one local lodges in 700 communities have been organized.

Five of the corporations in the steel industry elected to resist collective bargaining and undertook to destroy the steel workers' union. These companies filled their plants with industrial spies, assembled depots of guns and gas bombs, established barricades, controlled their communities with armed thugs, leased the police power of cities and mobilized the military power of a state to guard them against the intrusion of collective bargaining within their plants.

During this strike 18 steel workers were either shot to death or had their brains clubbed out by police, or armed thugs in the pay of the steel companies. In Chicago, Mayor [Edward] Kelly's police force was successful in killing ten strikers before they could escape the fury of the police, shooting eight of them in the back. One hundred sixty strikers were maimed and was successful in killing ten strikers before they could escape the fury of the police, shooting eight of them in the back. One hundred sixty strikers were maimed and injured by police clubs, riot guns and gas bombs and were hospitalized. Hundreds of strikers were arrested, jailed, treated with brutality while incarcerated and harassed by succeeding litigation. None but strikers were murdered, gassed, injured, jailed or maltreated. No one had to die except the workers who were standing for the right guaranteed them by the Congress and written in the law.

The infamous Governor [Martin L.] Davey, of Ohio, successful in the last election because of his reiterated promises of fair treatment to labor, used the military power of the Commonwealth on the side of the Republican Steel Company and the Youngstown Sheet and Tube Company. Nearly half of the staggering military expenditure incident to the crushing of this strike in Ohio was borne by the federal government through the allocation of financial aid to the military establishment of the state.

The steel workers have now buried their dead, while the widows weep and watch their orphaned children become objects of public charity. The murder of these unarmed men has never been publicly rebuked by any authoritative officer of the state or federal government. Some of them, in extenuation, plead lack of jurisdiction, but murder as a crime against the moral code can always be rebuked without regard to the niceties of legalistic jurisdiction by those who profess to be the keepers of the public conscience.

Shortly after Kelly's police force in Chicago had indulged in their bloody orgy, Kelly came to Washington looking for political patronage. That patronage was forthcoming and Kelly must believe that the killing of the strikers is no liability in partisan politics.

Meanwhile, the steel puppet Davey is still Governor of Ohio, but not for long I think—not for long. The people of Ohio may be relied upon to mete our political justice to one who has betrayed his state, outraged the public conscience and besmirched the public honor.

While the men of the steel industry were going through blood and gas in defense of their rights and their homes and their families, elsewhere on the far-flung C.I.O. front the hosts of labor were advancing and intelligent and permanent progress was being made. In scores of industries plant after plant and company after company were negotiating sensible working agreements.

The men in the steel industry who sacrificed their all were nor merely aiding their fellows at home but were adding strength to the cause of their comrades in all industry. Labor was marching toward the goal of industrial democracy and contributing constructively toward a more rational arrangement of our domestic economy.

Labor does not seek industrial strife. It wants peace, but a peace with justice. In the long struggle for labor's rights it has been patient and forbearing. Sabotage and destruction syndicalism have had no part in the American labor movement. Workers have kept faith in American institutions. Most of the conflicts, which have occurred have been when labor's right to live has been challenged and denied.

If there is to be peace in our industrial life let the employer recognize his obligation to his employees—at least to the degree set forth in existing statutes. Ordinary problems affecting wages, hours, and working conditions, in most instances, will quickly respond to negotiation in the council room.

The United States Chamber of Commerce, the National Association of Manufacturers, and similar groups representing industry and financial interests, are rendering a disservice to the American people in their attempts to frustrate the organization of labor and in their refusal to accept collective bargaining as one of our economic institutions.

These groups are encouraging a systematic organization of vigilante groups to fight unionization under the sham pretext of local interests. They equip these vigilantes with tin hats, wooden clubs, gas masks and lethal weapons and train them in the arts of brutality and oppression. They bring in snoops, finks, hatchet gangs and Chowderhead Cohens to infest their plants and disturb the communities.

Fascist organizations have been launched and financed under the shabby pretext that the C.I.O. movement is communistic. The real breeders of discontent and alien doctrines of government and philosophies subversive of good citizenship are such as these who take the law into their own hands.

No tin-hat brigade of goose-stepping vigilantes or bibble-babbling mob of blackguarding and corporation paid scoundrels will prevent the onward march of labor, or divert its purpose to play its natural and rational part in the development of the economic, political and social life of our nation.

Unionization, as opposed to communism, presupposes the relation of employment; it is based upon the wage system and it recognizes fully and unreservedly the institution of private property and the right to investment profit. It is upon the fuller development of collective bargaining, the wider expansion of the labor movement, the increased influence of labor in our national councils, that the perpetuity of our democratic institutions must largely depend.

The organized workers of America, free in their industrial life, conscious partners in production, secure in their homes and enjoying a decent standard of living, will prove the finest bulwark against the intrusion of alien doctrines of government.

Do those who have hatched this foolish cry of communism in the C.I.O. fear the increased influence of labor in our democracy? Do they fear its influence will be cast on the side of shorter hours, a better system of distributed employment, better homes for the under-privileged, social security for the aged, a fairer distribution of the national income?

Certainly the workers that are being organized want a voice in the determination of these objectives of social justice. Certainly labor wants a fairer share in the national income. Assuredly labor wants a larger participation in increased productive efficiency. Obviously the population is entitled to participate in the fruits of the genius of our men of achievement in the field of the material sciences.

Labor has suffered just as our farm population has suffered from a viciously unequal distribution of the national income. In the exploitation of both classes of workers has been the source of panic and depression, and upon the economic welfare of both rests the best assurance of a sound and permanent prosperity.

In this connection let me call attention to the propaganda which some of our industrialists are carrying on among the farmers. By pamphlets in the milk cans or attached to machinery and in countless other ways of direct and indirect approach, the farmers of the nation are being told that the increased price of farm machinery and farm supplies is due to the rising wage level brought about by the Committee for

Industrial Organization. And yet it is the industrial millions of this country who constitute the substantial market for all agricultural products.

The interest of the two groups are mutually dependent. It is when the pay roll goes down that the farmer's realization is diminished, so that his loans become overdue at the bank and the arrival of the tax collector is awaited with fear. On the other hand it is the prosperity of the farmer that quickness the tempo of manufacturing activities and brings buying power to the millions of urban and industrial workers.

As we view the years that have passed this has always been true and it becomes increasingly imperative that the farm population and the millions of workers in industry must learn to combine their strength for the attainment of mutual and desirable objectives and at the same time learn to guard themselves against the sinister propaganda of those who would divide and exploit them.

Under the banner of the Committee for Industrial Organization American labor is on the march. Its objectives today are those it had in the beginning: to strive for the unionization of our unorganized millions of workers and for the acceptance of collective bargaining as a recognized American institution.

It seeks peace with the industrial world. It seeks cooperation and mutuality of effort with the agricultural population. It would avoid strikes. It would have its rights determined under the law by the peaceful negotiations and contract relationships that are supposed to characterize American commercial life.

Until an aroused public opinion demands that employers accept that rule, labor has no recourse but to surrender its rights or struggle for their realization with its own economic power.

The objectives of this movement are not political in a partisan sense. Yet it is true that a political party which seeks the support of labor and makes pledges of good faith to labor must, in equity and good conscience, keep that faith and redeem those pledges.

The spectacle of august and dignified members of Congress, servants of the people and agents of the republic, skulking in hallways and closets, hiding their faces in a party caucus to prevent a quorum from acting upon a labor measure, is one that emphasizes the perfidy of politicians and blasts the confidence of labor's millions in politician's promises and statesmen's vows.

Labor next year cannot avoid the necessity of a political assay of the work and deeds of its so-called friends and its political beneficiaries. It must determine who are its friends in the arena of politics as elsewhere. It feels that its cause is just and that its friends should not view its struggle with neutral detachment or intone constant criticism of its activities.

Those who chant their praises of democracy but who lose no chance to drive their knives into labor's defenseless back must feel the weight of labor's woe even as its open adversaries must ever feel the thrust of labor's power.

Labor, like Israel, has many sorrows. Its women weep for their fallen and they lament for the future of the children of the race. It ill behooves one who has supped at labor's table and who has been sheltered in labor's house to curse with equal fervor and fine impartiality both labor and its adversaries when they become locked in deadly embrace.

I repeat that labor seeks peace and guarantees its own loyalty, but the voice of labor, insistent upon its rights, should not be annoying to the ears of justice or offensive to the conscience of the American people.

ELEANOR ROOSEVELT # 74

The Importance of Civil Liberties, 1940

First Lady Eleanor Roosevelt developed a reputation as an outspoken humanitarian and champion of civil rights during her lifetime. In this speech before the American Civil Liberties Union in Chicago, given on March 14, 1940, the first lady detailed some of her own experiences when seeing the results of privation or oppression. She witnessed how poverty had destroyed a family's hope for the future and how religious and racial prejudice had driven many from their homelands. For Roosevelt, this simply stood as a question of morality—that prejudice was unacceptable and poverty was abhorrent. The two could not be separated from threats to civil liberties as they robbed individuals of their ability to control their fates and dream of better lives.

Ladies and Gentlemen:

I am glad you gave an award to the press tonight, because that gave them the opportunity to tell us just what they could do. Now we have come here tonight because of civil liberties. I imagine a great many of you could give my talk far better than I could, because you have had first-hand knowledge in the things you have had to do in Chicago over the years to preserve civil liberties. Perhaps, however, I am more conscious of the importance of civil liberties in this particular moment of our history than anyone else, because as I travel through the country and meet people and see things that have happened to little people, I realize what it means to democracy to preserve our civil liberties.

All through the years we have had to fight for civil liberty, and we know that there are times when the light grows rather dim, and every time that happens democracy is in danger. Now, largely because of the troubled state of the world as a whole, civil liberties have disappeared in many other countries. It is impossible, of course, to be at war and to keep freedom of the press and freedom of speech and freedom of assembly. They disappear automatically. And so in many countries where ordinarily they were safe, today they have gone. In other countries, even before war came, not only freedom of the press and freedom of assembly, and freedom of speech disappeared, but freedom of religion disappeared. And so we know that here in this country, we have a grave responsibility. We are at peace. We have no reason for the fears which govern so many other peoples throughout the world; therefore, we have to guard the freedoms of democracy.

"Civil Liberties" emphasizes the liberty of the individual. In many other forms of governments the importance of the individual has disappeared. The individual lives for the state. Here in a democracy, the government still exists for the individual, but that does not mean that we do not have to watch and that we do not have to examine ourselves to be sure that we preserve the civil liberties for all our people, which are the basis of our democracy.

http://www.pbs.org/greatspeeches/timeline/e_roosevelt_s.html

Now, you know if we are honest with ourselves, in spite of all we have said, in spite of our Constitution, many of us in this country do not enjoy real liberty. For that reason we know that everywhere in this country every person who believes in democracy has come to feel a real responsibility to work in his community and to know the people of his community, and to take the trouble to try to bring about the full observance for all our people of their civil liberties.

I think I will tell you a little story that brought home to me how important it was that in every community there should be someone to whom people could turn, who were in doubt as to what were their rights under the law, when they couldn't understand what was happening to them. I happen to go every now and then to a certain mining community and in that mining community there are a number of people who came to this country many years ago. They have been here so many years that they have no other country. This is their country. Their children have been born here. They work here. They have created great wealth for this country, but they came over at a time when there was not very much feeling of social responsibility about giving them the opportunity to learn the language of the country to which they had come, or telling them how to become citizens, or teaching about the government of this country.

I had contact with a family where the man had been here over thirty-five years, and the first time I went to see him in his house it came about this way: I was standing with a group of people, and a young girl with arms full of packages came along the road. She stopped to look at me and said, "Why, you are Mrs. Roosevelt. My mama say, 'She is happy if you come to her house'." I said, "Where is her house?" "Up the run." So I walked with her and when I got to the house a Polish woman was sitting at the table. The girl walked in and said, "Mama, this is Mrs. Roosevelt," and the woman got up and threw both arms around me, and I was kissed on both cheeks. She told me she had been expecting me to come for a long time. She wanted me to come because she wanted me to see how really nice her house was, and we went through the four rooms, and it was nice. She had made crochet pieces which decorated every table. The bedspreads were things of real beauty. We admired everything together. We came back to the kitchen and she said, "You eat with us?" and I said, "No, I just had breakfast." She wouldn't let me leave without eating something, so we had a piece of bread there together.

Six months later I came back, and I went again to visit my friend. The minute I crossed the threshold, I knew something had happened in that house. It was quite dark. In a few minutes the old man came through from the back room, and he said; "Mrs. Roosevelt, you have come. I have wanted to ask you something for a long time. The mine, it close down, no more work. I work on W.P.A. for a time, and then they tell me I no citizen. Mrs. Roosevelt, I vote. I vote often. Why I no citizen?"

There was nobody that stood out in the community that he dared trust, that he felt he could go to find out what his rights were, or what he should do. Well, of course, it was true he had never become a citizen. His children were born in this country; they were citizens, but he was not. And they had lived, those two people, by being allowed by the county to take in four old men who would have gone otherwise to the county poor house. Six people were living on the allowance for those four old men. The allowance was pitifully small. As I looked at the stove at what they were going to have for supper, I realized the woman wouldn't again say, "Sit down and eat." There wasn't enough for a stranger, and that was the breakdown of her morale. It hurt you.

Something was wrong with the spirit of America that an injustice like that could happen to a man who, after all, worked hard and contributed to the wealth of the country. It should have been somebody's business, first of all, to see that he learned the English language well enough to find things out for himself. Secondly, when he was in trouble, to fight for his rights and to tell him how to go about to remedy what was wrong. I felt there was something wrong with any community where you had to wait many months for a stranger to come to listen to your story and help you straighten out what was a manifest injustice. He couldn't be on W.P.A. He could start out to become a citizen, and he could get relief and, at least, have the feeling that there was an interest on the part of someone in justice. I think that is, perhaps, one of the greatest things that the civil liberties committees do, and I wish we had one in every place throughout the country—one group of people who really care when things go wrong and do something when there is an infringement of the individual's rights.

There are many times when even with freedom of the press and freedom of speech, it is hard to get a hearing for certain causes. I often think that we, all of us, should think very much more carefully than we do about what we mean by freedom of speech, by freedom of the press, by freedom of assembly. I sometimes am much worried by the tendency that you find today in our country only to think that these are rights for the people who think as we do. Some people seem to think these rights are not for people who disagree with them. I believe that you must apply to all groups the right to all forms of thought, to all forms of expression. Otherwise, you practically refuse to trust people to choose for themselves what is wise and what is right, and in doing that you deny the possibility of a democratic form of government. You have to be willing to listen or to allow people to state any point of view they may have, to say anything they may believe, and trust that when everyone has had his say, when there has been free discussion and really free expression in an influenced press, in the end the majority of the people will have the wisdom to decide what is right. We have to have faith that even when the majority seems to decide as we think wrongly, we still believe the fundamental principles that we have laid down, and we wait for the day to come when the thing that we believe is right becomes the majority decision of the people.

Well, of course, that means that we have to have a real belief that people have sufficient intelligence to live in a democracy, and that is something which we are really testing out in this country today, because we are the only great democracy, and we are the only great democracy that is at peace and that can go on and live in what we consider a normal and free way of living. It is only here that people don't have to tremble when they say what they think. I don't know how many of you have read a book that I have been reading, but I think it is a most vivid picture of the kind of fear that has gradually come to all the people of Europe. It is *Stricken Field* by Martha Gellhorn, a young woman who was a war correspondent. The story was put in novel form and is about the taking over of Czechoslovakia. Certain people in Czechoslovakia were considered dangerous to the new regime—and the whole description is horrible of what they call "going underground," living in hiding, afraid to speak to each other, afraid to recognize each other on the streets, for fear they would be tortured to death. Only great fear could bring people to treat other people like that, and I can only say that it seems to me that we should read as vivid a story as this now, just to make us realize how important it is, that for no reason whatsoever, we allow ourselves to be dominated by fears so that we curtail civil liberties. Let us see that everybody who is really in danger in our community has, at least, his or her day in court. Constituted authority has to work under the law. When the law becomes something below the surface, hidden from the people, something which is underground, so to speak, and over which the people no longer hold control, then all of us are in danger.

Never before was it so important that every individual should carry his share of responsibility and see that we do obey the laws, live up to the Constitution, and preserve everyone of those precious liberties which leave us free as individuals. One of the things that we have to be particularly alive to today is the growth of religious prejudice and race prejudice. Those are two things which are a great menace because we find that in countries where civil liberties have been lost, both religious and race prejudice have been rampant. I think it would be well for us, if we could define what we mean when we say that we believe in religious freedom.

I sat at a desk in a political campaign once. I was running the office dealing with women for the National Democratic Committee. Over my desk came literature and material which I did not suppose any one would print in the United States, and much of it was written and published by people who belong to various religious denominations. It seems to me that the thing we must fix in our minds is that from the beginning, this country was founded on the right of all people to worship God as they saw fit, and if they do not wish to worship, they are not forced to worship. That is a fundamental liberty. When religion begins to take part in politics, we violate something which we have set up, which is a division between church and state.

As far as having respect for the religion of other people and leaving them to live their lives the way they wish, we should teach that to every child. Every child should know that his religion is his own and nobody else has the right to question it. In addition to that, I think we should begin much earlier to teach all the children of our nation what a wonderful heritage they have for freedom. For freedom from prejudice, because they live in a nation which is made up of a great variety of other nations. They have before them and around them every day the proof that people can understand each other and can live together amicably, and that races can live on an equal basis, even though they may be very different in background, very different in culture. We have an opportunity to teach our children how much we have gained from the coming to this land of all kinds of races, how much it has served in the development of the land. Somehow I think we have [also] failed in many ways in bringing it early enough to children how great is their obligation to the various strains that make up the people of the United States. Above all, there should never be race prejudice here; there should never be a feeling that one strain is better than another. Indians are the only real inhabitants of the country who have a right to say that they own this country! I think this is the reason that we should preserve freedom of mind on the things which are basic to civil liberties. And it should be easy for us to live up to our Constitution.

I am very much interested to find that in our younger generation, however, there is a greater consciousness of what civil liberties really mean, and I think that is one of the hopeful things in the world today, that youth is really taking a tremendous interest in the preservation of civil liberties. It is a very hard period in the world for youth because they are faced with new kinds of problems. We don't know the answers to many of the problems that face us today and neither do the young people, and the problems are very much more important to the young because they must start living. We have had our lives. The young people want to begin, and they can't find a way to get started. Perhaps that has made them more conscious of civil liberties. Perhaps that is why when you get a group of them together you find them fighting against the prejudices which have grown up in our country, against the prejudices which have made it hard for the minority groups in our country. The other night someone sent up a question to me: "What do you think should be done about the social standing of the Negro race in this country?" Well now, of course, I think the social situation is one that has to be dealt with by individuals. The real question that we have to face in this country is what are we doing about the rights of a big minority group as citizens in our democracy. That we have to face. Any citizen in this country is entitled to equality before the law; to equality of education; to equality at earning a living, as far as his abilities have made it possible for him to do; to equality of participation in government so that he or she may register their opinion in just the way that any other citizens do. Now those things are basic rights, belonging to every citizen in every minority group, and we have an obligation, I think, to stand up and be counted when it comes to the question of whether any minority group does not have those rights as citizens in this country. The minute we deny any rights of this kind to any citizen, we are preparing the way for the denial of those rights to someone else. We have to make up our minds what we really believe. We have to decide whether we believe in the Bill of Rights, in the Constitution of the United States, or whether we are going to modify it because of the fears that we may have at the moment.

Now I listened to the broadcast this afternoon with a great deal of interest. I almost forgot what a fight had been made to assure the rights of the working man. I know there was a time when hours were longer and wages lower, but I had forgotten just how long that fight for freedom, to bargain collectively, and to have freedom of assembly, had taken. Sometimes, until some particular thing comes to your notice, you think something has been won for every working man, and then you come across as I did the other day a case where someone had taken the law into his own hands and beaten up a labor organizer. I didn't think we did those things any more in this country, but it appears that we do. Therefore, someone must be always on the lookout to see that someone is ready to take up the cudgels to defend those who can't defend themselves. That is the only way we are going to keep this country a law-abiding country, where law is looked upon with respect and where it is not considered necessary for anybody to take the law into his own hands. The minute you allow that, then you have acknowledged that you are no longer able to trust in your courts and in your law-enforcing machinery, and civil liberties are not very well off when anything like that happens; so I think that after listening to the broadcast today, I would like to remind you that behind all those who fight for the Constitution as it was written, for the rights of the weak and for the preservation of civil liberties, we have a long line of courageous people, which is something to be proud of and something to hold on to. Its only value lies, however, in the fact that we profit by example and continue the tradition in the future. We must not let those people back of us down; we must have courage; we must not succumb to fears of any kind; and we must live up to the things that we believe in and see that justice is done to the people under the Constitution, whether they belong to minority groups or not. This country is a united country in which all people have the same rights as citizens. We are grateful that we can trust in the youth of the nation that they are going on to uphold the real principles of democracy and put them into action in this country. They are going to make us an even more truly democratic nation.

FRANKLIN D. ROOSEVELT **75**

The Four Freedoms, 1941

Franklin D. Roosevelt delivered this speech to Congress as a State of the Union address on January 6, 1941. While most State of the Union speeches, particularly in modern times, are broad summaries of the previous year and legislative agendas for the coming year, Roosevelt concentrated on one topic: the threat of war. By this time, Nazi Germany had overrun most of Europe, leaving only Great Britain to face them. The Japanese advanced throughout China. The president had recognized the threat to the United States early, but he needed to convince a nation that had largely chosen to withdraw from the international scene after the horrors of World War I to meet the new challenge. In this address, Roosevelt proposes the Lend-Lease program, which provided much needed weapons to the surviving Allies and may well have saved the war effort. But he also laid the ideological foundation on which the Allies would make their stand. He summarized the civil liberties of each individual around the world into four distinct freedoms: freedom of speech, freedom of religion, freedom from want, and freedom from fear. The United States could not ignore the threat from the Axis Powers not only to the independence of the nations of the world but the threat to freedoms. And for Roosevelt, freedom meant preserving the civil liberties of everyone throughout the world, else the security of freedom for all nations remained in jeopardy.

Mr. President, Mr. Speaker, members of the 77th Congress:

I address you, the members of this new Congress, at a moment unprecedented in the history of the union. I use the word "unprecedented" because at no previous time has American security been as seriously threatened from without as it is today. Since the permanent formation of our government under the Constitution in 1789, most of the periods of crisis in our history have related to our domestic affairs. And, fortunately, only one of these—the four-year war between the States—ever threatened our national unity. Today, thank God, 130,000,000 Americans in forty-eight States have forgotten points of the compass in our national unity.

It is true that prior to 1914 the United States often has been disturbed by events in other continents. We have even engaged in two wars with European nations and in a number of undeclared wars in the West Indies, in the Mediterranean and in the Pacific, for the maintenance of American rights and for the Principles of peaceful commerce. But in no case had a serious threat been raised against our national safety or our continued independence.

What I seek to convey is the historic truth that the United States as a nation has at all times maintained opposition—clear, definite opposition—to any attempt to lock us in behind an ancient Chinese wall while the procession of civilization went past.

http://www.ourdocuments.gov/doc.php?flash=true&doc=70

Today, thinking of our children and of their children, we oppose enforced isolation for ourselves or for any other part of the Americas.

That determination of ours, extending over all these years, was proved, for example, in the early days during the quarter century of wars following the French Revolution. While the Napoleonic struggles did threaten interests of the United States because of the French foothold in the West Indies and in Louisiana, and while we engaged in the War of 1812 to vindicate our right to peaceful trade, it is nevertheless clear that neither France nor Great Britain nor any other nation was aiming at domination of the whole world.

And in like fashion, from 1815 to 1914—ninety-nine years—no single war in Europe or in Asia constituted a real threat against our future or against the future of any other American nation. Except in the Maximilian interlude in Mexico, no foreign power sought to establish itself in this hemisphere. And the strength of the British fleet in the Atlantic has been a friendly strength; it is still a friendly strength.

Even when the World War broke out in 1941 it seemed to contain only small threat of danger to our own American future. But as time went on, as we remember, the American people began to visualize what the downfall of democratic nations might mean to our own democracy.

We need not overemphasize imperfections in the peace of Versailles. We need not harp on failure of the democracies to deal with problems of world reconstruction. We should remember that the peace of 1919 was far less unjust than the kind of pacification which began even before Munich, and which is being carried on under the new order of tyranny that seeks to spread over every continent today. The American people have unalterably set their faces against that tyranny. I suppose that every realist knows that the democratic way of life is at this moment being directly assailed in every part of the world—assailed either by arms or by secret spreading of poisonous propaganda by those who seek to destroy unity and promote discord in nations that are still at peace.

During sixteen long months this assault has blotted out the whole pattern of democratic life in an appalling number of independent nations, great and small. And the assailants are still on the march, threatening other nations, great and small. Therefore, as your President, performing my constitutional duty to "give to the Congress information of the state of the union," I find it unhappily necessary to report that the future and the safety of our country and of our democracy are overwhelmingly involved in events far beyond our borders.

Armed defense of democratic existence is now being gallantly waged in four continents. If that defense fails, all the population and all the resources of Europe and Asia, and Africa and Australasia will be dominated by conquerors. And let us remember that the total of those populations in those four continents, the total of those populations and their resources greatly exceeds the sum total of the population and the resources of the whole of the Western Hemisphere—yes, many times over.

In times like these it is immature— and, incidentally, untrue—for anybody to brag that an unprepared America, single-handed and with one hand tied behind its back, can hold off the whole world. No realistic American can expect from a dictator's peace international generosity, or return of true independence, or world disarmament, or freedom of expression, or freedom of religion—or even good business. Such a peace would bring no security for us or for our neighbors. Those who would give up essential liberty to purchase a little temporary safety deserve neither liberty nor safety.

As a nation we may take pride in the fact that we are soft-hearted; but we cannot afford to be soft-headed. We must always be wary of those who with sounding brass and a tinkling cymbal preach the "ism" of appeasement. We must especially beware of that small group of selfish men who would clip the wings of the American eagle in order to feather their own nests. I have recently pointed out how quickly the tempo of modern warfare could bring into our very midst the physical attack which we must eventually expect if the dictator nations win this war.

There is much loose talk of our immunity from immediate and direct invasion from across the seas. Obviously, as long as the British Navy retains its power, no such danger exists. Even if there were no British Navy, it is not probable that any enemy would be stupid enough to attack us by landing troops in the United States from across thousands of miles of ocean, until it had acquired strategic bases from which to operate. But we learn much from the lessons of the past years in Europe—particularly the lesson of Norway, whose essential seaports were captured by treachery and surprise built up over a series of years.

The first phase of the invasion of this hemisphere would not be the landing of regular troops. The necessary strategic points would be occupied by secret agents and by their dupes—and great numbers of them are already here and in Latin America. As long as the aggressor nations maintain the offensive they, not we, will choose the time and the place and the method of their attack. And that is why the future of all the American Republics is today in serious danger. That is why this annual message to the Congress is unique in our history. That is why every member of the executive branch of the government and every member of the Congress face great responsibility—great accountability.

The need of the moment is that our actions and our policy should be devoted primarily—almost exclusively—to meeting this foreign peril. For all our domestic problems are now a part of the great emergency. Just as our national policy in internal affairs has been based upon a decent respect for the rights and the dignity of all of our fellow men within our gates, so our national policy in foreign affairs has been based on a decent respect for the rights and the dignity of all nations, large and small. And the justice of morality must and will win in the end.

Our national policy is this:

First, by an impressive expression of the public will and without regard to partisanship, we are committed to all-inclusive national defense.

Secondly, by an impressive expression of the public will and without regard to partisanship, we are committed to full support of all those resolute people everywhere who are resisting aggression and are thereby keeping war away from our hemisphere. By this support we express our determination that the democratic cause shall prevail, and we strengthen the defense and the security of our own nation.

Third, by an impressive expression of the public will and without regard to partisanship, we are committed to the proposition that principles of morality and considerations for our own security will never permit us to acquiesce in a peace dictated by aggressors and sponsored by appeasers. We know that enduring peace cannot be bought at the cost of other people's freedom. In the recent national election there was no substantial difference between the two great parties in respect to that national policy. No issue was fought out on this line before the American electorate. And today it is abundantly evident that American citizens everywhere are demanding and supporting speedy and complete action in recognition of obvious danger.

Therefore, the immediate need is a swift and driving increase in our armament production. Leaders of industry and labor have responded to our summons. Goals of speed have been set. In some cases these goals are being reached ahead of time. In some cases we are on schedule; in other cases there are slight but not serious delays. And in some cases— and, I am sorry to say, very important cases—we are all concerned by the slowness of the accomplishment of our plans. The Army and Navy, however, have made substantial progress during the past year. Actual experience is improving and speeding up our methods of production with every passing day. And today's best is not good enough for tomorrow.

I am not satisfied with the progress thus far made. The men in charge of the program represent the best in training, in ability and in patriotism. They are not satisfied with the progress thus far made. None of us will be satisfied until the job is done. No matter whether the original goal was set too high or too low, our objective is quicker and better results. To give you two illustrations:

We are behind schedule in turning out finished airplanes. We are working day and night to solve the innumerable problems and to catch up.

We are ahead of schedule in building warships, but we are working to get even further ahead of that schedule.

To change a whole nation from a basis of peacetime production of implements of peace to a basis of wartime production of implements of war is no small task. And the greatest difficulty comes at the beginning of the program, when new tools, new plant facilities, new assembly lines, new shipways must first be constructed before the actual material begins to flow steadily and speedily from them.

The Congress of course, must rightly keep itself informed at all times of the progress of the program. However, there is certain information, as the Congress itself will readily recognize, which, in the interests of our own security and those of the nations that we are supporting, must of needs be kept in confidence. New circumstances are constantly begetting new needs for our safety. I shall ask this Congress for greatly increased new appropriations and authorizations to carry on what we have begun.

I also ask this Congress for authority and for funds sufficient to manufacture additional munitions and war supplies of many kinds, to be turned over to those nations which are now in actual war with aggressor nations. Our most useful and immediate role is to act as an arsenal for them as well as for ourselves. They do not need manpower, but they do need billions of dollars' worth of the weapons of defense. The time is near when they will not be able to pay for them all in ready cash. We cannot, and we will not, tell them that they must surrender merely because of present inability to pay for the weapons which we know they must have.

I do not recommend that we make them a loan of dollars with which to pay for these weapons—a loan to be repaid in dollars. I recommend that we make it possible for those nations to continue to obtain war materials in the United States, fitting their orders into our own program. And nearly all of their material would, if the time ever came, be useful in our own defense. Taking counsel of expert military and naval authorities, considering what is best for our own security, we are free to decide how much should be kept here and how much should be sent abroad to our friends who, by their determined and heroic resistance, are giving us time in which to make ready our own defense.

For what we send abroad we shall be repaid, repaid within a reasonable time following the close of hostilities, repaid in similar materials, or at our option in other goods of many kinds which they can produce and which we need. Let us say to the democracies: "We Americans are vitally concerned in your defense of freedom. We are putting forth our energies, our resources and our organizing powers to give you the strength to regain and maintain a free world. We shall send you in ever-increasing numbers, ships, planes, tanks, guns. That is our purpose and our pledge."

In fulfillment of this purpose we will not be intimidated by the threats of dictators that they will regard as a breach of international law or as an act of war our aid to the democracies which dare to resist their aggression. Such aid is not an act of war, even if a dictator should unilaterally proclaim it so to be. And when the dictators—if the dictators—are ready to make war upon us, they will not wait for an act of war on our part. They did not wait for Norway or Belgium or the Netherlands to commit an act of war. Their only interest is in a new one-way international law which lacks mutuality in its observance and therefore becomes an instrument of oppression. The happiness of future generations of Americans may well depend on how effective and how immediate we can make our aid felt. No one can tell the exact character of the emergency situations that we may be called upon to meet. The nation's hands must not be tied when the nation's life is in danger.

Yes, and we must prepare, all of us prepare, to make the sacrifices that the emergency—almost as serious as war itself—demands. Whatever stands in the way of speed and efficiency in defense, in defense preparations of any kind, must give way to the national need. A free nation has the right to expect full cooperation from all groups. A free nation has the right to look to the leaders of business, of labor and of agriculture to take the lead in stimulating effort, not among other groups but within their own groups.

The best way of dealing with the few slackers or trouble-makers in our midst is, first, to shame them by patriotic example, and if that fails, to use the sovereignty of government to save government. As men do not live by bread alone, they do not fight by armaments alone. Those who man our defenses and those behind them who build our defenses must have the stamina and the courage which come from unashakeable belief in the manner of life which they are defending. The mighty action that we are calling for cannot be based on a disregard of all the things worth fighting for.

The nation takes great satisfaction and much strength from the things which have been done to make its people conscious of their individual stake in the preservation of democratic life in America. Those things have toughened the fiber of our people, have renewed their faith and strengthened their devotion to the institutions we make ready to protect. Certainly this is no time for any of us to stop thinking about the social and economic problems which are the root cause of the social revolution which is today a supreme factor in the world. For there is nothing mysterious about the foundations of a healthy and strong democracy.

The basic things expected by our people of their political and economic systems are simple. They are:

Equality of opportunity for youth and for others.

Jobs for those who can work.

Security for those who need it.

The ending of special privilege for the few.

The preservation of civil liberties for all.

The enjoyment of the fruits of scientific progress in a wider and constantly rising standard of living.

These are the simple, the basic things that must never be lost sight of in the turmoil and unbelievable complexity of our modern world. The inner and abiding strength of our economic and political systems is dependent upon the degree to which they fulfill these expectations.

Many subjects connected with our social economy call for immediate improvement. As examples:

We should bring more citizens under the coverage of old-age pensions and unemployment insurance.

We should widen the opportunities for adequate medical care.

We should plan a better system by which persons deserving or needing gainful employment may obtain it.

I have called for personal sacrifice, and I am assured of the willingness of almost all Americans to respond to that call. A part of the sacrifice means the payment of more money in taxes. In my budget message I will recommend that a greater portion of this great defense program be paid for from taxation than we are paying for today. No person should try, or be allowed to get rich out of the program, and the principle of tax payments in accordance with ability to pay should be constantly before our eyes to guide our legislation.

If the congress maintains these principles the voters, putting patriotism ahead pocketbooks, will give you their applause. In the future days which we seek to make secure, we look forward to a world founded upon four essential human freedoms.

The first is freedom of speech and expression—everywhere in the world.

The second is freedom of every person to worship God in his own way—everywhere in the world.

The third is freedom from want, which, translated into world terms, means economic understandings which will secure to every nation a healthy peacetime life for its inhabitants—everywhere in the world.

The fourth is freedom from fear, which, translated into world terms, means a world-wide reduction of armaments to such a point and in such a thorough fashion that no nation will be in a position to commit an act of physical aggression against any neighbor—anywhere in the world. That is no vision of a distant millennium. It is a definite basis for a kind of world attainable in our own time and generation. That kind of world is the very antithesis of the so-called "new order" of tyranny which the dictators seek to create with the crash of a bomb.

To that new order we oppose the greater conception—the moral order. A good society is able to face schemes of world domination and foreign revolutions alike without fear. Since the beginning of our American history we have been engaged in change, in a perpetual, peaceful revolution, a revolution which goes on steadily, quietly, adjusting itself to changing conditions without the concentration camp or the quicklime in the ditch. The world order which we seek is the cooperation of free countries, working together in a friendly, civilized society.

This nation has placed its destiny in the hands and heads and hearts of its millions of free men and women, and its faith in freedom under the guidance of God. Freedom means the supremacy of human rights everywhere. Our support goes to those who struggle to gain those rights and keep them. Our strength is our unity of purpose.

To that high concept there can be no end save victory.

FRANKLIN D. ROOSEVELT AND
WINSTON CHURCHILL

76

The Atlantic Charter, 1941

As war raged around the world in 1941, many feared that the free nations of the world would be consumed by the Nazi horror. Although the United States had yet to enter World War II in August 1941, Franklin Roosevelt realized that the nation would soon be drawn into the conflict. In a secret meeting in the Atlantic Ocean with British Prime Minister Winston Churchill, the two drew up a set of principles known as the Atlantic Charter. Signed on August 14, 1941, it became a statement of what the free world was fighting to preserve in the onslaught of the Axis war machine, including self-determination for all nations and peoples and justice for all.

The President of the United States of America and the Prime Minister, Mr. Churchill, representing His Majesty's Government in the United Kingdom, being met together, deem it right to make known certain common principles in the national policies of their respective countries on which they base their hopes for a better future for the world.

First, their countries seek no aggrandizement, territorial or other;

Second, they desire to see no territorial changes that do not accord with the freely expressed wishes of the peoples concerned;

Third, they respect the right of all peoples to choose the form of government under which they will live; and they wish to see sovereign rights and self government restored to those who have been forcibly deprived of them;

Fourth, they will endeavor, with due respect for their existing obligations, to further the enjoyment by all States, great or small, victor or vanquished, of access, on equal terms, to the trade and to the raw materials of the world which are needed for their economic prosperity;

Fifth, they desire to bring about the fullest collaboration between all nations in the economic field with the object of securing, for all, improved labor standards, economic advancement and social security;

Sixth, after the final destruction of the Nazi tyranny, they hope to see established a peace which will afford to all nations the means of dwelling in safety within their own boundaries, and which will afford assurance that all the men in all lands may live out their lives in freedom from fear and want;

Seventh, such a peace should enable all men to traverse the high seas and oceans without hindrance;

Eighth, they believe that all of the nations of the world, for realistic as well as spiritual reasons must come to the abandonment of the use of force. Since no future peace can be maintained if land, sea or air armaments continue to be employed by nations which threaten, or may threaten, aggression outside of their frontiers, they believe, pending the establishment of a wider and permanent system of general security, that the disarmament of such nations is essential. They will likewise aid and encourage all other practicable measure which will lighten for peace-loving peoples the crushing burden of armaments.

Franklin D. Roosevelt

Winston S. Churchill

77

Preamble to the Charter of the United Nations, 1945

In June 1945, just as World War II was coming to an end, delegates from across the globe met in San Francisco, California, at the United Nations Conference on International Organization to create a new international peacekeeping organization, the United Nations. The delegates hoped that this organization would succeed where the League of Nations failed, hobbled by the absence of the United States. The Preamble mirrored the Constitution of the United States, emphasizing for whom the organization was dedicated—to we the people. The principles of democracy and human rights that the United States had exported to the rest of the world had now been firmly embraced by the other nations of the world through the demands of their own peoples for freedom or seeing what they had nearly lost to fascism as a result of World War II. The Preamble reaffirms American principles of freedom of speech, freedom of religion, peace, and liberty on a new international scale.

www.un.org

WE THE PEOPLES OF THE UNITED NATIONS DETERMINED

- to save succeeding generations from the scourge of war, which twice in our lifetime has brought untold sorrow to mankind, and
- to reaffirm faith in fundamental human rights, in the dignity and worth of the human person, in the equal rights of men and women and of nations large and small, and
- to establish conditions under which justice and respect for the obligations arising from treaties and other sources of international law can be maintained, and
- to promote social progress and better standards of life in large freedom,

AND FOR THESE ENDS

- to practice tolerance and live together in peace with one another as good neighbours, and
- to unite our strength to maintain international peace and security, and
- to ensure, by the acceptance of principles and the institutions of methods, that armed force shall not be used, save in the common interest, and
- to employ international machinery for the promotion of the economic and social advancement of all peoples,

HAVE RESOLVED TO COMBINE OUR EFFORTS TO ACCOMPLISH THESE AIMS

Accordingly, our respective Governments, through representatives assembled in the city of San Francisco, who have exhibited their full powers found to be in good and due form, have agreed to the present Charter of the United Nations and do hereby establish an international organization to be known as the United Nations.

HUBERT H. HUMPHREY **78**

The Sunshine of Civil Rights, 1948

Americans began to reexamine its position on civil rights in the years following World War II. The system of segregation in the South had become a glaring exception to the principle of equality and liberty in a nation that prided itself on these principles. At the Democratic National Convention in Philadelphia, on

http://www.americanrhetoric.com/speeches/huberthumphey.html; http://www.pbs.org/greatspeeches/timeline/h_humphrey_s2.html

July 14, 1948, the argument boiled over. Southern conservatives blistered at the suggestion that the Jim Crow system should change, while progressives argued that a free nation must include all races. Minneapolis Mayor Hubert H. Humphrey, soon to be a U. S. Senator from Minnesota and vice-president from 1965 to 1969, took to the podium and delivered a rousing address in defense of the civil rights plank being introduced into the Democratic platform. He spoke to a noisy convention crowd, but made a lasting impression by stating that a nation could not hide behind legal niceties to strip away the civil rights of a whole segment of the population.

Mr. Chairman, fellow Democrats, fellow Americans:

I realize that in speaking in behalf of the minority report on civil rights as presented by Congressman DeMiller of Wisconsin that I am dealing with a charged issue—with an issue which has been confused by emotionalism on all sides of the fence. I realize that there are here today friends and colleagues of mine, many of them—who feel just as deeply and keenly as I do about this issue and who are yet in complete disagreement with me.

My respect and admiration for these men and their views was great when I came to this convention. It is now far greater because of the sincerity, the courtesy, and the forthrightness with which many of them have argued in our prolonged discussions in the platform committee.

Because of this very great respect—and because of my profound belief that we have a challenging task to do here—because good conscience, decent morality, demands it—I feel I must rise at this time to support a report—the minority report— a report that spells out our democracy, a report that the people of this country can and will understand and a report that they will enthusiastically acclaim on the great issue of civil rights!

Now let me say this at the outset that this proposal is made for no single region. Our proposal is made for no single class, for no single racial or religious groups in mind. All of the regions of this country, all of the states have shared in our precious heritage of American freedom. All the states and all the regions have seen at least some of the infringements of that freedom—all people—get this—all people, white and black, all groups, all racial groups have been the victims at times in this nation of—let me say—vicious discrimination.

The masterly statement of our keynote speaker, the distinguished United States Senator from Kentucky, Alben Barkley, made that point with great force. Speaking of the founder of our party, Thomas Jefferson, he said this, and I quote from Alben Barkley:

> He did not proclaim that all the white, or the black, or the red, or the yellow men are equal; that all Christian or Jewish men are equal; that all Protestant and Catholic men are equal; that all rich and poor men are equal; that all good and bad men are equal.
>
> What he declared was that all men are equal; and the equality which he proclaimed was the equality in the right to enjoy the blessings of free government in which they may participate and to which they have given their support.

Now these words of Senator Barkley's are appropriate to this convention—appropriate to this convention of the oldest, the most truly progressive political party in America. From the time of Thomas Jefferson, the time when that immortal American doctrine of individual rights, under just and fairly administered laws, the Democratic party has tried hard to secure expanding freedoms for all citizens. Oh, yes, I know, other political parties may have *talked* more about civil rights, but the Democratic party has surely *done* more about civil rights.

We have made progress, we have made great progress, in every part of this country. We've made great progress in the South, we've made it in the West, in the North, and in the East, but we must now focus the direction of that progress towards the realization of a full program of civil rights to all. This convention must set out more specifically the direction in which our party efforts are to go.

We can be proud that we can be guided by the courageous trail blazing of two great Democratic presidents. We can be proud of the fact that our great and beloved immortal leader Franklin Roosevelt gave us guidance. And we be proud of the fact—we can be proud of the fact—that Harry Truman has had the courage to give to the people of America the new emancipation proclamation!

It seems to me—it seems to me, that the Democratic party needs to make definite pledges of the kinds suggested in the minority report to maintain the trust and the confidence placed in it by the people of all races and all sections of this country.

Sure, we're here as Democrats. But my good friends, we're here as Americans—we're here as the believers in the principle and the ideology of democracy, and I firmly believe that as men concerned with our country's future, we must specify in our platform the guarantees which we have mentioned in the minority report.

Yes, this is far more than a party matter. Every citizen in this country has a stake in the emergence of the United States as a *leader* in the free world. That world is being challenged by the world of slavery. For us to play our part effectively, we must be in a morally sound position.

We can't use a double standard—there's no room for double standards in American politics—for measuring our own and other people's policies. Our demands for democratic practices in other lands will be no more effective than the guarantee of those practices in our own country.

Friends, delegates, I do not believe that there can be any compromise on the guarantees of the civil rights which we have mentioned in the minority report.

In spite of my desire for unanimous agreement on the entire platform, in spite of my desire to see everybody here in honest and unanimous agreement, there are some matters which I think must be stated clearly and without qualification. There can be no hedging—the newspaper headlines are wrong! There will be no hedging, and there will be no watering down—if you please—of the instruments and the principals of the civil-rights program!

To those who say, my friends, to those who say, that we are rushing this issue of civil rights. I say to them we are 172 years late! To those who say—to those who say that this civil-rights program is an infringement on states' rights, I say this: the time has arrived in America for the Democratic party to get out of the shadow of state's rights and to walk forthrightly into the bright sunshine of human rights!

People, people—human beings—this is the issue of the 20th century. People of all kinds, all sorts of people, and these people are looking to America for leadership, and they're looking to America for precept and example.

My good friends—my fellow Democrats—I ask you for a calm consideration of our historic opportunity.

Let us not forget—let us do forget—the evil passions and the blindness of the past. In these times of world economic, political, and spiritual—above all spiritual—crisis, we cannot—and we must not—turn from the path so plainly before us. That path has already lead us through many valleys of the shadow of death. And now is the time to recall those who were left on that path of American freedom.

For all of us here, for the millions who have sent us, for the whole two-billion members of the human family—our land is now, more than ever before, the last best hope on earth. And I know that we can—and I know that we shall—begin here the fuller and richer realization of that hope—that promise of a land where all men are truly free and equal, and each man uses his freedom and equality wisely well.

My good friends, I ask my party, I ask the Democratic party, to march down the *high* road of progressive democracy. I ask this convention, I ask this convention, to say in unmistakable terms that we proudly hail, and we courageously support, our President and leader Harry Truman in his great fight for civil-rights in America!

79

Brown v. Board of Education, U.S. Supreme Court, 1954

The Brown v. Board of Education *case arose from the plight of Linda Brown, a 9-year-old African-American girl in Topeka, Kansas, who was forced to attend a segregated school across town even though she lived only four blocks from a white school. With the help of Thurgood Marshall of the National Association for the Advancement of Colored People, her parents sued the school district. NAACP leaders had been looking for a case to challenge the constitutionality of segregation for some time. Brown's case was combined with several others, and in 1954, the Supreme Court issued its unanimous decision: segregation was inherently unconstitutional and had no place in American public schools. It set the stage for many bitter confrontations in the future as white districts fought desegregation, but the case became an important statement on the equality of all school children and the principle that free individuals cannot be forced to live separately or denied opportunities because of their race.*

http://caselaw.lp.findlaw.com/scripts/getcase.pl?court=us&vol=347&invol=483

BROWN v. BOARD OF EDUCATION, 347 U.S. 483 (1954)

347 U.S. 483

BROWN ET AL. v. BOARD OF EDUCATION OF TOPEKA ET AL.

APPEAL FROM THE UNITED STATES DISTRICT COURT FOR THE DISTRICT OF KANSAS. * No. 1.

Argued December 9, 1952. Reargued December 8, 1953.

Decided May 17, 1954.

Segregation of white and Negro children in the public schools of a State solely on the basis of race, pursuant to state laws permitting or requiring such segregation, denies to Negro children the equal protection of the laws guaranteed by the Fourteenth Amendment—even though the physical facilities and other "tangible" factors of white and Negro schools may be equal. Pp. 486–496.

(a) The history of the Fourteenth Amendment is inconclusive as to its intended effect on public education. Pp. 489–490.

(b) The question presented in these cases must be determined, not on the basis of conditions existing when the Fourteenth Amendment was adopted, but in the light of the full development of public education and its present place in American life throughout the Nation. Pp. 492–493.

(c) Where a State has undertaken to provide an opportunity for an education in its public schools, such an opportunity is a right which must be made available to all on equal terms. P. 493.

(d) Segregation of children in public schools solely on the basis of race deprives children of the minority group of equal educational opportunities, even though the physical facilities and other "tangible" factors may be equal. Pp. 493–494.

(e) The "separate but equal" doctrine adopted in Plessy v. Ferguson, 163 U.S. 537 , has no place in the field of public education. P. 495. [347 U.S. 483, 484]

(f) The cases are restored to the docket for further argument on specified questions relating to the forms of the decrees. Pp. 495–496.

Robert L. Carter argued the cause for appellants in No. 1 on the original argument and on the reargument. Thurgood Marshall argued the cause for appellants in No. 2 on the original argument and Spottswood W. Robinson, III, for appellants in

---

*Together with No. 2, Briggs et al. v. Elliott et al., on appeal from the United States District Court for the Eastern District of South Carolina, argued December 9-10, 1952, reargued December 7-8, 1953; No. 4, Davis et al. v. County School Board of Prince Edward County, Virginia, et al., on appeal from the United States District Court for the Eastern District of Virginia, argued December 10, 1952, reargued December 7-8, 1953; and No. 10, Gebhart et al. v. Belton et al., on certiorari to the Supreme Court of Delaware, argued December 11, 1952, reargued December 9, 1953.

No. 4 on the original argument, and both argued the causes for appellants in Nos. 2 and 4 on the reargument. Louis L. Redding and Jack Greenberg argued the cause for respondents in No. 10 on the original argument and Jack Greenberg and Thurgood Marshall on the reargument.

On the briefs were Robert L. Carter, Thurgood Marshall, Spottswood W. Robinson, III, Louis L. Redding, Jack Greenberg, George E. C. Hayes, William R. Ming, Jr., Constance Baker Motley, James M. Nabrit, Jr., Charles S. Scott, Frank D. Reeves, Harold R. Boulware and Oliver W. Hill for appellants in Nos. 1, 2 and 4 and respondents in No. 10; George M. Johnson for appellants in Nos. 1, 2 and 4; and Loren Miller for appellants in Nos. 2 and 4. Arthur D. Shores and A. T. Walden were on the Statement as to Jurisdiction and a brief opposing a Motion to Dismiss or Affirm in No. 2. Paul E. Wilson, Assistant Attorney General of Kansas, argued the cause for appellees in No. 1 on the original argument and on the reargument. With him on the briefs was Harold R. Fatzer, Attorney General.

John W. Davis argued the cause for appellees in No. 2 on the original argument and for appellees in Nos. 2 and 4 on the reargument. With him on the briefs in No. 2 were T. C. Callison, Attorney General of South Carolina, Robert McC. Figg, Jr., S. E. Rogers, William R. Meagher and Taggart Whipple. [347 U.S. 483, 485]

J. Lindsay Almond, Jr., Attorney General of Virginia, and T. Justin Moore argued the cause for appellees in No. 4 on the original argument and for appellees in Nos. 2 and 4 on the reargument. On the briefs in No. 4 were J. Lindsay Almond, Jr., Attorney General, and Henry T. Wickham, Special Assistant Attorney General, for the State of Virginia, and T. Justin Moore, Archibald G. Robertson, John W. Riely and T. Justin Moore, Jr. for the Prince Edward County School Authorities, appellees.

H. Albert Young, Attorney General of Delaware, argued the cause for petitioners in No. 10 on the original argument and on the reargument. With him on the briefs was Louis J. Finger, Special Deputy Attorney General.

By special leave of Court, Assistant Attorney General Rankin argued the cause for the United States on the reargument, as amicus curiae, urging reversal in Nos. 1, 2 and 4 and affirmance in No. 10. With him on the brief were Attorney General Brownell, Philip Elman, Leon Ulman, William J. Lamont and M. Magdelena Schoch. James P. McGranery, then Attorney General, and Philip Elman filed a brief for the United States on the original argument, as amicus curiae, urging reversal in Nos. 1, 2 and 4 and affirmance in No. 10.

Briefs of amici curiae supporting appellants in No. 1 were filed by Shad Polier, Will Maslow and Joseph B. Robison for the American Jewish Congress; by Edwin J. Lukas, Arnold Forster, Arthur Garfield Hays, Frank E. Karelsen, Leonard Haas, Saburo Kido and Theodore Leskes for the American Civil Liberties Union et al.; and by John Ligtenberg and Selma M. Borchardt for the American Federation of Teachers. Briefs of amici curiae supporting appellants in No. 1 and respondents in No. 10 were filed by Arthur J. Goldberg and Thomas E. Harris [347 U.S. 483, 486] for the Congress of Industrial Organizations and by Phineas Indritz for the American Veterans Committee, Inc.

MR. CHIEF JUSTICE WARREN delivered the opinion of the Court.

These cases come to us from the States of Kansas, South Carolina, Virginia, and Delaware. They are premised on different facts and different local conditions, but a common legal question justifies their consideration together in this consolidated opinion.[1] [347 U.S. 483, 487]

In each of the cases, minors of the Negro race, through their legal representatives, seek the aid of the courts in obtaining admission to the public schools of their community on a nonsegregated basis. In each instance, [347 U.S. 483, 488] they had been denied admission to schools attended by white children under laws requiring or

---

[1]In the Kansas case, Brown v. Board of Education, the plaintiffs are Negro children of elementary school age residing in Topeka. They brought this action in the United States District Court for the District of Kansas to enjoin enforcement of a Kansas statute which permits, but does not require, cities of more than 15,000 population to maintain separate school facilities for Negro and white students. Kan. Gen. Stat. 72-1724 (1949). Pursuant to that authority, the Topeka Board of Education elected to establish segregated elementary schools. Other public schools in the community, however, are operated on a nonsegregated basis. The three-judge District Court, convened under 28 U.S.C. 2281 and 2284, found that segregation in public education has a detrimental effect upon Negro children, but denied relief on the ground that the Negro and white schools were substantially equal with respect to buildings, transportation, curricula, and educational qualifications of teachers. 98 F. Supp. 797. The case is here on direct appeal under 28 U.S.C. 1253. In the South Carolina case, Briggs v. Elliott, the plaintiffs are Negro children of both elementary and high school age residing in Clarendon County. They brought this action in the United States District Court for the Eastern District of South Carolina to enjoin enforcement of provisions in the state constitution and statutory code which require the segregation of Negroes and whites in public schools. S. C. Const., Art. XI, 7; S. C. Code 5377 (1942). The three-judge District Court, convened under 28 U.S.C. 2281 and 2284, denied the requested relief. The court found that the Negro schools were inferior to the white schools and ordered the defendants to begin immediately to equalize the facilities. But the court sustained the validity of the contested provisions and denied the plaintiffs admission [347 U.S. 483, 487] to the white schools during the equalization program. 98 F. Supp. 529. This Court vacated the District Court's judgment and remanded the case for the purpose of obtaining the court's views on a report filed by the defendants concerning the progress made in the equalization program. 342 U.S. 350 . On remand, the District Court found that substantial equality had been achieved except for buildings and that the defendants were proceeding to rectify this inequality as well. 103 F. Supp. 920. The case is again here on direct appeal under 28 U.S.C. 1253. In the Virginia case, Davis v. County School Board, the plaintiffs are Negro children of high school age residing in Prince Edward county. They brought this action in the United States District Court for the Eastern District of Virginia to enjoin enforcement of provisions in the state constitution and statutory code which require the segregation of Negroes and whites in public schools. Va. Const., 140; Va. Code 22-221 (1950). The three-judge District Court, convened under 28 U.S.C. 2281 and 2284, denied the requested relief. The court found the Negro school inferior in physical plant, curricula, and transportation, and ordered the defendants forthwith to provide substantially equal curricula and transportation and to "proceed with all reasonable diligence and dispatch to remove" the inequality in physical plant. But, as in the South Carolina case, the court sustained the validity of the contested provisions and denied the plaintiffs admission to the white schools during the equalization program. 103 F. Supp. 337. The case is here on direct appeal under 28 U.S.C. 1253. In the Delaware case, Gebhart v. Belton, the plaintiffs are Negro children of both elementary and high school age residing in New Castle County. They brought this action in the Delaware Court of Chancery to enjoin enforcement of provisions in the state constitution and statutory code which require the segregation of Negroes and whites in public schools. Del. Const., Art. X, 2; Del. Rev. Code 2631 (1935). The Chancellor gave judgment for the plaintiffs and ordered their immediate admission to schools previously attended only by white children, on the ground that the Negro schools were inferior with respect to teacher training, pupil-teacher ratio, extracurricular activities, physical plant, and time and distance involved [347 U.S. 483, 488] in travel. 87 A. 2d 862. The Chancellor also found that segregation itself results in an inferior education for Negro children (see note 10, infra), but did not rest his decision on that ground. Id., at 865. The Chancellor's decree was affirmed by the Supreme Court of Delaware, which intimated, however, that the defendants might be able to obtain a modification of the decree after equalization of the Negro and white schools had been accomplished. 91 A. 2d 137, 152. The defendants, contending only that the Delaware courts had erred in ordering the immediate admission of the Negro plaintiffs to the white schools, applied to this Court for certiorari. The writ was granted. The plaintiffs, who were successful below, did not submit a cross-petition.

permitting segregation according to race. This segregation was alleged to deprive the plaintiffs of the equal protection of the laws under the Fourteenth Amendment. In each of the cases other than the Delaware case, a three-judge federal district court denied relief to the plaintiffs on the so-called "separate but equal" doctrine announced by this Court in Plessy v. Ferguson, 163 U.S. 537 . Under that doctrine, equality of treatment is accorded when the races are provided substantially equal facilities, even though these facilities be separate. In the Delaware case, the Supreme Court of Delaware adhered to that doctrine, but ordered that the plaintiffs be admitted to the white schools because of their superiority to the Negro schools.

The plaintiffs contend that segregated public schools are not "equal" and cannot be made "equal," and that hence they are deprived of the equal protection of the laws. Because of the obvious importance of the question presented, the Court took jurisdiction.[2] Argument was heard in the 1952 Term, and reargument was heard this Term on certain questions propounded by the Court.[3] [347 U.S. 483, 489]

Reargument was largely devoted to the circumstances surrounding the adoption of the Fourteenth Amendment in 1868. It covered exhaustively consideration of the Amendment in Congress, ratification by the states, then existing practices in racial segregation, and the views of proponents and opponents of the Amendment. This discussion and our own investigation convince us that, although these sources cast some light, it is not enough to resolve the problem with which we are faced. At best, they are inconclusive. The most avid proponents of the post-War Amendments undoubtedly intended them to remove all legal distinctions among "all persons born or naturalized in the United States." Their opponents, just as certainly, were antagonistic to both the letter and the spirit of the Amendments and wished them to have the most limited effect. What others in Congress and the state legislatures had in mind cannot be determined with any degree of certainty.

An additional reason for the inconclusive nature of the Amendment's history, with respect to segregated schools, is the status of public education at that time.[4] In the South, the movement toward free common schools, supported [347 U.S. 483, 490] by general taxation, had not yet taken hold. Education of white children was largely in the hands of private groups. Education of Negroes was almost nonexistent,

---

[2]344 U.S. 1, 141 , 891.

[3]345 U.S. 972 . The Attorney General of the United States participated both Terms as amicus curiae.

[4]For a general study of the development of public education prior to the Amendment, see Butts and Cremin, A History of Education in American Culture (1953), Pts. I, II; Cubberley, Public Education in the United States (1934 ed.), cc. II-XII. School practices current at the time of the adoption of the Fourteenth Amendment are described in Butts and Cremin, supra, at 269-275; Cubberley, supra, at 288-339, 408-431; Knight, Public Education in the South (1922), cc. VIII, IX. See also H. Ex. Doc. No. 315, 41st Cong., 2d Sess. (1871). Although the demand for free public schools followed substantially the same pattern in both the North and the South, the development in the South did not begin to gain momentum until about 1850, some twenty years after that in the North. The reasons for the somewhat slower development in the South (e. g., the rural character of the South and the different regional attitudes toward state assistance) are well explained in Cubberley, supra, at 408-423. In the country as a whole, but particularly in the South, the War [347 U.S. 483, 490] virtually stopped all progress in public education. Id., at 427-428. The low status of Negro education in all sections of the country, both before and immediately after the War, is described in Beale, A History of Freedom of Teaching in American Schools (1941), 112-132, 175-195. Compulsory school attendance laws were not generally adopted until after the ratification of the Fourteenth Amendment, and it was not until 1918 that such laws were in force in all the states. Cubberley, supra, at 563-565.

and practically all of the race were illiterate. In fact, any education of Negroes was forbidden by law in some states. Today, in contrast, many Negroes have achieved outstanding success in the arts and sciences as well as in the business and professional world. It is true that public school education at the time of the Amendment had advanced further in the North, but the effect of the Amendment on Northern States was generally ignored in the congressional debates. Even in the North, the conditions of public education did not approximate those existing today. The curriculum was usually rudimentary; ungraded schools were common in rural areas; the school term was but three months a year in many states; and compulsory school attendance was virtually unknown. As a consequence, it is not surprising that there should be so little in the history of the Fourteenth Amendment relating to its intended effect on public education.

In the first cases in this Court construing the Fourteenth Amendment, decided shortly after its adoption, the Court interpreted it as proscribing all state-imposed discriminations against the Negro race.[5] The doctrine of [347 U.S. 483, 491] "separate but equal" did not make its appearance in this Court until 1896 in the case of Plessy v. Ferguson, supra, involving not education but transportation.[6] American courts have since labored with the doctrine for over half a century. In this Court, there have been six cases involving the "separate but equal" doctrine in the field of public education.[7] In Cumming v. County Board of Education, 175 U.S. 528 , and Gong Lum v. Rice, 275 U.S. 78 , the validity of the doctrine itself was not challenged.[8] In more recent cases, all on the graduate school [347 U.S. 483, 492] level, inequality was found in that specific benefits enjoyed by white students were denied to Negro students of the same educational qualifications. Missouri ex rel. Gaines v. Canada, 305 U.S. 337 ; Sipuel v. Oklahoma, 332 U.S. 631 ; Sweatt v. Painter, 339

---

[5]Slaughter-House Cases, 16 Wall. 36, 67-72 (1873); Strauder v. West Virginia, 100 U.S. 303, 307-308 (1880): "It ordains that no State shall deprive any person of life, liberty, or property, without due process of law, or deny to any person within its jurisdiction the equal protection of the laws. What is this but [347 U.S. 483, 491] declaring that the law in the States shall be the same for the black as for the white; that all persons, whether colored or white, shall stand equal before the laws of the States, and, in regard to the colored race, for whose protection the amendment was primarily designed, that no discrimination shall be made against them by law because of their color? The words of the amendment, it is true, are prohibitory, but they contain a necessary implication of a positive immunity, or right, most valuable to the colored race—the right to exemption from unfriendly legislation against them distinctively as colored—exemption from legal discriminations, implying inferiority in civil society, lessening the security of their enjoyment of the rights which others enjoy, and discriminations which are steps towards reducing them to the condition of a subject race." See also Virginia v. Rives, 100 U.S. 313, 318 (1880); Ex parte Virginia, 100 U.S. 339, 344-345 (1880).

[6]The doctrine apparently originated in Roberts v. City of Boston, 59 Mass. 198, 206 (1850), upholding school segregation against attack as being violative of a state constitutional guarantee of equality. Segregation in Boston public schools was eliminated in 1855. Mass. Acts 1855, c. 256. But elsewhere in the North segregation in public education has persisted in some communities until recent years. It is apparent that such segregation has long been a nationwide problem, not merely one of sectional concern.

[7]See also Berea College v. Kentucky, 211 U.S. 45 (1908).

[8]In the Cumming case, Negro taxpayers sought an injunction requiring the defendant school board to discontinue the operation of a high school for white children until the board resumed operation of a high school for Negro children. Similarly, in the Gong Lum case, the plaintiff, a child of Chinese descent, contended only that state authorities had misapplied the doctrine by classifying him with Negro children and requiring him to attend a Negro school.

U.S. 627 ; McLaurin v. Oklahoma State Regents, 339 U.S. 637 . In none of these cases was it necessary to re-examine the doctrine to grant relief to the Negro plaintiff. And in Sweatt v. Painter, supra, the Court expressly reserved decision on the question whether Plessy v. Ferguson should be held inapplicable to public education.

In the instant cases, that question is directly presented. Here, unlike Sweatt v. Painter, there are findings below that the Negro and white schools involved have been equalized, or are being equalized, with respect to buildings, curricula, qualifications and salaries of teachers, and other "tangible" factors.[9] Our decision, therefore, cannot turn on merely a comparison of these tangible factors in the Negro and white schools involved in each of the cases. We must look instead to the effect of segregation itself on public education.

In approaching this problem, we cannot turn the clock back to 1868 when the Amendment was adopted, or even to 1896 when Plessy v. Ferguson was written. We must consider public education in the light of its full development and its present place in American life throughout [347 U.S. 483, 493] the Nation. Only in this way can it be determined if segregation in public schools deprives these plaintiffs of the equal protection of the laws.

Today, education is perhaps the most important function of state and local governments. Compulsory school attendance laws and the great expenditures for education both demonstrate our recognition of the importance of education to our democratic society. It is required in the performance of our most basic public responsibilities, even service in the armed forces. It is the very foundation of good citizenship. Today it is a principal instrument in awakening the child to cultural values, in preparing him for later professional training, and in helping him to adjust normally to his environment. In these days, it is doubtful that any child may reasonably be expected to succeed in life if he is denied the opportunity of an education. Such an opportunity, where the state has undertaken to provide it, is a right which must be made available to all on equal terms.

We come then to the question presented: Does segregation of children in public schools solely on the basis of race, even though the physical facilities and other "tangible" factors may be equal, deprive the children of the minority group of equal educational opportunities? We believe that it does.

In Sweatt v. Painter, supra, in finding that a segregated law school for Negroes could not provide them equal educational opportunities, this Court relied in large part on "those qualities which are incapable of objective measurement but which make for greatness in a law school." In McLaurin v. Oklahoma State Regents, supra, the Court, in requiring that a Negro admitted to a white graduate school be treated like all other students, again resorted to intangible considerations: "... his ability to study, to engage in discussions and exchange views with other students, and, in

[9]In the Kansas case, the court below found substantial equality as to all such factors. 98 F. Supp. 797, 798. In the South Carolina case, the court below found that the defendants were proceeding "promptly and in good faith to comply with the court's decree." 103 F. Supp. 920, 921. In the Virginia case, the court below noted that the equalization program was already "afoot and progressing" (103 F. Supp. 337, 341); since then, we have been advised, in the Virginia Attorney General's brief on reargument, that the program has now been completed. In the Delaware case, the court below similarly noted that the state's equalization program was well under way. 91 A. 2d 137, 149.

general, to learn his profession." [347 U.S. 483, 494] Such considerations apply with added force to children in grade and high schools. To separate them from others of similar age and qualifications solely because of their race generates a feeling of inferiority as to their status in the community that may affect their hearts and minds in a way unlikely ever to be undone. The effect of this separation on their educational opportunities was well stated by a finding in the Kansas case by a court which nevertheless felt compelled to rule against the Negro plaintiffs:

> "Segregation of white and colored children in public schools has a detrimental effect upon the colored children. The impact is greater when it has the sanction of the law; for the policy of separating the races is usually interpreted as denoting the inferiority of the negro group. A sense of inferiority affects the motivation of a child to learn. Segregation with the sanction of law, therefore, has a tendency to [retard] the educational and mental development of negro children and to deprive them of some of the benefits they would receive in a racial[ly] integrated school system"[10]

Whatever may have been the extent of psychological knowledge at the time of Plessy v. Ferguson, this finding is amply supported by modern authority.[11] Any language [347 U.S. 483, 495] in Plessy v. Ferguson contrary to this finding is rejected.

We conclude that in the field of public education the doctrine of "separate but equal" has no place. Separate educational facilities are inherently unequal. Therefore, we hold that the plaintiffs and others similarly situated for whom the actions have been brought are, by reason of the segregation complained of, deprived of the equal protection of the laws guaranteed by the Fourteenth Amendment. This disposition makes unnecessary any discussion whether such segregation also violates the Due Process Clause of the Fourteenth Amendment.[12]

Because these are class actions, because of the wide applicability of this decision, and because of the great variety of local conditions, the formulation of decrees in these cases presents problems of considerable complexity. On reargument, the consideration of appropriate relief was necessarily subordinated to the primary question—the constitutionality of segregation in public education. We have now announced that such segregation is a denial of the equal protection of the laws. In order that we may have the full assistance of the parties in formulating decrees, the cases will be restored to the docket, and the parties are requested to present further argument on Questions 4 and

---

[10]A similar finding was made in the Delaware case: "I conclude from the testimony that in our Delaware society, State-imposed segregation in education itself results in the Negro children, as a class, receiving educational opportunities which are substantially inferior to those available to white children otherwise similarly situated." 87 A. 2d 862, 865.

[11]K. B. Clark, Effect of Prejudice and Discrimination on Personality Development (Midcentury White House Conference on Children and Youth, 1950); Witmer and Kotinsky, Personality in the Making (1952), c. VI; Deutscher and Chein, The Psychological Effects of Enforced Segregation: A Survey of Social Science Opinion, 26 J. Psychol. 259 (1948); Chein, What are the Psychological Effects of [347 U.S. 483, 495] Segregation Under Conditions of Equal Facilities?, 3 Int. J. Opinion and Attitude Res. 229 (1949); Brameld, Educational Costs, in Discrimination and National Welfare (MacIver, ed., (1949), 44-48; Frazier, The Negro in the United States (1949), 674-681. And see generally Myrdal, An American Dilemma (1944).

[12]See Bolling v. Sharpe, post, p. 497, concerning the Due Process Clause of the Fifth Amendment.

5 previously propounded by the Court for the reargument this Term.[13] The Attorney General [347 U.S. 483, 496] of the United States is again invited to participate. The Attorneys General of the states requiring or permitting segregation in public education will also be permitted to appear as amici curiae upon request to do so by September 15, 1954, and submission of briefs by October 1, 1954.[14]

It is so ordered.

DWIGHT D. EISENHOWER **80**

Farewell Address, 1961

President Dwight D. Eisenhower, a popular president and formerly the Allied Supreme Commander during World War II, had faced many challenges in his life. In this speech delivered on January 17, 1961, just before he left the presidency, he recounted the successes of his eight years as president, thanked the nation for the honor of the presidency, and left with a few warnings about the future. The threat from communism and totalitarianism from beyond America's shores was clear, but threats to America's freedom, Eisenhower believed, existed in the United States—not from subversion but from inaction. Most memorable from this address, he warned of the buildup of an elite which he referred to as the "military-industrial complex." Scientific knowledge was in danger of outpacing human morality and wisdom, particularly in the field of nuclear weapons, which could destroy American freedom in a panicked defense of security or destroy civilization in an ill-advised war.

My fellow Americans:

Three days from now, after half a century in the service of our country, I shall lay down the responsibilities of office as, in traditional and solemn ceremony, the authority of the Presidency is vested in my successor.

[13]"4. Assuming it is decided that segregation in public schools violates the Fourteenth Amendment "(a) would a decree necessarily follow providing that, within the [347 U.S. 483, 496] limits set by normal geographic school districting, Negro children should forthwith be admitted to schools of their choice, or "(b) may this Court, in the exercise of its equity powers, permit an effective gradual adjustment to be brought about from existing segregated systems to a system not based on color distinctions? "5. On the assumption on which questions 4 (a) and (b) are based, and assuming further that this Court will exercise its equity powers to the end described in question 4 (b), "(a) should this Court formulate detailed decrees in these cases; "(b) if so, what specific issues should the decrees reach; "(c) should this Court appoint a special master to hear evidence with a view to recommending specific terms for such decrees; "(d) should this Court remand to the courts of first instance with directions to frame decrees in these cases, and if so what general directions should the decrees of this Court include and what procedures should the courts of first instance follow in arriving at the specific terms of more detailed decrees?"

[14]See Rule 42, Revised Rules of this Court (effective July 1, 1954). [347 U.S. 483, 497]

Farewell Address, 1961, http://www.ourdocuments.gov/doc.php?flash=true&doc=90

This evening I come to you with a message of leave-taking and farewell, and to share a few final thoughts with you, my countrymen.

Like every other citizen, I wish the new President, and all who will labor with him, Godspeed. I pray that the coming years will be blessed with peace and prosperity for all.

Our people expect their President and the Congress to find essential agreement on issues of great moment, the wise resolution of which will better shape the future of the Nation.

My own relations with the Congress, which began on a remote and tenuous basis when, long ago, a member of the Senate appointed me to West Point, have since ranged to the intimate during the war and immediate post-war period, and, finally, to the mutually interdependent during these past eight years.

In this final relationship, the Congress and the Administration have, on most vital issues, cooperated well, to serve the national good rather than mere partisanship, and so have assured that the business of the Nation should go forward. So, my official relationship with the Congress ends in a feeling, on my part, of gratitude that we have been able to do so much together.

II

We now stand ten years past the midpoint of a century that has witnessed four major wars among great nations. Three of these involved our own country. Despite these holocausts America is today the strongest, the most influential and most productive nation in the world. Understandably proud of this pre-eminence, we yet realize that America's leadership and prestige depend, not merely upon our unmatched material progress, riches and military strength, but on how we use our power in the interests of world peace and human betterment.

III

Throughout America's adventure in free government, our basic purposes have been to keep the peace; to foster progress in human achievement, and to enhance liberty, dignity and integrity among people and among nations. To strive for less would be unworthy of a free and religious people. Any failure traceable to arrogance, or our lack of comprehension or readiness to sacrifice would inflict upon us grievous hurt both at home and abroad.

Progress toward these noble goals is persistently threatened by the conflict now engulfing the world. It commands our whole attention, absorbs our very beings. We face a hostile ideology-global in scope, atheistic in character, ruthless in purpose, and insidious in method. Unhappily the danger it poses promises to be of indefinite duration. To meet it successfully, there is called for, not so much the emotional and transitory sacrifices of crisis, but rather those which enable us to carry forward steadily, surely, and without complaint the burdens of a prolonged and complex struggle-with liberty at stake. Only thus shall we remain, despite every provocation, on our charted course toward permanent peace and human betterment.

Crises there will continue to be. In meeting them, whether foreign or domestic, great or small, there is a recurring temptation to feel that some spectacular and costly action could become the miraculous solution to all current difficulties. A huge increase in newer elements of our defense; development of unrealistic programs to cure every ill in agriculture; a dramatic expansion in basic and applied research—these and many other possibilities, each possibly promising in itself, may be suggested as the only way to the road we wish to travel.

But each proposal must be weighed in the light of a broader consideration: the need to maintain balance in and among national programs-balance between the private and the public economy, balance between cost and hoped for advantage-balance between the clearly necessary and the comfortably desirable; balance between our essential requirements as a nation and the duties imposed by the nation upon the individual; balance between action of the moment and the national welfare of the future. Good judgment seeks balance and progress; lack of it eventually finds imbalance and frustration.

The record of many decades stands as proof that our people and their government have, in the main, understood these truths and have responded to them well, in the face of stress and threat. But threats, new in kind or degree, constantly arise. I mention two only.

IV

A vital element in keeping the peace is our military establishment. Our arms must be mighty, ready for instant action, so that no potential aggressor may be tempted to risk his own destruction.

Our military organization today bears little relation to that known by any of my predecessors in peace time, or indeed by the fighting men of World War II or Korea. Until the latest of our world conflicts, the United States had no armaments industry. American makers of plowshares could, with time and as required, make swords as well. But now we can no longer risk emergency improvisation of national defense; we have been compelled to create a permanent armaments industry of vast proportions. Added to this, three and a half million men and women are directly engaged in the defense establishment. We annually spend on military security more than the net income of all United States corporations.

This conjunction of an immense military establishment and a large arms industry is new in the American experience. The total influence-economic, political, even spiritual—is felt in every city, every state house, every office of the Federal government. We recognize the imperative need for this development. Yet we must not fail to comprehend its grave implications. Our toil, resources and livelihood are all involved; so is the very structure of our society.

In the councils of government, we must guard against the acquisition of unwarranted influence, whether sought or unsought, by the military-industrial complex. The potential for the disastrous rise of misplaced power exists and will persist.

We must never let the weight of this combination endanger our liberties or democratic processes. We should take nothing for granted only an alert and knowledgeable citizenry can compel the proper meshing of huge industrial and military machinery of defense with our peaceful methods and goals, so that security and liberty may prosper together.

Akin to, and largely responsible for the sweeping changes in our industrial-military posture, has been the technological revolution during recent decades.

In this revolution, research has become central; it also becomes more formalized, complex, and costly. A steadily increasing share is conducted for, by, or at the direction of, the Federal government.

Today, the solitary inventor, tinkering in his shop, has been over shadowed by task forces of scientists in laboratories and testing fields. In the same fashion, the free university, historically the fountainhead of free ideas and scientific discovery, has experienced a revolution in the conduct of research. Partly because of the huge costs involved, a government contract becomes virtually a substitute for intellectual curiosity. For every old blackboard there are now hundreds of new electronic computers.

The prospect of domination of the nation's scholars by Federal employment, project allocations, and the power of money is ever present and is gravely to be regarded. Yet, in holding scientific research and discovery in respect, as we should, we must also be alert to the equal and opposite danger that public policy could itself become the captive of a scientific-technological elite.

It is the task of statesmanship to mold, to balance, and to integrate these and other forces, new and old, within the principles of our democratic system-ever aiming toward the supreme goals of our free society.

V

Another factor in maintaining balance involves the element of time. As we peer into society's future, we-you and I, and our government-must avoid the impulse to live only for today, plundering, for our own ease and convenience, the precious resources of tomorrow. We cannot mortgage the material assets of our grandchildren without risking the loss also of their political and spiritual heritage. We want democracy to survive for all generations to come, not to become the insolvent phantom of tomorrow.

VI

Down the long lane of the history yet to be written America knows that this world of ours, ever growing smaller, must avoid becoming a community of dreadful fear and hate, and be, instead, a proud confederation of mutual trust and respect.

Such a confederation must be one of equals. The weakest must come to the conference table with the same confidence as do we, protected as we are by our moral, economic, and military strength. That table, though scarred by many past frustrations, cannot be abandoned for the certain agony of the battlefield.

Disarmament, with mutual honor and confidence, is a continuing imperative. Together we must learn how to compose differences, not with arms, but with intellect and decent purpose. Because this need is so sharp and apparent I confess that I lay down my official responsibilities in this field with a definite sense of disappointment. As one who has witnessed the horror and the lingering sadness of war-as one who knows that another war could utterly destroy this civilization which has been so slowly and painfully built over thousands of years-I wish I could say tonight that a lasting peace is in sight.

Happily, I can say that war has been avoided. Steady progress toward our ultimate goal has been made. But, so much remains to be done. As a private citizen, I shall never cease to do what little I can to help the world advance along that road.

VII

So—in this my last good night to you as your President—I thank you for the many opportunities you have given me for public service in war and peace. I trust that in that service you find somethings worthy; as for the rest of it, I know you will find ways to improve performance in the future.

You and I—my fellow citizens—need to be strong in our faith that all nations, under God, will reach the goal of peace with justice. May we be ever unswerving in devotion to principle, confident but humble with power, diligent in pursuit of the Nation's great goals.

To all the peoples of the world, I once more give expression to America's prayerful and continuing inspiration:

We pray that peoples of all faiths, all races, all nations, may have their great human needs satisfied; that those now denied opportunity shall come to enjoy it to the full; that all who yearn for freedom may experience its spiritual blessings; that those who have freedom will understand, also, its heavy responsibilities; that all who are insensitive to the needs of others will learn charity; that the scourges of poverty, disease and ignorance will be made to disappear from the earth, and that, in the goodness of time, all peoples will come to live together in a peace guaranteed by the binding force of mutual respect and love.

JOHN F. KENNEDY **81**

Inaugural Address, 1961

On January 20, 1961, John F. Kennedy took the oath of office and assumed the presidency. As he assumed office, the United States and the Soviet Union remained bitter rivals and teetered on the brink of war. Kennedy foresaw his administration as an instrument to protect freedom against oppression around the world. For this, he declared, free men must be willing to act for the cause of liberty. Liberty was a natural right, but it could be taken away by the force of arms as had occurred in eastern Europe. In a memorable line, he called on Americans to rally to the cause of building a better nation and a freer world, to "ask not what your country can do for you—ask what you can do for your country."

Vice President Johnson, Mr. Speaker, Mr. Chief Justice, President Eisenhower, Vice President Nixon, President Truman, Reverend Clergy, fellow citizens:

We observe today not a victory of party but a celebration of freedom—symbolizing an end as well as a beginning—signifying renewal as well as change. For I have sworn

John F. Kennedy, *JFK: In His Own Words,* Maureen Harrison and Steve Gilbert, eds. (New York: Barnes and Noble Books, 1993): 17–21 before you and Almighty God the same solemn oath our forebears prescribed nearly a century and three-quarters ago.

The world is very different now. For man holds in his mortal hands the power to abolish all forms of human poverty and all forms of human life. And yet the same revolutionary beliefs for which our forebears fought are still at issue around the globe—the belief that the rights of man come not from the generosity of the state but from the hand of God.

We dare not forget today that we are the heirs of that first revolution. Let the word go forth from this time and place, to friend and foe alike, that the torch has been passed to a new generation of Americans—born in this century, tempered by war, disciplined by a hard and bitter peace, proud of our ancient heritage—and unwilling to witness or permit the slow undoing of those human rights to which this nation has always been committed, and to which we are committed today at home and around the world.

Let every nation know, whether it wishes us well or ill, that we shall pay any price, bear any burden, meet any hardship, support any friend, oppose any foe to assure the survival and the success of liberty.

This much we pledge—and more.

To those old allies whose cultural and spiritual origins we share, we pledge the loyalty of faithful friends. United there is little we cannot do in a host of cooperative ventures. Divided there is little we can do—for we dare not meet a powerful challenge at odds and split asunder.

To those new states whom we welcome to the ranks of the free, we pledge our word that one form of colonial control shall not have passed away merely to be replaced by a far more iron tyranny. We shall not always expect to find them supporting our view. But we shall always hope to find them strongly supporting their own freedom—and to remember that, in the past, those who foolishly sought power by riding the back of the tiger ended up inside.

To those people in the huts and villages of half the globe struggling to break the bonds of mass misery, we pledge our best efforts to help them help themselves, for whatever period is required—not because the communists may be doing it, not because we seek their votes, but because it is right. If a free society cannot help the many who are poor, it cannot save the few who are rich.

To our sister republics south of our border, we offer a special pledge—to convert our good words into good deeds—in a new alliance for progress—to assist free men and free governments in casting off the chains of poverty. But this peaceful revolution of hope cannot become the prey of hostile powers. Let all our neighbors know that we shall join with them to oppose aggression or subversion anywhere in the Americas. And let every other power know that this Hemisphere intends to remain the master of its own house.

To that world assembly of sovereign states, the United Nations, our last best hope in an age where the instruments of war have far outpaced the instruments of peace, we renew our pledge of support—to prevent it from becoming merely a forum for invective—to strengthen its shield of the new and the weak—and to enlarge the area in which its writ may run.

Finally, to those nations who would make themselves our adversary, we offer not a pledge but a request: that both sides begin anew the quest for peace, before the dark powers of destruction unleashed by science engulf all humanity in planned or accidental self-destruction.

We dare not tempt them with weakness. For only when our arms are sufficient beyond doubt can we be certain beyond doubt that they will never be employed.

But neither can two great and powerful groups of nations take comfort from our present course—both sides overburdened by the cost of modern weapons, both rightly alarmed by the steady spread of the deadly atom, yet both racing to alter that uncertain balance of terror that stays the hand of mankind's final war.

So let us begin anew—remembering on both sides that civility is not a sign of weakness, and sincerity is always subject to proof. Let us never negotiate out of fear. But let us never fear to negotiate.

Let both sides explore what problems unite us instead of belaboring those problems which divide us.

Let both sides, for the first time, formulate serious and precise proposals for the inspection and control of arms—and bring the absolute power to destroy other nations under the absolute control of all nations.

Let both sides seek to invoke the wonders of science instead of its terrors. Together let us explore the stars, conquer the deserts, eradicate disease, tap the ocean depths and encourage the arts and commerce.

Let both sides unite to heed in all corners of the earth the command of Isaiah— to "undo the heavy burdens... (and) let the oppressed go free."

And if a beachhead of cooperation may push back the jungle of suspicion, let both sides join in creating a new endeavor, not a new balance of power, but a new world of law, where the strong are just and the weak secure and the peace preserved.

All this will not be finished in the first one hundred days. Nor will it be finished in the first one thousand days, nor in the life of this Administration, nor even perhaps in our lifetime on this planet. But let us begin.

In your hands, my fellow citizens, more than mine, will rest the final success or failure of our course. Since this country was founded, each generation of Americans has been summoned to give testimony to its national loyalty. The graves of young Americans who answered the call to service surround the globe.

Now the trumpet summons us again—not as a call to bear arms, though arms we need—not as a call to battle, though embattled we are—but a call to bear the burden of a long twilight struggle, year in and year out, "rejoicing in hope, patient in tribulation"—a struggle against the common enemies of man: tyranny, poverty, disease and war itself.

Can we forge against these enemies a grand and global alliance, North and South, East and West, that can assure a more fruitful life for all mankind? Will you join in that historic effort?

In the long history of the world, only a few generations have been granted the role of defending freedom in its hour of maximum danger. I do not shrink from this responsibility—I welcome it. I do not believe that any of us would exchange places with any other people or any other generation. The energy, the faith, the devotion which we bring to this endeavor will light our country and all who serve it—and the glow from that fire can truly light the world.

And so, my fellow Americans: ask not what your country can do for you—ask what you can do for your country.

My fellow citizens of the world: ask not what America will do for you, but what together we can do for the freedom of man.

Finally, whether you are citizens of America or citizens of the world, ask of us here the same high standards of strength and sacrifice which we ask of you. With a good conscience our only sure reward, with history the final judge of our deeds, let us go forth to lead the land we love, asking His blessing and His help, but knowing that here on earth God's work must truly be our own.

MARTIN LUTHER KING, JR. **82**

Letter from Birmingham Jail, 1963

Dr. Martin Luther King, Jr. wrote this letter as he sat in an Alabama jail in 1963 for participating in protests against the Jim Crow system that relegated African-Americans and minorities to second-class citizens. He wrote this letter in response to a number of critics in the African-American community who feared that the protests that King was invited to lead would spark violent repercussions for African-Americans in Birmingham. King was not allowed access to any paper, so he wrote this dramatic statement on scraps of newspaper in the jail and had them smuggled out and reassembled for public display. In this letter, King describes the reality of life for minorities in the United States in 1963 and why he had to act. In a land of freedom, the state could not demand that honest, law-abiding citizens be mandated to have fewer freedoms than others simply because of skin color. Justice and equality of all before the law was King's motivation and his passion as he led the civil rights movement until his murder in 1968.

April 16, 1963

MY DEAR FELLOW CLERGYMEN:

While confined here in the Birmingham City Jail, I came across your recent statement calling our present activities "unwise and untimely." Seldom, if ever, do I pause to answer criticism of my work and ideas. If I sought to answer all the criticisms that cross my desk, my secretaries would be engaged in little else in the course of the day, and I would have no time for constructive work. But since I feel that you are men of genuine goodwill and your criticisms are sincerely set forth, I would like to answer your statement in what I hope will be patient and reasonable terms.

I think I should give the reason for my being in Birmingham, since you have been influenced by the argument of "outsiders coming in." I have the honor of serving as president of the Southern Christian Leadership

Martin Luther King, Jr. "Letter From Birmingham Jail," *Why We Can't Wait* (New York: Signet, 1963): 64–84

Conference, an organization operating in every Southern state, with headquarters in Atlanta, Georgia. We have some eighty-five affiliate organizations all across the South—one being the Alabama Christian Movement for Human Rights. Whenever necessary and possible we share staff, educational and financial resources with our affiliates. Several months ago our local affiliate here in Birmingham invited us to be on call to engage in a nonviolent direct action program if such were deemed necessary. We readily consented and when the hour came we lived up to our promises. So I am here, along with several members of my staff, because I have basic organizational ties here.

Beyond this, I am in Birmingham because injustice is here. Just as the eighth century prophets left their little villages and carried their "thus saith the Lord" far beyond the boundaries of their home towns; and just as the Apostle Paul left his little village of Tarsus and carried the gospel of Jesus Christ to practically every hamlet and city of the Graeco-Roman world, I too am compelled to carry the gospel of freedom beyond my particular home town. Like Paul, I must constantly respond to the Macedonian call for aid.

Moreover, I am cognizant of the interrelatedness of all communities and states. I cannot sit idly by in Atlanta and not be concerned about what happens in Birmingham. Injustice anywhere is a threat to justice every-where. We are caught in an inescapable network of mutuality, tied in a single garment of destiny. Whatever affects one directly affects all indi-rectly. Never again can we afford to live with the narrow, provincial "outside agitator" idea. Anyone who lives inside the United States can never be considered an outsider anywhere in this country.

You deplore the demonstrations that are presently taking place in Birmingham. But I am sorry that your statement did not express a similar concern for the conditions that brought the demonstrations into being. I am sure that each of you would want to go beyond the superficial social analyst who looks merely at effects, and does not grapple with underlying causes. I would not hesitate to say that it is unfortunate that so-called demonstra-tions are taking place in Birmingham at this time, but I would say in more emphatic terms that it is even more unfortunate that the white power structure of this city left the Negro community with no other alternative.

In any nonviolent campaign there are four basic steps: 1) Collection of the facts to determine whether injustices are alive. 2) Negotiation. 3) Self-purification and 4) Direct action. We have gone through all of these steps in Birmingham. There can be no gainsaying of the fact that racial injustice engulfs this community.

Birmingham is probably the most thoroughly segregated city in the United States. Its ugly record of police brutality is known in every section of this country. Its unjust treatment of Negroes in the courts is a notorious reality. There have been more unsolved bombings of Negro homes and churches in Birmingham than any city in this nation. These are the hard, brutal and unbelievable facts. On the basis of these conditions, Negro leaders sought to negotiate with the city fathers. But the political leaders consistently refused to engage in good faith negotiation.

Then came the opportunity last September to talk with some of the leaders of the economic community. In these negotiating sessions certain promises were made by the merchants—such as the promise to remove the humiliating racial signs from the stores. On the basis of these promises Rev. Shuttlesworth and the leaders of the Alabama Christian Movement for Human Rights agreed to call a moratorium on any type of demonstrations. As the weeks and months unfolded we realized that we were the victims of a broken promise. The signs remained. Like so many experiences of the past we were confronted with blasted hopes, and the dark shadow of a deep disappointment settled upon us. So we had no alternative except that of preparing for direct action, whereby we would present our very bodies as a means of laying our case before the conscience of the local and national community. We were not unmindful of the difficulties involved. So we decided to go through a process of self-purification. We started having workshops on nonviolence and repeatedly asked ourselves the questions: "Are you able to accept blows without retaliating?" "Are you able to endure the ordeals of jail?" We decided to set our direct-action program around the Easter season, realizing that with the exception of Christmas, this was the largest shopping period of the year. Knowing that a strong economic withdrawal program would be the by-product of direct action, we felt that this was the best time to bring pressure on the merchants for the needed changes. Then it occurred to us that the March election was ahead and so we speedily decided to postpone action until after election day. When we discovered that Mr. Connor was in the run-off, we decided again to postpone action so that the demonstrations could not be used to cloud the issues. At this time we agreed to begin our nonviolent witness the day after the run-off.

This reveals that we did not move irresponsibly into direct action. We too wanted to see Mr. Connor defeated; so we went through postponement after postponement to aid in this community need. After this we felt that direct action could be delayed no longer.

You may well ask: "Why direct action? Why sit-ins, marches, etc.? Isn't negotiation a better path?" You are exactly right in your call for negotiation. Indeed, this is the purpose of direct action. Nonviolent direct action seeks to create such a crisis and establish such creative tension that a community that has constantly refused to negotiate is forced to confront the issue. It seeks so to dramatize the issue that it can no longer be ignored. I just referred to the creation of tension as a part of the work of the nonviolent resister. This may sound rather shocking. But I must confess that I am not afraid of the word tension. I have earnestly worked and preached against violent tension, but there is a type of constructive nonviolent tension that is necessary for growth. Just as Socrates felt that it was necessary to create a tension in the mind so that individuals could rise from the bondage of myths and half-truths to the unfettered realm of creative analysis and objective appraisal, we must see the need of having nonviolent gadflies to create the kind of tension in society that will help men to rise from the dark depths of prejudice and racism to the majestic heights of understanding and brotherhood. So the purpose of the direct action is to create a situation so crisis-packed that it will inevitably open the door to negotiation. We, therefore, concur with you in your call for negotiation. Too long has our beloved Southland been bogged down in the tragic attempt to live in monologue rather than dialogue.

One of the basic points in your statement is that our acts are untimely. Some have asked, "Why didn't you give the new administration time to act?" The only answer that I can give to this inquiry is that the new Birmingham administration must be prodded about as much as the outgoing one before it acts. We will be sadly mistaken if we feel that the election of Mr. Boutwell will bring the millennium to Birmingham. While Mr. Boutwell is much more articulate and gentle than Mr. Connor, they are both segregationists, dedicated to the task of maintaining the status quo. The hope I see in Mr. Boutwell is that he will be reasonable enough to see the futility of massive resistance to desegregation. But he will not see this without pressure from the devotees of civil rights. My friends, I must say to you that we have not made a single gain in civil rights without determined legal and nonviolent pressure. History is the long and tragic story of the fact that privileged groups seldom give up their privileges voluntarily. Individuals may see the moral light and voluntarily give up their unjust posture; but as Reinhold Niebuhr has reminded us, groups are more immoral than individuals.

We know through painful experience that freedom is never voluntarily given by the oppressor; it must be demanded by the oppressed. Frankly, I have never yet engaged in a direct action movement that was "well timed," according to the timetable of those who have not suffered unduly from the disease of segregation. For years now I have heard the words [sic] "Wait!" It rings in the ear of every Negro with a piercing familiarity. This "Wait" has almost always meant "Never." We must come to see with the distinguished jurist of yesterday that "justice too long delayed is justice denied."

We have waited for more than three hundred and forty years for our constitutional and God-given rights. The nations of Asia and Africa are moving with jet-like speed toward the goal of political independence, and we still creep at horse and buggy pace toward the gaining of a cup of coffee at a lunch counter. I guess it is easy for those who have never felt the stinging darts of segregation to say, "Wait." But when you have seen vicious mobs lynch your mothers and fathers at will and drown your sisters and brothers at whim; when you have seen hate filled policemen curse, kick, brutalize and even kill your black brothers and sisters with impunity; when you see the vast majority of your twenty million Negro brothers smothering in an airtight cage of poverty in the midst of an affluent society; when you suddenly find your tongue twisted and your speech stammering as you seek to explain to your six-year-old daughter why she can't go to the public amusement park that has just been advertised on television, and see tears welling up in her eyes when she is told that Funtown is closed to colored children, and see the depressing clouds of inferiority begin to form in her little mental sky, and see her begin to distort her little personality by unconsciously developing a bitterness toward white people; when you have to concoct an answer for a five-year-old son asking in agonizing pathos: "Daddy, why do white people treat colored people so mean?"; when you take a cross-country drive and find it necessary to sleep night after night in the uncomfortable corners of your automobile because no motel will accept you; when you are humiliated day in and day out by nagging signs reading "white" and "colored"; when your first name becomes "nigger," your middle name becomes "boy" (however old you are) and your last name becomes "John," and your wife and mother are never given the respected title "Mrs."; when you are harried by day and haunted by night by the fact that you are a Negro, living constantly at tip-toe stance never quite knowing what to expect next, and plagued with inner fears and outer resentments; when you are forever fighting a degenerating sense of "nobodiness"; then you will understand why we find it difficult to wait. There comes a time when the cup of endurance runs over, and men are no longer willing to be plunged into an abyss of despair. I hope, sirs, you can understand our legitimate and unavoidable impatience.

You express a great deal of anxiety over our willingness to break laws. This is certainly a legitimate concern. Since we so diligently urge people to obey the Supreme Court's decision of 1954 outlawing segregation in the public schools, it is rather strange and paradoxical to find us consciously breaking laws. One may well ask: "How can you advocate breaking some laws and obeying others?" The answer is found in the fact that there are two types of laws: There are *just* and there are *unjust* laws. I would agree with Saint Augustine that "An unjust law is no law at all."

Now, what is the difference between the two? How does one determine when a law is just or unjust? A just law is a man-made code that squares with the moral law or the law of God. An unjust law is a code that is out of harmony with the moral law. To put it in the terms of Saint Thomas Aquinas, an unjust law is a human law that is not rooted in eternal and natural law. Any law that uplifts human personality is just. Any law that degrades human personality is unjust. All segregation statutes are unjust because segregation distorts the soul and damages the personality. It gives the segregator a false sense of superiority, and the segregated a false sense of inferiority. To use the words of Martin Buber, the Jewish philosopher, segregation substitutes and "I-it" relationship for an "I-thou" relationship, and ends up relegating persons to the status of things. So segregation is not only politically, economically and sociologically unsound, but it is morally wrong and sinful. Paul Tillich has said that sin is separation. Isn't segregation an existential expression of man's tragic separation, an expression of his awful estrangement, his terrible sinfulness? So I can urge men to disobey segregation ordinances because they are morally wrong.

Let us turn to a more concrete example of just and unjust laws. An unjust law is a code that a majority inflicts on a minority that is not binding on itself. This is difference made legal. On the other hand a just law is a code that a majority compels a minority to follow that it is willing to follow itself. This is sameness made legal.

Let me give another explanation. An unjust law is a code inflicted upon a minority which that minority had no part in enacting or creating because

they did not have the unhampered right to vote. Who can say that the legislature of Alabama which set up the segregation laws was democratically
elected? Throughout the state of Alabama all types of conniving methods
are used to prevent Negroes from becoming registered voters and there are
some counties without a single Negro registered to vote despite the fact
that the Negro constitutes a majority of the population. Can any law set
up in such a state be considered democratically structured?

These are just a few examples of unjust and just laws. There are some
instances when a law is just on its face and unjust in its application. For
instance, I was arrested Friday on a charge of parading without a permit.
Now there is nothing wrong with an ordinance which requires a permit for
a parade, but when the ordinance is used to preserve segregation and to
deny citizens the First-Amendment privilege of peaceful assembly and
peaceful protest, then it becomes unjust.

I hope you can see the distinction I am trying to point out. In no sense
do I advocate evading or defying the law as the rabid segregationist would
do. This would lead to anarchy. One who breaks an unjust law must do it
openly, *lovingly*, (not hatefully as the white mothers did in New Orleans
when they were seen on television screaming "nigger, nigger, nigger") and
with a willingness to accept the penalty. I submit that an individual who
breaks a law that conscience tells him is unjust, and willingly accepts the
penalty by staying in jail to arouse the conscience of the community over its
injustice, is in reality expressing the very highest respect for law.

Of course, there is nothing new about this kind of civil disobedience.
It was seen sublimely in the refusal of Shadrach, Meshach and Abednego to
obey the laws of Nebuchadnezzar because a higher moral law was involved.
It was practiced superbly by the early Christians who were willing to face
hungry lions and the excruciating pain of chopping blocks, before submitting to certain unjust laws of the Roman empire. To a degree academic
freedom is a reality today because Socrates practiced civil disobedience.

We can never forget that everything Hitler did in Germany was "legal"
and everything the Hungarian freedom fighters did in Hungary was
"illegal." It was "illegal" to aid and comfort a Jew in Hitler's Germany. But
I am sure that if I had lived in Germany during that time I would have aided
and comforted my Jewish brothers even though it was illegal. If I lived in a
Communist country today where certain principles dear to the Christian
faith are suppressed, I believe I would openly advocate disobeying these
anti-religious laws. I must make two honest confessions to you, my
Christian and Jewish brothers. First, I must confess that over the last few
years I have been gravely disappointed with the white moderate. I have
almost reached the regrettable conclusion that the Negro's great stumbling
block in the stride toward freedom is not the White Citizen's Counciler or
the Ku Klux Klanner, but the white moderate who is more devoted to
"order" than to justice; who prefers a negative peace which is the absence of
tension to a positive peace which is the presence of justice; who constantly
says "I agree with you in the goal you seek, but I can't agree with your
methods of direct action;" who paternalistically feels he can set the

timetable for another man's freedom; who lives by the myth of time and who constantly advises the Negro to wait until a "more convenient season." Shallow understanding from people of goodwill is more frustrating than absolute misunderstanding from people of ill will. Lukewarm acceptance is much more bewildering than outright rejection.

I had hoped that the white moderate would understand that law and order exist for the purpose of establishing justice, and that when they fail to do this they become dangerously structured dams that block the flow of social progress. I had hoped that the white moderate would understand that the present tension in the South is merely a necessary phase of the transition from an obnoxious negative peace, where the Negro passively accepted his unjust plight, to a substance-filled positive peace, where all men will respect the dignity and worth of human personality. Actually, we who engage in nonviolent direct action are not the creators of tension. We merely bring to the surface the hidden tension that is already alive. We bring it out in the open where it can be seen and dealt with. Like a boil that can never be cured as long as it is covered up but must be opened with all its pus-flowing ugliness to the natural medicines of air and light, injustice must likewise be exposed, with all of the tension its exposing creates, to the light of human conscience and the air of national opinion before it can be cured.

In your statement you asserted that our actions, even though peaceful, must be condemned because they precipitate violence. But can this assertion be logically made? Isn't this like condemning the robbed man because his possession of money precipitated the evil act of robbery? Isn't this like condemning Socrates because his unswerving commitment to truth and his philosophical delvings precipitated the misguided popular mind to make him drink the hemlock? Isn't this like condemning Jesus because His unique God-Consciousness and never-ceasing devotion to His will precipitated the evil act of crucifixion? We must come to see, as the federal courts have consistently affirmed, that it is immoral to urge an individual to withdraw his efforts to gain his basic constitutional rights because the quest precipitates violence. Society must protect the robbed and punish the robber.

I had also hoped that the white moderate would reject the myth of time. I received a letter this morning from a white brother in Texas which said: "All Christians know that the colored people will receive equal rights eventually, but it is possible that you are in too great of a religious hurry. It has taken Christianity almost 2000 years to accomplish what it has. The teachings of Christ take time to come to earth." All that is said here grows out of a tragic misconception of time. It is the strangely irrational notion that there is something in the very flow of time that will inevitably cure all ills. Actually time is neutral. It can be used either destructively or constructively. I am coming to feel that the people of ill-will have used time much more effectively than the people of good will. We will have to repent in this generation not merely for the vitriolic words and actions of the bad people, but for the appalling silence of the good people. We must come to see that human progress never rolls in on wheels of inevitability. It comes through the tireless efforts and persistent work of men willing to be co-workers with God, and without this hard work time itself becomes an ally of the forces of social stagnation. We must use time creatively, and forever realize that the time is always ripe to do right. Now is the time to make real the promise of democracy, and transform our pending national elegy into a creative psalm of brotherhood. Now is the time to lift our national policy from the quicksand of racial injustice to the solid rock of human dignity.

You spoke of our activity in Birmingham as extreme. At first I was rather disappointed that fellow clergymen would see my nonviolent efforts as those of the extremist. I started thinking about the fact that I stand in the middle of two opposing forces in the Negro community. One is a force of complacency made up of Negroes who, as a result of long years of oppression, have been so completely drained of self-respect and a sense of "somebodiness" that they have adjusted to segregation, and, of a few Negroes in the middle class who, because of a degree of academic and economic security, and because at points they profit by segregation, have unconsciously become insensitive to the problems of the masses. The other force is one of bitterness, and hatred comes perilously close to advocating violence. It is expressed in the various black nationalist groups that are springing up over the nation, the largest and best-known being Elijah Muhammad's Muslim movement. This movement is nourished by the contemporary frustration over the continued existence of racial discrimination. It is made up of people who have lost faith in America, who have absolutely repudiated Christianity, and who have concluded that the white man is an incurable "devil." I have tried to stand between these two forces saying that we need not follow the "do-nothingism" of the complacent or the hatred and despair of the black nationalist. There is the more excellent way of love and nonviolent protest. I'm grateful to God that, through the Negro church, the dimension of nonviolence entered our struggle. If this philosophy had not emerged, I am convinced that by now many streets of the South would be flowing with floods of blood. And I am further convinced that if our white brothers dismiss as "rabble rousers" and "outside agitators" those of us who are working through the channels of nonviolent direct action and refuse to support our nonviolent efforts, millions of Negroes, out of frustration and despair, will seek solace and security in black-nationalist ideologies, a development that will lead inevitably to a frightening racial nightmare.

Oppressed people cannot remain oppressed forever. The urge for freedom will eventually come. This is what happened to the American Negro. Something within has reminded him of his birthright of freedom; something without has reminded him that he can gain it. Consciously and unconsciously, he has been swept in by what the Germans call the *Zeitgeist*, and with his black brothers of Africa, and his brown and yellow brothers of Asia, South America and the Caribbean, he is moving with a sense of cosmic urgency toward the promised land of racial justice. Recognizing this vital urge that has engulfed the Negro community, one should readily understand public demonstrations. The Negro has many pent up resentments and latent frustrations. He has to get them out. So let him march sometime; let him have his prayer pilgrimages to the city hall; understand why he must have sit-ins and freedom rides. If his repressed emotions do not come out in these nonviolent ways, they will come out in ominous expressions of violence. This is not a threat; it is a fact of history. So I have not said to my people "get rid of your discontent." But I have tried to say that this normal and healthy discontent can be channelized through the creative outlet of nonviolent direct action. Now this approach is being dismissed as extremist. I must admit that I was initially disappointed in being so categorized.

But as I continued to think about the matter I gradually gained a bit of satisfaction from being considered an extremist. Was not Jesus an extremist for love—"Love your enemies, bless them that curse you, pray for them that despitefully use you." Was not Amos an extremist for justice—"Let justice roll down like waters and righteousness like a mighty stream." Was not Paul an extremist for the gospel of Jesus Christ—"I bear in my body the marks of the Lord Jesus." Was not Martin Luther an extremist—"Here I stand; I can do none other so help me God." Was not John Bunyan an extremist—"I will stay in jail to the end of my days before I make a butchery of my conscience." Was not Abraham Lincoln an extremist—"This nation cannot survive half slave and half free." Was not Thomas Jefferson an extremist—"We hold these truths to be self-evident, that all men are created equal." So the question is not whether we will be extremist but what kind of extremist will we be. Will we be extremists for hate or will we be extremists for love? Will we be extremists for the preservation of injustice—or will we be extremists for the cause of justice? In that dramatic scene on Calvary's hill, three men were crucified. We must not forget that all three were crucified for the same crime—the crime of extremism. Two were extremists for immorality, and thusly fell below their environment. The other, Jesus Christ, was an extremist for love, truth and goodness, and thereby rose above his environment. So, after all, maybe the South, the nation and the world are in dire need of creative extremists.

I had hoped that the white moderate would see this. Maybe I was too optimistic. Maybe I expected too much. I guess I should have realized that few members of a race that has oppressed another race can understand or appreciate the deep groans and passionate yearnings of those that have been oppressed and still fewer have the vision to see that injustice must be rooted out by strong, persistent and determined action. I am thankful, however, that some of our white brothers have grasped the meaning of this social revolution and committed themselves to it. They are still all too small in quantity, but they are big in quality. Some like Ralph McGill, Lillian Smith, Harry Golden and James Dabbs have written about our struggle in eloquent, prophetic and understanding terms. Others have marched with us down nameless streets of the South. They have languished in filthy roach-infested jails, suffering the abuse and brutality of angry policemen who see them as "dirty nigger lovers." They, unlike so many of their moderate brothers and sisters, have recognized the urgency of the moment and sensed the need for powerful "action" antidotes to combat the disease of segregation.

Let me rush on to mention my other disappointment. I have been so greatly disappointed with the white church and its leadership. Of course, there are some notable exceptions. I am not unmindful of the fact that each of you has taken some significant stands on this issue. I commend you, Rev. Stallings, for your Christian stand on this past Sunday, in welcoming Negroes to your worship service on a non-segregated basis. I commend the Catholic leaders of this state for integrating Spring Hill College several years ago.

But despite these notable exceptions I must honestly reiterate that I have been disappointed with the church. I do not say that as one of those negative critics who can always find something wrong with the church. I say it as a minister of the gospel, who loves the church; who was nurtured in its bosom; who has been sustained by its spiritual blessings and who will remain true to it as long as the cord of life shall lengthen. I had the strange feeling when I was suddenly catapulted into the leadership of the bus protest in Montgomery several years ago, that we would have the support of the white church. I felt that the white ministers, priests and rabbis of the South would be some of our strongest allies. Instead, some have been out-right opponents, refusing to understand the freedom movement and mis-representing its leaders; all too many others have been more cautious than courageous and have remained silent behind the anesthetizing security of the stained-glass windows.

In spite of my shattered dreams of the past, I came to Birmingham with the hope that the white religious leadership of this community would see the justice of our cause, and with deep moral concern, serve as the channel through which our just grievances would get to the power structure. I had hoped that each of you would understand. But again I have been disappointed. I have heard numerous religious leaders of the South call upon their worshippers to comply with a desegregation decision because it is the *law*, but I have longed to hear white ministers say, "follow this decree because integration is morally *right* and the Negro is your brother." In the midst of blatant injustices inflicted upon the Negro, I have watched white churches stand on the sideline and merely mouth pious irrelevancies and sanctimonious trivialities. In the midst of a mighty struggle to rid our nation of racial and economic injustice, I have heard so many ministers say, "Those are social issues with which the gospel has no real concern." And I have watched so many churches commit themselves to a completely other-worldly religion which made a strange distinction between body and soul, the sacred and the secular.

So here we are moving toward the exit of the twentieth century with a religious community largely adjusted to the status quo, standing as a tail-light behind other community agencies rather than a headlight leading men to higher levels of justice. I have traveled the length and breadth of Alabama, Mississippi and all the other southern states. On sweltering summer days and crisp autumn mornings I have looked at her beautiful churches with their lofty spires pointing heavenward. I have beheld the impressive outlay of her massive religious education buildings. Over and over again I have found myself asking: "What kind of people worship here? Who is their God? Where were their voices when the lips of Governor Barnett dripped with words of interposition and nullification? Where were they when Governor Wallace gave the clarion call for defiance and hatred? Where were their voices of support when tired, bruised and weary Negro men and women decided to rise from the dark dungeons of complacency to the bright hills of creative protest?"

Yes, these questions are still in my mind. In deep disappointment, I have wept over the laxity of the church. But be assured that my tears have been tears of love. There can be no deep disappointment where there is not deep love. Yes, I love the church; I love her sacred walls. How could I do otherwise? I am in the rather unique position of being the son, the grandson and the great-grandson of preachers. Yes, I see the church as the body of Christ. But, oh! How we have blemished and scarred that body through social neglect and fear of being nonconformists.

There was a time when the church was very powerful. It was during that period when the early Christians rejoiced when they were deemed worthy to suffer for what they believed. In those days the church was not merely a thermometer that recorded the ideas and principles of popular opinion; it was a thermostat that transformed the mores of society. Whenever the early Christians entered a town the power structure got disturbed and immediately sought to convict them for being "disturbers of the peace" and "outside agitators." But they went on with the conviction that they were "a colony of heaven," and had to obey God rather than man. They were small in number but big in commitment. They were too God-intoxicated to be "astronomically intimidated." They brought an end to such ancient evils as infanticide and gladiatorial contest.

Things are different now. The contemporary church is often a weak, ineffectual voice with an uncertain sound. It is so often the arch supporter of the status quo. Far from being disturbed by the presence of the church, the power structure of the average community is consoled by the church's silent and often vocal sanction of things as they are.

But the judgement of God is upon the church as never before. If the church of today does not recapture the sacrificial spirit of the early church, it will lose its authentic ring, forfeit the loyalty of millions, and be dismissed as an irrelevant social club with no meaning for the twentieth century. I am meeting young people every day whose disappointment with the church has risen to outright disgust.

Maybe again, I have been too optimistic. Is organized religion too inextricably bound to status-quo to save our nation and the world? Maybe I must turn my faith to the inner spiritual church, the church within the church, as the true *ecclesia* and the hope of the world. But again I am thankful to God that some noble souls from the ranks of organized religion have broken loose from the paralyzing chains of conformity and joined us as active partners in the struggle for freedom. They have left their secure congregations and walked the streets of Albany, Georgia, with us. They have gone through the highways of the South on tortuous rides for freedom. Yes, they have gone to jail with us. Some have been kicked out of their churches, and lost support of their bishops and fellow ministers. But they have gone with the faith that right defeated is stronger than evil triumphant. These men have been the leaven in the lump of the race. Their witness has been the spiritual salt that has preserved the true meaning of the Gospel in these troubled times. They have carved a tunnel of hope though the dark mountain of disappointment.

I hope the church as a whole will meet the challenge of this decisive hour. But even if the church does not come to the aid of justice, I have no despair about the future. I have no fear about the outcome of our struggle in Birmingham, even if our motives are presently misunderstood. We will reach the goal of freedom in Birmingham and all over the nation, because the goal of America is freedom. Abused and scorned though we may be, our destiny is tied up with the destiny of America. Before the pilgrims landed at Plymouth we were here. Before the pen of Jefferson etched across the pages of history the majestic words of the Declaration of Independence, we were here. For more than two centuries our fore-parents labored in this country without wages; they made cotton king; and they built the homes of their masters in the midst of brutal injustice and shameful humiliation—and yet out of a bottomless vitality they continued to thrive and develop. If the inexpressible cruelties of slavery could not stop us, the opposition we now face will surely fail. We will win our freedom because the sacred heritage of our nation and the eternal will of God are embodied in our echoing demands.

I must close now. But before closing I am impelled to mention one other point in your statement that troubled me profoundly. You warmly commended the Birmingham police force for keeping "order" and "preventing violence." I don't believe you would have so warmly commended the police force if you had seen its angry violent dogs literally biting six unarmed, nonviolent Negroes. I don't believe you would so quickly commend the policemen if you would observe their ugly and inhuman treatment of Negroes here in the city jail; if you would watch them push and curse old Negro women and young Negro girls; if you would see them slap and kick old Negro men and young boys; if you will observe them, as they did on two occasions, refuse to give us food because we wanted to sing our grace together. I'm sorry that I can't join you in your praise for the police department.

It is true that they have been rather disciplined in their public handling of the demonstrators. In this sense they have been rather publicly "nonviolent." But for what purpose? To preserve the evil system of segregation. Over the last few years I have consistently preached that nonviolence demands that the means we use must be as pure as the ends we seek. So I have tried to make it clear that it is wrong to use immoral means to attain moral ends. But now I must affirm that it is just as wrong, or even more so, to use moral means to preserve immoral ends. Maybe Mr. Connor and his policemen have been rather publicly nonviolent, as Chief Pritchett was in

Albany, Georgia, but they have used the moral means of nonviolence to maintain the immoral end of flagrant racial injustice. T. S. Eliot has said that there is no greater treason than to do the right deed for the wrong reason.

I wish you had commended the Negro sit-inners and demonstrators of Birmingham for their sublime courage, their willingness to suffer and their amazing discipline in the midst of the most inhuman provocation. One day the South will recognize its real heroes. They will be the James Merediths, courageously and with a majestic sense of purpose, facing jeering and hostile mobs and with the agonizing loneliness that characterizes the life of the pioneer. They will be old oppressed, battered Negro women, symbolized in a seventy-two year old woman of Montgomery, Alabama, who rose up with a sense of dignity and with her people decided not to ride the segregated buses, and responded to one who inquired about her tiredness with ungrammatical profundity; "my feet is tired, but my soul is rested." They will be the young high school and college students, young ministers of the gospel and a host of their elders courageously and nonviolently sitting-in at lunch counters and willingly going to jail for conscience's sake. One day the South will know that when these disinherited children of God sat down at lunch counters they were in reality standing up for the best in the American dream and the most sacred values in our Judaeo-Christian heritage, and thusly, carrying our whole nation back to those great wells of democracy which were dug deep by the founding fathers in the formulation of the Constitution and the Declaration of Independence.

Never before have I written a letter this long, (or should I say a book?). I'm afraid it is much too long to take your precious time. I can assure you that it would have been much shorter if I had been writing from a comfortable desk, but what else is there to do when you are alone for days in the dull monotony of a narrow jail cell other than write long letters, think strange thoughts, and pray long prayers?

If I have said anything in this letter that is an overstatement of the truth and is indicative of an unreasonable impatience, I beg you to forgive me. If I have said anything in this letter that is an understatement of the truth and is indicative of my having a patience that makes me patient with anything less than brotherhood, I beg God to forgive me.

I hope this letter finds you strong in the faith. I also hope that circumstances will soon make it possible for me to meet each of you, not as an integrationist or a civil rights leader, but as a fellow clergyman and a Christian brother. Let us all hope that the dark clouds of racial prejudice will soon pass away and the deep fog of misunderstanding will be lifted from our fear-drenched communities and in some not too distant tomorrow the radiant stars of love and brotherhood will shine over our great nation with all their scintillating beauty.

Yours for the cause of Peace and Brotherhood,

Martin Luther King, Jr.

© Estate of Martin Luther King, Jr.

JOHN F. KENNEDY **83**

National Address on Civil Rights, 1963

On June 11, 1963, President John F. Kennedy delivered a nationwide, televised address on the growing civil rights crisis in the United States. This latest confrontation had been sparked as the governor of Alabama called in the Alabama National Guard to blockade the University of Alabama to prevent desegregation in defiance of a federal court order to the contrary. Years of segregation and oppression of minorities in the United States was boiling over as demonstrations flared across the South. Kennedy's address supported the morality of these efforts and called for equality among the races. The civil rights movement became the focal point on the debate over American freedom in the 1960s as more groups rose up demanding their share of the American Dream and basic American liberties.

Good evening my fellow citizens:

This afternoon, following a series of threats and defiant statements, the presence of Alabama National Guardsmen was required on the University of Alabama to carry out the final and unequivocal order of the United States District Court of the Northern District of Alabama. That order called for the admission of two clearly qualified young Alabama residents who happened to have been born Negro.

That they were admitted peacefully on the campus is due in good measure to the conduct of the students of the University of Alabama, who met their responsibilities in a constructive way.

I hope that every American, regardless of where he lives, will stop and examine his conscience about this and other related incidents. This Nation was founded by men of many nations and backgrounds. It was founded on the principle that all men are created equal, and that the rights of every man are diminished when the rights of one man are threatened.

Today we are committed to a worldwide struggle to promote and protect the rights of all who wish to be free. And when Americans are sent to Viet-Nam or West Berlin, we do not ask for whites only. It ought to be possible, therefore, for American students of any color to attend any public institution they select without having to be backed up by troops.

It ought to be possible for American consumers of any color to receive equal service in places of public accommodation, such as hotels and restaurants and theaters and retail stores, without being forced to resort to demonstrations in the street, and it ought to be possible for American citizens of any color to register to vote in a free election without interference or fear of reprisal.

http://www.cs.umb.edu/jfklibrary/j061163.htm

It ought to be possible, in short, for every American to enjoy the privileges of being American without regard to his race or his color. In short, every American ought to have the right to be treated as he would wish to be treated, as one would wish his children to be treated. But this is not the case.

The Negro baby born in America today, regardless of the section of the Nation in which he is born, has about one-half as much chance of completing a high school as a white baby born in the same place on the same day, one-third as much chance of completing college, one-third as much chance of becoming a professional man, twice as much chance of becoming unemployed, about one-seventh as much chance of earning $10,000 a year, a life expectancy which is 7 years shorter, and the prospects of earning only half as much.

This is not a sectional issue. Difficulties over segregation and discrimination exist in every city, in every State of the Union, producing in many cities a rising tide of discontent that threatens the public safety. Nor is this a partisan issue. In a time of domestic crisis men of good will and generosity should be able to unite regardless of party or politics. This is not even a legal or legislative issue alone. It is better to settle these matters in the courts than on the streets, and new laws are needed at every level, but law alone cannot make men see right.

We are confronted primarily with a moral issue. It is as old as the scriptures and is as clear as the American Constitution.

The heart of the question is whether all Americans are to be afforded equal rights and equal opportunities, whether we are going to treat our fellow Americans as we want to be treated. If an American, because his skin is dark, cannot eat lunch in a restaurant open to the public, if he cannot send his children to the best public school available, if he cannot vote for the public officials who will represent him, if, in short, he cannot enjoy the full and free life which all of us want, then who among us would be content to have the color of his skin changed and stand in his place? Who among us would then be content with the counsels of patience and delay?

One hundred years of delay have passed since President Lincoln freed the slaves, yet their heirs, their grandsons, are not fully free. They are not yet freed from the bonds of injustice. They are not yet freed from social and economic oppression. And this Nation, for all its hopes and all its boasts, will not be fully free until all its citizens are free.

We preach freedom around the world, and we mean it, and we cherish our freedom here at home, but are we to say to the world, and much more importantly, to each other that this is the land of the free except for the Negroes; that we have no second-class citizens except Negroes; that we have no class or caste system, no ghettoes, no master race except with respect to Negroes?

Now the time has come for this Nation to fulfill its promise. The events in Birmingham and elsewhere have so increased the cries for equality that no city or State or legislative body can prudently choose to ignore them.

The fires of frustration and discord are burning in every city, North and South, where legal remedies are not at hand. Redress is sought in the streets, in demonstrations, parades, and protests which create tensions and threaten violence and threaten lives.

We face, therefore, a moral crisis as a country and as a people. It cannot be met by repressive police action. It cannot be left to increased demonstrations in the streets. It cannot be quieted by token moves or talk. It is time to act in the Congress, in your State and local legislative body and, above all, in all of our daily lives.

It is not enough to pin the blame of others, to say this a problem of one section of the country or another, or deplore the fact that we face. A great change is at hand, and our task, our obligation, is to make that revolution, that change, peaceful and constructive for all.

Those who do nothing are inviting shame as well as violence. Those who act boldly are recognizing right as well as reality.

Next week I shall ask the Congress of the United States to act, to make a commitment it has not fully made in this century to the proposition that race has no place in American life or law. The Federal judiciary has upheld that proposition in the conduct of its affairs, including the employment of Federal personnel, the use of Federal facilities, and the sale of federally financed housing.

But there are other necessary measures which only the Congress can provide, and they must be provided at this session. The old code of equity law under which we live commands for every wrong a remedy, but in too many communities, in too many parts of the country, wrongs are inflicted on Negro citizens and there are no remedies at law. Unless the Congress acts, their only remedy is in the street.

I am, therefore, asking the Congress to enact legislation giving all Americans the right to be served in facilities which are open to the public—hotels, restaurants, theaters, retail stores, and similar establishments.

This seems to me to be an elementary right. Its denial is an arbitrary indignity that no American in 1963 should have to endure, but many do.

I have recently met with scores of business leaders urging them to take voluntary action to end this discrimination and I have been encouraged by their response, and in the last 2 weeks over 75 cities have seen progress made in desegregating these kinds of facilities. But many are unwilling to act alone, and for this reason, nationwide legislation is needed if we are to move this problem from the streets to the courts.

I am also asking the Congress to authorize the Federal Government to participate more fully in lawsuits designed to end segregation in public education. We have succeeded in persuading many districts to desegregate voluntarily. Dozens have admitted Negroes without violence. Today a Negro is attending a State-supported institution in every one of our 50 States, but the pace is very slow.

Too many Negro children entering segregated grade schools at the time of the Supreme Court's decision 9 years ago will enter segregated high schools this fall, having suffered a loss which can never be restored. The lack of an adequate education denies the Negro a chance to get a decent job.

The orderly implementation of the Supreme Court decision, therefore, cannot be left solely to those who may not have the economic resources to carry the legal action or who may be subject to harassment.

Other features will also be requested, including greater protection for the right to vote. But legislation, I repeat, cannot solve this problem alone. It must be solved in the homes of every American in every community across our country.

In this respect I want to pay tribute to those citizens North and South who have been working in their communities to make life better for all. They are acting not out of a sense of legal duty but out of a sense of human decency.

Like our soldiers and sailors in all parts of the world they are meeting freedom's challenge on the firing line, and I salute them for their honor and their courage.

My fellow Americans, this is a problem which faces us all—in every city of the North as well as the South. Today there are Negroes unemployed, two or three times as many compared to whites, inadequate in education, moving into the large cities, unable to find work, young people particularly out of work without hope, denied equal rights, denied the opportunity to eat at a restaurant or lunch counter or go to a movie theater, denied the right to a decent education, denied almost today the right to attend a State university even though qualified. It seems to me that these are matters which concern us all, not merely Presidents or Congressmen or Governors, but every citizen of the United States.

This is one country. It has become one country because all of us and all the people who came here had an equal chance to develop their talents.

We cannot say to 10 percent of the population that you can't have that right; that your children cannot have the chance to develop whatever talents they have; that the only way that they are going to get their rights is to go into the streets and demonstrate. I think we owe them and we owe ourselves a better country than that.

Therefore, I am asking for your help in making it easier for us to move ahead and to provide the kind of equality of treatment which we would want ourselves; to give a chance for every child to be educated to the limit of his talents.

As I have said before, not every child has an equal talent or an equal ability or an equal motivation, but they should have an equal right to develop their talent and their ability and their motivation, to make something of themselves.

We have a right to expect that the Negro community will be responsible, will uphold the law, but they have a right to expect that the law will be fair, that the Constitution will be color blind, as Justice Harlan said at the turn of the century.

This is what we are talking about and this is a matter which concerns this country and what it stands for, and in meeting it I ask the support of all our citizens.

Thank you very much.

JOHN F. KENNEDY **84**

Ich bin ein Berliner, 1963

In this stirring address to the people of West Berlin, Kennedy delivered one of his most famous speeches. In the Cold War world divided between communists and democrats, Kennedy affirmed what the free nations stood for: the right of individuals to make their own choices in their lives and for freedom to flourish, it had

John F. Kennedy, *JFK: In His Own Words*, Maureen Harrison and Steve Gilbert, eds. (New York: Barnes and Noble Books, 1993): 277–279

*to extend to all individuals. For Kennedy, equality and self-determination were
the very essence of freedom.*

Two thousand years ago—Two thousand years ago, the proudest boast was *"civis
Romanus sum!"* Today in the world of freedom, the proudest boast is *"Ich bin ein Berliner!"*

There are many people in the world who really don't understand—or say they
don't—what is the greatest issue between the free world and Communist world. Let
them come to Berlin!

There are some who say that "communism is the wave of the future." Let them
come to Berlin!

And there are some who say in Europe and elsewhere, "we can work with the
Communists." Let them come to Berlin!

And there are even a few who say "yes, that it's true, that communism is an evil
system, but it permits us to make economic progress." *Lass' sie nach Berlin en kommen!*
Let them come to Berlin!

Freedom has many difficulties, and democracy is not perfect. But we have never
had to put a wall up to keep our people in, to prevent them from leaving us!

I want to say on behalf of my countrymen who live many miles away on the other
side of the Atlantic, who are far distant from you, that they take the greatest pride
that they have been able to share with you, even from a distance the story of the last
eighteen years.

I know of no town, no city, that has been besieged for eighteen years that still
lives with the vitality and the force and the hope and the determination of the city of
West Berlin!

While the wall is the most obvious and vivid demonstration of the failures of
the communist system, all the world can see, and we take no satisfaction in it. For it
is an offense not only against humanity, separating families, dividing husbands and
wives and brothers and sisters and dividing a people who wished to be joined
together!

What is true of this city is true to Germany: Real lasting peace in Europe can
never be assured as long as one German out of four is denied the elementary right of
free men, and that is to make a free choice.

In eighteen years of peace and good faith this generation of Germans has earned
the right to be free, including the right to unite their families and their nation in lasting peace with goodwill to all people.

You live in a defended island of freedom, but your life is part of the main. So let
me ask you, as I close, to lift your eyes beyond the dangers of today to the hopes of
tomorrow, beyond the freedom merely of this city of Berlin and all your country of
Germany, to the advance of freedom everywhere, beyond the wall, to the day of peace
with justice, beyond yourselves and ourselves to all mankind.

Freedom is indivisible, and when one man is enslaved, no man is free. When all
are free, then we look forward to that day when this city will be joined as one, and this
country and this great continent of Europe, in a peaceful and hopeful globe. When
that day finally comes, as it will, the people of West Berlin can take sober satisfaction
in the fact that they were in the front lines for almost two decades.

All free men, wherever they may live, are citizens of Berlin. And therefore, as a
free man, I take pride in the words *"Ich bin ein Berliner!"*

MARTIN LUTHER KING, JR. **85**

I Have a Dream, 1963

Some 250,000 people gathered at the Lincoln Memorial in Washington, DC, on August 28, 1963, as part of a civil rights demonstration to hear one of the most moving civil rights addresses of all time. Televised nationally, "I Have a Dream" became one of the most famous speeches of the twentieth century, and one of the most quoted. In this address, Dr. Martin Luther King, Jr., voices the hopes and dreams of the civil rights movement—equality and brotherhood. King argued that the prejudice and hatred that had reduced minorities to second-class citizens left minorities short of a state of total freedom and would not reach that state until they reached total equality before the law.

I am happy to join with you today in what will go down in history as the greatest demonstration for freedom in the history of our nation.

Five score years ago, a great American, in whose symbolic shadow we stand today, signed the Emancipation Proclamation. This momentous decree came as a great beacon light of hope to millions of Negro slaves, who had been seared in the flames of withering injustice. It came as a joyous daybreak to end the long night of their captivity.

But one hundred years later, the Negro still is not free. One hundred years later, the life of the Negro is still sadly crippled by the manacles of segregation and the chains of discrimination. One hundred years later, the Negro lives on a lonely island of poverty in the midst of a vast ocean of material prosperity. One hundred years later, the Negro is still languished in the corners of American society and finds himself an exile in his own land.

So we've come here today to dramatize a shameful condition. In a sense, we've come to our nation's capital to cash a check. When the architects of our Republic wrote the magnificent words of the Constitution and the Declaration of Independence, they were signing a promissory note to which every American was to fall heir. This note was a promise that all men—yes, black men as well as white men—would be guaranteed the unalienable rights of life, liberty, and the pursuit of happiness.

It is obvious today that America has defaulted on this promissory note insofar as her citizens of color are concerned. Instead of honoring this sacred obligation, America has given the Negro people a bad check, a check which has come back marked "insufficient funds." But we refuse to believe that the bank of justice is bankrupt. We refuse to believe that there are insufficient funds in the great vaults of opportunity of this nation. So we've come to cash this check—a check that will give us upon demand the riches of freedom and the security of justice.

We have also come to this hallowed spot to remind America of the fierce urgency of "now." This is no time to engage in the luxury of cooling off or to take the tranquilizing drug of gradualism. Now is the time to make real the promises of

Martin Luther King, *I Have a Dream* (New York: Scholastic Press, 1997)

democracy. Now is the time to rise from the dark and desolate valley of segregation to the sunlit path of racial justice. Now is the time to lift our nation from the quicksands of racial injustice to the solid rock of brotherhood. Now is the time to make justice a reality for all of God's children.

It would be fatal for the nation to overlook the urgency of the moment. This sweltering summer of the Negro's legitimate discontent will not pass until there is an invigorating autumn of freedom and equality. Nineteen sixty-three is not an end, but a beginning. And those who hope that the Negro needed to blow off steam and will now be content will have a rude awakening if the nation returns to business as usual. And there will be neither rest nor tranquility in America until the Negro is granted his citizenship rights. The whirlwinds of revolt will continue to shake the foundations of our nation until the bright day of justice emerges.

But there is something that I must say to my people who stand on the warm threshold which leads into the palace of justice. In the process of gaining our rightful place we must not be guilty of wrongful deeds. Let us not seek to satisfy our thirst for freedom by drinking from the cup of bitterness and hatred.

We must forever conduct our struggle on the high plane of dignity and discipline. We must not allow our creative protest to degenerate into physical violence. Again and again we must rise to the majestic heights of meeting physical force with soul force. The marvelous new militancy which has engulfed the Negro community must not lead us to a distrust of all white people, for many of our white brothers, as evidenced by their presence here today, have come to realize that their destiny is tied up with our destiny. And they have come to realize that their freedom is inextricably bound to our freedom. We cannot walk alone.

As we walk, we must make the pledge that we shall always march ahead. We cannot turn back.

There are those who are asking the devotees of civil rights, "When will you be satisfied?" We can never be satisfied as long as the Negro is the victim of the unspeakable horrors of police brutality. We can never be satisfied as long as our bodies, heavy with the fatigue of travel, cannot gain lodging in the motels of the highways and the hotels of the cities. We cannot be satisfied as long as the Negro's basic mobility is from a smaller ghetto to a larger one. We can never be satisfied as long as our children are stripped of their selfhood and robbed of their dignity by signs stating "For Whites Only." We cannot be satisfied as long as a Negro in Mississippi cannot vote and a Negro in New York believes he has nothing for which to vote. No, no, we are not satisfied, and we will not be satisfied until justice rolls down like waters and righteousness like a mighty stream!

I am not unmindful that some of you have come here out of great trials and tribulations. Some of you have come fresh from narrow jail cells. Some of you have come from areas where your quest—quest for freedom left you battered by the storms of persecution and staggered by the winds of police brutality. You have been the veterans of creative suffering. Continue to work with the faith that unearned suffering is redemptive.

Go back to Mississippi, go back to Alabama, go back to South Carolina, go back to Georgia, go back to Louisiana, go back to the slums and ghettos of our Northern cities, knowing that somehow this situation can and will be changed. Let us not wallow in the valley of despair.

I say to you today, my friends, so even though we face the difficulties of today and tomorrow, I still have a dream. It is a dream deeply rooted in the American dream. I have a dream that one day this nation will rise up and live out the true meaning of its creed: "We hold these truths to be self-evident; that all men are created equal."

I have a dream that one day on the red hills of Georgia the sons of former slaves and the sons of former slave owners will be able to sit down together at the table of brotherhood.

I have a dream that one day even the state of Mississippi, a state sweltering with the heat of injustice, sweltering with the heat of oppression, will be transformed into an oasis of freedom and justice.

I have a dream that my four little children will one day live in a nation where they will not be judged by the color of their skin but by the content of their character.

I have a dream today!

I have a dream that one day, down in Alabama, with its vicious racists, with its governor having his lips dripping with the words of interposition and nullification, one day right there in Alabama little black boys and black girls will be able to join hands with little white boys and white girls as sisters and brothers. . . . I have a dream today!

I have a dream that one day every valley shall be exalted, every hill and mountain shall be made low, the rough places will be made plain and the crooked places will be made straight, and the glory of the Lord shall be revealed, and all flesh shall see it together!

This is our hope. This is the faith that I go back to the South with. With this faith, we will be able to hew out of the mountain of despair a stone of hope. With this faith we will be able to transform the jangling discords of our nation into a beautiful symphony of brotherhood. With this faith we will be able to work together, to pray together, to struggle together, to go to jail together, to stand up for freedom together, knowing that we will be free one day!

This will be the day . . . this will be the day when all of God's children will be able to sing with new meaning. "My country 'tis of thee, sweet land of liberty, of thee I sing. Land where my fathers died, land of the Pilgrims' pride, from every mountainside, let freedom ring," and if America is to be a great nation, this must become true.

So let freedom ring! From the prodigious hilltops of New Hampshire, let freedom ring. From the mighty mountains of New York, let freedom ring, from the heightening Alleghenies of Pennsylvania!

Let freedom ring from the snowcapped Rockies of Colorado!

Let freedom ring from the curvaceous slopes of California! But not only that.

Let freedom ring from Stone Mountain of Georgia!

Let freedom ring from Lookout Mountain of Tennessee!

Let freedom ring from every hill and mole hill of Mississippi. From every mountainside, let freedom ring, and when this happens . . . when we allow freedom ring, when we let it ring from every village and every hamlet, from every state and every city, we will be able to speed up that day when all of God's children, black men and white men, Jews and Gentiles, Protestants and Catholics, will be able to join hands and sing in the words of the old Negro spiritual, "Free at last! Free at last! Thank God Almighty, we are free at last!"

LYNDON B. JOHNSON **86**

State of the Union Address, 1964

In the weeks following the assassination of John F. Kennedy, the new president, Lyndon Johnson, focused the nation's attention on a new political crusade, taking many of Kennedy's foundering proposals and pushing them through Congress. Johnson's 1964 State of the Union address also became known as the "War on Poverty" speech in which he launched his Great Society programs to eradicate poverty in the United States. Johnson's own painful memories of poverty in Texas energized him to use the collective strength of the nation to fight the ancient curse of want. The declaration of war on poverty took only a brief part of the speech but became the heart of Johnson's domestic proposals. For Johnson, the blessings of freedom could not exist in an environment where children did not have enough to eat and parents wondered where the family's next meal would come from. Congress was convinced that free men and women must have the right to rise out of poverty and passed many of Johnson's proposals, bringing millions out of poverty between 1964 and 1967.

Mr. Speaker, Mr. President, Members of the House and Senate, my fellow Americans:

I will be brief, for our time is necessarily short and our agenda is already long.

Last year's congressional session was the longest in peacetime history. With that foundation, let us work together to make this year's session the best in the Nation's history.

Let this session of Congress be known as the session which did more for civil rights than the last hundred sessions combined; as the session which enacted the most far-reaching tax cut of our time; as the session which declared all-out war on human poverty and unemployment in these United States; as the session which finally recognized the health needs of all our older citizens; as the session which reformed our tangled transportation and transit policies; as the session which achieved the most effective, efficient foreign aid program ever; and as the session which helped to build more homes, more schools, more libraries, and more hospitals than any single session of Congress in the history of our Republic.

All this and more can and must be done. It can be done by this summer, and it can be done without any increase in spending. In fact, under the budget that I shall shortly submit, it can be done with an actual reduction in Federal expenditures and Federal employment.

We have in 1964 a unique opportunity and obligation—to prove the success of our system; to disprove those cynics and critics at home and abroad who question our purpose and our competence.

If we fail, if we fritter and fumble away our opportunity in needless, senseless quarrels between Democrats and Republicans, or between the House and the Senate,

Lyndon B. Johnson, *Public Papers of the Presidents of the United States: Lyndon B. Johnson, 1963–64*, vol. I (Washington, D.C.: Government Printing Office, 1965): 112–118 or between the South and North, or between the Congress and the administration, then history will rightfully judge us harshly. But if we succeed, if we can achieve these goals by forging in this country a greater sense of union, then, and only then, can we take full satisfaction in the State of the Union.

II

Here in the Congress you can demonstrate effective legislative leadership by discharging the public business with clarity and dispatch, voting each important proposal up, or voting it down, but at least bringing it to a fair and a final vote.

Let us carry forward the plans and programs of John Fitzgerald Kennedy—not because of our sorrow or sympathy, but because they are right.

In his memory today, I especially ask all members of my own political faith, in this election year, to put your country ahead of your party, and to always debate principles; never debate personalities.

For my part, I pledge a progressive administration which is efficient, and honest and frugal. The budget to be submitted to the Congress shortly is in full accord with this pledge.

It will cut our deficit in half—from $10 billion to $4,900 million. It will be, in proportion to our national output, the smallest budget since 1951.

It will call for a substantial reduction in Federal employment, a feat accomplished only once before in the last 10 years. While maintaining the full strength of our combat defenses, it will call for the lowest number of civilian personnel in the Department of Defense since 1950.

It will call for total expenditures of $97,900 million—compared to $98,400 million for the current year, a reduction of more than $500 million. It will call for new obligational authority of $103,800 million—a reduction of more than $4 billion below last year's request of $107,900 million.

But it is not a standstill budget, for America cannot afford to stand still. Our population is growing. Our economy is more complex. Our people's needs are expanding.

But by closing down obsolete installations, by curtailing less urgent programs, by cutting back where cutting back seems to be wise, by insisting on a dollar's worth for a dollar spent, I am able to recommend in this reduced budget the most Federal support in history for education, for health, for retraining the unemployed, and for helping the economically and the physically handicapped.

This budget, and this year's legislative program, are designed to help each and every American citizen fulfill his basic hopes—his hopes for a fair chance to make good; his hopes for fair play from the law; his hopes for a full-time job on full-time pay; his hopes for a decent home for his family in a decent community; his hopes for a good school for his children with good teachers; and his hopes for security when faced with sickness or unemployment or old age.

III

Unfortunately, many Americans live on the outskirts of hope—some because of their poverty, and some because of their color, and all too many because of both. Our task is to help replace their despair with opportunity.

This administration today, here and now, declares unconditional war on poverty in America. I urge this Congress and all Americans to join with me in that effort.

It will not be a short or easy struggle, no single weapon or strategy will suffice, but we shall not rest until that war is won. The richest Nation on earth can afford to win it. We cannot afford to lose it. One thousand dollars invested in salvaging an unemployable youth today can return $40,000 or more in his lifetime.

Poverty is a national problem, requiring improved national organization and support. But this attack, to be effective, must also be organized at the State and the local level and must be supported and directed by State and local efforts.

For the war against poverty will not be won here in Washington. It must be won in the field, in every private home, in every public office, from the courthouse to the White House.

The program I shall propose will emphasize this cooperative approach to help that one-fifth of all American families with incomes too small to even meet their basic needs.

Our chief weapons in a more pinpointed attack will be better schools, and better health, and better homes, and better training, and better job opportunities to help more Americans, especially young Americans, escape from squalor and misery and unemployment rolls where other citizens help to carry them.

Very often a lack of jobs and money is not the cause of poverty, but the symptom. The cause may lie deeper in our failure to give our fellow citizens a fair chance to develop their own capacities, in a lack of education and training, in a lack of medical care and housing, in a lack of decent communities in which to live and bring up their children.

But whatever the cause, our joint Federal-local effort must pursue poverty, pursue it wherever it exists—in city slums and small towns, in sharecropper shacks or in migrant worker camps, on Indian Reservations, among whites as well as Negroes, among the young as well as the aged, in the boom towns and in the depressed areas.

Our aim is not only to relieve the symptom of poverty, but to cure it and, above all, to prevent it. No single piece of legislation, however, is going to suffice.

We will launch a special effort in the chronically distressed areas of Appalachia.

We must expand our small but our successful area redevelopment program.

We must enact youth employment legislation to put jobless, aimless, hopeless youngsters to work on useful projects.

We must distribute more food to the needy through a broader food stamp program.

We must create a National Service Corps to help the economically handicapped of our own country as the Peace Corps now helps those abroad.

We must modernize our unemployment insurance and establish a high-level commission on automation. If we have the brain power to invent these machines, we have the brain power to make certain that they are a boon and not a bane to humanity.

We must extend the coverage of our minimum wage laws to more than 2 million workers now lacking this basic protection of purchasing power.

We must, by including special school aid funds as part of our education program, improve the quality of teaching, training, and counseling in our hardest hit areas.

We must build more libraries in every area and more hospitals and nursing homes under the Hill-Burton Act, and train more nurses to staff them.

We must provide hospital insurance for our older citizens financed by every worker and his employer under Social Security, contributing no more than $1 a month during the employee's working career to protect him in his old age in a dignified manner without cost to the Treasury, against the devastating hardship of prolonged or repeated illness.

We must, as a part of a revised housing and urban renewal program, give more help to those displaced by slum clearance, provide more housing for our poor and our elderly, and seek as our ultimate goal in our free enterprise system a decent home for every American family.

We must help obtain more modern mass transit within our communities as well as low-cost transportation between them.

Above all, we must release $11 billion of tax reduction into the private spending stream to create new jobs and new markets in every area of this land.

IV

These programs are obviously not for the poor or the underprivileged alone. Every American will benefit by the extension of social security to cover the hospital costs of their aged parents. Every American community will benefit from the construction or modernization of schools, libraries, hospitals, and nursing homes, from the training of more nurses and from the improvement of urban renewal in public transit. And every individual American taxpayer and every corporate taxpayer will benefit from the earliest possible passage of the pending tax bill from both the new investment it will bring and the new jobs that it will create.

That tax bill has been thoroughly discussed for a year. Now we need action. The new budget clearly allows it. Our taxpayers surely deserve it. Our economy strongly demands it. And every month of delay dilutes its benefits in 1964 for consumption, for investment, and for employment.

For until the bill is signed, its investment incentives cannot be deemed certain, and the withholding rate cannot be reduced—and the most damaging and devastating thing you can do to any businessman in America is to keep him in doubt and to keep him guessing on what our tax policy is. And I say that we should now reduce to 14 percent instead of 15 percent our withholding rate.

I therefore urge the Congress to take final action on this bill by the first of February, if at all possible. For however proud we may be of the unprecedented progress of our free enterprise economy over the last 3 years, we should not and we cannot permit it to pause.

In 1963, for the first time in history, we crossed the 70 million job mark, but we will soon need more than 75 million jobs. In 1963 our gross national product reached the $600 billion level—$100 billion higher than when we took office. But it easily could and it should be still $30 billion higher today than it is.

Wages and profits and family income are also at their highest levels in history—but I would remind you that 4 million workers and 13 percent of our industrial capacity are still idle today.

We need a tax cut now to keep this country moving.

V

For our goal is not merely to spread the work. Our goal is to create more jobs. I believe the enactment of a 35-hour week would sharply increase costs, would invite inflation, would impair our ability to compete, and merely share instead of creating employment. But I am equally opposed to the 45- or 50-hour week in those industries where consistently excessive use of overtime causes increased unemployment.

So, therefore, I recommend legislation authorizing the creation of a tripartite industry committee to determine on an industry-by-industry basis as to where a higher penalty rate for overtime would increase job openings without unduly increasing costs, and authorizing the establishment of such higher rates.

VI

Let me make one principle of this administration abundantly clear: All of these increased opportunities—in employment, in education, in housing, and in every field—must be open to Americans of every color. As far as the writ of Federal law will run, we must abolish not some, but all racial discrimination. For this is not merely an economic issue, or a social, political, or international issue. It is a moral issue, and it must be met by the passage this session of the bill now pending in the House.

All members of the public should have equal access to facilities open to the public. All members of the public should be equally eligible for Federal benefits that are financed by the public. All members of the public should have an equal chance to vote for public officials and to send their children to good public schools and to contribute their talents to the public good.

Today, Americans of all races stand side by side in Berlin and in Viet Nam. They died side by side in Korea. Surely they can work and eat and travel side by side in their own country.

VII

We must also lift by legislation the bars of discrimination against those who seek entry into our country, particularly those who have much needed skills and those joining their families.

In establishing preferences, a nation that was built by the immigrants of all lands can ask those who now seek admission: "What can you do for our country?" But we should not be asking: "In what country were you born?"

VIII

For our ultimate goal is a world without war, a world made safe for diversity, in which all men, goods, and ideas can freely move across every border and every boundary.

We must advance toward this goal in 1964 in at least 10 different ways, not as partisans, but as patriots.

First, we must maintain—and our reduced defense budget will maintain—that margin of military safety and superiority obtained through 3 years of steadily increasing both the quality and the quantity of our strategic, our conventional, and our antiguerilla forces. In 1964 we will be better prepared than ever before to defend the cause of freedom, whether it is threatened by outright aggression or by the infiltration practiced by those in Hanoi and Havana, who ship arms and men across international borders to foment insurrection. And we must continue to use that strength as John Kennedy used it in the Cuban crisis and for the test ban treaty—to demonstrate both the futility of nuclear war and the possibilities of lasting peace.

Second, we must take new steps—and we shall make new proposals at Geneva—toward the control and the eventual abolition of arms. Even in the absence of agreement, we must not stockpile arms beyond our needs or seek an excess of military power that could be provocative as well as wasteful.

It is in this spirit that in this fiscal year we are cutting back our production of enriched uranium by 25 percent. We are shutting down four plutonium piles. We are closing many nonessential military installations. And it is in this spirit that we today call on our adversaries to do the same.

Third, we must make increased use of our food as an instrument of peace—making it available by sale or trade or loan or donation-to hungry people in all nations which tell us of their needs and accept proper conditions of distribution.

Fourth, we must assure our pre-eminence in the peaceful exploration of outer space, focusing on an expedition to the moon in this decade—in cooperation with other powers if possible, alone if necessary.

Fifth, we must expand world trade. Having recognized in the Act of 1962 that we must buy as well as sell, we now expect our trading partners to recognize that we must sell as well as buy. We are willing to give them competitive access to our market, asking only that they do the same for us.

Sixth, we must continue, through such measures as the interest equalization tax, as well as the cooperation of other nations, our recent progress toward balancing our international accounts.

This administration must and will preserve the present gold value of the dollar.

Seventh, we must become better neighbors with the free states of the Americas, working with the councils of the OAS, with a stronger Alliance for Progress, and with all the men and women of this hemisphere who really believe in liberty and justice for all.

Eighth, we must strengthen the ability of free nations everywhere to develop their independence and raise their standard of living, and thereby frustrate those who prey on poverty and chaos. To do this, the rich must help the poor—and we must do our part. We must achieve a more rigorous administration of our development assistance, with larger roles for private investors, for other industrialized nations, and for international agencies and for the recipient nations themselves.

Ninth, we must strengthen our Atlantic and Pacific partnerships, maintain our alliances and make the United Nations a more effective instrument for national independence and international order.

Tenth, and finally, we must develop with our allies new means of bridging the gap between the East and the West, facing danger boldly wherever danger exists, but being equally bold in our search for new agreements which can enlarge the hopes of all, while violating the interests of none.

In short, I would say to the Congress that we must be constantly prepared for the worst, and constantly acting for the best. We must be strong enough to win any war, and we must be wise enough to prevent one.

We shall neither act as aggressors nor tolerate acts of aggression. We intend to bury no one, and we do not intend to be buried.

We can fight, if we must, as we have fought before, but we pray that we will never have to fight again.

IX

My good friends and my fellow Americans: In these last 7 sorrowful weeks, we have learned anew that nothing is so enduring as faith, and nothing is so degrading as hate.

John Kennedy was a victim of hate, but he was also a great builder of faith—faith in our fellow Americans, whatever their creed or their color or their station in life; faith in the future of man, whatever his divisions and differences.

This faith was echoed in all parts of the world. On every continent and in every land to which Mrs. Johnson and I traveled, we found faith and hope and love toward this land of America and toward our people.

So I ask you now in the Congress and in the country to join with me in expressing and fulfilling that faith in working for a nation, a nation that is free from want and a world that is free from hate—a world of peace and justice, and freedom and abundance, for our time and for all time to come.

LYNDON B. JOHNSON **87**

The American Promise, 1965

Lyndon Johnson was known mainly for his mastery of the legislative process rather than his oratory. But this 1965 address on civil rights was considered to be one his finest speeches. In this message before Congress, Johnson calls for the passage of legislation that would become the Voting Rights Act of 1965. The Voting Rights Act ended literacy tests and other devices used in the South to deny African-Americans the right to vote. Johnson called this legislation a duty of the government to protect the rights of minorities. A free people must have their voices heard by the government, and Johnson was determined to uphold this principle. This principle was not a matter of legal language but a matter of right and wrong and of freedom against hatred and terror.

Mr. Speaker, Mr. President, Members of the Congress:

I speak tonight for the dignity of man and the destiny of democracy. I urge every member of both parties, Americans of all religions and of all colors, from every section of this country, to join me in that cause.

At times history and fate meet at a single time in a single place to shape a turning point in man's unending search for freedom. So it was at Lexington and Concord. So it was a century ago at Appomattox. So it was last week in Selma, Alabama.

There, long-suffering men and women peacefully protested the denial of their rights as Americans. Many were brutally assaulted. One good man, a man of God, was killed.

Lyndon B. Johnson, *Public Papers of the Presidents of the United States: Lyndon Johnson*, Vol. 1 (Washington, D.C.: Government Printing Office, 1965), 281

There is no cause for pride in what has happened in Selma. There is no cause for self-satisfaction in the long denial of equal rights of millions of Americans. But there is cause for hope and for faith in our democracy in what is happening here tonight. For the cries of pain and the hymns and protests of oppressed people have summoned into convocation all the majesty of this great Government—the Government of the greatest Nation on earth.

Our mission is at once the oldest and the most basic of this country: to right wrong, to do justice, to serve man.

In our time we have come to live with moments of great crisis. Our lives have been marked with debate about great issues; issues of war and peace, issues of prosperity and depression. But rarely in any time does an issue lay bare the secret heart of America itself. Rarely are we met with a challenge, not to our growth or abundance, our welfare or our security, but rather to the values and the purposes and the meaning of our beloved Nation.

The issue of equal rights for American Negroes is such an issue. And should we defeat every enemy, should we double our wealth and conquer the stars, and still be unequal to this issue, then we will have failed as a people and as a nation. For with a country as with a person, "What is a man profited, if he shall gain the whole world, and lose his own soul?"

There is no Negro problem. There is no Southern problem. There is no Northern problem. There is only an American problem. And we are met here tonight as Americans—not as Democrats or Republicans—we are met here as Americans to solve that problem.

This was the first nation in the history of the world to be founded with a purpose. The great phrases of that purpose still sound in every American heart, North and South: "All men are created equal"—"government by consent of the governed"—"give me liberty or give me death." Well, those are not just clever words, or those are not just empty theories. In their name Americans have fought and died for two centuries, and tonight around the world they stand there as guardians of our liberty, risking their lives. Those words are a promise to every citizen that he shall share in the dignity of man. This dignity cannot be found in a man's possessions; it cannot be found in his power, or in his position. It really rests on his right to be treated as a man equal in opportunity to all others. It says that he shall share in freedom, he shall choose his leaders, educate his children, and provide for his family according to his ability and his merits as a human being.

To apply any other test—to deny a man his hopes because of his color or race, his religion or the place of his birth—is not only to do injustice, it is to deny America and to dishonor the dead who gave their lives for American freedom.

The Right to Vote

Our fathers believed that if this noble view of the rights of man was to flourish, it must be rooted in democracy. The most basic right of all was the right to choose your own leaders. The history of this country, in large measure, is the history of the expansion of that right to all of our people.

Many of the issues of civil rights are very complex and most difficult. But about this there can and should be no argument. Every American citizen must have an equal right to vote. There is no reason which can excuse the denial of that right. There is no duty which weighs more heavily on us than the duty we have to ensure that right. Yet the harsh fact is that in many places in this country men and women are kept from voting simply because they are Negroes.

Every device of which human ingenuity is capable has been used to deny this right. The Negro citizen may go to register only to be told that the day is wrong, or the hour is late, or the official in charge is absent. And if he persists, and if he manages to present himself to the registrar, he may be disqualified because he did not spell out his middle name or because he abbreviated a word on the application.

And if he manages to fill out an application he is given a test. The registrar is the sole judge of whether he passes this test. He may be asked to recite the entire Constitution, or explain the most complex provisions of State law. And even a college degree cannot be used to prove that he can read and write.

For the fact is that the only way to pass these barriers is to show a white skin. Experience has clearly shown that the existing process of law cannot overcome systematic and ingenious discrimination. No law that we now have on the books—and I have helped to put three of them there—can ensure the right to vote when local officials are determined to deny it.

In such a case our duty must be clear to all of us. The Constitution says that no person shall be kept from voting because of his race or his color. We have all sworn an oath before God to support and to defend that Constitution. We must now act in obedience to that oath.

Guaranteeing the Right to Vote

Wednesday I will send to Congress a law designed to eliminate illegal barriers to the right to vote.

The broad principles of that bill will be in the hands of the Democratic and Republican leaders tomorrow. After they have reviewed it, it will come here formally as a bill. I am grateful for this opportunity to come here tonight at the invitation of the leadership to reason with my friends, to give them my views, and to visit with my former colleagues.

I have had prepared a more comprehensive analysis of the legislation which I had intended to transmit to the clerk tomorrow but which I will sub-mit to the clerks tonight. But I want to really discuss with you now briefly the main proposals of this legislation. This bill will strike down restrictions to voting in all elections—Federal, State, and local—which have been used to deny Negroes the right to vote.

This bill will establish a simple, uniform standard which cannot be used, however ingenious the effort, to flout our Constitution.

It will provide for citizens to be registered by officials of the United States Government if the State officials refuse to register them.

It will eliminate tedious, unnecessary lawsuits which delay the right to vote. Finally, this legislation will ensure that properly registered individuals are not prohibited from voting.

I will welcome the suggestions from all of the Members of Congress—I have no doubt that I will get some—on ways and means to strengthen this law and to make it effective. But experience has plainly shown that this is the only path to carry out the command of the Constitution.

To those who seek to avoid action by their National Government in their own communities; who want to and who seek to maintain purely local control over elections, the answer is simple:

Open your polling places to all your people.

Allow men and women to register and vote whatever the color of their skin.

Extend the rights of citizenship to every citizen of this land.

The Need For Action

There is no constitutional issue here. The command of the Constitution is plain. There is no moral issue. It is wrong—deadly wrong—to deny any of your fellow Americans the right to vote in this country.

There is no issue of States rights or national rights. There is only the struggle for human rights.

I have not the slightest doubt what will be your answer.

The last time a President sent a civil rights bill to the Congress it contained a provision to protect voting rights in Federal elections. That civil rights bill was passed after 8 long months of debate. And when that bill came to my desk from the Congress for my signature, the heart of the voting provision had been eliminated.

This time, on this issue, there must be no delay, no hesitation and no compromise with our purpose.

We cannot, we must not, refuse to protect the right of every American to vote in every election that he may desire to participate in.

And we ought not and we cannot and we must not wait another 8 months before we get a bill. We have already waited a hundred years and more, and the time for waiting is gone.

So I ask you to join me in working long hours—nights and weekends, if necessary—to pass this bill. And I don't make that request lightly. For from the window where I sit with the problems of our country I recognize that outside this chamber is the outraged conscience of a nation, the grave concern of many nations, and the harsh judgment of history on our acts.

We Shall Overcome

But even if we pass this bill, the battle will not be over. What happened in Selma is part of a far larger movement which reaches into every section and State of America. It is the effort of American Negroes to secure for themselves the full blessings of American life.

Their cause must be our cause too. Because it is not just Negroes, but really it is all of us, who must overcome the crippling legacy of bigotry and injustice.

And we shall overcome.

As a man whose roots go deeply into Southern soil I know how agonizing racial feelings are. I know how difficult it is to reshape the attitudes and the structure of our society.

But a century has passed, more than a hundred years, since the Negro was freed. And he is not fully free tonight.

It was more than a hundred years ago that Abraham Lincoln, a great President of another party, signed the Emancipation Proclamation, but emancipation is a proclamation and not a fact.

A century has passed, more than a hundred years, since equality was promised. And yet the Negro is not equal.

A century has passed since the day of promise. And the promise is unkept. The time of justice has now come. I tell you that I believe sincerely that no force can hold it back. It is right in the eyes of man and God that it should come. And when it does, I think that day will brighten the lives of every American.

For Negroes are not the only victims. How many white children have gone uneducated, how many white families have lived in stark poverty, how many white lives have been scarred by fear, because we have wasted our energy and our substance to maintain the barriers of hatred and terror?

So I say to all of you here, and to all in the Nation tonight, that those who appeal to you to hold on to the past do so at the cost of denying you your future.

This great, rich, restless country can offer opportunity and education and hope to all: black and white, North and South, sharecropper and city dweller. These are the enemies: poverty, ignorance, disease. They are the enemies and not our fellow man, not our neighbor. And these enemies too, poverty, disease and ignorance, we shall overcome.

An American Problem

Now let none of us in any sections look with prideful righteousness on the troubles in another section, or on the problems of our neighbors. There is really no part of America where the promise of equality has been fully kept. In Buffalo as well as in Birmingham, in Philadelphia as well as in Selma, Americans are struggling for the fruits of freedom.

This is one Nation. What happens in Selma or in Cincinnati is a matter of legitimate concern to every American. But let each of us look within our own hearts and our own communities, and let each of us put our shoulder to the wheel to root out injustice wherever it exists.

As we meet here in this peaceful, historic chamber tonight, men from the South, some of whom were at Iwo Jima, men from the North who have carried Old Glory to far corners of the world and brought it back without a stain on it, men from the East and from the West, are all fighting together without regard to religion, or color, or region, in Viet-Nam. Men from every region fought for us across the world 20 years ago.

And in these common dangers and these common sacrifices the South made its contribution of honor and gallantry no less than any other region of the great Republic—and in some instances, a great many of them, more.

And I have not the slightest doubt that good men from everywhere in this country, from the Great Lakes to the Gulf of Mexico, from the Golden Gate to the harbors along the Atlantic, will rally together now in this cause to vindi-cate the freedom of all Americans. For all of us owe this duty; and I believe that all of us will respond to it. Your President makes that request of every American.

Progress Through the Democratic Process

The real hero of this struggle is the American Negro. His actions and protests, his courage to risk safety and even to risk his life, have awakened the conscience of this Nation. His demonstrations have been designed to call attention to injustice, designed to provoke change, designed to stir reform.

He has called upon us to make good the promise of America. And who among us can say that we would have made the same progress were it not for his persistent bravery, and his faith in American democracy.

For at the real heart of battle for equality is a deep-seated belief in the democratic process. Equality depends not on the force of arms or tear gas but upon the force of moral right; not on recourse to violence but on respect for law and order.

There have been many pressures upon your President and there will be others as the days come and go. But I pledge you tonight that we intend to fight this battle where it should be fought: in the courts, and in the Congress, and in the hearts of men.

We must preserve the right of free speech and the right of free assembly. But the right of free speech does not carry with it, as has been said, the right to holler fire in a crowded theater. We must preserve the right to free assembly, but free assembly does not carry with it the right to block public thoroughfares to traffic. We do have a right to protest, and a right to march under conditions that do not infringe the constitutional rights of our neighbors. And I intend to protect all those rights as long as I am permitted to serve in this office.

We will guard against violence, knowing it strikes from our hands the very weapons which we seek—progress, obedience to law, and belief in American values. In Selma as elsewhere we seek and pray for peace. We seek order. We seek unity. But we will not accept the peace of stifled rights, or the order imposed by fear, or the unity that stifles protest. For peace cannot be purchased at the cost of liberty.

In Selma tonight, as in every—and we had a good day there—as in every city, we are working for just and peaceful settlement. We must all remember that after this speech I am making tonight, after the police and the FBI and the Marshals have all gone, and after you have promptly passed this bill, the people of Selma and the other cities of the Nation must still live and work together. And when the attention of the Nation has gone elsewhere they must try to heal the wounds and to build a new community.

This cannot be easily done on a battleground of violence, as the history of the South itself shows. It is in recognition of this that men of both races have shown such an outstandingly impressive responsibility in recent days—last Tuesday, again today.

Rights Must Be Opportunities

The bill that I am presenting to you will be known as a civil rights bill. But, in a larger sense, most of the program I am recommending is a civil rights program. Its object is to open the city of hope to all people of all races.

Because all Americans just must have the right to vote. And we are going to give them that right.

All Americans must have the privileges of citizenship regardless of race. And they are going to have those privileges of citizenship regardless of race. But I would like to caution you and remind you that to exercise these privileges takes much more than just legal right. It requires a trained mind and a healthy body. It requires a decent home, and the chance to find a job, and the opportunity to escape from the clutches of poverty.

Of course, people cannot contribute to the Nation if they are never taught to read or write, if their bodies are stunted from hunger, if their sickness goes untended, if their life is spent in hopeless poverty just drawing a welfare check.

So we want to open the gates to opportunity. But we are also going to give all our people, black and white, the help that they need to walk through those gates.

The Purpose of the Government

My first job after college was as a teacher in Cotulla, Texas, in a small Mexican-American school. Few of them could speak English, and I couldn't speak much Spanish. My students were poor and they often came to class without breakfast, hungry. They knew even in their youth the pain of prejudice. They never seemed to know why people disliked them. But they knew it was so, because I saw it in their eyes. I often walked home late in the afternoon, after the classes were finished, wishing there was more that I could do. But all I knew was to teach them the little that I knew, hoping that it might help them against the hardships that lay ahead.

Somehow you never forget what poverty and hatred can do when you see its scars on the hopeful face of a young child.

I never thought then, in 1928, that I would be standing here in 1965. It never even occurred to me in my fondest dreams that I might have the chance to help the sons and daughters of those students and to help people like them all over this country. But now I do have that chance—and I'll let you in on a secret—I mean to use it. And I hope that you will use it with me.

This is the richest and most powerful country which ever occupied the globe. The might of past empires is little compared to ours. But I do not want to be the President who built empires, or sought grandeur, or extended dominion.

I want to be the President who educated young children to the wonders of their world. I want to be the President who helped to feed the hungry and to prepare them to be taxpayers instead of taxeaters.

I want to be the President who helped the poor to find their own way and who protected the right of every citizen to vote in every election.

I want to be the President who helped to end hatred among his fellow men and who promoted love among the people of all races and all regions and all parties. I want to be the President who helped to end war among the brothers of this earth. And so at the request of your beloved Speaker and the Senator from Montana; the majority leader, the Senator from Illinois; the minority leader, Mr. McCulloch, and other Members of both parties, I came here tonight—not as President Roosevelt came down one time in person to veto a bonus bill, not as President Truman came down one time to urge the passage of a railroad bill—but I came down here to ask you to share this task with me and to share it with the people that we both work for. I want this to be the Congress, Republicans and Democrats alike, which did all these things for all these people.

Beyond this great chamber, out yonder in 50 States, are the people that we serve. Who can tell what deep and unspoken hopes are in their hearts tonight as they sit there and listen. We all can guess, from our own lives, how difficult they often find their own pursuit of happiness, how many problems each little family has. They look most of all to themselves for their futures. But I think that they also look to each of us. Above the pyramid on the great seal of the United States it says—in Latin—"God has favored our undertaking."

God will not favor everything that we do. It is rather our duty to divine His will. But I cannot help believing that He truly understands and that He really favors the undertaking that we begin here tonight.

Robert F. Kennedy **88**

The Value of Dissent, 1968

Sen. Robert F. Kennedy, a New York Democrat and brother of the slain president, delivered this address at Vanderbilt University in Nashville, Tennessee, on March 21, 1968. As he did throughout his short presidential campaign, he touched on the morality of fighting poverty and standing up against the forces of social stagnation. As the United States plunged into chaos with civil rights demonstrations and protests against the Vietnam War, Kennedy spoke in favor of the right to dissent. By 1968, the debate on civil liberties had become a debate on how far criticism of the government could extend. Many Americans bristled at any suggestion that the United States had fallen short of its principles. Kennedy argued that a man could love his country and still criticize questionable policies; that a man scrutinizes his government because he loves his country.

When we are told to forego all dissent and division, we must ask: Who is it that is truly dividing the country? It is not those who call for change; it is those who make present policy who divide our country; those who bear the responsibility for our present course; those who have removed themselves from the American tradition, from the enduring and generous impulses that are the soul of the nation . . .

Those who now call for an end to dissent, moreover, seem not to understand what this country is all about. For debate and dissent are the very heart of the American process. We have followed the wisdom of Greece: "all things are examined and brought into question. There is no limit set to thought."

For debate is all we have to prevent past errors from leading us down the road to disaster. How else is error to be corrected, if not by the informed reason of dissent? Every dictatorship has ultimately strangled in the web of repression it wove for its people, making mistakes that could not be corrected because criticism was prohibited . . .

A second purpose of debate is to give voice and recognition to those without the power to be heard. There are millions of Americans living in hidden places, whose

Robert F. Kennedy, *RFK: Collected Speeches*, Edwin O. Guthman and C. Richard Allen, eds. (New York: Viking, 1993): 331–333 faces and names we never know. But I have seen children starving in Mississippi, idling their lives away in the ghetto, living without hope or future amid the despair on Indian reservations, with no jobs and little hope. I have seen proud men in the hills of Appalachia, who wish only to work in dignity—but the mines are closed, and the jobs are gone and no one, neither industry or labor or government, has cared enough to help. Those conditions will change, those children will live, only if we dissent. So I dissent, and I know you do too.

A third reason for dissent in not because it is comforting, but because it is not—because it sharply reminds us of our basic ideals and true purpose. Only broad and fundamental dissent will allow us to confront—not only material poverty—but the poverty of satisfaction that afflicts us all . . .

So if we are uneasy about our country today, perhaps it is because we are truer to our principles than we realize, because we know that our happiness will not come from the goods we have, but from the good we do together . . .

We say with [French playwright Albert] Camus: "I should like to be able to love my country and still love justice." . . .

So I come here today, to this great university, to ask your help—not for me—for your country and for the future of your world. You are the people, as President Kennedy said, who have "the least ties to the present and the greatest ties to the future." I urge you to learn the harsh facts that lurk behind the mask of official illusion with which we have concealed our true circumstances, even from ourselves. Our country is in danger: Not just form foreign enemies; but above all, from our own misguided policies, and what they can do to this country, There is a contest, not for the rule of America, but for the hear of America. In these next eight months, we are going to decide what this country will stand for, and what kind of men we are. So I ask for your help, in the cities and homes of this state, in the towns and farms, contributing your concern and your action, warning of the danger of what we are doing, and the promise of what we can do. I ask you, as thousands of young men and women are doing all over this land, to organize yourselves, and then go forth and work for new policies—work to change our direction—and thus restore our place at the point of moral leadership, in our country, in our own hearts, and all around the world.

BARBARA JORDAN **89**

Defending the Constitution, 1974

As Congress began considering drawing up impeachment charges against President Richard Nixon in regard to the Watergate break-in and cover-up, U. S. Rep. Barbara Jordan of Texas, the first African-American woman elected to Congress from that state, delivered a powerful address on the constitution to the House Judiciary Committee. She emphasized one component of free government: the

www.pbs.org/greatspeeches; http://gos.sbc.edu/j/jordan3.html

sanctity and inviolability of the justice system and that freedom is in danger where justice and the due process of law are threatened. No one can be free so long as others, particularly government officials, believe that they are above the law. Because of Nixon's actions in this regard, he was forced to resign from the presidency just weeks after this July 1974 speech.

Mr. Chairman:

I join my colleague Mr. [New York Congressman Charlie] Rangel in thanking you for giving the junior members of this committee the glorious opportunity of sharing the pain of this inquiry. Mr. Chairman, you are a strong man and it has not been easy but we have tried as best we can to give you as much assistance as possible.

Earlier today, we heard the beginning of the Preamble to the Constitution of the United States, "We, the people." It is a very eloquent beginning. But when the document was completed on the seventeenth of September 1787 I was not included in that "We, the people." I felt somehow for many years that George Washington and Alexander Hamilton just left me out by mistake. But through the process of amendment, interpretation and court decision I have finally been included in "We, the people."

Today, I am an inquisitor; I believe hyperbole would not be fictional and would not overstate the solemnness that I feel right now. My faith in the Constitution is whole, it is complete, it is total. I am not going to sit here and be an idle spectator to the diminution, the subversion, the destruction of the Constitution.

. . . The subject of its jurisdiction are those offenses which proceed from the misconduct of public men. That is what we are talking about. In other words, the jurisdiction comes from the abuse or violation of some public trust. It is wrong, I suggest, it is a misreading of the Constitution, for any member here to assert that for a member to vote for an article of impeachment means that that member must be convinced that the President should be removed from office.

The Constitution doesn't say that. The powers relating to impeachment are an essential check in the hands of this body, the legislature, against and upon the encroachment of the Executive. In establishing the division between the two branches of the legislature, the House and the Senate, assigning to the one the right to accuse and to the other the right to judge, the framers of this Constitution were very astute. They did not make the accusers and the judges the same person.

We know the nature of impeachment. We have been talking about it awhile now. It is chiefly designed for the President and his high ministers to somehow be called into account. It is designed to "bridle" the Executive if he engages in excesses. It is designed as a method of national inquest into the conduct of public men. The framers confined in the Congress the power, if need be, to remove the President in order to strike a delicate balance between a President swollen with power and grown tyrannical and preservation of the independence of the Executive. The nature of impeachment is a narrowly channeled exception to the separation of powers maxim; the federal convention of 1787 said that. It limited impeachment to high crimes and misdemeanors and discounted and opposed the term, "maladministration." "It is to be used only for great misdemeanors," so it was said in the North Carolina ratification convention. And in the Virginia ratification convention: "We need one branch to check the others."

The North Carolina ratification convention: "No one need to be afraid that officers who commit oppression will pass with immunity.

"Prosecutions of impeachments will seldom fail to agitate the passions of the whole community," said Hamilton in the *Federalist Papers*, number 65. "And to divide it into parties more or less friendly or inimical to the accused." I do not mean political parties in that sense.

The drawing of political lines goes to the motivation behind impeachment; but impeachment must proceed within the confines of the constitutional term, "high crime and misdemeanors."

Of the impeachment process, it was Woodrow Wilson who said that "nothing short of the grossest offenses against the plain law of the land will suffice to give them speed and effectiveness. Indignation so great as to overgrow party interest may secure a conviction; but nothing else can."

Common sense would be revolted if we engaged upon this process for petty reasons. Congress has a lot to do: Appropriations, tax reform, health insurance, campaign finance reform, housing, environmental protection, energy sufficiency, mass transportation. Pettiness cannot be allowed to stand in the face of such overwhelming problems. So today we are not being petty. We are trying to be big, because the task we have before us is a big one.

This morning, in a discussion of the evidence, we were told that the evidence which purports to support the allegations of misuse of the CIA by the President is thin. We are told that that evidence is insufficient. What that recital of the evidence this morning did not include is what the President did know on June 23, 1972. The President did know that it was Republican money, that it was money from the Committee for the Re-election of the President, which was found in the possession of one of the burglars arrested on June 17.

What the President did know on June 23 was the prior activities of E. Howard Hunt, which included his participation in the break-in of Daniel Ellsberg's psychiatrist, which included Howard Hunt's participation in the Dita Beard ITT affair, which included Howard Hunt's fabrication of cables designed to discredit the Kennedy Administration.

We were further cautioned today that perhaps these proceedings ought to be delayed because certainly there would be new evidence forthcoming from the President of the United States. There has not even been an obfuscated indication that this committee would receive any additional materials from the President. The committee subpoena is outstanding and if the President wants to supply that material, the committee sits here. The fact is that on yesterday, the American people waited with great anxiety for eight hours, not knowing whether their President would obey an order of the Supreme Court of the United States.

At this point, I would like to juxtapose a few of the impeachment criteria with some of the President's actions.

Impeachment criteria: James Madison, from the Virginia ratification convention. "If the President be connected in any suspicious manner with any person and there is grounds to believe that he will shelter him, he may be impeached."

We have heard time and time again that the evidence reflects payment to the defendants of money. The President had knowledge that these funds were being paid and that these were funds collected for the 1972 presidential campaign. We know that the President met with Mr. Henry Petersen twenty-seven times to discuss matters related to Watergate, and immediately thereafter met with the very persons who were implicated in the information Mr. Petersen was receiving and transmitting to the President. The words are, "If the President be connected in any suspicious manner with any person and there be grounds to believe that he will shelter that person, he may be impeached."

Justice [Joseph] Story: "Impeachment is intended for occasional and extraordinary cases where a superior power acting for the whole people is put into operation to protect their rights and rescue their liberties from violations."

We know about the Houston plan. We know about the break-in of the psychiatrist's office. We know that there was absolute, complete direction in August 1971 when the President instructed Ehrlichman to "do whatever is necessary." This instruction led to a surreptitious entry into Dr. Fielding's office. "Protect their rights." "Rescue their liberties from violation."

The South Carolina ratification convention impeachment criteria: Those are impeachable "who behave amiss or betray their public trust."

Beginning shortly after the Watergate break-in and continuing to the present time, the President has engaged in a series of public statements and actions designed to thwart the lawful investigation by government prosecutors. Moreover, the President has made public announcements and assertions bearing on the Watergate case which the evidence will show he knew to be false. These assertions, false assertions; impeachable, those who misbehave. Those who "behave amiss or betray their public trust."

James Madison, again at the constitutional convention: "A President is impeachable if he attempts to subvert the Constitution."

The Constitution charges the President with the task of taking care that the laws be faithfully executed, and yet the President has counseled his aides to commit perjury, willfully disregarded the secrecy of grand jury proceedings, concealed surreptitious entry, attempted to compromise a federal judge while publicly displaying his cooperation with the process of criminal justice. "A President is impeachable if he attempts to subvert the Constitution."

If the impeachment provision in the Constitution of the United States will not reach the offenses charged here, then perhaps that eighteenth century Constitution should be abandoned to a twentieth century paper shredder.

Has the President committed offenses and planned and directed and acquiesced in a course of conduct which the Constitution will not tolerate? This is the question. We know that. We know the question.

We should now forthwith proceed to answer the question.

It is reason, and not passion, which must guide our deliberations, guide our debate, and guide our decision.

Mr. Chairman, I yield back the balance of my time.

JIMMY CARTER   **90**

Human Rights and Foreign Policy, 1977

In June 1977, President Jimmy Carter delivered a stirring address at Notre Dame University on the subject of human rights in American foreign policy. In a world threatened by nuclear annihilation by the world's superpowers, Carter averred that the United States could not allow itself to sacrifice the freedom of one nation to preserve its own, even for a short-term political or strategic gain. Human rights, Carter argued, were universal rights. In the years following his presidency, Carter won acclaim for his continuing efforts to bring peace to the nations of the world, winning the Nobel Peace Price in 2002.

Nation: to provide more efficiently for the needs of our people, to demonstrate—against the dark faith of our times—that our Government can be both competent and more humane.

But I want to speak to you today about the strands that connect our actions overseas with our essential character as a nation. I believe we can have a foreign policy that is democratic, that is based on fundamental values, and that uses power and influence, which we have, for humane purposes. We can also have a foreign policy that the American people both support and, for a change, know about and understand.

I have a quiet confidence in our own political system. Because we know that democracy works, we can reject the arguments of those rulers who deny human rights to their people.

We are confident that democracy's example will be compelling, and so we seek to bring that example closer to those from whom in the past few years we have been separated and who are not yet convinced about the advantages of our kind of life.

We are confident that the democratic methods are the most effective, and so we are not tempted to employ improper tactics here at home or abroad.

We are confident of our own strength, so we can seek substantial mutual reductions in the nuclear arms race.

And we are confident of the good sense of American people, and so we let them share in the process of making foreign policy decisions. We can thus speak with the voices of 215 million, and not just of an isolated handful.

Democracy's great recent successes—in India, Portugal, Spain, Greece—show that our confidence in this system is not misplaced. Being confident of our own future, we are now free of that inordinate fear of communism which once led us to embrace any dictator who joined us in that fear. I'm glad that that's being changed.

Jimmy Carter, *Public Papers of the Presidents of the United States: Jimmy Carter*, vol. 1 (Washington, D.C.: Government Printing Office, 1977), 95

For too many years, we've been willing to adopt the flawed and erroneous principles and tactics of our adversaries, sometimes abandoning our own values for theirs. We've fought fire with fire, never thinking that fire is better quenched with water. This approach failed, with Vietnam the best example of its intellectual and moral poverty. But through failure we have now found our way back to our own principles and values, and we have regained our lost confidence.

By the measure of history, our Nation's 200 years are very brief, and our rise to world eminence is briefer still. It dates from 1945, when Europe and the old international order lay in ruins. Before then, America was largely on the periphery of world affairs. But since then, we have inescapably been at the center of world affairs.

Our policy during this period was guided by two principles: a belief that Soviet expansion was almost inevitable but that it must be contained, and the corresponding belief in the importance of an almost exclusive alliance among non-Communist nations on both sides of the Atlantic. That system could not last forever unchanged. Historical trends have weakened its foundation. The unifying threat of conflict with the Soviet Union has become less intensive, even though the competition has become more extensive.

The Vietnamese war produced a profound moral crisis, sapping worldwide faith in our own policy and our system of life, a crisis of confidence made even more grave by the covert pessimism of some of our leaders.

In less than a generation, we've seen the world change dramatically. The daily lives and aspirations of most human beings have been transformed. Colonialism is nearly gone. A new sense of national identity now exists in almost 100 new countries that have been formed in the last generation. Knowledge has become more widespread. Aspirations are higher. As more people have been freed from traditional constraints, more have been determined to achieve, for the first time in their lives, social justice.

The world is still divided by ideological disputes, dominated by regional conflicts, and threatened by danger that we will not resolve the differences of race and wealth without violence or without drawing into combat the major military powers. We can no longer separate the traditional issues of war and peace from the new global questions of justice, equity, and human rights.

It is a new world, but America should not fear it. It is a new world, and we should help to shape it. It is a new world that calls for a new American foreign policy—a policy based on constant decency in its values and on optimism in our historical vision.

We can no longer have a policy solely for the industrial nations as the foundation of global stability, but we must respond to the new reality of a politically awakening world.

We can no longer expect that the other 150 nations will follow the dictates of the powerful, but we must continue—confidently—our efforts to inspire, to persuade, and to lead.

Our policy must reflect our belief that the world can hope for more than simple survival and our belief that dignity and freedom are fundamental spiritual requirements. Our policy must shape an international system that will last longer than secret deals.

We cannot make this kind of policy by manipulation. Our policy must be open; it must be candid; it must be one of constructive global involvement, resting on five cardinal principles.

I've tried to make these premises clear to the American people since last January. Let me review what we have been doing and discuss what we intend to do.

First, we have reaffirmed America's commitment to human rights as a fundamental tenet of our foreign policy. In ancestry, religion, color, place of origin, and cultural background, we Americans are as diverse a nation as the world has even seen. No common mystique of blood or soil unites us. What draws us together, perhaps more than anything else, is a belief in human freedom. We want the world to know that our Nation stands for more than financial prosperity.

This does not mean that we can conduct our foreign policy by rigid moral maxims. We live in a world that is imperfect and which will always be imperfect—a world that is complex and confused and which will always be complex and confused.

I understand fully the limits of moral suasion. We have no illusion that changes will come easily or soon. But I also believe that it is a mistake to undervalue the power of words and of the ideas that words embody. In our own history, that power has ranged from Thomas Paine's "Common Sense" to Martin Luther King, Jr.'s "I Have a Dream."

In the life of the human spirit, words are action, much more so than many of us may realize who live in countries where freedom of expression is taken for granted. The leaders of totalitarian nations understand this very well. The proof is that words are precisely the action for which dissidents in those countries are being persecuted.

Nonetheless, we can already see dramatic, worldwide advances in the protection of the individual from the arbitrary power of the state. For us to ignore this trend would be to lose influence and moral authority in the world. To lead it will be to regain the moral stature that we once had.

The great democracies are not free because we are strong and prosperous. I believe we are strong and influential and prosperous because we are free.

Throughout the world today, in free nations and in totalitarian countries as well, there is a preoccupation with the subject of human freedom, human rights. And I believe it is incumbent on us in this country to keep that discussion, that debate, that contention alive. No other country is as well-qualified as we to set an example. We have our own shortcomings and faults, and we should strive constantly and with courage to make sure that we are legitimately proud of what we have.

Second, we've moved deliberately to reinforce the bonds among our democracies. In our recent meetings in London, we agreed to widen our economic cooperation, to promote free trade, to strengthen the world's monetary system, to seek ways of avoiding nuclear proliferation. We prepared constructive proposals for the forthcoming meetings on North-South problems of poverty, development, and global well-being. And we agreed on joint efforts to reinforce and to modernize our common defense.

You may be interested in knowing that at this NATO meeting, for the first time in more than 25 years, all members are democracies. Even more important, all of us reaffirmed our basic optimism in the future of the democratic system. Our spirit of confidence is spreading. Together, our democracies can help to shape the wider architecture of global cooperation.

Third, we've moved to engage the Soviet Union in a joint effort to halt the strategic arms race. This race is not only dangerous, it's morally deplorable. We must put an end to it. I know it will not be easy to reach agreements. Our goal is to be fair to both sides, to produce reciprocal stability, parity, and security. We desire a freeze on further modernization and production of weapons and a continuing, substantial reduction of strategic nuclear weapons as well. We want a comprehensive ban on all nuclear testing, a prohibition against all chemical warfare, no attack capability against space satellites, and arms limitations in the Indian Ocean.

We hope that we can take joint steps with all nations toward a final agreement eliminating nuclear weapons completely from our arsenals of death. We will persist in this effort.

Now, I believe in detente with the Soviet Union. To me it means progress toward peace. But the effects of detente should not be limited to our own two countries alone. We hope to persuade the Soviet Union that one country cannot impose its system of society upon another, either through direct military intervention or through the use of a client state's military force, as was the case with Cuban intervention in Angola.

Cooperation also implies obligation. We hope that the Soviet Union will join with us and other nations in playing a larger role in aiding the developing world, for common aid efforts will help us build a bridge of mutual confidence in one another.

Fourth, we are taking deliberate steps to improve the chances of lasting peace in the Middle East. Through wide-ranging consultation with leaders of the countries involved—Israel, Syria, Jordan, and Egypt—we have found some areas of agreement and some movement toward consensus. The negotiations must continue.

Through my own public comments, I've also tried to suggest a more flexible framework for the discussion of the three key issues which have so far been so intractable: the nature of a comprehensive peace—what is peace; what does it mean to the Israelis; what does it mean to their Arab neighbors; secondly, the relationship between security and borders—how can the dispute over border delineations be established and settled with a feeling of security on both sides; and the issue of the Palestinian homeland.

The historic friendship that the United States has with Israel is not dependent on domestic politics in either nation; it's derived from our common respect for human freedom and from a common search for permanent peace.

We will continue to promote a settlement which all of us need. Our own policy will not be affected by changes in leadership in any of the countries in the Middle East. Therefore, we expect Israel and her neighbors to continue to be bound by United Nations Resolutions 242 and 338, which they have previously accepted.

This may be the most propitious time for a genuine settlement since the beginning of the Arab-Israeli conflict almost 30 years ago. To let this opportunity pass could mean disaster not only for the Middle East but, perhaps, for the international political and economic order as well.

And fifth, we are attempting, even at the risk of some friction with our friends, to reduce the danger of nuclear proliferation and the worldwide spread of conventional weapons.

At the recent summit, we set in motion an international effort to determine the best ways of harnessing nuclear energy for peaceful use while reducing the risks that its products will be diverted to the making of explosives.

We've already completed a comprehensive review of our own policy on arms transfers. Competition in arms sales is inimical to peace and destructive of the economic development of the poorer countries.

We will, as a matter of national policy now in our country, seek to reduce the annual dollar volume of arms sales, to restrict the transfer of advanced weapons, and to reduce the extent of our coproduction arrangements about weapons with foreign states. And just as important, we are trying to get other nations, both free and otherwise, to join us in this effort.

But all of this that I've described is just the beginning. It's a beginning aimed towards a clear goal: to create a wider framework of international cooperation suited to the new and rapidly changing historical circumstances.

We will cooperate more closely with the newly influential countries in Latin America, Africa, and Asia. We need their friendship and cooperation in a common effort as the structure of world power changes.

More than 100 years ago, Abraham Lincoln said that our Nation could not exist half slave and half free. We know a peaceful world cannot long exist one-third rich and two-thirds hungry.

Most nations share our faith that, in the long run, expanded and equitable trade will best help the developing countries to help themselves. But the immediate problems of hunger, disease, illiteracy, and repression are here now.

The Western democracies, the OPEC nations, and the developed Communist countries can cooperate through existing international institutions in providing more effective aid. This is an excellent alternative to war.

We have a special need for cooperation and consultation with other nations in this hemisphere—to the north and to the south. We do not need another slogan. Although these are our close friends and neighbors, our links with them are the same links of equality that we forge for the rest of the world. We will be dealing with them as part of a new, worldwide mosaic of global, regional, and bilateral relations.

It's important that we make progress toward normalizing relations with the People's Republic of China. We see the American and Chinese relationship as a central element of our global policy and China as a key force for global peace. We wish to cooperate closely with the creative Chinese people on the problems that confront all mankind. And we hope to find a formula which can bridge some of the difficulties that still separate us.

Finally, let me say that we are committed to a peaceful resolution of the crisis in southern Africa. The time has come for the principle of majority rule to be the basis for political order, recognizing that in a democratic system the rights of the minority must also be protected.

To be peaceful, change must come promptly. The United States is determined to work together with our European allies and with the concerned African States to shape a congenial international framework for the rapid and progressive transformation of southern African society and to help protect it from unwarranted outside interference.

Let me conclude by summarizing: Our policy is based on an historical vision of America's role. Our policy is derived from a larger view of global change. Our policy is rooted in our moral values, which never change. Our policy is reinforced by our material wealth and by our military power. Our policy is designed to serve mankind. And it is a policy that I hope will make you proud to be Americans.

CESAR CHAVEZ

91

Eulogy for Rufino Contreras, 1979

The United Farm Workers was formed in the 1960s by migrant farm workers upset over low pay, racial discrimination, and dangerous working conditions they faced. Most of these migrant farm workers were of Hispanic heritage, and many were immigrants or the children of immigrants. Under the leadership of Cesar Chavez, himself a migrant farm worker who rose through the ranks of the movement, the union won a few modest gains in pay scales, working conditions across the Southwest, and recognition of their union. Still, the union faced violent opposition in the face of their nonviolent protests. On February 10, 1979, Rufino Contreras, a twenty-seven year old who had joined the strike to ask for better pay and working conditions for lettuce workers, was shot and killed. Chavez delivered this address at the funeral of Contreras in February 1979 in Calexico, California, near the Mexican border. In his eulogy, Chavez touches on a theme he would repeat often, "What is the worth of a man?" He answered this through his work by defending the sanctity of human life and the right of hard-working individuals to earn a living.

February 10, 1979, was a day of infamy for farm workers. It was a day without joy. The sun didn't shine. The birds didn't sing. The rain didn't fall.

Why was this such a day of evil? Because on this day greed and injustice struck down our brother Rufino Contreras.

What is the worth of a man? What is the worth of a farm worker? Rufino, his father and brother together gave the company 20 years of their labor. They were faithful workers who helped build up the wealth of their boss, helped build up the wealth of his ranch.

What was their reward for their service and their sacrifice? When they petitioned for a more just share of what they themselves produced, when they spoke out against the injustice they endured, the company answered them with bullets; the company sent hired guns to quiet Rufino Contreras.

Capital and labor together produce the fruit of the land. But what really counts is labor: the human beings who torture their bodies, sacrifice their youth and numb their spirits to produce this great agricultural wealth—a wealth so vast that it feeds all of America and much of the world. And yet the men, women and children who are the flesh and blood of this production often do not have enough to feed themselves.

But we are here today to say that true wealth is not measured in money or status or power. It is measured in the legacy that we leave behind for those we love and those we inspire.

In that sense, Rufino is not dead. Wherever farm workers organize, stand up for their rights and strike for justice, Rufino Contreras is with them.

Rufino lives among us. It is those who have killed him and those who have conspired to kill him that have died; because the love, the compassion, the light in their hearts have been stilled.

Why do we say that Rufino still lives? Because those of us who mourn him today and bring him to his rest rededicate ourselves to the ideals for which he gave his life. Rufino built a union that will someday bring justice to all farm workers.

If Rufino were alive today, what would he tell us? He would tell us, "Don't be afraid. Don't be discouraged." He would tell us, "Don't cry for me, organize!"

This is a day of sorrow, but it is also a day of hope. It is a time of sadness because our friend and brother is dead. It is a time of hope because we are certain that Rufino today enjoys the justice in heaven that was denied him on earth.

It is our mission to finish the work Rufino has begun among us, knowing that true justice for ourselves and our opponents is only possible before God, who is the final judge.

MARIO CUOMO   **92**

A Tale of Two Cities, 1984

Gov. Mario Cuomo of New York delivered this stunning address to the Democratic National Convention in San Francisco on July 16, 1984. In this speech, he attacked Ronald Reagan's speech at the Republican National Convention that Cuomo and many Democrats believed overlooked major social problems of poverty in the United States. In this rousing address, Cuomo asserts that one of the most essential duties of a free nation is to provide everyone with an opportunity to escape poverty. For individuals to be free, they must have the freedom of opportunity and freedom of economic mobility which would give individuals control over their destinies. And since governments are responsible for protecting freedom, governments must provide individuals with the means to move upward economically. This was part of a major debate on American social policy in the latter decades of the twentieth century, of whether the government should protect this freedom of opportunity by actively working with individuals to relieve poverty or by standing aside.

On behalf of the great Empire State and the whole family of New York, let me thank you for the great privilege of being able to address this convention. Please allow me to skip the stories and the poetry and the temptation to deal in nice but vague rhetoric. Let me instead use this valuable opportunity to deal immediately with the questions that should determine this election and that we all know are vital to the American people.

Ten days ago, President Reagan admitted that although some people in this country seemed to be doing well nowadays, others were unhappy, and even worried, about themselves, their families and their futures.

Mario M. Cuomo, "A Tale of Two Cities," *More Than Words* (New York: St. Martin's Press, 1993): 22–31

The President said that he didn't understand that fear. He said, "Why, this country is a shining city on a hill."

The President is right. In many ways we are "a shining city on a hill."

But the hard truth is that not everyone is sharing in this city's splendor and glory. A shining city is perhaps all the President sees from the portico of the White House and the veranda of his ranch, where everyone seems to be doing well.

But there's another city, another part of the shining city, the part where some people can't pay their mortgages, and most young people can't afford one, where students can't afford the education they need, and middle class parents watch the dreams they hold for their children evaporate.

In this part of the city, there are more poor than ever, more families in trouble, more and more people who need help but can't find it. Even worse: There are elderly people who tremble in the basements of their houses there, and there are poor who sleep in the city's streets, in the gutter, where the glitter doesn't show. There are ghettos where thousands of young people, without an education or a job, give their lives away to drug dealers every day.

There is despair, Mr. President, in faces you don't see, in the places you don't visit in your shining city. In fact, Mr. President, this is a nation—Mr. President, you ought to know that this nation is more of a "Tale of Two Cities," than it is just a "shining city on a hill."

Maybe, if you visited more places, Mr. President, you'd understand. Maybe if you went to Appalachia where some people still live in sheds, and to Lackawanna [New York] where thousands of unemployed steel workers wonder why we subsidize foreign steel; maybe if you stopped in at a shelter in Chicago and talked with some of the homeless there.

Maybe Mr. President, if you asked a woman who'd been denied the help she needs to feed her children because you say we need the money to give a tax break to a millionaire, or for a missile we couldn't afford to use—maybe then you'd understand. Maybe, Mr. President, but I'm afraid not. Because, the truth is, this is how we were warned it would be.

President Reagan told us from the very beginning that he believed in a kind of social Darwinism. Survival of the fittest. "Government can't do everything," we were told. So it should settle for taking care of the strong and hope that economic ambition and charity will do the rest. Make the rich richer and what falls from the table will be enough for the middle class and those trying to make it, to work their way into the middle class.

The Republicans called it "trickle-down" when [President Herbert] Hoover tried it. Now they call it "supply-side." It's the same shining city for those relative few who are lucky enough to live in its good neighborhoods. But for the people who are excluded—but for the people who are locked out—all they can do is stare from a distance at that city's glimmering towers.

The Republicans believe the wagon train will not make it to the frontier unless some of our old, some of our young, and some of our weak are left behind by the side of the trail.

The strong—the strong they tell us—will inherit the land!

We Democrats believe that we can make it all the way with the whole family intact. We have. More than once.

Ever since Franklin Roosevelt lifted himself from his wheelchair to lift this nation from its knees, wagon train after wagon train to new frontiers of education, housing, peace. The whole family aboard. Constantly reaching out to extend and enlarge the family. Lifting them up into the wagon on the way. Blacks and Hispanics, people of every ethnic group, and Native Americans—all those struggling to build their families and claim some small share of America.

We Democrats must unite so that the entire nation can. Surely the Republicans won't bring the country together. Their policies divide the nation into the lucky and the left out, the royalty and the rabble.

The Republicans are willing to treat this division as victory. They would cut this nation in half, into those temporarily better off and those worse off than before, and call that division "recovery."

. . . We believe we must be the family of America, recognizing that at the heart of the matter we are bound one to another, that the problems of a retired school teacher in Duluth are our problems. That the future of the child in Buffalo is our future. The struggle of a disabled man in Boston to survive, to live decently, is our struggle. The hunger of a woman in Little Rock, our hunger. The failure anywhere to provide what reasonably we might, to avoid pain, is our failure.

For fifty years, we Democrats created a better future for our children using traditional democratic principles as a fixed beacon, giving us direction and purpose, but constantly innovating, adapting to new realities. [Franklin] Roosevelt's alphabet programs, [President Harry] Truman's NATO and the G.I. Bill of Rights, Kennedy's intelligent tax incentives and the Alliance for Progress, Johnson's civil rights, Carter's human rights and the nearly miraculous Camp David Accord. Democrats did it, and Democrats can do it again.

And we can do it again, if we do not forget, forget that this entire nation has profited by these progressive principles. That they helped lift up generations to the middle class and higher. That they gave us a chance to work, to go to college, to raise a family, to own a house, to be secure in our old age, and before that to reach heights that our own parents would not have dared to dream of.

That struggle to live with dignity is the real story of the shining city, and it's a story, ladies and gentlemen, I didn't read in a book or learn in a classroom. I saw it and lived it, like many of you. I watched a small man with thick calluses on both hands work fifteen and sixteen hours a day. I saw him once literally bleed from the bottoms of his feet, a man who came here uneducated, alone, unable to speak the language, who taught me all I needed to know about faith and hard work and simple eloquence of his example. I learned about our obligation to each other from him and from my mother. And they asked to be protected in those moments when they would not be able to protect themselves. This nation and its government did that for them.

And that they were able to build a family and live in dignity and see one of their children go from behind their little grocery store in South Jamaica, on the other side of the tracks were he was born, to occupy the highest seat in the greatest state in the greatest nation, in the only world we know, is an ineffably beautiful tribute to the democratic process.

And, ladies and gentlemen, on January 20, 1985, it will happen again. Only on a much, much grander scale. We will have a new President of the United States, a Democrat born not to the blood of kings but the blood of pioneers and immigrants.

We will have America's first woman Vice-President, the child of immigrants, and she will open with one magnificent stroke a whole new frontier for the United States. It will happen, if we make it happen—if you and I make it happen.

I ask you, ladies and gentlemen, brothers and sisters, for the good of all of us—for the love of this great nation, for the family of America—for the love of God, please, make this nation remember how futures are built.

Thank you and God bless you.

1984 Democratic National Convention Keynote Address, ©1984 by Mario Cuomo.

CESAR CHAVEZ **93**

Address to the Commonwealth Club of California, 1984

On November 9, 1984, Cesar Chavez gave this address before the prestigious Commonwealth Club in San Francisco, California. He reiterates many of the ideas he had expressed through his years as president of the United Farm Workers. He recounts the plight of farm workers who had little education or opportunity to improve themselves, little money for food, and having to work bare-handed in fields wet with pesticides. His union thus became more than just a labor union or a civil rights movement, but a demand for these laborers to claim a piece of the American Dream. Ultimately, he makes the cause of the union one of freedom—the freedom to organize, the freedom to live without fear or oppression, and the freedom to live in dignity.

Twenty-one years ago last September, on a lonely stretch of railroad track paralleling U.S. Highway 101 near Salinas, 32 Bracero farm workers lost their lives in a tragic accident.

The Braceros had been imported from Mexico to work on California farms. They died when their bus, which was converted from a flatbed truck, drove in front of a freight train.

Conversion of the bus had not been approved by any government agency. The driver had "tunnel" vision.

Most of the bodies lay unidentified for days. No one, including the grower who employed the workers, even knew their names.

Today, thousands of farm workers live under savage conditions—beneath trees and amid garbage and human excrement—near tomato fields in San Diego County, tomato fields which use the most modern farm technology.

Vicious rats gnaw on them as they sleep. They walk miles to buy food at inflated prices. And they carry in water from irrigation pumps.

Child labor is still common in many farm areas.

As much as 30 percent of Northern California's garlic harvesters are under-aged children. Kids as young as six years old have voted in state-conducted union elections since they qualified as workers.

Some 800,000 under-aged children work with their families harvesting crops across America. Babies born to migrant workers suffer 25 percent higher infant mortality than the rest of the population.

Malnutrition among migrant worker children is 10 times higher than the national rate.

Farm workers' average life expectancy is still 49 years—compared to 73 years for the average American.

All my life, I have been driven by one dream, one goal, one vision: To overthrow a farm labor system in this nation which treats farm workers as if they were not important human beings.

Farm workers are not agricultural implements. They are not beasts of burden—to be used and discarded.

That dream was born in my youth. It was nurtured in my early days of organizing. It has flourished. It has been attacked.

I'm not very different from anyone else who has ever tried to accomplish something with his life. My motivation comes from my personal life—from watching what my mother and father went through when I was growing up; from what we experienced as migrant farm workers in California.

That dream, that vision, grew from my own experience with racism, with hope, with the desire to be treated fairly and to see my people treated as human beings and not as chattel.

It grew from anger and rage—emotions I felt 40 years ago when people of my color were denied the right to see a movie or eat at a restaurant in many parts of California.

It grew from the frustration and humiliation I felt as a boy who couldn't understand how the growers could abuse and exploit farm workers when there were so many of us and so few of them.

Later, in the '50s, I experienced a different kind of exploitation. In San Jose, in Los Angeles and in other urban communities, we—the Mexican American people—were dominated by a majority that was Anglo.

I began to realize what other minority people had discovered: That the only answer—the only hope—was in organizing. More of us had to become citizens. We had to register to vote. And people like me had to develop the skills it would take to organize, to educate, to help empower the Chicano people.

I spent many years—before we founded the union—learning how to work with people.

We experienced some successes in voter registration, in politics, in battling racial discrimination—successes in an era when Black Americans were just beginning to assert their civil rights and when political awareness among Hispanics was almost non-existent.

But deep in my heart, I knew I could never be happy unless I tried organizing the farm workers. I didn't know if I would succeed. But I had to try.

All Hispanics—urban and rural, young and old—are connected to the farm workers' experience. We had all lived through the fields—or our parents had. We shared that common humiliation.

How could we progress as a people, even if we lived in the cities, while the farm workers—men and women of our color—were condemned to a life without pride? How could we progress as a people while the farm workers—who symbolized our history in this land—were denied self-respect?

How could our people believe that their children could become lawyers and doctors and judges and business people while this shame, this injustice was permitted to continue?

Those who attack our union often say, "It's not really a union. It's something else: A social movement. A civil rights movement. It's something dangerous."

They're half right. The United Farm Workers is first and foremost a union. A union like any other. A union that either produces for its members on the bread and butter issues or doesn't survive.

But the UFW has always been something more than a union—although it's never been dangerous if you believe in the Bill of Rights.

The UFW was the beginning! We attacked that historical source of shame and infamy that our people in this country lived with. We attacked that injustice, not by complaining; not by seeking hand-outs; not by becoming soldiers in the War on Poverty.

We organized!

Farm workers acknowledged we had allowed ourselves to become victims in a democratic society—a society where majority rule and collective bargaining are supposed to be more than academic theories or political rhetoric. And by addressing this historical problem, we created confidence and pride and hope in an entire people's ability to create the future.

The UFW's survival—its existence—was not in doubt in my mind when the time began to come—after the union became visible—when Chicanos started entering college in greater numbers, when Hispanics began running for public office in greater numbers—when our people started asserting their rights on a broad range of issues and in many communities across the country.

The union's survival—its very existence—sent out a signal to all Hispanics that we were fighting for our dignity, that we were challenging and overcoming injustice, that we were empowering the least educated among us—the poorest among us.

The message was clear: If it could happen in the fields, it could happen anywhere—in the cities, in the courts, in the city councils, in the state legislatures.

I didn't really appreciate it at the time, but the coming of our union signaled the start of great changes among Hispanics that are only now beginning to be seen.

I've traveled to every part of this nation. I have met and spoken with thousands of Hispanics from every walk of life—from every social and economic class. One thing I hear most often from Hispanics, regardless of age or position—and from many non-Hispanics as well—is that the farm workers gave them hope that they could succeed and the inspiration to work for change.

From time to time you will hear our opponents declare that the union is weak, that the union has no support, that the union has not grown fast enough. Our obituary has been written many times.

How ironic it is that the same forces which argue so passionately that the union is not influential are the same forces that continue to fight us so hard.

The union's power in agriculture has nothing to do with the number of farm workers under union contract. It has nothing to do with the farm workers' ability to contribute to Democratic politicians. It doesn't even have much to do with our ability to conduct successful boycotts.

The very fact of our existence forces an entire industry—unionized and non-unionized—to spend millions of dollars year after year on improved wages, on improved working conditions, on benefits for workers.

If we're so weak and unsuccessful, why do the growers continue to fight us with such passion?

Because so long as we continue to exist, farm workers will benefit from our existence—even if they don't work under union contract.

It doesn't really matter whether we have 100,000 members or 500,000 members. In truth, hundreds of thousands of farm workers in California—and in other states— are better off today because of our work.

And Hispanics across California and the nation who don't work in agriculture are better off today because of what the farm workers taught people about organization, about pride and strength, about seizing control over their own lives.

Tens of thousands of the children and grandchildren of farm workers and the children and grandchildren of poor Hispanics are moving out of the fields and out of the barrios—and into the professions and into business and into politics. And that movement cannot be reversed!

Our union will forever exist as an empowering force among Chicanos in the Southwest. And that means our power and our influence will grow and not diminish. Two major trends give us hope and encouragement.

First, our union has returned to a tried and tested weapon in the farm workers' non-violent arsenal—the boycott!

After the Agricultural Labor Relations Act became law in California in 1975, we dismantled our boycott to work with the law.

During the early- and mid-'70s, millions of Americans supported our boycotts. After 1975, we redirected our efforts from the boycott to organizing and winning elections under the law.

The law helped farm workers make progress in overcoming poverty and injustice. At companies where farm workers are protected by union contracts, we have made progress in overcoming child labor, in overcoming miserable wages and working conditions, in overcoming sexual harassment of women workers, in overcoming dangerous pesticides which poison our people and poison the food we all eat. Where we have organized, these injustices soon pass into history.

But under Republican Governor George Deukmejian, the law that guarantees our right to organize no longer protects farm workers. It doesn't work anymore.

In 1982, corporate growers gave Deukmejian one million dollars to run for governor of California. Since he took office, Deukmejian has paid back his debt to the growers with the blood and sweat of California farm workers.

Instead of enforcing the law as it was written against those who break it, Deukmejian invites growers who break the law to seek relief from the governor's appointees.

What does all this mean for farm workers?

It means that the right to vote in free elections is a sham. It means that the right to talk freely about the union among your fellow workers on the job is a cruel hoax. It means the right to be free from threats and intimidation by growers is an empty promise.

It means the right to sit down and negotiate with your employer as equals across the bargaining table—and not as peons in the field—is a fraud. It means that thousands of farm workers—who are owed millions of dollars in back pay because their employers broke the law—are still waiting for their checks.

It means that 36,000 farm workers—who voted to be represented by the United Farm Workers in free elections—are still waiting for contracts from growers who refuse to bargain in good faith.

It means that, for farm workers, child labor will continue. It means that infant mortality will continue. It means malnutrition among our children will continue. It means the short life expectancy and the inhuman living and working conditions will continue. Are these make-believe threats? Are they exaggerations?

Ask the farm workers who are still waiting for growers to bargain in good faith and sign contracts. Ask the farm workers who've been fired from their jobs because they spoke out for the union. Ask the farm workers who've been threatened with physical violence because they support the UFW.

Ask the family of Rene Lopez, the young farm worker from Fresno who was shot to death last year because he supported the union.

These tragic events forced farm workers to declare a new international boycott of California table grapes. That's why we are asking Americans once again to join the farm workers by boycotting California grapes.

The Louis Harris poll revealed that 17 million American adults boycotted grapes. We are convinced that those people and that good will have not disappeared.

That segment of the population which makes our boycotts work are the Hispanics, the Blacks, the other minorities and our allies in labor and the church. But it is also an entire generation of young Americans who matured politically and socially in the 1960s and '70s—millions of people for whom boycotting grapes and other products became a socially accepted pattern of behavior.

If you were young, Anglo and on or near campus during the late '60s and early '70s, chances are you supported farm workers.

Fifteen years later, the men and women of that generation of are alive and well. They are in their mid-30s and 40s. They are pursuing professional careers. Their disposable income is relatively high. But they are still inclined to respond to an appeal from farm workers. The union's mission still has meaning for them.

Only today we must translate the importance of a union for farm workers into the language of the 1980s. Instead of talking about the right to organize, we must talk about protection against sexual harassment in the fields. We must speak about the right to quality food—and food that is safe to eat.

I can tell you that the new language is working; the 17 million are still there. They are responding—not to picketlines and leafletting alone, but to the high-tech boycott of today—a boycott that uses computers and direct mail and advertising techniques which have revolutionized business and politics in recent years.

We have achieved more success with the boycott in the first 11 months of 1984 that we achieved in the 14 years since 1970.

The other trend that gives us hope is the monumental growth of Hispanic influence in this country and what that means in increased population, increased social and economic clout, and increased political influence.

South of the Sacramento River in California, Hispanics now make up more than 25 percent of the population. That figure will top 30 percent by the year 2000. There are 1.1 million Spanish-surnamed registered voters in California; 85 percent are Democrats; only 13 percent are Republicans.

In 1975, there were 200 Hispanic elected officials at all levels of government. In 1984, there are over 400 elected judges, city council members, mayors and legislators. In light of these trends, it is absurd to believe or suggest that we are going to go back in time—as a union or as a people!

The growers often try to blame the union for their problems—to lay their sins off on us—sins for which they only have themselves to blame.

The growers only have themselves to blame as they begin to reap the harvest from decades of environmental damage they have brought upon the land—the pesticides, the herbicides, the soil fumigants, the fertilizers, the salt deposits from thoughtless irrigation—the ravages from years of unrestrained poisoning of our soil and water.

Thousands of acres of land in California have already been irrevocably damaged by this wanton abuse of nature. Thousands more will be lost unless growers understand that dumping more poisons on the soil won't solve their problems—on the short term or the long term.

Health authorities in many San Joaquin Valley towns already warn young children and pregnant women not to drink the water because of nitrates from fertilizers which have contaminated the groundwater.

The growers only have themselves to blame for an increasing demand by consumers for higher quality food—food that isn't tainted by toxics; food that doesn't result from plant mutations or chemicals which produce red, luscious-looking tomatoes—that taste like alfalfa.

The growers are making the same mistake American automakers made in the '60s and '70s when they refused to produce small economical cars—and opened the door to increased foreign competition.

Growers only have themselves to blame for increasing attacks on their publicly-financed hand-outs and government welfare: Water subsidies; mechanization research; huge subsidies for not growing crops.

These special privileges came into being before the Supreme Court's one-person, one-vote decision—at a time when rural lawmakers dominated the Legislature and the Congress. Soon, those hand-outs could be in jeopardy as government searches for more revenue and as urban taxpayers take a closer look at farm programs—and who they really benefit.

The growers only have themselves to blame for the humiliation they have brought upon succeeding waves of immigrant groups which have sweated and sacrificed for 100 years to make this industry rich. For generations, they have subjugated entire races of dark-skinned farm workers.

These are the sins of the growers, not the farm workers. We didn't poison the land. We didn't open the door to imported produce. We didn't covet billions of dollars in government hand-outs. We didn't abuse and exploit the people who work the land. Today, the growers are like a punch-drunk old boxer who doesn't know he's past his prime. The times are changing. The political and social environment has changed. The chickens are coming home to roost—and the time to account for past sins is approaching. I am told, these days, why farm workers should be discouraged and pessimistic: The Republicans control the governor's office and the White House. They say there is a conservative trend in the nation.

Yet we are filled with hope and encouragement. We have looked into the future and the future is ours!

History and inevitability are on our side. The farm workers and their children— and the Hispanics and their children—are the future in California. And corporate growers are the past!

Those politicians who ally themselves with the corporate growers and against the farm workers and the Hispanics are in for a big surprise. They want to make their careers in politics. They want to hold power 20 and 30 years from now.

But 20 and 30 years from now—in Modesto, in Salinas, in Fresno, in Bakersfield, in the Imperial Valley, and in many of the great cities of California—those communities will be dominated by farm workers and not by growers, by the children and grandchildren of farm workers and not by the children and grandchildren of growers. These trends are part of the forces of history that cannot be stopped. No person and no organization can resist them for very long. They are inevitable.

Once social change begins, it cannot be reversed.

You cannot uneducate the person who has learned to read. You cannot humiliate the person who feels pride. You cannot oppress the people who are not afraid anymore. Our opponents must understand that it's not just a union we have built. Unions, like other institutions, can come and go.

But we're more than an institution. For nearly 20 years, our union has been on the cutting edge of a people's cause—and you cannot do away with an entire people; you cannot stamp out a people's cause.

Regardless of what the future holds for the union, regardless of what the future holds for farm workers, our accomplishments cannot be undone. "La Causa"—our cause—doesn't have to be experienced twice.

The consciousness and pride that were raised by our union are alive and thriving inside millions of young Hispanics who will never work on a farm!

Like the other immigrant groups, the day will come when we win the economic and political rewards which are in keeping with our numbers in society. The day will come when the politicians do the right thing by our people out of political necessity and not out of charity or idealism.

That day may not come this year. That day may not come during this decade. But it will come, someday!

And when that day comes, we shall see the fulfillment of that passage from the Book of Matthew in the New Testament, "That the last shall be first and the first shall be last."

And on that day, our nation shall fulfill its creed—and that fulfillment shall enrich us all.

Thank you very much.

RONALD REAGAN **94**

Tear Down This Wall, 1987

In this famous speech in West Berlin on June 12, 1987, Ronald Reagan re-emphasized what was at stake in the struggle of democracy against communism. On some levels, the speech is a sequel to John F. Kennedy's "Ich Bin Ein Berliner Speech" of 1963. This speech, however, became a stirring challenge to the Soviet Union to let the people of Germany live according to their own will and own consciences, and more important, prove their commitment to their own people by tearing down the ugly reminders of oppression in their midst.

Thank you very much.

[West German] Chancellor Kohl, Governing Mayor [of West Berlin] Diepgen, ladies and gentlemen: Twenty-four years ago, President John F. Kennedy visited Berlin, speaking to the people of this city and the world at the city hall. Well, since then two other presidents have come, each in his turn, to Berlin. And today I, myself, make my second visit to your city.

We come to Berlin, we American Presidents, because it's our duty to speak, in this place, of freedom. But I must confess, we're drawn here by other things as well: by the feeling of history in this city, more than 500 years older than our own nation; by the beauty of the Grunewald and the Tiergarten; most of all, by your courage and determination. Perhaps the composer, Paul Linke, understood something about American Presidents. You see, like so many Presidents before me, I come here today because wherever I go, whatever I do: *"Ich hab noch einen koffer in Berlin."* [I still have a suitcase in Berlin.]

Our gathering today is being broadcast throughout Western Europe and North America. I understand that it is being seen and heard as well in the East. To those listening throughout Eastern Europe, I extend my warmest greetings and the good will of the American people. To those listening in East Berlin, a special word: Although I cannot be with you, I address my remarks to you just as surely as to those standing here before me. For I join you, as I join your fellow countrymen in the West, in this firm, this unalterable belief: *Es gibt nur ein Berlin.* [There is only one Berlin.]

Behind me stands a wall that encircles the free sectors of this city, part of a vast system of barriers that divides the entire continent of Europe. From the Baltic, south, those barriers cut across Germany in a gash of barbed wire, concrete, dog runs, and guardtowers. Farther south, there may be no visible, no obvious wall. But there remain armed guards and checkpoints all the same—still a restriction on the right to travel, still an instrument to impose upon ordinary men and women the will of a totalitarian state. Yet it is here in Berlin where the wall emerges most clearly; here, cutting across your city, where the news photo and the television screen have imprinted this brutal division of a continent upon the mind of the world. Standing before the Brandenburg Gate, every man is a German, separated from his fellow men. Every man is a Berliner, forced to look upon a scar.

[West German] President von Weizsäcker has said: "The German question is open as long as the Brandenburg Gate is closed." Today I say: As long as this gate is closed, as long as this scar of a wall is permitted to stand, it is not the German question alone that remains open, but the question of freedom for all mankind. Yet I do not come here to lament. For I find in Berlin a message of hope, even in the shadow of this wall, a message of triumph.

In this season of spring in 1945, the people of Berlin emerged from their air-raid shelters to find devastation Thousands of miles away, the people of the United States reached out to help. And in 1947 Secretary of State—as you've been told—George Marshall announced the creation of what would become known as the Marshall Plan. Speaking precisely 40 years ago this month, he said: "Our policy is directed not against any country or doctrine, but against hunger, poverty, desperation, and chaos."

In the Reichstag a few moments ago, I saw a display commemorating this 40th anniversary of the Marshall Plan. I was struck by the sign on a burnt-out, gutted structure that was being rebuilt. I understand that Berliners of my own generation can remember seeing signs like it dotted throughout the Western sectors of the city. The sign read simply: "The Marshall Plan is helping here to strengthen the free world." A strong, free world in the West, that dream became real. Japan rose from ruin to become an economic giant. Italy, France, Belgium—virtually every nation in Western Europe saw political and economic rebirth; the European Community was founded.

In West Germany and here in Berlin, there took place an economic miracle, the Wirtschaftswunder. [Former West German leaders] Adenauer, Erhard, Reuter, and other leaders understood the practical importance of liberty—that just as truth can flourish only when the journalist is given freedom of speech, so prosperity can come about only when the farmer and businessman enjoy economic freedom. The German leaders reduced tariffs, expanded free trade, lowered taxes. From 1950 to 1960 alone, the standard of living in West Germany and Berlin doubled.

Where four decades ago there was rubble, today in West Berlin there is the greatest industrial output of any city in Germany—busy office blocks, fine homes and apartments, proud avenues, and the spreading lawns of park land. Where a city's culture seemed to have been destroyed, today there are two great universities, orchestras and an opera, countless theaters, and museums. Where there was want, today there's abundance—food, clothing, automobiles—the wonderful goods of the Ku'damm. From devastation, from utter ruin, you Berliners have, in freedom, rebuilt a city that once again ranks as one of the greatest on Earth. The Soviets may have had other plans. But, my friends, there were a few things the Soviets didn't count on: *Berliner herz, Berliner humor, ja, und Berliner schnauze.* [Berliner heart, Berliner humor, yes, and a Berliner schnauze.]

In the 1950's [Soviet Premier Nikita] Khrushchev predicted: "We will bury you." But in the West today, we see a free world that has achieved a level of prosperity and well-being unprecedented in all human history. In the Communist world, we see failure, technological backwardness, declining standards of health, even want of the most basic kind—too little food. Even today, the Soviet Union still cannot feed itself. After these four decades, then, there stands before the entire world one great and inescapable conclusion: Freedom leads to prosperity. Freedom replaces the ancient hatreds among the nations with comity and peace. Freedom is the victor.

And now the Soviets themselves may, in a limited way, be coming to understand the importance of freedom. We hear much from Moscow about a new policy of reform and openness. Some political prisoners have been released. Certain foreign news broadcasts are no longer being jammed. Some economic enterprises have been permitted to operate with greater freedom from state control. Are these the beginnings of profound changes in the Soviet state? Or are they token gestures, intended to raise false hopes in the West, or to strengthen the Soviet system without changing it? We welcome change and openness; for we believe that freedom and security go together, that the advance of human liberty can only strengthen the cause of world peace.

There is one sign the Soviets can make that would be unmistakable, that would advance dramatically the cause of freedom and peace. General Secretary [Mikhail] Gorbachev, if you seek peace, if you seek prosperity for the Soviet Union and Eastern Europe, if you seek liberalization: Come here to this gate! **Mr. Gorbachev, open this gate! Mr. Gorbachev, tear down this wall!**

I understand the fear of war and the pain of division that afflict this continent, and I pledge to you my country's efforts to help overcome these burdens. To be sure, we in the West must resist Soviet expansion. So we must maintain defenses of unassailable strength. Yet we seek peace; so we must strive to reduce arms on both sides. Beginning 10 years ago, the Soviets challenged the Western alliance with a grave new threat, hundreds of new and more deadly SS-20 nuclear missiles, capable of striking every capital in Europe. The Western alliance responded by committing itself to a counterdeployment unless the Soviets agreed to negotiate a better solution; namely, the elimination of such weapons on both sides. For many months, the Soviets refused to bargain in earnestness. As the alliance, in turn, prepared to go forward with its counterdeployment, there were difficult days—days of protests like those during my 1982 visit to this city—and the Soviets later walked away from the table.

But through it all, the alliance held firm. And I invite those who protested then, I invite those who protest today, to mark this fact: Because we remained strong, the Soviets came back to the table. And because we remained strong, today we have within reach the possibility, not merely of limiting the growth of arms, but of eliminating, for the first time, an entire class of nuclear weapons from the face of the Earth. As I speak, NATO ministers are meeting in Iceland to review the progress of our proposals for eliminating these weapons. At the talks in Geneva, we have also proposed deep cuts in strategic offensive weapons. And the Western allies have likewise made far-reaching proposals to reduce the danger of conventional war and to place a total ban on chemical weapons. While we pursue these arms reductions, I pledge to you that we will maintain the capacity to deter Soviet aggression at any level at which it might occur. And in cooperation with many of our allies, the United States is pursuing the Strategic Defense Initiative research to base deterrence not on the threat of offensive retaliation, but on defenses that truly defend; on systems, in short, that will not target populations, but shield them. By these means we seek to increase the safety of Europe and all the world. But we must remember a crucial fact: East and West do not mistrust each other because we are armed; we are armed because we mistrust each other—And Our differences are not about weapons but about liberty. When President Kennedy spoke at the City Hall those 24 years ago freedom was encircled, Berlin was under siege. And today, despite all the pressures upon this city, Berlin stands secure in its liberty. And freedom itself is transforming the globe. In the Philippines, in South and Central America, democracy has been given a rebirth.

Throughout the Pacific, free markets are working miracle after miracle of economic growth. In the industrialized nations a technological revolution is taking place—a revolution marked by rapid, dramatic advances in computers and telecommunications.

In Europe, only one nation and those it controls refuse to join the community of freedom. Yet in this age of redoubled economic growth, of information and innovation, the Soviet Union faces a choice: It must make fundamental changes, or it will become obsolete. Today thus represents a moment of hope. We in the West stand ready to cooperate with the East to promote true openness, to break down barriers that separate people, to create a safer, freer world.

And surely there is no better place than Berlin, the meeting place of East and West, to make a start. Free people of Berlin: Today, as in the past, the United States stands for the strict observance and full implementation of all parts of the Four Power Agreement of 1971. Let us use this occasion, the 750th anniversary of this city, to usher in a new era, to seek a still fuller, richer life for the Berlin of the future. Together, let us maintain and develop the ties between the Federal Republic and the Western sectors of Berlin, which is permitted by the 1971 agreement. And I invite Mr. Gorbachev: Let us work to bring the Eastern and Western parts of the city closer together, so that all the inhabitants of all Berlin can enjoy the benefits that come with life in one of the great cities of the world. To open Berlin still further to all Europe, East and West, let us expand the vital air access to this city, finding ways of making commercial air service to Berlin more convenient, more comfortable, and more economical. We look to the day when West Berlin can become one of the chief aviation hubs in all central Europe.

With our French and British partners, the United States is prepared to help bring international meetings to Berlin. It would be only fitting for Berlin to serve as the site of United Nations meetings, or world conferences on human rights and arms control or other issues that call for international cooperation. There is no better way to establish hope for the future than to enlighten young minds, and we would be honored to sponsor summer youth exchanges, cultural events, and other programs for young Berliners from the East. Our French and British friends, I'm certain, will do the same. And it's my hope that an authority can be found in East Berlin to sponsor visits from young people of the Western sectors.

One final proposal, one close to my heart: Sport represents a source of enjoyment and ennoblement, and you may have noted that the Republic of Korea (South Korea) has offered to permit certain events of the 1988 Olympics to take place in the North. International sports competitions of all kinds could take place in both parts of this city. And what better way to demonstrate to the world the openness of this city than to offer in some future year to hold the Olympic games here in Berlin, East and West?

In these four decades, as I have said, you Berliners have built a great city. You've done so in spite of threats, the Soviet attempts to impose the East-mark, the blockade. Today the city thrives in spite of the challenges implicit in the very presence of this wall. What keeps you here? Certainly there's a great deal to be said for your fortitude, for your defiant courage. But I believe there's something deeper, something that involves Berlin's whole look and feel and way of life, not mere sentiment. No one could live long in Berlin without being completely disabused of illusions. Something instead, that has seen the difficulties of life in Berlin but chose to accept them, that continues to build this good and proud city in contrast to a surrounding totalitarian presence that refuses to release human energies or aspirations. Something that speaks with a powerful voice of affirmation, that says yes to this city, yes to the future, yes to freedom. In a word, I would submit that what keeps you in Berlin is love both profound and abiding.

Perhaps this gets to the root of the matter, to the most fundamental distinction of all between East and West. The totalitarian world produces backwardness because it does such violence to the spirit, thwarting the human impulse to create, to enjoy, to worship. The totalitarian world finds even symbols of love and of worship an affront. Years ago, before the East Germans began rebuilding their churches, they erected a secular structure: the television tower at Alexander Platz. Virtually ever since, the authorities have been working to correct what they view as the tower's one major flaw, treating the glass sphere at the top with paints and chemicals of every kind. Yet even today when the Sun strikes that sphere—that sphere that towers over all Berlin the light makes the sign of the cross. There in Berlin, like the city itself, symbols of love, symbols of worship, cannot be suppressed.

As I looked out a moment ago from the Reichstag, that embodiment of German unity, I noticed words crudely spray-painted upon the wall, perhaps by a young Berliner, "This wall will fall. Beliefs become reality." Yes, across Europe, this wall will fall. For it cannot withstand faith; it cannot withstand truth. The wall cannot withstand freedom. And I would like, before I close, to say one word. I have read, and I have been questioned since I've been here about certain demonstrations against my coming. And I would like to say just one thing, and to those who demonstrate so. I wonder if they have ever asked themselves that if they should have the kind of government they apparently seek, no one would ever be able to do what they're doing again.

Thank you and God bless you all.

BILL CLINTON **95**

Religious Liberty in America, 1995

Just as the nation's earliest concerns centered on religious freedom, the late twentieth century found America with those concerns once again. President Bill Clinton addressed those concerns before a group of students at James Madison High School in Vienna, Virginia, as he defended the Religious Freedom Restoration Act of 1993. Clinton thanks a number of local officials in the audience and a young student who introduced him as he begins his speech. In this address, Clinton praises religious toleration and diversity as a source of spiritual strength for the nation and that by allowing everyone to explore their own conscience, they do not have to live in fear of persecution but can learn to trust neighbors of different faiths.

Thank you, Secretary [of Education Richard] Riley, for the introduction, but more for your outstanding leadership of the Department of Education and the work you have done not only to increase the investment of our country in education, but also to lift the quality and the standards of education and

http://clinton1.nara.gov/White_House/EOP/OP/html/book3-plain.html

to deal forthrightly with some of the more difficult, but important issues in education that go to the heart of the character of the young people we build in our country.

Superintendent Spillane, congratulations on your award and the work you are doing here in this district. Dr. Clark, Ms. Lubetkin. To Danny Murphy, I thought he gave such a good speech I could imagine him on a lot of platforms in the years ahead. He did a very fine job.

Mayor Robinson, and to the Board of Supervisors—Chair Katherine Hanley, and to all the religious leaders, parents, students who are here; the teachers; and especially to the James Madison teachers, thank you for coming today.

Last week at my alma mater, Georgetown, I had a chance to do something that I hope to do more often as President, to have a genuine conversation with the American people about the best way for us to move forward as a nation and to resolve some of the great questions that are nagging at us today. I believe, as I have said repeatedly, that our nation faces two great challenges: first of all, to restore the American dream of opportunity, and the American tradition or responsibility; and second, to bring our country together amidst all of our diversity in a stronger community so that we can find common ground and move forward together.

In my first two years as President I worked harder on the first question, how to get the economy going, how to deal with the specific problems of the country, how to inspire more responsibility through things like welfare reform and child support enforcement. But I have come to believe that unless we can solve the second problem we'll never really solve the first one. Unless we can find a way to honestly and openly debate our differences and find common ground, to celebrate all the diversity of America and still give people a chance to live in the way they think is right, so that we are stronger for our differences, not weaker, we won't be able to meet the economic and other challenges before us. And therefore, I have decided that I should spend some more time in some conversations about things Americans care a lot about and that they're deeply divided over.

Today I want to talk about a conversation—about a subject that can provoke a fight in nearly any country town or on any city street corner in America—religion. It's a subject that should not drive us apart. And we have a mechanism as old as our Constitution for bringing us together.

This country, after all, was founded by people of profound faith who mentioned Divine Providence and the guidance of God twice in the Declaration of Independence. They were searching for a place to express their faith freely without persecution. We take it for granted today that that's so in this country, but it was not always so. And it certainly has not always been so across the world. Many of the people who were our first settlers came here primarily because they were looking for a place where they could practice their faith without being persecuted by the government.

Here in Virginia's soil, as the Secretary of Education has said, the oldest and deepest roots of religious liberty can be found. The First Amendment was modeled on Thomas Jefferson's Statutes of Religious Liberty for Virginia. He thought so much of it that he asked that on his gravestone it be said not that he was President, not that he had been Vice President or Secretary of State, but that he was the founder of the University of Virginia, the author of the Declaration of Independence and the author of the Statues of Religious Liberty for the state of Virginia.

And of course, no one did more than James Madison to put the entire Bill of Rights in our Constitution, and especially, the First Amendment.

Religious freedom is literally our first freedom. It is the first thing mentioned in the Declaration of Independence. And as it opens, it says Congress cannot make a law that either establishes a religion or restricts the free exercise of religion. Now, as with every provision of our Constitution, that law has had to be interpreted over the years, and it has in various ways that some of us agree with and some of us disagree with. But one thing is indisputable: the First Amendment has protected our freedom to be religious or not religious, as we choose, with the consequence that in this highly secular age the United States is clearly the most conventionally religious country in the entire world, at least the entire industrialized world.

We have more than 250,000 places of worship. More people go to church here every week, or to synagogue, or to a mosque or other place of worship than in any other country in the world. More people believe religion is directly important to their lives than in any other advanced, industrialized country in the world. And it is not an accident. It is something that has always been a part of our life.

I grew up in Arkansas which is, except for West Virginia, probably the state that's most heavily Southern Baptist Protestant in the country. But we had two synagogues and a Greek Orthodox church in my hometown. Not so long ago in the heart of our agricultural country in Eastern Arkansas one of our universities did a big outreach to students in the Middle East, and before you know it, out there on this flat land where there was no building more than two stories high, there rose a great mosque. And all the farmers from miles around drove in to see what the mosque was like and try to figure out what was going on there.

This is a remarkable country. And I have tried to be faithful to that tradition that we have of the First Amendment. It's something that's very important to me.

Secretary Riley mentioned when I was at Georgetown, Georgetown is a Jesuit school, a Catholic school. All the Catholics were required to teach theology, and those of us who weren't Catholic took a course in world's religion, which we called Buddhism for Baptists. And I began a sort of love affair with the religions that I did not know anything about before that time.

It's a personal thing to me because of my own religious faith and the faith of my family. And I've always felt that in order for me to be free to practice my faith in this country, I had to let other people be as free as possible to practice theirs, and that the government had an extraordinary obligation to bend over backwards not to do anything to impose any set of views on any group of people or to allow others to do it under the cover of law.

That's why I was very proud—one of the proudest things I've been able to do as President was to sign into law the Religious Freedom Restoration Act in 1993. And it was designed to reverse the decision of the Supreme Court that essentially made it pretty easy for government, in the pursuit of its legitimate objectives, to restrict the exercise of people's religious liberties. This law basically said—I won't use the legalese—the bottom line was that if the government is going to restrict anybody's legitimate exercise of religion they have to have an extraordinarily good reason and no other way to achieve their compelling objective other than to do this. You have to bend over backwards to avoid getting in the way of people's legitimate exercise of their religious convictions. That's what that law said.

This is something I've tried to do throughout my career. When I was governor, for example, we were having—of Arkansas in the '80s—you may remember this—there were religious leaders going to jail in America because they ran child care centers that they refused to have certified by the state because they said it undermined their ministry. We solved that problem in our state. There were people who were prepared to go to jail over the home schooling issue in the '80s because they said it was part of their religious ministry. We solved that problem in our state.

With the Religious Freedom Restoration Act we made it possible, clearly, in areas that were previously ambiguous for Native Americans, for American Jews, for Muslims to practice the full range of their religious practices when they might have otherwise come in contact with some governmental regulation.

And in a case that was quite important to the Evangelicals in our country, I instructed the Justice Department to change our position after the law passed on a tithing case where a family had been tithing to their church and the man declared bankruptcy, and the government took the position they could go get the money away from the church because he knew he was bankrupt at the time he gave it. And I realized in some ways that was a close question, but I thought we had to stand up for the proposition that people should be able to practice their religious convictions.

Secretary Riley and I, in another context, have also learned as we have gone along in this work that all the religions obviously share a certain devotion to a certain set of values which make a big difference in the schools. I want to commend Secretary Riley for his relentless support of the so-called character education movement in our schools, which is clearly led in many schools that had great troubles to reduce dropout rates, increased performance in schools, better citizenship in ways that didn't promote any particular religious views but at least unapologetically advocated values shared by all major religions.

In this school, one of the reasons I wanted to come here is because I recognize that this work has been done here. There's a course in this school called Combatting Intolerance, which deals not only with racial issues, but also with religious differences, and studies times in the past when people have been killed in mass numbers and persecuted because of their religious convictions.

You can make a compelling argument that the tragic war in Bosnia today is more of a religious war than an ethnic war. The truth is, biologically, there is no difference in the Serbs, the Croats and the Muslims. They are Catholics, Orthodox Christians and Muslims, and they are so for historic reasons. But it's really more of a religious war than an ethnic war when properly viewed. And I think it's very important that the people in this school are learning that and, in the process, will come back to that every great religion teaches honesty and trustworthiness and responsibility and devotion to family, and charity and compassion toward others.

Our sense of our own religion and our respect for others has really helped us to work together for two centuries. It's made a big difference in the way we live and the way we function and our ability to overcome adversity. The Constitution wouldn't be what it is without James Madison's religious values. But it's also, frankly, given us a lot of elbow room. I remember, for example, that Abraham Lincoln was derided by his opponents because he belonged to no organized church. But if you read his writings and you study what happened to him, especially after he came to the White House, he might have had more spiritual depth than any person ever to hold the office that I now have the privilege to occupy.

So we have followed this balance, and it has served us well. Now what I want to talk to you about for a minute is that our Founders understood that religious freedom basically was a coin with two sides. The Constitution protected the free exercise of religion, but prohibited the establishment of religion. It's a careful balance that's uniquely American. It is the genius of the First Amendment. It does not, as some people have implied, make us a religion-free country. It has made us the most religious country in the world.

It does not convert—let's just take the areas of greatest controversy now—all the fights have come over 200 years over what those two things mean: What does it mean for the government to establish a religion, and what does it mean for a government to interfere with the free exercise of religion. The Religious Freedom Restoration Act was designed to clarify the second provision—government interfering with the free exercise of religion and to say you can do that almost never. You can do that almost never.

We have had a lot more fights in the last 30 years over what the government establishment of religion means. And that's what the whole debate is now over the issue of school prayer, religious practices in the schools and things of that kind. And I want to talk about it because our schools are the places where so much of our hearts are in America and all of our futures are. And I'd like to begin by just sort of pointing out what's going on today and then discussing it if I could. And, again, this is always kind of inflammatory; I want to have a noninflammatory talk about it.

First of all, let me tell you a little about my personal history. Before the Supreme Court's decision in Engel against Vitale, which said that the state of New York could not write a prayer that had to be said in every school in New York every day, school prayer was as common as apple pie in my hometown. And when I was in junior high school, it was my responsibility either to start every day by reading the Bible or get somebody else to do it. Needless to say, I exerted a lot of energy in finding someone else to do it from time to time, being a normal 13-year-old boy.

Now, you could say, well, it certainly didn't do any harm; it might have done a little good. But remember what I told you. We had two synagogues in my hometown. We also had pretended to be deeply religious and there were no blacks in my school, they were in a segregated school. And I can tell you that all of us who were in there doing it never gave a second thought most of the time to the fact that we didn't have blacks in our schools and that there were Jews in the classroom who were probably deeply offended by half the stuff we were saying or doing—or maybe made to feel inferior.

I say that to make the point that we have not become less religious over the last 30 years by saying that schools cannot impose a particular religion, even if it's a Christian religion and 98 percent of the kids in the schools are Christian and Protestant. I'm not sure the Catholics were always comfortable with what we did either. We had a big Catholic population in my school and in my hometown. But I did that—I have been a part of this debate we are talking about. This is a part of my personal life experience. So I have seen a lot of progress made and I agreed with the Supreme Court's original decision in *Engel v. Vitale*.

Now, since then, I've not always agreed with every decision the Supreme Court made in the area of the First Amendment. I said the other day I didn't think the decision on the prayer at the commencement, where the Rabbi was asked to give the nonsectarian prayer at the commencement—I didn't agree with that because I didn't think it any coercion at all. And I thought that people were not interfered with. And I didn't think it amounted to the establishment of a religious practice by the government. So I have not always agreed.

But I do believe that on balance, the direction of the First Amendment has been very good for America and has made us the most religious country in the world by keeping the government out of creating religion, supporting particular religions, interfering, and interfering with other people's religious practices.

What is giving rise to so much of this debate today I think is two things. One is the feeling that the schools are special and a lot of kids are in trouble, and a lot of kids are in trouble for nonacademic reasons, and we want our kids to have good values and have a good future.

Let me give you just one example. There is today, being released, a new study of drug use among young people by the group that Joe Califano was associated with— Council for a Drug-Free America—massive poll of young people themselves. It's a fascinating study and I urge all of you to get it. Joe came in a couple of days ago and briefed my on it. It shows disturbingly that even though serious drug use is down overall in groups in America, casual drug use is coming back up among some of our young people who no longer believe that it's dangerous and have forgotten that's it's wrong and are basically living in a world that I think is very destructive.

And I see it all the time. It's coming back up. Even though we're investing money and trying to combat it in education and treatment programs, and supporting things like the DARE program. And we're breaking more drug rings than every before around the world. It's almost—it's very disturbing because it's fundamentally something that is kind of creeping back in.

But the study shows that there are three major causes for young people not using drugs. One is they believe that their future depends upon their not doing it; they're optimistic about the future. The more optimistic kids are about the future, the less likely they are to use drugs.

Second is having a strong, positive relationship with their parents. The closer kids are to their parents and the more tuned in to them they are, and the more their parents are good role models, the less likely kids are to use drugs.

You know what the third is? How religious the children are. The more religious the children are, the less likely they are to use drugs.

So what's the big fight over religion in the schools and what does it mean to us and why are people so upset about it? I think there are basically three reasons. One is, people believe that—most Americans believe that if you're religious, personally religious, you ought to be able to manifest that anywhere at any time, in a public or private place. Second, I think that most Americans are disturbed if they think that our government is becoming anti-religious, instead of adhering to the firm spirit of the First Amendment—don't establish, don't interfere with, but respect. And the third thing is people worry about our national character as manifest in the lives of our children. The crime rate is going down in almost every major area in America today, but the rate of violent random crime among very young people is still going up.

So these questions take on a certain urgency today for personal reasons and for larger social reasons. And this old debate that Madison and Jefferson started over 200 years ago is still being spun out today basically as it relates to what can and cannot be done in our schools, and the whole question, specific question, of school prayer, although I would argue it goes way beyond that.

So let me tell you what I think the law is and what we're trying to do about it, since I like the First Amendment, and I think we're better off because of it, and I think that if you have two great pillars—the government can't establish and the government can't interfere with—obviously there are going to be a thousand different factual cases that will arise at any given time, and the courts from time to time will make decisions that we don't all agree with, but the question is, are the pillars the right pillars, and do we more or less come out in the right place over the long run.

The Supreme Court is like everybody else, it's imperfect—and so are we. Maybe they're right and we're wrong. But we are going to have these differences. The fundamental balance that has been struck it seems to me has been very good for America, but what is not good today is that people assume that there is a positive-antireligious bias in the cumulative impact of these court decisions with which our administration—the Justice Department and the Secretary of Education and the President—strongly disagree. So let me tell you what I think the law is today and what I have instructed the Department of Education and the Department of Justice to do about it.

The First Amendment does not—I will say again—does not convert our schools into religion-free zones. If a student is told he can't wear a yarmulke, for example, we have an obligation to tell the school the law says the student can, most definitely, wear a yarmulke to school. If a student is told she cannot bring a Bible to school, we have to tell the school, no, the law guarantees her the right to bring the Bible to school.

There are those who do believe our schools should be value-neutral and that religion has no place inside the schools. But I think that wrongly interprets the idea of the wall between church and state. They are not the walls of the school.

There are those who say that values and morals and religions have no place in public education; I think that is wrong. First of all, the consequences of having no values are not neutral. The violence in our streets—not value neutral. The movies we see aren't value neutral. Television is not value neutral. Too often we see expressions of human degradation, immorality, violence and debasement of the human soul that have more influence and take more time and occupy more space in the minds of our young people than any of the influences that are felt at school anyway. Our schools, therefore, must be a barricade against this kind of degradation. And we can do it without violating the First Amendment.

I am deeply troubled that so many Americans feel that their faith is threatened by the mechanisms that are designed to protect their faith. Over the past decade we have seen a real rise in these kind of cultural tensions in America. Some people even say we have a culture war. There have been books written about culture war, the culture of disbelief, all these sort of trends arguing that many Americans genuinely feel that a lot of our social problems today have arisen in large measure because the country led by the government has made an assault on religious convictions. That is fueling a lot of this debate today over what can and cannot be done in the schools.

Much of the tension stems from the idea that religion is simply not welcome at all in what Professor Carter at Yale has called the public square. Americans feel that instead of celebrating their love for God in public, they're being forced to hide their faith behind closed doors. That's wrong. Americans should never have to hide their faith. But some Americans have been denied the right to express their religion and that has to stop. That has happened and it has to stop. It is crucial that government does not dictate or demand specific religious views, but equally crucial that government doesn't prevent the expression of specific religious views.

When the First Amendment is invoked as an obstacle to private expression of religion it is being misused. Religion has a proper place in private and a proper place in public because the public square belongs to all Americans. It's especially important that parents feel confident that their children can practice religion. That's why some families have been frustrated to see their children denied even the most private forms of religious expression in public schools. It is rare, but these things have actually happened.

I know that most schools do a very good job of protecting students' religious rights, but some students in America have been prohibited from reading the Bible silently in study hall. Some student religious groups haven't been allowed to publicize their meetings in the same way that nonreligious groups can. Some students have been prevented even from saying grace before lunch. That is rare, but it has happened and it is wrong. Wherever and whenever the religious rights of children are threatened or suppressed, we must move quickly to correct it. We want to make it easier and more acceptable for people to express and to celebrate their faith.

Now, just because the First Amendment sometimes gets the balance a little bit wrong in specific decisions by specific people doesn't mean there's anything wrong with the First Amendment. I still believe the First Amendment as it is presently written permits the American people to do what they need to do. That's what I believe. Let me give you some examples and you see if you agree.

First of all, the First Amendment does not require students to leave their religion at the schoolhouse door. We wouldn't want students to leave the values they learn from religion, like honesty and sharing and kindness, behind the schoolhouse door—behind at the schoolhouse door, and reinforcing those values is an important part of every school's mission.

Some school officials and teachers and parents believe that the Constitution forbids any religious expression at all in public schools. That is wrong. Our courts have made it clear that that is wrong. It is also not a good idea. Religion is too important to our history and our heritage for us to keep it out of our schools. Once again, it shouldn't be demanded, but as long as it is not sponsored by school officials and doesn't interfere with other children's rights, it mustn't be denied.

For example, students can pray privately and individually whenever they want. They can say grace themselves before lunch. There are times when they can pray out loud together. Student religious clubs in high schools can and should be treated just like any other extracurricular club. They can advertise their meetings, meet on school grounds, use school facilities just as other clubs can. When students can choose to read a book to themselves, they have every right to read the Bible or any other religious text they want.

Teachers can and certainly should teach about religion and the contributions it has made to our history, our values, our knowledge, to our music and our art in our country and around the world, and to the development of the kind of people we are. Students can also pray to themselves—preferably before tests, as I used to do.

Students should feel free to express their religion and their beliefs in homework, through art work, during class presentations, as long as it's relevant to the assignment. If students can distribute flyers or pamphlets that have nothing to do with the school, they can distribute religious flyers and pamphlets on the same basis. If students can wear T-shirts advertising sports teams, rock groups or politicians, they can also wear T-shirts that promote religion. If certain subjects or activities are objectionable to their students or their parents because of their religious beliefs, then schools may, and sometimes they must, excuse the students from those activities.

Finally, even though the schools can't advocate religious beliefs, as I said earlier, they should teach mainstream values and virtues. The fact that some of these values happen to be religious values does not mean that they cannot be taught in our schools.

All these forms of religious expression and worship are permitted and protected by the First Amendment. That doesn't change the fact that some students haven't been allowed to express their beliefs in these ways. What we have to do is to work together to help all Americans understand exactly what the First Amendment does. It protects freedom of religion by allowing students to pray, and it protects freedom of religion by preventing schools from telling them how and when and what to pray. The First Amendment keeps us all on common ground. We are allowed to believe and worship as we choose without the government telling any of us what we can and cannot do.

It is in that spirit that I am today directing the Secretary of Education and the Attorney General to provide every school district in America before school starts this fall with a detailed explanation of the religious expression permitted in schools, including all the things that I've talked about today. I hope parents, students, educators and religious leaders can use this directive as a starting point. I hope it helps them to understand their differences, to protect student's religious rights, and to find common ground. I believe we can find that common ground.

This past April a broad coalition of religious and legal groups—Christian and Jewish, conservative and liberal, Supreme Court advocates and Supreme Court critics—put themselves on the solution side of this debate. They produced a remarkable document called "Religion in Public Schools: A Joint Statement of Current Law." They put aside their deep differences and said, we all agree on what kind of religious expression the law permits in our schools. My directive borrows heavily and gratefully from their wise and thoughtful statement. This is a subject that could have easily divided the men and women that came together to discuss it. But they moved beyond their differences and that may be as important as the specific document they produced.

I also want to mention over 200 religious and civic leaders who signed the Williamsburg Charter in Virginia in 1988. That charter reaffirms the core principles of the First Amendment. We can live together with our deepest differences and all be stronger for it.

The charter signers are impressive in their own right and all the more impressive for their differences of opinion, including Presidents Ford and Carter; Chief Justice Rehnquist and the late Chief Justice [Warren] Burger; Senator [Bob] Dole and former Governor [Michael] Dukakis; [former Secretary of Education and moral philosopher] Bill Bennett and Lane Kirkland, the president of the AFL-CIO; [television producer and liberal activist] Norman Lear and [conservative activist] Phyllis Schlafly signed it together—Coretta Scott King and Reverend James Dobson.

These people were able to stand up publicly because religion is a personal and private thing for Americans which has to have some public expression. That's how it is for me. I'm pretty old-fashioned about these things. I really do believe in the constancy of sin and the constant possibility of forgiveness, the reality of redemption and the promise of a future life. But I'm also a Baptist who believes that salvation is primarily personal and private, that my relationship is directly with God and not through any intermediary.

People—other people can have different views. And I've spent a good part of my life trying to understand different religious views, celebrate them and figure out what brings us together.

I will say again, the First Amendment is a gift to us. And the Founding Fathers wrote the Constitution in broad ways so that it could grow and change, but hold fast to certain principles. They knew—they knew that all people were fallible and would make mistakes from time to time. And I have—as I said, there are times when the Supreme Court makes a decision, if I disagree with it, one of us is wrong. There's another possibility: both of us could be wrong. That's the way it is in human affairs.

But what I want to say to the American people and what I want to say to you is that James Madison and Thomas Jefferson did not intend to drive a stake in the heart of religion and to drive it out of our public life. What they intended to do was to set up a system so that we could bring religion into our public life and into our private life without any of us telling the other what to do.

This is a big deal today. One county in America, Los Angeles County, has over 150 different racial and ethnic groups in it—over 150 different. How many religious views do you suppose are in those groups? How many? Every significant religion in the world is represented in significant numbers in one American county, and many smaller religious groups—in one American county.

We have got to get this right. We have got to get this right. And we have to keep this balance. This country needs to be a place where religion grows and flourishes.

Don't you believe that if every kid in every difficult neighborhood in America were in a religious institution on the weekends, the synagogue on Saturday, a church on Sunday, a mosque on Friday, don't you really believe that the drug rate, the crime rate, the violence rate, the sense of self-destruction would go way down and the quality of the character of this country would go way up?

But don't you also believe that if for the last 200 years we had had a state governed religion, people would be bored with it, think that it would—they would think it had been compromised by politicians, shaved around the edges, imposed on people who didn't really content to it, and we wouldn't have 250,000 houses of worship in America? I mean, we wouldn't.

It may be perfect—imperfect, the First Amendment, but it is the nearest thing ever created in any human society for the promotion of religion and religious values because it left us free to do it. And I strongly believe that the government has made a lot of mistakes which we have tried to roll back in interfering with that around the edges. That's what the Religious Freedom Restoration Act is all about. That's what this directive that Secretary Riley and the Justice Department and I have worked so hard on is all about. That's what our efforts to bring in people of different religious views are all about. And I strongly believe that we have erred when we have rolled it back too much. And I hope that we can have a partnership with our churches in many ways to reach out to the young people who need the values, the hope, the belief, the convictions that comes with faith, and the sense of security in a very uncertain and rapidly changing world.

But keep in mind we have a chance to do it because of the heritage of America and the protection of the First Amendment. We have to get it right.

Thank you very much.

Bibliography

"Against Slavery," *Connecticut Gazette*, March 11, 1774.

"Ain't I A Woman?," *Anti-Slavery Standard*, May 2, 1863.

"Ain't I A Woman? (Alternate Version)," *Anti-Slavery Bugle*, June 21, 1851.

"AmericanRhetoric," http://www.americanrhetoric.com/speeches/huberthumphey.html;
http://www.americanrhetoric.com/speeches/johnlewisrightsoflabor.htm

"Archives of the West," http://www.pbs.org/weta/thewest/resources/archives/six/jospeak.htm.

"The Avalon Project, Yale University," http://www.yale.edu/lawweb/avalon.htm

Bahite, Russel D. and David W. Levy, eds. *FDR's Fireside Chats*. New York: Penguin Books, 1992.

Baker, Liva. *The Justice from Beacon Hill: The Life and Times of Oliver Wendell Holmes*. New York: HarperCollins, 1991.

Bartley, Numan V. *The New South, 1945–1980*. Baton Rouge, Louisiana State University Press, 1995.

Brown, Richard D., ed. *Major Problems in the Era of the American Revolution, 1760–1791*, 2nd ed. Boston: Houghton Mifflin, 2000.

Cantrell, Gregg, Arnoldo DeLeon, and Robert Calvert. *The History of Texas*, 3rd ed. Wheeling, IL: Harlan Davidson, 2002.

Carleton, Mabee. *Sojourner Truth, Slave, Prophet, Legend*. New York: University Press, 1993.

Carter, Jimmy. *Public Papers of the Presidents of the United States: Jimmy Carter*, vol. I. Washington, D.C.: Government Printing Office, 1977.

Channing, William Ellery. *The Works of William Ellery Channing*, 2nd ed. Boston: James Munroe and Co., 1843.

Congressional Globe, 31st Congress, 1st Session. Washington, D.C.: Government Printing Office, 1850.

Cooper, John M. *Pivotal Decades*. New York: W. W. Norton, 1990.

Cuomo, Mario M. *More Than Words*. New York: St. Martin's Press, 1993.

Dickinson, John. "Letters From a Farmer in Pennsylvania," *Empire and Nation*, Forrest McDonald, ed. Englewood Cliffs, NJ: Prentice Hall, 1962.

Divine, Robert A., et al. *America Past and Present*, 4th ed. New York: Harper Collins, 1995.

Documenting the American South, http://docsouth.unc.edu.

Donald, David Herbert. *Lincoln*. New York: Simon and Schuster, 1995.

Douglass, Frederick. "An Appeal to Congress for Impartial Suffrage," *Atlantic Monthly* 19 (January 1867): 112–117.

———."The Color Line," *North American Review* 132 (June 1881): 567–577.

Dubofsky, Melvyn and Foster Rhea Dulles. *Labor in America: A History*, 7th ed. Wheeling, IL: Harlan Davidson, 2004.

Elkins, Stanley and Eric McKittrick. *The Age of Federalism*. New York: Oxford University Press, 1993.

Fee, Chester Anders. *Chief Joseph: The Biography of a Great Indian*, New York: Wilson-Erickson, 1936.

"Findlaw: Cases and Codes," http://caselaw.lp.findlaw.com/scripts/getcase.pl?court=us&vol=347&invol;=483

Fink, Leon, ed. *Major Problems in the Gilded Age and Progressive Era*. Lexington, MA: D.C. Heath and Co., 1993.

Flexner, James Thomas. *Washington: The Indispensable Man*. Boston: Little, Brown, 1974.

Franklin, Benjamin. *The Autobiography and Other Writings*, Peter Shaw, ed. New York: Bantam, 1982.

———. *The Papers of Benjamin Franklin*, Leonard W. Labaree, et al., eds. New Haven, CT: Yale University Press, 1962.

Franklin, John Hope and Alfred A. Moss, Jr. *From Slavery to Freedom*, 8th ed. New York: A. A. Knopf, 2000.

Freidel, Frank. *Franklin D. Roosevelt: A Rendezvous with Destiny*. Boston: Little, Brown, 1990.

Gaustad, Edwin S. *Liberty of Conscience: Roger Williams in America*. Grand Rapids, MI: W.B. Eerdmans, 1991.

Giglio, James N. *The Presidency of John F. Kennedy*. Lawrence, KS: University Press of Kansas, 1991.

"Gitlow v. New York," http://caselaw.lp.findlaw.com/scripts/getcase.pl?navby=CASE&court=US&vol=268&page=652.

Goodwin, Doris Kearns. *Lyndon Johnson and the American Dream*. New York: Harper and Row, 1976.

———. *No Ordinary Time*. New York: Simon and Schuster, 1994.

"Great American Speeches," www.pbs.org/greatspeeches

Hall, Kermit, ed. *Major Problems in American Constitutional History*. Lexington, MA: D. C. Heath, 1992.

Hawkins, Hugh, ed. *Booker T. Washington and His Critics: Black Leadership in Crisis*. Lexington, MA: D. C. Heath, 1974.

Hicks, John D. *The Populist Revolt, A History of the Farmers' Alliance and the People's Party*. Minneapolis: University of Minnesota Press, 1931.

Hoffert, Sylvia A. *A History of Gender in America*. Upper Saddle Rive, NJ: Prentice Hall, 2003.

"Inaugural Address of Theodore Roosevelt," http://www.bartleby.com/124/pres42.html

"Inaugural Address of Woodrow Wilson," http://www.bartleby.com/124/pres44.html

Isaacson, Walter. *Benjamin Franklin*. New York: Simon and Schuster, 2003.

Jefferson, Thomas. *The Life and Selected Writings of Thomas Jefferson*, Adrienne Koch and William Peden, eds. New York: Modern Library, 1993.

"John F. Kennedy Presidential Library," http://www.cs.umb.edu/jfklibrary/j061163.htm

Johnson, Lyndon B. *Public Papers of the Presidents of the United States: Lyndon B. Johnson, 1963–64*, Vol. I. Washington, D.C.: Government Printing Office, 1965.

Kennedy, John F. *JFK: In His Own Words*, Maureen Harrison and Steve Gilbert, eds. New York: Barnes and Noble Books, 1993.

Kennedy, Robert F. *RFK: Collected Speeches*, Edwin O. Guthman and C. Richard Allen, eds. New York: Viking, 1993.

Ketcham, Ralph, ed. *The Anti-Federalist Papers and the Constitutional Convention Debates*. New York: Penguin, 1986.

Kierner, Cynthia A. *Revolutionary America, 1750–1815*. Upper Saddle River, NJ: Pearson, 2003.

King, Martin Luther. *Why We Can't Wait*. New York: Signet, 1963.

———. *I Have a Dream*. New York: Scholastic Press, 1997.

Lawrence, Mason, ed. *Against Slavery: An Abolitionist Reader*. New York: Putnam Penguin, 2000.

Lincoln, Abraham. *Selected Writings of Abraham Lincoln*, Herbert Mitgang, ed. New York: Bantam, 1992.

"Massachusetts History Society," http://www.masshist.org/adams/manuscripts_1.cfm

McCullough, David. *John Adams*. New York: Simon and Schuster, 2001.

———. *Truman*. New York: Simon and Schuster, 1992.

McFeely, William S. *Frederick Douglass*. New York: Norton, 1991.

McPherson, James M. *The Battle Cry of Freedom: The Civil War Era*. New York: Oxford University Press, 1997.

Moore, Jacqueline M. *Booker T. Washington, W.E.B. Du Bois, and the Struggle for Racial Uplift*. Wilmington, DE: Scholarly Resources, 2003.

Morris, Edmund. *Theodore Rex*. New York: Random House, 2001.

"National Archives," www. ourdocuments. gov; http://clinton1.nara.gov/White_House/EOP/OP/html/book3-plain.html.

Nerburn, Kent. *Chief Joseph and the Flight of the Nez Perce: The Untold Story of an American Tragedy*. New York: HarperSanFrancicso, 2005.

Paine, Thomas. *The Crisis*. Albany, NY: Charles R. and George Webster, 1792.

———. *Rights of Man*. New York: Doubleday, 1973.

Potter, David M. *The Impending Crisis, 1848–1861*. New York: Harper and Row, 1976.

Pringle, Henry F. *Theodore Roosevelt*. New York: Harcourt, Brace, 1956.

"Religious Freedom," http:/ /religiousfreedom. lib. virginia. edu

Read, James H. *Power Versus Liberty: Madison, Hamilton, Wilson, and Jefferson*. Charlottesville, VA: University Press of Virginia, 2000.

Remini, Robert V. *Daniel Webster: The Man and His Time*. New York: W. W. Norton, 1997.

Riley, Glenda. *Inventing the American Woman: An Inclusive History*. Wheeling, IL: Harlan Davidson, 2001.

Roland, Charles P. *An American Iliad: The Story of the Civil War*. Lexington, KY: University Press of Kentucky, 1991.

Rossiter, Clinton, ed. *The Federalist Papers*. New York: Penguin, 1961.

Sewall, Samuel. *The Selling of Joseph; A Memorial*. Boston: Bartholomew Green and John Allen, 1700.

———. *The Selling of Joseph; A Memorial*. Sidney Kaplan, ed. Amherst, MA: University of Massachusetts Press, 1969.

"Speech Before the House Judiciary Committee," http://gos.sbc.edu/j/jordan3.html

"The Speeches of Daniel Webster," http://www.dartmouth.edu/~dwebster/speeches/bunker-hill.html

"The Speeches of Ronald Reagan," http://www.presidentreagan.info/speeches/brandenburg_gate.cfm

Stanton, Elizabeth Cady. *A History of Woman Suffrage*. Rochester, NY: Fowler and Wells, 1889.

Thomas, Evan. *Robert Kennedy: His Life*. New York: Simon and Schuster, 2000.

Thompson, John A. *Woodrow Wilson*. New York: Longman, 2002.

Tindall, George Brown and David E. Shi. *America: A Narrative History*, 6th ed. New York: W. W. Norton, 2004.

"The Unanimous Declaration of Independence Made by the Delegates of the People of Texas in General Convention at the town of Washington on the 2nd day of March 1836," *Telegraph and Texas Register*, March 12, 1836.

"United Farm Workers," www.ufw.org

"United Nations," www.un.org

"United States Information Bureau," http://usinfo.state.gov/usa/infousa/facts.htm

"University of Virginia Library," www.lib.uvirginia.edu/etext/ETC.html

"U.S. History.org," http://www.ushistory.org

Vance, Zebulon B. *The Duties of Defeat: An Address Delivered Before the Two Literary Societies of the University of North Carolina, June 7, 1866*. Raleigh, NC: William B. Smith and Co., 1866.

Washington, Booker T. *The Booker T. Washington Papers*, Louis R. Harlan, ed. Urbana: University of Illinois Press, 1974.

Wildes, Harry Emerson. *William Penn*. New York: MacMillan, 1974.

Wilentz, Sean, ed. *Major Problems in the Early Republic, 1787–1848*. Lexington, MA: D. C. Heath, 1992.

Woodward, C. Vann. *Origins of the New South*. Baton Rouge, LA: Louisiana State University Press, 1971.

———. *The Strange Career of Jim Crow*. New York: Oxford University Press, 1955.

"The Zenger Trial: An Account, by Douglas Linder (2001)," http://www.law.umkc.edu/faculty/projects/ftrials/zenger/journalissues3.html.